KNOWLEDGE:
ITS CREATION, DISTRIBUTION, AND
ECONOMIC SIGNIFICANCE

VOLUME III

THE ECONOMICS
OF INFORMATION AND
HUMAN CAPITAL

KNOWLEDGE:
ITS CREATION, DISTRIBUTION, AND
ECONOMIC SIGNIFICANCE

VOLUME III

THE ECONOMICS
OF INFORMATION AND
HUMAN CAPITAL

BY FRITZ MACHLUP

PRINCETON UNIVERSITY PRESS

CONTENTS

ANALYTICAL TABLE OF CONTENTS

FOREWORD

In breadth and depth, this is a unique book in economic scholarship. The historical roots of the ideas are richly documented. The analysis is based on theory and evidence. What is said is lucid. The advances in the economics of information, and in human capital, are presented clearly both for economists and for intelligent general readers who are not concerned about the technicalities of economics.

To appreciate the complexity of modern economics, it is necessary to see that its achievements have in large measure been made possible by the division of labor in what economists do. Economics has become highly specialized. The nature of this specialization has had the consequence that most economists present their specific contributions to serve those economists who specialize in the same part of economics. Economists no longer can manage to stay abreast of all economics. Rare is the economist these days who takes on the task of integrating the theoretical and empirical advances of the various specialized parts. Economic literature that is readily understandable by concerned general readers is becoming a lost art.

The hallmark of the work of Professor Fritz Machlup is in its comprehensive scholarship, in relating each of his specific studies to the general core of economics, in seeking the linkage between theory and evidence, and in his command of the art of writing. I think of Alfred Marshall, Joseph Schumpeter, Jacob Viner, and Harry Johnson for a corresponding set of talents.

For over two decades Machlup has devoted his research to the economic significance of the increases in the production of knowledge and its distribution. His 1962 book, *The Production and Distribution of Knowledge* (Princeton University Press), is a major contribution. In my review of that book I called attention to its specific merits and I noted that above all, "Machlup is every inch an economist."

Machlup continued to pursue the economic significance of knowledge with the help of competent assistance. We now have this important book, which was fortunately completed before his untimely death. It is not restricted to the economics published in English. It deals critically with many aspects of economic theory. It brings to bear the findings of a vast number of studies pertaining to economic information and human capital. The content of the text and the rich extensive footnotes are a veritable intellectual gold mine.

July 1983   Theodore W. Schultz

ACKNOWLEDGMENTS

FRITZ MACHLUP preferred to thank those who had helped him with the research and writing of his books only after the reading of proofs and the preparation of the index were done. Although his death on January 30, 1983, made it impossible for him to write the acknowledgments for this volume himself, he did leave lists to aid in the task. *The Economics of Information and Human Capital*, Volume III in his series *Knowledge: Its Creation, Distribution, and Economic Significance*, has had a long history and there are many to thank.

Nine agencies have sponsored Fritz Machlup's research for his series on knowledge: the National Science Foundation, the National Endowment for the Humanities, the Ford Foundation, the John and Mary Markle Foundation, the Alfred P. Sloan Foundation, the National Institute of Education, the Exxon Education Foundation, the Earhart Foundation, and the Spencer Foundation. The support of all of these agencies should be acknowledged in Volume III.

Most of Part Two, "Knowledge as Human Capital," was written before Part One. The semifinal drafts of all ten chapters of Part Two were sent in the summer of 1980 to three experts on human capital—Mark Blaug, Elchanan Cohn, and W. Lee Hansen. Their comments and suggestions, and those of Jacob Mincer, who read the manuscript for the Press, were especially helpful in the preparation of the final draft in 1982. For Part One, "The Economics of Knowledge and Information," advice on Chapter 7, "Empirical Research, Theoretical Analysis, Applied Inquiry," was sought from Moses Abramovitz, Alfred W. Coats, Emile Grunberg, Mark Perlman, and Julian Simon. Other chapters in Part One have benefited from comments by Jess Benhabib, Clive Bull, Roman Frydman, Leonid Hurwicz, Mark Perlman, and Andrew Schotter.

Our research team has included over seventy assistants through the years, although only a few have contributed material for Volume III. The help of Jalalledin Jalali for Part One and of O'Young Kwon and Rosa Schupbach for Part Two should be acknowledged here. Mary Taylor Huber provided assistance for chapters in both parts and made comments and suggestions on the manuscript as a whole. Peggy Riccardi, editor for Volumes I and II, has also edited Volume III and has taken on the tasks of reading proofs and of preparing the index.

MARY TAYLOR HUBER
Senior Research Assistant
Princeton University   to Fritz Machlup

VOLUME III

THE ECONOMICS
OF INFORMATION AND
HUMAN CAPITAL

CHAPTER 1

Introduction

I BEGIN with a declaration of independence for each of the volumes completed or planned for this series. They all deal with knowledge, its creation and distribution, and several deal also with the economic significance of the generation and dissemination of knowledge; but each volume can be sampled or read, understood, and perhaps even enjoyed, by people who have not read any of the preceding volumes and do not plan to read any of the forthcoming ones.

I do not mean to say that readers would not benefit from becoming familiar with the intellectual offerings in the other volumes. I feel fairly certain that all readers can gain valuable insights from the epistemological discussions in Volume I, *Knowledge and Knowledge Production*, especially in the chapter on "The Known and the Knowing." Similarly, the intellectual history offered in Volume II, *The Branches of Learning*, should be of interest to most, especially to those with a penchant for our cultural and, particularly, our academic heritage. Yet, I cannot honestly say that a knowledge of such matters is a prerequisite for understanding economic problems, including those to be discussed in the present volume.

The declaration of independence that I have made for each volume can only with certain qualifications be repeated for each chapter of this volume. What will be discussed in the next twenty chapters does hang together, and the reader of any chapter in this book will surely find it helpful to have read or browsed through the preceding chapters. Yet, I have made a conscious effort to approach independence even for the different chapters of this volume. An author should not impose upon his readers a moral or pragmatic obligation to read his book from cover to cover. Instead, he should make it easy for the reader to skip one or more chapters and still read with almost full understanding any of the subsequent chapters. An attempt to write semi-independent, self-contained chapters may call for more repetition than would be desirable in a continuous presentation of the arguments. In my own reading experience I have preferred repetitiveness to the parsimonious rule "saying it once is enough" forcing me to go back to earlier chapters to find the argument needed for comprehension of a proposition. I have lost much more time hunting for passages that the author evidently wanted me to remember (but my memory actually had not retained) than I have lost reading the "repeats" of the ideas pertinent to a specific point. I cannot expect everybody to share my preference for reiteration, but those who dislike repetition ought to tolerate it in the thought that it is helpful to others.

Noneconomists and Nonspecialized Economists

These remarks in defense of repetitiveness suggest that I am not writing for the specialist. A specialist who is well read—not all are—is likely to find much of the "stuff" I offer just "old hat," unless he is a *narrow* specialist, one specialized not in the economics of information but in a sub-subspecialty, such as the economics of futures markets or wage contracts or public goods. Such a sub-subspecialist may welcome a chance of joining a quick and easy sightseeing tour through the territory neighboring the one he has made his bailiwick. In any case, this "tourist guide" through the economics of knowledge and information is not intended to give specialists new insights. Instead, it is to tell intelligent noneconomists and nonspecialized economists, and also economists specialized in other areas, what kinds of things are discussed in the economics of knowledge and information. So many people have told me that they have not the vaguest notion of what may be talked about under that heading that I have concluded I should try to tell them.

This is not an easy task, because most of the modern literature in this field is not written in English or any other natural language. It is written in algebra. Noneconomists who never look into economic journals may be surprised to learn that in most of them few pages can be found without equations, formulas, and a great variety of mathematical notations. Sometimes a page has more lines in algebra than in English. I have set for myself the task of writing without a single line of algebra, even where this constraint should make it impossible to give a proper presentation of an author's ideas. Much gets lost in translation, and this may be true also for translations from algebra into English. In some instances, however, authors may be surprised to see their writings paraphrased in English and nevertheless conveying what they believed to be ineffable in words.

The "And" Between Knowledge and Information

In the title of the present volume, I have abbreviated "Economics of Knowledge and Information" by omitting "Knowledge." This omission is to satisfy an aesthetic norm: book designers find long titles awkward to fit on the title page, on the dust cover, and on the spine of the volume. However, for describing our subject it is more helpful to mention knowledge as well as information. To explain what may seem to be a pleonastic duplication I must repeat comments made on several occasions in Volume I about the semantic and conceptual relationships between knowledge and information.

The semanticist will note that the verbs "to inform" and "to know" have different meanings: informing is a process or activity, whereas knowing is a state of mind. To be consistent, one would use the noun "information" to denote the process or activity, and the noun "knowledge" for the state of knowing. On the other hand, both nouns are used also for the *contents* (the sense, not the size) of what people know or are being informed about. With reference to the contents, dictionaries define "information" as certain kinds of knowledge, but never "knowledge" as a kind of information. Thus, one speaks of general and enduring *knowledge* but of particular (concrete) or timely *information*, often of only transitory relevance. Some writers who dislike subtle distinctions use the two words as equivalents. Others would prefer to speak of *stocks* of knowledge and *flows* of information, a usage more in conformance with the verb forms of the words.

That in everyday parlance people sense a difference may be seen from the fact that in railroad stations, airports, department stores, and libraries we expect to find a booth or counter marked INFORMATION, but never one marked KNOWLEDGE. In later volumes of my work I shall discuss "information services," not "knowledge services." On the other hand, we would frown on education programs that fill the student's head with loads of "information"; we want them to disseminate "knowledge" of enduring value and to develop a taste or thirst for more knowledge, not just information. Thus we must take account of the fact that often the two words are not interchangeable. This forces me to resort to the pleonastic phrase "knowledge and information" even where the first term alone would suffice.[1]

[1] I wish to take this opportunity to refer to a pertinent speech by the Librarian of Congress, protesting against the current habit of equating libraries, "our Fortresses of Knowledge," with providers of "information services." "While knowledge is orderly and cumulative, information is random and miscellaneous. We are flooded by messages from the instant—everywhere in excruciating profusion. . . . information tends to drive knowledge out of circulation." Dr. Boorstin deplores that our "Knowledge-Institutions," the universities, colleges, and libraries, are being starved while information services are sold by a booming industry. "While the Information Industry flourishes and seeks new avenues of growth, . . . our Knowledge-Institutions go begging, . . . we see the Knowledge-Industry being transformed, and even to some extent displaced, by an Information-Industry." Daniel J. Boorstin, "Remarks . . . at the White

Noneconomists coming from one of the various disciplines concerned with information—librarians, computer scientists, information managers, and other information professionals—and sampling this book in order to find out what economists have to say about information will have sensed from the preceding paragraphs that the word "information" does not mean here what it means to them. They may be thinking of problems such as the cost and prices of information products and services. Specialists in mathematical information theory will be less surprised, because they realize that they use the term for an altogether different conception. I shall not fuss here about definitions; attempts to define may in this instance obscure rather than clarify matters. After a few paragraphs the reader will be better informed about the meanings intended by economists who write about the role of information than he would if he tried to decode or decrypt the usually esoteric definitions.

The Economics of Knowledge and Information

The economics of knowledge and information, regarded as a specialty in the study of economics, is—as I have said—divided into many subspecialties.[2] In my classification presented in Chapter 10 of this volume, I distinguish 17 subspecialties, but it should be understood that through mergers or splits one could, with no less justification, divide the relevant literature into, say, 12 or 21 subgroups. In the chapters that I devote to this literature I shall not attempt to furnish an exhaustive survey. All I can do is to select some of the

House Conference on Library and Information Services," *Special Libraries*, Vol. 71 (February 1980), pp. 113-116.

[2] A good many economists are not aware of the wide scope of the economics of knowledge and information. As a matter of fact, many firmly believe that it has only one theme—though it is a different theme that they think "it" is. I have encountered the following beliefs: (1) "It" deals with the optimization of a communication system; it provides a benefit-and-cost analysis for alternative organizations. (2) "It" is a merger of decision theory, operations research, and team theory, all concerned with management of large organizations of business or government. (3) "It" analyzes the problem of the decentralized use of widely dispersed information, its possible centralization for application in central planning; it compares the results of free markets with those of centralized decision-making. (4) "It" deals with the creation and utilization of new technology; the incentives for research, development, invention, innovation, diffusion, and utilization of new knowledge. (5) "It" analyzes the consequences of variable uncertainty and asymmetrically distributed information for prices, quantities, and qualities of products and services in various markets. (6) "It" provides a statistical analysis of the allocation of resources to the creation and dissemination of knowledge and information and, in particular, measures the size of the "information" sector relative to the gross national product. Needless to say, all of these concerns are part of the total, but none can reasonably be regarded as the sole concern of the specialty.

topics that have become conspicuous by the large number of re-spected economic analysts attracted to them.

Most economists have been interested chiefly in the role of infor-mation in the performance of markets and in the formation of market prices. In Chapters 3 and 4, I discuss problems relating to futures markets, insurance markets, product markets, labor markets, and financial markets. In Chapters 5 and 6, I deal with problems of public decisions, public goods, new knowledge (especially technological innovations), dispersed knowledge and central planning. Chapter 7 is a methodological essay on empirical research, theoretical analysis, and applied inquiry, with special consideration of the economics of knowledge and information. Chapter 8 is given to an examination of the types of "economic agents" assumed to "interact" as they respond to new information by revising their expectations of future developments.

A factual report on the extraordinary expansion of the specialized literature on the economics of knowledge and information is pre-sented in Chapter 9, followed by a new classification that I have developed for it. Chapter 11, with a sample bibliography, testing the usefulness of the new classification scheme by assigning more than 1,000 titles of books and articles to appropriate slots, completes Part One of the volume.

I want to make an admission with regard to a few of the issues selected for inclusion in the various chapters of Part One. I consider some of the theories or hypotheses to be rather "far out" in several respects. That they are speculations about constructs without ac-ceptable empirical referents would not make them irrelevant or un-interesting; but some are, as I understand them, based on mutually incompatible assumptions. (To mention one example: the theory of "rational expectations," alluded to in several chapters and discussed in greater detail in Chapter 8.) The fact that the theories in question are fashionable among many mathematical economic theorists and command much space in the learned journals has impressed me sufficiently to include them in my survey. Other theories, however, also "far out" in my judgment, are not included, because they have not (or not yet) gained sufficient attention among fellow economists. They are, as I see them, too fantastical (ambitious) to merit discussion at this time. (As an example I mention the theory of "interdepend-ence of intellectual, ethical, and economic development."[3]

[3] Wilhelm Krelle, "The General Interdependence of the Intellectual, Ethical and Economic Development," *Economic Essays* [Graduate Institute of Economics, Na-tional Taiwan University], Vol. 9 (May 1980), pp. 49-74. Krelle develops a mathe-matical model linking the distribution of knowledge, the distribution of ability, and

Knowledge and Human Capital

The seventeenth and last subject group in the new classification proposed in Part One accommodates writings on "human capital." I give this topic a special place by devoting it to the whole of Part Two, "Knowledge as Human Capital."

The connection between knowledge and human capital is easily understood if one realizes that capital is formed by investment, that investment in human resources is designed to increase their capacity (to produce, to earn, to enjoy life, etc.), and that improvements of capacity, as a rule, result from the acquisition of knowledge. Such knowledge may be in the nature of "knowing *what*" or of "knowing *how*."

Chapter 12, the first in Part Two, is an attempt to "rehearse" some of the essential conceptions of the theory of capital, as it developed as a theory of physical capital goods. I thought it would not be appropriate to embark on a discussion of the theory of human capital before getting acquainted or reacquainted with capital theory in general. Chapter 13 contains a report on a proposal to distinguish four types of capital (two nonhuman and two human); but it also includes an argument why a trichotomy, based on three possible sites of knowledge, is more helpful. Knowledge may be (1) embodied in physical goods, (2) embodied in individual persons ("knowledge carriers"), and (3) nonembodied either in products or in persons. Thus, we can distinguish three categories of capital: material capital; human capital; and nonmaterial, nonhuman capital. The chief method of forming human capital is learning through schooling or training.

Capital can be quantified only by valuation, private or social. In Chapter 14 the sources of valuation are examined, with special emphasis on attempts to estimate private and social benefits and costs of investment in education. Chapter 15, on "Human Capacity, Created by Nature and Nurture," ventures into heatedly contested territory, the possibility of attributing human capacity to either genetic endowment or conscious improvements. The controversies about intelligence tests and similar achievement tests are examined in this context. Chapter 16 explores "The Route from Investments to Returns" and the various influences on ability, capacity, performance,

---

the distribution of value judgments in society to determine demand, production, and investment. To model such interdependencies could be interesting, but it is visionary to think that such a model could be helpful in econometric forecasting, chiefly by endogenizing what have hitherto been recognized to be unreliable (and probably unknowable) exogenous variables. Krelle proposes "a dynamic, stochastic system of difference equations which simultaneously determines the economic variables and the changes of value judgments, information and abilities" (p. 73).

and earnings. Such influences include family effects, school effects, teacher effects, peer-group effects, and various cross-effects and re-cursive dependencies. Empirical analyses, attempting to isolate some of the effects, particularly those of incremental schooling, are sur-veyed in Chapter 17, titled "Production Functions: The Choice of Variables."

Chapter 18 treats the role of "credentialism" in determining dif-ferential earnings of labor: does longer school attendance increase the graduates' productivity and efficiency, or does it merely help employers to screen job seekers? A complex set of problems is treated in Chapter 19: "Depreciation of Knowledge Stocks and Human Cap-ital." The pragmatic significance of the "appropriate" rate of depre-ciation is a controversial question. The problems discussed in Chap-ter 20 are perhaps too intricate for the purposes of this volume. They include heroic attempts to use available statistical data to construct profiles of lifetime earnings that exhibit the implicit costs of training on the job, and implicit net earnings that reflect additional learning as well as gradual depreciation of acquired skills. Chapter 21, the last in this volume, reviews various estimates of rates of return to investment in schooling.

Some of my critical readers may question whether it is really nec-essary and appropriate to bring the issue of genetic versus environ-mental factors (in determining differential abilities) into the agenda of this volume. I submit that this discussion could not properly be dodged. The concept of increased or improved capacity implies the contrary notion of "unimproved" capacity, or "raw natural re-sources," because additions can sometimes be appraised only by knowing magnitudes or values "before" and "after." This suggests that, in the context of human-capital formation, the notion of genetic endowment versus acquired abilities has to be dealt with, in disre-gard of the taboo frequently imposed on explorations of the issue. I mention this detail in the introduction to the volume in order to explain why more than economics will be involved in the discus-sions.

Still, the interdisciplinary character of my work will be less in evidence in the present volume than it was in the preceding two and will be in several of the subsequent seven. As I see the shape of the work at this juncture, this Volume III contains more economics than any of the rest.

Economic Statistics and the Bottom Line

The announcement that this volume is largely devoted to econom-ics may mislead some readers about the scope of the discussions presented. If they expect to be told here how many dollars were spent in the United States in 1978 or 1980 for producing knowledge, they will be disappointed. No economic statistics will be supplied in this volume.

I know from countless telephone calls and personal conversations that many of my readers are impatient to hear about the size of the output of the knowledge industries, its growth over the years, and, particularly, the relative share of knowledge production in the gross national product. In my book, *The Production and Distribution of Knowledge in the United States*, I produced scores of statistical tables about the size and growth of various branches of knowledge industries; and, in a formidable tabulation on pages 354 to 357, I furnished an aggregation, with figures for the year 1958, in fifty-six lines, seven columns, and with several subtotals. This set of economic statistics was followed by computations of various ratios. One finding caught the attention of many readers, because it was surprising to them (as it had been to me), namely, that "total knowledge production in 1958 was almost 29 per cent of adjusted GNP—provided all our estimates are accepted, our conclusions granted, our omissions disregarded." Another finding was equally "sensational": that the growth rate of knowledge production was two-and-one-half times the growth rate of the production of all other goods and services in the nation's total product.[4]

Ever since I published these findings people have been asking me for updates and current figures. Other researchers have presented projections and estimates for later years, and one widely quoted investigation for the year 1967 gave 46 per cent of GNP as the share of "information activity."[5] This estimate, by Marc Porat, was based on somewhat different concepts and techniques and was therefore not strictly comparable with my findings for 1958. A more recent study, by Michael Rubin, updated the figures for only the "primary information sector" and found its share in the GNP almost unchanged for 1972 from the 1967 share.[6]

[4] Fritz Machlup, *The Production and Distribution of Knowledge in the United States* (Princeton: Princeton University Press, 1962), pp. 362 and 374.

[5] Marc Uri Porat, *The Information Economy*, Vol. I, *Definition and Measurement* (Washington, D.C.: U.S. Department of Commerce, Office of Telecommunications, 1977). Porat distinguished a "primary information sector," comprising "those firms which supply the bundle of information goods and services exchanged in a market context" and a "secondary information sector" which produces information services for "internal consumption," for example, in government for use by the government, and in firms that do not sell information (p. 51). In 1967, the primary sector accounted for 25.1 per cent of GNP, the secondary sector for 21.1 per cent.

[6] Michael Rogers Rubin and Elizabeth Taylor, "The U.S. Information Sector and

The tasks I have set myself for my present research include, of course, the calculation of up-to-date estimates, perhaps for 1978 or 1980; but much will have to be done before I come to "aggregates" for some sixty branches in the knowledge-producing sector. My technique calls for separate estimates that are based on data not always available from the product accounts or the input-output statistics of the Bureau of Economic Analysis in the U.S. Department of Commerce. Data from the census of manufactures are needed for some branches of knowledge production; for others the population census has to be consulted; in other instances, special statistics of the Office of Education, of professional organizations, of trade associations, and many other sources, furnish the bases of my estimates. The findings will be reported in great detail, with full explanations of adjustments (for example, for suspected double-counting) in Volumes V to VIII of this work, and will be summarized and aggregated in Volume IX.*

I consider the estimates for particular branches of the knowledge sector far more interesting than the "sum total." No decisions should be based on the total cost of knowledge production, whereas there may be important decisions about education at various levels or in different divisions, about research, telecommunication, computers, and so forth, and for these decisions detailed statistical breakdowns may be essential. I fully understand the fascination that a single figure such as the share of knowledge production in the GNP may have for some observers of the economic scene. What I do not quite understand is why they are so eager to know whether that figure is 49 or 51 per cent, or even 47 or 53 per cent. These differences do not really matter for any important judgments regarding economic or political developments. We are not faced here with an election won by majority vote where it would be of the essence for the knowledge sector to go above 50 per cent.

These comments on the eagerness to "see the bottom line" have been prompted by expressions of disappointment about my dilatory treatment of the statistical aspects of the production of knowledge. One of my friendly readers found it "tantalizing" to be treated to so many "delicious hors d'oeuvres" before coming to the entrees and

GNP: An Input-Output Study," *Information Processing & Management*, Vol. 17 (No. 4, 1981), p. 164. The share of the "primary" sector is given as 24.8 per cent of GNP in 1972 as against 25.1 per cent in 1967, not a significant difference.

* These estimates will not now appear as planned in Volumes V through IX. However, the more than 100 tables being prepared by Michael Rubin in collaboration with Fritz Machlup will be published, with commentary by Michael Rubin and Mary Huber, as an extensive appendix to a reprint edition of Fritz Machlup's 1962 volume, *The Production and Distribution of Knowledge in the United States* (Princeton: Princeton University Press, 1962).—Ed.

the rest of the full-course dinner. Although I am flattered that the early dishes that I am serving are called delicious, I am not happy about their being regarded as hors d'oeuvres. In my view, epistemological problems or the intellectual history of the classification of learning or the presentation of the more esoteric issues of the economics of information are not any less important than the statistical inquiries that yield estimates of the share of knowledge production in the gross national product.

With this pronouncement I have come back full circle to the statement with which I started this introduction: the declaration of independence for this and any other volume of this work.

Such independence, however, should not be mistaken for a lack of coherence. To be sure, the different volumes may appeal to different groups of readers. For example, I expect that the present volume will have more interest to economists than to statisticians or historians, and that the volume on education will have a market somewhat different from that of the volume on the media of communication. For this reason I am making a major effort to preserve the "independence" of each volume in the sense that it is interesting also to readers who have not read the previous volumes. But the unity of the theme is not thereby reduced.

PART ONE
_____

The Economics
of Knowledge and
Information

THERE HAS never been any doubt about the
commanding role that knowledge and
information play in human action in general
and economic action in particular; and the
inherent uncertainty of information and
knowledge has never been seriously questioned.
In the last twenty years the analysis of the
economics of knowledge and information has
become an area of specialization. Chief emphasis
has been on the complexities that may arise
from the fact that information, new or old, may
be inordinately uncertain, incomplete, partial,
biased, misleading, costly, available to some but
not to others, or giving rise to expectations,
warranted or unwarranted, of various future
developments. The ten chapters in the first part
of this volume are mainly designed to survey,
clarify and, most of all, to simplify some of the
relevant literature. Chapters 7 and 8 concentrate
on methodology; Chapter 9 presents evidence
for the new specialty's recent growth; and
Chapters 10 and 11 deal with its classification.

CHAPTER 2

OLD ROOTS AND NEW GROWTH

CHOICE is at the core of economics. This is quite explicit in pure economic theory, with its emphasis on the "logic of choice" and the "economic principle"; but it is true also at all levels of applied economics, from problems regarding consumers' decisions and business management to problems of public policy, welfare economics, and benefit-and-cost analysis. Of course, not *blind* choice but *informed* choice underlies economic decision-making and intelligent human action, however imperfect the decisionmakers' accumulated knowledge and obtainable information may be. Thus, stocks of knowledge and flows of information guide the choices and decisions that result in economic action. This is by no means a new discovery; it has always been obvious and taken for granted.

Since economists in earlier times never questioned the role of knowledge and information in economic action—and hence also in the analysis of the *results* of economic action—they did not often take the trouble of writing about it extensively. But to suggest that the older literature is silent about the role of knowledge and information would be to falsify the history of economic thought. From reading the economic journals of the last ten or twenty years one may gain the impression that the subject of incomplete, erroneous, and uncertain knowledge is a very recent addition to economic analysis. In view of this misapprehension it will be appropriate to begin this chapter with a sampling of old writings—old origins of reputedly new ideas in economic theory. The main task, however, assigned to this chapter and the next will be to present an overview of the area named "economics of knowledge and information." The best way to understand what is meant by such a heading is to look at the kinds of problems discussed under it and to see how economists deal with them.

Strong Roots in Old Writings

One of the significant achievements of economic theory in the twentieth century—the analysis of "measurable utility" of probable, or expected, gains in games of chance—has a strong root in a work, published in 1738, by Daniel Bernouilli.[1] The economics of insurance and insurable risks, involving the probability of mass occurrences and the impossibility of knowing the consequences for individual economic agents, was examined by several nineteenth-century writers, including Antoine-Augustin Cournot in 1843.[2] Adam Smith discussed in many passages of his *Wealth of Nations* (1776) the effects that different degrees of "risk" in alternative employments of labor and capital tend to have upon wages and profits in different trades and occupations. He also considered the possible gains and losses from investments in "experimentation," in agriculture as well as in manufacture, and probed into the formation of human capital through educational investment improving the productivity of labor.[3]

Some schools of thought, especially the Austrian school of economics, beginning with Carl Menger in 1871, have consistently placed major emphasis on subjective judgments based on the individual actors' partial, erroneous, and always uncertain knowledge. The first chapter of Menger's *Principles* contains a section with the title "Time and Error," in which he discussed the inevitability of ignorance, error, and uncertainty in every phase of the economic process.[4] Although he regarded the uncertainty of knowledge of all "causal connections in production," that is, technology, as one of the most essential elements in "economic uncertainty," he saw in the advance of that knowledge the most important force in the increase of economic welfare. Individual agents' subjective valuations of goods and services in view of their expected future usefulness have remained heart and soul of Austrian economics from Menger to the present. This emphasis on uncertain expectations can be traced through a

---

[1] Daniel Bernouilli, "Specimen Theoriae novae de mensura sortis," in *Commentarii academiae scientiarum imperialis Petropolitanae*, Vol. 5 (St. Petersburg: Imperial Academy of Sciences, 1738); English translation by Louise Sommers, "Exposition of a New Theory on the Measurement of Risk," *Econometrica*, Vol. 22 (January 1954), pp. 23-36.

[2] Antoine-Augustin Cournot, *Exposition de la théorie des chances et des probabilités* (Paris: Hachette, 1843).

[3] Adam Smith, *An Inquiry into the Nature and Causes of the Wealth of Nations* (London: Strahan and Cadell, 1776).

[4] Carl Menger, *Grundsätze der Volkswirtschaftslehre* (Vienna: Braumüller, 1871), pp. 21-26: — One wonders whether economists trained in the last 30 or 40 years have ever read any of the old literature. To give just one example, a statement by a first-rate economist: "It is only since Stigler's (1961) work on 'The Economics of Information' that economists have worried about how individuals should and do behave when imperfectly informed of the consequences of their actions." Michael Rothschild, "Models of Market Organization with Imperfect Information: A Survey," *Journal of Political Economy*, Vol. 81 (November-December 1973), p. 1286.

long line of Austrians, no matter whether they wrote about time-preference, saving, and capital formation (Böhm-Bawerk, 1889),[5] entrepreneurial vision and innovation in production and distribution (Schumpeter, 1912),[6] uncertainty of expectations and the demand for money balances (Mises, 1912),[7] or about the dispersion of knowledge among masses of individuals and the impossibility of the transfer of such knowledge to a centralized planning agency (Hayek, 1937, 1945).[8]

To include some fundamental ideas in a comprehensive treatise of a scientific subject such as economics is one thing; to make them the focal point of a monograph is another. A monograph often exhibits the key words in its title. (This is even more likely in the case of a specialized article.) To illustrate the difference with two important works of American authors: Irving Fisher in his treatise on *The Rate of Interest*[9] was not any less aware of the significance of risk and uncertainty than was Frank Knight in his monograph on *Risk, Uncertainty, and Profit*.[10] Note, incidentally, that these works were published six to eight decades before a specialized literature on the economics of knowledge and information developed.

These samples should suffice for the moment to confirm the statement that economic theories on the role of knowledge and infor-

[5] Eugen von Böhm-Bawerk, *Kapital und Kapitalzins*, Vol. 2, *Positive Theorie des Kapitales* (Jena: Gustav Fischer, 1889), English translation: *Capital and Interest*, Vol. 2, *Positive Theory of Capital* (South Holland, Ill.: Libertarian Press, 1959).

[6] Joseph A. Schumpeter, *Die Theorie der wirtschaftlichen Entwicklung* (Munich and Leipzig: Duncker & Humblot, 1912), English translation by Redvers Opie, *The Theory of Economic Development* (Cambridge, Mass.: Harvard University Press, 1934).

[7] Ludwig von Mises, *Die Theorie des Geldes und der Umlaufsmittel* (Munich and Leipzig: Duncker & Humblot, 1912), English translation by H. E. Batson, *The Theory of Money and Credit* (London: Jonathan Cape, 1934; new ed., New Haven: Yale University Press, 1953).

[8] Friedrich A. Hayek, "Economics and Knowledge," *Economica*, N.S., Vol. 4 (February 1937), pp. 33-54; Friedrich A. Hayek, "The Use of Knowledge in Society," *American Economic Review*, Vol. 35 (September 1945), pp. 519-530; reprinted in Friedrich A. Hayek, *Individualism and Economic Order* (Chicago: University of Chicago Press, 1948), pp. 79-91.

[9] Irving Fisher, *The Rate of Interest* (New York: Macmillan, 1907). For a discussion of expectations regarding future needs and future incomes upon current time-preference, see p. 103; for discussions of individual and "average expectations," of risk takers and their "coefficients of caution," of the uncertainty surrounding new inventions and discoveries, and of speculation, risk pooling, and concentration of knowledge, see pp. 212-217. Let me quote: "Risk is due to partial knowledge. Our present acts must be controlled by the future, not as it actually is, but as it looks to us through the veil of chance" (p. 213).

[10] Frank H. Knight, *Risk, Uncertainty, and Profit* (Boston: Houghton Mifflin, 1921; reprinted, London: London School of Economics, 1933).

mation in economic processes are not inventions of the last ten, twenty, or thirty years. There will be further opportunities in later parts of this and subsequent chapters to refer to writers who contributed to the economics of knowledge long before this area of study became a recognized specialty of economic science.[11]

Informed Choices Presuppose Information, But Not Complete Knowledge

Instead of saying that informed choices presuppose information one may just as well say that knowledgeable choices presuppose knowledge. It should be understood, however, that knowledge and information are always incomplete and uncertain, particularly because all knowledge and information relevant for economic choices, decisions, and actions refer to the future. Even if knowledge relates to the past and the present—to current conditions or circumstances— it is relevant for current decisions only insofar as decisionmakers assume that these conditions or circumstances will remain unchanged or will change in expected (vaguely "predictable") ways.

Who are the decisionmakers, the economic agents in question? Apart from the most distinguished undistinguished decisionmaker, economic man, neoclassical economic theory in its most elementary models distinguishes only two categories of economic decisionmakers: households and firms. In more elaborate models, economic theorists distinguish consumers, laborers, job seekers, landowners, savers, investors, asset holders, producers, traders, financial intermediaries, entrepreneurs, managers, cartel leaders, legislators, regulatory authorities, fiscal authorities, monetary authorities, and other agencies, groups, or individuals exerting political as well as economic power.[12] It is possible to arrange all these types of decisionmakers into three categories: households, business firms, and gov-

---

[11] Among the economists of the 20th century who have stressed the role of information and communication in the economic process, Harold A. Innis has received honorable mention by Kenneth Boulding, though without reference to a particular publication. I quote Boudling: "Up to the present I can think of only one economist of any standing whose prime concern has been with the impact of communications on the economy—the late Harold A. Innis—and he was never able to present his thought in a way that carried weight among professional economists. Nevertheless, the study of the sources and spread of economic information, the way in which information changes the subjective knowledge of the economic environment of various actors and so affects their economic behaviour—these may well be the keys to a successful dynamic economics that will enable us to solve the highly mysterious problem of the rates of transmission of economic behaviour through the economy. . . ." Kenneth Boulding, "Notes on the Information Concept," *Exploration* [Toronto], Vol. 6 (1955), pp. 111-112.

[12] A more detailed list can be found below in Chapter 8.

ernment, but not without some strain. The difficulties are greatest with regard to saving decisions, investment decisions, and asset-holding decisions. Decisions to save, for example, are made by consumers, business firms, and government; and decisions to invest are made by households, by workers training on the job and workers seeking jobs, by landowners, business firms of all kinds, and government in all its manifestations.

This preliminary list of economic agents suffices for most problems of economic theory, but surely not for all. Are thieves, robbers, and muggers to be regarded as entrepreneurs, workers, business firms, or private tax authorities? They certainly make informed decisions about the use of their time and about the most appropriate operating techniques; many do their work largely on the night shift, taking account of differential probabilities of being caught; they invest in different weapons in accordance with their acquired skills; and they adjust to changes of circumstances, especially changes in the law and its enforcement.

Two distinctions are often overlooked at the peril of misunderstanding the basic methodological status of the theories in question: the distinction between an economic agent's spontaneous action and his response or reaction to new information; and the distinction between a "real" decisionmaker in a concrete situation at a particular time and place and an ideal-typical (imaginary) decisionmaker in a typical (but merely assumed) situation, where the analyst for the sake of simplicity and clarity abstracts from all specific circumstances of any concrete case in time and place.

The distinction between spontaneous *action* and typical *response* to new information is of strategic importance because the degrees of incompleteness and uncertainty of the "old knowledge" and the "new information" may be very different: the old knowledge of the given state of affairs may be vague and unreliable, whereas the report of a new event or a change in conditions may be relatively clear, reliable, and for all practical purposes complete. A firm in the manufacturing industry, for example, may have a rather vague knowledge of its cost conditions and its markets, but the news of an increase in an excise or sales tax, or of an increase in wage rates, is relatively free from uncertainty. Critics of marginal analysis in the theory of the firm have often contended that all inferences drawn from geometric or algebraic models featuring revenue functions (sales-opportunity curves) and cost functions (production-opportunity curves) are questionable on grounds of insufficient knowledge and crippling uncertainty. These critics have failed to comprehend that the model usually has a very limited objective: to indicate the direction in which the optimal price charged and optimal quantity produced by the firm would change if one of the curves were to shift in a certain direction. The exact shape of the curves and their exact positions in geometric space are usually not of great relevance in this exercise. Only the direction of the shift of one or both of the curves matters, at least under most (assumed) constellations. The shift is dictated by the *new*, relatively certain information: the managers of the firm, in our example, cannot fail to learn of the change in taxes or wage rates. The initial shapes and positions of the curves, depicting the firm's incomplete and uncertain knowledge of cost and market conditions, may make little difference to the conclusion derived from their assumed shift.

The distinction between concrete *cases* (involving real persons) and ideal-typical *constructions* (with imagined persons) is tied up with the difference between empirical and theoretical analyses. For behavioral research one will want to find out just what the decisionmakers really know, or believe they know, about the circumstances that supposedly bear upon their actions in particular instances. For abstract-theoretical analysis, on the other hand, one constructs heuristic ideal (imaginary) types of decisionmakers and equips them with just the kind of (ideal-typical) knowledge that they would need to function properly in the theoretical model.[13] Whether and to what extent these mental constructions are really heuristic, that is, useful in explaining *observed* changes in empirical magnitudes, can be seen only by comparing them with the *inferred* changes of theoretical magnitudes. Such comparisons may be regarded as testing the applicability of the theoretical model, but not as verification.[14] One of the difficulties of the comparison of observed and inferred changes in economic variables is the fact that it is impossible to ascertain that the *actual* knowledge of real decisionmakers corresponds, at least approximately, to the *assumed* knowledge of the ideal-typical decisionmakers in the model. Yet, this is not so troublesome as it would be if knowledge of the "entire state of affairs" were of strategic importance. For most practical purposes, as we have seen, only the knowledge of the *change* in circumstances matters; the assumption that information about such a change reaches the decisionmakers is not at all unrealistic.[15]

[13] For a more detailed discussion, see below, Chapter 7.

[14] Fritz Machlup, "The Problem of Verification in Economics," *Southern Economic Journal*, Vol. 22, pp. 1-21; reprinted in Fritz Machlup, *Methodology of Economics and Other Social Sciences* (New York: Academic Press, 1978), pp. 137-157.

[15] Almost the entire literature in this area fails to distinguish between the existing vague and uncertain knowledge of the entire state of affairs and a rather unambiguous

The distinction between knowledge of states and knowledge of changes is helpful also in comprehending the issue of objective versus subjective knowledge. It should be clear, on methodological grounds, that only subjective knowledge can be regarded as the basis of decision-making. No matter what an objective observer may know about all sorts of things, a decisionmaker cannot act on that knowledge unless he, too, has it or acquires it. If we want to use our theories for explanations or predictions of observable events or data of the real world, we must find some bridge between the knowledge claimed by the objective observer and the subjective knowledge of the (actual or imaginary) decision-making agent. Such bridges are not easily established for knowledge of entire states of affairs, but they exist for pieces of information about substantive changes in the economic environment. For example, an increase in taxes or wages can reasonably be assumed to be as well known to the person who has to pay it as to the economist who discusses its economic consequences.

Subjective and Objective Knowledge

The preceding remarks on subjective and objective knowledge call for a clarification. Strictly speaking, knowledge is never objective, least of all knowledge of the future. Such knowledge is always in the nature of subjective expectations. The only tenable distinction we can make is between different types of persons claiming knowledge of the future. There are, on the one hand, those who act on the basis of their expectations or uncertain knowledge, and they may be considered as interested parties or participants. There are, on the other hand, some observers or analysts who are absolutely disinter-

---

and relatively certain piece of information about a *new* event or *change* in the situation. Even one of the most astute contributors to this area of study, Alan Coddington, writes as if this distinction did not exist or did not matter:

> If we attempt to understand economic life by supposing that in it men apply reason to their circumstances, the question naturally arises: what *can* men know about their circumstances? Or even: what *do* men know about their circumstances? Having answered these questions we could then go on to ask: what happens when men apply reason to this knowledge? In fact, economic theory has not proceeded in this manner, but the other way round. Instead of asking how reason can be applied to the knowledge that men can or do have of their economic circumstances, it asks how reason can be applied to circumstances which are perfectly known. The problems of what can be known and how it can come to be known—problems of ignorance, uncertainty, risk, deception, delusion, perception, conjecture, adaptation and learning—are then tackled as a complication or refinement on the theory.

Alan Coddington, "Creaking Semaphore and Beyond: A Consideration of Shackle's 'Epistemics and Economics,' " *British Journal for the Philosophy of Science*, Vol. 26 (June 1975), p. 151.

ested—or *nonparticipants*, neither taking, recommending, nor suggesting any action based on their expectations. We may call their expectations "objective" knowledge, even though it may, in fact, be less reliable than the subjective knowledge of interested agents.

As long as economic theory is used only to explain or predict some observable changes as consequences of specified events or of changes in the economic environment, the suggested scheme will serve its purpose; that is to say, we need not bother with incompleteness and uncertainty of the knowledge of given states of affairs and can do our job, assuming that *changes* in these states are ordinarily known full well to the agent, who makes his decision in response to them. The chosen models will usually yield unambiguous inferences regarding the direction in which the dependent economic variables will change in adjustment to the new information. Things become more complex and, indeed, questionable if the economist looks for findings that include an evaluation of the changes involved, that is, a judgment that things are getting better or worse. For such purposes it is not admissible to say that precise knowledge of an entire state of affairs does not matter and that the new information about a specific change in circumstances is all that matters. If decisionmakers merely guess the actualities and potentialities that exist in their world, and if we are aware of the fact that their guesses of the present and their conjectures of the future may be sadly incorrect, it is pretentious to claim knowledge about an improvement or deterioration of the actual state of affairs that may result from an adjustment, however rational, to a change of a single element in the totality of the economic environment. A rational response of a business firm to an increase in tax rates could put the firm into the best possible position only if the initial position, before the tax increase and before the firm's response to it, had been optimal with regard to the total state of the firm's environment—something that neither the decisionmakers within nor the observers outside the firm could know with any degree of certainty.

Positive and Evaluative Propositions

Despite continuous efforts of methodologists to caution against the confusion of positive with evaluative (normative) economics, many writers have remained deaf to the warnings and insensitive to the differences in the assumptions required for the two departments of discourse. This insensitivity is difficult to understand in view of the manifest differences between the questions asked. In positive economics, the typical question is "what is most likely to happen as a result of a particular change," say, of a reduction in the import quota for a certain commodity. In normative economics, the typical question is "will a particular change (for example, the reduction of that import quota) increase the economic welfare of the nation"? To answer the second question, much more knowledge is required both on the part of the decisionmakers and on the part of the economic analysts. Many propositions in the literature regarding the role of uncertainty are seriously inadequate because they fail to specify which kind of problem is under examination.

Not only is the role of uncertainty different in positive and normative propositions, but there is also the serious question about the "adequacy" or "aptness" of the decisionmakers' knowledge. Assume that all producers of a certain product misjudge the cost conditions under which they produce and the market conditions under which they can purchase their inputs and sell their outputs. (Of course, whether or not the objective analyst's [nonparticipant's] judgment regarding the participants' misjudgments is "correct" can rarely, if ever, be tested. Much of the knowledge involved relates to the future and is, moreover, hypothetical in that at best only one of many hypothetical functional associations can ever be shown to confirm or disconfirm a stated knowledge claim.) Allowing the assumption of general "misjudgment," we can only conclude that the producers will act according to their own lights, not according to the "superior" lights of the nonparticipating outside observers (the "scientific egg-heads without practical experience"). Hence, the results of a change in conditions will depend, at least in the short run, only on the "mistaken" knowledge of the agents, not on the "true facts" as seen by those who (supposedly) "really know" but do not act.

Objective and Subjective Rationality

The reference to "participants" acting on the basis of knowledge judged to be mistaken by nonparticipating (and thus "objective") observers invites comments on the concept of rationality. In Austrian economics it has always been clear that a theory of economic action, and also of the results of economic actions and reactions, can be based only on *subjective rationality*, that is, on consistency between the individual's intentions and purposes and his ideas of how these purposes could be attained—no matter whether these ideas are correct or incorrect in the opinion of objective (scientific) analysts.[16]

---

[16] Max Weber, the great interpreter of methodological individualism and subjectivism, coined rather awkward terms to distinguish objectively rational action and subjectively rational action. He called the former *richtigkeitsrationales Handeln*, the latter *zweckrationales Handeln*, which may be rendered in English (though not very adequately) as correct-rational and purposive-rational acting, respectively. Max Weber,

Not all economists, however, embraced the teachings of method-ological individualism and subjectivism, and some have clung to a notion of objective rationality, a rationality based on "true" knowl-edge, or at least knowledge as correct as it could possibly be at the current stage of scientific enlightenment. Those who entertain this notion have difficulty reconciling observed results of economic ac-tions based on decisionmakers' subjective beliefs, conjectures, and expectations with theoretical conclusions inferred from models that include assumptions of objective rationality. This particular diffi-culty is a gratuitous consequence of a methodological position suc-cessfully set aside more than a hundred years ago. Herbert Simon believes that the notion of objective rationality, or "substantive ra-tionality," as he calls it, has been set aside only very recently. The opposite of substantive rationality, in Simon's analysis, is not sub-jective but *procedural* rationality, associated with decisionmakers' procedures to acquire more complete or more certain knowledge or to cope more successfully with existing uncertainty.[17]

The emphasis on procedural rationality indicates a concern, not with *what* the decisionmakers know (believe, expect) but with *how* they go about acquiring knowledge and using knowledge for their decision-making. Procedures employed in intelligence operations, information processing, and cognitive routines designed to reach economic decisions (or, more specifically, business decisions) could be either built into abstract-theoretical models or made the subject of concrete-empirical research. Simon did both, but he was less con-

---

"Über einige Kategorien der verstehenden Soziologie," *Logos*, Vol. 4 (1913); reprinted in *Gesammelte Aufsätze zur Wissenschaftslehre*, 3d ed. (Tübingen: J.C.B. Mohr [Paul Siebeck], 1968 [1st ed. 1922]), p. 433 — Weber found the notion of correct rationality—objective rationality, in my terminology—so unsuitable for explanatory purposes that he dropped it in all his later writings. Only subjective rationality, consistency of the decisionmaker's aims and his beliefs, conjectures, and expectations, remained in the center of Weber's sociology.

[17] "As economics becomes more concerned with procedural rationality, it will nec-essarily have to borrow from psychology or build for itself a far more complete theory of human cognitive processes than it has had in the past." (Note the future tense!) Herbert Simon, "From Substantive to Procedural Rationality," in Spiro J. Latsis, ed., *Method and Appraisal in Economics* (Cambridge: At the University Press, 1976), p. 144.
My own position on the need to study the modes of thinking of decisionmakers where "only a few actors are involved" was clearly stated in my book *The Economics of Sellers' Competition* (Baltimore: Johns Hopkins University Press, 1952), for ex-ample, on p. 413. But as early as 1939 I wrote that "in order to explain the price of rubber-tires it may be necessary to interpret the actions of the late Mr. Firestone and a few other gentlemen." Fritz Machlup, "Evaluation of the Practical Significance of the Theory of Monopolistic Competition," *American Economic Review*, Vol. 29 (June 1939), p. 235.

cerned with constructing models of ideal-typical decisionmakers adopting ideal-typical cognitive procedures than with urging and promoting case studies of actual business firms to find out what procedures were being followed by selected executives and managers when they considered and agreed on specific actions. It is not yet clear how the findings of such empirical case studies could become reliable bases for inductive generalizations, especially if we learn that procedures differ widely from firm to firm, from personality to personality, and from time to time. The findings may become significant if and when we can establish that certain types of strategic procedures are associated with certain types of business organizations, business conditions, and easily identifiable personality traits.

This kind of empirical study has become known as "behavioral research of the firm" and some interesting work has been published, though not yet of the sort that would permit predictions any more specific or more accurate than the more traditional theory of the firm using the presumably "empty" assumptions of intentionally profit-maximizing responses to new information.[18] The conventional general theory of the firm does not deny that people in corporate management responsible for important decisions make costly efforts to improve their knowledge, to reduce the potential consequences of error, and to mitigate the incidence of risk and uncertainty.[19] But for predicting the directions in which prices and outputs are likely to change as a result of, say, an increase in the import tariff for a commodity produced and sold by a large number of firms, no sophisticated qualifications regarding actions designed to reduce the impact of uncertainty are either needed or helpful. We should again recall the distinction between spontaneous economic actions and reactions provoked by new information about a specified change in conditions.

Coping with Uncertainty or Reducing It

Economic decisionmakers as a rule seek more knowledge when they think that the cost of acquiring it will be less than the disad-

[18] Fritz Machlup, "Theories of the Firm: Marginalist, Behavioral, Managerial," *American Economic Review*, Vol. 57 (March 1967), pp. 1-33, esp. pp. 25-26; reprinted in Fritz Machlup, *Methodology*, pp. 391-423, esp. pp. 415-416.

[19] Herbert Simon ("Rationality," pp. 143-144) distinguishes four kinds of actions to reduce or cope with uncertainty: "(i) intelligence actions to improve the data on which forecasts are based, to obtain new data, and to improve the forecasting models; (ii) actions to buffer the effects of forecast errors; holding inventories, insuring, and hedging, for example; (iii) actions to reduce the sensitivity of outcomes to the behavior of competitors; steps to increase product and market differentiation, for example; (iv) actions to enlarge the range of alternatives whenever the perceived alternatives involve high risk."

vantages due to their ignorance and uncertainty. This does not mean that additional knowledge will always result in diminished uncertainty; instead, it may show, for example, that the distribution of probabilities is more dispersed than the seeker of the information has thought. Thus, his new knowledge may make him actually more uncertain than he had been without it.[20] Similarly, a resolute decisionmaker may feel quite safe and certain in the possession of the knowledge he believes to have, and hence not anxious to seek more information, although from the point of view of some nonparticipants—"objective observers"—he may be quite uninformed or misinformed. Certainty and uncertainty, like most essential variables in the economic analysis of human action, are subjective. (Some theorists, eager to express their "objective" judgments, may wish to distinguish "unwarranted" from "warranted certainty.")

When the cost of obtaining additional information is regarded as too high, the rational decisionmaker will not act to acquire it, but instead will "passively" accommodate himself to the existing uncertainty. This recognition led some surveyors of the literature on the subject to divide it into "the economics of uncertainty" and "the economics of information." The former is concerned with "terminal actions," where the decisionmaker "may be said to adapt to the fact of uncertainty," the latter with "non-terminal or informational actions," where "a final decision is deferred while awaiting or actively seeking new evidence which will, it is anticipated, reduce uncertainty."[21]

A similar distinction was proposed to contrast "the existence of knowledge-deficiency" with "the provision of knowledge-surrogates." The former "covers such things as risk, uncertainty, mistakenness, ignorance, deception and delusion." Knowledge-surrogates include "conjecture, expectation, perception, learning, adaptation and so on. 'Knowledge' itself does not appear on the list, for we can

[20] If Irving Fisher contended that "risk varies inversely with knowledge" he surely thought of objective knowledge and objective risk—neither of which are what matters in the decision-making by an economic agent, who acts on the basis of what he thinks he knows and on the risks he perceives. As said in the text above, subjective risk may increase with increasing subjective knowledge. The quoted phrase is from Irving Fisher, *The Rate of Interest* (New York: Macmillan, 1907), p. 217.

[21] Jack Hirshleifer and John G. Riley, "The Analytics of Uncertainty and Information—An Expository Survey," *Journal of Economic Literature*, Vol. 17 (December 1979), pp. 1377-1378. In an earlier (stylistically infelicitous) statement, Hirshleifer transferred the adjectives characterizing the two types of decisionmaker to the two types of analysis: "the economics of information is active where the economics of uncertainty is passive." Jack Hirschleifer, "Where Are We in the Theory of Information?" *American Economic Review*, Vol. 63 (Suppl. May 1973), p. 31.

have knowledge only of the past; the reasoning which underlies conduct relates to future, as yet non-existent, states of affairs."[22] The separation of knowledge proper from knowledge surrogates reflects a restrictiveness in the definition of knowledge that reminds us of language analysts insisting on several layers of truth tests. Yet, even knowledge of the past could rarely, if ever, pass such tests. A businessman's knowledge of the past is neither complete nor certain but often inaccurate and vague; sometimes this "knowledge" is no more than a set of forever untestable hypotheses. He may have accounting records of purchases, sales, wages, and prices (often a bit arbitrary because of discounts, rebates, commissions, extra charges, taxes, bad debts, etc.), but he can never have anything approaching knowledge in a strict sense about his cost curves (for quantities not actually produced) or demand or revenue curves (for quantities not actually sold). The most relevant pieces of his knowledge of the *past* are what Coddington would call perceptions and conjectures (or what others would call postdictions or retrodictions); they are just as uncertain as the businessman's predictions and expectations of *future* possibilities and probabilities. We should either demote *all* empirical knowledge to the rank of "knowledge surrogates" or accept a wide concept of knowledge that includes beliefs, conjectures, and expectations of any degree of uncertainty. It is largely a matter of convenience: we save space by opting for a wide concept of knowledge, dropping the word "surrogate."

Taking Account of Uncertainty

The expression "taking account of uncertainty" is ambiguous even if the reference is to existing uncertainty not reducible by any search for additional knowledge. For it is not clear *who* is "taking account"—the economic *agent* in his choosing and decision-making or the economic *analyst* in his theorizing about results of economic activities. As a matter of fact, both the agent and the analyst take account of uncertainty, the former in judging the consequences of his alternative actions and deciding on taking that which seems to be the most promising or least unsatisfactory, and the latter in judging the consequences that the most likely actions taken by various economic agents are likely to have upon magnitudes considered significant in "positive" economic analysis. It hardly needs saying that the two sides of the problem hang together: the economic agents' assumptions and decisions and the economic analysts' research programs.

[22] Coddington, "Creaking Semaphore," pp. 152-153.

It is helpful to distinguish between uncertainty of knowledge and uncertainty of the knower. All knowledge about the real world is uncertain, including knowledge acquired by experience, but especially "knowledge" about the continuation of "known" circumstances, and, most of all, "knowledge" about future events. Forecasts can be made, if at all, only with some "per cent probability" of realization. Equally important as any estimates of probability, if not more important, may be the feeling of uncertainty on the part of the knower. He may be confident about what he thinks he knows or he may be rather unsure, or even full of doubts. The degree of his awareness of the uncertainty of his knowledge and the degree of his hesitations, doubts, and fears—risk *awareness* and risk *aversion*—are separate parts of his subjective uncertainty, which is again quite different from the "real" or "objective" uncertainty of the continuation of current conditions, of perceived changes, and expected future events.

An example from everyday life may help us see these differences. We have planned a weekend excursion, but learn from a friend that he remembers having listened to the weatherman on the radio forecasting a 30 per cent probability of rain. Several uncertainties are piled on one another: (1) the 30 per cent chance, if correctly foreseen, still means that it will either rain or not, indeed, that there may be perfect weather; (2) the weatherman may have erred and, on the basis of all objective indications, should have stated that the probability of rain was as low as 15 per cent (or perhaps as high as 50 per cent); (3) our friend who told us about the forecast may have misheard or misremembered what was said on the radio; and (4) quite apart from these uncertainties, that is, even if we do not doubt that there was no error in the reported probabilities, some of us may decide to change our plans, go elsewhere or stay home, or to go ahead with our original plans. These possibilities depend on how optimistic we are—after all, there is a 70 per cent chance of no rain—or how much we hate to get wet.

In transferring this four-part fugue of considerations from everyday life to business life, we must take note of at least three differences. First, in the economy there is usually no official forecaster who would announce the "objective" probability of "bad weather" for a particular undertaking. Second, there is not just one numerical probability but a distribution of probabilities of profits and losses of various magnitudes. (Such distributions of probabilities refer not only to investment decisions but to business decisions of any sort, since every decision may affect net revenue positively or negatively within a wide or a narrow range.) Third, whereas the individuals' reactions to the weather forecast will not affect the probability of rain, reactions to economic forecasts, say, to forecasts of a movement of stock prices, may affect the probability of such movement.

Despite these differences, it remains true that different economic agents may, in the same "objective" situation and faced with the same information, reach different estimates of the probability distribution of outcomes, and may even with the same expectations of "odds" reach different decisions. Thus we find that the same information will induce different expectations, that the same expectations will be entertained with different degrees of confidence, and that the same expectations entertained with the same degree of confidence may still lead to different decisions depending on the venturesomeness or timidity of the decisionmaker.

This need not demolish economic theory "under uncertainty." Indeed, there is no useful economic theory without uncertainty.[23] Just as consumers have different preferences and producers have different costs, all economic agents have different estimates of probability distributions, different risk awareness, different risk aversion. Such differences will as a rule not affect the direction of change induced by new information; the idea that the exact magnitude of induced change of any economic variable is determinate does not hold anyway, at least not in most instances. Economists are overly ambitious if they undertake to predict numerically exact effects of anything. They had better realize the limits of their foresight.[24]

It is sometimes said that economists "assume away" or "disregard" the existence of uncertainty. If this is true, it can refer only to the economist's teaching to beginning students. A teacher cannot expect to have his students grasp everything at once; he presents his material step by step, but he will never, if he is worth his salt, leave the

[23] It may make sense, for didactic purposes, to speak of "decision-making under uncertainty," but the expression "judgment under uncertainty" is almost meaningless. What judgment would ever be required in the absence of uncertainty? The word "judging" implies that someone is faced with uncertain probabilities, risks, incomplete information, and often also lack of confidence in particular estimations. Yet, we find the expression "judgment under uncertainty" in the literature of economics, of decision theory, and sometimes of mathematical psychology.

[24] The illustration of the effect of the weather forecast upon the weekend excursionists may help. If a thousand persons have signed up for the excursion, the number of those who will cancel after the chance of rain is announced will vary directly with the reported probability of rain; perhaps the approximate number of cancellations can be estimated if the proportions of optimists and pessimists, hardy and timid souls, are known. These proportions may vary among different regions and towns, and also for different seasons, age groups, types of excursion, etc., etc. The general direction of response to the weather report, however, is unquestionable: a decline in the number of participants.

students with the illusion that knowledge is ever complete and certain. (If he is an Austrian economist, he will probably in the very first lesson mention the inevitability of ignorance and uncertainty on the part of economic decisionmakers.) There are great differences, however, in the ways in which economic theorists have dealt with uncertainty.

In a book published in 1952 I pursued an approach I still consider pedagogically effective, though perhaps too simplistic at the present (1980) state of sophistication.[25] Since this chapter is offered largely for the benefit of nonspecialists, I am reproducing under the next two side-headings my oversimplification of almost thirty years ago.

Maximum Profit versus Security

For teaching purposes it is usually expedient provisionally to abstract from "uncertainty" and to assume that all alternative possibilities—revenues and costs of all outputs—are equally certain. When the assumption of uncertainty is introduced, some serious complications can be avoided by employing the trouble-saving device of correcting each uncertain value by a "safety margin." The more uncertain the expectation of a revenue the more of a safety margin must be deducted, and the more uncertain the estimate of a cost the more of a safety margin must be added, in order to make all revenue and cost expectations comparable. These procedures avoid or evade difficulties either by defining them away or by assuming them resolved. It is only permissible, however, to do this after one has satisfied oneself that the simplified model remains useful for the explanation of a real world in which information is very incomplete, uncertainty very large, and the willingness to bear uncertainty very different between different persons and different periods.

Some, overly anxious to discard or reform "old" theory, have quickly assumed it to be necessary in a very direct and explicit way to take account of the presence of uncertainty and the aversion to risk. They have proposed to do this by postulating a "security motive" operating separately from the "profit motive." Business conduct is then assumed to be oriented towards two separate goals, maximum profits and security, with the former severely limited by the importance the latter has for the survival of the business firm. According to this view, since firms are willing to sacrifice profit opportunities for the sake of greater security, it is misleading, or even patently incorrect,

[25] Machlup, *Sellers' Competition*, pp. 51-56. I have changed two sentences of the original text.

to base the theory of the firm upon the postulate of profit maximization.

It is highly questionable whether the separation of profit and security as quasi-independent goals is a useful device in the analysis of business conduct. Will not any move that promises profits without risks increase security *pari passu* with profits? Will not any move that involves great risk imply as great a risk to profits as it does to security? Is it not the risk of loss that creates the danger to security? Is it possible or sensible to talk about profit expectations and consistently to exclude the possibilities of loss?

The old proverbial inequality[26] stating that a bird in hand is better than two in the bush or ten in the wood well illustrates the point that "profit maximization" does not mean what its narrow interpreters contend it means. The bird catcher who wishes to maximize the number of birds in hand, but prefers one safely in hand to two potential victims in the bush, implicitly admits that his confidence in his catching ability is not great; he may catch two, one, or none, but apparently the chance of getting two does not compensate him for the risk of getting none. The distribution of possible outcomes in the case of the ten birds in the wood overlaps with that of the second choice in that it includes the possibilities of getting two, one, or none; but it also includes several other possibilities—up to a catch of ten birds. But the probabilities of such a lucky catch are deemed to be low and the bird catcher prudently resigns himself to the safe possession of one bird in hand. This, after weighing all the odds and chances, is obviously the maximum he expects he will have. It would be rather silly to say that the pursuit of the maximization principle would make him go after the ten birds and that it is the quest for security that causes him to pass up the "better" opportunities. No one, to change the example, attempting to maximize his profits will knowingly prefer a chance in a lottery promising a prize of a million dollars to one in a lottery promising only half a million if in the first case the chance is one in a million while it is ten in a million for the second.

To be sure, the optimist and the pessimist, the gambler and the timid soul, the man with large reserves and the one without, may have different inclinations towards taking chances. The risk of a loss that could endanger the survival of a firm is very different from the same risk of the same loss if the men in charge could stand it without batting an eye. But does this imply that it is easier to analyze business

[26] "A bird in hand is worth two in the bush." Miguel de Cervantes, *Don Quixote*, Chap. 4. "Better one byrde in hand than ten in the wood." John Heywood, *Proverbes*, Part I, Chap. 11.

conduct by separating the profit motive from the security motive? All it does imply is that for certain problems—by no means for all or many—it may be expedient to develop a model with a "preference function" for risk bearing, so that the propensity to take chances can be set against the opportunity of making profits and losses with various distributions of the odds.[27]

Again indulging in my penchant for analogies, I wish to caricature the dilemma of an automobilist wavering between the goals of attaining maximum speed regardless of risk—which might mean for him to drive at 120 miles per hour—and maximum safety—which might mean to stand still, perhaps at home in his garage. If the goal, however, is to minimize the time it takes him to arrive at his destination, he will surely weigh the risks and drive at varying speeds depending on circumstances. Admittedly, it may be pertinent to add other motives—enjoying the countryside, chatting or petting with his passenger, avoiding the tension of high-speed driving, etc.—if one is to explain the conduct of particular drivers in particular situations. But for an explanation of the effects that various typical occurrences are likely to have upon a driver's conduct—for example, a narrow S-curve, a bumpy stretch of the road, heavy traffic—we shall not go wrong if we take maximum speed (minimum time) in reaching his destination as the only basic assumption. The typical driver knows that he will not get there at all if he takes the curves too fast or if his car breaks down after hitting too vehemently the bumps in the pavement. In short, the postulate of maximum speed in reaching the destination comprises the risks of delays and suffices for the explanation of the most typical responses of automobile operators. Similarly, the postulate of maximum profit comprises the risks of losses and suffices for the explanation of the most typical responses of business operators.

Maximum Profit versus Most-Favored Odds

Those who revolt against the single rule of the principle of profit maximization but are willing to recognize it as one of two or more governors of business conduct still recognize that the principle makes sense and, to some extent, works. Other revolutionaries are more radical and want the principle to be thrown out altogether. They deny that "profit maximization" makes any sense as a guide to action where there is uncertainty.[28]

---

[27] See, for example, Leonid Hurwicz, "Theory of the Firm and of Investment," *Econometrica*, Vol. 14 (1946), p. 110.

[28] Gerhard Tintner, "The Theory of Choice under Subjective Risk and Uncertainty," *Econometrica*, Vol. 9 (1941), pp. 298-304; Armen A. Alchian, "Uncertainty, Evolution,

Where foresight is uncertain, each action that may be chosen is identified with a "distribution" of potential outcomes—not with a unique outcome—and these distributions are overlapping. There is no such thing as "maximizing" a distribution of possible outcomes. At best, the actor may select among the alternatives that action whose "outcome distribution" is *optimal* according to his preference scheme.[29]

All this may or must be granted. Yet, the conclusions are not those that the critics have drawn. All that follows, in my opinion, is that the expression "profit maximization" should be understood to stand for "selection of the action with the optimum distribution of potential outcomes" according to the businessman's outlook and preferences. This reinterpretation of the maximum as an optimum—which still is a maximum in nonpecuniary terms—does no harm to the theory of the firm as an output and price adjuster. It neither reduces the theory to "empty tautologies" nor vitiates the generalizations derived from it.

Those who raise the cry "empty tautologies" apparently have in mind the impossibility for an outside observer to establish the exact risk-aversion preference scheme and the risk-distribution estimates of a businessman, and the resulting impossibility of testing the theory through "concrete cases." They forget that the outside observer would not have much more positive information about profit expectations in "concrete cases" if businessmen were "absolutely certain" about their revenue and cost estimates. They also forget that it is not the purpose of the theory of the firm to predict the prices or outputs a particular firm would decide upon in an objectively described situation. The real purpose is to explain the general effects upon prices and outputs that particular kinds of changes of conditions would tend to have. The model of the firm faced with uncertainty is neither more nor less "empty" than the model without the accessories for uncertainty. It merely is more consistent with our knowledge of the way businessmen think.[30]

---

and Economic Theory," *Journal of Political Economy*, Vol. 58 (1950), pp. 211-221. Alchian states that "where foresight is uncertain, 'profit maximization' is meaningless as a guide to specifiable action" (p. 211).

[29] Alchian, "Uncertainty," p. 212.

[30] Let me try to make these considerations more concrete by providing an illustration. Assume that an increase in the excise tax for gasoline by 5 cents a gallon is announced. It is *almost certain* (but never absolutely certain) that the cost of gasoline, and thus of driving a car or fueling another engine, will be higher than it would be without the tax increase. It is *quite uncertain*, however, that the cost of gasoline to the buyer will increase by 5 cents a gallon (indeed, there are good reasons for concluding that the increase will be smaller, though nobody can know for sure by how

Those who believe that the generalizations about price and output which we derive from the theory of the firm are "vitiated" by the recognition of the significance of uncertainty in the decision-making of the businessman would have a point if one or both of the following possibilities were shown to be likely: (a) if the changes of conditions whose effects are analyzed were to affect the businessman's propensity to bear uncertainty significantly and in a haphazard, unpredictable way; (b) if they were to change the distribution of potential outcomes of alternative moves significantly and in a haphazard, unpredictable way. Neither of these possibilities, however, is at all likely to occur in connection with events of the type ordinarily analyzed. For example, the imposition of an excise tax would neither substantially change a firm's willingness to take chances, nor would it affect the probability distribution of net-revenue opportunities in an unpredictable way.[31] Likewise, an increase in the price of a productive factor or an increase in the demand for the product would tend to affect these probability distributions in definite directions and ordinarily in determinate degrees; and there is no reason for assuming that these changes would seriously reshape the risk-aversion preference scheme of the businessman. Hence, it is unnecessary to know just what this preference scheme was like in the first place, or just what the distribution of the net-revenue opportunities relating to all the alternative moves was before the change in conditions. The theory is to explain how the change may affect prices and outputs, not what they were before and will be afterwards. This explanation is accomplished by "assuming" an initial equilibrium position and "determining" intermediate or final equilibrium positions in accordance with the assumed changes in conditions. This is how models, mental or physical, are supposed to work.[32]

Bearing Risk and Uncertainty

The preceding discussion was rather general with regard to types of risk or uncertainty; it used bird catchers, automobile drivers, and businessmen as examples of actors taking account of uncertainty. A more discriminating cast of actors may give a better idea of the scope

---

much). It is *not certain*, moreover, that the cost of driving automobiles or of fueling other engines will be more expensive than it was before the tax increase, for some offsetting changes may occur. Whatever the outcome, it is never certain—neither for the economic agent nor for the economic analyst.

[31] Exceptions are conceivable and in such a case one would have to admit that little or nothing can be said about it.

[32] Of course, not everything that is sound for the Economics of Adjustment is equally sound for the Economics of Welfare. The difference in aims and claims dictates a difference in some basic methodology.

of the problems involved. We should, however, first note the distinction Frank Knight proposed between risk and uncertainty.

Johann Heinrich von Thünen, in his great work *Der isolirte Staat* (1826), distinguished between insurable and uninsurable risks.[33] Frederick B. Hawley, in his book *Enterprise and the Productive Process* (1907) defined profit as "residual and uncertain" income from business enterprise and explained it as a reward for the entrepreneurs' bearing of risk.[34] Finally, Frank Knight, in his *Risk, Uncertainty, and Profit* (1921) saw a "fundamental difference between a determinate uncertainty or risk and an indeterminate, unmeasurable one"[35] and proposed to distinguish between "measurable risk and unmeasurable uncertainty."[36] This distinction is useful, but unfortunately it has lately fallen into disuse. Too many economists these days treat the two terms as equivalent, perhaps in deference to common usage in business language. Thus, they speak of foreign-exchange risks, which surely are not measurable, and of risk aversion, when exposure to nonmeasurable uncertainty is involved.

Is it possible to separate subjective risk estimates and risk aversion not only in theory but also through actual measurements? For ordinary business decisions no operations can be devised to separate the effects of (a) different ways of calculating the chances of success or failure, (b) different judgments of the distribution of probabilities of gains and losses of various magnitudes, (c) different degrees of confidence in the accuracy of these estimates, (d) different preferences for risk taking, that is, attractions of or aversions to risk exposure, and (e) different wealth and incomes, and consequently different capacities to afford losses (without going broke). For some very special decisions, there is a way of getting around this problem to some extent: the most notorious example is playing in a lottery for which the odds and the mathematical expectation of winnings are known and can be trusted without question. In this case the first three uncertainties and doubts are eliminated and replaced by a mathematical expectation which the gambler accepts. This leaves only two factors that are unknown, the personal preference for (or aversion to) taking risks and the capacity to bear losses. These two

[33] Johann Heinrich von Thünen, *Der isolirte Staat* [in modern spelling, *Der isolierte Staat*] (Hamburg: Perthes, 1826). The relevant distinctions are in Volume II (or Part 2) of the third edition, published in 1850. See edition by Heinrich Waentig (Jena: Gustav Fischer, 1930), pp. 478-483; edition by Walter Braeuer and Eberhard E. A. Gerhardt (Darmstadt: Wissenschaftliche Buchgesellschaft, 1966), Part 2, pp. 83-89.

[34] Frederick Hawley, *Enterprise and the Productive Process* (New York: Putnam, 1907), p. 24.

[35] Knight, *Risk, Uncertainty, and Profit*, p. 46.

[36] Ibid., p. 20.

factors cannot be easily separated, because the capacity to afford losses depends not only on accumulated wealth and past income but also on future incomes. With some ingenious devices—such as the "permanent-income hypothesis"—it may be possible to isolate risk-preference functions. By standardizing the capacity to bear losses and varying the mathematical expectations of wins and losses, risk-preference functions can be calculated.[37]

Another case for which mathematical expectations can be calculated is insurance. In the lottery, the calculation was based on the stipulated number of lots and the stipulated schedule of prizes. In the case of life insurance the risks can be measured on the basis of actuarial experience, that is, the mortality tables drawn from the records of the past. In the case of insurance against damages from ordinary accidents the risks can be measured on the basis of long-term records of experience—on the assumption that the observed frequencies of accidents and sizes of damages can be projected into the future and will not change. In the case of lotteries the mathematical expectations are the same for every buyer of chances and, if all tickets are sold, unambiguously calculable for the seller. This is not so, however, in the case of insurance. The insurer may have a stronger reason for projecting past experience into the future than have different actual and potential buyers of insurance. Many of the latter entertain hopes that their risks are less than those of the masses. They consequently decide that the cost of insurance would be too high relative to their estimates of risk exposure or their smaller aversion to risk bearing. The two factors that keep them from buying insurance cannot, however, be separated: low risk estimates and low risk aversion. (A more detailed discussion of the so-called "informational economics of insurance" will be found in the next chapter.)

Totally different in nature are the chances of gains and losses by

[37] "Risk-aversion" is not a given quantity or ratio, say, a trade-off between a certain and a risky or uncertain income, something like a choice between an unconditional bonus of $1,000 payable immediately and a prize of $3,000 on the condition that today's Dow Jones index of industrial shares will not be below a specified level. Any trade-off between certain and risky income is a function of many variables, including present wealth, present liquidity, expected income, expected publicity of the decisionmaker's choice, presence of particular persons at the time he makes his decision, his state of health, his monetary mood, and so forth. A member of the research department of a large bank attempted to ascertain the risk-aversion functions of the top executives of the bank's management. He subjected them to a variety of questions. The vice chairman found to his embarrassment that he answered the same questions one way when he was alone, another way when some colleagues were present, and differently again when the chairman gave him his proxy: he became more averse to (hypothetical) risk-taking when he had to answer for his superior. Nothing came of this experiment.

holders of securities. The uncertainty borne by those who "play the stock market" is notorious; a prodigious literature deals with insiders' and outsiders' information about corporate developments, with financial analysis, brokers' and market-makers' practices, cyclical fluctuations of stock prices, random walks, spectral analysis, and several other topics related to speculation in securities.

Although all buyers of corporate securities are investors in financial assets, the uncertainty of stock-market speculation is different in character from the "investor's risk" (or rather uncertainty) borne by those who decide on placing their capital funds in particular companies that look especially promising. Again different is the lender's risk (or uncertainty), which may depend not only on the borrower's liquidity, solvency, and character, but also on legal institutions and political situations.

Most intensively analyzed has been entrepreneurial uncertainty, although the emphasis has shifted in recent years. From uncertainty as the explanation of profits of enterprise, the analysts' interest has shifted to the various foci of uncertainty in the firms' costs and revenues, especially in the expectations of opportunities to acquire labor and other inputs (supply risks), and opportunities to sell the outputs (demand risks). The transformation of these uncertainties into safety margins in calculations of prospective costs and in sales-and-revenue expectations of firms prior to their investment plans, and the emergence of pure profits as a result of such cautious calculations by potential newcomers considering entry into an industry, was discussed by me in an article in 1942.[38]

Uncertainty in the expectations of business firms is conveniently broken down into three major parts: producer's uncertainty, buyer's uncertainty, and seller's uncertainty. *Uncertainty in production* may be due to vagaries of the physical environment, technological malfunctions, governmental interferences, or labor troubles resulting in work stoppages. Examples that come to mind most easily: weather conditions affecting crops, water supply, energy supply; technological malfunctions of generators, motors, transformers, transmissions, equipment of any kind; legislative and administrative impositions, ordinances, regulatory requirements, prohibitions; labor troubles such as strikes, slowdowns, absenteeism.[39] *Buyer's uncertainty*, or un-

---

[38] Fritz Machlup, "Competition, Pliopoly, and Profit," *Economica*, N.S., Vol. 9 (February and May 1942), pp. 1-23, 153-173; later included in Machlup, *Sellers' Competition*, esp. pp. 245-251.

[39] Hirshleifer coined the expression "event uncertainty" to denote the decision-maker's problem with things that may go wrong but are seen as "exogenous data." He contrasts it with "market uncertainty," which is due to actions and reactions of

certainty in input procurement, relates chiefly to markets for raw materials and intermediate products needed in production; potential disappointments may come from price boosts, shortages, inadequate qualities, or delays in delivery. *Seller's uncertainty* concerns the selling opportunities for the firm's products; this is probably the most serious of the uncertainties confronted by entrepreneurial and managerial decisionmakers, and it is surely the one most extensively and intensively explored and discussed by economists.

It will be important in all discussions of the effects of uncertainty to distinguish three aspects: (1) the effects on the thinking, decisions, and actions of the individual economic agent, here the business firm; (2) the effects on the interactions of members of groups, such as the industry (firms supplying competing products) or the market (suppliers and buyers), and on the resulting prices, quantities, and qualities of goods and services; and (3) the effects on economic welfare. Not in all discourses, oral or published, are these distinctions made; the derivation of the effects on prices, quantities, and qualities is often combined, without any warning, with implicit evaluations from the point of view of "society."

Much more has to be said about uncertainty and its effects on sellers and buyers. Most of the next two chapters will be devoted to this theme. The present chapter, however, may be concluded with a discourse on the role of "more and better information" on economics and on the economy.

Information: Its Effects on Economics and on the Economy

Can we distinguish between the roles information is seen to play in economics, on the one hand, and in the economy, on the other? Yes, we can and we shall.[40]

The question about a role (or effect) of anything in (or on) the economy can be answered only by an inquiry called "economics." Indeed, "the economy" is an abstract concept, or mental construct, formed in economics and nothing can be said about the economy except by talking economics. Still, economics looks at certain records of data, and new information may affect both the data and our ways of looking at them. Hence it is perfectly sound to make the distinction: information, say, its speed, accuracy, scope, coverage, and so

---

other economic agents and, because of conjectural interaction, are considered "endogenous variables." Hirshleifer and Riley "Analytics of Uncertainty," pp. 1376-1378.

[40] The next pages were presented at a conference on "The Role of Information in Economics and in the Economy," on 7 November 1980 at Northwestern University, sponsored by the Division of Information Science and Technology, National Science Foundation.

on, makes a difference to what people—economic agents—do; and it makes a difference to how other people—economic observers and analysts—observe, conceptualize, theorize. As a matter of fact, information may play different roles in the thinking and doing of both economic *agents* and economic *analysts*.

I can see two influences of information upon economics: *theoretical* economics is changed by the increased emphasis economists place on knowledge, information, ignorance, uncertainty, and so forth, and by computerized methods of simulation and, hence, of ascertaining the effects of different assumptions underlying the theoretical models; and *empirical* economics is changed by the amount of data available and by the speed, and indeed the practical possibility, of processing such masses of data.

That the distinction between the roles of information in economics and in the economy makes good sense can be seen from a simple deliberation. It is possible that the development of new information services, information machines, and information systems changes many things in the production and distribution of goods, in the organization of firms, in the habits of households, and so forth, without forcing the analyst to change his constructs, models, and general theories. It is equally possible that the analyst, under the influence of developments in the technology and/or supply of information, changes his modes of analyzing even if economic agents have not changed their modes of acting; he may change some of his favorite assumptions, his choice of data, and his techniques of treating his data.

What was said in these paragraphs can expediently be shown in a more systematic, more visible arrangement:

EFFECTS OF INFORMATION ON ECONOMICS

A. On theoretical analysis:
  (1) Novel *constructs*, *models*, and *assumptions* regarding knowledge, ignorance, uncertainty, expectations and their revisions, etc.
  (2) Better techniques of *simulation* through processing large quantities of assumed numerical pseudodata.

B. On empirical research:
  (3) New techniques of *obtaining* data through interrogation, for example, survey research, polling, and, more seldom, through experimentation.
  (4) Better techniques of *collecting* and *retrieving* recorded (documented) data, textual or numerical.

(5) Better techniques of *processing* large quantities of stored data, textual or numerical.

C. On scope and division of the field:

(6) *Addition of new specialties* in economics dealing with old and new problems regarding the creation and dissemination of knowledge, including such matters as demand, cost, supply, benefits, and externalities in the provision of information services.

(7) *Extension of old specialties* in economics to analyze changes in the economy due to new or radically improved information services and information machines.

EFFECTS OF INFORMATION ON THE ECONOMY

(1) Speedier communication allowing *faster responses in related markets* in different countries and different economic sectors.

(2) More effective and efficient dissemination of economic data, public and private, allowing *faster revisions of expectations*, adaptive or rational, on.the part of economic agents.

(3) Electronic communication in monetary or financial sectors increasing the speed in the *transfer of money funds and other assets* and affecting the functioning of money markets, foreign-exchange markets, securities markets, and commodities markets.

(4) Required heavy investments in very expensive equipment for information processing, especially computers, thereby diverting increasing shares of the total *investment into fixed assets*, possibly raising the incentives to invest, but perhaps crowding out investment in other capital goods, with undetermined end-results on factor productivity.

(5) Changes in the types of skills required for the functioning of electronic data-processing and communication, resulting in changes in relative rates of earnings and in the *educational and occupational structure of the labor force*.

(6) Automation of many previously manually controlled technical processes with the result that the *ratio of white-collar to blue-collar workers* tends to increase.

(7) Increasing dependence of management, staff, production personnel, suppliers, customers, government officials, clients, and the public at large on the proper functioning of electronic data processing and data retrieval from electronic memories with possibly serious consequences for the *bureaucratization of the economy and society*.

These are only a few examples of the consequences of the so-called information revolution for the economy as a whole. Particular developments can be seen in many specific sectors of the economy, most clearly in the information-machine industry (computers; calculators; copiers; word-processing, typing and composing machines; printing presses; control devices for many manufacturing industries) and in telecommunications. The revolution in teaching is still to come, provided the resistance of teachers can be overcome.

The effects of the information revolution included in the list above are all in the nature of long-run developments. The last of the seven propositions has also implications for *noneconomic* developments and for economic *short-run* possibilities. Certain political long-run developments have been predicted, referring to the power structure of society, sometimes called "postindustrial society"—a set of speculations accepted by many, but surely not all, political philosophers. The economic short-run possibilities relate to the increasing dependence of the information economy on the uninterrupted supply of electricity. The computerized economy is far more vulnerable to breakdowns in the provision of electric power than an economy that is less dependent on nearly continuous flows of masses of up-to-the-minute information. The risks of breakdowns, blackouts, and "downs" are quite real but probably do not seriously reduce the long-run benefits that society can derive from the new technology of information.

CHAPTER 3

INFORMATION AND PRICES: FUTURES, INSURANCE, AND PRODUCT MARKETS

IN THIS CHAPTER and the next we will survey those areas of the economic theory of knowledge and information that relate to the significance of information in the working of various markets for goods and services and, particularly, in the formation of market prices. The problems analyzed are chiefly those raised by the acquisition of new and timely information; and some of the complexities arise from the fact that such information may be highly uncertain, incomplete, biased, misleading, costly, available to some but not to others, and giving rise to expectations of further changes.

I should repeat that it is not my intention in this survey to touch on all themes now covered in publications, seminars, and lecture courses on the economics of knowledge and information. Nor do I want to treat any of the selected themes in any but cursory fashion. No attempt is made in these chapters to break new ground, extend the frontiers of economic knowledge, give specialists new insights, or present an outline of the field. What then are these chapters designed to do? They are, as I noted in my Introduction, designed "to tell intelligent noneconomists and nonspecialized economists what kinds of things are discussed in the economics of knowledge and information."

"Market information" or, more correctly, information obtainable to or obtained by actual and potential sellers and buyers, will occupy us in these chapters. We shall begin with a discussion of sellers' uncertainty and proceed to the subject of advertising. We shall then deal with futures markets, including the forward-exchange markets, with insurance markets, and with product markets. Labor markets and financial markets will be treated in the next chapter.

SELLER'S UNCERTAINTY

One may wonder why *seller*'s uncertainty is singled out here for special treatment. Is seller's uncertainty more important or problematic than the uncertainty of buyers of goods and services, of seekers of jobs, of investors or speculators? No, but it happens that the theory of the firm has developed a conceptual apparatus in which market positions are distinguished according to considerations "typical" for the seller visualizing his sales opportunities. "Demand as seen by the seller" is inherently uncertain, and the variables on which it is believed to depend are characteristically different under different market positions.

The Seller's Market Position

Under pure competition (alternatively called perfect polypoly, or atomistic competition), where the seller is a "price taker and quantity adjuster" expecting that he can sell at the current market price any quantity he may care to offer, seller's uncertainty is confined to future market prices. The seller cannot, acting alone, influence either spot prices (for prompt delivery) or futures (for delivery at specified dates in the future). Yet, these prices can vary and often are expected to vary: hence, uncertainty. Governments sometimes intervene in order to stabilize these "excessively competitive" prices; such attempts may, but usually do not, reduce seller's uncertainty. As a matter of fact, experiences with price-stabilization schemes have been poor, and recent discussions have dealt with business exposure to "regulatory risks."

Under most other forms of competition, seller's uncertainty is far more complicated, because the quantity he thinks he can sell depends on the price he charges (monopolistic competition, imperfect and perfect monopoly) and, as a rule, his sales depend also on prices charged and quantities sold by his competitors. If he includes among his considerations the possible and the most probable reactions of his rival sellers to his own actions, the cognitive processes of reaching decisions become quite involved; "conjectural variations," in the terminology of Ragnar Frisch, encumber the oligopolist's decision-making on selling policies. Needless to say, the uncertainty of sales expectations under unorganized and uncoordinated oligopoly is quite severe; in order to reduce such uncertainty—and the losses resulting from "price wars" and "cutthroat competition"—oligopolists try to form coalitions, collusive agreements, and cartels regulating (limiting, restricting, eliminating) competition in the market. In some countries, particularly the United States, collusion, agreements "in restraint of trade," and "concerted action" to limit competition, are unlawful, but it has not been possible to prevent such activities. It is very difficult to prove concerted action if it takes the form of announcements of prices (which competitors can be "expected" to imitate) or of systems of delivered prices where published freight rates are "guiding" the competitors' identical quotations of prices c.i.f. place of destination (basing-point systems).[1] Collusion of this sort is not explicit—there may be no letters or memoranda in the files and no evidence of the conspirators meeting officially or socially ("even for merriment and diversion," as Adam Smith wrote in 1776)— but conformance with implied agreements can be arranged by public announcements and other seemingly innocent signals.

Noncollusive Duopoly

The special case of noncollusive duopoly—only two sellers without collusion—has been given much attention in the literature, chiefly because it was analyzed as early as 1838 by the great mathematical economist Cournot, and invited critical modifications by other mathematicians and mathematical economists. Cournot's assumptions were rather peculiar; two of them, which were partly explicit, partly implicit in Cournot's own exposition, were formulated (in my 1952 volume) as follows:

> —The two sellers are assumed to be totally uninformed about each other's policies: each believes that, regardless of his own actions and their effects on the market price, the other would go on producing the same output that he just happens to produce. This belief is absolutely unfounded because in fact each seller regularly adjusts his output, whenever the situation changes, in order to maximize his profits as he sees them in the light of his erroneous belief about the other seller's policy. No experience to the contrary will shake this belief; each will adhere to it religiously and make his own decisions—concerning his output volume—on that basis.[2]
> —The two sellers, so ill-informed about each other's policy, are astoundingly well informed about the aggregate demand in the market. Not only the omniscient economists know this demand schedule—the two sellers know it also. This might be considered as a rather queer coincidence, because one cannot even say that they may have learned about the

[1] Systems of delivered prices usually involve discriminatory net prices f.o.b. place of origin. Under the basing-point system of pricing this discrimination is inherent in the system, an incidental result of the scheme to eliminate price competition. Fritz Machlup, The Basing-Point System, (Philadelphia: Blakiston, 1949).

[2] Justifying this assumption about the rather stupid beliefs of the two sellers about each other, Cournot said merely that "men cannot be supposed to be free from error and lack of forethought." Antoine Augustin Cournot, Researches into the Mathematical Principles of the Theory of Wealth (New York: Macmillan, 1927), p. 83; translated by Nathaniel T. Bacon from Recherches sur les principes mathématiques de la théorie des richesses (Paris: Hachette, 1838).

demand schedule by a trial-and-error method of output changes. For if they could learn by trial and error the exact reactions of the buyers in the market to the changes in output and the associated price changes, they surely could learn also each other's reactions to these changes.[3]

The assumptions made by Cournot's critics were equally unreasonable. (Note that my charge is not that they were unrealistic; unrealistic, even counterfactual, assumptions can be very useful.) They imply that each seller believes his rival would not react to his own moves although he himself regularly reacts to the moves of his rival. How can one imagine sensible people would imperviously stick to delusions that are exposed at every step they make? Modern theory of duopoly has adopted more reasonable ways to deal with the problem of two, or a few, persons trying to anticipate the moves and countermoves of their rivals. The development of the mathematical theory of games of strategy has put the theories of oligopoly on an altogether new track, though it has become increasingly doubtful that this track will lead to a determinate solution of the problem of noncollusive pricing.

The essential difference between theories of "conjectural variations" and the application of the theory of games is this: In the former theories it is assumed that each seller acts on the basis of some anticipations, however vague and uncertain, of his rivals' reactions to his own actions. In the theory of games each participant acts in such a way as to obtain a result that would be the best, or the least bad, in any event, including the most unfavorable countermoves the rivals may make to his move. He will adopt one of two kinds of "good strategies," either "pure" or "mixed" strategies. In the latter, a player plays "several strategies at random, so that only their probabilities are determined. . . . By this device the opponent cannot possibly find out what the player's strategy is going to be, since the player does not know it himself."[4] In my opinion, it is questionable whether these mixed strategies are of great importance in oligopolistic behavior. An oligopolist, more often than not, will not mind if his competitors find out what his own strategy is. Indeed, he often prefers them to understand the intent of his moves, because misunderstandings may lead to costly conflict.[5]

My skepticism regarding the fruitfulness of the application of game

[3] Fritz Machlup, *The Economics of Sellers' Competition* (Baltimore: Johns Hopkins University Press, 1952), pp. 372-373.

[4] John von Neumann and Oskar Morgenstern, *The Theory of Games and Economic Behavior*, 2d ed. (Princeton: Princeton University Press, 1947), p. 146.

[5] The preceding paragraph reproduces almost verbatim a passage from my *Economics of Sellers' Competition*, pp. 429-430.

theory to the problem of oligopolistic pricing has lately been shared by several writers. Herbert Simon regards attempts of finding determinate solutions of the oligopoly problem on the basis of the principle of profit maximization without empirical knowledge of the particular procedures of oligopolistic decision-making as "the permanent and ineradicable scandal of economic theory." And he adds: "Game theory, initially hailed as a possible way out, provided only a rigorous demonstration of how fundamental the difficulties really are."[6]

ADVERTISING

Sellers in positions of pure (atomistic) competition need never do anything to attract more buyers or larger orders, since—by definition—they can sell all they care to offer for sale at the market price. Sellers in more usual positions—monopolistic or oligopolistic competition—may find it advantageous to advertise in order to increase sales. Advertisements are designed to inform potential buyers where the products in question can be acquired, at what prices—presumably lower than from competitors—and in what special quality— presumably better than from competitors. In any case, the advertiser produces information, which may be new to the recipients of the message or may merely repeat (reinforce) what they were told before. As a matter of fact, the information may also be misleading or false, at least with regard to the claims about the quality of the products.

The Economics of Advertising

The economics of advertising is encumbered by the evaluative zeal of some of its analysts. There are those who see advertising as an unquestionable social blessing and those who see it as an unmitigated evil. Protagonists of advertising are convinced that everybody will be better off as a result of the information received, and that qualities will be improved and prices reduced thanks to advertising. Antagonists are sure that monopolists use advertising to manipulate consumers' tastes, to betray consumers' trust, and to enrich themselves

[6] Herbert Simon, "From Substantive to Procedural Rationality," in Spiro J. Latsis, ed., *Method and Appraisal in Economics* (Cambridge: At the University Press: 1976), pp. 140-141. — For an excellent statement on the "disillusionment" of game theorists with the usefulness of their apparatus for solving these problems as long as it was "totally lacking in any institutional detail," see Andrew Schotter and Gerhard Schwödiauer, "Economics and the Theory of Games: A Survey," *Journal of Economic Literature*, Vol. 18 (June 1980), pp. 479-527, esp. p. 480.

by excessive prices charged to the consumers.[7] Besides strong partisan views of the welfare effects of advertising, the literature contains also findings of "positive economics," based on theoretical analysis and empirical research.

One such issue relates to the firm deciding on its best selling policy. The firm has to combine three interrelated variables in an optimal fashion: selling price, product quality, and advertising expenditure. Price reduction, quality improvement, and increase in the advertising budget cannot reasonably be regarded as sheer substitutes, because they are partly complementary in their effects. True, a quality improvement in lieu of high advertising expenditures may, in the long run, increase sales, but the results may be much faster and better if customers are informed, by more advertising, about the quality improvement. The optimal combination of attractive pricing, improved quality, and effective advertising can be found in theory by geometric or algebraic techniques, provided the decisionmakers in the firm "know" how customers will react to each change in any of the variables. Such knowledge can at best be very vague, incomplete, and uncertain. What the seller can know with much greater certainty is how the best combination will change if competitors reduce their prices, if the cost of producing a top-quality product increases, or if the cost of advertising goes up. Thus we run again into the problem of the serious uncertainty of determining the optimum position, and the far less serious uncertainty of determining the direction in which elements in an apparent optimum position will change as a result of new information about changes in cost or demand conditions.

The analysis of optimal advertising budgets is far more meaningful with dynamic than with static adjustments. This is almost self-evident: none of the variables that affect sales will do so without delay. It takes a while for all potential buyers to learn of price reductions

---

[7] A convenient list of charges against advertising, compiled by Kirzner, includes (1) offenses against aesthetic, ethical, and moral standards, (2) misinformation, ranging from exaggeration to fraud, (3) manipulation of consumers' tastes, (4) reduction of competition and creation of monopoly positions, (5) wasteful expenditures, leading to higher prices and lower real output. Kirzner evaluates the charges and shows that few of them stand up to unbiased analysis. Israel M. Kirzner, "Advertising," *The Freeman*, Vol. 22 (September 1972), pp. 515-528. The issue of manipulation of consumers' tastes through "Madison Avenue type" of advertising by large producers of consumer goods has been addressed in the following (rather tendentious) comment: "The formation of wants is a complex process. No doubt wants are modified by Madison Avenue. They also are modified by Washington, by university faculties, and by churches. And it is not at all clear . . . that Madison Avenue has the advantage when it comes to false claims and exaggeration." Harold Demsetz, "The Technostructure, Forty-Six Years Later," *The Yale Law Journal*, Vol. 77 (1968), p. 810.

and to react to them; it may take even longer for them to become aware and convinced of quality improvements; and it stands to reason that consumer response to advertising will, as a rule, increase over time. The possibilities of alternative timing in the adjustment of the three variables raise challenging problems of dynamic optimization.[8]

Effects on Buyers

Just how does advertising affect actual and potential buyers? According to one answer, the advertisement either better informs buyers about the ways in which they can *satisfy* their given tastes or it *changes* their tastes. The second possibility would apply only to goods and services offered to consumers. Many writers assume that almost all advertising is for consumer goods, but this is not always true. Even if one disregards the large advertising expenditures by government departments and agencies (the U.S. Department of Defense is reported to be the largest single advertiser), one cannot overlook the fact that many producers of producers goods, of, for example, machinery and instruments, spend as large a percentage of their total sales on advertising as do producers that cater directly to consumers.

It has been proposed to distinguish between "search goods" and "experience goods." The consumer evaluates the quality of search goods by inspecting them before he makes the purchase; he evaluates the quality of experience goods through actual use after purchase.[9] Advertisements for search goods normally contain direct information about the qualities of the products so that the consumer can undertake his search and inspection more efficiently. Advertising for experience goods is chiefly designed to "signal" to the consumer that the producer invests large sums to establish and maintain the reputation of the product—investments that can pay off only if the firm continues to produce goods of high quality, thereby securing "repeat sales."[10] The importance of repeat sales of experience goods for the functioning of the market economy can hardly be exaggerated.

[8] Machlup, *Sellers' Competition*, pp. 182-197; Robert Dorfman and Peter O. Steiner, "Optimal Advertising and Optimal Quality," *American Economic Review*, Vol. 44 (December 1954), pp. 826-836; Marc Nerlove and Kenneth J. Arrow, "Optimal Advertising under Dynamic Conditions," *Economica*, Vol. 39 (May 1962), pp. 88-93; John M. Scheidell, *Advertising, Prices, and Consumer Reaction: A Dynamic Analysis* (Washington, D.C.: American Enterprise Institute, 1978).

[9] Phillip Nelson, "Information and Consumer Behavior," *Journal of Political Economy*, Vol. 78 (March-April 1970), pp. 311-329; and "Advertising as Information," *Journal of Political Economy*, Vol. 82 (July-August, 1974), pp. 729-754.

[10] James M. Ferguson, "Introduction" to Charles W. Baird, *Advertising by Professionals* (Los Angeles: International Institute for Economic Research, 1977), p. 3.

The good experiences of a satisfied customer are, of course, the logical counterpoint of the bad experiences that may induce a buyer to look for another source of supply. The cost of bad experiences and the risk of more bad experiences, added to the cost of search (time, effort, and money outlays), are part of the "full price" paid for the product; and this price may include also the cost of advertising defrayed by the producer or seller. It has been argued that "advertising affects the demand for goods because it lowers the gap between the market price received by the seller and the full price borne by the buyer—a gap that exists because of the buyer's cost of obtaining information about the characteristics of varieties of products and sellers, and the costs of adjusting to disappointing . . . purchases."[11] This does not necessarily mean that the information conveyed by advertisements is always "true" and reliable. It does, however, shift the role of advertising from a device for taste-changing to an element in the determination of prices paid and quantities sold.

This shift in the conception of advertising from "manipulation of tastes" to "provision of knowledge" need not be regarded as a matter of ideology. To be sure, Kenneth Galbraith sees advertising as the businessmen's way of creating "wants that previously did not exist." Galbraith holds that "outlays for the manufacturing of a product are not more important in the strategy of modern business enterprise than outlays for the manufacturing of demand for the product."[12] When Stigler and Becker oppose the distinction between "persuasive" and "informative" advertising, they do so on the basis of a time-honored methodological principle: not to introduce more variables where a few could do the job of explaining the data.[13] They argue that many observations that are ordinarily explained by differences and changes in tastes can easily be explained without them, that is, with just the set of variables conventionally used in the theory of demand, in particular, prices and incomes.[14] Tastes are "treated . . . as stable over time."[15] A good's "utility depends not only on the quantity of the good but also the consumer's knowledge of its true or alleged properties"; and it is now assumed that this knowledge,

[11] Isaac Ehrlich and Lawrence Fisher, "The Derived Demand for Advertising: A Theoretical and Empirical Investigation," American Economic Review, Vol. 72 (June 1982), p. 366.

[12] John Kenneth Galbraith, The Affluent Society (Boston: Houghton Mifflin, 1958), pp. 155-156.

[13] This rule, in general methodology, has been known as "Occam's Razor" or "the principle of parsimony."

[14] George J. Stigler and Gary S. Becker, "De Gustibus Non Est Disputandum," American Economic Review, Vol. 67 (March 1977), pp. 76-90.

[15] Ibid., p. 76.

"whether real or fancied, is produced by the advertising of producers and perhaps also the own search of households."[16]

The principle of parsimony need not overrule other principles of methodology. Those who feel strongly that advertising is not only a means to inform consumers but may in addition serve to develop or change their tastes are not necessarily out of order. Self-analysis and interrogation may, at least in certain instances, support the hypothesis that advertising has actually created wants that had not existed before. Still, it would not be easy to prove that these wants had not been latent or dormant, waiting to be awakened by the emerging knowledge that there was now an opportunity to satisfy them.

Effects on Market Constellation

Another effect of advertising on the buyer may be the development of consumer loyalty to the advertised brand. Such loyalty reduces the buyers' sensitivity to changes in price; this implies a reduction in the price elasticity of demand for the particular, more differentiated product. Lower elasticities suggest higher selling prices. This incentive to keep prices higher may or may not be offset by other effects of heavy advertising, for example, economies of scale facilitated by the large sales volume of the advertising firm.

Impressive research efforts have been devoted to the question of whether higher degrees of industrial concentration, and hence presumably greater market power, are associated with larger ratios of advertising expenditures to sales. Between 1964 and 1976 no fewer than twenty-three empirical studies on this relationship were published.[17] Some of these studies took the concentration index as the dependent variable, others made the advertising ratio the dependent variable. Whatever coefficients of regression were found—and several of them were statistically insignificant—it is by no means clear whether advertising is supposed to lead to concentration and monopoly power or whether firms that control larger shares of the market are shown to spend more on advertising. Connected with these issues is the question whether the large advertising budgets of existing firms discourage newcomers from entering the industry. The requirement of investing millions of dollars in advertising to conquer for a new product a modest share in the market may be a serious obstacle to entry: outsiders will not attempt to break into a field dominated by a few large firms with vast investments in advertising.

The advertising expenditures of producers and traders pay for a

---

[16] Ibid., p. 84.

[17] Stanley I. Ornstein, *Industrial Concentration and Advertising Intensity* (Washington, D.C.: American Enterprise Institute, 1977), pp. 68-73.

substantial part of the mass media of communication. In the United States the cost of the electronic media—radio and television broadcasting—is almost entirely paid by commercial advertisers. Of the print media, magazines and newspapers derive a major portion of their gross income from the sale of advertising space, and even some learned journals rely on revenues from commercial advertising as a welcome contribution to their operating cost. How would subscription rates and the numbers of subscribers be affected if the income from advertising were cut or eliminated? If advertising is considered by some social critics as a wasteful and undesirable activity, would the imposition of a tax on advertising be indicated as a remedy? What consequences could be expected from such taxation? Who would ultimately pay for such a tax? The advertiser? The consumer of advertised goods? The buyer of newspapers and magazines?

Some aspects of advertising are regulated by the government. The Federal Trade Commission attempts to stop false or misleading advertising. The economic questions regarding such regulatory activities relate chiefly to the benefits of preventing fraudulent and deceptive advertising, and to the costs of enforcing the promulgated prohibitions and remedies. Estimating the benefits of such regulation is particularly difficult, because in many instances market forces might suffice to terminate the unscrupulous dissemination of misinformation before widespread and irreparable damage is suffered by the consuming public. These questions, like many others in the economics of advertising, are unsolved and controversial.

Some economists have expressed concern about the possibility of ruinous competition arising from a combination of consecutive price cutting with informative advertising. Sellers, believing in the immediate effectiveness of advertising a slight reduction in price—a reduction they could not make were they not convinced that the "ads" can bring in the customers—may set out to conquer the entire market, or at least the lion's share of it. This could induce a sequence of competitive price-cutting until average revenue (per unit) was down to minimum average cost exclusive of the cost of advertising. Thus, producers would break even, except for their outlays for advertising, and therefore would suffer a net loss. This scenario was called the "advertising paradox."[18] The paradox was resolved by replacing the notion of "equilibrium with one uniform market price" with that of an "equilibrium price distribution."[19] Retail stores will

[18] Joseph E. Stiglitz, "Equilibrium in Product Markets with Imperfect Information," *American Economic Review*, Vol. 69 (Suppl. May 1979), p. 344.

[19] The use of "equilibrium" as an adjective modifying all sorts of things has become part of the economists' jargon. For the benefit of noneconomists, I should try to

charge different prices. Those charging low prices will have higher sales, those charging higher prices will be satisfied with lower sales, and none will have an incentive to change his position.[20] If, besides the dispersion of advertised prices, advertising expenses, and sales volumes, there is also a dispersion of product qualities and consumers' preferences, the supposed paradox disappears without leaving a trace.

FUTURES MARKETS

From a discussion of advertising, that is, dissemination of information about *differentiated* products supplied by firms in monopolistic or oligopolistic competition, we now turn to a discussion of futures markets—markets in which exclusively *nondifferentiated*, standardized commodities are traded, ordinarily (though not always) under conditions of pure competition. An earlier reference to expectations of particular "spot prices in the future" as distinguished from "present prices of futures" suggests the need of such a discussion of this theme. In any case, interactions between spot and futures markets are the subject of lively discussions in the economics of information.

Hedging and Speculation

Contracts for future delivery at agreed dates and specified prices are bought and sold in futures markets. Transactors are usually divided into hedgers, trying to reduce risks, and speculators, willing to bear the risks associated with possible price changes. A holder of an asset or a producer of a staple product can, by selling it forward, escape the risk of loss. A producer who has accepted advance orders for his output can by means of forward purchases protect himself against price increases of needed raw materials. An exporter who

---

elaborate. By "equilibrium price distribution" writers mean that there may be a dispersion of prices charged for the same or very similar (and therefore mutually substitutable) goods at the same time in stores not far apart from one another, and that this dispersion is sustainable in the sense that, in absence of changes in relevant circumstances—costs, incomes, tastes, prices of other goods and services, new information about existing or impending conditions, and so forth—no inherent tendency for a change in the given dispersion of prices exists. "Existence" of such an equilibrium does not refer to any concrete time or place but only to the idealizations of fictitious posssibilities (states and processes) in the theorist's mind. More on this in Chapter 8.

[20] Gerard R. Butters, "Equilibrium Distributions of Sales and Advertising Prices," *Review of Economic Studies*, Vol. 44 (October 1977), pp. 465-492.

expects to be paid in foreign currency can avoid the foreign-exchange risks by selling it in the forward market. Although it is conceivable that hedgers' supply is exactly matched by other hedgers' demand, such matching is ordinarily quite unlikely to happen. Differences may then be taken care of by speculators absorbing the hedgers' excess supply or meeting the hedgers' excess demand. Thus, the risk averters are helped out by professional (and occasionally also amateur) risk bearers.

The characterization of some transactions as "hedging" or "speculation" is to some extent arbitrary. In normal circumstances, producers and traders may carry the risks of possible changes in prices and exchange rates without even thinking about them; in times of serious fluctuations, however, the desire for risk coverage is increased. If firms that have normally carried these risks as parts of their general exposure to uncertainty suddenly come to the markets in search of futures contracts ("forward cover"), they are likely to be taken for speculators. Assume, for example, that large corporations, having for several years carried uncovered foreign positions, say, direct investments abroad, learn about ongoing or planned monetary policy and become nervous about the exchange risks; their attempts to cover these positions by borrowing the foreign currencies in question, or by selling the currencies in the forward market, may easily be interpreted, not as hedging operations, but as speculation. In strict observance of the accepted definitions, the corporations are *implicit speculators* as long as they are carrying their foreign positions uncovered, and become *explicit hedgers* when they act to cover their positions.

Hedging can eliminate a possible loss, but only by eliminating also a chance of profit. For example, the producer of a product, or any holder of an asset, who sells it (or an equivalent asset) in the futures market at a fixed price protects himself thereby against the possible loss from a price fall; but he foregoes an extra profit he might make if the spot price in the future were to rise. Speculators of the explicit sort have been called "pure speculators": their exposure to risk is not implied in "doing business" in an industry defined by criteria other than carrying open positions, long or short. Pure speculators are specialists in information, insights, foresight, and risk bearing. Any new single transaction by the pure speculator constitutes either the taking of a bet with *another speculator* who happens to entertain a contrary (or at least sufficiently different) opinion about the development of the particular market or the provision of forward cover sought by *hedgers* desiring to reduce their exposure to risk. In comparison with the hedger, the speculator has a lower risk aversion and/or he believes himself to have better foreknowledge of price developments. In other words, the speculator estimates his risk (in the sense of a probability) to be smaller and he is less averse to assume risks of given magnitudes. Although he collects from hedging businessmen a premium for the risk he takes, by reducing their uncertainty he reduces their cost of doing business.

Although individual speculators, favored by better information than the rest or by special foresight or by good luck, may make large profits, this need not be true for speculators as a group. For example, an empirical study of wheat prices in the 1920s concluded "as a statement of historical fact, that speculators in wheat futures as a group have in the past [a ten-year period] carried the risks of price changes on hedged wheat and have received no reward for the service, but paid heavily for the privilege."[21] This is by no means an exceptional case. Indeed, if large numbers of speculators operate in vigorous competition, everyone "seeking to take on a large commitment and make a big profit," the result under conditions of "perfect equilibrium" of the group, will be a net profit of zero.[22] In other words, "speculation under competition tends to yield nothing but interest on the money invested."[23] If this finding of positive economics is accepted, the verdict of evaluative economics can only be in favor of speculation as an activity beneficial to particular groups of producers and consumers. Does it say anything about the "economy as a whole"?

If speculators suffer losses, and producers and consumers of certain products benefit from the speculators' operations, does this imply that a net benefit accrues to the "economy as a whole"? Not if the speculators are counted as members of the same economy, and the producers' and consumers' gains are at the expense of the speculators. The question is then whether the gains are equal to the losses, or are larger or smaller. An analogy to transfer payments would suggest that gains and losses compensate each other, but an analogy to subsidies would not suggest this result, inasmuch as the price effects involved may influence the allocation of resources. The losses of the speculators, effective in reducing the cost of doing business, may operate like subsidies to the industry affected and result in more resources being allocated to it than would be optimal for "the econ-

[21] Holbrook Working, "Financial Results of Speculative Holding of Wheat," *Wheat Studies*, Vol. 7 (July 1931), p. 435. Quoted from Anne E. Peck, comp., *Selected Writings of Holbrook Working* (Chicago: Board of Trade, 1977), p. 10.

[22] John Burr Williams, "Speculation and the Carryover," *Quarterly Journal of Economics*, Vol. 50 (May 1936), p. 443.

[23] Ibid., p. 445.

omy." Moreover, the losses of the speculators may indicate that they bought at relatively high prices and sold at relatively low prices, which would imply that price fluctuations had been wider than they would have been without the speculators' misjudgments. If losses of speculators reflect a destabilizing influence of their operations, and if "unwarranted price fluctuations" are harmful to "the economy," the verdict of the welfare economist would be against the speculators. If all this sounds bewildering, then it sounds precisely as an evaluation of a complex process *should* sound.[24]

Premiums and Discounts, Carrying Costs and Inventories

Empirical and theoretical economists have long been puzzled by the fact that futures are quoted sometimes below and sometimes above the current price. In the foreign-exchange market one speaks of a "premium" if the forward rate is above the current spot price, and of a "discount" if it is below. In the commodity markets one speaks of a "positive carrying charge" or (in Europe) a "contango," and an "inverse carrying charge" or "backwardation."

Some writers believed that a positive difference, a contango, was "normal," because there are usually some stocks of commodities held in storage and no rational businessman would carry stocks unless he expected to be reimbursed for at least the cost of carrying them, including storage, spoilage, handling, interest, and risk. Other writers believed that an inverse (negative) carrying charge, a backwardation, was "normal," because producers and holders of a commodity prefer to avoid the risk of prices falling during the months ahead and therefore, as rational risk averters, would offer to sell contracts for future delivery of the commodity at a slightly reduced price.[25]

These contradictory generalizations are no longer accepted; whether quotations of futures are above or below current prices depends on several factors, some of which may pull one way or the other. For example, the past crop may have been unusually poor, or, on the other hand, it may have been a "bumper crop"; reports of conditions affecting the next crop may promote expectations for an average, a poor, or again a bumper crop. Some stocks of the commodity are

[24] The issues looked less bewildering to Nicholas Kaldor, "Speculation and Economic Stability," *Review of Economic Studies*, Vol. 7 (October 1939), pp. 1-27; reproduced with revisions in Kaldor, *Essays on Economic Stability and Growth* (Glencoe, Ill.: Free Press, 1960), pp. 17-58. Kaldor held that under certain conditions and within certain ranges, speculation is destabilizing and harmful.

[25] For a very persuasive exposition of the theory of normal backwardation see John Maynard Keynes, *A Treatise of Money*, Vol. II (London: Macmillan, 1930), pp. 142-144.

being carried in storage even if the price is expected to fall; these are "necessary working stocks" held to meet the contingency of customers' demands before the new crop becomes available. Economists have spoken of the "convenience yield" of these stocks held in the face of a future price below the current. Thus, the existence of stocks of commodities neither depends on the existence of positive carrying charges nor does it indicate irrational conduct.[26] The existence of inverse carrying charges, similarly, is far more often explained by special circumstances than by risk aversion on the part of producers and holders of commodities; expectations of favorable conditions for the next crop, for imports, or for other increases in supply after a particular date are most often the main factor explaining the backwardation, the low price of the future of the particular commodity.

The most commonsense generalization is that carrying charges will be inverse when stocks are relatively low and increased supplies are expected to come forth later; and carrying charges will be positive when stocks are relatively large and no unusually heavy increases in supply are expected. This generalization, however, refers chiefly to nonperishable crop commodities. There are perishable crop commodities for which the risk of spoilage is too high for long periods of storing; where storage is impossible, too expensive, or too risky, seasonable variations in price can be very wide. Most commodities traded in futures markets are eminently storable, but some—for example, metals—are subject to fluctuations in demand far more than to fluctuations in supply. For these commodities hardly any reliable generalizations have been developed. Not that traders and speculators in commodities operate without rules of thumb, but the existence of rumor mills, hunches, and supposed clairvoyance excludes the formulation of statements of any predictive value. A performance test of forecasts published in newsletters and advisory services can readily debunk the art of prognostication—except for periods of general money and price inflation, when forecasts of a rise can hardly fail to be correct over the long run.

The Future Spot Price and the Present Price of the Future

If expectations—of future demand, future supply, future government regulations, and so forth—are dominant factors in the determination of the price of any commodity for delivery at a stated future

---

[26] Accepted trade language is apt to confuse the reader. Carrying charges are not the same as carrying costs. The price difference between the May future and the September future is called carrying *charge*; the cost of storage, handling, interest, insurance, spoilage, and other risks is carrying *cost*. In many theoretical publications, however, the expression "carrying charges" is intended to refer to carrying costs.

date, are these expectations as a rule validated by the spot prices quoted when that date becomes the present? The answer is definitely no. This becomes immediately clear if one realizes that the "July future of wheat," to give an example, may have fluctuated from day to day over the ten months preceding July and that these fluctuations may have been over a considerable range. It is possible, or even likely, that in the course of these ten months the price of the July future was, by coincidence, on a few days equal to the price that eventually emerged when July came around and all open positions were closed. On all other days the price was different; since expectations change from day to day, only a small fraction of them can have been "correct."[27]

Some writers entertain the idea that one could find out what the "effective" expectations of the transactors were on any particular day by formulating an equation that expressed the actual price as a function of objectively given factors and some "expected" magnitudes. The fallacy behind this idea is the widespread but nevertheless erroneous belief that a price can express both the sellers' and the buyers' valuations. Clearly, at a given market price, the seller values what he gives up less than the buyer values what he acquires. Thus, the expectations entertained by the buyer are more optimistic than the expectations entertained by the seller. Moreover, the expectations of the nontransactors are left unconsidered in this approach, although they are of relevance in the determination of the elasticities of supply and demand. Also disregarded is the fact that there are intraday fluctuations of price; and the "fixing" of the price for the day, or for the morning or afternoon, is hardly representative of the expectations of those who bought or sold at a price above or below the final price or the one selected for the fixing. Finally, the specification of the algebraic function may fit the considerations of some types of transactor but not of others. In the case of cotton futures, information about the crops of the last few years, about past consumption, about the stocks in warehouses, and about open contracts may be generally known, as may be the official forecasts of the next crop. Speculators may discount these forecasts by different percentages; some may expect increases in demand next year, whereas others may not; some may expect larger exports or imports than others, some have better information than others regarding crops in

[27] Incidentally, the price at which the July future can be closed need not be the same as the spot price on July 1 for actual delivery. Wheat from the new crop "on track," whose owners want to avoid storage costs, may be cheaper than wheat in store. Indeed, in September, when elevators for wheat storage are full, wheat on track "without a home" may be much below the price of the September future.

other cotton-producing countries, and so forth. With these and other expectations influencing the bids and offers of market participants, it is difficult to see how an algebraic function can be specified that allows an identification of the variables.

Volatility of Spot and Futures Prices

Until recently it had been generally accepted that the existence of futures markets reduces the volatility of prices of commodities. As futures markets provide producers and consumers of the traded commodities opportunities to transfer, through hedging, some of the inevitable "price risks" to speculators willing to assume these risks, prices in both the spot and the futures markets are, presumably, made more stable. I had to qualify this statement for cases in which speculators misjudge the market situation and suffer losses. Such losses indicate that the fluctuations of prices have been wider than they would have been in the absence of the speculators' operations. On the other hand, if speculators have made profits, they evidently have bought the commodity when its price was low and sold it when its price was high, so that their operations must have moderated the price swings. This conclusion has recently been challenged on the basis of a different kind of argument.

The argument points to transactions costs. It assumes, correctly, I think, that the existence of futures markets reduces transactions costs; it further assumes that low transactions costs facilitate selling and buying at the slightest provocation; and it concludes that this greater sensitiveness to all sorts of information, including rumors, surmises, and vague conjectures, results in wider fluctuations of prices.[28] This is not an argument about "destabilizing speculation"; indeed, it may be an argument about "destabilizing hedging." The cheaper it is to change one's position in the market between "long" and "short," the greater will be the incentive to do so. As a matter of fact, this argument has been made with great vigor during recent debates about excessive fluctuations in the foreign-exchange market.

Forward-Exchange Markets

The most intensively explored futures markets are those for the exchange of currencies, the forward-exchange markets.[29] Published

---

[28] Joseph Abramoff, "The Inception of Commodities Futures Markets: Does It Cause Greater or Less Commodity Price Volatility?" Ph.D. dissertation, New York University, April 1982.

[29] In conventional terminology one speaks of a *forward* market for foreign currencies but a *futures* market for commodities. Yet, foreign currencies are traded also in some commodities exchanges, for example in Chicago, so that there exist also "futures

quotations of exchange rates, both spot and forward, are relatively reliable and comparable for different financial centers (though their locations in different time zones may prevent simultaneity of quotations); the markets are highly competitive (except where exchange restrictions impose controls and regulations); the traded "commodity" is standardized; and transactions costs are well known and relatively stable. These conditions facilitate research as far as interrelations of observed data are concerned, but the important influences of subjective knowledge—conjectures and expectations—are as difficult to explore in forward-exchange markets as they are in most other economic spheres.

As in all futures markets, the transactors are either hedgers or speculators, the latter taking risks, the former averting or reducing risks. The group of hedgers includes exporters and importers who want to cover their exchange risks—exporters by selling forward the expected foreign-exchange proceeds from their exports, importers by buying forward the expected foreign-exchange requirements to pay for their imports. Also among the hedgers are firms executing capital transactions, for example, debtors committed to debt service through payments in foreign currencies. An important group of hedgers are those engaged in "covered interest arbitrage," a business most germane to large banks and financial intermediaries with large foreign departments. Interest arbitrage takes advantage of differences in interest rates prevailing in the markets of different countries. Thus, when interest rates in London exceed those in New York, it pays banks to place in London funds borrowed in New York—provided they can cover themselves against a possible fall of the British pound sterling (or, what is the same thing, against a rise of the U.S. dollar). Uncovered interest arbitrage is very risky. Assume that the interest rate in London exceeds that in New York by 2 per cent per annum, or ½ per cent for 90 days; in this case a rise in the dollar by ½ per cent, say from $2.40 for one pound sterling to $2.388, would wipe out the gain from earning higher interest and would cause a loss of the transaction costs. Hence, interest arbitrageurs will want to cover their exchange risks; that is, they will hedge by selling the pound

---

markets for foreign exchange." Differences are chiefly that the futures are traded in the form of standard-size contracts with the "Exchange" (rather than a broker, dealer, bank, or a hedging or speculating firm); that in the futures market a margin requirement calls for deposits of cash, collateral, or guarantees; that the transactions are for set dates (only one closing date a month, rather than 30, 60, or 90 days from the transaction); and that the contracts are repurchased with U.S. dollars rather than fulfilled through actual delivery of the foreign currencies.

sterling in the forward market at the same time as they buy the spot sterling needed to lend out in London.

Competition in the foreign-exchange markets, both for spot and for forward exchange, and competition in the money markets (short-term credit markets) will lead to a matching of the spread between spot and forward exchange rates with the international interest differentials. The interest arbitrageurs, buying spot sterling and selling forward sterling for dollars, drive up the rate for spot sterling and depress the rate for forward sterling, until any further incentive for interest arbitrage disappears. It will disappear when the discount for 90-day sterling is equal to the interest differential that can be earned by borrowing in New York and lending in London. This matching of discounts (or premiums) of currencies in the forward exchange markets with positive (or negative) differences between the interest rates in their credit markets above (or below) those in the other country is called the principle of interest parity.[30]

The role of information in these operations is too obvious to require elaboration. The simultaneous transactions in the spot and forward exchange market call for price information available in the same room, and this is normally the case since the spot dealer and the forward dealer usually sit at the same long table in the bank's foreign-exchange department (and often one and the same person deals in both markets). Both dealers are in telephone contact with the dealers at other banks or currency brokers. For the transactions in the money markets long-distance communication, probably by telephone, is needed; the time difference may be somewhat inconvenient, since office hours in London are almost over when the New York bankers get to their offices, but this time gap is not a serious obstacle to the expeditious translation of information into action.

The role of information is far more complex with regard to the speculators' deliberations. The speculators' economic survival depends on their success in correctly guessing the emergence of a discrepancy between the present forward rate and the future spot

---

[30] This is one of the rare economic theories that can be more or less successfully confirmed in empirical tests, because the operational concepts correspond relatively closely to the theoretical constructs involved. Why only "relatively closely," why not completely? Because exchange rates, both spot and forward, vary several times during the day, and the actual rates at which the operations were transacted need not be the rates reported in the newspapers. The interest-rate differentials are even more arbitrary: the banks in question may have borrowed from large depositors in New York or in the Federal Funds market, and may have placed the funds in British Treasury bills, in commercial paper, or what not. The researcher has a choice of rates to use for his empirical test, but he can never know whether the chosen proxy is the most suitable.

rate. For example, the speculator who has bought forward sterling from the hedging interest-arbitrageur will make a profit only if he is able to sell these sterling 90 days later, when they are about to be delivered, at a spot rate above the forward rate contracted with the hedger. In order to form expectations regarding future movements in exchange rates, speculators will have to rely on a variety of data about trends and oscillations in rates, commodity prices, trade, and so forth, and on policy announcements, as well as on expert interpretations of these data and announcements. Such cogitations were relatively easy as long as countries were safely on the gold standard or under strict regimes of fixed exchange rates with only narrow bands around par values. Under a regime of managed flexible rates with substantial differences in the countries' inflation rates, the formation of expectations regarding the movement of exchange rates becomes a rather mysterious matter.

New information—unexpected "news"—plays a "predominant role" in the determination of exchange rates. Recent writers have decomposed the effects of news into those that alter the expected future spot rate and those that lead to a reassessment of the interest-rate differential. Empirical research is confronted with the difficulty of quantifying the news. In any case, it seems plausible to hold that "current exchange rates already reflect current expectations about the future, while changes in the current exchange rates reflect primarily changes in these expectations which, by definition, arise from new information."[31]

One point should be emphatically noted. Some bankers and economists talk about interest parity and purchasing-power parity as if these were two closely connected components in the theories of the determination of foreign-exchange rates. This is a mistake. If unexpected relative changes in the purchasing power of different national moneys—that is, different annual rates of price inflation—affect foreign-exchange rates, they do so only over the long run and not even vaguely proportionally—never precisely, and never in the short run. Interest differentials, however, affect the spread between spot rates and forward rates almost instantaneously and with great precision, provided markets are free, with arbitrage unrestricted. Even substantial changes in foreign-exchange rates, no matter whether or not they are parallel with changes in commodity-price levels, will leave interest parity in full operation: spot and forward exchange rates will

[31] Rudiger Dornbusch, "Monetary Policy under Exchange Rate Flexibility," in *Managed Exchange-Rate Flexibility: The Recent Experience*, Federal Reserve Bank of Boston Conference Series No. 20 (1978).

move together, but the spread between them continues to be determined by interest parity.[32]

INSURANCE MARKETS

The analysis of insurance and insurance markets has even earlier origins than that of foreign-exchange markets. Insurance contracts presuppose probability theory; works on this subject by Barrois (1834) and Cournot (1843) are usually given among the early references.[33] But with the recent growth of mathematical analysis as well as abstract-theoretical economics, the literature on the "informational aspects" of the economics of insurance has produced many refinements and important extensions.[34]

Disparate Knowledge About Risks

Studies of markets commonly divide their attention between the supply of the object traded and the demand for it; thus, a study of insurance markets can be expected to treat of the demand side—the insured and those who want to buy insurance—and, separately, of the supply side—the insurers. Although such an approach would be quite appropriate, the nature of insurance as risk-pooling makes it possible to treat the insurance market as a risk-sharing arrangement among those who seek protection against risks for which mathematical expectations can be calculated on the basis of long-term experience. The fact that the seekers of insurance can get together and arrange for mutual insurance implies—according to some analysts—that the opportunities for oligopolistic or monopolistic schemes of providers of insurance are effectively limited, barring govern-

[32] Jacob A. Frenkel, "Flexible Exchange Rates, Prices, and the Role of 'News': Lessons from the 1970s," *Journal of Political Economy*, Vol. 89 (July-August 1981), pp. 700-701. Among the early writings on matters related to the functioning of, and interactions between, money markets and foreign-exchange markets are George Joachim Goschen's *Theory of Foreign Exchanges* (London: E. Wilson, 1861) and Walter Bagehot's *Lombard Street: A Description of the Money Market* (London: H. S. King, 1873).

[33] Théodore Barrois, *Essai sur l'application du calcul des probabilités aux assurances contre l'incendie* (Lille: Société royale des sciences de Lille, 1843); Antoine-Augustin Cournot, *Exposition de la théorie des chances et des probabilités* (Paris: Hachette, 1834). In the sample bibliography in Chapter 4.7 below, Barrois' work is listed under 3.3 Insurance, but Cournot's work under 9.2 Statistical Decision Theory.

[34] To cite just one source, I refer to Karl Borch, *The Mathematical Theory of Insurance: An Annotated Selection of Papers on Insurance Published 1960-1972* (Lexington, Mass.: Heath, 1974).

mental restrictions on competition. Thus, even where insurance companies are operated for profit, one may treat the provision of insurance as if it were under a system of mutual insurance, with the companies merely acting as intermediaries handling the managerial and administrative tasks required by the risk-sharing arrangement.[35]

A priori reasoning has led to simple formulas for the determinate size of premiums for insurance against specified risks: they would be equal to the mathematical expectations of indemnifiable damages according to the actuarial experience for the typical group of insured.[36] To this amount one has to add transactions costs plus an appropriate safety margin for the accumulation of a reserve to meet the contingency of an accidental bunching of damages within a short period. Under the strict definition of mutual insurance, however, reserve accumulation would be unnecessary, since the funds needed for the indemnification of those who suffer insured losses would be assessed and collected from all members. In line with qualifications advanced by Hirshleifer and Riley, the "equilibrium price," that is, "each person's premium/indemnity ratio must [slightly] exceed the odds that he will suffer a loss."[37]

The most interesting insurance problems from the standpoint of the economics of knowledge relate to the fact that the group of actually or potentially insured may be composed of subgroups with different risk distributions. Typical differences in probability distributions of different groups ("risk classes") may be due to natural or behavioral causes. To take examples from health and life insurance, natural causes may be differences in mortality, morbidity, or susceptibility associated with sex or race; behavioral causes may be drug addiction, smoking, excessive use of alcohol, sugar, or other unwholesome foods. Instead of natural and behavioral differences in risks, one may distinguish unavoidable and avoidable differences.

[35] John M. Marshall, "Insurance Theory: Reserves versus Mutuality," *Economic Inquiry*, Vol. 12 (December 1974), pp. 476-492. — The theoretical analysis of mutual insurance usually disregards some very "practical" considerations: the policyholders may be less cost-conscious than profit-minded stockholders often are, with the result that the administrators of "mutuals" are sometimes overpaid and undermonitored. See Andrew Tobias, *The Invisible Bankers: Everything the Insurance Industry Never Wanted You to Know* (New York: Simon & Schuster, 1982).

[36] "In insurance a basic assumption is that there will always exist a unique amount of money which is the lowest premium at which a company will undertake to pay a claim with a known probability distribution. This assumption establishes an equivalence between certain and uncertain events." Borch, *Mathematical Theory*, p. 90.

[37] Jack Hirshleifer and John G. Riley, "The Analytics of Uncertainty and Information: An Expository Survey," *Journal of Economic Literature*, Vol. 17 (December 1979), p. 1387.

(Whether exposure to pregnancy should be regarded as an avoidable or unavoidable risk—confined to women—is an open question.) Examples of avoidable risk exposure in the field of fire and theft insurance include failures to install loss-reducing equipment such as burglar alarms, double locks, smoke detectors, fire alarms, sprinkler systems, fire extinguishers, and so forth. The economic problems associated with these distinctions are usually discussed under the heading "adverse selection" and "moral hazard." Adverse selection refers to the case of an undifferentiated premium being charged to different risk classes, either because it would be impossible or too expensive to sort the seekers of insurance into the risk class to which they belong or because the differentiation of premiums is ruled out for political or legal reasons. Moral hazard refers to cases in which the promise of indemnification for losses acts as a disincentive for the insured to reduce the risks of damage.

Adverse Selection

Adverse selection is often a problem of different information being available to the insurer and the insured, the latter knowing his risk class whereas the insurer is ignorant of it. Actuarial experience for the whole population (of the potentially insured) yields a mathematical expectation of the average risk, overstating the risk for some subgroups and understating the risk for others. With the premium determined by the mathematical expectation of loss for the entire group, "the high-risk class would be getting a bargain, but the low-risk class may . . . be better off without any insurance."[38] If the low-risk people drop out, and only the high-risk people stay in the insurance pool, the actuarial experience of the risk pool will eventually reflect the probability of higher losses, and result in a higher "equilibrium premium." This result, however, is not inescapable, for, if risk aversion is large enough, even those with low risk expectations will buy insurance. Still, one cannot reasonably expect risk aversion always to offset all large differentials in risk estimates; thus the "best risks," that is, those with the lowest loss probabilities, may stay out of the pool if the insurance premium is determined by the average loss probabilities of a pool that includes too many with much higher loss probabilities.

The problem of adverse selection disappears if the insurer can, perhaps at a moderate cost, identify the members of the different risk classes and if he is willing and permitted to charge differential premiums. Identification of the sex of the insured is without cost, and

---

[38] Ibid., p. 1389.

differences in mathematical expectations of mortality and morbidity for male and female buyers of health and life insurance are matters of record. The major difference in medical expenses is due to pregnancy with either abortion or childbirth; in old-age pension or annuity insurance the difference lies in the longer life expectancy of women, which means annuity payments for several additional years. Thus, actuarial experience would dictate lower premiums for men than for women. Uniform premiums for both sexes imply that men subsidize the insurance of women.[39] This is a timely subject in view of vociferous political demands for "equal treatment" of women and men. If insurance is compulsory, adverse selection is not relevant, and the compulsory subsidization in the name of fairness may be deemed of minor relevance in terms of social benefits and costs.

Moral Hazard

Things are different with regard to moral hazard, because the subsidization of the careless and irresponsible by the cautious and solicitous is conducive to social waste. The probability of loss or damage can often be reduced by appropriate investments and appropriate conduct. If insurance can be purchased at the same premium regardless of the insured having procured installations that can prevent certain accidents or reduce the damages resulting from accidents, and regardless of his risk-increasing or risk-reducing conduct, the insured will find such investments and such conduct unnecessary. Why should a business firm, as a hard-nosed maximizer of money profits, install expensive equipment to prevent or reduce damages for which it will be fully indemnified? As far as the insurance company is concerned, why should it engage in expensive surveillance, inspecting and monitoring the installations and operations of the insured, if it can charge premiums in accordance with actuarial experiences of a group that includes the insolicitous and careless along with the rest? It seems that under these conditions insurance systems cannot but lead to social waste—unless remedial arrangements can be instituted.

Remedies have been of various sorts: differentiating premiums according to the installation of loss-preventing or loss-reducing equipment; inspection and monitoring of plant, equipment, and the observance of safety rules, with surcharges levied for deficiencies;

[39] Some advocates of equality have called differential premiums "discriminatory." The definition of economic discrimination hinges on the relation between prices and costs; price differentials that reflect cost differentials are not discriminatory. On the contrary, price uniformity in spite of clear cost differences is discriminatory in the economic sense.

the provision of fixed amounts deductible from any indemnity payments, so that the insured himself pays for the first x dollars or y per cent of each damage claim; the provision of co-insurance by the insured, limiting the indemnity to a certain percentage of the damage. None of these remedies, however, can completely remove the disincentives implied in insurance without perfectly accurate assessments of the underlying risks being reflected in the actual premiums.[40]

PRODUCT MARKETS

Problems of moral hazard and adverse selection encountered in insurance markets and identified as consequences of "asymmetrical" availability of information to sellers and buyers exist also in product markets, especially in connection with differences in the qualities of products. In insurance it is typically the seller who has less knowledge, since the buyer can be better informed about the risk class in which he belongs. In product markets, however, particularly in retail markets, buyers (households) are typically less informed than the sellers about aspects of product quality such as invisible defects, risks of malfunction, breakage, and decomposition.

Knowledge About Quality

One analyst of "quality uncertainty" spoke of "the market for lemons."[41] A "lemon" is the American slang word for a product, such as an automobile, that proves defective after a relatively short time of use. The buyer does not deliberately or knowingly purchase a lemon, but he may be aware of the fact that what he acquires will, with some degree of probability, turn out to be a lemon. His estimate of this probability may differ from that of the seller, and the inequality of the underlying knowledge may have consequences for the performance of the market mechanism, or rather for the ways in which market signals guide the seller's decisions.

Brand-new automobiles may turn out to be lemons. As a rule, sellers (producers and dealers) will have an opportunity to obtain—within several months after the introduction of a new model—statistical information about the proportion of new cars that have de-

[40] For the classical statement of the problem of moral hazard in insurance for medical care see Kenneth J. Arrow, "Uncertainty and the Welfare Economics of Medical Care," *American Economic Review*, Vol. 53 (December 1963), pp. 941-973, esp. pp. 961-962.

[41] George A. Akerlof, "The Market for 'Lemons': Quality Uncertainty and the Market Mechanism," *Quarterly Journal of Economics*, Vol. 84 (August 1970), pp. 488-500.

veloped defects. Buyers' information will be confined to rumors or, at best, to reports from consumer-research organizations. It has been argued that buyers' estimates of the lemon risk are typically more pessimistic than those of the sellers, but to me the reasons for this hypothesis are neither obvious nor cogent.

A stronger argument about inequality of knowledge can be made with regard to second-hand cars, especially if the reference is not to dealers but, at least in the first place, to individual owners and individual buyers. The owner who has driven his car for some time, perhaps for years, knows the strong and weak points in the automobile that he intends to sell; he knows, for example, that the brakes may soon need new linings and that the fuel pump has been giving trouble, but he knows also that he has recently replaced the muffler, that the engine is in fine shape, and that reliable repair work has been done on the transmission. The buyer knows little and believes even less. He is convinced there is a high risk that he will acquire a lemon. If buyers typically overestimate this risk and thus underestimate the value of second-hand automobiles, they will bid only low prices, and car owners will sell at these prices only when they themselves think little of the quality of their automobiles. A would-be seller who is not forced, for some personal reasons, to sell his car, will refuse to sell it for less than it is worth to him. Owners will hold on to better cars; only real lemons will be sold. As a result of the buyers' distrust, due to their less complete and more uncertain information, the share of automobiles of inferior quality in the second-hand market will be greater than it would be if information were not asymmetrical. To be sure, there are different price ranges, but the average quality of second-hand automobiles will be adjusted downward in every price category.

The case of dealers is different in that they are both buyers and sellers of second-hand automobiles. With regard to the selling side of their business, one may again point to an asymmetry in knowledge about quality: the dealers may be a little better informed than those to whom they sell. This difference in information is largely a difference in the cost of search: the dealer may have more reliable knowledge of the car's history (he may be well acquainted with the previous owner) and he may have more expertise in inspecting and testing each vehicle before sale. Buyers, aware of their inability to obtain a "fair" appraisal of the automobiles, and distrusting the sales talk of the dealer, are unwilling to buy except at discounts commensurate to their high risk estimate. At these low prices the dealers cannot but sell "cheaper," that is, poorer cars. The (subjective) "quality risk" assumed by the less informed buyer results in larger shares of lemons being sold in the market.

There are probably no easy ways to test this hypothesis empirically; or to test its implications. But in theory the implications are plausible. The implications are (1) that owners of cars, disinclined to sell them below their "real" value, keep them for more years than they would if the prices in the second-hand market were not unduly depressed owing to the inadequate information available to buyers; (2) that the volume of production of new cars is less than it would be if owners could sell their old cars at higher prices, that is, "trade them in" more favorably; (3) that, because owners keep their cars longer, the percentage of relatively older cars in the second-hand market is greater than it would be otherwise, a circumstance that increases both the objective and the subjective risk that the cars are lemons; and (4) that the welfare of the people involved in making, acquiring, and using automobiles could be increased if the information of buyers of second-hand cars were more complete. Against these implications the welfare analyst will have to set the extraordinarily large cost of securing to the buyers so much dependable information that they would no longer overestimate the risk of getting a lemon. Guarantees might serve as substitutes for full information where the sellers are producers; individual owners of old automobiles cannot be expected to assume the quality risk by giving guarantees to the buyers.[42]

In some other markets the disparity in sellers' and buyers' knowledge about product quality may be more pronounced, and the arguments about the consequences more cogent. Assume a product for which materials of different quality can be used, affecting the risk of defectiveness and the length of the service life of the product. The producer knows full well which material he has used, but the buyer may have no practicable, cost-efficient way to test the quality. If the products look alike and consumers can differentiate qualities only by trusting the word of the seller, producers originally inclined to use materials of highest quality may find it difficult to compete with the makers of cheaper products. If they cannot convince enough customers of the better quality of their product, they will be forced to switch to the inferior materials and produce goods of poorer quality. This theory may be applicable to products sold in rather excep-

---

[42] There was a time when it was a widespread practice for owners to trade-in their cars after one or at most two years of use. This meant that the second-hand market had a larger share of automobiles of relatively recent vintage. As a result, the objective risk of second-hand cars being lemons was smaller, and the subjective risk-estimates of the buyers were probably lower.

tional markets. In most markets, practices and institutions have developed to avoid the presumed deterioration of product qualities: brand names, trademarks, guarantees, and similar devices allow the consumer to select "reliable" producers, give the producer a strong incentive to safeguard his reputation, and enable the producer to obtain prices that pay for the better quality of the product he supplies.[43]

Seller's Guarantees and Liability

The economic analysis of "guarantees against product failure" has generated very interesting problems. One analyst suggested that a "product should be thought of as a bundle of characteristics: a price, a distribution over the space of possible product failures, and an insurance policy. Guarantees are a form of insurance against product failure.[44] At the same time, "guarantees will act as signals of reliability" and are thus one of the common "sources of information."[45] Guarantees offered voluntarily to all buyers by the producer may be costly to him: he may have to make free repairs, exchange the defective product, or take it back. These risks borne by the seller will raise the price of the product to the buyer. In some situations— perhaps because of governmental regulations or because there are only a few producers—the buyer may not have a choice and thus must pay for "nonvoluntary insurance" against product failure. From these facts several questions arise for students of welfare economics: are the costs optimal to the two parties concerned—that is, the cost of the guarantee to the producer, implicit in the "fines" or penalties for product failure, and the cost to the buyer, implicit in the higher price of the product? Is the distribution of the risk among all parties concerned—seller, buyer, and possibly a third party affected by an accident caused by a defective product—optimal from the point of view of society?

Answers to these questions will be controversial since people's preferences, including risk aversion, are far from uniform and there is no such thing as a community indifference curve. This does not

[43] I should perhaps inform the reader that the economists who have treated these problems in the learned journals have rarely explained their theories in plain English. They could not dispense with algebra and systems of simultaneous equations and inequalities, involving ordinal or even cardinal utility, to prove the supposed failure of unregulated markets to serve the welfare of the community. My commonsense exposition cannot possibly convey to the reader the more sophisticated arguments or propositions of mathematical analysis.

[44] Michael Spence, "Consumer Misperceptions, Product Failure and Producer Liability," *Review of Economic Studies*, Vol. 44 (October 1977), p. 561.

[45] Ibid., p. 571.

prevent legislators, regulators, juries, and judges from imposing their own preferences on others on the conviction that they know what is best for society. The principle of caveat emptor, "let the buyer be on guard," a principle going back to Roman law and widely accepted until the first half of the twentieth century, has in many respects been abandoned for the opposite rule, to make the seller liable for product failures. The ideology of "consumerism," which has led to a fast spread of regulatory agencies and to policing the producers' performance, is firmly based on the notion of disparity in knowledge. The present popular idea is that less informed buyers of consumer goods and services ought to be protected against misperceptions. Although improvements in the availability of information (on weights and measures, ingredients, directives, warnings against malfunctions and other dangers) may be helpful, producer liability has been thought to provide the most effective protection. The benefits consumers may derive from such protection are manifest; its cost, however, is not adequately appreciated and not sufficiently researched.[46]

One disadvantage of guaranteeing minimum standards of quality is that the variety of products available in the market may be reduced. Some consumers might prefer to buy goods of lower quality at lower prices—but cannot find them. Among the more important problems of consumer protection by means of possibly costly guarantees is the possibility of moral hazard. The notion of moral hazard, first developed in connection with insurance contracts and premiums, is fully relevant with regard to the implicit insurance through guarantees

[46] Three dicta may be quoted to show what some specialists think about these questions:

A. "The effect of consumer misperceptions is that demand votes are miscast, and the supply-side produces the wrong products. . . . Demand will provide inappropriate incentives for producers to supply product reliability. The same dollar votes will fail to cause the supply of adequate levels of consumer protection against the residual risks, in the form of guarantees and other forms of voluntary liability, undertaken by producers." Spence, "Consumer Misperceptions," p. 561.

B. "It is often an implicit assumption in much of the legal and political literature on guarantees that a responsible firm should offer a complete guarantee against any random and unavoidable malfunctioning of its products. . . . such a doctrine is not in general compatible with the use of guarantees to secure an optimal allocation of risks. Optimality may require that some risks remain with the consumer. . . . profit-maximizing firms will overguarantee their products. . . ." And "guarantees as market signals . . . are overproduced by profit-oriented firms." Geoffrey Heal, "Guarantees and Risk Sharing," *Review of Economic Studies*, Vol. 44 (October 1977), p. 560.

C. ". . . although clearly the traditional presumption of caveat emptor has no basis within welfare economics when information is costly, the full implications of various attempts at consumer protection need to be examined carefully within a well-artic-ulated model of product market equilibrium . . . before their desirability can be correctly assessed." Stiglitz, "Equilibrium," p. 344.

against product failure. The probability of product failure is strongly affected by such factors as careless use and insufficient maintenance of the product acquired. This fact may have significant implications for conclusions arrived at by the welfare economists.[47]

Searching for the Best Buy

It would be unreasonable to assume that buyers know without cost or effort where to find the "best buy"—the best combination of price and quality of the goods and services they desire to purchase. Even where product and quality are undifferentiated, prices may be different and the buyer must "shop around" if he wants to get the lowest price. For most frequency distributions of price quotations one can confidently expect that more shopping-around will yield a lower lowest price, but that the expectation of finding a still lower price decreases as increasing numbers of suppliers are asked for their quotations. In technical language, search activity is subject to the "law of diminishing returns." The optimum amount of search is at the point where the cost of asking one more seller for his asking price equals the expected reduction of the lowest quote received.[48]

If quality is not uniform, the "best buy" is not just the lowest price, but the best combination of price and quality. If the cost of shopping around is considerable and the cost of testing quality before the purchase is substantial, consumers will find it cheaper to pay the prices asked by the seller and accept his assurance that the qualities of his products are unexcelled. Sellers aware of the "search aversion" of their customers may raise prices at least by amounts equal to the buyers' presumed cost of search, a cost in money, time, and convenience. Thus, even though the number of sellers is very large, all individual shopkeepers, counting on the search aversion of customers, may behave as if they were monopolistic competitors and thus charge higher than competitive prices, "quasi-monopoly prices."[49]

Some rather "unexpected" results should be expected to occur in some circumstances. Assume again that the number of shopkeepers is so large that none of them thinks that a reduction of his price would be so widely noticed as to attract an increase in business sufficient to make price reduction a profitable move. In this case it might pay a group of them to get together and form a chain or similar

---

[47] ". . . in its moral hazard's presence, there is an optimal degree of consumer misperception, an interesting case of two informational gaps sometimes being better than one." Spence, "Consumer Misperceptions," p. 571.

[48] George Stigler, "The Economics of Information," *The Journal of Political Economy*, Vol. 69 (May-June 1961), pp. 214-216.

[49] Stiglitz, "Equilibrium," pp. 339-340.

group of "thrift shops" or "cut-rate stores" that would become highly visible and attract shoppers who would seek out these cheaper suppliers. The case is unexpected in that it contradicts the rule that prices are lower if sellers are more numerous and independent. The explanation of the "paradoxical" outcome lies in the wider spread of information about the price policies adopted by the allied sellers and in the implied reduction in the buyers' cost of search for lower prices.

Quite apart from the existence of chains of cheaper stores, there may, in fact, be two or more classes of stores: low-price stores for shoppers with low search costs and/or low search aversion, and high-price stores for shoppers with high search costs or aversion. If there are very many buyers who are well informed and refuse to pay more than the lowest possible price, the market may become more competitive, and even buyers who are neither informed nor seeking information about the cheapest sources of supply may receive the benefit of lower prices. (A case of "external benefits": buyers who do not incur any search costs benefit from the shopping practices of those who do.)[50]

Economists have developed highly technical propositions about "optimal search rules." Following George Stigler's general theory of search, according to which search will be continued up to the point where additional search costs become equal to the gain expected from it, builders of algebraic models have investigated the relationships between search activity, search costs, price dispersions assumed to exist before the search, price dispersions discovered in the course of the search, reservation price (the maximum the buyer is willing to pay) before the search and subsequently affected by early search experience, and so forth.[51] These pieces of analysis, mostly purely theoretical, though interspersed with reverent bows to realism, ordinarily refer to retail markets, where individual householders trade with relatively small shopkeepers. The present fashion of analyzing these markets contrasts with the propensity of earlier economists to minimize problems of retail distribution and to emphasize wholesale trade and markets for interindustry trade. This is not to say that the disregard of retail distribution constituted a better allocation of the economists' time. Economists deal not only with the

[50] Steven Salop and Joseph Stiglitz, "Bargains and Ripoffs: A Model of Monopolistically Competitive Price Dispersion," *Review of Economic Studies*, Vol. 44 (September 1977), p. 494.

[51] Michael Rothschild, "Searching for the Lowest Price Where the Distribution of Prices is Unknown," *Journal of Political Economy*, Vol. 82 (July-August 1974), pp. 689-711.

practically most important problems but with any that appear intellectually attractive. The consumer's sequential search for the "best buy" can be a fascinating topic for research and analysis. For example, one learns that greater dispersion of prices charged for the same good can be expected to lower the searcher's reservation price as well as the expected cost of his search, but that the resulting increase in search activity is likely to affect the attitudes of some storekeepers and will tend to reduce the degree of price dispersion.[52] One also learns that shoppers "who fail to find low prices in their initial searches despair of ever finding them and become willing to accept high prices."[53] This is commonsense reasoning, but well worth pointing out.

Screening and Signaling

Searching as a market-related activity is not necessarily confined to would-be buyers; would-be sellers, too, engage in search activities, designed to seek the best outlets for whatever they have to offer. Indeed, job search, the search by suppliers of labor services for good buyers—employers—is an important subspecialty within the special field of the economics of information and will be reported on later in this chapter.

Two somewhat related activities of market parties have been explored: screening and signaling, the one designed to obtain, the other to transmit information. Sellers wanting to send messages about themselves and about the quality of their goods or services to potential buyers engage in signaling; buyers intent upon learning more about the sellers and the goods and services offered engage in screening.[54] The theory of signaling has formulated general propositions concerning the use of signals. Thus, "for a signal to be effective, it must be unprofitable for sellers of low-quality products to imitate

---

[52] Ibid., p. 692.

[53] Ibid., p. 700.

[54] "What I call signals, taking the seller's point of view, others have called screening or sorting, looking at things from the buyers' standpoint." Michael Spence, "Informational Aspects of Market Structure: An Introduction," *Quarterly Journal of Economics*, Vol. 90 (November 1976), p. 592. Spence's notion that the seller "signals" and the buyer "screens" is not in conformance with the general view of the function of screening. Also sellers of various services engage in screening; for example, the suppliers of loans and other forms of credit, the sellers of insurance, and the sellers of schooling (especially private higher education) screen the would-be buyers of their services. Some suppliers do both signaling and screening; for example, private schools and colleges signal the quality of their offerings and screen the quality of applicants for admission. — For comments on the semantics of "screening" see below, Chapter 18.

it."[55] This applies to the use of high price quotations as signals of high quality of products. A low-quality producer selling to permanent or long-term customers will find it counterproductive to imitate the price signals of competitors who offer better qualities. The misrepresentation implied in the high price would soon be found out and, hence, sellers prefer to abstain from using or continuing to use the wrong signals.

Two major types of signaling mechanisms have been distinguished: "contingent contracts" and "exogenously costly signals." With the contingent contracts we are back at the sellers' guarantees for the quality of their product. Guarantees, we recall, serve simultaneously to redistribute risk (among buyer and seller) and to transmit information (about the seller's confidence in his product). In instances in which the seller has *full knowledge* of the quality of his product, whereas the buyer can only rely on what he is told, the seller's contingent penalty for deviation of actual from guaranteed quality would never have to be paid. In instances, however, in which the seller knows at best a *probability* of the product being perfect or defective, penalty payments will be inevitable. The judgment of welfare economics is different in the two cases. In the former, "with no seller uncertainty, contingent contracts are efficient signaling mechanisms. There are penalties, but no one pays them" and the situation becomes, "in terms of resource allocation, indistinguishable from an equilibrium with perfect symmetric information."[56] In the second case, where quality is a random fact, and thus not known with certainty to either seller or buyer, one cannot maintain that the sharing of the risk of product failure is optimal from the point of view of society.

Exogenously costly signals—an infelicitous term—are defined as signals the costs of which are independent of buyer behavior. It is held that the transmission of information by means of these signals involves "a real social cost" and that "the performance of a market in which there is this type of signal can, in principle, be improved by taxing the signaling activity."[57]

Quality Competition

If producers can compete with one another by offering lower prices for given qualities or better qualities at given prices or a combination of both, the question suggests itself whether, in general, price competition or quality competition is "more effective" in attracting buy-

[55] Ibid., p. 592.
[56] Ibid., p. 594.
[57] Ibid., p. 597.

ers and in increasing economic welfare. Most economists are prepared to presume that price competition will be more effective because
price differences are more visible and more easily measurable than
differences in the quality of the products. Such an answer, however,
is somewhat primitive, for, precisely because of the greater visibility
of "price shading," sellers under conditions of oligopoly—conscious
of the rivals' possibly punishing reactions—may find quality competition the only practical way of attracting more buyers. Where each
seller is self-conscious, knowing that his rivals are watching him
and may quickly react to any competitive price move of his, he may
reason that certain improvements in the quality of his product cannot
be quickly imitated by his competitors. Even in fields of polypolistic
competition—among many small-scale producers—quality competition has sometimes been common practice. In some markets, such
as in the women's apparel and women's dress industries, conventional "price lines" were adopted, and manufacturers competed by
offering "better and bigger values" at fixed prices. Thus, it is not safe
to rely on simple generalizations about the economic significance of
quality competition.[58]

A serious difficulty lies in the fact that quality and, especially,
differences in quality may not be measurable. Whereas the quantity
of output can for most products be measured in physical terms,
quality often cannot be measured, chiefly because it has too many
dimensions. What matters for some materials may be smoothness,
flexibility, durability, toxic risks, resistance to water, pressure, or
stress, and so forth; for some appliances it may be the probability of
malfunction, of risk to users or others, or durability, outward appearance, size, and so forth; for automobiles it may be size, weight,
speed, fuel economy, maintenance cost, probability of malfunction,
longevity, riding comfort, style, and so on.

Some economic analysts have attempted to simplify their arguments by disregarding the fact that quality is multifaceted. Some
have made the convenient assumption that quality was a simple
function of production cost (usually average cost per unit of output,
sometimes incremental cost in excess of the cost per unit of the
lowest-quality product). This expedient, however, runs counter to
the fact that quality improvements require sometimes the installation
of equipment at a fixed cost, sometimes outlays proportional to the
quantity produced, and sometimes increasing or decreasing variable
costs. Even worse, the expedient neglects the possibility of some

[58] I have examined various types of quality competition in my book *The Economics of Sellers' Competition*, pp. 162-182 and 449-461.

producers making better products at lower costs. Thus, process inventions, innovations reducing the cost of making a product of given quality, would, if cost were taken as an index of quality, be misinterpreted as deterioration of quality.

It is true that it is usually possible for producers to improve the quality of their product by spending more on it; obversely, they may be able to economize by making an inferior product. But it is also possible to increase production cost and yet get a product of poorer quality. The idea of "measuring" or "expressing" differences in quality by differences in production cost is not acceptable except under very specific conditions.

Buyers Judging Quality by Price

Much analytical effort has been expended to analyze the problems that arise from buyers' inability to judge the quality of products by costless inspection before purchase. Economists examining these problems have sometimes failed to make the necessary distinctions between different types of products and types of buyers and have thoughtlessly generalized findings that applied only to particular buyers of particular kinds of products. If the buyers are business firms processing intermediate products acquired continuously or periodically, they have ordinarily suitable means of testing the quality of their inputs; indeed, in some industries the buyers of inputs know more about quality than their suppliers do. But even if the buyers are householders acquiring consumer goods regularly or frequently, they may well be capable of learning how to judge quality, perhaps not by sophisticated tests, but by experience, their own as well as the communicated experience of other householders. Thus, the problem of buyers' near-ignorance with respect to quality is important only in instances where householders buy the product only once in a long while, with intervals too long to permit a learning process leading to a modicum of judgment of quality.

In these instances it is possible that buyers are inclined to judge quality by price, that is, that they simply assume that a higher price asked by the seller is a "signal" of a better quality. Theorists must, of course, analyze the implications of this assumption, and they have done so with rigorous algebraic arguments. The results are common sense: if buyers really take the asking price as the only indication of the quality of the product and if there is no other way for them to distinguish an inferior from a superior product, producers will have no incentive to expend costs or efforts to produce high-quality products. Only the least-costly quality will be produced.

The theorists reaching this conclusion should, however, proceed beyond the demonstration of its internal consistency and validity and ask themselves whether the underlying conditions would be likely to persist. Would not the parties on the two sides of the market have incentives to change the conditions in such ways that quality competition would become feasible? We have learned that several effective signals of quality differentials, other than price differentials, have developed: trademarks, trade names, brands, guarantees; and, perhaps most importantly, the sellers' goodwill earned by a history of reliable service over long periods of satisfactory repeat sales.

CHAPTER 4

LABOR MARKETS AND
FINANCIAL MARKETS

THAT LABOR MARKETS and financial markets are treated in a separate chapter in this survey of the economics of knowledge and information should not indicate a thematic break. The reason for the break is merely a concern that few readers like to go over so many pages in one sitting and may prefer to have a breather at an appropriate point. Refreshed, we can now proceed.

LABOR MARKETS

Problems of information are of special importance in the working of the labor market: searching, signaling, and screening are activities affecting the supply of and demand for labor, the dispersion of wage rates, the rate of unemployment of workers with particular skills as well as of labor in general, the participation of persons of working age in the labor force, and other matters that bear on the operation of the labor markets. Much of recent economic analysis of these issues goes back to Stigler's general theory of search published in his article of 1961 and, in particular, to its sequel of 1962, "Information in the Labor Market."[1] The theory of job search has since developed into an intensively cultivated subspecialty. A survey article, published in two parts in 1976, provided a bibliography of 122 entries or, if we eliminate duplications in the second part, 102 items.[2] Of these 102 items, 80 were published between 1971 and 1976. The flow of publications in this subspecialty has been accelerating since then.

[1] George J. Stigler, "The Economics of Information," *Journal of Political Economy,* Vol. 69 (May-June 1961), pp. 213-225; and "Information in the Labor Market," *Journal of Political Economy,* Vol. 70 (September-October 1962), pp. 94-104.

[2] Steven A. Lippman and John J. McCall, "The Economics of Job Search: A Survey. Part I, Optimal Job Search Policies," *Economic Inquiry,* Vol. 14 (June 1976), pp. 15-189; and "The Economics of Job Search: A Survey. Part II, Empirical and Policy Implications of Job Search," *Economic Inquiry,* Vol. 14 (September 1976), pp. 347-368.

Search for Workers and Search for Jobs

Whereas most of the recent research has focused on job search, that is, on jobless workers' search for employment and employed workers' search for better jobs, one should not overlook the employers' searches for suitable workers. Search is definitely a two-way activity. And it need not always be a systematic, organized activity. "Information networks in labor markets" may be formal—for example, labor exchanges operated by governments (federal or state), trade unions, schools, colleges, universities, and profit-making employment agencies—or informal, such as referrals by word of mouth and hiring at the gate.[3] An employer can extend the search for suitable workers by interviewing additional numbers of job seekers or he can intensify the search by obtaining more information about those already screened.[4] Employers often prefer to use the informal information network, which may be costless and may procure more qualified and more reliable workers. Employers paying relatively low wages will more likely use the more expensive services of employment exchanges.[5]

Analyses of workers' search for jobs must first distinguish between an unemployed worker seeking any "acceptable" job and an employed worker seeking a better job than he has; and also between a "discouraged worker," who is unemployed but has given up searching, and a "contented worker," who is employed and satisfied with his job and, hence, not searching either.[6] Thus, just as the ranks of those actively searching for jobs include employed as well as unemployed workers, so do the ranks of those who are not searching. Of course, transfers among the four subgroups are frequent. Exogenous changes and information about these changes will affect the constituency of each subgroup, and subjective factors, such as aversion to risk-bearing and to exposure to uncertainty will influence individual decisions.

Major exogenous conditions affecting the number of those searching for jobs are (a) the "time efficiency" of search—how much time will it take to find an acceptable job (how many hours a week and how many weeks)—(b) the given "wage distribution" (the average of wage offers and their dispersion), and (c) the height of unem-

[3] Albert Rees, "Information Networks in Labor Markets," *American Economic Review*, Vol. 56 (Suppl. May 1966), pp. 559-566.

[4] Ibid., p. 560. — Three cheers for one of the rare economists who uses language properly and does not confuse intensive with extensive!

[5] Ibid., p. 563.

[6] Stephen McCafferty, "A Theory of Semi-Permanent Wage Search," *Southern Economic Journal*, Vol. 45 (July 1978), pp. 46-62.

ployment compensation. The time efficiency of search, in turn, will depend on the vacancy rate: the more vacancies the less time it will take to find a job.[7] "Wage distribution" is not easy to define, because if the dispersion of wage offers is wide, the jobs at the lower end of the wage scale may be deemed unacceptable, and the average may therefore not be relevant. In a rough way, however, it is reasonably clear what is meant: if potential wage offers are higher, job seekers will be inclined to wait longer and continue to search for a more attractive job. In other words, their "reservation wage" or "acceptance wage," or the lowest wage offer acceptable to them, will be higher if job opportunities look good.[8] That the level of unemployment compensation is a major factor in the determination of the number of job holders to quit and look for something better, and also in the determination of the length of time the unemployed will continue their job search, is obvious. The higher the unemployment compensation, the lower will be the "search intensity" (or, more simply, the less will be the search effort) of the job seekers and the higher will be their "reservation wages," the lowest wage offers they are prepared to accept. "Search unemployment" is increased as a result.

Although changes in the relevant factors are likely to affect the size of search unemployment, the direction of the influence is sometimes unpredictable. It seems clear that higher search costs will reduce the lowest wage acceptable to the job seeker and hence will reduce the duration of search and, consequently, the rate of search unemployment.[9] Yet, the higher cost of search (in terms of time and leisure to be sacrificed) may also reduce the effort devoted to the

[7] The use of the concept of "time efficiency of search," by combining hours per week and number of weeks devoted to the search, allows a simplification of the argument in that it merges two approaches to the problem: models of sequential search, based on the assumption of one contact made per period with the effort extended until the searcher finds it optimal to stop; and models of optimizing the number of potential employers contacted per period. It is unnecessarily clumsy to work with such constraining assumptions; the job seeker can make several contacts a week, sacrificing leisure if he is unemployed, or leisure and working time if he is employed; but there are limits to this concentrated effort, and the job seeker may have to extend the search for more weeks. For an exposition of the analytical problems involved, see Jess Benhabib and Clive Bull, "Job Search: The Choice of Intensity," *Journal of Political Economy* (forthcoming, 1983).

[8] An employed worker will hold out for a much better-paying job before he is ready to quit his old job; he finds that "the foregone possibility of continuing search" for something still better is "a cost of accepting an offer." McCafferty, "Wage Search," p. 48.

[9] John J. McCall, "Economics of Information and Job Search," *Quarterly Journal of Economics*, Vol. 84 (February 1970), pp. 117-119.

task, which may prolong the search. This offset is not likely to be sufficient, however, to neutralize the effect of the search cost upon the lowest acceptable wage. Another ambiguity in net effects may be found in instances in which the variance of wage offers increases. The consequent increase in the "marginal expected returns to search" may induce some job seekers to increase their search efforts but also to raise the lowest acceptable wage. For more risk-averse job seekers, however, the opposite may be more likely, which leaves the net effect undetermined.[10]

Wage Differentials and Discrimination

Why wages, at any moment of time, differ for different occupations, different regions, and different workers is far less puzzling than the fact that many economists seem seriously puzzled by the differences. Perhaps a habit of thought, the assumption of "homogeneous" labor in oversimplified models designed to explain the distributive shares going to the "three" factors of production, has made the explanation of differential earnings of labor a special problem of "advanced" economic theory. Or, perhaps, an egalitarian passion has made equal pay (for unequal work) an objective of social justice and has led to a conviction that differences in wages are evidence of discrimination and exploitation. No doubt, wage differentials *may* be discrimina-tory—if they exceed or fall short of the differences in the workers' marginal products—but the *absence* of wage differences is almost *certainly* discriminatory in a world in which individuals differ in strength, ability, age, training, industry, perseverance, motivation, and trustworthiness, and in which conditions of supply and demand are subject to change.[11]

Adam Smith, in 1776, was not puzzled by the existence of wage differentials; he devoted a chapter of his great book to the question of "inequalities arising from the nature of the employments" and "inequalities occasioned by the policy" of governments.[12] Smith found

[10] McCafferty, "Wage Search," pp. 52-53.

[11] "Comprehensive definitions of price discrimination will always be clumsy be-cause they must include price making by buyers as well as price making by sellers and they must refer not only to discriminatory price differentials for the same goods and services but also to discriminatory price uniformities or price similarities for different goods and services. For in most practical cases the goods and services subject to discriminatory treatment are not homogeneous and the discrimination can be dem-onstrated only by comparing their prices with what they cost the seller or what they are worth to the buyer." Fritz Machlup, *The Political Economy of Monopoly* (Balti-more: Johns Hopkins University Press, 1952), p. 136.

[12] Adam Smith, *An Inquiry into the Nature and Causes of the Wealth of Nations* (London: Strahan and Cadell, 1776; Routledge, 1903), pp. 77 and 93.

five "principal circumstances" causing inequalities: "I. The agree-ableness or disagreeableness of the employments themselves; II. The easiness and cheapness, or the difficulty and expense of learning them; III. The constancy or inconstancy of employment in them; IV. The small or great trust which must be reposed in those who exercise them; and V. The probability or improbability of success in them."[13] Smith discussed these causes of wage differentials in detail. The second cause, the cost and time of training and learning, has become a specialty in economics, the theory of human capital. The third, fourth, and fifth of the listed causes are all related to experience-ratings and information. Workers prefer steady jobs; they will have to be compensated by higher hourly rates in occupations that offer only seasonal, weather-dependent, or otherwise "inconstant" em-ployment. For jobs that call for special trustworthiness, only a se-lected few will be suitable, and their compensation will be accord-ingly high. Occupations in which the prospects of success are highly uncertain will be chosen only if the gains of the winners are high enough to offset the probability of failing. Risk averters are not at-tracted to these occupations for they call for "contempt of risk" and "presumptuous hope of success."[14]

Smith discussed three types of public policy that were causing inequalities in wages: (1) "Exclusive privileges" are "restraining the competition in some employments to a smaller number than would otherwise be disposed to enter into them"; (2) Subsidies for the training of certain professions are "increasing the competition in some employments beyond what it naturally would be"; and (3) Policies "obstructing the free circulation of labour," that is, reducing occupational and regional mobility, favor workers in some occupa-tions or regions and depress wages in others.[15] Smith mentioned, with regard to the first, restrictions on the number of apprentices and unnecessarily long terms of apprenticeship.[16] He also cited re-strictive municipal regulations and producers' conspiracies to raise prices.[17] His major examples of the second were ministers of the church and teachers.[18]

These three types of public policy seem to be sufficient cause to create large differentials in wages, but they are regarded as inade-quate to explain why the mean earnings of black workers in the

[13] Ibid., Routledge ed., p. 77.
[14] Ibid., p. 84.
[15] Ibid., pp. 107-113.
[16] Ibid., pp. 93-97.
[17] Ibid., p. 102.
[18] Ibid., pp. 103-107.

United States in 1967 were only about 65 per cent of those of whites. A few factors contributing to this difference in earnings can be easily explained. A small part is due to larger unemployment rates in occupations in which black workers are concentrated. Another small part is due to the different age distribution of white and nonwhite labor: the average age of nonwhites is lower, and earnings of the young are generally lower. That larger percentages of black workers are employed in low-wage occupations is often attributed to differences in school years completed. This difference has almost disappeared for those who are now leaving school, but it will not be reduced soon for black workers of all ages, since the older ones have had less schooling as well as inferior schooling.[19] To the extent that for these and other reasons the marginal productivity of black labor is below that of white labor, the differential in wages cannot be attributed to currently practiced discrimination. Yet, an evaluation of the relevant factors may, according to analysts, account for only 50 or 60 per cent of the difference and thus leave the remainder to be explained.[20] Can racial discrimination be the explanation?

[19] Kenneth J. Arrow, "Models of Job Discrimination," in Anthony H. Pascal, ed., *Racial Discrimination in Economic Life* (Lexington, Mass.: Heath, 1972), pp. 84-85. — That it takes so long for the effects of discriminatory schooling to disappear from mean differential earnings has several consequences that have not always been considered. For example, in a recent paper James P. Smith offers an interesting explanation for the conspicuous improvement of relative incomes received by male black workers between 1960 and 1970. Although incomes of young and middle-aged blacks did increase in that period to reduce the gap between black and white labor, Smith attributes a large portion of the improvement in the ratio for blacks of all ages to the retirement or death of the oldest cohorts, those born (and hardly schooled) between 1890 and 1900. In other words, attrition of the age groups with the lowest earnings can explain an improvement of relative mean earnings even if the earnings ratios in other age groups remained unchanged. James P. Smith, "Race and Human Capital," Paper prepared for a session of the National Academy of Education, May 1982 (not yet published).

[20] If average earnings of black workers are or were 65 per cent of those of whites, and if of this difference of 35 per cent some 18 to 21 percentage points are explained by factors other than discrimination, the remainder to be explained is 14 to 17 per cent. This seems to be consistent with several other findings cited by John S. Pettengill, *Labor Unions and the Inequality of Earned Income* (Amsterdam and New York: North-Holland, 1980). He refers to a finding that in 1967 black men "with no education" earned about 85 per cent of what white men with no education earned. This reference is to Albert Wohlstetter and Sinclair Coleman, "Race Differences in Income," in Anthony H. Pascal, ed., *Racial Discrimination in Economic Life* (Lexington, Mass.: Heath, 1972), but without a page reference, and I was unable to verify it. He further cites a comparison of earnings of black and white men with similar scores on the Armed Forces Qualifying Test, showing a differential of 20 per cent. Dave M. O'Neill, "The Effect of Discrimination on Earnings: Evidence from Military Test Score Results," *Journal of Human Resources*, Vol. 5 (Fall 1970), again without page reference. I assume

Racial Discrimination in Wages and Jobs

Let us distinguish wage discrimination—paying less for equal performance—from job discrimination—excluding certain groups from
jobs for which they would be no less suitable than the workers who
are hired. If equally qualified black labor is available in perfectly
elastic supply of wage rates below those paid to whites, it is hard to
explain why an employer should refrain from hiring blacks and thus
forego the opportunity of reducing his cost of production. To use
higher-paid labor where cheaper labor would perform equally well
seems to be an expensive luxury, not consistent with the usually
assumed business objective of maximizing profits.[21] If several employers indulged their distaste for black skin and employed whites
only, some more-profit-motivated entrepreneurs could, by employing cheaper black labor, capture the market for their product. If the
antiblack employers did not then give up their discriminatory hiring
policy, they would be driven out of business. Only if they were
sheltered by monopoly positions, protected against competition from
expanding or newly entering firms, could the discriminating firms
continue to afford their "discriminating" taste. Their managers would
not maximize profits but, instead, their personal utility; they would
be sacrificing pecuniary gains (and also the gratification of seeing
their business grow) in order to satisfy their preferences for white
skin.

Some economists do not believe that firms really have to sacrifice
profits if they indulge in wage or job discrimination, or that they
must abandon such discrimination if they want to maximize profits.
One theory of wage discrimination consistent with profit maximization refers to firms in monopsonistic positions as employers of two
or more substitutable kinds of labor.[22] These firms are faced with a
scarce supply of labor, scarce in the sense that employers can get

---

that Pettengill took this figure from Table 4 on p. 483. He cites another comparison,
between young black and white men of the same age, experience, education, hours
worked, marital status, and a test score measuring "knowledge of work opportunities,"
showing a differential of only 10 per cent. Charles R. Link and Edward C. Ratledge,
"Social Returns to Quantity and Quality of Education: A Further Statement," *Journal
of Human Resources*, Vol. 10 (Winter 1975), pp. 78-89. I was unable to find in this
source any statement to the effect cited by Pettengill. Incidentally, the small differential of only 10 per cent cannot be taken as evidence for a contention that racial
discrimination is unimportant, since young blacks do not as a rule have equal opportunities to acquire the same work experience as young whites.

[21] Gary S. Becker, *The Economics of Discrimination* (Chicago: University of Chicago
Press, 1957).

[22] Joan Robinson, *The Economics of Imperfect Competition* (London: Macmillan,
1932), pp. 292-304, esp. pp. 302-303.

more workers of a certain type only by paying more to them as well as to those already on their payroll. (Such a rising supply curve, or average labor-cost curve, for the individual firm—a condition that can exist when there are not many other firms around interested in cheaper labor—logically implies that marginal labor cost, that is, the cost of employing more workers, is higher than average labor cost. To hire additional workers costs the firm more than it has to pay them.) Profits will then be higher if employment of labor available under such conditions is kept lower. This theory is valid for the situation described, but one cannot reasonably suppose that such situations actually exist in sufficient frequency to explain wage discrimination against black labor. Black labor is rarely that scarce; as a rule it is quite plentiful in the sense that firms can find more of it at the going wage rate.[23]

More Arguments About Racial Discrimination

Several other arguments have been advanced against economists' conclusions that wage discrimination, that is, wage differentials in excess of differences in productive efficiency, would be unprofitable in normal circumstances and that employers indulging in such discrimination would sooner or later become unfit to survive. The arguments range from highly abstract modeling of special situations to broad sociological generalizations; in addition we are furnished references to historical periods when wage and job discrimination was reduced or suspended for a few years.[24]

If employers' personal preferences "were the sole cause of wage differences, it [would be] hard to believe that competitive forces are

[23] Besides the case of monopsonistic wage discrimination, discussed above, two other cases with similar results should be mentioned: collusive and noncollusive oligopsony of employers. For nontechnical explanations see my book *The Political Economy of Monopoly* (Baltimore: Johns Hopkins University Press, 1952), pp. 351-379, esp. pp. 352-362. My views regarding the frequency with which situations similar to those described in theoretical models are likely to occur in reality have changed over the years.

[24] All these kinds of argumentation are employed by dedicated fighters against discrimination whose analysis of the problem is in the service of their good cause. I am citing Barbara R. Bergmann, "Occupational Segregation, Wages and Profits When Employers Discriminate by Race or Sex," *Eastern Economic Journal*, Vol. 1 (April and July 1974), pp. 103-110; and "Reducing the Pervasiveness of Discrimination," in Eli Ginzberg, ed., *Jobs for Americans* (Englewood Cliffs, N.J.: Prentice-Hall, 1976), pp. 120-141. Bergmann's historical illustration is in the latter essay, where she points to the employment experience of the United States in World War II, a period of "acute labor shortage." "Very little if anything was said at the time about the lack of training of blacks, or their lack of good education or their poor work incentives" (p. 137).

inadequate to eliminate wage differentials."[25] One can, however, conceive of conditions leading to a lasting coexistence of all-black and all-white work forces at different firms—hence job discrimination but not wage discrimination. One conceivable condition making for an "equilibrium" with fully segregated firms would be the existence of strong racial preferences on the part of white workers, who would "condescend" to work in a desegregated plant or department but only with reduced effort and efficiency or only for higher pay. In this case, the profit motive would sustain the continuation of job discrimination against blacks. A strong force preserving such discrimination is the slow amortization of "personnel investment," that is, the cost of hiring, training, and firing workers. Even if the employer "himself has no racial feelings, the wage rate in full equilibrium will equal the marginal product of labor less the return on the personnel investment."[26] Only a sufficiently large wage differential would induce a firm to accept the loss of the personnel investment sunk into its white work force and make the new personnel investment required for the switch to a black work force.

Another explanation of persistent racial discrimination consistent with profit maximization and market competition has been proposed as part of a "formal model of caste equilibrium." Caste equilibrium "is defined as a state of the economy in which caste customs are obeyed, yet no single individual, by behaving differently, can make himself better off."[27] The point is that in a caste society strict rules dictate not only a code of behavior but also the punishment for infractions of the code. An employer hiring an "outcaste" will become an outcaste himself, ostracized and boycotted by white workers, suppliers, customers, and all with whom he has to deal in his business. Such a system can perpetuate discrimination unless a large coalition of its opponents "can break the equilibrium."[28] As long as the system survives, people "can predict from knowledge" of caste

---

[25] Arrow, "Models," p. 92. — Blacks are only 15 per cent of the labor force; the presence of even relatively few profit-motivated firms would suffice to eliminate racial wage discrimination. More specifically, if the managements of firms employing 15 or more per cent of the labor force thought larger profits to be preferable to the satisfaction of any antiblack taste, wages of equally efficient blacks and whites would soon be equal. The process of gradual equalization through market competition can, however, be retarded by trade unions enforcing equal wage rates for all, since initial wage differentials are needed to make it more profitable to employ black instead of white workers. John S. Pettengill, *Labor Unions*, p. 196.

[26] Ibid., p. 95.

[27] George Akerlof, "The Economics of Caste and of the Rat Race and Other Woeful Tales," *Quarterly Journal of Economics*, Vol. 90 (November 1976), p. 611.

[28] Ibid., p. 614.

relations how third parties would treat them in the case of infractions of the rules. "Such predictions can lead to an equilibrium in which all expectations are met and economic incentives favor obedience to the caste code—even in the extreme case where employers' tastes are totally neutral regarding the observance of caste customs."[29]

More plausible than the explanations of wage and job discrimination through models featuring employers' tastes, workers' tastes, or social caste codes are explanations based on prejudices concerning the quality of labor. The quality of labor differs widely and some differences cannot be easily discerned. The personnel officer of a large firm can look into the applicants' ages and school credentials and take these as indicators of some of their qualifications, but several other ingredients of quality can neither be judged from easily observed indicators nor tested except in time-consuming performance tests. "Skin color is a cheap source of information" for those who believe that the average qualifications of different racial groups are different.[30] Relying on the experiences of others or on his own, the employer may have come to the conclusion that the statistical probability of getting a good worker—steady, punctual, responsive, as well as hard-working—from the pool of applicants is lower for blacks than for whites. This is quite consistent with the possibility that many of the black applicants are superior, not only to many of the white ones, but also to the average whites. But how can they be selected from the pool? With no other criteria of selection available, statistical probability seems to be a reasonable consideration to go by, and this is prejudicial to the blacks.

A sad consequence of judging individuals by statistical averages or distributions of the group to which they belong is that it may lead to serious inefficiencies (quite apart from injustices). If a worker does not improve his chances of employment at better terms by investing in himself through more schooling and training, the incentive for self-improvement is impaired.[31] A vicious circle may result: the low average quality of the group will be reduced further if the practice of judging individuals by the group average removes incentives for self-improvement.[32]

[29] Ibid., p. 610. — The moral and political problems of a caste society are sometimes discussed under the heading of ethnic (or social) pluralism. An interesting point of view—regarding the "fundamental tension between pluralism and democracy"—is discussed in Stephen Steinberg's book on The Ethnic Myth: Race, Ethnicity, and Class in America (New York: Atheneum, 1981), p. 258.

[30] Arrow, "Models," p. 96.

[31] Akerlof, "Economics of Caste," p. 607.

[32] Arrow, "Models," p. 97. — Arrow points to the similarity of this process to the principle of "adverse selection" in insurance. See Chapter 3 above.

Lower Earnings of Women

Explanations of the substantial differentials that exist in wages and earnings of women relative to men may rely on some of the same theories as are used to explain differentials between black and white workers. The caste theory, however, would be utterly implausible. No sane person will maintain that suppliers or customers would inflict severe punishment on employers of women as "social out-castes." On the other hand, employers' ingrained tastes and male coworkers' preferences may well play a role in job discrimination; and employers' prejudices regarding the productive efficiency, suitability, or constancy of women workers could be significant factors in wage discrimination. Such prejudices may be due to insufficient or faulty information or, alternatively, to correct statistical probabilities regarding the composition of the female labor force. The latter, we recall, has been designated as "statistical discrimination."

In 1946 mean annual earnings of women, from wages and salaries, were 56 per cent of those of men; by 1969 they had further declined to 47 per cent. Virtually all of this gap between mean earnings can be explained as the combined effect of some independent variables not including sex—although the differences in some of these variables for men and women may in turn be seen as effects of attitudes or institutions biased against women. The major factors accounting for the observed differentials in mean annual earnings are (1) the number of hours worked during the year; (2) the amount of schooling and the subjects studied; (3) the amount of relevant job experience; (4) the occupation; (5) the type of employer. If women and men worked the same numbers of hours, had the same schooling in the same subjects, had the same job experience in terms of hours per year, years of employment, and uninterrupted stretches of employment, in the same occupations performed for the same types of employers, the labor earnings would be the same for women as for men.[33] In actual fact, there are systematic differences in all five factors affecting men's and women's earnings.

[33] "Indeed, Department of Labor surveys found that the differential almost disappears when men's and women's earnings are compared within detailed job classifications and within the same establishment." Barry R. Chiswick and June A. O'Neill, eds., *Human Resources and Income Distribution: Issues and Policies* (New York: Norton, 1977), p. 156. Contrast this statement with the following one: "Virtually all studies which have been done put the proportion of the sex differential and the race differential due to discrimination at greater than 50 percent." Barbara R. Bergmann, "Reducing the Pervasiveness of Discrimination," p. 129. The apparent contradiction between the two statements vanishes if each of the factors "explaining" some portion of observed differences in annual earnings is in turn related to some kind of discrimination, past or current, with varying proportions attributed to natural and cultural elements, sometimes even 100 per cent to prejudicial environmental influences.

The first factor, the difference in the number of hours worked per year, accounted in 1969 for 16 percentage points, so that women's mean annual earnings would have been 63 per cent of those of men, not the observed 47 per cent.[34] The second factor, differences in years of schooling completed, accounted in earlier years for another few points—4 per cent of the mean earnings of men in 1946—but by 1969 the school experience of women, measured in years of schooling, had caught up with that of men, so that none of the difference in mean earnings could be explained by this factor. But for college-educated workers, and hence those working in jobs requiring higher educational attainments, there was a conspicuous difference in subjects studied: men had majored largely in engineering, physical sciences, and business; women in education, humanities, and fine arts. The men's preparation therefore was for higher-paid occupations than was the preparation of women. That these differences did not show up more visibly in men's and women's mean earnings was due to the fact that in the lowest ranges of earnings, in occupations with low educational requirements, we find overwhelming majorities of men. The fact that 83 per cent of all managers and administrators were men whereas 97 per cent of stenographers, typists, and secretaries were women is statistically, in the determination of mean earnings, neutralized by the fact that 86 per cent of all farm laborers and 87 per cent of all janitors and sextons were men. Still, if one is interested in the upper ranges of skills and earnings, the difference in the choices of subjects taken in high school and college is of considerable significance.

The third factor is of great importance: men and women of the same ages have, on the average, very different amounts of relevant job experience.[35] Three facts may be behind this difference: (a) many

---

[34] Council of Economic Advisors. — The decline in mean annual earnings of women as a percentage of those of men from 56 in 1946 to 47 in 1969 was largely due to a larger increase of women in the labor force who worked fewer hours per week and fewer days and weeks per year.

[35] As I use the self-explanatory term "job experience," I should perhaps report on the use of an unintelligible jargon word probably meant as an equivalent. It is connected with the widespread misuse of the term "labor market." A reader confronted with the expression "labor market behavior" may ponder which of three possible meanings is intended: (1) the behavior of the labor market, (2) the behavior of [organized] labor in the market, (3) the behavior of one or more laborers or job seekers in the job market; yet, as the reader can find out if he endures, the particular author means none of the above nor anything that has to do with the market, nor with labor as a group or organization, nor with anyone's behavior in offering labor, offering a job, or negotiating wage rates or terms of employment. Instead, by "labor market behavior" the author means the job experience of a worker, that is, in how many jobs and for how many months or years a particular worker has worked up to now. Solomon William Polachek, "Sex Differences in College Major," *Industrial and Labor Relations*

women work fewer days and weeks per year, (b) many women enter the labor market for their first job later in life and thus are beginners at an age at which men have accumulated some years of job experience, and (c) many women interrupt their careers in order to have children and take care of them. This third element, job interruption for one, two, or even more years, is especially weighty; it explains approximately half of the gap between men's and women's earnings. We shall have to return to this point after we have completed going through our preliminary list.

Differences in the types of occupation open to women compared with those that seem to be "reserved" for men—the fourth factor— are often mentioned as chief explanation for the supposedly discriminatory gap in earnings. If the focus is on mean earnings of *all* members of the labor force, the gap due to occupational differences hardly exists, but in the upper ranges of the spectrum of skills and earnings, it is significant. (This is another point calling for further comment, to be made presently.) The last of the five factors enumerated, differences in the type of employer—size of organization, big corporations versus small firms—is probably connected with the conditions that strongly determine the differences in factors 3c and 4, the inconstancy of employment of women and the choices of studies preparing them for jobs.

A sixth factor, not so easily joined with the others in a regression analysis, is the lower geographic mobility of married women. They cannot, as a rule, move to the place where their job opportunities are most favorable, because they feel compelled to seek work near the location where the husband is employed. Indeed, when the husband moves to a better job, the wife, in order to keep the family together, may have to give up a good job for an inferior one near their new residence. If women stay with their husbands, and follow them when they move to better jobs, because they want to maximize family income and the husband's earnings are larger than theirs, the gap between the two increases. If, on the other hand, the woman's attachment to her husband is only a matter of tradition, convention, or religious commitment, and not the result of her pecuniary con-

---

Review, Vol. 31 (July 1978), p. 499. The same and other writers talk about "market work," skipping the word labor, but they do not mean the work *of* the market, or anybody's work *in* the market—such as time spent in job search—but, instead, work in paid employment. Jacob Mincer and Solomon Polachek, "Women's Earnings Reexamined," *Journal of Human Resources*, Vol. 13 (Winter 1978), p. 118. Thus, the phrase "persons who spend less time in market work" is supposed to mean persons with less time spent in paid jobs. The term "market work" evidently is designed to exclude students' homework, wives' housework, private scholars' research work, and all other work not included in payroll statistics.

siderations, the critical observer's verdict may be different. If the observer sees "discrimination" whenever a wage differential is not attributable to differences in potential productivity but instead to what he regards as social prejudice, he may have a point in support of his charge.

Discrimination Against Women

A statistical analysis that regresses mean annual earnings of the entire labor force on the first five factors mentioned can "explain" virtually the entire difference between men's and women's earnings without using gender (sex) as an independent variable. Some scientistic interpreters might take this statistical result as evidence against the existence or effectiveness of economic or social discrimination against women. Such a conclusion, however, would be naive, first, because statistical covariations (correlations, regressions, etc.) cannot establish or confirm causal relationships, and second, because, as I said before, some of the explanatory variables may in turn have come to be what they are as a result of discriminatory practices, institutions, or traditions. This can be maintained with impressive degrees of conviction with respect to the educational preparation (subjects studied) of women, the occupational choices of women, and the type of employers for whom women work.

The difference in the choices of subjects studied by men and women in school on the secondary and tertiary levels can well be attributed to entrenched prejudices about sex roles in our society. No biological, physiological, or other genetic differences dictate why women should take less course work in mathematics, physics, engineering, or business and, instead, flock into courses on teacher preparation, literature, and fine arts. No matter whether teachers, counselors, parents, or classmates are responsible for steering female students away from studies that would prepare them for occupations that require scarcer skills and offer higher rewards, or whether the students' choices are regarded as determined by their own tastes and preferences freely exercised in full knowledge of the sacrifice in future earnings, the educational choices in question are based on actual or putative discrimination. This discrimination may take several forms: strong, though unwarranted, beliefs in the genotypic capacity of females to master subjects demanding more abstract mental performance; strong cultural tabus against women becoming intellectuals and career seekers instead of taking care of babies and attending to household chores; and warranted or unwarranted beliefs that the more lucrative occupations for which the subjects in question have to be studied are virtually closed to women, so that the effort of preparing for them would be wasted. All these attitudes can be reasonably characterized as prejudiced and in effect discriminatory.

To the extent that young women's choices of courses of study are motivated only by their personal tastes and preferences, and not by such feelings as "what good would they do me in this world of job discrimination," one may say that the observed self-selection is not a matter of social discrimination against women. There is no way to determine this except through interrogation of students, and I know of no conclusive surveys of this sort.[36] In any case, some social psychologists and sociologists could attribute any "developed tastes" of young women to the lasting impressions of traditional "sex roles" assigned to them as children by parents, friends, and playmates.

As to the occupational choices of women, apart from the educational preparation for the occupations in question, suspicions of (past or present) discrimination seem even more strongly warranted. It is no coincidence that in 1970 only 1.6 per cent of all engineers, 3.6 per cent of all architects, 4.9 per cent of all lawyers and judges, and 9.3 per cent of all physicians, but as many as 82.0 per cent of all librarians, 92.0 per cent of all dietitians, 97.3 per cent of registered nurses, and 83.7 per cent of elementary-school teachers were women. These disproportions, shown in the official statistics of the United States, were clearly the consequences of discrimination in the past. That all the low figures had been even lower in 1960, and all the high figures even higher, suggests that women's shares are becoming less disproportionate. There can be little doubt that the low shares reflect restricted access of women to particular occupations. Indeed the fact that women have been kept out of certain occupations and therefore restricted to other occupations, open to both sexes, has reduced the supply of labor in the former and increased it in the latter, and thereby contributed to the maintenance of differences in the rates of pay in different occupations.

The figures thus far quoted are all for professional and technical workers, but the numbers for salaried managers and administrators reflect even more restrictive selections: there are many low-percentage shares of women in managerial positions, and no high shares at all. (One of the highest shares of women in managerial jobs is 40.2 per cent as building superintendents. Among the low shares of women

---

[36] Some (unreliable) clues can be derived from the findings, reported by Bruce K. Eckland, "Subject Index for Use with the 1970 Survey Questionnaire," Working Paper No. 2 (Chapel Hill: Institute for Research in the Social Sciences, University of North Carolina, 1972), quoted in Polachek, "Sex Differences," p. 502. The question "attended college because college graduates earn more" was checked chiefly by men, the question "attended college to marry well" was favored by women.

is "public administrators and postal inspectors": 6.1 per cent.) Only two explanations other than job discrimination merit consideration in this context: the actual or anticipated inconstancy in women's dedication to career work and, perhaps closely associated with the first, women's self-selection, which in these cases means self-exclusion from occupations that require degrees of constant involvement and undivided attention that are not compatible with women's roles as mothers.

The same explanations may possibly be suggested to account for the fact that relatively more women than men work in middle-sized and small establishments. In many smaller establishments women can more easily arrange for a few days off or for temporary leaves of absence, interruptions not always tolerated in large organizations. Whether employers prefer workers who promise greater constancy in holding and performing their jobs or whether female workers prefer employers who may be less insistent on such continuity, a pattern of job distribution will follow that apppears structured by the workers' sex.

Job Experience of Women: Later, Shorter, and Discontinuous

Differences in job experience of men and women are measurable and significant. They are reasonable indicators of workers' probable efficiency and general qualifications, and hence they are nondiscriminatory causes of differentials in compensation. The facts are that, on the average, women enter the labor force later in life, that their accumulated job experience is shorter, and that it has been reduced in effectiveness by discontinuities. All these facts are connected with childbearing and child rearing, functions imposed by nature and only in some minor aspects by culture.

Some analysts have used age as a statistical proxy for postschool experience. Yet, life experience is not the same as job experience and does not contribute as much to productive capacity, the essence of human capital. Neither age, the number of years since birth, nor the number of years since leaving school is an acceptable indicator of job qualification. If women enter the labor force only after their children no longer need them, they are beginners, in any job other than mothering, at an age at which men have had a chance to accumulate job experience. The competitive market pays for job experience but not for mothering, notwithstanding the private and social value of the latter.[37]

[37] The effect of delayed entry into the labor force is reflected by the systematic widening of the gap between men's and women's earnings for higher age groups. At ages 20 to 24, working women earn 70 per cent of men's annual earnings; at ages 45

Women's job experience is shorter than that of men, not only because of its later beginning but also because of its interruptions. This would be true even if interruptions were not also eroding some of the productive capacities acquired in paid jobs. The simple fact that women work fewer hours and weeks per year, and sometimes leave their jobs for one or more years in order to take care of their children, results in smaller accumulations of human capital, at least of that part of it that is represented by earning capacity.

Now add to the lateness and shortness of women's job experience the undeniable fact that interruptions in the use of productive capacity on the job may result in its deterioration. In contrast to some physical capital, which deteriorates through use (wear and tear), human capital deteriorates chiefly through nonuse. The notion of atrophy of human capacity as a result of significant interruptions in its use was developed by Jacob Mincer. On the basis of ingenious computations with data on wages and earnings he estimated that a one-year interruption resulted in a lowering of average money wages by 1 per cent; a two-year interruption, by 3.6 per cent; and a three-year interruption, by 19 per cent. (Corrected for simultaneous rates of price inflation, the reduction in real wages associated with a three-year interruption was shown to be 13 per cent.)[38]

Atrophy through job interruptions is more severe for higher skills. In other words, productive capacity deteriorates faster in occupations demanding more schooling and training and paying higher rates of compensation. This atrophy through job interruption has a twofold effect upon earnings of women: *actual* interruptions reduce their rates of pay, and *anticipated* interruptions reduce the incentives to prepare for jobs that promise better pay and therefore greater losses from discontinuity. This suggests that women who anticipate that they will want to stay home from work for shorter or longer periods of time will find the returns to the investment required for preparing for better-paying occupations substantially reduced and unattractive. Hence, these jobs are attractive only to those who can count on working in them without serious interruptions, that is, to men and to only those women who do not plan to have children and take care of them.[39]

---

to 54, they earn only 59 per cent. The main cause is that women enter the labor market at higher ages as beginners. Chiswick and O'Neill, *Human Resources*, pp. 26-31.

[38] Mincer and Polachek, "Women's Earnings Re-examined," p. 123. According to the data for the same sample, 15 per cent of the women holding jobs in both 1967 and 1971 had "one interruption," 8 per cent had two, and 2 per cent had three. (I assume "one interruption" is to mean a "one-year interruption.")

[39] Ibid., pp. 131-132.

A more general statement about women in different types of employment can be made if one, in accordance with Gary Becker's proposal, distinguishes three types of jobs, different in the kind and amount of learning experience they offer to the worker. There is (A) the job that gives the worker a highly specific experience, usable only in the particular occupation in the particular firm; (B) the job that gives the worker a rather general experience, transferable to employment in the other firms; and (C) the job that gives the worker little learning that would make him gradually more valuable to the current employer or to the other employers in the same or other industries.[40] Commonsense reasoning suggests that employers will be willing to pay for the training period in Type A jobs, where the workers over time become more valuable to them, but not to others, so that employers need not fear that the trained employees will quit for other jobs. Yet, this consideration cannot be extended to female workers, who may quit in order to work on mothering or to move away with their husbands. Thus, employers will "discriminate" against women, though this cannot be regarded as discrimination in the economic sense, since one cannot expect employers to invest in the training of employees they are likely to lose before the investment has paid off. In Type B jobs, providing general and transferable training, employers will not pay for the cost of training new workers; that is, novices in this kind of employment will have to pay for their training by accepting low starting wages. Women, anticipating that they may want to quit before long, that is, before the pay would become higher (reflecting the more qualified labor), will not want to accept this type of job. Type C jobs, providing no particularly valuable training and hence costing little either to employers or to employees, pay higher wages than Type B jobs pay to beginners but are no-growth, dead-end jobs. These are the jobs available as well as acceptable to female workers.

These reflections offer a reasonable explanation for the very unequal distribution of jobs and for the observed fact that women are chiefly in jobs that neither require nor provide valuable learning experience.[41]

The Significance of Information and Knowledge

The question may be raised again why the analysis of women's wages and of differentials between men's and women's earnings from

[40] These ideal-typical distinctions will be further discussed in Part Two of this volume; see Chapter 13.

[41] For a clear exposition of these ideas see Isabel V. Sawhill, "The Economics of Discrimination Against Women: Some New Findings," *The Journal of Human Resources*, Vol. 8 (Summer 1973), pp. 383-396, esp. pp. 338-394.

labor is seen as a part of the economics of knowledge and information. (Not that the subject was taken away from those professing
labor economics or the economics of income distribution, but the
modern specialists in the economics of information have claimed
special competence in dealing with some of the problems involved.)

These claims can be sustained on the basis of the following considerations: schooling, choice of subjects studied, and training on
the job are among the chief factors regarded as responsible for the
observed outcomes; choices of occupations and employers by job-
seeking women, and choices of suitable workers by employers are
made on the basis of information and informed expectations regarding a variety of probability estimates. Occupations and employers
are selected with a view to skill requirements and probable returns
to the necessary investments in human capital under various conditions, such as individual dedication to and constancy in the paid
work or, alternatively, anticipations of work interruptions or divided
allegiance to career and to family. Workers are selected by employers
with a view to the statistical (group) probability of productive efficiency, dedication, and constancy. Women who are determined to
put career ambitions ahead of family concerns will escape prejudicial
"statistical discrimination" only by transmitting the right signals to
employers, indicating that they are not to be judged by the average
qualification of the group but by their exceptional characteristics.[42]

These few lines—with their references to schooling and training,
to job seekers' and employers' information and expectations, to private investments in human capital, to adverse selection of occupations resulting in "statistical discrimination," and to signals transmitted by especially qualified workers determined to break out of
the confines of typecasting and statistical group averages—amply
justify the incorporation of these "labor problems" in the special
field of economics of knowledge and information. It would be wrong,
however, to think that these are the only labor problems assigned to
the new specialty. In order to show that the overlap between labor
economics and information economics is much wider, I present the
case of the formation of expectations of upward pressures of wage
costs leading to so-called "rational" anticipations and responses on
the part of employers deciding on investment and price policies.

Wage Push in the Short Run and the Long

The question is whether upward pressures of wage rates by trade
unions will in the long run change income distribution in favor of

---

[42] No value judgment is intended here. The "exceptional" characteristics refer merely
to a self-selected difference from the average of the statistical aggregate.

labor at the expense of profits and property incomes. This question has been debated for more than a century. "The one side is just as firmly convinced that strong bargaining increases the workers' share in the national product at the expense of capitalists as the other side is convinced that in the long run the workers in unions with greater bargaining power obtain their gains at the expense of workers in weaker unions or no unions."[43] The "visible evidence" in support of the union argument seems strong, but it refers only to *money* wages of particular labor *groups* in the *short* run. The issue is whether one may legitimately ascribe to successful trade-union actions an increase in the *real* wages of labor *as a whole* in the *long* run. Statistical analysis has not been capable of deciding the question. "By and large, the annual changes in the relative share of labor income are associated most closely with changes in business activity and corporation profits—labor's share being the highest in the worst depression years with serious unemployment, and lowest in prosperity years with high levels of employment and profits."[44]

If empirical evidence is not conclusive, reliance on theoretical reasoning is all that is left to the contenders. Those who hold that wage pressures by strong unions redistribute the national product largely at the expense of members of weaker unions or no unions, or of the unemployed labor force, but not at the expense of profits, point to long-run adjustments to the wage boost: higher prices in the higher-wage industries, lower rates of investment in the lower-profit industries, reduced job opportunities in the industries paying the increased wages, larger numbers of job seekers in the more open industries paying lower wages, and larger numbers of unemployed. Those on the other side of the argument do not have much respect for such long-run theorizing. Assume, for example, "that the wage increases secured by collective bargaining can temporarily encroach upon profits; that the adjustments, which eventually shift the incidence from the owners of enterprise to consumers and unorganized workers, take time; and that, before this time is over, the unions act again and secure another advance in wage rates; would this not invalidate the theory? If the trade unions never allow the economy enough time for the adjustments to work themselves out, if they move again and again and always stay ahead of the game, is it not the short-run theory that should be applied? Since there will always be a short run, are not the short-run effects the ones that really count?

"These are highly suggestive questions and one is easily persuaded to answer them affirmatively. But what they really call for is an

[43] Machlup, *Political Economy of Monopoly*, p. 394.
[44] Ibid., p. 397.

examination of the meaning of 'long-run' adjustments in this context. Probing into this, we can see that it covers very different things, some of which may take a lifetime of a plant whereas others may take no more than the reaction time of an alert businessman. We can see, moreover, that adjustment periods have no fixed clock time or calendar time, but may become shorter and shorter as the same sort of stimulus recurs and the pattern of response remains essentially the same. The stimuli are the wage pressures by trade unions, the responses are investment decisions and price decisions by business- men. At first it could be assumed that it would take many years— namely, until the replacement of deteriorated equipment becomes necessary—for the forced wage cost increases to be followed by re- duced investment in the affected industries. As time goes on, how- ever, one will have to assume that entrepreneurs include trade-union wage pressures in their expectations, so that their investment deci- sions reflect, not past 'disappointments,' but rather 'anticipations' of future cost increases. In other words, investments may be adjusted or even overadjusted to union wage pressures long in advance. Price decisions, which first are assumed to wait for the determination of the exact effects upon production cost or even for the emergence of inflated demands for products, may later have to be assumed to be coincident with, if not anticipatory of, the acceptance of a new wage contract fixing increased rates of pay.

"In brief, what in an analytical model is regarded as the short run may be without relevance to reality, and what in the model is called the long run may refer to adjustments that in reality may not be long delayed but, instead, may be practically instantaneous or even in advance of the impulse that 'causes' them."[45]

The kind of reasoning in which the long-run outcome of a series of sequential steps in a process of adjustment "modeled" by eco- nomic theorists becomes the expectation of economic agents re- sponding immediately (if not in advance) to some disequilibrating events, has now been promoted to the theory of (so-called) "rational expectations." This theory, alluded to in the context of several themes in this volume, will be critically examined in Chapter 8. The criti- cisms to be raised there against some of the assumptions and im- plications of the theory do not, however, invalidate the simple hy- pothesis proposed by me in 1952, according to which economic agents can learn from experience to form expectations and to respond to certain events so speedily that the short-run effects are squeezed out and the long-run effects become the "instant impact." The point

---

[45] Ibid., pp. 408-409.

is that the employers' expectations of future wage pressures by strong labor unions will raise product prices and reduce investments in plant capacity—adjustments that, as a rule, would follow unexpected wage increases only after a long lapse of time.[46]

FINANCIAL MARKETS

In most markets there is little doubt about the object of trade, about what is supplied and what is demanded. In a product market, for example, despite all varieties in quality, size, weight, delivery terms, and so forth, the general convention leaves no doubt: on the supply side, producers, traders, or their agents offer the specified product for sale (or hire) against money (or promises of money), and on the demand side, users (processors, consumers), traders, or their agents seek to purchase that product with money (or promises of money). Language is sometimes less clear with regard to the job market: the supply of jobs is a demand for labor, and the demand for jobs is a supply of labor. Yet, few readers allow themselves to be confused by this ambiguity; most of them translate statements about the job markets into statements about the labor market and see on the supply side workers offering their labor for sale (hire) against money, and on the demand side employers promising to pay money for certain types of labor. Confusion, however, reigns in common parlance as well as in specialists' discourse about financial markets; in some financial markets money to be paid immediately is traded against money to be paid later, and it can be quite bothersome to ascertain which of the two is meant to be the object of supply and demand.

Whether it is *present* money or the promise of money in the *future* that is supplied and demanded in the market depends often on the form in which the promises of future money are certified. If these promises are in the form of negotiable long-term debentures or obligations, such as bonds, or of equity (ownership) shares, such as stocks, the markets in which the securities are traded regard these promises of future money (payments of interest, dividends, or principal) as the objects supplied and demanded. Present money is paid and received in exchange for the securities purchased and sold. This is not common practice, however, in all markets for long-term credit.

---

[46] My views on profitability, investment, and industrial employment seem to be entirely consistent with such recent theories as those rigorously formulated by Edmond Malinvaud, *The Theory of Unemployment Reconsidered* (Oxford: Blackwell, 1977). See also his article "Wages and Unemployment," *Economic Journal*, Vol. 92 (March 1982), pp. 1-12.

In the primary mortgage market, for example, the loanable funds, the present money offered as mortgage funds, are the objects of supply and demand, and the mortgage is merely the legal interest in the real property that serves as security for the long-term debt. The sides are reversed in the secondary mortgage market, where previously created mortgages are bought and sold, and present money is paid and received in exchange. In short-term credit markets, however, it is always the present money that is the object of supply and demand; the future money is simply the promised repayment of the loans granted and taken. In the money market the time interval between present money being borrowed and lent and future money being repaid and collected is very short, sometimes—as in the case of overnight money—less than twenty-four hours. Still, supply and demand in this market refers to the present money, not to the promises to repay the loans.

Even with regard to the money market, where the immediate funds as well as the promises to repay are regarded as liquid, economists cannot resist the use of confusing terminology; they like to speak of the demand for money to borrow and of the demand for money to hold, the former a "market demand" or "flow demand" for short-term credit, the latter a "stock demand" (not a market demand) for cash balances, including check deposits in commercial banks. To be sure, the concept of a stock demand for money balances plays a role in the explanation of the flow demand for, and flow supply of, credit; but it should be understood that only the latter—the flows—are market phenomena.[47]

The semantic problems regarding financial markets can be solved with a modicum of care and good will. Would that the substantive economic problems could be solved that easily! Information, imperfect knowledge, risk, and uncertainty play different roles in the

[47] I cannot in good conscience fail to warn the reader about the deplorable lack of terminological discipline in the discipline of economics, or in plain language, the growing incidence of word theft. During the last twenty years the term "money market," which had enjoyed a stable meaning for at least 200 years, was stolen and misappropriated to designate an altogether different concept that involves no market at all. What is now inappropriately named "money market" is to represent some total of preferences of owners of wealth to *hold* in their portfolios stocks of a variety of assets— to hold, not to sell or to buy as one does in a market.

To be sure, changes in the "stock supply" or in the "stock demand" for whatever it is that can be purchased or sold may explain changes in the "flow supply" or in the "flow demand" for the good or asset in question. That all four constructs can be represented in the form of functions or curves does not make them all into "market functions"; only flow functions picture market conditions. The inappropriateness of the new terminology is compounded by the fact that the object of trade in this misnamed "money market" is *not* money.

different credit and capital markets; indeed, the information sought, produced, offered, disseminated, and acquired by the parties involved—by lenders and borrowers of liquid funds, by buyers, brokers, and sellers of old securities, by issuers, underwriters, and buyers of new securities—is usually about quite different matters, so that it is not easy to formulate general propositions fitting all financial markets. The biggest differences are probably between customer-loan markets, on the one hand, and securities markets, on the other. That the suppliers of present money expect their returns (earnings) in very different forms—interest, dividend, appreciation and capital gain—is only part of the story.

Customer Market for Loans

The characteristic property of the customer market for loans is that it involves personal relations, usually negotiations, between lender and borrower, even where the market as a whole is reasonably competitive.[48] The supply of loanable funds to the individual borrower is never perfectly elastic, and the borrower is therefore never in a position of "pure competition"; he is, in the jargon of economic theory, a "monopsonistic competitor" for loanable funds. This means that his cost of borrowing—interest rate and other expenses—is higher for larger amounts than for smaller, with the result that the marginal cost of borrowing is higher than the average cost.[49] The positions and upward slopes of the curves representing the average and marginal costs of borrowing will depend on the information the lender has about the borrower and his credit standing. In particular, he may want to know all that can be learned about the borrower's assets, liabilities, credit history, past and current production and sales, inventories, past and current incomes, past growth, present investment plans, prospective orders, expected selling prices of his products, organizing and management abilities, technological competence, labor relations, standing with suppliers, customers, competitors, auditors, character and experience of management personnel, and sim-

[48] Arthur M. Okun, *Prices and Quantities: A Macroeconomic Analysis* (Washington, D.C.: Brookings Institution, 1981), p. 188 — I shall not distinguish in these brief observations between consumer loans and business loans, and between commercial loans (with maturity of less than a year) and term loans (with maturity exceeding a year).

[49] To realize that the borrower is hardly ever in a position of "pure competition"—where he can borrow without limit, that is, as much as he may want at a given rate of interest—is not to condemn such an unrealistic assumption as worthless for all purposes. Such a model may have its uses, for example, to help explain why it is essentially counterfactual and why quantitative rationing of loans is practically inevitable as far as most borrowers are concerned.

ilar "data" that may bear on the borrower's business practices, integrity, reliability, earning capacity, and risk exposures.

It is on the basis of such information that the supplier of loanable funds decides on the upper limit of his lending to a particular would-be borrower. A lender may dislike differentiating the interest rate among different clients, lest he may get angry complaints about "unfair" discrimination; he will, instead, differentiate by the sizes of the loans he offers. He will lend only $20,000 to one customer but $200,000 or even $2,000,000 to others, whom he considers to be better risks. The would-be borrower, on the other hand, may be shopping around for the loan or loans he needs or can profitably use in his business or in his private affairs. He will often find that he may obtain larger amounts if he is prepared to pay higher interest rates (inclusive of other costs of borrowing). But even if he has no such choice—no possible trade-off between the size of loans obtainable and his cost of borrowing—there will still be an increasing cost of funds sought for any particular purpose whenever alternative uses of funds compete for the funds at his disposal.[50]

The kinds of knowledge, of new information, and of revised expectations that influence the decisions of the borrowers are fundamentally different from those influencing the lenders. This hardly needs saying, but I say it here because it does not hold for some other financial markets. On the stock market, for example, virtually the same kinds of information affect potential buyers and potential sellers of existing securities; by and large, the question relates to the chances that prices of, or returns on, certain shares of stock will rise or fall. In the customer market for loans, however, the parties on the two sides of the market decide and act on the basis of very different considerations—with perhaps one exception, namely, the promise of returns to the project for which the would-be borrower alleges to

---

[50] Two ways of reasoning are commonly used in theoretical models and their graphical representation. The user of funds, say, a business firm, may think of *all possible* uses and arrange them in descending order of expected profitability. This would yield decreasing marginal productivity (or marginal "efficiency") of investment funds. Alternatively, he may think of a *particular* investment project of his, to which he may allocate increasing amounts; each additional dollar, or lump of money, would involve some stinting on his other projects; but since he would reduce alternative allocations of funds first to the *least* profitable uses and then to *more* profitable (more promising) projects, the opportunity cost of additional funds devoted to the particular project under consideration would be increasing. Thus, the marginal cost of funds to any project is increasing even when the interest rate that lenders charge to the firm is invariant. These considerations apply to all kinds of users of funds, not just to those in the customer market; they are equally relevant to firms raising funds in the capital markets.

seek finance. However, the fact that both lender and borrower may look into this information bearing on the probable returns to a particular project is not of great importance. The lender is more interested in the existing assets and the ongoing returns to the previous investments of the seeker of new funds; moreover, he knows that money is "fungible" and that the funds supposed to finance a carefully specified project may in fact free the borrower's funds for other purposes. No banker worth his salt will be so naive as to believe that the soundness of his loan will depend on the merits of the "new" project described by a would-be borrower. The larger the firm that seeks a loan, the less will its alleged uses of the new funds bear on the lender's considerations. My conclusion is that the possible exception to the rule—that lenders and borrowers look for different information—does not seem to be of importance. The two parties in the customer market for loans are interested in *different* kinds of information.

Credit Rationing

Many of the economic problems associated with the commercial-loan market have been discussed in the literature under the heading of credit rationing. The practice of quantitative rationing of credit, however, is not confined to the customer-loan market; it is applied on three levels: (1) rationing of central-bank credit by fixing a limit to the level or growth of either the total of loans outstanding or the total of all debt assets (loans and securities) held by the central bank; (2) rationing of central-bank lending to any particular commercial bank (or other borrower); and (3) rationing of credit by a commercial bank to any particular borrower.[51] The problems of credit rationing on these three levels are quite different, and so are the types of information sought and evaluated by the parties concerned.[52] What is common to all types of credit rationing is the interrelation between "availability" and "cost."[53]

[51] A fourth practice, an alternative to rationing of central-bank credit to (or borrowing by) commercial banks, is the imposition of limits to commercial *lending*.

[52] Dwight M. Jaffee, *Credit Rationing and the Commercial Loan Market* (New York: Wiley, 1971). This author has attempted to analyze the problems of credit rationing at all levels, which involves both macroeconomic and microeconomic data and theory.

[53] Rationing through quantitative allocation is a technique of distributing a limited supply and thus to some extent an alternative to the setting of prices. Would it perhaps suffice, in the case of bank credit, to set the quantity, that is, the amount of credit available, and leave the price, the rate of interest, unchanged? Assume the interest rate for commercial loans were fixed at 6 per cent per year, but commercial banks were able to purchase in the market at a price of 50 long-term bonds, paying 6 per cent a year on the nominal value of 100. The actual yield of the bonds would then

Personal and Impersonal Markets

Having discussed some problems of information with regard to the market for commercial loans, the most "personal" of the financial markets, I may execute a double somersault landing at the other extreme, the stock market, which for the bulk of day-to-day transactions is the most "impersonal" financial market. In the typical organized stock exchange only members do the trading, chiefly on behalf of others. The actual sellers do not know to whom they sell and the actual buyers do not know from whom they buy. Even their broker, as a rule, does not know, except in the rare instance when he is "market maker" for a particular stock and can match selling orders and buying orders of his own customers. This anonymity of sellers and buyers does not hold with regard to new issues. The floating of new stock issues involves negotiations with an underwriter or a consortium of underwriters; much information is exchanged between the issuer of stock and the underwriter; and the problems are of a different nature than those in the trading of existing shares of stock.

Most analyses of the stock market are concerned with the trading aspects in a largely impersonal market for long-term securities. As a matter of fact, the records of prices and trade volumes in the stock market present so many problems and puzzles that one can hardly be surprised by the large volume of the literature or by the large variations in hypotheses offered to explain observations and to furnish predictions.

The Stock Market

The stock exchange—the market for equity securities (shares of the capital stock) of business corporations—serves several purposes; economic analysis of the functioning of this capital market often has its focus on only one or two of the functions, in disregard of the others. One may concentrate on several different aspects: (1) one may see it as the source of liquid funds for corporate enterprises issuing new shares to raise money capital needed for "real" investment; (2) one may examine it as a source of funds for stockholders who want to liquidate their holdings and get out of the market to use their proceeds for other purposes, perhaps to purchase consumer

---

be almost twice that obtainable from commercial loans. The bank would be tempted to cut the availability of funds loanable to their customers to zero. In these circumstances, the fixing of interest rates would surely not have the desired effects. For centuries politicians all over the world have failed to take account of the fungibility of money and have pressured governments to hold interest rates down to untenable levels.

durables like residential housing or automobiles; (3) one may regard it as the institution that—by allowing the switching of stocks from current holders to new holders without affecting the liquidity position of the firm whose shares are being traded—overcomes the illiquidity of capital invested in fixed assets by giving stock buyers a somewhat more liquid asset salable at any time (though not necessarily at the original purchase price) and thereby secures to business firms access to investible funds that would otherwise not be available; (4) one may study it as a large price-generating apparatus for corporate equity, giving signals to attract capital funds to firms, industries, and economic sectors that are judged to be growing and becoming more profitable, and dissuading holders of investible funds from channeling them towards less profitable or even declining industries; or (5) one may imagine it as a huge gambling casino giving risk-loving bettors chances to try their superior insights, or their good luck, to make large capital gains at the risk of losing much of their stake.

The last two of these functions—generating the right prices to guide investors, and providing a forum for the price-guessing contests of stock-market players—are connected: the bids or offers based on the judgments of all market participants, be they investors or speculators, determine the prices of the stocks traded. This is not to say that each player who acquires a particular stock has done his own analysis of its "real value" or its prospect for a rise; many, perhaps most buyers of common stock rely on advice by professional investment analysts, stockbrokers, or supposedly well-informed friends and acquaintances. Several mutually conflicting theories "explain" the processes by which buyers, sellers, advisers, and tipsters reach the judgments that determine the decisions to buy or sell and, consequently, the movements of stock prices. Perhaps though, the alternative techniques of valuating stocks or predicting changes in their prices are used simultaneously by different groups operating in the stock exchange. This would make it even harder to explain why stock prices have moved as they have, or to predict how they would move in the future, especially in the short run.

The problem under discussion concerns the selection of particular stocks and their prices relative to the prices of other stocks or to some averages reflecting movements of the market as a whole. Thus, cyclical or secular movements of some index of stock prices are not pertinent to the present discussion; what matters here are the prices of the shares of selected companies.[54]

[54] Economists analyzing "modern portfolio theory" attempt to estimate differences

Following one of the most intelligent and most intelligible expositions of the mysteries of stock pricing, we may distinguish four positions:[55] A. The future price, or at least the relative price movement, of a particular stock can be predicted by a "fundamental" analysis of its "intrinsic" value, a value based on a "firm foundation" of the growth rate of earnings, the length of time for which this growth rate is expected to last, the ratio of dividend payout, the degree of risk (or price volatility), and the market rates of interest. This position is called the "firm-foundation theory" of stock valuation.[56] B. The future price of the stock can be predicted by a "technical" analysis of its past record, especially by charting the prices at which it sold during the last year or two and observing "trends," "resistance levels," "support levels," and even more fanciful constellations, such as "head-and-shoulder positions" and "double bottoms." The technical analysts and chartists reject the "firm-foundation theory" as too logical for speculators whose actions are based almost entirely on psychological sentiments. This position has been called the "castle-in-the-air theory" of stock speculation.[57] C. The future price of a stock is unpredictable (just as the future position of a molecule in its random walk cannot be foreseen). The past records of stock-price movements contain no useful information, since the probability of a price going up or down is not affected by the direction of the preceding change or changes. This position is the "narrow random-walk theory."[58] Fundamental analysis also is regarded as unhelpful, chiefly because—according to a widely held theory about "efficient markets"—all publicly available information is already reflected in the current price. In these circumstances, a random guess is as good as, or better than, any analysis based on public information. This position is the "broad form" of the random-walk theory.[59] D. Special situations can sometimes be identified either by means of inside information (which

---

in the risks borne by holders of different kinds of stock; it is taken for granted that bearing higher risks is associated with earning higher gross rates of return. Many of the "risk measures" proposed by analysts relate to observed variations in the price of particular stocks. Movements of the general index of stock-market prices account for a "systematic" risk, whereas movements of the price of a particular stock account for an "unsystematic" risk. Thus, to focus the analysis on the prices of shares of selected companies is to concentrate on the "unsystematic risk," or the residual after eliminating the systematic risk of variations due to cyclical or secular movements of the entire market. See Burton G. Malkiel, "Risk and Return: A New Look," National Bureau of Economic Research, Working Paper No. 700 (June 1981).

[55] Burton G. Malkiel, *A Random Walk Down Wall Street* (New York: Norton, 1973).
[56] Ibid., pp. 73-92.
[57] Ibid., pp. 22-25, 97-107, 122-135.
[58] Ibid., pp. 114-135.
[59] Ibid., pp. 167-170.

in the United States it is illegal to use) or by detecting instances in which the market has been slow in recognizing the prospects of a particular stock. Whereas the market is usually very "efficient" in absorbing and reflecting almost immediately any new information, some developments in particular firms or industries are gradual and may have remained undetected by all but the most alert and eager detective-analysts. If their guesses are correct and they purchase the stock before the market "catches on," they stand to make substantial gains.

Three of the described positions, A, C, and D, are not really mutually exclusive, especially if one distinguishes between a very short and a not so short run. Random walk, price movements according to fundamental valuations, and gains of the specially informed stock buyer are all compatible with one another. Paul Samuelson demonstrated that the random walk of prices observed in the stock market "can be deduced rigorously from a model which hypothesizes that a stock's present price is set at the expected discounted value of its future dividends, where the future dividends are supposed to be random variables generated according to any general (but known) stochastic process."[60] Thus, there is no incompatibility in principle (a) "between the so-called random-walk model and the fundamentalists' model," and (b) "between behavior of stock's prices that behave like random walk at the same time that there exist subsets of investors who can do systematically better than the average investors." The systematic speculative gains that go to a small number of stock-market transactors are due to their access to "more or better information or a better way of evaluating existing information."[61]

Information Affects Prices, and Prices Convey Information

There is a two-way relationship between information and the movement of stock prices: new information affects stock prices, and stock prices convey information. This double relationship need not take the form of a feedback loop; the two influences may work quite independently.

[60] Paul A. Samuelson, "Proof That Properly Discounted Present Values of Assets Vibrate Randomly," *Bell Journal of Economics*, Vol. 4 (Autumn 1973), p. 369. Reproduced in *The Collected Scientific Papers of Paul A. Samuelson*, Vol. IV (Cambridge, Mass.: MIT Press, 1977), p. 465.

[61] Ibid., in the *Bell Journal of Economics*, p. 373; in *Collected Papers*, Vol. IV, p. 469. — The quoted remarks seem to agree with common sense, but many of the economists' discussions in the learned journals are so technical and esoteric that persons with insufficient training in higher mathematics will find the arguments incomprehensible. I have followed the principle to leave aside all expositions that I was unable to translate into plain English.

The effect of new information upon stock prices is not questioned by any observer. The question is only how quickly prices react to new information. It is the speed of this reaction that is implied in the definition of (what is misnamed) an "efficient market." Unfortunately, "the definitional statement that in an efficient market prices 'fully reflect' available information is so general that it has no empirically testable implications."[62] The construct "available information" has no unambiguous empirical counterpart. One may, of course, arbitrarily decide that "published information" is the relevant operational concept. Empirical testing has been done on the reaction of recorded stock prices to public announcements of annual earnings, dividend payments, stock splits, awards of large contracts, the initiation or settlement of lawsuits, and so forth. It is on the basis of such tests that most researchers have come to conclude and confirm that the stock market is "highly efficient" and that stock prices hardly move at all when a previously announced action eventually takes place. In other words, the actions had been anticipated and fully reflected in the price of the particular stock. Specialists in the theory of stock-market prices have coined the term "fair-game models" in the analysis of market conditions in which prices are in full conformance with "expected returns." I must warn, however, that "expected returns" does not mean returns expected by you and me, or even by a sample of stockholders or brokers, but has a purely mathematical definition.[63] In order to avoid misunderstandings, one may distinguish between "subjective" and "objective" expectations—but bear in mind that among the variables that determine objective expectations are some rather arbitrary proxies for incurably subjective factors.

To see how things work, assume that a corporation announces an increase in its dividend payments. Whether a corporation pays to its shareholders larger or smaller percentages of its earnings would not affect the total market value of the firm were it not for the information effects of the action.[64] Managements may take actions chiefly to achieve information effects, for example, they may raise dividends in the hope that the decision will "convey important information to

[62] Eugene F. Fama, "Efficient Capital Markets: A Review of Theory and Empirical Work," *Journal of Finance*, Vol. 25 (May 1970), pp. 383-417.

[63] A reader not of a mathematical bent may sympathize with me in disliking the use of the word "expected" for things that in fact not a single person really expects. A "mathematical expectation" need not be what any individual concerned with the matters in question actually expects.

[64] Merton H. Miller and Franco Modigliani, "Dividend Policy, Growth, and the Valuation of Shares," *Journal of Business*, Vol. 34 (October 1961), pp. 411-433.

the market concerning management's assessment of the firm's long-run earning and dividend-paying potential."[65] Going still another step back, we note that the news that management is going to propose to its stockholders' meeting the approval of a stock split—say, the distribution of one new share to the holders of two existing shares—may immediately raise the price of the existing stock because of "implied information." The point is that stock splits are often regarded as opportune when management anticipates higher earnings and accordingly higher dividend payments. The experience that "in the past stock splits have very often been associated with substantial dividend increases" has taught the market to expect such increases.[66] The re-evaluation of the shares in question will thus take place when the split is proposed; it will not wait until the split is effected, or increased dividend payments are announced.

The reverse flow of information, emanating from relative prices and price movements of corporate stocks and going to owners and users of investible funds, has been the subject of rather firmly held but not always clearly articulated theories. The basic idea, evidently, is that higher (or rising) stock prices attract additional funds towards financial investment in the companies that issued the shares and at the same time induce their managers to use such funds for additional real investment.[67] As a rule, higher prices tend to *reduce* the quantity demanded; why then should higher stock prices *increase* the demanded number of more expensive shares? Also as a rule, higher prices tend to increase the quantity supplied; this rule seems to work: there may in fact be a spate of management decisions to issue and offer new shares at the higher prices. Yet, we need a more complete understanding of the considerations that underlie these decisions. If the rise in the price of shares, and consequently the issue price of new shares, is such that the ratio of price to expected earnings is increased, this implies that the proceeds from a new issue are relatively cheap funds for the company. Moreover, they involve special gains for the owners of the old shares, that is, for the owners of the firm before its expansion. The managers' interest in the expansion

[65] Eugene F. Fama, Lawrence Fisher, Michael C. Jensen, and Richard Roll, "The Adjustment of Stock Prices to New Information," *International Economic Review*, Vol. 10 (February 1969), pp. 2-3.

[66] Ibid., p. 20.

[67] "In theory, the stock market is supposed to provide the signals for firms to make the correct investment decisions." Joseph E. Stiglitz, "Information and Capital Markets," in Cathryn Cootner and William F. Sharpe, eds., *Financial Economics: Essays in Honor of Paul H. Cootner* (Englewood Cliffs, N.J.: Prentice-Hall, 1982), p. 118.

needs little explaining: their emoluments, their influence, and their prestige stand to gain.

The question of the demand for new shares at increased prices requires more thought. If an increase in the price of a stock leads investors to expect the rise to continue—say, because the "momentum will be maintained"—a speculative increase in the demand for shares is "explained." In the past investors and speculators have observed that new stock issues have in most instances been followed by increases in their market prices substantially above the issue prices. Hence, one can well understand that many will want to benefit from such quick appreciations, either as speculators eager to make a short-term capital gain or as investors wanting to buy the stock "cheap" and hold it for future income. Whether these investors will actually find that they receive extraordinary returns to their investment depends on whether the company's earnings continue to increase so that the issue price of the new shares has not yet anticipated the long-term profits of the enterprise. In any case, however, it is not the *higher* price but the expectation of a *rising* price of the stock that attracts additional funds.

In characterizing the two flows of information as independent of each other, I did not mean to rule out possible feedback relations. It has been suggested, for example, that the production of relevant information for the use of financial investors may lead to an increase in the price of a stock, and this increase, in turn, may affect the considerations and decisions of the firm's management to undertake additional real investment.[68]

The Hypothesis of the So-Called Efficient Market

A few times in the preceding sections references were made to a theory or hypothesis about "efficient" markets. I took pains to place quotation marks around the adjective because I wanted to indicate that this has been an inappropriate choice of words. In an analysis of a market it is essential to distinguish (1) prevalent types of decision-making by the actual or potential sellers and buyers from (2) the existing trading arrangements for the execution of their offers and bids. Whether sellers and buyers are smart and alert or indolent and slow is one thing; it is another thing whether the organization of the market is such that the orders of the would-be sellers and

---

[68] ". . . information produced for investors' use on personal account affect firms' production-investment decisions (and thus allocations of resources) via the information's effects on the prices of firms' ownership shares." Nicholas J. Gonedes, "Information Production and Capital Market Equilibrium," *Journal of Finance*, Vol. 30 (June 1975), p. 862.

buyers are properly executed, and bids, offers, and transactions are speedily and accurately reported. The term "efficiency" is reasonably employed in commenting on the organization of the market; it is unreasonable for an analyst to call the market "efficient" because he finds that sellers and buyers respond quickly to opportunities implied in available information.[69]

Leaving aside my semantic reservations, I must also call in question the underlying fundamental assumption of financial analysts positing that securities markets are "efficient" in terms of zero lags in customers' responses to new information. The notion of "efficient" stock markets hypothesizes that actual or potential holders of corporate stock react *instantly* to new information that might affect the prospects of future returns. There are weaker and stronger forms of the hypothesis, relating largely to the type of information available to the public: is it only public information, such as items reported in the daily press, or is it also rumored information, as from tipsters considered close to "insiders," or is it any and all information of possible relevance—restricted, rumored, or publicized? The implication of the strongest form of the hypothesis is that, since the price of the stock in question jumps or drops immediately, without any delay, to the "correct" level, there is not a chance ever to make money by buying an "undervalued" stock or selling an "overvalued" one. In an "efficient" market, stocks are never undervalued or overvalued.

I am raising the charge of misplaced concreteness: analysts may be well served by models of equilibrium as long as they do not believe that equilibria can be observed in the real world. As I shall argue in

---

[69] Shorter or longer time lags in the reactions of consumers of certain goods and holders of certain assets to received information relevant to expected "utilities" or "returns" to be derived from the goods and assets are not felicitously referred to by "efficiency" or "inefficiency" of the "market." Should the market for cigarettes be called "inefficient" because most consumers have long disregarded the well-publicized risk of cancer from cigarette smoke? If I have failed to sell my shares in a corporation the impending bankruptcy of which had been reported to me by a reliable source, and if I have failed to deliver bonds that, almost a year earlier, had been called for redemption, I admit that I was careless, indolent, preoccupied with other things; but should we say that my lack of prompt response has made the particular capital markets inefficient? It makes more sense, I submit, if one reserves the rating of inefficiency for situations involving the technical operation of the markets. For example, if lack of communication makes it difficult to find out the prices at which securities were offered, bid, or traded; if brokers allow several days to pass before they carry out their customer's orders; if the telephone connections between brokers' offices and the floor of the securities exchange are poor or entirely out of order; if brokers are sloppy in recording and reporting market transactions; or if various obstacles reduce the "transparency" of the market or the capability of potential buyers or sellers to obtain access to the market.

another chapter, equilibria are always in the future—in an imagined future—never in the present—in an observable present. Moreover, I charge the analysts who apply the hypothesis of instantaneous equilibration to the real world with a naive faith in the insiders' or outsiders' ability to interpret new information so unambiguously that they all come to the same expectation or prediction of future earnings and risks. Even among the executives of a well-run corporation, different degrees of optimism and pessimism will lead to divergent forecasts of future net returns. It is absurd to believe that even the best-informed insiders would arrive at the same estimates of future gross earnings, net revenues, interest-rate fluctuations, and all other variables essential in calculating the present value of a share of stock. Yet, the hypothesis of the implications of "market efficiency" has been analyzed and discussed in a rich flow of research papers offering econometric "tests" of its validity and empirical applicability.[70]

[70] For a sophisticated test, which is found to be inconsistent with the hypothesis and is thus taken to disconfirm it, see Robert J. Shiller, "The Use of Volatility Measures in Assessing Market Efficiency," *The Journal of Finance*, Vol. 36 (May 1981), pp. 291-304. — A reader of the manuscript of this chapter, who provided me with helpful comments, suggested that, "A discussion of the evidence on the efficient markets hypothesis would be welcome. This is a very powerful theory which says roughly that if prices weren't martingales there would be simple ways to make money. Therefore prices should follow a martingale. Recent evidence [however] suggests that prices vary too much for them to be martingales. How is one to explain this fact? It is an important outstanding puzzle in the economics of information."

I have not included anything about martingales in the text, for the simple reason that I expect few of my readers to know the meaning of this term. No textbook in economics explains or uses the term. It is defined in mathematics dictionaries and encyclopaedias and in some recent texts on probability theory and stochastic processes, but all these definitions employ mathematical symbols. The only definitions in English words, without mathematical terms, are in dictionaries. *Webster's* defines a martingale as "any of several systems of betting in which a player increases his stake, usually by doubling each time he loses a bet." The *Oxford* defines it as "a system in gambling which consists of doubling the stake when losing in the hope of eventually recouping oneself." These applications of the term are not what my reader had in mind. More sophisticated definitions do not emphasize the specific betting aspect of the concept but are more generally couched in terms of random functions, mathematical expectations, "Markov processes," "Wiener processes," and "Poisson processes." A few examples are given in English sentences: "The first example of a martingale is a symmetric random walk over integer-valued points on a straight line"; and it is suggested that "a martingale is something intermediate between a process with independent increments and zero mean and a process with uncorrelated increments." A. D. Wentzell, *A Course in the Theory of Stochastic Processes* (New York: McGraw-Hill, 1981), pp. 108 and 109.

As to the substantive point made by my reader, about prices following a martingale or not following a martingale, I see no puzzle in the theory of market prices except for theorists who believe that observed prices are equilibrium prices. To me it is quite clear, and I will explain it in Chapter 8 of this volume, that equilibria are only mental

If the Stock Exchange Were a Pure Gambling Casino

Since the bulk of all transactions in the stock exchange consists of purchases and sales of existing stock among individuals who happen to "have different opinions about the probability distributions of the outcomes," it may be helpful to examine the operations of such a "pure exchange market" under simplified conditions:[71] (1) Gambling is a zero-sum game in that no one can gain except at the expense of others, and no one can lose without benefiting others. (This assumption disregards brokers' commissions, state taxes, capital-gains taxes, price inflations with fictitious gains for all, etc.) (2) Buyers, holders, and sellers of shares are rational in some sense related to "reasonableness" and conformance with "objectively" sound principles. (This is a meaning of rationality rejected by Max Weber and many others, who recognized only subjective rationality, no matter how foolish the actor's conduct may appear to others. The "modern" meaning refers to full attention to all observable events and available information, including "mathematical expectations" based on some "unbiased" interpretation of the facts.) (3) Holders of shares of stock are averse to exposure to risk. (This assumption disregards that many buyers of stock actually like to take risks, just as every buyer of a chance in a lottery knows that the risk of losing his stake is overwhelming; the small hope of winning one of the large prizes is enough to attract the bettors and gamblers. The "mathematical expectation" of winning is far below the price of the chance; after all, the organization—government, agency—wants to make a substantial net revenue from running the lottery. The same holds true for owning and for "playing" betting machines such as "one-armed bandits.") (4) It is possible to acquire information at a cost, and some of it may even be "perfect information." (This assumption disregards that perfect information about the future cannot exist in business or any other human affairs.)

If these conditions were assumed to prevail, one could logically deduce that the uninformed would not wish to trade in the stock

---

constructs of possible help in the explanation of directions and changes in directions in the movements of prices and quantities. There are lags of various lengths in the responses of different economic agents to any new information. The idea of "instantaneous adjustment" may be helpful in concept formation but should not be taken seriously in concrete cases. New information is sometimes acted upon quickly, sometimes very slowly; sometimes a latecomer will lose money because expectations overshoot the most plausible values, sometimes they will still make money several weeks after the "news" was received. This is no puzzle to someone who knows that people are not all alike.

[71] An ingenious analysis of this sort was made by Joseph Stiglitz in "Information and Capital Markets."

market, that the informed would have no one to trade with, and that no one would spend a cent to become better informed.[72] Since all of us know that plenty of trading is going on in the stock exchange, why go through this laborious mental exercise? The reason is simply to prove that the assumptions are contrary to fact. If many people trade in the stock market, evidently some of them are not rational (in the modern sense), some of them are not risk-averse, and some are buying and receiving information at a cost. In addition, some of them believe themselves to be better informed than others, many entertain different opinions about the prospective returns to particular stocks, some enter the market for the first time, some have lost so much that they get out of the market, some have been lucky and are optimistic about their supposedly superior foresight, some have to place large incomes and savings in whatever assets look decent, some have to liquidate their stocks in order to meet other obligations, and so on. It stands to reason that differences in risk-aversion and in reasonableness play a major role, and that differences in information and interpretative skill are also significant factors in explaining gambling and trading in the stock market. In any case, "the stock market is clearly not a pure gambling market."[73]

If the Stock Market Were Like a Beauty Contest

Before we undertake to learn a little more about the kinds of information available to investors and speculators in the stock market, we should take note, or refresh our memory, of what John Maynard Keynes said about the problem created by the "increase in the proportion of the equity in the community's aggregate capital investment which is owned by persons" ignorant of financial analysis and swayed by ephemeral and really "non-significant" events.[74] No paraphrase can match Keynes' delightful prose:

> A conventional valuation which is established as the outcome of the mass psychology of a large number of ignorant individuals is liable to change violently as the result of a sudden fluctuation of opinion due to factors which do not really make much difference to the prospective yield; since

[72] Ibid., pp. 121-131.

[73] Ibid., p. 131.

[74] John Maynard Keynes, The General Theory of Employment, Interest and Money (London: Macmillan, and New York: Harcourt Brace, 1936), p. 153. (The publishers' permission to reproduce these passages from pp. 154, 155, 157 is gratefully acknowledged.)

there will be no strong roots of conviction to hold it steady.
. . .

. . . It might have been supposed that competition between
expert professionals, possessing judgment and knowledge
beyond that of the average private investor, would correct
the vagaries of the ignorant individual left to himself. It
happens, however, that the energies and skill of the professional investor and speculator are mainly occupied otherwise. For most of these persons are, in fact, largely concerned, not with making superior long-term forecasts of the
probable yield of an investment over its whole life, but with
foreseeing changes in the conventional basis of valuation a
short time ahead of the general public. They are concerned,
not with what an investment is really worth to a man who
buys it "for keeps", but with what the market will value it
at, under the influence of mass psychology, three months
or a year hence. Moreover, this behaviour is not the outcome
of a wrongheaded propensity. It is an inevitable result of an
investment market organised along the lines described. For
it is not sensible to pay 25 for an investment of which you
believe the prospective yield to justify a value of 30, if you
also believe that the market will value it at 20 three months
hence.

Thus the professional investor is forced to concern himself with the anticipation of impending changes, in the news
or in the atmosphere, of the kind by which experience shows
that the mass psychology of the market is most influenced.
. . .

. . . professional investment may be likened to those newspaper competitions in which the competitors have to pick
out the six prettiest faces from a hundred photographs, the
prize being awarded to the competitor whose choice most
nearly corresponds to the average preferences of the competitors as a whole; so that each competitor has to pick, not
those faces which he himself finds prettiest, but those which
he thinks likeliest to catch the fancy of the other competitors, all of whom are looking at the problem from the same
point of view. It is not a case of choosing those which, to
the best of one's judgment, are really the prettiest, nor even
those which average opinion genuinely thinks the prettiest.
We have reached the third degree where we devote our

intelligences to anticipating what average opinion expects
the average opinion to be. . . .

Keynes' description of the working of the stock market was widely
accepted and often quoted with full approval, but some regarded it
as a parody of the real thing.[75] The idea that the masses of ignorant
investors and speculators actually look at the financial pictures of
as many as a hundred corporate bodies (or faces) and pick the ones
they think will be picked by other "voters" in the "beauty contest"
as the ones most likely to be thought the prettiest, not by themselves
but by other students of mass psychology, is untenable. If there is
any serious picking and choosing, it is done by a small minority of
stock analysts, brokers, speculators, and investors; the others look
at much smaller samples of stocks—if they look at all and do not
just follow the advice of their broker and tipster.

It is true that mass reactions to events of the day, to political and
economic news, may cause vibrations, oscillations, and fluctuations
in stock prices; these influences, however, affect chiefly the prices
of the most widely held stocks and thereby the general level of stock
prices. After what we have learned about the well-nigh inevitable
random walk of prices in organized markets, and about the popular
sensitivity to news that is of no real relevance to the future economic
performance of the companies whose shares show oscillations in
price, we wonder whether it is really the news that prompts the
stock-market transactions. It seems more likely that the financial
reporters of the daily newspapers and their "authoritative" sources
feel obliged to give some "plausible" story to explain each up or
down registered in the market. These stories are usually without
foundation. Neither the reporters nor their sources know who sold
or bought what stocks and, still less, for what reasons: stock prices
declined yesterday? "Of course, because" of the announcement of
the larger deficit in the trade balance. The market showed greater
strength the next day? "Of course, because" of the report that the
rate of unemployment was down by one-tenth of 1 per cent for the
past quarter-year. These newspaper explanations of all the ups and
downs of stock prices in their random walk are unfounded inventions, but they induce even those who ought to know better to embark
on speculations about the "ignorant speculators' " activities and about

[75] "In this kind of world, there is a sucker born every minute—and he exists to buy
your shares at a higher price than you paid for them. . . . All the smart investor has
to do is beat the gun—get in at the very beginning. This theory might less charitably
be called the 'greater-fool theory.' It's perfectly all right to pay three times what a
stock is worth as long as later on you can find some innocent to pay five times what
it's worth." Malkiel, *Random Walk*, p. 24.

the damage these activities inflict upon the economy by "distorting" the implied information that stock prices ought to convey to investors.[76]

Information, Screens, and Signals

The question about the determination of relative stock prices has remained controversial. However, the dominant theory, espoused by leading economists writing in the learned journals, suggests that incentives to seek and to supply *pertinent* information about the relative performance of share-issuing corporations exist and are to some extent effective. This does not mean that all such information is correct, unbiased, and as complete as it could be. Indeed, the system provides also incentives to supply misinformation, and one cannot reasonably conclude that relative stock prices correctly reflect the relative earnings potentials of the firms as judged by the most qualified, best-informed, and genuinely honest appraisers.

What kind of information about stock companies is generally available to financial investors? To mention only the best-known sources, there are the quarterly, semiannual, and annual financial statements; annual statements audited by certified public accountants; annual (or more frequent) reports by the managements of the companies; prospectuses for new issues of equity or debt securities; periodic evaluations by appraising and accrediting houses; periodic evaluations by the financial analysts of large brokerage firms; occasional interviews of management by financial analysts; and, of course, current news items in daily, weekly, and monthly papers. Individual investors have developed preferences for some special indicators of the firms' prospects of future earnings, such as the current flow and the backlog of orders; the rate of investment undertaken in the recent past and planned for the near future; the expenditures for research and development; the awards of patents of invention; the debt-equity ratio; plans for dividend payments, stock splits, or mergers; the growth of sales, of assets, or of net income; changes in management personnel; the percentage of the firm's equity owned by the firm's officers or by the entire management; and so on and so forth.

Knowing that investors are in the habit of screening the stock companies by criteria of that sort, managers have learned to signal to the market the firm's state of health as reflected in these criteria.

[76] These strictures against naive financial journalism should not be taken as applying to well-trained reporters on financial markets. There is little doubt, for example, that changes in the cost and availability of credit are likely to affect securities prices, and that reported movements in monetary aggregates, expected to affect the credit policy of the central bank, may be quickly reflected in the prices of bonds and stocks.

For example, they try to signal the management's confidence of the company's future by exhibiting large percentages of the company's shares owned by the executive officers.[77] Similarly, if the debt-equity ratio is used by investors in screening alternative stock acquisitions, firms are likely to send a favorable signal to the market, even if the "favorable" debt-equity ratio may not be in the best interest of the firm. In brief, the signals may convey misinformation and, moreover, may be costly to the signaling company.

One controversial question relates to the cost and amount of information sought and/or supplied in a pure exchange market. If there are incentives to the acquisition of information for the use of buyers and holders of shares, such information, though costly, has no social value, since the private benefits of the informed are at the expense of the uninformed—and therefore redistributive, with no gain to society.[78] Earlier it had been argued that in an "efficient market," where prices reflect all new information almost without delay, no incentive to acquire information would exist so that no information would be produced even if society could clearly benefit from it.[79] The two views contradict each other, and it has turned out that both are wrong, for, in general, "where individuals differ, there will be some incentives for acquiring information, but if information is costly, market prices reflect the information of the informed individuals only imperfectly."[80]

Asset Risk as Judged by the Dispersion of Analysts' Forecasts

A very special flow of information has recently been given prominence as a possibly important factor in the explanation of different rates of return on different securities: the analyses and forecasts furnished by financial analysts.

It has long been regarded as plausible in theory and confirmed by actual fact that higher rates of return can be obtained on investments in securities that are regarded as exposing the holder to greater risks. Yet, what facts are indicative of differences in risk? Greater risk is involved in holding securities that fluctuate widely than in holding

---

[77] This point is emphasized by Stiglitz, who however adds that the managers of "bad" firms will be induced to imitate those of "good" firms in signaling to the market this supposed indicator of self-confidence. Stiglitz, "Information," pp. 120, 147, 153, 154, 156.

[78] Eugene F. Fama and Arthur B. Laffer, "Information and Capital Markets," *Journal of Business*, Vol. 44 (July 1971), pp. 289-298; Jack Hirshleifer, "Where Are We in the Theory of Information?" *American Economic Review*, Vol. 63 (Suppl. May 1973), pp. 34-35.

[79] For references, see the literature cited above in footnotes 62, 64, 65, and 70.

[80] Stiglitz, "Information," p. 120.

less sensitive securities, because greater losses will be realized if the holder is forced to liquidate his securities portfolio at a time when the market is weak. Greater variability of price is usually judged by the past performance of the security, its so-called "beta" measure. The question is whether past betas are really good predictors of future betas. It is easy to see why some financial analysts sometimes conclude that certain stocks with a past record of wide price fluctuations will perform much better in the future. The degree of price variability in the past may be different from that expected to prevail in the future; that is to say, the specific experience with the stocks in question need not be accepted as a valid indicator of the future risks.

Rejecting the beta measure as a valid indicator of comparative risk for different asset portfolios, Burton Malkiel has recently searched for more reasonable risk indicators. Looking at several eligible candidates for this position, he came up with a new one: the dispersion of views among Wall Street security analysts concerning the future earnings and dividend growth of a stock.[81] The dispersion in analysts' forecasts may measure specific risks as well as a variety of systematic risks.[82]

Not that unanimity of forecasters assures that their forecasts will eventually prove correct! They may be all wrong. But the risks an investor "assumes," and which determine his willingness to acquire and hold particular assets, are subjective ex ante judgments, and these judgments may be strongly affected by the dispersion in the opinions of persons regarded as well informed and judicious. The more they disagree among themselves, the greater the risk attached to the investment, and hence the lower its market price relative to reported earnings.

The Total Asset Portfolio

Despite the length of our discussions of the role of information in financial markets, we have concentrated on only two polar types: the markets for commercial loans and for corporate stocks. The omission of several other financial markets of great practical importance may be regarded as deplorable. Criticism may be especially justified in view of the recent interest in general theories of "capital-asset pricing," "portfolio preferences," and "asset-portfolio equilibrium."

Instead of extending the present survey to the literature of other financial markets—say, mortgage loans, money-market funds, government bonds, and so forth—we might look into the literature on

---

[81] Malkiel, "Risk and Return."
[82] See footnote 54 above for the meaning of systematic and unsystematic risk.

portfolio selection. Even this, however, had better be deferred to a later chapter. Since the research and analysis of asset portfolios has been in terms of an "optimum mix" and "portfolio equilibrium," it seems preferable to return to the subject of portfolio selection after we have examined the nature and significance of equilibrium concepts in economic analysis. This means postponement until Chapter 8.

CHAPTER 5

PUBLIC DECISIONS AND
PUBLIC GOODS

THE TWO PRECEDING CHAPTERS have reviewed issues discussed in the literature of the economics of information that emphasized market phenomena, market processes, and market results. In this chapter and in the one that follows the review will be continued, but the accent will be more on social and political valuations and on procedures that may qualify as "nonmarket techniques" of obtaining information about individual valuations for purposes of public choice. This statement may sound mysterious, but it will become clearer as we proceed. The point is that in some areas public decisions are inevitable, and many political economists agree that public choices should, if possible, respect and reflect the individual preferences of those affected by public action. The verb "should" in the preceding sentence signals to the reader that we have crossed the frontier and entered normative or prescriptive economics. However, we need not stay there. To investigate whether certain procedures for eliciting information and for arriving at decisions are inherently consistent and also compatible with stated objectives is part of positive, not normative, economics. We shall encounter, in this chapter, problems that straddle the frontier, but in general we can indulge in theory without politics, though the opposite would not be possible.

PUBLIC DECISION-MAKING

In most of the topics discussed in the preceding chapters, information was seen primarily as a factor explaining *private* expectations, decisions, and actions as they impinge on supply and demand and thus affect prices, production, and consumption. Now we shall turn our attention to the role of information in *public* decision-making.

These decisions may relate to a variety of tasks that governments have found appropriate to assume: to modify (or "correct") market prices that are suspected of sending wrong signals to producers and consumers; to provide incentives and disincentives that would change the calculations of producers and consumers in a supposedly preferred direction; to regulate industries that would otherwise produce too much or too little of certain products or byproducts; and to establish and operate industries that would not be operated in a "desirable" way, or not at all, by private enterprise.

Market Failure

The term "market failure" has become widely accepted as the designation for sets of circumstances in which political economists or welfare economists do not trust the free market, or free-market prices, to produce results consistent with the "social optimum."

The most frequent case of market failure occurs in situations in which prices and revenues obtained by producers do not fully reflect the marginal benefits that society at large derives from the output, or in situations in which the costs incurred and borne by the producers do not fully reflect the marginal sacrifices that society at large has to suffer as a result of the productive activity in question. In the economists' terminology, these are the instances in which social and private marginal benefits, and social and private marginal costs (sacrifices, injuries), deviate from each other; in other words, they are instances of "external" benefits, not reflected in the producer's internal revenue, and of "external" costs, not reflected in the producer's internal cost calculations.[1]

A simple way of comprehending the notion of "externalities" is to think of joint production, where the byproduct escapes into the air, either benefiting people who do not pay for it or injuring people who do not receive compensation. If the byproduct is beneficial, but the beneficiaries can neither be made to pay for value received nor be excluded from its enjoyment, they are "free riders," and the producer's revenue is smaller than society's benefit. If the byproduct is harmful, but the injured can neither collect damages nor be protected against the harm, they are "innocent victims," and the producer's cost is smaller than society's sacrifice. Beneficiaries not paying for benefits received, and victims not compensated for injuries suffered,

[1] Noneconomists, possibly baffled by the adjective "marginal," may be assured that this is not an instance of dispensable jargon, especially since its equivalents, "incremental," "additional," or "differential" are not any easier to understand. The nouns "benefits," "revenue," "product," "utility," "costs," etc., have to be modified by adjectives if it is to become clear whether one means "total," "average," or "marginal." Average is the total divided by the number of units; marginal is the increase of the total due to adding one unit (the last unit or an additional unit). For example, if the total cost of producing 100 units is $1,000, and the total cost of producing 101 units is $1,007, the average cost is $10 or $9.97, respectively, whereas the marginal cost is $7.00. Thinking in terms of marginal values, that is, thinking in terms of "the difference it makes," is the key to economic reasoning.

as a result of the producer's operations, exemplify the concepts of external benefits and external costs, respectively. (Alternative terms are "third-party effects" or "spillover effects.")

Producing Too Little or Too Much

The optimum output from the point of view of the profit-seeking producer is that volume at which his long-run marginal revenue is equal to his long-run marginal cost.[2] If there are external benefits from his production, society might be better off with a larger output; if there are external costs from his production, society might be better off with a smaller output, or perhaps without any output at all. By coincidence, the two externalities may offset each other; otherwise, the welfare economist may say that too little or too much is being produced, relative to the social optimum, depending on whether external marginal benefits exceed or fall short of external marginal cost.

When the verdict of the welfare economist holds that marginal social benefits from any productive activity exceed its marginal social costs, the prescription is for public measures designed to increase output beyond the volume that maximizes the private net benefits of the producer. In a private-enterprise economy, where command performances are ruled out, the prescribed measures may consist of government-made spurs, baits, or bribes (subsidies) of various sorts. In the opposite case, bans, curbs, fines, or taxes may be prescribed and imposed to reduce the volume of the particular output below that which maximizes the producer's private net benefits. Such a restrictive prescription would be appropriate, in the welfare economist's view, where marginal social benefits fall short of marginal social costs and therefore the particular output is too large, in that it absorbs too much of the society's resources; society would be better off with less of the particular good or service.[3]

Judgments of this sort presuppose the availability of a large stock and wide flow of knowledge. But, undoubtedly, the knowledge and information that shape producer's decisions are different in essential

[2] Noneconomists may need to be told that as long as marginal revenue exceeds marginal cost, an increase in output will increase total profit; if marginal revenue is below marginal cost, a reduction of output will allow higher profit; profit is maximized at the level of output at which marginal revenue and marginal cost are equal. In a case in which output is not perfectly divisible, profit is at a maximum at the level of output at which marginal revenue exceeds marginal cost by the smallest possible amount.

[3] The idea of government measures altering the producer's marginal revenue or cost, say, through subsidies or taxes varying with output, is of course to induce the firm to make the desired adjustments in its production.

respects from the knowledge and information that shape the decisions of legislators, governmental administrators, and their advisers,
including welfare economists. The increases in revenue and cost that
managers in a business firm expect to be associated with a small
increase in output can be figured out in thought processes demanding
far less subtlety and fantasy than are required for the benefit-and-
cost analyses in which policy advisers and those responsible for
policy decisions ought to engage before they can feel reasonably sure
about the consequences of the measures adopted.[4] Moreover, one
should not forget another difference between private and social benefit-and-cost calculations: any miscalculations of the business managers will lead to losses (or reductions in profits) that the firm has
to absorb and the stockholders have to shoulder, probably holding
the managers responsible; in contradistinction, miscalculations in
the formulation of public policy may lead to social losses and reductions in real national income without any blame being put on
those responsible for the adoption of the ill-advised policies.

These differences do not always disturb the theorists as they "model"
the effects of public measures designed to remedy or counteract
market failures due to externalities. As long as the models are entirely
formal and the modelers shy away from substituting real numbers
for their algebraic symbols, actual deficiencies in the knowledge base
and lack of access to needed information may not matter. One can
solve theoretical problems by *assuming* that the essential variables
are known. However, to apply these solutions when in fact the variables are unknown, is to indulge in sheer "pretence of knowledge."[5]
Still, misgivings regarding the actual implementation of schemes of
public policy need not keep the economic theorist from analyzing
hypothetical relations among variables, some supposedly "given,"
others dependent.

There is an additional difficulty in this kind of theorizing. Among
the various algebraic functions that compose the theorist's model,
one function is sometimes taken for granted: the "objective function," that is, the equation that defines the goals, or objectives, of

---

[4] There is nearly general agreement on the judgment that public decisionmakers,
especially in regulatory agencies created to protect health and safety and to prevent
damage to the environment, fail to make appropriate use of available scientific (including economic) information. They tend to disregard scientific evidence and find
themselves "stuck with visceral estimates and political accommodations as the only
basis for policy." Lester B. Lave, *The Strategy for Social Regulation: Decision Frameworks for Policy* (Washington, D.C.: The Brookings Institution, 1981), p. 6.

[5] Friedrich A. von Hayek, "The Pretence of Knowledge," Nobel Memorial Lecture,
December 11, 1974, *Les Prix Nobel en 1974* (Stockholm: The Nobel Foundation, 1975),
pp. 249-258.

the decisionmakers. In the case of decisions regarding the most appropriate public policy, the objective function has to express the social goals to be attained or furthered. This is not a simple matter: the notion of a *given* "social welfare" function is illusive.[6]

The Social Optimum

Many advocates of particular public policies, recommending this or that measure as most likely to lead to the social optimum, forget that there is no agreement regarding the hierarchy of social goals. Does maximum social utility mean that an increase in national product is always "good" even if it leads to more inequality in its distribution? Does it allow the principle of "fairness"—for example, letting the most efficient creators of new ideas reap and keep the rewards of their labors and ingenuity—to have precedence over the greatest possible increase in total production?

Sometimes the same people who fume and roar against monopoly profits, or any sort of profit, support strong and long protection of patent monopolies in order to let inventors and investors enjoy the fruits of their labors and venturesomeness. Sometimes the same people who resent gross inequalities of income find it intolerable to have high profits of patent holders eroded by competitive imitation of the new products and processes. Sometimes the same people who abhor inherited wealth and privilege want copyright protection to last long enough for the great-grandnieces of authors to earn royalties on books written by their great ancestor. How can all these conflicting goals be reconciled and fused in a definition of the social optimum and how can the welfare economist know what kind of public policy will serve the nation best? Does the information needed by the policymakers include a fair ranking and mixing of the conflicting social goals according to nonexplicit value judgments of uninformed majorities?

---

[6] "In fact, there exists [sic] three thoroughly different concepts of such a Social Welfare Function. They are conveniently distinguished by the Kantian labels of Categorical, Pragmatical and Technical." Serge-Christophe Kolm, "The Optimal Production of Social Justice," in Julius Margolis and Henri Guitton, eds., *Public Economics*, Proceedings of a Conference held [in Biarritz] by the International Economic Association (London: Macmillan, 1969), p. 169. — Kolm illustrates his distinctions by referring to works of well-known economists and suggesting that the categorical function is the object of Arrow's study, the pragmatical function is what Bergson and Samuelson have had in mind, and the technical function enables the economist "to use maximisation computation techniques" and helps in "decentralising the work of a team or of a hierarchy" (pp. 169-170). I suspect that Kolm's distinctions are not acceptable to many fellow welfarers.

Social versus Private Choices

Some of my rhetorical questions and some of my critical comments regarding social decision-making, social objectives, and social optima probably reflect a bias in favor of individualistic and in opposition to collectivist values and choices. However, my strictures against the collectivist position or my overenthusiasm for the individualistic stance call for qualifications.

The meaning of private benefit-and-cost considerations would be unambiguous only if the manager of the private business firm were its sole owner and risk-bearer, so that his decisions and actions would affect only his own fortunes, never the fortunes of the creditors and stockholders (that is, those who have provided the funds for the firm to acquire its assets), and if the head of the private household were choosing and acting exclusively for himself, not for any members of his family. But undoubtedly these are counterfactual assumptions. Business managers make decisions about the use of other people's money, and the financial consequences of bad decisions are often suffered by those who have provided some of the invested funds. Heads of households frequently leave spending decisions to spouses or children; or they make decisions for the supposed benefit (but perhaps actual harm) of members of their family. A parent's choices are often resented by the children, who may strongly disagree with the parent's "superior knowledge" of what is good for them. And they may suffer lasting consequences from inappropriate decisions regarding their education and training for careers.

The problems of optimal choices for a family may be less serious than those for a community or a nation, but an element of "choosing for others" is present in the optimization of household objectives or maximization of the householder's utility. The problems are less serious because the householder's expenditure decisions involve ordinarily only his own income and wealth. The conceptual and logical problems are considerably more complex when a municipal council has to make decisions on behalf of the community, spending taxpayers' money in ways helpful to some members of the community but harmful to others.

Although these qualifications may have attenuated the sharp contrast between the concepts of private and social optimization, they have not removed it.[7]

---

[7] Jack Wiseman argues forcefully against the "concepts of a community welfare that in some sense transcends the apperceptions of individuals." According to the "organic" view of social welfare, "certain 'public choice' (allocative and redistributive) decisions would properly be reserved to the group which had somehow been decided to have special insight into the social welfare of the whole." Against this view Wise-

In view of the complexity of the issues involved in this discussion about private and public decision-making, I may try to put the arguments in slightly different form. In the pure theory of microeconomics, decisions about offering and bidding, selling and buying, are made by the persons directly affected, that is, the persons suffering disutilities, enjoying utilities, sacrificing alternative benefits, spending their own income or wealth. At all levels of decision-making, however, delegation of the decision-making power is possible, and in some instances practically unavoidable. In a rich household, an employed housekeeper may make decisions on behalf of family members; in a business firm, executive directors and managers make decisions on behalf of the firm's owners, perhaps unknown (anonymous) stockholders; and in a municipality, state, or nation, legislators and bureaucrats make decisions on behalf of residents, citizens, or subjects, voting or nonvoting. If decision-making can be delegated at all levels, one wonders why so much fuss is made about the "fundamental" contrast between ideological individualism and collectivism.[8] One rather obvious answer turns on the relative closeness or distance between those who deputize and who act as deputies: the housekeeper is in immediate contact with the members of the household; the business managers receive periodical, if not continual, messages from the major stockholders; the legislators and bureaucrats, however, receive their mandates only after lengthy intervals and only rather vaguely, often in contradictory ways.[9]

---

man upholds "the individualistic paradigm." For "neither logic nor history give credence to the view that there exists an identifiable 'special group', within societies, specially qualified to exercise choices on behalf of others." Jack Wiseman, "The Choice of Optimal Social Expenditures," in Karl W. Roskamp, *Public Choice and Public Finance* (Paris: Editions Cujas, 1980), p. 252. — Wiseman's own suggestions, however, do not spare the individual the encroachments on his liberties by the bureaucracies of the "groups" to which he belongs and which he has trusted with operating a system of "voluntary coercion" (p. 260).

[8] Ideological individualism is not the same as methodological individualism. The latter refers to methods of analysis or research programs, chiefly to the principle that in the explanations of economic phenomena we have to go back to the actions (or inaction) of individuals, since groups or "collectives" cannot act except through the actions of individual members. Ideological individualism refers to political objectives.

[9] Some economists question the assumption that governments are particularly anxious to serve the public good and/or are really knowledgeable about what the public interest demands. For example, according to one author, "The theoretical analysis of government behavior does not indicate that any government would care to respond to policy suggestions, no matter what the arguments, unless its members see a personal political benefit." This author contrasts his "idea of the actual operation of government organizations as opposed to the idealized concept usually assumed by economists. The key notion is that in analyzing governmental and bureaucratic behavior, one must recognize that each of the individual members of these organizational groups opti-

No matter how antagonistic the ideological individualist is to all public decision-making, he cannot help admitting that there are *some* decisions that have to be made collectively—by a government, an authority, or a bureaucracy, acting "preferably" on the basis of a voting mechanism conveying information about the preferences of the members of the community. The reason for this admission is that *some* goods or services wanted by most or all individuals would not be produced if only price signals emerging from free competitive markets were guiding the allocation of productive resources.

Public or Social Goods

The existence of goods or services that are generally wanted but made available only as a result of group action has rarely, if ever, been denied. For beginning students of economics, the best-known example is probably the lighthouse in Adam Smith's presentation of "legitimate" exceptions to the principle of laissez faire.[10] Smith's analysis of this case was, understandably, not sufficiently subtle by present-day standards of economic theorizing, but the development of sophisticated "theories of public goods" began already in the last quarter of the nineteenth century, or about a hundred years ago.[11] The latest stage of theoretical analysis began some forty years ago.[12]

---

mizes his own utility function subject to the constraints imposed upon him." James B. Ramsey, *Bidding and Oil Leases* (Greenwich, Conn.: Jai Press, 1980), pp. xx and 4. — Another author warns that "an economist should no more expect the government to serve the public good as he sees it than he expects the industrial corporation or the trade union to serve the public good." Melvyn B. Krauss, "Recent Developments in Customs Union Theory: An Interpretive Survey," *Journal of Economic Literature*, Vol. 10 (June 1972), p. 434.

[10] According to Smith, the government has the "duty of erecting and maintaining certain public works and certain public institutions, which it can never be for the interest of any individual . . . to erect and maintain, because the profit could never repay the expense to any individual . . . though it may frequently do much more than repay it to a great society." Adam Smith, *An Inquiry into the Nature and Causes of the Wealth of Nations* (London: Routledge, 1903 [1st ed., 1776]), p. 540.

[11] Maffeo Pantaleone, "Contributo alla teoria del riparto delle spese pubbliche," *Rassegna Italiana* (15 October 1883); Emil Sax, *Grundlegung der theoretischen Staatswissenschaft* (Vienna: Hölder, 1887); Ugo Mazzola, *I dati scientifici della finanza pubblica* (Rome: Loescher, 1890); Knut Wicksell, *Finanztheoretische Untersuchungen und das Steuerwesen Schwedens* (Jena: Fischer, 1896); Erik Lindahl, *Die Gerechtigkeit der Besteuerung* (Lundi: Gleerup, 1919); Emil Sax, "Die Werungstheorie der Steuer, "*Zeitschrift für Volkswirtschaft und Sozialpolitik*, N.S., Vol. 4 (1924), pp. 191-240. For English translations of some of these works, see Richard A. Musgrave and Alan T. Peacock, eds., *Classics in the Theory of Public Finance* (London: Macmillan, for the International Economic Association, 1958).

[12] Richard A. Musgrave, "The Voluntary Exchange Theory of Public Economy,"

The expositions in this literature are all rather technical; they are made even more complicated by inconsistent terminologies, employing different terms for the same concept and the same terms with different meanings.

Private versus Public Goods

The expressions "public goods," "social goods," "communal goods," and "collective consumption goods" sometimes refer to the same notion, sometimes to different notions; they are contrasted with "private goods" or "individual goods." One source states that "individual goods are characterized by *divisibility*. They can be divided into small units over which particular persons can be given exclusive possession. . . . Social goods, on the other hand, are not divisible into units that can be the unique possession of individuals. Rather, they tend to become part of the general environment—available to all persons within that environment."[13] This set of terms and definitions, though one of the clearest, is not generally accepted. The most widely used terms are "private" versus "public" goods—despite the endeavor of a major contributor to the literature to use the term "public goods" for a wider concept comprising "social goods" as well as other kinds of goods, such as "mixed goods" and "merit goods."[14]

The adjectives "private" and its contraries modifying the noun

---

Quarterly Journal of Economics, Vol. 53 (February 1939), pp. 213-237; Howard R. Bowen, "The Interpretation of Voting in the Allocation of Economic Resources," Quarterly Journal of Economics, Vol. 58 (November 1943), pp. 27-48; Paul A. Samuelson, "The Pure Theory of Public Expenditure," Review of Economics and Statistics, Vol. 36 (November 1954), pp. 387-389; Samuelson, "Diagrammatic Exposition of a Theory of Public Expenditure," Review of Economics and Statistics, Vol. 37 (November 1955), pp. 350-356; Samuelson, "Aspects of Public Expenditure Theories," Review of Economics and Statistics, Vol. 40 (November 1958), pp. 332-338; Richard A. Musgrave, The Theory of Public Finance (New York: McGraw-Hill, 1959); James M. Buchanan and Milton Z. Kafoglis, "A Note on Public Goods Supply," American Economic Review, Vol. 53 (June 1963), pp. 403-414; Leif Johansen, Public Economics (Amsterdam: North-Holland, 1965); James M. Buchanan, The Demand and Supply of Public Goods (Chicago: Rand McNally, 1968); Paul A. Samuelson, "Pure Theory of Public Expenditures and Taxation," in Margolis and Guitton, eds., Public Economics. Proceedings of a Conference held [in Biarritz] by the International Economic Association (London: Macmillan, 1969), pp. 98-123; Richard A. Musgrave, "Provision for Public Goods," in Margolis and Guitton, eds., Public Economics (1969), pp. 124-144; Richard A. Musgrave and Peggy B. Musgrave, Public Finance in Theory and Practice, 3d ed. (New York: McGraw-Hill, 1980).

[13] Bowen, "Interpretation," p. 27.

[14] Musgrave, Theory of Public Finance, pp. 9-15, 42-49; 1969, pp. 124, 139, 143-144; Musgrave and Musgrave, Public Finance, pp. 77-87.

"good" may refer to four different notions: to the production of the good, to the provision of the good to its users, to its distribution (and acquisition), or to its use. Let us make these differences clear, beginning with the first two.

Private versus public production is quite clear: the good is *produced* either in a private enterprise or in one operated by the government or a public agency; if the product is a service, it is performed either by private individuals, self-employed or employed by private firms, or by employees of a governmental department or agency. Whether the good or service is *provided* privately or publicly is a question of finance, namely, who pays for the production of the good or the performance of the service. It is easy to understand that many goods and services are provided (paid for) by the government (national, state, or local) but produced in the private sector. In many countries the share of private production in the national production is larger than the share of private provision (financing), because governments pay for many goods and services that are privately produced and performed. A few illustrations may be helpful: research and development (R and D) *performed* by private firms and private organizations exceeds privately *funded* R and D, because government funds pay for substantial parts of privately performed R and D; a municipality may provide for the collection of trash and garbage, but these services may be performed by private business firms; a state may provide highways, but private firms may build them; a nation may provide for national defense, but the mortars, tanks, cannons, and rifles may be produced by a private defense industry; finally, the school system may be provided (financed) by the government but possibly operated by private schools paid with government vouchers or subsidized in other ways.

The other two proposed criteria of what are called "private" goods refer, on the one hand, to their *distribution* (or acquisition or possession) and, on the other hand, to their *use* (or consumption). With regard to the former, the essential point is the possibility or practicability of excluding those who fail to pay for the service or benefit received. The good is designated as "private" if the benefit can be withheld from nonpayers; it is designated as "public" if exclusion of nonpayers is impossible, impractical, or inordinately expensive. In the fourth definition the criterion refers to the possibility or impossibility that more than one individual can simultaneously benefit from using the good or service without any additional cost to anybody. The good is "private" if it can be used (enjoyed, consumed) at any one time by only one person (or firm); it is a "public" good if it can be used, without extra cost to anybody, by more than one person (or firm).

In order to reduce the likelihood of misunderstandings if the same term "public" is employed by some for goods and services that can be easily withheld from nonpayers and by others for goods and services that can without extra cost be used by more than one person, it has been proposed to speak of "public" goods when nonpayers cannot be excluded from their use, but of "social" goods when a second, or any additional, person (producer or consumer) can use (enjoy) the good without additional costs being imposed on anybody. Unfortunately, no alternative terms have been proposed for "private," which, therefore, could mean either "nonpublic" or "nonsocial"; moreover, because the majority of writers have ignored the proposal, one finds in much of the current literature "public goods" in any of the four meanings.

According to a well-meant terminological proposal, "social goods are goods the consumption of which is nonrival."[15] Alas, this sentence defines one unknown term by another, equally unknown. The intended meaning cannot, as far as I see, be expressed in one word; so let us not be stingy, but lavish as many words on the concept as it takes to define it intelligibly. As a polar opposite a good or service is called "private" if its use or enjoyment by one person makes it impossible for another person to use it at the same time. (You cannot swallow the same cookie that I am swallowing; you cannot wear my shoes while I am wearing them; and you cannot use your eyeglasses while I have them sitting on my nose.) By contradistinction, a good or service is called "public" or "social" if its use by one person does not preclude its being used simultaneously by other persons (usually, though not always, located nearby) without causing any additional cost, in terms of money, effort, or inconvenience to providers or to other users. (You can look at the clock on the church tower at the same time as I look without inconveniencing me in the least; you can walk on the same sidewalk as I walk without getting in my way; the same lamps that light the streets for me light them also for you for the same total cost; you can enjoy looking at the same trees, flowers, and sculptures as I without causing me or anybody else any additional costs; you can listen to the same program on the radio or TV as I and it will not cost any more than it would if you did not; you can appreciate simultaneously with me, and at the same total cost, the unlittered streets after the street cleaners and trash collectors have done their jobs.) Now, to try a definition: public (or, if you will, social) goods are those that can be used and enjoyed at the same time

[15] Musgrave and Musgrave, *Public Finance*, p. 56. — For some reason most writers speak of "consumption"; "use" would be the better term. Moreover, most writers speak of person; "user" would be more appropriate, especially since the public good may be used by producing *firms*.

by additional people (beneficiaries) without any addition to total cost. In more technical language, the marginal cost of letting more people (persons or firms) benefit from the given good or service is zero.[16]

Congestion and "Mixed Goods"

It would be too clumsy always, in deference to alternative terminological tastes, to say "social, or public, goods." I trust the reader will do what the readers of the specialized literature have been forced to do, namely, to accept the two adjectives as synonyms in many contexts.

The definition offered at the end of the preceding section holds only for the polar case of a "pure public good" or ("purely social good"), for, if additional users are admitted without limit, congestion may eventually cause increments to total cost, chiefly in the form of inconvenience or loss of time. If too many drivers crowd a street or bridge, its total investment cost may remain unchanged (and "average fixed cost" would decline), but the slowdown in traffic, which may be first merely a nuisance, may soon constitute an increase in variable cost to all users of the existing facility.[17] In addition, maintenance costs may be higher if use is much increased.

When the consequences of congestion become serious, the economic analyst may demote the service rendered by the public facility from the rank of a purely social good to that of an impure one, or a "mixed" good, or "ambiguous" good. On normative grounds, he may agree that it might be a good idea—"good" for the maximum benefit to the members of the user group—if user fees were charged in order to reduce the number of users and thus alleviate the congestion. Where no congestion is likely to arise—say, in use of the benefits from a good broadcasting program—some welfare economists are inclined to vote against charging any price for the use of the public

[16] The Musgraves speak of "consumption" where I say "use." No real distinction is intended; I just do not like to say that I "consume" the light given from the street lamps, or the cleaned streets on which I walk. Samuelson defines a public good as "one with the property of involving a 'consumption externality,' in the sense of entering into two or more persons' preference functions simultaneously." Samuelson, "Public Expenditures and Taxation," p. 102. In his earliest article he had considered "the 'external economies' or 'jointness of demand' intrinsic in the very concept of collective goods and governmental activities." Samuelson, "Pure Theory of Public Expenditure," p. 389.

[17] Students of microeconomic theory of production will remember that joint products may be complements or substitutes in production depending on the utilization of existing "fixed" productive capacity. In the same way, a positive externality may become a negative one when overcrowding of the public facility sets in.

facility. They would propose that the investment costs of establishing it and the operating costs of running it be paid out of "general tax revenues."

Exclusion of Free Riders

The question of charging user fees raises another problem, namely, whether it is physically or economically practicable to exclude "free riders," that is, users who do not pay for the service. Notwithstanding the fact that some earlier writers have employed the expression "public goods" to denote goods or services that could not be withheld from nonpaying users, the problem is a different one. The question of "nonexcludability" (an ugly word, which some writers of textbooks have found themselves unable to exclude) is separate from the question of zero marginal cost of including more people in the circle of users. There can be nonsocial goods—goods for which the addition of more users does raise the total cost to providers or other users—that cannot be kept from new beneficiaries who, since they cannot be excluded, will not be prepared to pay for them. (An example would be an overcrowded street, a purely social good before it was congested by a surfeit of users, where techniques to collect user charges would be too expensive to install or to operate.) Incidentally, that it is not feasible to exclude free riders from the use on nonsocial goods—for which allocation by the market might otherwise be the most efficient way to distribute the scarce services—is sometimes regarded as another instance of "market failure."

The opposite case, where it would be feasible to exclude nonpaying users from access to a public (social) good, raises interesting issues of policy. Many welfare economists argue that it would be "allocative inefficiency" to exclude users for nonpayment of charges if their use were not causing any incremental cost. In their opinion, when marginal cost is zero, the price charged to users should be zero too—or total utility would not be maximized. On the other hand, with the selling price zero, total revenue likewise is zero, and investment, maintenance, and operations of the facility can be paid for only by appropriations from general funds. The consequences of raising the needed funds by taxation may be just as harmful or "inefficient" as the charging of a price to the beneficiaries of the service. No cogent general case can be made for the free distribution of a good or service—even though marginal cost is zero—if total costs are positive and have to be covered somehow. Where it is possible to exclude nonpaying users, charging the beneficiaries need not be any less economical or less equitable than charging the general taxpayers, many of whom may neither directly nor indirectly benefit from the service.

The exclusion of nonpaying users ("free riders") by means of fees or prices for goods or services that could be provided at a zero marginal cost may be inefficient per se. This does not imply, however, that normative economics would necessarily prescribe that the use of the public facilities in question be free to all comers. Where all possible outcomes are inefficient, the task of the welfare economist is to explore the *comparative* inefficiencies of the practically attainable solutions. I shall come back to this point, although it is not our major concern in this study; after all, this is not a discussion of economic policy but a survey of the bearing of information on the problem of public goods.

The Demand for Public Goods

The essentials of the problem of public goods can be seen most clearly in the extreme case where it is not feasible or it is too expensive to exclude free riders *and* where the marginal cost of accommodating more users is zero. Allocation through the free market is, in this case, out of the question. Still open to question, however, is whether the provision of the facility is really wanted by the members of the community and, if so, in what size or capacity. Among the usual examples of essentially public services are police force, court system, street lights, street paving and cleaning, fire department, control of air pollution, control of infectious diseases, national security forces.[18] The basic idea is that all or almost all members of communities, states, or nations have (or "should" have) a demand for the facilities or services in question, and whatever size of facility, or quantity of services, is provided will be available to all. Even if some of the beneficiaries were willing to do with less than what the authorities decide to provide, there would be no way to vary the magnitude available to each according to individual tastes or valuations. The economist feels called upon to devise a model that suggests how the socially optimal size of the public facility can be determined.

It is not surprising that such models will assign a major role in the decision problem to the demand curve, the curve that shows the

[18] The examples illustrate slightly different issues. Whereas street lights may be "pure public goods," street paving may be subject to wear and tear through greater use; the size of the police force is variable and can without great difficulties be adjusted to the size of the population; control of infectious diseases requires coercion, as voluntary participation in an immunization program may be ineffective. Nevertheless, all these cases have common elements of the "public-good problem." The theory of public goods cannot fit all instances of the real world without adaptation to special circumstances.

relations between quantities demanded by consumers (users) and the prices that reflect their valuations. There is, however, a significant difference between the demand for private goods and the demand for public goods, especially in the way in which the demand curves of individual consumers (users) are aggregated in a total demand curve. In a market for private goods the demand curves of all potential individual buyers are *added laterally*, that is, the *quantities demanded* are added to show how total demand varies with price; where this aggregate demand curve intersects the supply curve for the good or service in question, the market price will be established. This market price will be the same for all buyers, but the quantities acquired by different individuals will differ. This is not so in the case of a social or public service: in any given situation the quantity provided is invariable and each individual user can have the benefit of all that is provided. Of course, the potential user may not really need it or want it, but it is there for everyone to partake of to the extent desired. But the marginal utility (or the valuation in money or in a numéraire) of the fixed amount of services available to each individual may differ widely according to tastes, incomes, prices of other goods and services, and other circumstances. The individual demand curves may be *added vertically*, so that the resulting curve would show the *total amount* of money the users would be willing to pay if they had to pay for the amounts of services available. Where this schedule of vertical sums of hypothetical price-offers (pseudo-demand prices) intersects with the supply curve (or cost curve) for the service, the optimizing political decisionmakers can, if they are omniscient, find the quantity of the public services that ought to be provided.[19]

This elegant solution of the decision problem is of course not even vaguely operational or applicable to problems of the real world.[20]

[19] Following the expositions in the most widely cited sources, the formulation in the text above assumes that the users of the public good are *consumers* and their valuations are seen as being based on marginal *utility*. A more general formulation would extend the principle to users that are *firms* using the services of the public good as inputs in their various *production activities* and valuing these inputs on the basis of their marginal *productivity*. Among the few writers who formulated their arguments, not in terms of collective consumption, but instead in terms of collective use in production by profit-maximizing business firms—that is, for public goods used as inputs for producing private goods—are Keimei Kaizuka, "Public Goods and Decentralization of Production," *Review of Economics and Statistics*, Vol. 47 (February 1965), pp. 118-120; and Theodore Groves and Martin Loeb, "Incentives and Public Inputs," *Journal of Public Economics*, Vol. 4 (August 1975), pp. 212-226.

[20] For a clear exposition of this theoretical solution see Howard R. Bowen in *Toward Social Economy* (New York: Rinehart, 1948), p. 177. The basic principles are formulated in Paul A. Samuelson, "Pure Theory of Public Expenditure," "Diagrammatic

The demand curves of the *potential* buyers of *public* services are imaginary to a much greater extent than the relevant ranges of the demand curves of *actual* buyers of *private* goods and services. About private goods or services one may say that buyers reveal their essential preferences when they offer to purchase various quantities at given prices. Nothing of this sort is revealed about the demand for public services for which no price is asked and no price is set.

Unrevealed Preference for Public Goods and Services

In a world of only private goods—with no "collective goods"—competitive market pricing can act in the manner of an "analogue calculating machine."[21] On the one hand, "perfect competition among productive enterprises would ensure that goods are produced at minimum costs and are sold at proper marginal costs, with all factors receiving their proper marginal productivities; and on the other hand, each individual, in seeking as a competitive buyer to get to the highest level of indifference subject to given prices and tax, would be led as if by an Invisible Hand to the grand solution of the social maximum position."[22]

In a world with public goods—collective goods—the allocation of resources among alternative uses is no longer so well guided by the invisible hand, for "no decentralized pricing system can serve to determine optimally these [best] levels of collective consumption. Other kinds of 'voting' or 'signalling' would have to be tried. But . . . now it is in the selfish interest of each person to give *false* signals, to pretend to have less interest in a given collective consumption activity than he really has."[23] If each user of a collective facility or public service had to contribute to its cost according to the private benefit that he derives or expects to derive from it, he would have a virtually irresistible incentive to understate that benefit. The summation of the stated or declared marginal valuations of the public services would be less, probably substantially less, than the "true" benefits accruing to the users.

It is well known that in most countries large numbers of taxpayers "cheat" on their declarations of taxable incomes. They do so in full

---

Exposition," and "Aspects," cited in footnote 12 above. See also James M. Buchanan (1968); and John G. Head and Carl S. Shoup, "Public Goods, Private Goods and Ambiguous Goods," *Economic Journal*, Vol. 79 (September 1969), pp. 567-572.

[21] Samuelson, "Pure Theory of Public Expenditure," p. 388.

[22] Ibid. The "tax" in the last sentence was a "lump-sum tax for each individual so selected . . . as to lead to the "best state of the world," taking account of some "interpersonal normative" conditions for an equitable distribution.

[23] Ibid., pp. 388-389.

knowledge of the illegality of understating their incomes and of the risk of penalties if they are "caught." It is hardly thinkable that beneficiaries of public goods and services would honestly "declare" the value of the free benefits received by them, a value that no one could ever prove to be understated. Some would merely be "conservative" in their estimates, others would be "pessimistic," and others would be plainly "cheating." There is no chance that the personal valuations of the free services would be revealed truthfully if the confessor had to pay a tax, fee, or price proportionate to the declared value.

Some theorists have labored hard to find a strategy or mechanism that would induce the user of public goods to reveal his true preferences and valuations. One rather esoteric approach has employed the theory of games, with each "player" making his declarations of expected benefits on the basis of assumptions about the most likely counterdeclarations by the other players. Some game theorists think they have found a solution for the case of two players, each finding it best to tell the truth.[24] The prospects, however, of generalizing this solution to a game among n persons do not look promising.

A "Pseudo-Demand Algorithm"

Before we proceed to a discussion of voting mechanisms designed to convey to public decisionmakers the kinds of information they would need to provide the public goods and services that the people really want, and in amounts in which they want them, it may be helpful to some readers if we looked once more into the important difference between genuine and pseudo-demand functions. Neither of the two are actually known to any single mind or any data bank, but there is a difference in the hypothetical possibility of some points or ranges becoming "revealed" in a relevant sense. A curve showing an individual's demand for a particular good may be interpreted either as the schedule of quantities he would purchase at various prices or as the schedule of prices he might offer for various quantities. The individual will readily reveal how much he is willing to buy at any given price—indeed, this is what he does in the market whenever he learns what price he will have to pay—whereas he would not be willing to reveal how much he would be willing to pay for any given quantity—for he could not be sure that he was not offering a higher price than would be necessary for getting what he wants.

This difference explains why the economist speaks of *revealed* preferences in the competitive market for private (nonpublic) goods, and of *nonrevealed* preferences on which the determination of the optimal quantities of public goods to be provided by public authorities ought to be based. It explains also why the unrevealed-demand curve is called a pseudo-demand curve. And, hence, it explains why one writer on the subject began his article by writing: "The classic problem of public goods is to devise a set of rules such that persons, in following their own self-interest, would provide information that revealed the optimal expenditure on a public good."[25] In other words, the problem is how to induce beneficiaries of public services to reveal their true preferences.

Paul Samuelson proposed a "pseudo-demand algorithm to compute equilibrium" consistent with the social optimum. Since the consumer (or user) of public goods "has every reason not to provide us with a revelatory demand function," *a referee*, "appointed by the planning authority" and knowing the consumers' indifference functions, might calculate for every one of them correct pseudo-demand functions for both private and public goods under a variety of conditions. Among these conditions would be the fixed (but not uniform) "pseudo-tax-prices" at which the referee "pretends" the consumer "can buy as much or as little of the public goods as he pleases."[26]

Samuelson is under no illusion regarding the practical implementation of such a fantastic scheme. But he is right in assuming that his elucidation is helpful. It helps us understand that, although the perfectly competitive market for pure private goods can work in the manner of an "analogue calculating machine," the public "referees" estimating the unrevealed benefits obtained by the individual users of public services can at best work as fanciful parts in an imaginary system using a "pseudo-demand algorithm" in fictitious computations of the socially optimal position.[27] With regard to practical applications of the algorithm, Samuelson realizes that our knowledge is, and may perhaps remain, insufficient for any decision-making about providing, pricing, or taxing public goods if such decisions should have a valid and plausible claim to social optimality.[28]

[25] T. Nicolaus Tideman, "the Efficient Provision of Public Goods," in Selma J. Mushkin, ed., *Public Prices for Public Products* (Washington, D.C.: The Urban Institute, 1972), p. 111.

[26] Samuelson, "Public Expenditures and Taxation," pp. 103-104.

[27] Ibid., p. 102.

[28] Ibid., p. 107.

Voting as a Substitute for Individual Consumer Choice

Howard Bowen has suggested that "the closest substitute for consumer choice is voting."[29] But "closest" may still be far from "close." To be sure, some very ingenuous economists have argued that a perfect system of voting could be devised to secure information about the voters' preferences that supposedly are behind the "pseudo-demand schedules" for particular public services. Some of these writers have advanced the theory that *simultaneous* voting for expenditures and for taxes would achieve the social optimum, especially if unanimity, or *approximate unanimity*, were required.[30]

Bowen's acceptance of voting as a substitute of individual consumer choices in competitive markets was based on four assumptions: (1) that all individuals in the community actually vote (with secret ballots) and express their true preferences (without tactical or strategic conjectures regarding the possible consequences of their own votes and the expected votes by others); (2) that the costs to the community of the various possible quantities of public services are fully known; (3) that the cost of the public services actually provided "will be divided equally among all the citizens"; and (4) that all individual demand curves are "distributed symmetrically" around the modal demand.[31] This fourth assumption presupposes that the individuals' "tastes or desires" are "distributed according to the normal law of error" and that "all individuals must be potentially in an equal position to benefit from the social good."[32] If voters can choose among various quantities in which the good or service is to be made available, the majority vote is likely to correspond to the modal demand and the outcome will approximate the point at which the pseudo-demand curve and the average-cost curve intersect. In Bowen's view, "the modal vote provides direct information as to the most economical amount" of the public service to be provided.[33]

For instances in which the public service is already being provided and only "increments to existing outputs" are to be decided, Bowen considers individual voting on the magnitude of the increment. In a sequence of consecutive votes one can expect that a large majority in favor of an expansion will indicate that further expansion will bring the size of the operation closer to the social optimum. The

[29] Bowen, "Interpretation," p. 33.

[30] Such views, entertained by Knut Wicksell and Leif Johansen, were found untenable by Paul Samuelson. See his "Expenditures and Taxation," pp. 105-107.

[31] Bowen, "Interpretation," p. 34.

[32] Ibid., pp. 35-36.

[33] Ibid., p. 38. — Bowen suggested a different procedure of taxation if the social good is produced under conditions of increasing cost.

best-possible position is reached when about one-half of the people are for further expansion and one-half are opposed to it. Note, however, that in all this voting the cost assessment, or tax on each individual will be the same, not varied with the user's subjective estimate of the benefit he derives from the public service.

This uniformity of price (user fee, tax assessment) is in crass contradiction to the original formulation of the problem. There it was contended that an essential difference was to be found in the *uniform price but varying quantities in the case of private goods* and *the uniform quantity but varying prices (or marginal valuations) in the case of public goods.* In the voting scheme just described, both the quantity and the (cost-covering) price of the public good were uniform for all members of the community. The price charged conformed, not to the user's individual valuations of benefits received, but only to the unweighted *average valuation* by all members.[34]

Conformance of the price charged with the *average* benefit obtained by the users of the public goods does not satisfy the requirements of a "Pareto optimum" and, still less, the requirements of a social-welfare optimum in any accepted sense. If some users of a public service pay less than the marginal subjective value they derive from it while others are forced to pay (in taxes) more than what the service is worth to them, the fact that underpayments and overpayments are approximately equal, and thus cancel out, does not constitute a convergence to optimality. The only sustainable claim for the system is that *total* expenditures for the public good in question may converge to the level consistent with maximum efficiency—although the system would most likely have unintended redistributive side effects and would not even be efficient by the Pareto standard.[35]

---

[34] An exception was proposed only for instances where groups within the community could be distinguished that were quite differently positioned as to opportunities of taking advantage of the public service provided. In such instances, differential assessments of the cost to different groups could be made, but not according to the users' tastes and votes, but according to objective criteria of accessibility. With variable cost assessments (user fees, prices) there is a risk that "the results of the voting will tend to be unreliable." Ibid., p. 48.

[35] Assume a general equilibrium that is perfectly Pareto-efficient (that is, it is not possible to devise a change in the allocation of factors or products that would increase any person's satisfaction without reducing the satisfaction of some other person or persons). If, starting from such a position, outputs of various goods, though produced in unchanged quantities, were redistributed among different consumers, the system would no longer be in equilibrium and, still less, "Pareto-efficient": trades that benefit both parties to the exchange would become possible and attractive.

Other Voting Schemes for Getting Preferences Revealed

In a more recent paper—thirty years after Bowen's—another strong argument was made in support of majority voting as a means of eliciting valid information usable for public decisions on the "correct" quantity of public goods to be provided. According to the author, Nicolaus Tideman, the task is to design "a voting procedure in which there are no obvious gains from lying."[36] As in Bowen's scheme, the tax assessment to each individual for covering the cost of the project would be uniform, that is, the same absolute amount would be charged to every member of the community; only if there are differences among groups with respect to their ability to take advantage of the services provided would cost assessments be different, according to the differential opportunity to benefit; but they would still be uniform within each group. The voting according to this proposal would essentially be about "marginal changes in expenditure" on the public good in question. Tideman's scheme, however, has been found wanting; we shall briefly come back to it after making a few distinctions that have to be comprehended before any such proposals can be intelligently discussed.

Many different voting schemes for public choices regarding the provision of public goods have been proposed in the last fifteen or twenty years. The authors are in full agreement on the need for "demand-revealing mechanisms or procedures" because the free market can perform the task of eliciting people's valuations only for private (nonpublic, nonsocial, noncollective) goods and services. There is agreement also on the difficulty of obtaining true and honest information from voters because they have an inherent incentive to hide their true valuations of the benefits they expect to receive from the public undertaking on which they are supposed to vote.[37]

Voting schemes for public projects differ in several essentials. For example, a single project may be on the ballot in a stated magnitude (expressed perhaps in terms of a bond issue to raise the required funds) to be voted on by yes or no, accepted or rejected; alternatively,

[36] Tideman, "Efficient Provision," p. 112.

[37] The words "voting" and "polling" are often used as synonyms, which makes sense if virtually the entire population participates; if only the members of samples are asked for their preferences, rankings, or valuations, polling is the more appropriate term. Polling ought to be distinguished by the relative size of the sample and by the technique of selecting it. Various types of opinion searches are known under such headings as mailed-questionnaire technique, interviewing procedures, and survey-research methods. All these systems have been used with limited success but never, as far as I know, for the purpose of revealing the marginal valuations of public goods by prospective beneficiaries.

two or more options may be offered. If voters are to choose among options, four types of procedure are available to elicit the people's preferences in different degrees of explicitness: (1) Vote yes on only one of the options (thereby implying negative votes on the others). (2) Rank all options, giving 1 to the most favored, 2 to the second-best, and so on. (3) State how much money you would be willing to pay to secure adoption of your most-preferred option instead of the second-best, and how much you would be willing to pay for this second to be adopted instead of the third, and so forth. (4) State how much money each of the options would be worth to you. (Note that the payments or valuations mentioned in the third and fourth questions are all strictly hypothetical and remain anonymous if balloting is secret.)

Any answers to the fourth question imply answers to the first three: as the ballot informs the authorities or the election commission of the *total* value that each of the options reportedly has to the voters, it informs also about the *differential* values, which the third question is designed to elicit, and about the ranking that would result from the answers to the second question.[38]

Illustrated by a simple example, the problem is for the authorities, for example, a city council, to decide whether or not to build an expensive public facility serving all, or a majority, of its residents, but to build it only if the residents really find it worth what it costs. Even if the required funds can be borrowed, there would be an annual cost for debt service (interest and gradual repayment), for maintenance, and for operating expenses. Let us assume that two alternative sizes of the facility are under consideration, so that the choice is among three options: the large size, the small size, or none at all. The decisionmakers, in this case the city council, are determined to let the people "dictate" the decision by revealing how much the services of the public good are worth to them. This revelation should come by way of a voting procedure so designed that the responses are not falsified by "strategic" thinking of voters or respondents who may believe that *overstating* their relative preferences might help

[38] Among the proponents of the third procedure are T. Nicolaus Tideman in "The Efficient Provision of Public Goods," and T. Nicolaus Tideman and Gordon Tullock, "A New and Superior Process for Making Social Choices," *Journal of Political Economy*, Vol. 84 (September 1976), pp. 1145-1159. The fourth procedure was proposed by Theodore Groves and Martin Loeb, "Incentives and Public Inputs," *Journal of Public Economics*, Vol. 4 (August 1975), pp. 211-226; Theodore Groves and John Ledyard, "Optimal Allocation of Public Goods: A Solution to the 'Free Rider' Problem," *Econometrica*, Vol. 45 (May 1977), pp. 783-809; and Theodore Groves and John O. Ledyard, "Some Limitations of Demand Revealing Processes," *Public Choice*, Vol. 29 (Suppl. Spring 1977), pp. 107-124.

them to get their most-favored scheme adopted or that *understating* might help them to get a lower tax assessed.

Most balloting procedures on public choices invite (and this is a challenge to the proponents' ingenuity) voting on the basis of "strategic conjectures"—guessing the most likely votes of other voters and leaning against the wind by trying to vote against the putative majority—with the result that the outcome sends to the authorities messages that do not reflect the voters' true judgments on the merits of the options. To reduce the risk of misinformation, proponents of demand-revealing voting procedures have devised all sorts of schemes purported to elicit truthful information, schemes that usually sacrifice secret ballots and the anonymity of the voters. Although the descriptions are usually couched in algebraic language and supported by "rigorous" mathematical demonstrations, almost every one of the schemes, however "superior" each is to its predecessors, has later been shown to be deficient. In particular, "whatever social benefit demand-revealing processes provide by reducing somewhat the potential for strategic voting is counterbalanced by the social cost they generate by eliminating anonymity."[39]

Some of the voting schemes, including the ones by Tideman and Tullock,[40] actually provide premiums for voters who supply complete information regarding their preferences and penalties for voters whose vote can be shown to have changed the majority vote (something that may easily happen when there are only three voters, as in their illustration, but hardly ever when the number of voters is in the thousands or hundreds of thousands). Such payments to or by individual voters are possible only if the ballot is open, not secret. There are, of course, degrees of secrecy: the individual responses may be secret to fellow respondents but open to the authorities, open to the polling authority but secret to the tax authorities, and so forth. Any departure from full secrecy, however, would raise serious doubts in the minds of the voters; the thought that a system of premiums or penalties to individual voters would operate as a truth elixir seems to be politically naive.

A few of the members of the elite group of "public-good specialists" have begun to register some misgivings and to formulate what they conceive to be "limitations" of the validity of the proposals and

[39] William H. Riker, "Is 'a New and Superior Process' Really Superior?" *Journal of Political Economy*, Vol. 87 (August 1979), pp. 875-890; the quoted clauses are from p. 889.

[40] Tideman, "Efficient Provision," p. 20, and Tideman and Tullock, "New and Superior Process," p. 26.

the practical operability of the proposed mechanisms.[41] One such limitation is due to the recognition that the "correct" decision on the level of production of any public good—a correct decision based on correctly revealed preferences—will not typically lead to efficient allocations of resources; indeed, it has been shown that a simple procedure by majority vote may result in a more efficient allocation (judged by the Pareto standard). A serious limitation lies in the fact that the voter or respondent, in revealing his preference, cannot anticipate the income effects of the execution of the public decision and subsequent allocation. An additional problem arises from the possibility that mechanisms that induce "honest responses on an individual level" may not be "immune to cooperative behavior"; moreover, even on the individual level, "the incentive to reveal one's true tastes decreases with the size of the population."[42]

Alternatives to Voting

It has become very popular to associate a process of voting with the objective of having the people's preferences determine the allocation of factors and products. For private goods, people vote with dollars; for public goods, they vote with ballots, so that "the economy" is guided entirely by the free will of individual "voters," expressed either in the marketplace or in the election booth. To put the issue of "revealed demand" in this metaphoric language is probably persuasive: the market demand for private goods is symbolized as a system of "voting" in which money replaces the ballot; and the voters' majority vote for public goods is symbolized as a system of getting consumer preferences revealed through ballots replacing "money demand." Metaphors have their uses, but they are not perfect substitutes for reasoned arguments.

In any case, voting is not the only way to find out about consumers' preferences. As a matter of fact, alternatives to voting as a demand-revealing procedure have been proposed. Closest to general voting is the polling of individuals in representative samples. Instead of asking the entire adult citizenship to respond—with or without special incentives to participate and to respond truthfully to all questions—one may be satisfied with selecting random samples on the assumption that they are representative of the entire population. The results obtained from the samples can then be "blown up" to estimate the worth of the proposed projects to the entire community, state, or nation.

[41] Groves and Ledyard, "Some Limitations of Demand," pp. 107-124.

[42] Jerry Green and Jean-Jacques Laffont, "On the Revelation of Preferences for Public Goods," *Journal of Public Economics*, Vol. 8 (August 1977), p. 80.

Some imaginative alternatives to voting as a preference-revealing process have been invented by theoretical analysts for the purpose of elucidating the essential problems to their colleagues and students, but not as practical proposals for actual implementation. As an example, we may recall the system of teams of "referees" digging out the unrevealed valuations from all the persons whose preferences are supposed to be taken into account by the public decisionmakers.[43]

An alternative procedure, mentioned by some economists but not analyzed in any detail, involves a bargaining process. Not bargaining among all individuals involved, which would be clearly impossible in any system (except in a symbolic sense in the free market for private goods), but bargaining among "representatives of various social groups." It is assumed that the members of the groups have sufficiently similar preferences to constitute a united front supporting a consolidated program of choosing among all available options and have succeeded in informing their representatives sufficiently well to enable them to bargain with the representatives of other groups and achieve the right compromises. The bargaining discussions and the negotiations will have to follow appropriate and clearly stipulated "institutional rules" if the outcome is to reflect the preferences of all individuals in the population.[44]

Finally, there is what I like to call the "sequential bidding process," or the "continuous feedback shuttle," between free economic agents and neutral planning agencies. The basic idea is that the planners follow no preferences of their own but merely process the information "coming in" in the form of individual responses to tentative bids and offers. Some writers call this mechanism or procedure "the planning process," a designation borrowed from participants in discussions of socialism in which most people have been inclined to give the authorities a good deal more authority than that of applying fixed rules to (free) peoples' responses to questions.[45]

It is, therefore, hardly surprising that the theory of decision-making about public goods and the theory of planning under socialism have been merged, at least in the heads of some highly sophisticated writers. As long as economists were thinking of public goods as rare

[43] See above in this chapter, the section on "A Pseudo-Demand Algorithm."

[44] For descriptions of the bargaining approach to the determination of an optimum program in a world in which "information on wants and technological possibilities is a priori decentralized," see various writings by Edmond Malinvaud. For brief references see Edmond Malinvaud, "A Planning Approach to the Public Good Problem," *The Swedish Journal of Economics*, Vol. 73 (March 1971), p. 97, and in the section on "A Procedure with Mutual Concessions," pp. 102-104.

[45] For a more detailed description of the sequential bidding or "planning process" see below, Chapter 6.

exceptions in a world of competitive markets trading private goods—
a few lighthouses versus virtually all other goods—and as long as
socialists were thinking of a central planning agency making all
decisions in a comprehensive plan of producing that which, according to its own knowledge and wisdom, "was best for the people,"
the theory of public goods and the theory of socialist planning were
miles apart. But now that some modern economists have adopted
the view that pure private goods are exceptions in a world of largely
public goods, and many socialist economists have chosen to abandon
authoritarian planning for a system of either real or simulated markets in which the individual tastes and preferences of all the people
should be fully reflected in economic decision-making, the rationale
for a merger of two kinds of theoretical models seems persuasive.[46]

Another intellectual integration has coincided with this convergence: the frontiers between positive and normative economics have
become blurred and, for some observers, have disappeared. The distinction between positive study of "what is" and normative study
of "what ought to be" now seems less categorical than it has long
been made out to be by strict methodologists.[47]

Public Goods Privately Sold Above Marginal Cost

The frontiers between the positive and the normative domains of
economics are carefully observed by many analysts and policy advisers. An example will shed some light on these frontiers and, in
addition, on the frontiers between abstract and applied theory.

Public goods have been defined as those that can be enjoyed by
more than one person at zero marginal cost. Maximum efficiency has
been defined in terms of equality of price, marginal utility, and marginal cost. If marginal cost is zero, a price above zero would restrict
sales and output to a volume below maximum efficiency; on the

[46] "The government (which could be thought of as a computer) chooses according
to fixed rules the level of public goods to be provided and the taxes to be levied on
consumers based on market prices for all goods and the information ("messages")
communicated by consumers." Groves and Ledyard, "Optimal Allocation," p. 784.

[47] "The recent development in the analysis of collective consumption has interest
for both aspects of economic theory. On the one hand it aims at being 'positive,' i.e.,
at explaining how the provision for public goods is actually decided in our societies.
On the other hand it is also "normative" when it suggests ways for a better organization
of social decisions in such matters. The two aspects are often simultaneously involved,
the border line being more difficult to draw in this subject than in many others. Indeed
by its very nature public consumption requires that some direct agreement be reached
between those taking part in the government of the community. We do not find in
this field the clear distinction between the positive study of an equilibrium resulting
from individual behavior and the normative study of an optimum program for the
society as a whole." Malinvaud, "A Planning Approach," p. 96.

other hand, if the price is zero, private enterprise will have no incentive to provide the good. All these statements follow from definitions and conventional (fundamental) postulates; can policy recommendations reasonably be based on definitional resolutions? Not if methodological principles are well understood.

Some economists, however, are prepared, or even anxious, to make the jump from definitions, analytical postulates, and mere mental constructions to normative propositions and prescriptions for public policy. They accept, as if it were a natural law, the maxim that public goods be provided by public enterprise at zero prices. Economists who know both economic analysis and the ways of the real world try to avoid such naiveté. Paul Samuelson, in one of his classic pieces, has been explicit in "warning that a *public good* should not *necessarily* be run by public rather than private enterprise."[48] And, in an acerbic reply to a writer who had misread Samuelson's intentions, he explained that definitions, aiding the understanding of abstract relationships, should not be used to support particular economic policies.[49] In emphasizing his warning Samuelson did in effect support the point made by Jora Minasian, that "the *theory* of public goods is of little help in distinguishing those goods that are best provided via community action from those that should be left to individual decisions and preferences."[50] Neither the condition of zero marginal cost of additional use nor the difficulty of excluding nonpaying beneficiaries should be taken as definitive indication for making the public good or service available free of charge to all comers. Several countervailing considerations may carry weight.[51]

[48] Samuelson, "Public Expenditures and Taxation," p. 108.

[49] "The merits or demerits of subscription TV cannot be settled by an appeal to abstract reasoning or principles. Imperfections of one arrangement must be weighed against imperfections of another. Value judgments must enter into the final resolution: one category of citizens stand probably to gain, and one to lose; there is no feasible mechanism by which the gainers can efficiently compensate the losers; nor is there a presumption that they ought to compensate if they could, or ought not to either. . . . [O]ne [cannot] decide what market or social mechanisms should be used for an activity by *first* deciding whether it is a private or is a public good. Instead, in terms of how important are its various features (externalities or lack of same, etc.), society decides what degree of market autonomy or public decision-making shall be applied to it." Paul A. Samuelson, "Public Goods and Subscription TV: Correction of the Record," *The Journal of Law and Economics*, Vol. 7 (October 1964), p. 83.

[50] Jora R. Minasian, "Television Pricing and the Theory of Public Goods," *The Journal of Law and Economics*, Vol. 7 (October 1964), p. 78. In a postscript Minasian offers this conclusion: "The fact that a solution raises price above marginal cost provides no reason for rejecting it" (p. 80).

[51] The free-rider problem and the no-extra-cost problem should be kept more strictly apart than is done in much of the literature. Samuelson is among the most careful in

Multiple Services from a Given Facility

Where the analysis of the most essential relationships is as complicated as in the case of the optimal provision and pricing of a public good or service, one cannot reasonably complain about "unduly simplifying assumptions" being made for the sake of easier treatment and better comprehension. Thus, one should probably accept without objection or qualification the assumption that a public facility of a *given size*, or a *given quantity* of the public good in question, is provided for the use by the community. On the other hand, many of us can understand a problem better if we are aware of some of the more realistic aspects that the simplified models disregard. We may appreciate the simplification much more if we know what is being left out in the models used for analysis. Some of the models are not equipped to take account of the variability of the size of the facility or of the quantity of the service provided.

Some of the analytical models omit the variability of the clientele, or of the groups interested in the service or capable of enjoying its benefits. For example, some sports facilities may be useless to many physically handicapped; certain educational services may be out of reach of the aurally or linguistically handicapped; throughways and autostradas may be of no concern to those who have no automobile and do not travel; but many public goods are so designed that minor modifications can substantially enlarge or reduce the circle of beneficiaries. (I have previously referred to analysts who did allude to differences in potential users' opportunities to take advantage of the available services.)

Another issue is the variety of services that can be rendered by a given facility. A given resource (facility) may be capable of yielding more than one kind of service, and different users of the facility may be interested in, and appreciate (positively or negatively), one or two but not necessarily all the different services potentially available.

To recapitulate, the analyst of the problems of the provision, valuation, and pricing of public goods may choose to take account of

---

pointing to the distinction; he teaches it even to beginning students of economics. Thus, he writes in his textbook that even if the lighthouse could collect a toll charge from every ship that uses its benefit, this "fact would not necessarily make it socially optimal for this service to be provided like a private good at a market-determined individual price. Why not? Because it costs socially zero extra cost to let one extra ship use the service; hence any ship discouraged from these waters by the requirement to pay a positive price will represent a social economic loss." Paul A. Samuelson, *Economics*, 8th ed. (New York: McGraw-Hill, 1970), p. 151, footnote 5. — On the other hand, he does not oppose pay-television on such grounds. See above, footnote 49.

variabilities in the *scale* of the proposed facility, in the spectrum of *clients*, and in the *composition* of services obtainable from the resource; and he may take note of the possible interrelations among these three factors in the public choices in question.

The lighthouse near dangerous rocks and shoals in an ocean bay gives only one physical service, warning lights to the navigators of ships. A river dam for flood control may give only one kind of service, protection against flooding, though many dams also serve other purposes. A school system, however, may serve many different purposes, and it is often an oversimplification to put all services rendered by the system under the heading "education."[52] On the other hand, a public program for immunization (vaccination or other kinds of innoculation) may be regarded as yielding one physically or physiologically distinct service, protection against infectious disease (which has the special feature that every member of the community benefits from the immunization of his fellow members because it makes his own protection much safer).

The existence of multipurpose public goods invites a discussion not included in any of the writings that have come to my attention. Some who have written about public goods and the unrevealed valuations of their services by the beneficiaries have chosen for their illustration a public park in a densely populated city. They have not, however, distinguished the variety of services yielded by the park,

[52] Some writers take it for granted that the public-school system is a public good. This is by no means certain; surely not if the schools are used to capacity or are even overcrowded. There may be a minimum size of school, with zero marginal cost with respect to *some* "fixed" factors, but beyond that size one cannot count on zero marginal cost for the accommodation of additional students.

The danger of misunderstanding any terminology that uses English words to denote technical concepts in a special field is great; indeed, misunderstandings are unavoidable if noneconomists believe that they can know without special effort what economists mean, for example, by "public good." To furnish such an example let me quote from a recent article written jointly by a historian of education and a political scientist. They state that "schooling is a public rather than private good, and hence its base of support and governance must extend well beyond those who directly benefit (for example, school employees and students and their families). If education were simply a consumer good—like clothes, a matter of individual taste—there would be little sense in seeking common ground. But the schooling of all affects the future of all, at least indirectly." David Tyack and Elisabeth Hansot, "Conflict and Consensus in American Public Education," *Daedalus*, Vol. 110 (Summer 1981), p. 23. If the writers had learned the economists' jargon, they would have realized that the existence of "externalities" such as third-party benefits does not suffice to transform a private good into a public good, that public goods can be (either or both) consumption goods and investment goods, and that education is usually regarded as investment from the public as well as from the private point of view, and almost never as "simply a consumer good."

a task to which I shall address myself forthwith.[53] Not that any new and important insights will be obtained from this exercise; but it will allow the reader to comprehend without toil and tears some homely implications of the theory that would not normally be derived from inspecting a system of simultaneous equations.

The Park, the Birdwatchers, and the Lovers

According to widely accepted definitions, a park is a public good even if it is privately owned and not open to the public. This is so by virtue of the fact that other persons—though perhaps not very many—*could* be admitted to the park and *could* enjoy it without any extra cost to the owner or rightful users. That is to say, zero marginal cost is the criterion of a public good, at least under the most authoritative definition. Other definitions have stressed the principle of exclusion, or rather nonexcludability, as a characteristic of a public good, but this is now out of fashion. That unauthorized persons *can* be excluded from privately owned parks follows from the fact that they actually *are* effectively excluded in any number of instances. In some large cities—London, New York, and others—there are parks owned by clubs and associations and open only to members and their families and guests. Finally, there is the possibility of parks being open to the public upon payment of an admission charge. That people can be excluded from using the public good, or from using some or all of its services, may be an important issue of public policy, but theorists have found it preferable to separate this question from the analysis of the potential benefits to potential users.

The cost of building and maintaining the park is assumed to be fixed, no matter who bears it—the private owner (an individual person or a voluntary association) or the local government—and no matter how it is financed—out of the owners' income and wealth, private gifts, loans, general taxes, admission charges, and so forth. To be sure, that the cost is taken to be fixed is again a simplifying, partly counterfactual assumption: for, if the park is visited by many, the care of the lawn and paths and the removal of litter may cause extra expenses. Even the assumption that a park of a given size can yield a fixed bundle of services is unrealistic, because some services become quickly impaired through congestion. (Too many joggers or ball players may impinge on the peaceful rest sought by readers and sunbathers; in the economist's language, some of the services rendered by the facility are technically complementary up to a point

---

[53] That I am "using" a park for paradigmatic purposes does not add an additional service yielded by that public good, for my idealized park is only a mental construction, not a real park with flowers, birds, and bees.

but become substitutes as soon as overcrowding sets in.) This implies that a public good may stop being a public good when it is used by so many that they get in each other's way: the park is a public good only as long as it has ample extra space for additional users. I shall treat it as satisfying this condition and I shall also abstract from the marginal maintenance cost associated with heavy use and abuse.

A list of services offered by the park to a variety of users might include better air for people within the park, for people living or working in buildings adjacent to the park, and for people within a radius of a mile or so around the park; more sunlight for people within the park and for people in buildings adjacent to the park in rooms facing the park; beauty in the form of lawns, flowers, shrubs, and trees for people within the park and for people overlooking or looking into the park; beauty in the form of some tasteful sculptures for those who appreciate the fine arts; the joy of sight and sound of birds for people within the park and for people in buildings adjacent to the park to whom the birds pay frequent visits on balconies and windowsills; pleasant paths and lawns for strollers, walking alone, or in company conversing undisturbed by the hurly-burly of the city (and perhaps by the fear of being overheard); tracks and courses for joggers and runners; playgrounds for children and sports fans; restful places for readers and dozers, lying in the sun or under a shady tree; cozy nooks for lovers sheltered by sympathetic shrubs and bushes; and probably several other nice things—less noise, less dust—appreciated by different users of the park.[54]

With so many different services yielded, the users' benefits from a park of a given "size" in terms of square measure, investment outlay, or annual maintenance cost cannot unambiguously be estimated ex ante. A question asked in a referendum whether the government should provide a park at a construction cost of $500,000 cannot be answered meaningfully, let alone truthfully, before voters are shown a blueprint with explanations about its expected capacity to cater to breathers of good air, birdwatchers, strollers, joggers, dozers, lovers, and others. Although these complications do not impair the validity of the theory of revealed and unrevealed preferences, they certainly rule out any thoughts of practical implementation of

---

[54] The shrubs and bushes provide also hiding places for muggers—an external benefit of a rather special kind, closely associated with larger negative effects on other users of the public facility. (This note was suggested by Mary Huber.) The birds on the windowsills are also sometimes unwelcome for the mess they deposit. Some of my friends and fellow expositors of the theory of public goods would disapprove of my list of possible benefits and would replace it by an expression like $b = (b_1, b_2, \ldots b_n)$.

schemes for extracting unrevealed valuations. The benefits accruing to the different users of the many-sided public facility can never be measured or estimated. A system of admission prices could possibly lead to a partial disclosure of buyers' satisfactions, but such a system would not be consistent with Pareto optimality (efficiency)—let alone, optimality of "social welfare"—since, with positive prices and zero marginal cost, the facility would surely be "underutilized." If no admission prices are charged and the cost of the public project is covered by taxes, the problem of efficient and equitable tax assessments is unsolved, especially if taxes are imposed on people who never take advantage of any of the potential services offered.

Degrees of Externality

It has been suggested that the essence of the concept of public goods should be seen in their "consumption externalities."[55] This kind of externality means that the benefits available from the good in question could be enjoyed by two or more persons simultaneously. Once the good exists and can be used by one person, its benefits could also be available, without extra cost, to one, two, or more others; "could," provided others are not deliberately excluded. There are theorists who object to this meaning of externality of benefits and who would restrict the term to situations where the desired (or undesired) effects of the use of the good by one person *actually* affect some others. In other words, if a user of a good *prevents* any shared use by others and *prevents* benefits (or ill effects) afforded by the use of the good from spilling over to other persons, then the term "externality" (or external effects) seems out of place, at least to readers and students who like to hold the term to its original meaning. Yet I see no strong reasons for rejecting the employment of the term to denote *potential* effects, and, hence, for objecting to having potential external benefits declared as the criterion of a public (or social) good.[56]

There is, however, another kind of externality, a kind well illustrated by our paradigmatic park. Whereas most of the services of the park can be enjoyed only by persons within it, some services accrue

[55] Samuelson, in "Public Expenditures and Taxation," p. 102.

[56] I do not see, however, why Samuelson speaks only of "*consumption* externality" and not of *general* externality in the provision and use of goods and services. External effects in production are at least as important as those in consumption, and the implications for "productivity functions" are as significant, if not more so, as those for "preference functions." Perhaps Samuelson, in defining public goods, meant "consumption" to include productive use, and "preference" or "utility" to include productivity considerations. (At one place Samuelson states that "a public good is one that enters two or more persons' utility." Ibid., p. 108.)

to persons outside, to "external" beneficiaries in the literal sense of the word. The breathers of better air in buildings adjacent to the park, or not too far from it; the recipients of better sunlight in rooms facing the park; the persons in buildings overlooking the park, or the passers-by looking into it, enjoying the trees and bushes; the birdwatchers nearby; these are at least four kinds of outside beneficiaries, obtaining really external effects of the existence of the park.

These effects are external also in the conventional economic sense: the owners, operators, or users of the park can neither control these effects nor collect pecuniary compensation for the benefits rendered. Whereas the owners or operators of the park could, by charging admission fees to visitors of the park, create money revenues for themselves, they cannot collect from passers-by; and the only way to "internalize" the benefits accruing to persons living or working in the vicinity of the park would be to buy the surrounding land and buildings before the park is built. Otherwise the owners of the real property around the park will be the lucky recipients of "unearned increments" in the form of higher rents and higher land values. These are "external effects" in the original, much narrower, sense of the term.

The theory of public expenditures and taxation can accommodate some of these old-fashioned (Pigovian) externalities more easily than the newfangled ones (the Samuelsonian "consumption externalities"), because the external benefits accruing to the occupants of the nearby buildings are likely to show up in increased market values of the well-sited real estate and can be captured by the authorities through appropriate tax assessments. The presence of market prices for land and buildings affords the theorists as well as the tax authorities the advantages of revealed preferences on the part of the external beneficiaries, advantages theorists and tax authorities are denied by the public-good character of the services enjoyed by those inside the park, that is, persons who will not reveal the subjective value of what they obtain.

Psychic Public Goods

Some public goods are facilities rendering material or tangible services. A municipal or regional water supply system with excess capacity may be used as an example. Most public goods, however, render nontangible services, though there is the undecided conceptual question whether the designation "public good" should be given to the physical *facilities* providing the intangible services or rather to the *services* provided. This question has not been given much attention in the literature on public goods. Perhaps it does not matter whether the lighthouse (and its crew) or the light beam that it sends is regarded as the public good. In some instances even more candidates may vie for the title "public good." Think of the medical facilities and the attending technicians that supply inoculations; the inoculations that provide protection against infectious diseases; and the protection enjoyed by the inoculated individuals (and even by some noninoculated) thanks to the whole public-health program, inclusive of the law, law enforcement, or propaganda campaign that coerce or induce people to be inoculated. The program, the facilities, the inoculations, and the protection, each may be a reasonable candidate for the characterization as "public good."

Analogous questions have been raised with regard to private goods. Do we, as consumers, want bread or rather the nutritional and gustatory services that it renders? Do we want shoes or rather the protection they afford against cold and injury? Several activities may be required between the acquisition of a physical consumer good and the consumer's final want satisfaction. Think of food items, purchased at the store, carried home, prepared for cooking, cooked, served, carved or cut, and finally chewed and swallowed, all before they can render the desired nutritional services. These questions—of precisely what it is that satisfies our wants—have been raised and discussed but usually put aside as unimportant for most analytical purposes. Nevertheless, the fact that consumer goods may be tangible objects rendering intangible services, and that really the latter are what satisfies our wants can hardly be denied.

In the case of public goods, however, another kind of intangibility may exist and call for our attention: some public goods may have only what I propose to call an "awareness effect." Needless to say, for anything to be appreciated and valued as a "good," awareness of its being good for something is a logical prerequisite. One may wish to distinguish between physical, chemical, and other qualities of a good and purely psychic additions to its value through awareness effects of various kinds. Advertising, for example, may make an otherwise unchanged product a more highly valued good merely because its users are made aware, perhaps falsely, of some special feature of the product. Sometimes the information or awareness effect may account for a large part of the value of the good. In the case of some goods, information, knowledge, and awareness are not merely part but the whole of what makes them goods, that is, useful and valuable. And in certain cases the "usefulness" may not in any but a very indirect sense affect the recipients of the information, the persons becoming aware of something: they may simply be glad to hear it or read it.

Illustrations may clarify the distinctions here proposed. Financial information is surely intangible, but it may do something for the material circumstances of the informed. Education, to the extent that it conveys *practical* knowledge, may increase the future earning power of the educated; and to the extent that it produces solely *intellectual* knowledge, it may increase the capacity of the educated to enjoy life. Entertainment does not affect either the material circumstances of the entertained or their future life-enjoying capacity, but it gives them an immediate pleasure; such "*pastime* knowledge" may have an economic value as well as a moral value to its recipient.[57] Finally, there is a kind of information that makes the recipients "feel good" for reasons that have little or nothing to do with their direct personal well-being, present or future; it is information that "pleases their soul" in that it conveys a realization of some objectives of a group with which the recipients identify. For example, they may learn about something that appeals to their ethical, religious, or political persuasions; or that flatters their pride as members of a group, be it a club, an institution, or as residents of a town or province, or citizens of a country or nation. Awareness of some event or change of conditions may create, for members of a particular group, feelings of satisfaction or gratification, even if their own circumstances are not affected by that event or change of conditions. This information, then, is a public good—zero marginal cost with respect to additional recipients of the information—that derives its value exclusively from the "awareness effect."

I am not the inventor of this conceptual class of public goods. Some writers on international trade have referred to this source of satisfaction due to public awareness when they have tried to explain why nations protect inefficient domestic producers against foreign competition. Many citizens derive "psychic incomes" from the thought that the goods they consume are not imported but are made in their own country.[58] "Their good feeling or happiness is comparable to that derived from having a winning football team, a native or resident composer of world fame, or a generally admired natural world wonder."[59] A good feeling produced by a piece of information about the

---

[57] In Volume I, *Knowledge and Knowledge Production*, I distinguished these classes of knowledge on p. 108.

[58] Harry G. Johnson, "An Economic Theory of Protectionism, Tariff Bargaining, and the Formation of Customs Unions," *Journal of Political Economy*, Vol. 73 (May-June 1965), p. 258. Also Charles A. Cooper and Benton F. Massell, "A New Look at Customs Union Theory," *Economic Journal*, Vol. 75 (December 1965), pp. 742-747.

[59] Fritz Machlup, *A History of Thought on Economic Integration* (London: Macmillan, 1977), p. 267.

group of which the individual happens to be a member is different from the good feeling produced by something that affects the individual directly, perhaps something that keeps him warm, smells good, tastes good, keeps him healthy, or protects him from bodily harm, from damage to his property, or from threats to his freedom.

I have not found appropriate terms to distinguish the various kinds of intangible goods that are appreciated chiefly or exclusively for the awareness effects upon the recipients. Where the awareness effect is only a small addition to effects that can possibly be perceived with one of the five senses, the problems of economic analysis are minor. Where the awareness effect dominates, analysis becomes complicated, especially if a part of the effect derives from expectations of future effects on the recipients themselves, or on their capacities to earn or to enjoy, and another part derives from merely "soul-pleasing" information about fellow club members or fellow citizens.

Here is an illustration of one of these "mixed" kinds of awareness. Assume, for example, that the community is considering an expensive project of subsidized housing for the poor, and that the worth of the project to the residents of the city is to be ascertained. The nonpoor residents may be affected by a hoped-for reduction in the crime rate, a hoped-for reduction in morbidity (through better disease control, reduced pollution, etc.), and an expected improvement in the city's appearance (attractive buildings replacing ugly slums); but they may also be gratified by the expectation of better living conditions for the poor.[60] The last ingredient of the mixture of hopes and expectations is the one I call "soul-pleasing" information; its value depends on a developed sense of "social conscience."[61]

One more example of a psychic public good might be a project designed to achieve a more equal distribution of the national income by means of a system of taxes and bonuses. The social cost consists of the expense of the bureaucratic apparatus collecting taxes and dispensing benefit payments and of the possible reduction in national income due to the disincentive effects of higher taxes. The worth of the project to individual residents or voters is determined by how they expect to be directly affected as taxpayers or recipients of transfer payments and by how they value the egalitarian policy. Those who would expect neither to pay higher taxes nor to receive

---

[60] I have omitted some possibly negative effects, such as adverse changes in the flow of street traffic.

[61] The term "altruism" has been used in the analyses of situations of this kind. See, for example, Emil Sax, "Die Wertungstheorie der Steuer," *Zeitschrift für Volkswirtschaft und Sozialpolitik*, N.S., Vol. 4, 1924, p. 212.

benefit payments would value the project entirely on the basis of their socioeconomic philosophy.

Pragmatic Implications of the Theory of Public Goods

After this lengthy discourse on the economics of public goods—with allusions to sophisticated mathematical models, imaginative schemes to elicit truthful information on expected utilities, ingenious systems of voting, taxing, and bribing for the sake of maximizing social-welfare functions, but also with some lighthearted illustrations designed to relieve the strain of dead-earnest theorizing—the reader may ask "so what?" Are there any pragmatic implications of the theory of public goods and, if so, what are they?

Some goods (services) would not be provided by private enterprise if it were not for special incentives created by public or collective agencies. If users or beneficiaries of these goods cannot be excluded for nonpayment or cannot be made to pay what the goods are worth to them, private enterprise cannot be expected to produce what is clearly wanted. If, on the other hand, nonpayers can be excluded and a price can be collected, production will be smaller than would be "socially optimal," because additional output could be had at no extra cost but is offered for sale only at a positive price. In such circumstances it has been considered good policy for the state to provide incentives in the form of subsidies to producers or consumers or, alternatively, to have the state take over the task of providing the good.

If the number of public goods is small relative to the mass of private goods, the schemes adopted for the provision of the public goods need not seriously disturb or distort the free-market economy. There is a danger of waste and distortion if people attempt to remedy or counteract every instance of "market failure," because the likelihood of failure in public decision-making and of bureaucratic failure in implementing these decisions may be much greater. Some deviations from "ideal output" may be far less serious than the inefficiencies, wastes, and distortions involved in attempts to counteract the market failures. If some public goods are produced in the private sector and offered in the market at prices in excess of marginal cost (where nonpayers can be excluded without excessive cost), the consequent underproduction (relative to the social optimum) may constitute shortfalls far more tolerable than the wastes due to public schemes for avoiding them.

The situation is perhaps different if public goods are the rule and private goods the exception—something not easily discernible, because many goods are semiprivate and semipublic. This is especially true for goods (services) produced in facilities that cannot be efficiently established at small scale; when such facilities are underutilized, so that marginal cost does not include any return to the investment that created them, the public-good character may prevail, but it declines and eventually vanishes as excess capacity disappears.

Some economists have proposed a very different kind of solution to the problem of public goods: a "planning approach" that would work for both public and private goods. The idea is that a central board would engage in a systematic dialogue with all individual economic agents and thereby generate responses to the board's probes. The agents' responses would be offers to sell or buy certain quantities of a good or service at a price held out by the board or, alternatively, to pay certain prices for a quantity of a good or service to be provided by the board. Inasmuch as a scheme of central price setting or quantity fixing would work for public as for nonpublic goods, its discussion may well be joined with that of central planning. A "planning approach to the public-good problem" may with equal justification be examined in a section on central planning or in a section on public goods.[62] I choose to defer the discussion to the next chapter, to the section on "Dispersed Knowledge and Central Planning."

[62] Mary Huber has questioned the consistency of this unequal treatment: why examine the "voting approach to the public-good problem" under the heading of "public goods" but the "planning approach" under "central planning"? My reply is that the voting approach could not possibly be considered for more than a handful of goods whereas the planning approach could, at least in theory, work for any number—all the millions that exist.

CHAPTER 6

New Knowledge,
Dispersed Information, and
Central Planning

THE DISCUSSIONS of "Public Decisions and Public Goods" in the preceding chapter are fully pertinent to the topics dealt with in the present chapter; indeed it might have made better sense to have the discourse on these closely related issues pressed into one chapter. It would have been, however, an excessively long chapter, which few readers could finish in one sitting. If the reader wants a break, it may be expedient to suggest an appropriate place for it. A break at this point can be well defended: in the discussion of public choice—at least up to the section on psychic public goods—the role of knowledge and information was "instrumental," an "input" in the process of choice; in the discussion that follows in the first half of this chapter, knowledge plays a double role, for it will be both input and output, in that knowledgeable and informed choices about the production of knowledge will be examined. The role of information in decisions about streets, parks, and lighthouses was investigated in the previous chapter; now we shall investigate the role of information and knowledge in decisions about generating *new* knowledge. In the second section of this chapter, we shall examine another aspect of knowledge: its dispersion among many different minds and the controversy about the possibility of centralizing or socializing it.

KNOWLEDGE AS A PUBLIC GOOD

If a public or social good is defined as one that can be used by additional persons without causing any additional cost, then knowledge is such a good of the purest type. To seek knowledge, to create, acquire, transmit, or retrieve knowledge—all these activities are ordinarily associated with effort or sacrifice of some sort; that is, they are not without cost. To use existing knowledge, however, may be costless.

That the use of existing knowledge can be without marginal cost is often disbelieved because such use is ordinarily associated with activities that require labor, materials, or other scarce resources. For example, to make a paper airplane requires the use of paper and labor besides the use of knowledge, and every additional paper airplane costs again paper and labor. No *additional knowledge*, however, is needed; the same knowledge that enables the youngster to make his first airplane will serve him to make his sixth and his twelfth airplane. (He may even learn more "by doing" and with increased skill need less time per airplane, but this is a different matter; perhaps some of the "excessively long" time it took him to make the first few units of output should be regarded as cost of acquiring some "how-to knowledge." The point to grasp and to remember is that the same amount of knowledge that is used to make m units of output will serve to make m + 1 units, and the same knowledge that is used by n persons (producers) can enable n + 1 persons to make the same product. There may be a cost of the transfer of knowledge, of teaching it and learning it, but there is no additional cost of using it once it has been acquired.

Existing Knowledge versus New Knowledge

If the marginal cost of using existing knowledge is zero, but the cost of creating new knowledge is high, a serious dilemma arises. Maximum efficiency in the use of existing knowledge requires that no restriction be placed on that use; hence, the price of using existing knowledge has to be zero. Maximum efficiency in the use of resources to *create* new knowledge requires that the opportunity cost of all needed resources can be expected to be fully recovered by the value of the knowledge created; this will be possible only if the pecuniary benefits attributable to the use of the new knowledge are actually captured or requisitioned to pay for the cost of creating it; this requires that a "price" be paid for the use of the knowledge. Such a price can be maintained only if the use of the new knowledge is restricted. In brief, only the expectation of a positive price of the use of knowledge will secure the allocation of resources to the creation of knowledge, but only a zero price will secure the efficient use of the knowledge once it has been created.

This dilemma has challenged the analytical intelligence of economists for hundreds of years, even though it has been only during the last fifty years or so that they recognized that it is the general dilemma of the provision and utilization of public goods. They have also learned that there is no solution that is satisfactory in a normative sense. The provision of the public good requires resources, but the cost of these resources can be recovered from the users of the public good (or its services) only if the use is restricted.

In pursuing this analysis and deliberating on its welfare-economic aspects we are in danger of overgeneralizing. A special kind of knowledge, namely, technological and other commercially useful knowledge of enduring value, has been given an unduly paradigmatic place in the universe of knowledge; the normative dilemma associated with that kind of knowledge is not present or not serious in connection with most other kinds of knowledge. The bulk of the stock of intellectual and practical knowledge has been around for years and decades, and even centuries; the bulk of *new* knowledge, currently created (say, in the last year), is not of enduring relevance and thus does not raise the problem of securing the continuity of a stream of pecuniary revenues deriving from its use. Knowledge expected to become obsolete or irrelevant after a relatively short time may be very much worth producing and acquiring for current use, but the policy problem of keeping eager users from using it is not very significant. Even where such knowledge (or "information") is commercially produced and distributed, it is not difficult to exclude nonpayers—free riders—from immediate access; and delayed access is without value because of the ephemeral service life of this information.

Just what then troubles the welfare economist about the "public-good character" of knowledge? It is in the class of knowledge sometimes called "industrial property," chiefly novel technological inventions resulting from heavy expenditures for research and/or development, which—without subsidies—cannot be recovered except if the use of the invention is restricted for several years.[1] It may help our sense of proportions if we can see how much the R and D expenditures in the United States weigh in the total annual cost of creating and transmitting knowledge. In 1958, public and private expenditures for R and D accounted for 8.1 per cent of the total cost of "knowledge production."[2] Included in the expenditures for research were those for basic research in all fields, including some that had nothing to do with the creation of new technological knowledge

[1] "Inventions . . . , once they have been made and developed, require no maintenance and no replacement. The marginal cost of using them is zero even in the long run; and 'perfectly competitive pricing' would not permit recovery of any part of the investment cost." Fritz Machlup, *An Economic Review of the Patent System*, Study No. 15 of the Subcommittee on Patents, Trademarks, and Copyrights of the Committee on the Judiciary, U.S. Senate, 85th Cong., 2d Session, pursuant to S. Res. 236 (Washington, D.C.: U.S. Government Printing Office, 1958), p. 59.

[2] Fritz Machlup, *The Production and Distribution of Knowledge in the United States* (Princeton: Princeton University Press, 1962), p. 361.

or any knowledge of industrial or practical use. More recent estimates show even smaller magnitudes. Figures based on somewhat different techniques of calculation, in 1967, give the share of R and D in the total of "information activities" as 4.5 per cent.[3] Thus, if new industrial technology is the knowledge for which the public-good dilemma is most critical, we may take comfort from the fact that it relates only to a small part of society's production of knowledge.

New technology may be the most interesting class of knowledge in the present context, but there are also other kinds that are affected by the public-good dilemma. Recorded reference works, texts in books and journals, music, graphics, and other printed matter may be in this category. The marginal cost of an additional copy may contain the cost of paper, binding, distribution and delivery services, and other incremental outlays for required resources; but no additional inputs are required from authors, editors, artists, composers, compositors, and other producers of the published knowledge, so that no additional costs are incurred for these once-for-all activities. If the selling price for the output includes nothing to pay for "fixed" inputs, no pecuniary compensations can be paid to the persons who have provided them. Temporary monopoly rights for the sale of the products are needed to secure prices above marginal cost and, hence, to provide incomes to those who have contributed their "knowledge-producing services."

Broadcasting is another class of knowledge-producing activities that, if the rule "price not to exceed marginal cost" were imposed, would be left without any revenue for services rendered: radio and television stations can serve additional listeners and viewers without additional cost. In this case, where the customers provide their own appliances, the total cost to the broadcaster is independent of the size of the audience within a given area, which implies zero marginal cost per customer. Alternative solutions are to sell subscriptions at a monopoly price, to sell broadcasting time to advertisers, to cover the cost through subsidies paid from tax revenues, or to combine any or all of these revenue-raising techniques.

These examples may have served as an appropriate transition from

---

[3] Marc Uri Porat, The Information Economy (Washington, D.C.: U.S. Department of Commerce, Office of Telecommunications, 1977). The statistics provided in these nine volumes do not yield this information directly, because the input-output tables of the Bureau of Economic Analysis do not supply the appropriate data. We may take, however, Porat's figure of $368.1 billion for total expenditures for information in 1967 and compare with it the expenditures reported in the tables of the National Science Foundation of $16.5 billion for the total of governmental, business, and private R and D activities. This yields a share of 4.5 per cent, much smaller than in 1958.

the section on social or public goods to a section on new knowledge. Important as it is to see the theoretical connections among the different areas in the economics of knowledge and information, we should not linger on the topical transition but, instead, move on to an analysis of the incentives to generate and use new knowledge.

•

GENERATION AND USE OF NEW KNOWLEDGE

Arguments supporting or opposing the practice of granting monopoly privileges for the exclusive use of technological inventions constitute one of the oldest themes in economic analysis. *Special* monopoly grants by kings and other rulers to private inventors and innovators were known in the fourteenth century.[4] The first *general* promise of exclusive rights to inventors was made in a statute enacted in 1474 by the Republic of Venice. In the sixteenth century, patents were issued by German princes, some of whom had a well-reasoned policy of granting privileges on the basis of a careful consideration of the utility and novelty of the inventions and of the burden that would be imposed on the country by excluding others from the use of these inventions and by enabling the patentees to charge higher prices.

An English court in 1603, in the "Case of Monopolies," declared void under common law a monopoly on playing cards, for which no new knowledge was involved; and the Statute of Monopolies of 1623/1624 prohibited exclusive rights to trade—except patent monopolies to the "first and true inventor" of a "new manufacture." In the United States of America, the Constitution of 1787 gave to Congress the power "to promote the Progress of Science and useful Arts, by securing for limited Times to Authors and Inventors the exclusive Right to their respective Writings and Discoveries." Under this power the Congress passed the patent law in 1790.

Promote Inventions, Restrict Their Use

We are confronted here with an economic theory explicitly stated and translated into political and legal action at least six hundred years ago and restated hundreds of times: the theory that the *generation* of technological knowledge can be promoted by promises of restrictions on its *use*. Economists have never rejected the theory, but they have often disagreed on the *net* effects of the system of monopoly grants by means of patents of invention. Such net effects

---

[4] For references, see my study, *An Economic Review of the Patent System*, p. 2. — A few sentences from this study are reproduced in the text above.

are impossible to estimate, because they presuppose answers to un-answerable questions: How many inventions would *not* be made and developed if no promises were given that the inventor or his assignee or licensee would be protected against competition from imitators? How much output is *not* produced when competitors are not allowed to use the superior production processes or to make and sell the novel products protected by patents? Both the benefits society stands to gain and the losses it stands to suffer can be appraised only by comparing actual with fictitious situations, with no clues, let alone evidence, available for such comparisons.[5]

Naive empiricists, looking at "the record" and refusing to "spec-ulate," might simply count the number of patent applications or the number of patents issued and make the positive pronouncement that all these inventions for which patents were sought or obtained were "evidently" made thanks to the incentive provided by the patent system. These positivists seem untroubled by the possibility and strong probability that many of the inventions filed with the patent office may have been made in any case, that is, also in the absence of a patent system, and many others would have been made only a little later, so that the patent incentive could be credited at best for the gains due to the earlier emergence of the invention.[6] On the other

[5] During the 1940s and 1950s I was working on a book on "The Economics of the Patent System." Several other commitments retarded the progress. By 1950 I had completed seven chapters. Later I expanded the scope of the undertaking and changed the title to "The Economics of Invention, Innovation, and the Patent System." The outline provided for 31 chapters, of which about one-half were in various stages of completion by 1957. Upon request of John C. Stedman, associate counsel of Senator Joseph C. O'Mahoney, I used some of the material for Study No. 14, prepared for the Subcommittee on Patents, Trademarks, and Copyrights, Committee of the Judiciary, U.S. Congress, Senate (Washington: Government Printing Office, 1958). Upon invi-tation of Simon Kuznets I used parts of two chapters of my manuscript for the paper "The Supply of Inventors and Inventions," presented at the Conference on *The Rate and Direction of Inventive Activity*, organized by the National Bureau of Economic Research. An abbreviated version of the paper was published in the volume of pro-ceedings. (Princeton: Princeton University Press, 1962), a full version in the *Welt-wirtschaftliches Archiv*, Vol. 85 (No. 2, 1960), pp. 210-254. Two articles in the *Hand-wörterbuch der Sozialwissenschaften* (1962) and the article "Patents" in the *International Encyclopedia of the Social Sciences* (1968) were among the byproducts of my labors. The original manuscript, however, of several hundred pages, has been waiting for me to find the time to complete the work—which I now realize will never come.

[6] My remarks about "naive empiricists" should not be taken as denying the im-portance of findings from truly competent empirical research in this area. In a study reported after I had written this chapter, Edwin Mansfield and his associates have gained significant insights on imitation costs and inventions that would have been made also without patent incentives: "Patents do tend to increase imitation costs, particularly in the drug industry; but excluding drugs, patent protection did not even

hand, it is conceivable that the naive empiricist fails to credit the system for unrecorded contributions to progress. For example, the hope for patent monopolies may have induced research and development that actually led to useful inventions that were not patented, either because the inventors chose not to apply or because the patent office refused to award the patents. Similarly, nonpatented inventions—not included in any patent statistics—may have been inspired by patented technology.[7]

In a benefit-and-cost analysis of the patent system, the cost side includes some items that are accessible to empirical estimation, for example, the operating cost of the patent system. Most items, however, are just as inaccessible as those on the benefit side. Losses due to the limited use made of the patented technology (because of the exclusion of competitors and, consequently, because of product prices above the competitive level); losses due to the strengthening of firms' market power that may go with strong patent positions; and losses due to possible delays in the development and/or use of inventions; none of these can be read from any records. Confronted with these obstacles to analysis, I have suggested that, although "it may be impossible to estimate the total benefits and costs of the patent system, one may attempt to analyze the marginal benefits and costs of particular moderate changes in the duration, scope, or strength of patented protection."[8] One cannot hope to produce any "positive" numerical data to back up an analysis of this sort but must rely on abstract models of "probable" behavior on the basis of "plausible" expectations of "typical" businessmen. Businessmen will form "rational" expectations by interpreting past experiences and current information in the light of theories, sound or unsound, and in the shade of their personal dispositions and moods.

Pessimistic and Optimistic Monopolists and Competitors

That the theory of technological progress should be so strongly affected by methodological subjectivism may be surprising to readers not liberated from the prejudices of scientism. Subjectivist explanation of business conduct is essential in the theory of monopolistic

---

seem essential for the development and introduction of at least three-fourths of the patented innovations studied here. From the point of view of public policy, this obviously is an interesting finding." Edwin Mansfield, Mark Schwartz, and Samuel Wagner, "Imitation Costs and Patents: An Empirical Study," *Economic Journal*, Vol. 91 (December 1981), p. 917.

[7] Fritz Machlup, "Patents," *International Encyclopedia of the Social Sciences* (New York: Macmillan and The Free Press, 1968), Vol. 11, pp. 461-472, esp. pp. 469-471.

[8] Ibid., p. 470; and also Study No. 14, U.S. Congress, Senate (1958), pp. 79-80.

decision-making, where it makes a great difference whether the monopolist is confident that his market position will last, or will last under certain conditions, or whether he expects that his favorable position will be gone before long.[9]

A pessimistic monopolist is like a man suffering from an inferiority complex: he is a monopolist whose position we regard as safe—because we, as outside observers, find the probability of newcomers invading his bailiwick to be very small—but who himself is convinced that newcomers' competition will arise any moment to spoil his business. His judgment and our judgment disagree. If *he* should be right, the case would be without great social significance, because his monopoly would be finished. But if *we* are right in regarding his monopoly position as firm and safe for a long time, his conduct is apt to be rather unfortunate from the point of view of society, for he will try to make the most of his supposedly monopoly position by charging "what the traffic will bear."

For the pessimistic monopolist we can plausibly generalize that open avenues of technological advance will remain untried. Investment in industrial research, development, and innovation will not appear promising in view of the supposedly imminent advent of competition. Inventions will be suppressed if the time for the amortization of the required new investments seems too short.

On the other hand, there is the possibility of the opposite error, the overoptimistic entrepreneur who underestimates the actual degree of pliopoly (ease of entry into his field) and overestimates the safe period. He need not be an actual monopolist, nor even imagine that he is one; it suffices that he believes it will take his competitors—imitators or makers of substitutes—longer than it actually does to start competing with him. This optimism is the best promoter of technical progress. Progress calls for both innovation and imitation. If firms anticipate rapid imitation, they will not risk expensive innovations. But if imitation is rapid while the firms expect it to be slow, society will gain the benefit of innovation as well as of rapid imitation.

To buy innovation by paying with unnecessarily long delays in imitation—through patent protection for many years—is a poor bargain for society to make. Imitation always and necessarily lags behind innovation. It will be best from the point of view of society if innovators optimistically overestimate this lag. If they expect the lag to be longer than it actually is, innovation will be enhanced and

[9] Fritz Machlup, *The Economics of Sellers' Competition* (Baltimore: Johns Hopkins University Press, 1952), pp. 554-556. The next six paragraphs in the text above are reproduced, with some clauses inserted, from the cited pages.

imitation will not be delayed. That it may create this socially whole-some illusion on the part of innovators is the strongest justification for a well-designed patent system.

Let us return to our pessimistic monopolist and make sure that we do not confuse him with the seller in a position of imperfect monopoly. The latter hopes to maintain his position if he is cautious in his policy, particularly if he avoids appearing too prosperous, and perhaps also if he tries to make his position secure by introducing new technology. The pessimistic monopolist does not believe mod-eration in his price policies will avert competition or that he can avert competition by technological innovations. Since he expects com-petitors to break into his market in any event, he sees no sense in moderation in pricing and no sense in risking large investments. He will pursue a short-run policy of exploiting his position while he can. He will not want to pass up profit opportunities he thinks will be gone before long.

From the point of view of society, pessimistic monopolists are the worst possible type. *Confident* monopolists may after all be "do-gooders" and, although there is no presumption that policies which people believe to be "good for society" really turn out to be so, there is at least a chance that they are. Moreover, the attention that con-fident monopolists are apt to pay to expected long-run developments, especially to the long-term growth of demand, may to some extent offset the essentially restrictive effects of monopolistic business op-eration. Sellers under *imperfect* monopoly are somehow limited in exploiting their position lest they invite its termination. But the *pessimistic* monopolists see no good reason or argument that would keep them from pursuing the most restrictive policies.

The following conclusions may be drawn from these considera-tions as they bear on the social benefits and costs of the patent system: If firms are pessimistic about the protection that patents will give them against competition from imitators, they will be less eager to invest in research, development, and inventive activity; and, with respect to the patents they obtain, they will be more restrictive in utilizing the patented technology, that is, fearing that the patents may be declared invalid, or that it will be difficult to enforce their exclusive rights against infringing competitors, they will try "to make hay while the sun shines"—to charge "what the traffic will bear" before competition spoils their market. In other words, the incentive effects of the patent system will be unduly limited, but the restrictive effects on the use of new technology will be unduly strong. The opposite result can be expected if firms are hopeful that the patent system affords them safe protection. In these circumstances they are likely to be keen on investment in inventive activity and not unduly restrictive in their pricing policies.

If one understands that the effects of the patent system, as of many other legal, political, and social institutions, depend on subjective dispositions and changing moods of people, one will not be surprised if economists are unable to pronounce with confidence and honesty on the "great social net benefits" or the "inordinate costs of protection" of exclusive rights.

Underproduction of New Technology

If competition from newcomers and imitators were so brisk and so effective that all profits or all margins above variable costs were wiped out in almost no time, no investment in inventive and innovative activity would seem attractive. This self-evident conclusion led some economic theorists to make the pronouncement that "perfect competition" would stop all technological progress. This pronouncement is not "illogical"; indeed, it follows from a special definition of perfect competition: if one defines it, not as a process in time, but as a timeless jump from one "equilibrium position" to another, prices will cover only "necessary" costs, or opportunity costs, not "sunk" costs. Even if one chooses a less formal (not analytical) definition but merely exaggerates the speed with which unrestricted newcomers' and imitators' competition works in reality, one may come to the conclusion that unrestrained competition would annihilate businessmen's propensity to invest in inventive and innovative activity. If potential investors in invention and innovation had to expect almost immediate imitation and competition to drive the price of their products instantly down to the level at which no margin above unavoidable costs would be left, they surely would decide against such investment. After all, the probability would be overwhelming that all their outlays for research, development, and innovation would be lost.[10]

[10] Joseph Schumpeter presented forceful arguments in support of monopolistic restrictions and patent monopolies to promote innovation. Monopoly power of big business would give firms the funds, the capacity, and the incentives for the inventive and innovative activities on which technical progress depends. A strong patent system would be a helpful addition to the innovators' need for temporary protection against the "perennial gale" of competition. High profits due to restrictive business policies "provide the baits that lure capital on to untried trails," which lead to new techniques of production and organization. Thus, ". . . the protection afforded by patents and so on [for example, cartel arrangements, agreements in restraint of trade] is, in the conditions of a profit economy, on balance a propelling and not an inhibiting factor." Joseph A. Schumpeter, *Capitalism, Socialism, and Democracy* (New York: Harper, 1942), pp. 84 and 88, respectively. Schumpeter's theory of the need for monopolistic

Disregarded in this argument is the fact that, in reality, there is a "natural" lag of imitation behind innovation. The first question to be raised on this count is whether that lag is sufficient to make innovative investment attractive, at least to some extent. A second question is whether artificial brakes and obstacles to the working of competition, such as the existence of monopolistic positions in many industries and the existence of a patent system, can add to the natural lag an "artificial" lag sufficient to give innovative investors the time needed to recover their investments and make a profit even when investment outlays are large. A third question is whether, despite the slowing down of imitators' competition by means of these brakes, the production of new technology is seriously below the optimum level (identified by the Pareto standard). In brief, admitted that under conditions approaching perfect competition (from imitators and newcomers) the volume of inventive and innovative investment, induced by expectations of a natural lag of competitive imitation behind innovation, is not negligible (and may be considerable), there would still be underinvestment in the creation of new technological knowledge. Even with an artificial lengthening of that lag by means of monopolistic brakes, including grants of patent monopolies, the rate of investment in inventive and innovative activities may still be below the optimum. Why is this so and how serious is the underinvestment, and the consequent underproduction of new technology, likely to be?

Several reasons have been given why there would be underproduction of technological ideas even under a patent system: inventive activity is always risky—the chances of success are quite unpredictable—and all risky activities are underexploited; patent protection is only partially effective—the chances of having patent rights successfully enforced are again unpredictable—and hence the expectations of appropriating the benefits from a successful invention are highly uncertain; and whatever schemes are devised for the exploitation of patent rights—exclusive use, royalties under licensing contracts, and so forth—are likely to fail in capturing all the benefits for investors in inventive and innovative efforts.[11]

protection of capitalistic innovators has been praised by some, rejected by others. For a survey of the literature on this issue, see Morton I. Kamien and Nancy L. Schwartz, "Market Structure and Innovation: A Survey," *Journal of Economic Literature*, Vol. 13 (March 1975), pp. 1-37.

[11] Kenneth J. Arrow, "Economic Welfare and the Allocation of Resources for Invention," in Richard Nelson, ed., *The Rate and Direction of Inventive Activity: Economic and Social Factors*, Universities—National Bureau for Economic Research Committee (Princeton: Princeton University Press, 1962), pp. 609-625.

The benefits not captured by producers of the improved technology—the external benefits from producing new knowledge—accrue to consumers. Thus, as in all cases of external benefits, private (the firms') marginal revenues will be less than social marginal benefits, with the result that too little, from society's point of view, is invested in innovative effort.

The Consumers' Free Rides

To translate economic jargon into plain English, let us try to understand how the benefits "society" derives from the availability of a new technique of production may be divided between producers and consumers. The gains to the producers who have created and developed the new knowledge are called internal benefits, internal to the firm; the gains to consumers are external, outside the firm whose venturesomeness has led to the new knowledge.

Think of an invention of a new machine for use in manufacturing a widely consumed product. An innovative firm spends large amounts of capital funds for research, development, design, experimentation, casting, machine manufacture, installation, alterations, and so forth, until finally the machine is in operation to make the product. The cost of labor and material per unit of output produced with the new machine is below what it used to be with the old process of production. If the patent system does not work for this innovator, and his competitors can procure and operate the same kind of machine, market prices will soon reflect the reduced production cost of the final product. The cost of production will, of course, include the price of the new machines, since imitators will not get them "for free" but will have to pay for them; their costs, however, will not include any outlays for the original research, development, experimentation, and so on. The innovator, having a slight headstart, may recover a small portion of his investment, but if the imitators are quick and competition is vigorous, prices will before long be down to a level that covers, besides labor and material, the machine cost per unit of output, but not any costs that the imitators need not incur. The imitators will not profit once product prices are down to the "competitive level"; the innovator will have lost a portion of the investment he made in developing the new technique. Who gains from the technological advance? The consumer, of course, since he has to pay less per unit for the product than he had to pay before the technique was in general use.

I now invite the reader to join me in a little mental experiment. Think of a demand curve of the usual form, sloping down from the upper left to the lower right, with prices of the product on the vertical axis and quantities on the horizontal. Mark two points on that curve, one depicting the situation before the introduction of the new technique, the other, farther down, the situation after the reduced production cost allows consumers to buy larger quantities at a lower price. Horizontal lines from the two points on the demand curve to the price axis will circumscribe a slice that represents the benefits accruing to the consumers if the price of the product is reduced. Visualize now what happens if the price is not reduced, perhaps because a tight patent monopoly succeeds in keeping competitors from using the new technique and allows the innovative producer to keep up the price and "capture" the margin between current cost and price, and to thereby recover some or all of the investment he had sunk into the innovative efforts. The same slice (minus the little triangle at the right end) depicts the producer's return to his investment if he can fully exploit his patent monopoly.[12]

The graphic representation of the benefits derived from the new production technique helps distinguish internal and external benefits; if the "slice" made possible by the reduction in current production cost goes to the innovating producer, it represents internal benefits; if it goes to consumers, it represents external benefits. Associated with this difference is also a different distribution of income. I resort now to a trick that enables us to eliminate the distributive consequences of the innovation: assume that the product in question is consumed by everybody and that everybody holds, in proportion to his consumption, shares in the company that makes the product

---

[12] A note for those who care about such things as little triangles: If the producer does not reduce his selling price, he cannot expect to increase his sales. If total demand is unchanged and the volume of sales remains the same as before, but the current cost per unit of output is now down to the level marked by the lower point, the increase in net revenue collected by the producer is equal to the unchanged quantity times the per-unit-cost reduction. This is the rectangular slice between the two horizontal lines but without the little triangle bordered by the demand curve that connects the two points, the lower of which represents an increased quantity purchased by consumers.

The conditional clause—"if he can fully exploit his patent monopoly"—requires a more technical explanation, which is largely directed to readers advanced in economic theory. "Full exploitation" of a monopoly position may, in pure theory encompassing extreme and fanciful situations, imply "price discrimination of the first degree," where each consumer pays for each unit the highest price he would be prepared to pay, so that (if it were not for the income effects of price changes) the seller could confiscate, as it were, the entire area under the demand curve. In this case, the monopolist, exercising price discrimination of the first (highest) degree, would capture not only the rectangles that symbolize subsequent cost reductions, but also the triangles at the right end of each rectangle. (I apologize for this digression, which probably makes no sense at all to most readers but is perhaps necessary to prove to my fellow economists that I can be unintelligible even without using mathematical notations.)

and has undertaken the investment in researching and developing the new cost-reducing technology. Thus, the consumers of this product are at the same time owners of the company that produces it. If the cost-reducing invention is patented and the innovation cannot be imitated without the patentee's authorization, the shareholder-customers have the choice of receiving the stream of benefits from the superior technology either in the form of increased dividends or in the form of reduced prices of the good. Since they are producers as well as consumers of the same product, the benefits from the new knowledge have in effect become "internalized." If the consumers' income elasticity of demand for the particular product is positive, so that they would want to use a portion of the dividend increase to purchase more of the product, they would be well advised to opt for a reduced product price. (The differential advantage would be relatively small; it is related only to the mysterious little triangle previously mentioned in a parenthesis and vaguely explained in a footnote.)

Joint Producers' and Consumers' Interests

The didactic trick of merging the interests of consumers and shareholders, and thereby changing them from hypothetical adversaries into partners in the same enterprise, may help us further in examining the optimality of decisions *before* any allocations to inventive and innovative efforts are made. One of the reasons for suspecting underinvestment in technological improvements has been that some of the benefits would be external, flowing to consumers rather than to the owners of the producing firm. The fusion of consumer and stockholder should dispose of the externality problem and show how the allocation of resources to technology-improving activities may be affected by a joint maximization of the merged benefits. Thus, the shareowners, thinking of their interests both as consumers and as owners of the producing firm, are called upon to decide how much should be spent on risky searches for technological inventions and venturesome innovations that, if successful, would reduce the cost of production. Would they vote for larger allocations? They would be told, of course, that the funds required for the investments (R and D expenditures) would have to come out of current and future dividends—current if they were taken directly out of current profits (or reducing profits if R and D is charged as current expense), future if the funds were borrowed in the market (sequestering or garnishing future earnings for the payment of interest and repayment of principal). The decision to invest in the hope for a good return in the future would clearly be viewed as a decision to give up current consumption (paid for from current dividends) in exchange for a chance of larger future consumption (made possible either through larger future dividends or through lower prices of consumable product).

The stockholders, with their stereoscopic vision as both owners and customers of the firm, would take their interests as consumers into account when they consider the possible benefits from innovative investment. If the investment is successful, they would get the full benefit, be it through lower prices or through higher dividends. This is very different from the opportunities seen by a firm closely held by a few noncustomers; these owners would have to treat the benefits to consumers as external, as outside their profit-and-loss calculations. One may conclude that the allocations of resources to inventive and innovative activities would be smaller with the separation of consumer and producer interests.

A possibly offsetting factor might be seen in differences between business managers and small stockholders in their risk estimates and risk aversion. If the stockholders delegate to the management the power to make all decisions about the uses of funds, then the differences need not matter; but if the stockholders had to vote on whether risky outlays should be made at the expense of profits and dividends in the near and medium-term future, they might be more cautious and more niggardly in their allocations. (Their "time preference"—favoring present consumption over promises of future consumption—is probably greater if they reveal it in direct voting than if they let the elected directors express it on their behalf.) The management's propensity to invest and to spend for purposes of exploration and innovation is probably much higher than a small stockholder's propensity to make such outlays, simply because the managers do not have to sacrifice present consumption or other benefits; directing and overseeing larger investments and bolder projects may even increase their present emoluments. They can easily be daring and enterprising with other people's money.

It is impossible to say how significantly stockholders' propensities, as reflected in their direct decision-making, would differ from their "realized" propensities reflected in the indirect decision-making delegated to their elected management. (Similar issues exist between direct and representative democracy.) It is reasonable to assume that allocations of resources to projects with uncertain returns in the distant future would be far more niggardly if the owners of corporations were to make their own decisions, instead of delegating this function to elected managers. However, some very astute observers of the economic scene, and analysts of corporate relations in particular, have concluded that management decisions do reflect the genuine preferences of the owners. For, according to these views, owners can always sell their shares of the companies they consider mismanaged (or managed in pursuit of objectives they do not approve) and acquire shares in companies managed for objectives they share.

Whatever else we may have learned from this discussion, we must have come to a sure understanding that in a model more representative of the real world—where consumers' benefits are not merged with those of the producers whose goods they purchase—large portions of the benefits expected to be derived from resource allocations to improvements in technology are external. Given such externality, there is likely to be underinvestment in technological advance and underproduction of productive knowledge. Still, this is not the last word: other factors, pulling in the opposite direction, have to be considered.

Advantages in Foreseeing Price Changes

One factor increasing the rewards from inventive and innovative activities is the opportunity of the insiders to make speculative gains from price changes associated with a change in production technique. These speculative gains are not net benefits to society but merely transfers of wealth from uninformed, or late-informed, persons to the best-informed ones. Inventors, or the firms with which they work, believing that their research and development efforts will succeed, are in good positions to foresee that certain goods and certain assets will become more valuable or less valuable when the new techniques become operative. Buying the goods and assets that are likely to appreciate, and perhaps selling short those that will lose in value, can bring substantial capital gains to the insiders. This theory has been proposed by Jack Hirshleifer.[13]

Hirshleifer illustrates his theory of inventors' speculative advantages by pointing to the opportunities for gainful speculation of which Eli Whitney could have taken advantage had he applied his information about the consequences of his cotton gin to anticipate changes in "the price of cotton, the value of slaves and of cotton-bearing land,

---

[13] Jack Hirshleifer, "The Private and Social Value of Information and the Reward to Inventive Activity," *American Economic Review*, Vol. 61 (September 1971), pp. 561-574, esp. pp. 570-571. Also "Where Are We in the Theory of Information?" *American Economic Review*, Vol. 63 (Suppl. May 1973), pp. 33-34; also Jack Hirshleifer and John G. Riley, "The Analytics of Uncertainty and Information: An Expository Survey," *Journal of Economic Literature*, Vol. 17 (December 1979), p. 1405.

the business prospects of firms engaged in cotton ware-housing and shipping, the site values of key points in the transport network that sprang up."[14]

Hirshleifer places much emphasis on these advantages "of the unique position of the innovator for forecasting and consequently capturing portions of the pecuniary effects" of the innovation. He even thinks it possible that the inventor's "position to reap speculative profits," in addition to his patent-protected share in the technological benefits, lead to overcompensation of the innovative efforts.[15]

Fishing for New Ideas, and the Rush to Invent

Another factor that possibly affects the production of technological knowledge and may offset partly, fully, or excessively the tendency to underproduce (because so large a part of the benefits is external, that is, uncaptured by the producer) has been identified by Yoram Barzel in a theory strongly supported by Hirshleifer.[16] As paraphrased by Hirshleifer, "undiscovered ideas are like fish in the sea, subject to the rule of capture. Since the patent right goes to the first in possession, with perfect patents competitive invention would be biased toward prematurity. The rule of capture leads to too many too small fish being caught!"[17] If there is free and easy entry into the fishing industry—no exclusive rights to fishing—and if there are property rights in fish caught, there will be overfishing from the point of view of society, since the population of fish is limited. Just as there would be a "rush to fish" before other fishermen catch too much of the "fugitive resource," there is a "rush to invent" before other inventors catch the best of what is still in the pool of undiscovered ideas. (Whereas the notion of an exhaustion of the pool of still undiscovered ideas is untenable if the time horizon is sufficiently wide, for any short period of time the assumption that the number of practically usable technological inventions is limited is quite sensible.[18])

---

[14] Hirshleifer, "Private and Social Value," p. 571.

[15] Ibid., pp. 571 and 572.

[16] Yoram Barzel, "Optimal Timing of Innovations," *Review of Economics and Statistics*, Vol. 50 (August 1968), pp. 348-355.

[17] Hirshleifer, "Where are We?" p. 33.

[18] I have shown elsewhere that there is no real contradiction between the proposition that "the more there is invented the easier it becomes to invent still more" and the opposite proposition that "the more there has been invented the less there is left to be invented,"—for they refer to different situations and different time horizons. Fritz Machlup, "The Supply of Inventors and Inventions," *Weltwirtschaftliches Archiv*, Vol. 85 (No. 2, 1960), pp. 236-237; reprinted in George Bitros, ed., *Selected Economic*

This rush to invent before others make the prize inventions of the time, and to secure patent protection for their exclusive use, may result in overallocation of resources in inventive and innovative activities. Some economists have concluded from these arguments that the distinction "between a right *in* an idea [more correctly, a right in the commercial use of an idea] and a right *of* engaging in search for an idea" might be recognized by proposing an appropriate change of institutions.[19] Instead of granting exclusive rights in the use of inventions, the state should auction off the rights of searching for specified inventions.[20] In such an auction, the "lowest-cost inventor" would probably make the highest bid for the right to produce the specified invention, and this would "solve" the problem of the rush to invent. Although I find playing with such ideas entertaining and instructive, I shudder at the thought that anybody might want to incorporate them in practical policy recommendations.

Perhaps we should report here the evaluation of the existing patent system by Harry Johnson at the end of a carefully developed argument.[21] He finds that, in general, the system of granting temporary monopoly rights in the use of inventions (1) does not encourage socially undesirable innovations, (2) provides insufficient incentive for some socially desirable innovations, (3) restricts the use of successful innovations once made, (4) is biased against more fundamental as compared with more superficial innovations, and against basic as compared with applied research, (5) encourages wasteful duplication of effort, (6) encourages, in particular circumstances, excessively rapid development and introduction of innovations, and (7) gives to large firms an advantage over small firms in terms of the returns to outlays for research and development.[22] Johnson, like all economic analysts before and after him, has no answer to the question "how serious in quantitative terms are the wastes and deficiencies involved in stimulating innovation by the conferment of temporary monopoly power through patents . . . , by comparison with the long-run benefits in terms of technical improvements and economic growth."[23]

Writings of Fritz Machlup (New York: New York University Press, 1976), pp. 465-466. This article is pertinent to several issues discussed in the text above.

[19] Hirshleifer and Riley, "Analytics of Uncertainty," p. 1405.

[20] Steven N. S. Cheung, "Property Rights and Invention," and "The Right to Invent and the Right to an Invention," University of Washington, Institute of Economic Research, Reports Nos. 79-11 and 79-13, 1979.

[21] Harry G. Johnson, *Aspects of Patents and Licenses as Stimuli to Innovation*. Bernhard-Harms Vorlesungen No. 7 (Kiel: Institut für Weltwirtschaft, Universität Kiel, 1976), pp. 25-36.

[22] Ibid., p. 35.

[23] Ibid., p. 36.

Confusing Uses of Terms and Figures

A debate about the patent system can easily become a comedy of errors because participants are often careless in the use of words. The most frequent confusion is between a patent and the invention it covers. A writer would say something about the use of the patent though he actually means the use of the patented invention. A patented *invention* is used if the patented product is made or the patented process is employed in production, of whatever it may be, for commercial purposes. A *patent* is used to enlist the aid of the courts in enjoining an infringer from using the patented invention; or to impress a partner in a negotiation and induce him to accept an agreement on contested issues.

The most perplexing confusions occur in discussions about the "value of patents." What the writer or speaker may have in mind is (a) the value of existing patents to their owners, (b) the value of existing patents to society, (c) the value of the patent system to society, (d) the value of patented inventions to their users, (e) the value of patented inventions to society, (f) the value of patent-induced inventions to society and perhaps other things. It is probably not necessary to explain these different "values," but perhaps it is helpful to state that to confuse an invention with the patent that excludes unauthorized persons from using it is like confusing a bridge with the tollgates that exclude many who might want to use it.[24] To say this is not to make an adverse value judgment about either patents or tollgates. To be sure, some economists have proposed the removal of all tollgates from existing bridges, but others have admitted that some important bridges would not be built were it not possible to look forward to the revenues to be collected in tolls from future users of the planned bridges.

The difference between inventions and patent rights to exclude others from using inventions has a bearing on the statistics of national wealth and the stock of capital. Domestic patents, although valuable assets to their private owners, are not part of the nation's wealth or capital stock. Inventions, however, may figure in the statistical accounts of the nation, though in a rather indirect way. National-income statistics record incomes generated by domestic productive activities or, in the product account, the goods and services produced to meet final demand by domestic consumers, business, government, and by foreigners. Final demand may be consumption or investment. Economists may regard inventions as final products, but the experts in charge of the national accounts in the United States have chosen not to do so; the "output" of research and development undertaken

---

[24] Machlup, *An Economic Review of the Patent System*, pp. 54-55.

by private business firms is treated as intermediate product, that is, cost of producing other products. In order to treat R and D uniformly, whether financed by business, by government, or by private nonprofit organizations, I shall in my own calculations treat all expenditures for R and D as investment, and therefore as part of the national product, no matter whether they have led to useful inventions or not. To cite a precedent for such a procedure: educational expenditures in the public-school system are generally treated as part of the national income regardless of whether or not they have led to certified learning achievements on the part of students.

As to statistics of national wealth, which are not computed by government statisticians but by several nonofficial scholars or organizations, practices regarding the treatment of accumulated technological knowledge vary. Again, there are no entries for an accumulated stock of inventions, but in several statistics a stock of accumulated R and D outlays, usually with some adjustment for depreciation, is recorded. In at least one statistical study of the nation's stock of capital, past outlays for R and D, adjusted for depreciation through obsolescence, are shown under a rubric of "intangible nonhuman capital."[25] Other sources prefer to treat the improvements in the nation's productive capacity through inventive activities as a formation of "human" capital. These questions will be discussed in Part II of this volume, on "Knowledge as Human Capital."

Expenditures for Research and the Growth of the Economy

That research promotes technological knowledge, invention, and innovation, and that innovation in turn promotes the growth of productivity is widely understood, or even taken for granted. Although individual research projects may fail to pan out, particular inventions may fail to become operable, and particular innovations may fail to improve productivity, an increase in the total research effort is apt, as a whole, to generate an increase in "average" productivity. Faith in this proposition is so great that most economists are convinced that the decline of the growth in productivity in the late 1970s, and its fall to zero in the early 1980s, can be explained to a large extent or even entirely by a slowdown in the growth of research expenditures. There is some controversy about the time lag between increased expenditures for research and the dependent increase in output of goods and services. Some analysts believe they can see an

[25] John W. Kendrick, *The Formation and Stock of Total Capital* (New York: National Bureau for Economic Research, 1976), p. 9.

instantaneous effect and, hence, can explain the decline in the "growth rate of productivity" by the reduction in research expenditures of the same year. Others find the disregard of a lag between research effort and effective exploitation of the new knowledge created by it quite unreasonable; they argue that one should not expect that the reaction of productivity growth to a change in research effort would become visible before several years.[26]

Both parties to this controversy seem to be thinking chiefly, or perhaps only, of the effects of research on productivity rather than of the reverse effects of the growth of economic activity upon research expenditures.[27] This direction of causality is direct and fast: when industrial activity is vigorous and growing, industry will be able and eager to invest in R and D; but when activity slows down, when profits decline or vanish, industry will retrench its investments, including its outlays for R and D. Whatever it may be that has increased the cost of production and retarded or stopped the growth of productivity, the reaction is not likely to be long delayed: research efforts will be diminished. Where government is a strong contributor to R and D, budgetary difficulties may compel it to cut its appropriations along with other programs. The annual statistics of economic magnitudes will then show both the growth of productivity and the nation's research expenditures reduced. Less alert observers of the data may misinterpret the simultaneous decline as supporting the hypothesis that the slowdown in R and D has caused an immediate decline in the growth of productivity.

The two-way link between productivity growth and research outlays may thus be seen as a feedback loop with peculiar timing, in that the effects in one direction—from factor productivity to R and D—may be quick and strong, whereas they may be delayed and weak in the opposite direction, from R and D to productivity. From a strictly long-run point of view, the mutual dependence may be ac-

[26] The hypothesis that the decline in the growth of productivity can be blamed on the R-and-D slowdown has been rejected in at least two excellent studies: Edward F. Denison, "Explanations of Declining Productivity Growth," *Survey of Current Business*, Vol. 59 (No. 8, Part II, August 1979), pp. 1-24; and Zvi Griliches, "R & D and the Productivity Slowdown," *American Economic Review*, Vol. 70, Papers and Proceedings (May 1980), pp. 343-352. Both papers supply references to writings that proclaimed the disconfirmed hypothesis.

[27] An explanation of a two-way link was given in my 1962 volume: "It is with respect to knowledge-production as social investment that one expects the two-way link between knowledge-production and national product, successful investment permitting faster growth of national product, and income growth permitting more investment in knowledge-production." Machlup, *Production and Distribution of Knowledge*, p. 365.

cepted as plausible, although the idea of "measuring" the effects of changes in research expenditures upon the growth of productivity is somewhat naive in view of the presence of dozens of other variables that may affect productivity.[28] Some important long-run tendencies, however, can be deduced from general and plausible propositions related to the difference between measurable, or at least quantifiable, outputs and nonquantifiable outputs. The output of physical goods is roughly measurable (excepting changes in quality), whereas the output of research-and-development activities is not. If that nonmeasurable output of R and D contributes to increases in the measurable output of physical goods and to a lowering of their production cost, whereas nothing of that sort happens to the R and D sector, the ratio between physical and nonphysical production is likely to change over time: the cost of R and D is likely to increase relative to the cost of material products.[29]

These considerations have nothing to do with inflationary increases of wages and prices. They refer to the relative costs of physical goods, produced with ever greater efficiency thanks to successful R and D, and the cost of R and D measured only by input—chiefly human labor—and not affected by any change in the ratio of input to nonmeasurable output. Not only is the intellectual output of researchers not measurable; there is no reason why their thought processes should become systematically more efficient over time. This unbalanced growth promises a secular decline in the growth of measured productivity per unit of factor since the size of the sector of the economy in which production becomes more efficient will decline relative to the sector in which efficiency is more or less circumscribed and, anyway, not subject to measurement.

For a better understanding of the meaning of "growth" in areas of production in which *output* cannot be measured, and most of the

---

[28] Edward Denison, in the paper cited, tried to assess, not measure, no fewer than "seventeen suggested reasons for the slowdown" in the growth of productivity (p. 20). R and D expenditures were judged to "have contributed little, if anything" to the slowdown, at most 0.1 percentage points (p. 7).

[29] William Baumol furnished an illuminating example of this tendency for the computing industry, in which "hardware," the physical machinery, is differentiated from "software," the programs and other ideas for the operation of the machinery. In the early 1970s the cost of computing was roughly 80 per cent for hardware and 20 per cent for software; during the ten years since then, hardware cost decreased 25 per cent per year while software cost (virtually pure labor) increased 6 per cent per year; as a result, the ratio is now reversed, that is, shares of hardware and software cost are now 20:80. Technological progress had brought down the cost of the computer at a spectacular rate; the cost of personnel needed for its operation had increased. William J. Baumol and Edward N. Wolff, "Feedback from Productivity Growth to R & D," *Scandinavian Journal of Economics*, Vol. 85 (forthcoming, 1983).

increase is in terms of expenditures for *input*, it may be helpful to go through a bit of hypothetical reasoning. Imagine an economy divided in two sectors, one, *A*, producing physical goods, the other, *B*, intangible services, *A* employing three fourths, *B* one fourth of the total labor force. Assume now an increase in productivity in sector *A* due to technological progress and a consequent increase in the physical output of sector *A* by, say, 10 per cent; assume further that all wages and salaries, in *A* and *B*, are increased by 10 per cent and that product prices remain unchanged. If there is no change in the allocation of resources, money expenditures will have increased by the same 10 per cent in both sectors. In Sector *A*, where "growth" is measured in terms of sales of output, an increased quantity of goods is sold at unchanged prices; in Sector *B*, where "growth" is measured in terms of payments for input, an unchanged quantity of labor is paid increased wages. Thus, the "real" increase in production in *A*, with no change in activity in *B*, results by way of adjustment in factor incomes in the same relative increase in expenditures for the intangible services of *B*. The "production" of intangible services by an unchanged quantity of labor with unchanged productivity will show the same percentage increase as the production of physical goods.

There is a reverse side to the coin. Increases in productivity in the performance of intangible services cannot be measured; indeed, most of them are in the form of improvements of quality, defying all attempts at quantification. No matter how "real," how substantial, how important they are, they need not be reflected in any increased money values of input—their only measure. As we have seen in the discussion of research and development, an increase in the efficiency and productivity of these activities may eventually result in increased productivity in industries producing physical goods, but the production of knowledge does not exhibit an increase on that score. This failure of "growth indices" to reflect improved efficiency in the production of intangible services has several implications. One of these relates to structural differences between economies: an economy with a large service-producing sector may not be able to "show off" with as large a physical growth rate as an economy that concentrates on the production of tangible goods, the increase of which is shown in the index of physical production and in GNP in constant dollars.[30]

These ideas, first expressed in my 1962 volume, have been further

[30] The last two paragraphs are a literal reproduction from my 1962 volume cited above, pages 375-376.

developed by William Baumol. In his recent paper, coauthored with Edward Wolff, he distinguishes between "a stagnant and a progressive" sector in the economy. "Inevitably, with the passage of time, the former must constitute more and more of . . . total cost." The progressive sector, with its cost falling, becomes successively smaller; the stagnant sector, with its cost (largely labor) rising, becomes larger; the combined cost will become "asymptotically stagnant." This reasoning suggests that "a slowing down of productivity growth may be a predictable consequence of the workings of the innovation mechanism that feeds it."[31]

The Transfer of Knowledge

The proposition that the *creation* of new knowledge may require valuable resources and hence have a high cost, private and social, whereas the *use* of existing knowledge may be possible without any additional cost, is perhaps too simple in that it disregards the problem of the *transfer* of knowledge. The distinction between recorded knowledge—for example, knowledge printed in books, journals, or patent claims—and knowledge in the heads of certain persons—for example, inventors, innovators, and imitators—suggests the need of different activities by which knowledge is transferred to those who want to make use of it. These activities may require the input of time, energy, and other resources.

The school system is designed to transfer knowledge from teachers, from books, and from electronic storage to the active minds of students; to teach students the skills needed to obtain access to stored knowledge in the future; and to stimulate their desire to acquire additional knowledge. Many kinds of information services have been developed in the last thirty years to facilitate the transfer of knowledge. In the case of new technological knowledge, difficulties of various sorts have made the problem of transferring it a subspecialty in economic research. Interpersonal, interfirm, interindustry, and international transfer of technology have been studied by academic scholars, public agencies, and private organizations.

It makes a difference for the ease of transfer whether the technological innovation can be described in words and pictures in detail sufficient to enable trained technicians to replicate the processes and produce the products in question. If some of the processes cannot be well described, and can be learned only by observing how they are done by those who know them, the transfer of the "know-how" is more costly, especially if the learners are in a distant part of the

---

[31] Baumol and Wolff, "Feedback."

world.[32] And much depends on the learners' receptiveness, which may be limited or underdeveloped. The transfer of technology is to a large extent "a person-to-person process"; if the recipient is not sufficiently prepared or not sufficiently motivated to absorb the knowledge, its transfer may be very difficult.[33]

The difficulties become almost insuperable if the owners of the know-how are determined to keep it secret. Such know-how may relate to patented as well as to unpatented techniques or products, notwithstanding the legal requirement of "full disclosure" in patents of invention. Processes that cannot be described in words cannot possibly be included in the claims formulated in the patent. It is said that an inventor has the choice between relying on patent protection or on protection of his secret technological knowledge.[34] Some, however, may be in the fortunate position of enjoying both protections if the patented invention cannot be "reduced to practice" (to use the trade jargon) without complementary know-how.

It is largely the question of secret know-how that gives rise to the political-economic problems of international transfer of knowledge. The owners of both patents and know-how are not prepared to share their secrets unless they can be sure of safe protection under their patents and possibly also ownership or co-ownership of the enterprises abroad in which their processes are used and their products produced. In view of this concatenation of circumstances, researchers need combined insights into the economics of patent protection, the economics of trade secrets, and the economics of multinational corporations.

A theory of the transfer of technological knowledge should not fail to distinguish different dispositions of the "haves" and the "have nots." If both are willing, that is, if the knowers are willing to share their secrets and the nonknowers are prepared and eager to learn, the transfer will surely be easier than if one of the parties were not willing. The knower cannot successfully convey his knowledge to

[32] "Much of the detailed knowledge . . . can more easily and in part exclusively be transferred by demonstration and training in actual operations." Ingvar Svennilson, "Technical Assistance: The Transfer of Industrial Know-How to Non-Industrialized Countries," in Kenneth Berrill, ed., Economic Development with Special Reference to East Asia (New York: St. Martin's Press, 1964), p. 408; quoted in Richard A. Easterlin, "Why isn't the Whole World Developed?" Journal of Economic History, Vol. 41 (March 1981), p. 4.

[33] On the "personal factor" in the successful diffusion of technological knowledge see Nathan Rosenberg, "Economic Development and the Transfer of Technology," Technology and Culture, Vol. 11 (October 1970), pp. 550-575.

[34] Steven N. S. Cheung, "Property Rights in Trade Secrets," Economic Inquiry, Vol. 20 (January 1982), pp. 40-53.

one who may "need" the know-how but is not prepared to comprehend and practice it.[35] On the other hand, the would-be recipient of
the know-how may be fully prepared and keenly interested, but little
can be done to achieve the transfer if the owner of the know-how is
not willing to give up his secrets. If the price that has to be paid for
persuading the knower to share his knowledge is very high, it may
be better to wait. Over time even the best-guarded technological
secrets are found out, or they may become obsolete.[36]

Nontechnological Commercially Useful Knowledge

Not all commercially useful new knowledge is technological. Business firms spend substantial amounts of effort and money on creating
and acquiring new knowledge that would be useful to them in non-
technological aspects of their operations. Most of this knowledge,
however, is only subjectively, not socially, new; and whatever really
new knowledge is developed in or for the firm is likely to be of the
transitory type usually referred to as "information." Some of this
information may be in the nature of a public good (in the sense that
others might use it without any increase in the total cost of its production), but only rarely is the need of it sufficiently urgent to cause
the uninformed to make a substantial effort to obtain it. Many trade
secrets remain secret because few outsiders try hard enough to elicit
the concealed knowledge. Of course, industrial espionage exists, but
it is usually directed towards gaining technological secrets.

The term "trade secret" may refer to technological or nontech-
nological knowledge; the concept includes any compilation of information—say, a list of customers—that gives a firm "an opportunity
to obtain an advantage over competitors who do not know or use
it."[37] The main point is that it serves "for continuous use in the
operation of the business"; thus "it differs from other secret information in a business . . . in that it is not simple information as to
single or ephemeral events in the conduct of the business."[38]

[35] ". . . the most important question about technology transfer in the long run is
whether the receiving side is able to absorb the technology it imports." Thane Gustafson, *Selling Russians the Rope*, Report of the Rand Corporation, 1981.

[36] The industrial development of a poor country does not substantially depend on
its access to the most recent advances in technology. The common technology of the
industrial world of twenty or thirty years ago would in most instances provide enough
scope for industrial development. Short supply of capital, and of entrepreneurial and
managerial talent, and insufficiencies of the economic "infrastructure" are, in my
opinion, much more confining limits to development than are the notorious restrictions on the access to the newest technological inventions.

[37] American Law Institute, *Restatement of Torts*, Section 757, Comment b (1939);
quoted by Steven N. S. Cheung, "Property Rights."

[38] American Law Institute, *Restatement of Torts*.

These "single or ephemeral events in the conduct of the business" are among that widely dispersed knowledge the disregard of which seriously, if not fatally, flaws most theories of central planning of the economy.

DISPERSED KNOWLEDGE AND CENTRAL PLANNING

In philosophical and sociological writings one encounters notions such as "social knowledge"[39] and "social stock of knowledge."[40] Those who coined and used such terms have not suggested that "society" can collectively plan or act on the basis of these aggregates of knowledge; on the contrary, they contrasted "social" with "individual knowledge" and the "social stock" with "private stocks of subjective knowledge" and stressed the dispersion of knowledge in individual people's minds. Only individuals can make decisions, either alone or in committees, for themselves or for others; and each individual knows only a minute fraction of what all contemporary individuals together know, no matter what efforts are made to devise information systems for making individual knowledge "centrally" available. Yet, some writers on economic planning have assumed that all relevant knowledge of individual economic agents can be reduced to numbers and that summaries or aggregates can be conveyed to central decisionmakers. This cannot be done; neither the division of knowledge nor the dispersion of knowledge can be overcome by the most advanced techniques of information-processing, and this impossibility cannot reasonably be disregarded in theories of economic planning.

The topic "central planning," because it involves the problem of conveying pertinent parts of dispersed "private" or "individual" knowledge to the "central mind" of the planning authority, has become an important subspecialty of the economics of knowledge and information. That the review of writings on this topic is being placed in the context of discussions of knowledge as a public good may seem odd to some of my readers. Several reasons, however, favor this order, and one of them is that "a central-planning approach" has been recommended as the best possible way to deal with the

[39] Bertrand Russell, *Human Knowledge: Its Scope and Limits* (New York: Simon & Schuster, 1948), p. 3. See my *Knowledge and Knowledge Production*, the first volume of this work, pp. 28-29.

[40] Alfred Schutz and Thomas Luckmann, *The Structures of the Life World*, translated by Richard M. Zaner and A. Tristam Engelhardt, Jr. (Evanston, Ill.: Northwestern University Press, 1973), Chaps. 3 and 4. See my *Knowledge and Knowledge Production*, pp. 167-168.

problem of providing public goods. If public goods are held to constitute so large a portion of total national product that a central-planning scheme is considered the appropriate way to deal with this problem, then it is reasonable to assume that the same bureaucracy will be employed to operate the mechanism for pricing all other products too.

The efficient provision of public goods is, of course, only one of several possible grounds on which central planning has been advocated.[41] The chief driving force has always been an "anticapitalist" mentality, a firm belief that the free-enterprise system is anarchic as well as exploitative, whereas socialism with central comprehensive planning is a rational, just, and efficient way to run the economy. The notion that the knowledge required for rational resource allocation is initially dispersed and unavailable to the central planners had not occurred to most advocates of planning before Friedrich Hayek clarified the implications of the division and dispersion of knowledge. "In contemporary economics the starting point for the discussion of information is Hayek's work, and its significance appears to have first occurred to him while studying the socialist controversy."[42]

Division and Dispersion of Knowledge

The central problem of economics, according to Hayek, "is how the spontaneous interaction of a number of people, each possessing only bits of knowledge, brings about a state of affairs . . . which could be brought about by deliberate direction only by somebody who possessed the combined knowledge of all those individuals."[43] In an

[41] Central planning in the form of central price setting for nonpublic goods has been seen as indicated chiefly because free-market prices would in many instances give "wrong" signals and thus lead to nonoptimal allocations of resources. The following instances figure most prominently among the reasons for "market failure": (1) indivisibility, (2) large sellers (and buyers) in monopolistic (monopsonistic) or oligopolistic (oligopsonistic) positions, (3) chronic externalities (spillover effects), and (4) increasing returns to scale. Although these and other market failures have been emphasized in hundreds of publications, the possibility of corresponding planning failures has rarely been examined. Yet, characteristically, the diagnosticians of market failures, especially those due to indivisibilities, monopolistic and oligopolistic positions, and externalities, have attempted to find techniques to correct them within the system of essentially free markets, say, through subsidies and taxes, evidently because they believed that the risk of inefficient outcomes would be greater with centralized decision-making.

[42] Benjamin N. Ward, The Socialist Economy: A Study of the Organizational Alternatives (New York: Random House, 1967), p. 25.

[43] Friedrich A. Hayek, "Economics and Knowledge," Economica, N.S., Vol. 4 (Feb-

attempt to solve this problem, Hayek distinguishes different ways in which individuals acquire the knowledge relevant to their interactions. Neither the knowledge they seek to learn at a cost to themselves nor the knowledge they acquire "as if it were by accident" plays the essential "equilibrating" or coordinating role; what matters in this respect is "the knowledge which he [the acting individual] is bound to acquire" as he attempts to carry out an original plan and finds "that the facts are different from what he expected."[44] It is the system of competitive market prices that acts to force individuals to revise their expectations and correct their original plans, and thereby "to co-ordinate the separate actions of different people."[45]

The price system acts as "a mechanism for communicating information"; and the "most significant fact about this system is the economy of knowledge with which it operates."[46] The great error that has allowed socialists to believe in the possibility of an efficient and consistent system of central economic planning is that they have identified the knowledge required for that task with scientific and technological knowledge, helpful in directing the processes of production, and with statistical knowledge, helpful in determining what to produce and how much. They have failed to see the need for the unorganized "knowledge of the particular circumstances of time and place," which cannot be conveyed in statistical form.[47] Let us see Hayek's argument in his own words:

> If we can agree that the economic problem of society is
> mainly one of rapid adaptation to changes in the particular
> circumstances of time and place, it would seem to follow
> that the ultimate decisions must be left to the people who
> are familiar with these circumstances, who know directly
> of the relevant changes and of the resources immediately
> available to meet them. We cannot expect that this problem
> will be solved by first communicating all this knowledge to
> a central board which, after integrating *all* knowledge, is-

ruary 1937), p. 49; reprinted in Hayek, *Individualism and Economic Order* (Chicago: University of Chicago Press, 1948), pp. 50-51. Hayek repeats this idea when he asks how "the combination of fragments of knowledge existing in different minds can bring about results which, if they were to be brought about deliberately, would require a knowledge on the part of the directing mind which no single person can possess." "Economics and Knowledge," p. 52; *Individualism*, p. 54.

[44] Hayek, "Economics and Knowledge," p. 51; *Individualism*, pp. 52-53.

[45] Friedrich A. Hayek, "The Use of Knowledge in Society," *American Economic Review*, Vol. 35 (September 1945), p. 526; reprinted in Hayek, *Individualism and Economic Order*, p. 85.

[46] Hayek, "Use of Knowledge," pp. 526-527; *Individualism*, p. 86.

[47] Hayek, "Use of Knowledge," p. 524; *Individualism*, p. 83.

sues its orders. We must solve it by some form of decentralization. But this answers only part of our problem. We need decentralization because only thus can we ensure that the knowledge of the particular circumstances of time and place will be promptly used. But the "man on the spot" cannot decide solely on the basis of his limited but intimate knowledge of the facts of his immediate surroundings. There still remains the problem of communicating to him such further information as he needs to fit his decisions into the whole pattern of changes of the larger economic system.

How much knowledge does he need to do so successfully? Which of the events which happen beyond the horizon of his immediate knowledge are of relevance to his immediate decision, and how much of them need he know?

There is hardly anything that happens anywhere in the world that *might* not have an effect on the decision he ought to make. But he need not know of these events as such, nor of *all* their effects. It does not matter for him *why* at the particular moment more screws of one size than of another are wanted, *why* paper bags are more readily available than canvas bags, or *why* skilled labor, or particular machine tools, have for the moment become more difficult to acquire. All that is significant for him is *how much more or less* difficult to procure they have become compared with other things with which he is also concerned, or how much more or less urgently wanted are the alternative things he produces or uses. It is always a question of the relative importance of the particular things with which he is concerned, and the causes which alter their relative importance are of no interest to him beyond the effect on those concrete things of his own environment.

Fundamentally, in a system where the knowledge of the relevant facts is dispersed among many people, prices can act to coördinate the separate actions of different people. It is worth contemplating for a moment a very simple and commonplace instance of the action of the price system to see what precisely it accomplishes. Assume that somewhere in the world a new opportunity for the use of some raw material, say tin, has arisen, or that one of the sources of supply of tin has been eliminated. It does not matter for our purpose—and it is very significant that it does not matter— which of these two causes has made tin more scarce. All that the users of tin need to know is that some of the tin they used to consume is now more profitably employed elsewhere, and that in consequence they must economize tin. There is no need for the great majority of them even to know where the more urgent need has arisen, or in favor of what other needs they ought to husband the supply. If only some of them know directly of the new demand, and switch resources over to it, and if the people who are aware of the new gap thus created in turn fill it from still other sources, the effect will rapidly spread throughout the whole economic system and influence not only all the uses of tin, but also those of its substitutes and the substitutes of these substitutes, the supply of all the things made of tin, and their substitutes, and so on; and all this without the great majority of those instrumental in bringing about these substitutions knowing anything at all about the original cause of these changes. The whole acts as one market, not because any of its members survey the whole field, but because their limited individual fields of vision sufficiently overlap so that through many intermediaries the relevant information is communicated to all. The mere fact that there is one price for any commodity—or rather that local prices are connected in a manner determined by the cost of transport, etc.—brings about the solution which (it is just conceptually possible) might have been arrived at by one single mind possessing all the information which is in fact dispersed among all the people involved in the process.[48]

I have spoken of "division and dispersion" of knowledge because I want to distinguish two different phenomena. Division of knowledge, like division of labor, refers to the fact that individuals have acquired different skills, mastered different specialties, and developed different interests and inclinations. Dispersion of knowledge refers to the "particular circumstances of time and place"; this is knowledge of momentary local situations, which may be knowledge of facts that relate only to the particular locality, to persons in the immediate environment, and also to people's current aspirations and desires—matters that are important for efficient allocation of resources but which cannot be included in reports to the planning commission.

[48] Hayek, "Use of Knowledge," p. 524-526; *Individualism*, pp. 83-86. (The reproduction of these paragraphs was kindly permitted by Hayek and the editor of the *American Economic Review*.)

Economic Calculation in Socialist Planning

Hayek's argument goes back to the claim, in 1920, by Ludwig von Mises that central planning under socialism, without markets and market prices, and "calculating" merely with "values" of goods determined by "socially necessary labor hours," could not produce efficient results consistent with the preferences of the planners, let alone of the people for whom they plan.[49] Socialist writers, from Karl Marx on, had almost regularly rejected any system of money prices for products and productive factors. Within a few years after Mises' challenge—and after the breakdown of the first attempts at planning without money and money prices in the Soviet Union—most socialist economists admitted that prices were necessary even for a centrally planned system if internally consistent allocations of resources were to be achieved; abstract blueprints were constructed for simulated markets with quasi-competitive prices coordinating all economic activities even if all enterprises were socialized.[50]

For many years the discussion concentrated on technical issues, such as whether the appropriate systems of simultaneous equations could be solved and whether all required computations could be made quickly enough, if at all.[51] In actual fact, these discussions did not address the essence of the Mises challenge. The issue is not whether calculations are possible and practicable with all available "data" but whether the relevant data could become available to the

---

[49] Ludwig von Mises, "Die Wirtschaftsrechnung im sozialistischen Gemeinwesen," *Archiv für Sozialwissenschaft und Sozialpolitik*, Vol. 47 (April 1920), pp. 86-121; included in Mises, *Die Gemeinwirtschaft* (Jena: Fischer, 1922; 2d ed., 1932); English translation, "Economic Calculation in the Socialist Commonwealth," in Friedrich A. Hayek, ed., *Collectivist Economic Planning* (London: Routledge, 1935), pp. 87-130; included in Mises, *Socialism* (London: Jonathan Cape, 1936).

[50] The best-known schemes for "market socialism" were those by Henry D. Dickinson, "Price Formation in a Socialist Community," *Economic Journal*, Vol. 43 (June 1933), pp. 237-250; Abba P. Lerner, "Economic Theory and Socialist Economy," *Review of Economic Studies*, Vol. 2 (October 1934), pp. 51-61; idem, "A Note on Socialist Economics, *Review of Economic Studies*, Vol. 4 (October 1936), pp. 72-76; and Oskar Lange, "On the Economic Theory of Socialism," *Review of Economic Studies*, Vol. 4 (October 1936 and February 1937), pp. 53-71 and 123-142, reprinted in Benjamin E. Lippincott, ed., *On the Economic Theory of Socialism* (New York: McGraw-Hill, 1938).

[51] If such questions were pertinent at a time before electronic computers were available, they are no longer, or may soon no longer be, pertinent. Leonid Hurwicz, in a private communication to me, dated March 12, 1982, suggests that, "considering the number of goods one should distinguish when time, place, and quality are taken into account, even modern electronic computers would lack adequate capacity and speed." Furthermore, "the Mises problem of the transmission of the relevant local knowledge (functions, sets, parameters) to the center would still be overwhelming in an economy where all calculations would be carried out centrally" (not as in market socialism).

central planning agency. The Mises challenge was that the information necessary for rational central planning could not be obtained and that market prices of privately owned means of production as well as of products are required for a rational allocation of resources.[52]

The misunderstandings arose largely because most participants in the discussion argued in terms of static equilibrium under "given" conditions, whereas the problem of efficient allocation becomes really important when conditions are changing. If nothing changes—if factor supply, factor qualities, production technology, organization, and consumer preferences remain unchanged—a central planning board can probably, by a system of trial and error in simulated markets, arrive at a set of "equilibrium prices" for all goods and services. Yet, this is not the problem in any "real" economy, capitalist or socialist. Adjustment to change is what matters; and the question is whether such adjustment can be accomplished with the same efficiency by a central agency that sets prices and/or quantities as it can by free "interactions" of independent economic agents pursuing their own aims and plans and competing with one another in free markets.

At the present juncture of the discussion, writers on the theory or practice of central economic planning no longer doubt that a price mechanism is an indispensable tool of the planners' task. The Mises challenge has definitely prevailed on this point, as it has also on a second: "decentralized procedures" are manifestly accepted by the present protagonists of planning.[53] Still controversial is the question

---

[52] Don Lavoie, "A Critique of the 'Standard' Account of the Socialist Calculation Debate," doctoral dissertation, New York University (June 1981).

[53] To avoid a misunderstanding we should note that the word "decentralization" has been used in two meanings: one, as a movement, or its result, from an earlier state of centralization, and, alternatively, as a state of dispersion not resulting from such a movement. Assume three possible constellations: (1) Knowledge is dispersed among a million people; (2) Knowledge is being centralized in the brains and records of a central authority; and (3) Knowledge is divided among the brains and records of geographically or functionally separated authorities. The first two constellations constitute polar opposites, the second being obviously the result of a process of "informational centralization," that is, of transmitting some of the initially dispersed knowledge to the central authority. The third constitutes a middle constellation: it may be the result of (incomplete) centralization, with information going from individual agents (units) to the various authorities, or it may be the result of decentralization, a reorganization of the economic regime by splitting the central (supreme) authority into several subauthorities. The latter kind of decentralization constitutes a *historical* change, a reapportionment of powers and responsibilities; it is not a flow of information from the "center" to subaltern authorities. These bureaus or boards still receive information from the million people, each of whom is the initial source of knowledge about his circumstances and preferences. With a view to this flow of information, the third constellation should not be characterized as "informational decentralization."

of the relative efficiency of *real* markets and *simulated* markets, that is, a comparative evaluation of, on the one hand, completely non-centralized decision-making (by private producers) coordinated by prices that affect producers' profits and reflect people's utilities, and on the other hand, decision-making by a central agency setting prices or determining quantities on the basis of responses (proposals, signals) received from respondents (consumers and enterprises). Although this is the question debated in the learned economic journals (usually in mathematical language), laymen and less advanced students of economics still cannot see why it should be so difficult for a central committee, with the aid of some good engineers, to prepare and execute an efficient economic plan for the nation.

The Efficiency of the Information System
Serving the Economic Process

By "economic process" most economists understand the process of allocating resources among a variety of uses in ways that do not involve waste and will achieve outcomes superior to all feasible alternatives. Superior in whose judgment? The simplest answer, "in the judgment of the dictator," is not acceptable to most of us; the answer "in the judgment of the majority of voters," is not acceptable either, because it relies on political ideology and disregards essentially economic criteria. The most widely accepted answer among economic theorists is "Pareto optimality," that is, an allocation for which there is no achievable alternative that could make anybody better off without making anybody else worse off in the judgment of those directly affected. (That there may be several different Pareto optima and no technique of finding an *optima optimorum*—the very best of the best allocations—is a disturbing thought to the welfare economist; alas, it is only one of his troubles.)

Different types of organization of the economic process require different "amounts" of information for efficient operation. The free-market system can work with a minimum of explicit communication. Producers, for example, need not tell anybody how much they produce, how they produce, what inputs they use, how much it costs them, or anything about their actual or potential circumstances. It is enough if they name the quantity they wish to buy or to sell, or the price they will pay or expect to receive. Consumers can be silent about everything except how much of a good or service they wish to buy. A completely planned economy, at the other extreme, would

---

Likewise, the first constellation, having neither a central authority nor several sub-authorities, is not characterized by informational decentralization but, instead, by unadulterated dispersion. Perhaps "noncentralization" would be the appropriate term.

require a most elaborate intercommunication system. The planning commission would need detailed information about available resources, production possibilities, and people's preferences. It is practically impossible to develop methods for collecting and conveying the necessary information about (a) resources, such as the different capabilities of millions of workers of different strength, intelligence, training, experience, and efficiency, (b) the production functions for millions of intermediate and final products in different qualities and combinations at different places under different managements in different existing and not yet existing productive facilities (machinery and other equipment), and (c) the preference maps of millions of households. Nothing of this sort has ever been tried or even seriously considered. Even if the people's preferences are disregarded on the strength of faith in the planners' "wisdom," enabling them to know what is good for the people, the indispensable information about available resources and potential outputs would still exceed by far the capacity of any conceivable message system. Indeed, not even the knowledge of all feasible production possibilities with existing equipment could be conveyed by the managers of the individual establishments to a central planning commission.[54]

As a matter of fact, information about production possibilities and about resource availabilities, though separable in theory, cannot be separated for practical purposes. There is no point in figuring out potential outputs of goods for which the available resources are not suitable and for which required inputs are out of reach of the particular establishments. Moreover, in the same industry, with the technology—a compendium of all known techniques—available to all managers, the input-output ratios for ostensibly the "same product" are different among the various establishments, simply because of undefinable differences in the qualities of ostensibly the "same factors," including labor, raw materials, equipment, organization, climate, and other locational elements.[55] Matching available resources

---

[54] ". . . , as has often been shown, the planning bureau cannot be aware of all the information needed for a perfect description of techniques. These are too numerous, complex, and diverse. Only the individual firms or highly specialized industry offices can have precise knowledge of the conditions governing production in their particular field. Some way must, therefore, be found for these firms and offices to participate in the preparation of the plan." Edmond Malinvaud, "Decentralized Procedures for Planning," in Edmond Malinvaud and Michael O. L. Bacharach, eds., *Activity Analysis in the Theory of Growth and Planning.* Proceedings of a Conference Held [at Cambridge] by the International Economic Association (London: Macmillan, 1967), p. 170.

[55] An example from my personal experience in industrial management may illustrate this statement. I supervised the operation of six cardboard mills in two adjacent provinces of Austria. Pulpwood, the only major raw material, came from the vicinity

with the most appropriate products and product qualities is a programming task that cannot be efficiently done except by people on the spot or by people in direct communication with them, that is in ongoing dialogues between local and only slightly removed decisionmakers, for example, between supervisors of individual plants and managers of the individual parent firm. Agencies or administrative bodies not directly in contact with the production supervisors, say, "industry offices," obtaining information from several firms will, as a rule, be insufficiently equipped to program efficient resource allocations and to make sound output decisions even for standardized products.

Most economic theorists have resigned themselves to these facts of economic life and have accepted the lesson that for the sake of efficiency and economy individual economic agents must be part of the economic process, not just as conveyors of information and recipients of instructions and commands, but as decisionmakers about uses of resources and about quantities and qualities of products. Theorists have examined the possibility of establishing efficient systems of noncentralized decision-making that can be alternatives, and perhaps even superior alternatives, to unrestricted free-market economies. The best-known designs of such an alternative were based on the neoclassical model of static equilibrium under pure (atomistic) competition—each firm taking all prices of factors and products as given and beyond its control, and adjusting its inputs and outputs in a way that would maximize its profits. The objective of profit maximization implies an attempt to produce at the lowest possible cost such quantities of output as would make marginal cost equal to the given price. (This is called the "parametric function" of price.) The capitalistic profit motive could, at least in theory, be replaced by a "Rule," imposed on all enterprises, public or private, to produce

of each mill; water power was the major source of energy; the same type of machines of approximately the same vintage was used in all mills; the labor force was of the same ethnic origin with the same schooling; technical supervisors were sometimes transferred among the mills. None the less, input-output ratios showed systematic differences: output per unit of labor, of energy, of pulpwood, etc., varied among the six mills, and even more so in comparison with analogous figures for mills operated by other firms (where variances were as much as 50 per cent). Since, though virtually the same production techniques were employed, the qualities of the ostensibly standardized product were not the same for some (though not all) of its uses, sound production programs called for judgments on the basis of completely dispersed information defying all attempts at meaningful centralization and aggregation. Of course, one *can* centralize and aggregate reams of figures, but the results of "planning" based on such "information" will be a mess.

that output that would equalize marginal cost to price.[56] This rule, if everything were to work as postulated by the "market socialists," would be superior to the capitalistic profit goal because it could avoid market failures due to monopolistic positions.

The idea behind the theory of market socialism is that in principle the planning authority is merely a price-setting authority which, in order to set the "right" prices, need not have much more information than any auctioneer requires and acquires in conducting an auction or similar schemes of competitive bidding in a free market. In effect, the official price setters would follow simple market-clearing procedures, raising a price to squeeze out any excess demand and reducing a price to eliminate excess supply. This sounds quite simple until a few questions are asked, such as these: How often are prices to be adjusted (daily, weekly, monthly?), by how much, under what rule or formula? Are the prices, and any contracts to sell or purchase at these prices, only tentative until an official "fixing" when all markets really appear to "clear" in a (short-run or long-run) equilibrium, or are all prices bid, offered, and accepted considered definitive even when they are on the path towards, but still distant from, equilibrium?

Before trying to indicate what kinds of answers have been suggested to some of these questions, I may offer a simplified description of one of the noncentralized planning approaches suggested in the literature. I propose to refer to it as the "feedback shuttle."

The Feedback Shuttle: Sequential Bidding Process

The scheme I have chosen for presentation happens to be one designed for a special purpose: to deal with the problem of public goods. This should not unduly disturb us, inasmuch as the basic procedures that Edmond Malinvaud has developed for his "planning approach to the public-good problem" are serviceable also for non-public goods; his scheme, moreover, is compatible with his earlier analysis of "decentralized procedures for planning," an analysis of the general problems of planning in recognition of the impossibility of devising a system of centralized comprehensive planning of the economy.[57]

[56] This rule, often referred to as the "Lerner-Lange Rule" was first proposed in the articles cited in footnote 50 above. The clearest formulation appears in Abba P. Lerner, *The Economics of Control: Principles of Welfare Economics* (New York: Macmillan, 1944).

[57] Malinvaud, "Decentralized Procedures," pp. 170-208; idem, "A Planning Approach to the Public Good Problem," *The Swedish Journal of Economics*, Vol. 73 (March 1971), pp. 96-112.

The essence of Malinvaud's blueprint is what he called "an iterative exchange of information between agents and a central administrative body."[58] It is assumed that the central agency, "the board," charged with the selection of the best program, does not possess the initially dispersed information needed for the appropriate selection. The needed information is supposed to become effective by means of a sequential exchange of "indicators," issued by the board, and responses in the form of "proposals" by the individual agents; on the basis of the proposals the board revises the indicators, to which the individuals respond again with revised proposals, and so on, and so forth, in a sequence of exchanges, which I have designated above as a feedback shuttle. The revisions should preferably be in small steps; "if revisions are made by infinitesimal steps, [the process] converges to an optimum."[59]

The question is whether the official indicators (probes or trial balloons) are to be *quantities* of goods and services or *prices* (and taxes). It is clear that the individuals' proposals will be prices in response to official offers of quantities, and quantities in response to official quotations of prices. Here the problem of true or untrue revelations becomes relevant: "By his demands on the market each individual reveals his needs and wants for private commodities. But [under most schemes] he sees no reason for reporting correctly his demand for collective consumption, because the latter will be provided even if he does not ask for it."[60] The "underreporting" in the individuals' responses would result in smaller than optimal "collective consumption," and the tendency towards underreporting will increase as the number of participants increases.[61] The institution of sequential revisions of the indicators is likely to remedy this situation, because "anyone reporting correctly cannot suffer from the revision of the program, at least if this revision is made by small steps," whereas "anyone reporting a false [proposal] could lose. . . ."[62] Thus, "reporting correctly . . . is the unique strategy that rules out a decrease of the [individual's] utility level."[63] The major point in this feedback shuttle is that it "uses as indicators quantities for the public goods and prices for the private goods."[64]

[58] Malinvaud, "Approach to the Public Good Problem," p. 97.
[59] Ibid., p. 106.
[60] Ibid.
[61] Ibid., p. 108.
[62] Ibid., p. 109.
[63] Ibid., p. 110.
[64] Ibid., p. 111. Malinvaud explains why the solution to the problem of public goods proposed by Erik Lindahl (Die Gerechtigkeit der Besteuerung [Lund: Gleerup, 1919]) was faulty. It used price (or tax) indicators and would result in an outcome that was both inefficient and inequitable.

In this, as in virtually all planning approaches that purport to take account of the people's preferences, the assumption is made that the devised process is capable of transferring essential parts of the noncentralized knowledge of millions of individual consumers in some usable form to the central administrative board; and that at least ultimately the dispersed knowledge of the people's preferences, factor endowments, and production opportunities is effectively reflected in the allocative equilibrium. This equilibrium is approached in a sequence of revisions of indicators (probes) and adjustments of responses (proposals) and is eventually reached when responses and indicators have become fully compatible and, thus, no further revisions of indicators are required. The notion that the equilibrium is actually reached distinguishes this planning scheme from the theoretical conceptions of those for whom equilibrium has only explanatory significance.

The "Language" of the Mechanism

Leonid Hurwicz has developed a set of terms denoting concepts he finds helpful in the analysis of information systems that serve to guide noncentralized decision-making by means of prices possibly determined by a central authority.[65] According to Hurwicz, "the final outcome of any adjustment process is a decision concerning resource allocation"; the process "takes place over time and includes the participation (in the form of various information processing and 'command' functions) of the various components of the economy."[66] The "complex of messages sent out or received" may contain proposals, responses, or commands, apart from other kinds of announcements. "A message is called a 'proposal' . . . if it describes a set of visible actions (resource transfers) that might conceivably be taken by some units," and "an adjustment process is called opera-

[65] Leonid Hurwicz, "Optimality and Informational Efficiency in Resource Allocation Processes," in Kenneth J. Arrow, Samuel Karlin, and Patrick C. Suppes, eds., *Mathematical Methods in the Social Sciences, 1959* (Stanford: Stanford University Press, 1960), pp. 27-46; idem, "Conditions for Economic Efficiency of Centralized and Decentralized Structures," in Gregory Grossman, ed., *Value and Plan: Economic Calculation and Organization in Eastern Europe* (Berkeley: University of California Press, 1960), pp. 162-175 and 182-183; idem, "Centralization and Decentralization in Economic Processes," in Alexander Eckstein, ed., *Comparison of Economic Systems: Theoretical and Methodological Approaches* (Berkeley: University of California Press, 1971), pp. 79-102; idem, "On the Dimensional Requirements of Informationally Decentralized Pareto-Satisfactory Processes," in Kenneth J. Arrow and Leonid Hurwicz, eds., *Studies in Resource Allocation Processes* (Cambridge: At the University Press, 1977), pp. 413-417.

[66] Leonid Hurwicz, "Conditions for Economic Efficiency," p. 167.

tional if every message is a proposal."[67] If every message is a proposal, the process is "privacy preserving," since it does not disclose internal information of the participating units (apart from revealed preferences and revealed expectations reflected in a proposal made or accepted [as I feel obliged to add to Hurwicz's statement]). Implied in noncentralization of the procedure is the feature of "anonymity": "the decision makers need not know who wants how much of their products or who can supply how much of the material, but merely how much of the product is demanded [from them] and what total amounts of materials are available [to them]."[68]

The concept of *tâtonnement*—a gradual groping towards market equilibria by means of tentative proposals and tentative responses during a phase of communication without binding transactions—is an integral part of Hurwicz's schemes. A binding decision, a real plan, is reached only after a sequence of "paper plans."[69] The same procedure of preliminary probing without real transactions is employed in Malinvaud's schemes. They provide for sequential price probes ("prospective indices") announced by the central "planning bureau," to which firms respond with quantity proposals, whereupon the bureau revises its price probe, to which firms again respond with duly adapted proposals regarding quantities to be taken or delivered.[70] In the case of public goods the position is reversed, with the planning bureau indicating quantities (or the size of facilities) and the interested users proposing prices.[71] There is a theoretical choice between continuous and iterative adjustment procedures, with

[67] Ibid., p. 168. The meaning of "operational" in this context is not clear without an illustration: The messages in an auction are called "operational" because the bidder's proposal may be acted upon immediately; on the other hand, messages describing cost functions to a planning board are "not operational," because they lead first to calculations, deliberations, and negotiations, not to acceptance or another final decision.

[68] Ibid., p. 170. — Joseph S. Berliner, paraphrasing these definitions, possibly with some regret about the implied restrictions on the powers of central authorities, writes: "Under the rule of anonymity, a planning board can issue no detailed orders to individual firms; it can issue only general instructions applying to all firms in a class. And under the rule of operationalism a planning board is enjoined from demanding internal information from firms, a requirement which alone would cripple its pretensions to centralized decision making." Berliner is no admirer of efficiency: "a real economic system may be miserably inefficient, and yet be vital, growing rapidly, and ebullient." Joseph S. Berliner, "Comment" [on Hurwicz's paper], in Gregory Grossman, ed., *Value and Plan: Economic Calculation and Organization in Eastern Europe* (Berkeley: University of California Press, 1960), p. 179.

[69] Leonid Hurwicz, "Centralization and Decentralization," pp. 85-86.

[70] Edmond Malinvaud, "Decentralized Procedures," pp. 179-186.

[71] Edmond Malinvaud, "A Planning Approach," pp. 79-102.

a presumed difference regarding the probability and speed of "convergence" towards equilibrium in an "optimum programme."[72] No formulas, however, have been proposed for adoption to guide the successive revisions of the tentative prices announced by the planning bureau.[73] As a matter of fact, no planning system ever adopted and actually operated has experimented with any of the noncentralized schemes of continuous or iterative probing for equilibrium values by efficient, let alone optimal, procedures.[74]

Reservations and Apprehensions

Some apprehensions regarding the efficiency, practicability, and cost of schemes of "planning through central pricing" have been voiced explicitly in the preceding pages, and others can probably be read from between the lines. A few reservations may perhaps be stated here in simple language.

One reservation refers to the implied stability of consumer preferences during periods of adjustment, or of groping towards equilibrium. It is highly probable that tastes change all the time, causing the hypothetical equilibrium to change long before the successive allocations and reallocations of resources have taken full account of the previous state of preferences. This reservation is satisfactorily answered by pointing out that changes in preferences can be accommodated by rule-conforming revisions of indicators and proposals just as easily as it can be done when preferences remain invariant. The free-market system for private goods appears to work in an analogous fashion, with daily revisions of bids and offers taking account of varying wants and tastes of consumers.[75]

[72] Malinvaud, "Decentralized Procedures," p. 184.

[73] Malinvaud suggests that "to increase the rapidity" of convergence, the planning bureau take "into account the information supplied by the firms at all the preceding stages and not merely the material transmitted at the latest stage. With the accumulation of information, the bureau will acquire a more and more precise knowledge of the technology of the firm" (Ibid., p. 197). In this scheme, operationality, privacy-preservation, and anonymity, as defined by Hurwicz, have been sacrificed: the planning bureau attempts to construct the production functions of the firms. The procedure implicitly assumes that technology or, at least, the circumstances of the firms have not changed over the months or years during which the information has been accumulated.

[74] Ibid., p. 186.

[75] Perhaps a difference can be seen between fully anonymous and privacy-preserving procedures and procedures with direct contacts among producers and consumers. Such direct contacts may result in greater sensitivity of production plans to changes in tastes. This point is related to the "second reservation" stated in the text. (I am indebted to Leonid Hurwicz for calling my attention to this connection between the two issues.)

A second reservation is far more serious and possibly fatal to the method of sequential bidding as a practically operational system that supposedly can translate dispersed and ever-changing preferences of consumers into central decision-making about resource allocations. This reservation refers to the fact that the knowledge of people's preferences is not only dispersed over millions of minds and not only subject to continual change, but that it has too many blank spaces to be transferred in the form of price-or-quantity responses. The described planning system cannot give the people what they want, because they themselves cannot know what they want if they do not know what they could have. A steady stream of innovations in a free-enterprise system keeps altering the "production possibilities," including those that relate to new products and new qualities of existing products. Imaginative entrepreneurs, stimulated by anticipations of (temporary) profits, present consumers with options that have not existed hitherto but are expected to arouse responses of a kind different from those symbolized in the customary models of market equilibrium and in models of allocative equilibrium. The availability of new products makes a market system quite unlike the scheme of official indicators of quantities or prices announced by a central board and private proposals of prices or quantities submitted in response by the consuming public. The organized feedback shuttle allowing informed decisions by a planning board does not give a proper place to the important phenomenon of product innovation.[76]

A third reservation refers to the important question of direct contacts between customers and producers, especially important when the customer is a processor of an intermediate product that comes in very many different qualities. It is easily forgotten that many intermediate products, materials fabricated into final or other intermediate products, are differentiated by dozens of quality dimensions, not "better" or "worse," but of different suitability for different uses.

The range of possible variations in quality will as a rule be greater for products made out of many component parts

---

[76] Product innovation is often associated with direct contact between producer and user. This raises the question whether the introduction of novel products is not linked with the phenomenon of "thin" markets and, hence, with models of monopolistic or otherwise imperfect competition. Such imperfections would result in "Pareto-inferior outcomes." (Again I must acknowledge valuable comments by Hurwicz on an earlier draft of this chapter.) On the other hand, Hayek would not be worried by such lapses from pure or perfect competition, for he sees the benefits of competition, not in some properties of static-equilibrium positions, but in the drive to explore and innovate. Friedrich A. Hayek, "Competition as a Discovery Procedure," in *New Studies in Philosophy, Politics, Economics and the History of Ideas* (Chicago: University of Chicago Press, 1978), pp. 179-190.

or ingredients than for products that combine fewer things. . . . Despite these "rules" we may find most remarkable ranges of quality differences in goods made out of relatively few component parts or ingredients or with relatively little precision, skill, or taste. Even with non-synthetic, non-composite materials more or less careful sorting and grading may cause significant differences in "quality." Fabrics that look identical to the layman may differ in a number of ways: the better [read: more suitable] grades may be washable, non-shrinking, non-fading, waterproof, holding shape, etc. Paper board may be more or less suited for various kinds of processing, such as bending, shaping, folding, grooving, pasting, printing, waterproofing, etc.[77]

To find the best-suited intermediate product, processors and fabricators have to engage in shopping around and have to be in direct contact with their suppliers. A central agency between suppliers and users may impose huge inefficiencies on the allocation process. Decisions on price and quantity of standardized staple commodities may conceivably be made by a market-replacing central board, but if each product comes in countless qualities the task for the central bureaucracy becomes practically impossible, quite apart from the administrative cost involved.

Before taking up the question of the administrative cost, we should first address the question whether the adjustment process "towards equilibrium" should be a programming scheme with all sequential steps merely "on paper" or "in the computer" with no binding contracts made during the groping phase or whether all probes and responses should be regarded as firm commitments resulting in trades at prices and for quantities that would not qualify as equilibria.

Tâtonnement: A Phase in Programming, a Sequence of Trades, or a Heuristic Fiction

Whether the feedback shuttle between central and individual decisions—the official probes and the individual proposals—should be sequences of *trials on paper* or rather of *definitive contracts* has been unambiguously answered by Hurwicz, Malinvaud, and a few others

---

[77] Fritz Machlup, *The Economics of Sellers' Competition*, pp. 453-454. — Book paper is only one of many different types of paper. But even within this type one can distinguish "40 product classes, 12 grades, 33 finishes . . . , 8 colors, . . . and 19 types of packing." Combining this with the different sizes, trims, and quantity classes, "a meticulous specification of product would distinguish between 170 and 180 million possible products in the book paper industry." Committee on Price Determination for the Conference on Price Research, *Cost Behavior and Price Policy* (New York: National Bureau of Economic Research, 1943), p. 333.

for their schemes of noncentralized planning: The *tâtonnement* was a phase in a programming process, and binding contracts were concluded only at the end of that phase, when the adjustment was complete. This is not, however, the only possible solution; one can imagine a scheme of sequential trades on the basis of firm bids and offers, with the planning board changing its quotations in a gradual adjustment to perceived imbalances between supply and demand—where the imbalance may be due in part to incomplete convergence and in part to new changes in conditions (resources, technology, tastes).

These alternatives in the use of *tâtonnement* in "practical" adjustment mechanisms discussed in the current literature on planning have some parallels in the use of *tâtonnement* in the theoretical analysis of adjustment discussed in the old literature on the working of free-market economies. In particular, Léon Walras, the originator of the concept, was careful to distinguish between the fictional "static state," where the sequence of trades in the markets could eventually reach general equilibrium, and the more realistic "dynamic state," where continuing changes in basic conditions would never allow equilibrium to be reached. In either case, *tâtonnement* as a concept was a heuristic fiction, and as a term was an analogy, perhaps a mere metaphor. It was not meant to be a realistic description of an observable process but, instead, a mental construction serving explanatory purposes. The market, more realistically conceived, would be "continually tending towards equilibrium without ever actually attaining it."[78]

One may have methodological qualms about a heuristic fiction, developed as a part of an explanatory theoretical system, being transformed into a practical procedure in a scheme of programming the actual allocation of productive resources. Such qualms need not, however, degenerate into stern objections. There is nothing wrong, logically, psychologically, or ethically, in taking an idea from a purely theoretical system and putting it to use in a practical-political scheme.

---

[78] "... in order to come ... more closely to reality, we must drop the hypothesis of an annual market period and adopt in its place the hypothesis of a continuous market. Thus, we pass from the static to the dynamic state. ... Such is the continuous market, which is perpetually tending towards equilibrium without ever actually attaining it, because the market has no other way of approaching equilibrium except by groping, and, before the goal is reached, it has to renew its efforts and start over again, all the basic data of the problem, e.g., the initial quantities possessed, the utilities of goods and services, the technical coefficients, the excess of income over consumption, the working capital requirements, etc., having changed in the meantime." Léon Walras, *Elements of Pure Economics*, translated by William Jaffé (Homewood, Ill.: Irwin, 1954; [1st French ed., Lausanne: Corbaz, 1974]), p. 380.

In the case in point, however, one may advise the transformers to take heed of the major reservation on which the pure theorists have insisted: that *tâtonnement* could be thought of as leading to equilibrium only if conditions stopped changing but could not be expected to do so if conditions kept changing.

The applied theorists, who examined *tâtonnement* processes as part of blueprints for noncomprehensive, noncentralized economic planning, have not yet given sufficient thought to optimal adjustment processes under conditions of continually ongoing change. But even for situations with only small and slow changes it is not clear whether the blueprints thus far developed are really workable, efficient, and otherwise desirable. Theoretical welfare economics does not equip us to decide these questions. Theoretical efficiency and practical efficiency are very different things, and "desirability" cannot be determined by economic arguments alone, in disregard of ethical and political values.

The Administrative Cost of Central Planning

The cost of administering virtually any scheme in which government is heavily involved has always aroused misgivings in my mind. These apprehensions are evidently not shared by all economists. Thus, Malinvaud finds that "the study of the cost of different procedures may well be of lesser significance. Cost does not appear to be a determining factor for the choice among the various procedures which may be considered as institutionally feasible. The rules to be followed by firms must be simple; if not, there would be a risk that they be poorly understood and incorrectly followed. As to the cost of the calculations to be undertaken at the central level, this will always be low in relation to the cost of the industrial decisions affected by the plan."[79]

The apparent unconcern about the cost of government bureaucracy can perhaps be explained by an assumption that larger expenditures at the level of the central government will reduce cost and/or increase efficiency at the level of industry. I find no evidence, empirical or theoretical, to support such an assumption. On the contrary, it seems likely that more extensive and more expensive assignments to the central administration will be paralleled by more extensive and less productive tasks imposed on the producing units. Experience in most countries has shown that paper work in governmental offices and paper work in industry reporting to government are positively correlated. Moreover, many of the rules and procedures imposed by

[79] Malinvaud, "Decentralized Procedures," pp. 178-179.

government offices are counterproductive. In the words of Leonid Hurwicz, "behavior rules," though intended to induce satisfactory strategies on the part of the enterprises, may in fact not be "incentive-compatible." In such cases, well-meant rules may influence the affected units to behave in ways different from what is intended.[80] In any case, the cost of the planning procedures cannot reasonably be shrugged away in an evaluation of the schemes proposed or adopted.[81]

[80] Hurwicz, "Centralization and Decentralization," pp. 86-88.

[81] Some economists do realize the immensity of the cost of the required communication between central agency and individual economic agents. In a brief note commenting on the article by Jacques H. Drèze and Dominique de la Vallée Poussin, "A Tâtonnement Process for Public Goods," *Review of Economic Studies*, Vol. 38 (April 1971), pp. 133-150, Iwao Nakatani observes that "communication between the central planner and other economic agents must involve *all* the consumers in the economy and that would be extremely costly in an economy with a large number of consumers." He proposes to modify the *tâtonnement* model by "sample surveys." The population is to be divided into "classes according to some similar and observable attributes which are considered to be correlated with preferences." Nakatani realizes, however, that a taxation scheme that would involve many individuals not included in the sample might cause considerable difficulties and inequities. Iwao Nakatani, "A 'Sample' Tâtonnement Process for Public Goods," *Osaka Economic Papers*, Vol. 31 (December 1981), pp. 115-120. I have referred to this note chiefly to show that some economists are seriously concerned about the cost of communication required for informed planning by central authorities.

CHAPTER 7

Empirical Research, Theoretical Analysis, Applied Inquiry

THE READER AND I may disagree on whether this chapter is really necessary, but perhaps I can persuade him that exposure to this sort of discourse can improve the social scientist's quality of life. Some of the literature on the economics of knowledge and information is "purely theoretical," some "entirely empirical," at least in the judgment of the academic community. But do we know what we mean by these opposites? Are we aware that "empirical" research can mean several very different things, and that "theoretical," also, has many shades of meaning? And what about the many papers that are intended to be both empirical and theoretical? These are questions of methodology, which is not everybody's cup of tea, but they are nevertheless worth addressing. Readers suffering from (or perhaps enjoying) chronic methodophobia are warned—though they would probably, even without warning, after the first few paragraphs decide to skip this chapter.

Empirical versus Theoretical

The contrast between empirical research and abstract-theoretical analysis is fundamental in that it holds for all sciences, natural and cultural; it applies to economics neither more nor less than to other social sciences; and within economics the distinction is relevant in all special fields, no matter how much or how little they stress the roles of knowledge and information. It will be useful to subdivide both empirical research and abstract-theoretical analysis into several approaches; and, with regard to economics, to distinguish different kinds or types of economic agents, no matter whether they are to be interrogated, observed, modeled, or fictionalized in ideal-typical fashion. Another distinction relates to the focus on either *particular* cases or *classes* of cases within spans of historical time. These differences can be illuminated, in conjunction with the discussion of the more fundamental distinctions and hence do not require an allocation of separate sections in the exposition that follows.

Purely empirical research works with *observational* entities, and all its terms are operationally defined. The opposite of operationally defined terms (or operational concepts) are purely *mental* constructs, that is, inventions of the mind removed from observational perceptions and apperceptions, with the terms defined with a degree of purity never found in any empirical reality. Stated most succinctly, empirical research deals with recorded *data*, that is, with records of observations, whereas abstract-theoretical analysis deals with pure *ideas*, primarily definitions, axioms, postulates, assumptions, and inferences. Henry Margenau, physicist and philosopher of science, spoke of the domain of observation and the domain of construction. No iron curtain separates the two domains. On the contrary, many bridges are supposed to connect the two, and one of the main concerns of methodology is the development of "rules of correspondence" between propositions in the domain of observation and propositions in the domain of construction.

Perhaps I have exaggerated the claim of purity when I spoke of *purely* empirical research and *purely* theoretical analysis. After all, empirical research, in selecting its data, in choosing the things to observe, is guided by hunches, called hypotheses or tentative theories, however vague and naive; and theoretical analysis in forming its constructs receives stimulation and clues from experience, however vague and naive. Moreover, empirical research with specific data is often intended to yield generalizations, however rough; and theoretical analysis is intended to be applied to some particular experiences, however qualified. Most importantly, an ever-increasing number of scientists want to maintain dual residence or citizenship in the two domains. Perhaps we should replace the metaphor of bridges between the two domains with the metaphor of a gray or neutral zone or domain, perhaps a "Middle Kingdom," populated by propositions linking data of observations, representing operational concepts, with models composed of theoretical constructs. Many researchers and analysts in the natural and social sciences believe that the Middle Kingdom is wider and richer than the two polar domains on either side.[1]

Perhaps we can avoid unnecessary misunderstandings if we immediately concede that empirical research when it is oriented towards theoretical interpretation and generalization, and theoretical analysis when it is oriented towards empirical testing, may be in-

---

[1] In Chinese the Middle Kingdom was sometimes called the "Flowery Kingdom." If my sources are correct, these expressions refer to the history of China between the third and fifth centuries. The designation "central" or "middle kingdom" has often been used as a metaphor in tripartitions of all sorts.

tended for assignment to the intermediate zone. Yet, even if this "desegregated" zone is considered the most pragmatic part of any discipline, we should begin with exploring the two extreme, mutually exclusive domains.

EMPIRICAL RESEARCH

One cannot successfully explore the three domains of scientific inquiry strictly one at a time; differences and contrasts cannot be fully comprehended without comparing one with the others. Hence, although I begin with an exploration of the empirical domain, the home of observed phenomena and recorded data, I shall often look across the frontier to the distant theoretical domain of abstract mental construction and to the neighboring Middle Kingdom of application and confluence of empirical and theoretical thought.

Types of Empirical Research

Empirical research can be subdivided according to several criteria, such as by the different *activities* that constitute it or the different *objectives* it is designed to serve. The major constituent activities are obtaining, checking, processing, and using data. The term "data" usually refers to records of observation, the things "given" to the researcher's sensory perception and cognitive reflection. The notion "getting the data" may seem ambiguous or even self-contradictory, since what is *given* to the researcher he need not set out to *get*. The apparent contradiction disappears when the meaning of the word "data" is not confined to *recorded* data, but extended to data yet to be obtained; "obtaining data" comprises both tasks: observing and recording. The even more popular phrase "collecting data" is no less ambiguous. Does it mean only the gathering of what already is on record—retrieval from storage—or does it include the first making of a record, like jotting down the result of a count? If we include the first production of a record, the first notation, as part of the act of "collecting data," we find that empirical research may comprise the following activities: observing, counting, measuring, recording, checking, cleaning, sorting, arranging, comparing, rearranging, probing, juxtaposing, correlating, and probably several more things done to or with the data, provided that these activities can be done without, or with only a modicum of, abstract-theoretical construction.

If data are what has been perceived and/or recorded, the question arises whether misperceived or misrecorded data are to be granted the designation "data." Should series of supposed facts that we suspect to be the results of optical illusions or fallacies of interpretation be called data? Moreover, if some of the recorded numbers—counts, measurements, instrument readings—have been "doctored" or even faked, are we to regard them as data? Are randomly generated numbers, obtained for appropriate purposes, empirical data? Are we to accord the designation "data" to sets of numbers that are not given to us by observation, experimentation, or any other experience but, instead, have been made up to simulate what we believe to be a possible, or perhaps even a likely or typical, constellation or sequence of things?

Answers to these questions are matters of convention: people may agree to allow or to disallow some of the things proposed as "data," and different groups of people may arrive at contrary conventions. Much should depend on the purpose for which the observations or pseudo-observations are recorded. If some numbers were "doctored" with the thought that errors made in the original record had to be corrected, such manipulation is not much different from cleaning the data to remove impurities and irrelevant and confusing "noise." If some numbers were "faked" with a view to presenting to processors and interpreters a more impressive fit of allegedly observed reality with preconceived regularities or favored hypotheses, the record is one of "faked data," but still data. On the other hand, if sets of numbers are produced and presented for no other purposes than to "model" and make a show of certain preconceived mathematical relationships, to exhibit nontrivial implications, or to provide opportunities for exercising one's logical or computational skills, then perhaps these records of assumed numbers had better not be regarded as data in empirical research.[2] If only exercise is intended, or if only "conceivable" relationships of unknown likelihood are to be demonstrated, and if no regular numerical relationships among data of observation can be inferred from the sets of numbers "given" to the analyst, his computational work cannot reasonably be regarded as empirical research.

Two activities are sometimes included in the list of possible constituents of empirical research: interpreting and explaining. There is an essential difference between "causal" explanation and "statistical" explanation. The latter may be regarded as empirical: indeed, those who "explain" by means of statistical operations, such as correlation or regression, warn, if they are conscientious, against taking

---

[2] Are finger exercises for the pianist regarded as music or just as means for improving muscular coordination and dexterity? They can be both—just as empirical research may be good practice of techniques and, at the same time, fertile of empirical findings.

the resulting coefficients as indicative of causal relations. Where interpretation or explanation involve notions of causality, either explicitly or only implicitly, the researcher's activity is "applied" inquiry; it belongs to the Middle Kingdom lying between the domains of observation and construction. A theoretical model is employed to interpret and explain a particular sequence and constellation of empirical data. The model comes from the domain of construction, the data come from the domain of observation; the empirical data become (more or less suitable) proxies for mental constructs of the abstract theory. This blending of the imports from the two outer domains should be characterized neither as empirical research nor as theoretical analysis.

Within the category of applied inquiry one may find that the *intentions* or *objectives* of the activities in question may determine whether the inquiry has more affinity to the domain of observation or to the domain of construction. If the prime purpose is to interpret or explain a concrete case, say, an event or situation identified by time and place, the application of theory to specific empirical data is more akin to empirical research. If, however, empirical data are employed to illustrate or test the usefulness (explanatory or predictive value) of an abstract theory and its generality, the work is more in the nature of an adjunct to, or complement of, theoretical analysis, though it should still be assigned to the middle domain of application.[3]

Empirical Research in the Social Sciences

What was said in the preceding section applies generally to all scientific and scholarly work. When we come to distinguish *sources of empirical data in the social sciences* we become aware of differences between inquiries into natural phenomena and social phenomena.[4] This is conspicuously clear with regard to the first three of the major sources of empirical data in the social sciences: (1) introspection, (2) interrogation, (3) search of documents, (4) controlled experimentation, and (5) imperfectly controlled observation.

---

[3] Is taxonomic work always empirical? Surely not; one may prepare taxonomies of purely mental constructs without any observational ingredients. Just think of the taxonomies of figures and moods in syllogistic reasoning or of principles in the calculus of classes. Indeed, some of the divisions and distinctions proposed in the present discussion are taxonomic exercises with nonobservables. People who think of taxonomies as being essentially empirical are overgeneralizing from their experiences in courses in zoology and botany.

[4] Fritz Machlup, *Methodology of Economics and Other Social Sciences* (New York: Academic Press, 1978). See esp. Chap. 12, pp. 309-332.

The first two sources cannot exist in the natural sciences, and the third can exist only in a metaphoric sense of "document," namely, if document is used for all sorts of marks, not only for written, printed, engraved, or recorded statements by human beings.

Long-standing controversies have been carried on with regard to introspection, the first on my list of sources of empirical data in the social sciences. *Introspective empiricism* has been rejected by adherents of rigid behaviorism. Strangely enough, interrogational and documentary empiricism have been accepted, although the original source is basically the same: the social agent's replies to interrogators' questions and the documents produced by or for the agent originate largely from his introspective reflections. Thus, consistency would require that the findings from interrogation and from searches of documents produced by or for him be likewise rejected by those who deny the "scientific" standing of introspection as admissible evidence. A simple trick, namely, the interpretation of audible or readable expressions of introspective thought as "public, observable behavior" (rather than as private cogitation), has succeeded in appeasing or satisfying some ardent behaviorists and fellow neopositivists. Incidentally, interrogational, documentary, experimental, and other observational empirical research programs for the study of social conduct and behavior have sometimes been grouped together as "behavioral" empiricism (not to be confused with "behaviorist" empiricism). This is quite appropriate in that all these approaches involve observation of individual persons as social or economic agents and in that they focus on their thinking, utterances, records, or responses to specified stimuli under specified conditions.

One may distinguish between inside (or internal) data and outside (or external) data. The former relate to the conduct, behavior, or attitudes of the social agents under observation, the latter to external *effects* possibly attributed or imputed to the conduct, behavior, or attitudes of the agents (individuals, specified groups, or anonymous groups). The word "effects" is ambiguous, however. External data may be the effects, the results, of the reporting, compiling, adding, averaging, etc., of internal data: for example, data on price movements in a country, region, or particular market are probably based on reports about a multitude of prices quoted or stated by individual transactors; likewise, data on changes in national income are based on millions of reports (tax returns, output figures, employment, etc.) from individuals speaking for households, business firms, or other organizations. Apart from these "effects" of individual *reporting* are the probable effects of individual *actions* upon the reported magnitudes, such as the effects of individual borrowing on total spending and employment. The difference should be clear: an increase in reported unemployment is, of course, the result of more persons reporting that they have been unsuccessful in finding a job; but in a different sense, in the sense now intended, the increase may be the effect of shutdowns or output cuts by manufacturing firms because of reduced profit opportunities, perhaps due to reduced demand or to increased wage rates, higher fuel cost, or stiffer taxes.

Corroboration, interpretation, and explanation, activities in which investigators engage once they have obtained their series of data, have special meanings in the social sciences. Corroboration may involve spot-checks and cross-checks with social agents or their records. Explanation may be either causal or merely "statistical." Statistical explanation, as I said earlier, does not imply any causal relations but is confined to observed (hence past) regularities in the relationship among series of statistical numbers (covariations, coefficients, or correlation or regression). These operations are still in the empirical domain. If, however, interpretation or explanation involve preconceptions or conclusions regarding causation, they call for ideal-typical construction; a significant correspondence has to be established between the observed "behavior" of the data and constructed (imagined) types of conduct of hypothesized (fictitious) social agents. Interpretation and explanation are thereby moved from the domain of observation into the mixed or integrated area of application.

Research on Economic Decision-Making

For the specific purpose of investigating decision-making by economic agents, a slightly modified list of alternative empirical research methods may be more acceptable. I shall omit here introspective empiricism, partly because I want to avoid offending any surviving orthodox believers in neopositivism, but chiefly because this often exiled inhabitant of the empirical domain can enter less obtrusively (and sometimes even welcomed) over the earlier-mentioned bridge built, under the rules of correspondence, between the domain of observation and the domain of construction; it enters in the guise of what I have called "imagined introspection,"[5] which I regard as an integral part of understanding human action.

Thus we may begin the list of research techniques for the study

[5] Fritz Machlup, *The Economics of Sellers' Competition* (Baltimore: Johns Hopkins University Press, 1952), pp. 423-424; and Fritz Machlup, "Operational Concepts and Mental Constructs in Model and Theory Formation," *Giornale degli Economisti*, N.S., Vol. 19 (September-October 1960), p. 580. Both are reproduced in Machlup, *Methodology*, pp. 94-95 and 186, respectively.

of economic decision-making with *interrogational empiricism*, stressing the interrogator's *direct contact* with real (live) decision-making persons who willingly submit to interrogation about their reasoning, motivations, experiences, expectations, doubts, and decisions. My second entry is *documentary empiricism*, which relies essentially on *indirect contact* with these persons through studying documents they have produced. Empiricism in the form of controlled experiments is rare in economics, though a few examples of *experiments in decision-making* have been reported. A separate entry may be allocated to research by means of more casual, less perfectly controlled types of *observation of decisionmakers and procedures* employed in reaching individual or collective decisions. All these research techniques relate to internal data.

Research techniques relating to external data may be classified according to the ways in which one can connect the data with the agents who are supposed to have played a role in bringing about (causing, inducing, influencing) the phenomena recorded. It may be possible to resort to *interrogational or documentary cross-checking* with living agents or with their internal records, respectively, to corroborate the claim (or hypothesis) that the external data somehow reflect the agents' actions. When such corroboration is not possible, the external data—prepared neither by nor for insiders—may nevertheless be attributed, hypothetically by means of *ideal-typical construction*, to decisionmakers' actions. There may or may not be opportunities for *potential recourse* to confirming or disconfirming testimony by actual decisionmakers. Finally, there is *statistical-correlational empiricism*, basing research exclusively on external data correlated with other sets of external data, that is, with objective records of events suspected of being causally connected, but with *no construction* of intervening ideal types of decision-making and *no recourse* to direct or indirect contact with real decisionmakers.

A more concise recapitulation of types of empirical work in getting or using internal and external data may be helpful:

(A) Internal data
   (1) obtained through interrogation in direct contact with real decisionmakers;
   (2) obtained through search of documents, and thus mainly indirect contact with real decisionmakers;
   (3) obtained through controlled experiments in decision-making;
   (4) obtained through imperfectly controlled observation of de-

cision-making (where the data are chiefly qualitative and procedural).

(B) External data

    (5) obtained outside the decision-making setting but allowing potential contacts with insiders for interrogational or documentary spot-checks;

    (6) supported by interpretations with the aid of ideal-typical constructions and with potential recourse to confirmation or corroboration by contacts with real decisionmakers;

    (7) supported by interpretations with the aid of ideal-typical constructions, but no recourse to confirmation or corroboration by contacts with real decisionmakers;

    (8) connected by way of statistical-correlational techniques, without supportive interpretations through ideal-typical constructions and also without recourse to confirmation or corroboration by contacts with real decisionmakers.

These rather cryptic characterizations of different techniques of research on economic decision-making will have to suffice for the present discussion. The elaboration that I attempted would spread over more pages than I dare to impose on the reader.[6]

ABSTRACT-THEORETICAL ANALYSIS

As we leave the domain of observation for an exploration of the domain of construction, we should recall attention to the unavoidable interdependence among these two domains. I shall first point to the difference between logical and psychological connections, and afterwards make a brief anticipatory comment about the middle domain, in which empirical concepts and abstract-theoretical constructs congregate and fraternize.

Logical Autonomy, Psychological Interdependence

Logical autonomy does not imply psychological self-sufficiency.[7] Some undercover relations between the a priori and the a posteriori

---

[6] Readers infected with methodolatry—a term coined by the philosopher Arthur Oncken Lovejoy—and therefore eager to read the omitted elaboration, running to 15 typewritten pages, may write to me for a complimentary copy.

[7] Another way of saying this would be that autarchy does not imply autarky. (The absence of the latter term from widely used dictionaries has long confused our typesetters, editors, and authors.)

may be illegitimate under the strict norms of formal logic, but they exist nonetheless, albeit as psychological ties. This is so because the processes of sensory perception and observation are constantly influenced and guided by invisible imports from the domain of theoretical construction, and the processes of abstract construction are constantly influenced by invisible imports from the domain of experience.

That we cannot even start observing without guidance from conceptualization (or construction of types) is an old story but so often forgotten that it cannot be retold too often. We can illustrate it best by asking a few elementary questions with regard to each activity designed to procure empirical data. Interrogation: what questions should be asked and of whom? Document search: what kinds of document should be selected and for what should they be searched? Experiments: just what kinds of experiments should be made? Observation: precisely what should be observed? Each of these questions can be answered only on the basis of theories, perhaps more modestly called hunches, hypotheses, or models.[8]

The same dependence prevails for all other activities concerning empirical data, including arranging data, cleaning them of impurities, correcting them for errors, and so forth. Sometimes it is believed that the search for covariances, the application of mathematical operations to test systematic relationships between series of data, is merely mechanical, not informed by theoretical construction. Yet, only a half-wit would earnestly look for coefficients of correlation among series of variables if he did not think that they may have something to do with one another. To regress one magnitude on a series of "factors" presupposes a hunch or theory that these factors might be good predictors, or even causes, of the dependent variable. This does not mean that the empirical researcher has committed himself to one and only one possible model; he may have a whole battery of models for trying them, one after the other, on his sets of data, in the hope of establishing strong or weak, positive or negative functional relations among the variables represented by his data. The choice of variables and the specification of the models are dictated by theoretical constructions, although these constructions, in turn, may have been induced by happenstance experiences, such as "seeing" something that has not previously been represented in any of the constructs incorporated in the theoretical model relating to the problem in question.

[8] "Facts must be *selected* for study on the basis of a hypothesis." Morris C. Cohen and Ernest Nagel, *An Introduction to Logic and Scientific Method* (New York: Harcourt Brace, 1934), p. 201.

Acceptance of the *psychological* dicta "no empirical data without prior theory" and "no theoretical construction without previous experience" does not contradict the *logical* principles concerning the different status of empirical data of observation and of abstract ideas of construction.[9]

[9] The literature on economic research and analysis offers a good many debates on this issue. The most famous is the *Methodenstreit* between Carl Menger and Gustav Schmoller, with Menger's *Untersuchungen über die Methode der Sozialwissenschaften und der Politischen Oekonomie insbesondere* (Leipzig: Duncker & Humblot, 1883), Gustav von Schmoller's review article "Zur Methodologie der Staats-und Sozialwissenschaften," *Jahrbuch für Gesetzgebung, Verwaltung und Volkswirthschaft im deutschen Reiche*, Vol. 7 (1883), pp. 239-258, and Menger's rejoinder *Die Irrthümer des Historismus in der deutschen Nationalökonomie* (Vienna: Alfred Hölder, 1884). For a balanced statement about the controversy, see John Nevill Keynes, *The Scope and Method of Political Economy* (London: Macmillan, 1891).

Another debate on the claims to "priority" of either theory or observation took place in *Critiques of Research in the Social Sciences: II. An Appraisal of Frederick C. Mills' The Behavior of Prices*, by Raymond T. Bye (New York: Social Science Research Council, 1940), with a rejoinder by Mills and a panel discussion in which Wesley C. Mitchell, Jacob Viner, and several others took part.

A sort of replay of the debate can be found in the exchange between Tjalling C. Koopmans, "Measurement without Theory," *Review of Economic Statistics*, Vol. 29 (August 1947), pp. 161-172, and Rutledge Vining, "Koopmans on the Choice of Variables to Be Studied and of Methods of Measurement," *Review of Economics and Statistics*, Vol. 31 (May 1949), pp. 77-94, with Koopman's "Reply," pp. 86-91.

A little known footnote in Wesley C. Mitchell's *Business Cycles: The Problem and Its Setting* (New York: National Bureau of Economic Research, 1927), pp. 59-60, had dealt with the same issue. It merits reproduction here:

[2] In his recent critique of current German studies of business cycles, Dr. Adolf Löwe makes the following comment upon the treatment of facts and theory in my earlier book upon business cycles:

As in all social-economic work, so in our narrower field, the analysis of facts forms the second chapter of an exposition. It must be preceded by a chapter on the theory of business cycles. Such is always the order in truth, even though the first chapter remains unwritten, and though (worse still) the writer is not conscious that his mind harbors a theory. For it is theory which provides the principles by which the irreproducible fullness of reality can be set in order; it is theory which formulates the questions which the facts must answer. (See "Der gegenwärtige Stand der Konjunkturforschung in Deutschland," in *Die Wirtschaftwissenshaft nach dem Kriege*, Festgabe für Lujo Brentano. Munich and Leipzig, 1925, vol. ii, p. 367. I have translated freely in an effort to preserve the vigor of the original.) . . .

Dr. Löwe's view of the relations between facts and theory in scientific work is a common one. But it seems to me over-schematic. Against the statement, "One cannot set economic facts in order unless one has a theory" (I should prefer to say "hypothesis"), can be put the statement, "One cannot form an economic theory unless one knows some facts." And both these statements overlook the fact that the two categories are not mutually exclusive. The theories with which science works cannot be conceived as

Segregation and Integration

The sharp distinction proposed here, on logical grounds, between concrete-empirical and abstract-theoretical domains is disapproved, or even rejected, by many philosophers, natural scientists, and social scientists. They oppose segregation even in logical categories. They may be satisfied, however, with a scheme that recognizes the middle domain as the most important one.

On my map, the domain of observation is inhabited by empirical, operational concepts; the domain of construction by mental, constitutive constructs of a purity neither observed nor observable. The desegregated domain in the middle allows visitors and immigrants from the segregated domains to mix: empirical concepts are tentatively substituted for nonoperationally defined terms in models originally proposed as hypotheses or heuristic fictions.

Perhaps we should guard against a confusion between two very different things. There is, on the one hand, a purposive bringing together, in the middle domain, of concrete-empirical concepts and

---

existing apart from the facts of human experience, and men can apprehend facts only in terms of the notions with which their minds are furnished. The more thoughtfully one considers the relations between these two phases of knowing, the less separable they become. Even on the basis of the crude usage which contrasts fact and theory, it is futile to debate which of the two comes first in the history of the race, in the life of an individual, in the growth of a science, or in the progress of an investigation. What is clear is that in scientific work these two blends, knowledge of fact and theoretical conceptions, keep stimulating, extending and enriching each other. An investigator who starts with what purports to be an exposition of theory is tacitly using the facts by which the ideas have been molded. And one who starts with what purports to be an exposition of facts, is tacitly using the theoretical conceptions by which facts have been apprehended. Whether it is better to begin a particular task by elaborating upon the theoretical conceptions employed, saying little about the facts for the moment; or to begin by elaborating upon the facts, saying little about theories for the moment, depends upon the problem in hand and upon the contribution which the investigator hopes to make toward its solution. In an investigation of moment, both the theory and the facts are elaborated at various stages of the proceedings, each by the aid of the other, and later workers start with a fact-theory blend improved by the new contribution.

It is clear that Mitchell's interest was in applied theory, in the Middle Kingdom where theoretical "notions" and recorded data are brought together; however, the theoretical constructions were often insufficiently specified, which gave rise to Koopman's criticism that Mitchell's work with data was "hypothesis-seeking" instead of "hypothesis-testing" and therefore excessively empirical in that it lacked the capacity to prove what tools of analysis were better or inferior for the purpose. Tjalling C. Koopmans, "A Reply," *Review of Economics and Statistics*, Vol. 31 (May 1949), p. 91.

abstract-theoretical constructs in attempts to apply theory either in case studies and historical studies or in tests of hypotheses. On the other hand, there are the connections discussed in the preceding subsection: the (often subconscious) psychological and evolutionary interdependence in concept formation, the mutual influences in forming empirical concepts in the domain of observation, and abstract-theoretical constructs in the domain of construction.

Perhaps the difference between the unavoidable "foreign influences" in the two autonomous, strictly segregated domains and the "deliberate integration" engineered in the desegregated central domain is less important than I believe it to be. Some philosophers of science oppose the separatism evidenced in my metaphoric description of scientific procedure and promote the integration of all types of reflective inquiry. To support my methodological distinctions I propose to offer an illustration of the independent existence of a scientific system displaying the structure of purely imaginary entities. This illustration will be the "hypothetico-deductive system of economic science."

Scarcity and Economy

According to one of the most widely accepted definitions, "economics is the science which studies human behavior as a relationship between ends and scarce means which have alternative uses." It studies how "different degrees of scarcity of different goods give rise to different ratios of valuation between them" and how "changes in conditions of scarcity, whether coming from changes in ends or changes in means—from the demand side or the supply side—affect these ratios."[10]

Scarcity of means that "have alternative uses" is the basic condition of economic conduct in that it forces people to make choices and, ideally, to economize and allocate "rationally," that is, in conformance with their preferences and their beliefs about causal relations. A wide range of implications of scarcity can be *deduced* from a small number of definitions, postulates, and assumptions; and if these assumptions are just that, namely, *assumed*—without any claims to being "empirically true" in a concrete situation—the entire chain from premises to inferences constitutes a theoretical construction logically (not psychologically) independent of any experience or ob-

---

[10] Lionel Robbins, *An Essay on the Nature and Significance of Economic Science* (London: Macmillan, 1932), p. 15. — Robbins cites several Austrian economists among earlier proponents of the fundamental notions underlying his definition.

servation. Many economists have taken strong positions regarding, on the one hand, the a priori nature of this hypothetico-deductive system or, on the other hand, its *empirical* foundation on introspective observation and unquestionable (perhaps objectively verifiable) experiences. This controversy becomes moot, and insistence on the a posteriori nature of economic theory becomes nonrelevant, if the methodological partition into empirical and theoretical domains, with a middle zone for proper correspondence between epistemic knowledge and ideal construction, is adopted.[11]

Economic science as a hypothetico-deductive system based on the assumptions of scarcity and rationality could flourish in the domain of construction even if real human beings were living in a world where no scarcity existed and all goods and services as well as time were abundant and, therefore, free. Of course, if the real world were a world of universal abundance, the construction of an imaginary system of scarcity would at best have the usefulness of play, a funthing. (If in such a world fun were also abundant, an additional piece of fun would be worthless too.) A fictitious construction of Paradise, where nothing is scarce, can give some intellectual pleasure to people living in a real world of scarcity, in a world, that is, where few things are free and persons with limited resources have to economize in their use.

The Austrian philosopher Felix Kaufmann composed a witty poem on the methodology of a purely fictitious scarcity-economics logically derived by an economic theorist who lives in Paradise, where

---

[11] Lionel Robbins has sometimes been interpreted as a follower of the aprioristic nature of economic science. This is not in conformance with his formulations, for he places much emphasis on the fact that scarcity is the "real" condition of human existence. Thus, he finds it

> conceivable that living creatures may exist whose "ends" are so limited that all goods for them are "free" goods, that no goods have specific significance.
>
> But, in general, human activity with its multiplicity of objectives has not this independence of time or specific resources. The time at our disposal is limited. There are only twenty-four hours in the day. We have to choose between the different uses to which they may be put. The services which others put at our disposal are limited. The material means of achieving ends are limited. We have been turned out of Paradise. We have neither eternal life nor unlimited means of gratification. Everywhere we turn, if we choose one thing we must relinquish others which, in different circumstances, we would wish not to have relinquished. Scarcity of means to satisfy given ends is an almost ubiquitous condition of human behaviour (pp. 14-15).

The passage is retained virtually without change in the revised (1935) edition of Robbins's book.

no scarcity can ever be experienced and hence no economic choices
can ever be made.

Der Nationalökonom im Paradies

Als unser Herr die weite Welt geschaffen,
Die Krokodile, Papageien und die Affen,
Da hat er in die Welt zu guter letzt
Den Wirtschaftswissenschaftler hingesetzt.

Nun sass der brave Mann im Paradiese
Mit einem ganz verzweifelten Gefriese,
"Weh mir, dass ich kein Material mehr hab',
"Es gibt kein Wirtschaften, denn nichts ist knapp.

"Mit Gütern wollt'ich planvoll disponieren
"Und dann mein Handeln streng analysieren
"Und schliesslich stolz sein, wenn ich sagen kann:
"So handle ich und das ist jedermann.

"Doch muss ich fruchtlos mein Gehirn zerplagen,
"Denn gar nichts gibt es hier sich zu versagen,
"Jeder Genuss ist allsogleich parat,
"Selbst mit der Zeit man nicht zu sparen hat.

Da sprach der Herr: "Du sollst nicht klagen derfen,
"Du kannst dir eine Theorie entwerfen,
"Das macht den Menschengeist ja so erlaucht,
"Dass er zum Denken nichts zu wissen braucht.

"Zwar kannst du niemals einen Satz erproben,
"Doch eben drum sollst du mich stündlich loben,
"So bleibt die Lehre aufrecht unentwegt,
"Wo nichts erprobt wird, wird nichts widerlegt.

Froh rief der Forscher: "Was war für ein Tor i,
"Von nun an denk' ich nur mehr a priori,
"Die Empirie, die bleibt mir völlig gleich,
"Hier gibt's ja keinen Anwendungsbereich."

Doch seit wir nicht im Paradies mehr wohnen,
Ist scharf zu scheiden zwischen Konventionen
Und Sätzen, deren Sinn darin besteht
Zu sagen, was in Wirklichkeit vorgeht.

The Economic Theorist in Paradise

When first the world was made by the Creator
With monkeys, parrots, and the alligator,
He fashioned as the last one on the list
The learned theoretical economist.

In Paradise now sat this worthy creature,
Perplexity inscribed on every feature:
"Woe unto me! For nothing here is scanty:
" 'Economy' is out when all is plenty.

"If things were scarce, I would economize
"And rationally allocate; then analyze
"My thoughts, and in the end I would proclaim
"My acts as typical, since all will act the same.

"In vain, alas, I put my mind to trial;
"Here is no scope to practice self-denial,
"Immediately on tap is every pleasure,
"And time itself you do not have to treasure."

Then spoke the Lord: "Complain thou not to me,
"Just go and fashion your own theory.
"The mind with such nobility is blessed
"That without knowledge it can function best.

"Sure, you can never test a single phrase.
"But just for that I do deserve much praise.
"Your theories will ever stand unmoved:
"What can't be tested, cannot be disproved."

"Fool that I was," the scholar shouted, "Glory,
"From now on will I think just a priori.
"Empiricism has lost all its might,
"What I assert can never be applied."

Since we no longer do in Eden dwell,
It's necessary to distinguish well
Conventions now from statements that contrive
To show just what goes on in real life.

The absence of empirical data of observation and of any personal experiences with such activities as economizing, maximizing, optimizing, satisficing, and rational decision-making need not prevent a speculative mind from imagining a world in which these activities would make good sense. The ingenious theoretical constructs would, however, have no empirical counterparts, and the theoretical findings would have no application to anything. The moral of Kaufmann's poem is that economists who do not live in Paradise and construct an economic science based on the assumption of scarcity have both a duty and an opportunity to compare their mental constructions (conventions) with the facts of experience in the empirical domain.[12]

This precept for theoretical analysts may, by some, be interpreted as a legacy of the neopositivistic creed, a commitment to empirical "verification" and a condemnation of unverifiable constructions as meaningless pseudopropositions. Such an interpretation would not be justified; the methodology of Felix Kaufmann can be characterized as conventionalism tempered by a search for evidence of applicability to specified empirical situations.[13] The original neopositivistic methodology, incidentally, with its insistence on physical confirmability, was later retracted. In one of his latest pronouncements, Rudolf Carnap states: "I regard as meaningful for me whatever I can, in principle, confirm subjectively"; and "everything I know, including what I know by introspection, is in principle confirmable by others on the basis of their observations."[14]

Counterfactual Assumptions

No rules are imposed on constructions of the mind as long as the construction takes place in the proper domain and is not designed to serve any specific purposes. There is thus an unlimited license for imagery and no "building code" restrains the architects' inventive fancy, provided that the figments of their imagination remain within the domain of construction. However, if they are produced for export

[12] Felix Kaufmann, "Der Nationalökonom im Paradies," translated as "The Economic Theorist in Paradise," unpublished collection of poems, Vienna, 1924-1935. Kaufmann was a philosopher who had the tolerance and flexibility enabling him to belong simultaneously to three learned circles committed to mutually contradictory methodological positions: the Vienna Circle (Moritz Schlick and Rudolf Carnap, representing logical positivism), the Freiburg School (Edmund Husserl, representing phenomenology), and the Mises Circle (Ludwig von Mises, representing apriorism). In the poem on "The Economic Theorist in Paradise" Kaufmann good-naturedly satirizes the aprioristic position. With the permission of Dr. Else Kaufmann, his widow, I have reproduced here both the original German text and an English translation (first rendered by Margaret F. W. Joseph, recently revised by Karl Aschaffenburg and myself).

[13] Felix Kaufmann, *Methodology of the Social Sciences* (New York: Oxford University Press, 1944).

[14] Rudolf Carnap, "Replies and Expositions," in Paul Arthur Schilpp, ed., *The Philosophy of Rudolf Carnap* (La Salle, Ill.: Open Court, 1963), p. 882.

to the zone of application, where they come into contact with products of real experience—empirical facts and recorded data—the abstract models and the constructs included in them had better be presentable, lest they be regarded as absurd or ridiculous monstrosities. To be useful for explanatory purposes, they have to be so designed that they can satisfy conventional rules of correspondence and can be associated in meaningful relations with concepts of experience, indeed, if possible, with data representing operationally defined terms. This does not mean, however, that the mental constructs should be "realistic" or that the assumptions adopted for a theoretical model must not be "contrary to fact."

Virtually all causal explanations include, as integral parts of the argument, counterfactual assumptions. If, for example, we want to understand how a specific piece of information affects the outcome of specified constellations and processes, we need to compare the informed decisions with those that would have been taken without the information. To give another example, if we want to understand the role of uncertainty regarding specific expectations, we have to see how our model works with and without such uncertainty. For a third example, the effect of mobility of labor can best be studied by assuming once "perfect mobility," then "perfect immobility," and also some selected degrees of mobility, perhaps defined by the cost of obtaining reliable information and by the cost of moving. Every one of these assumptions may be counterfactual, and some cannot *possibly* be anything but counterfactual. Hypothetical reasoning with counterfactual assumptions is a necessary part of any causal analysis.

The realization that unrealistic and counterfactual assumptions are indispensable in causal reasoning should not mislead the analyst into believing that "anything will do," or that *any* departure from reality will serve a useful purpose. Assumptions, realistic, unrealistic, or counterfactual, have to be *relevant* for the purpose, applicable to the case or problem at hand. Realism and relevance are very different things.[15] The most realistic assumption about some factor or variable may be completely irrelevant in a case in which this factor or variable plays no role whatsoever. And a flagrantly counterfactual assumption about a factor or variable may be highly relevant, indeed indispensable, where the influence of this factor or variable has to be assessed. Of course, assumptions can also be un-

---

[15] See, for example, Frank H. Knight, "Realism and Relevance in the Theory of Demand," *Journal of Political Economy*, Vol. 52 (November-December 1944), pp. 289-318; John Maurice Clark, "Realism and Relevance in the Theory of Demand," *Journal of Political Economy*, Vol. 54 (July-August 1946), pp. 347-353. Some pertinent observations are in Machlup, *Methodology*, pp. 78-79 and 186-187.

realistic as well as irrelevant. Far too often we find instances in which an economic analyst explicitly assumes "certainty" of expectations, even though this patently counterfactual assumption has no relevance to the particular case, either regarding the typical decision made or regarding the external effects of the typical actions taken. The inclusion of assumptions not relevant to the outcome narrows the applicability of the hypothesis or theory involved; as a rule, it is the lack of relevance, not the lack of realism, that reduces or destroys the usefulness of a theoretical construction.

Types of Theoretical Analysis in Economics

Subdivisions of abstract-theoretical analysis can be based on many different criteria, most of them serving little or no pragmatic purpose. Whether, for example, the language of exposition, especially the difference between *verbal and mathematical argument*, is a reasonably useful distinction depends on the numbers of readers excluded by their lack of mathematical preparation. (This distinction is still important, as a recent survey has shown.[16] One may expect, however, that for the next generation of economists the distinction will become irrelevant, because most graduate students in this field nowadays spend more time learning mathematics than learning economics.)

The very popular distinction between *microtheory and macrotheory* suffers from differing understandings of micro and macro and from the imposition of a dichotomy on a theoretical system that requires at least a trichotomy with the focus on (1) an individual decision-making unit (such as the firm), (2) a group of decision-making units (such as an industry or a market for a particular good), and (3) the economy as a whole. The dichotomy, micro and macro, makes economic theorists and their audiences wonder where "small" ends and "large" begins. Most economists have decided to use the pair of words for an altogether different distinction: microeconomics for theories of relative prices (including costs and selling prices) and the composition of factors and products (in firms, industries, markets, and the whole economy); and macroeconomics for theories of

---

[16] "The amount of mathematics in an article explains 30 per cent of the variation in the number of readers for AER [*American Economic Review*], 22 per cent for QJE [*Quarterly Journal of Economics*], 16 per cent for ReStat [*Review of Economics and Statistics*], and 20 per cent for JMCB [*Journal of Money, Credit, and Banking*]." Fritz Machlup; Kenneth Leeson; et al., *Information through the Printed Word*, Vol. 2: Journals (New York: Praeger, 1978), p. 282. The quoted sentence is from Part 4, "The Use of Journals," pp. 223-316, much of which was published in an article by Stephen Kagann and Kenneth W. Leeson, "Major Journals in Economics: A User Study," *Journal of Economic Literature*, Vol. 16 (September 1978), pp. 979-1003.

global magnitudes or aggregates (of heterogeneous things) such as national income, total investment, total consumption, and foreign balance, without regard to their composition.[17]

The distinction between micro- and macrotheories has been used in the economics of information in connection with explorations of causes and effects of changes in expectations. The role of information in arousing or altering expectations is under examination in both microeconomic and macroeconomic problems, but the emphasis on "dynamic expectations" has become a special feature in theories of fiscal and monetary policy, frequently referred to as macroeconomic policies. The development of "inflationary expectations" on the part of the masses of money holders responding to information about movements of prices and wages, and of currently revised expectations on the part of fiscal and monetary authorities responding to apparent feedback effects of their policy measures, have greatly stimulated this special branch of the economics of information and expectations.

A useful distinction on methodological grounds relates to the role different analysts of the causal nexus between exogenous changes (events, shocks, new information) and dependent changes (effects, adjustments, equilibration) assign to the *intervention of human minds*. I consider this distinction sufficiently important to deserve elaboration.

Theories Emphasizing or Bypassing the Intervention of the Mind

On one side are economic theories that presume interventions of human minds between the objective facts or events that are interpreted as causes and effects, and treat these interventions as essential parts of any explanations (and predictions) yielded by the theories. On the other side are economic theories that bypass and downplay these intervening variables and are satisfied to find (nonmediated) associations between recorded facts or events treated as independent

[17] For more than twenty years I have been trying to find a good Greek name for the economics of groups, the area between the genuine micro and the genuine macro. Perhaps "mesoeconomics" would be appropriate. At the present understanding of the terms—micro versus macro—the literature can be classified only according to the emphasis on relatives and aggregates, respectively; and this distinction becomes less relevant as we learn more about the complexities of the entire system of economic theory. See Fritz Machlup, "Micro- and Macro-Economics: Contested Boundaries and Claims of Superiority," in Machlup, *Essays in Economic Semantics* (New York: Prentice-Hall, 1963; New York University Press, 1975), pp. 97-144. The essay was first published in German: Machlup, *Der Wettstreit zwischen Mikro- und Makrotheorien in der Nationalökonomie* (Tübingen: Mohr-Paul Siebeck, 1960).

and dependent variables. Not that these analysts would explicitly deny the existence of mental processes between causal events and their (testable) results; but, if they concede the existence of cognitive intermediation between stimulating information and responsive action, they leave it out of the causal chain, possibly because of a methodological commitment to refuse "nonobservables" admission into their theories.

The distinction between these two types of theories is of special interest in the economics of knowledge and information. The responses of the human mind to certain occurrences may differ systematically in different circumstances, including the length of time during which economic agents have been exposed to particular experiences. Some commentators like to speak of "psychological" influences in economic reactions to given developments, and a few go so far as to say that "this is a psychological problem, not an economic one." There is little or no point in disputing the frontiers between psychology and economics in the analysis of economic decision-making. Indeed, scholars sometimes share the same views on the analysis of decision-making and yet disagree on whether one should allow it to be called psychological.[18]

Regardless of the name one gives a particular approach to the understanding of economic decision-making, it seems helpful and probably essential that in the analysis of certain problems the roles of information, knowledge, ignorance, error, expectations, risk, uncertainty, and so forth, be thoroughly explored. These explorations, to be sure, have to be empirical as well as theoretical, but at the moment we are talking about types of abstract-theoretical analysis and, hence, of mental constructs of the processes of decision-making and of the economic agents engaged in this activity. In abstract theory, the economic agents, seeking and receiving information and revising their expectations, are imaginary types (personal ideal types) equipped with precisely such intelligence as we find it heuristically expedient to assume they possess. Thus it involves no great strain on our imagination to add several functions to the fictitious mind at work, for example, a more sophisticated memory, a more subtle ca-

[18] Austrian economists have sometimes been called adherents to the psychological school of economic theory, but whatever "psychologizing" was introduced into the construct of decision-making was in the mode of Carl Menger, not of Sigmund Freud. I have tried to clarify the relationship between the psychology and the logic of concept formation and to exorcize "psychologism" from the subjective "meant meanings" inherent in the mind-presuming constructs called "ideal types." See my essay "The Ideal Type: A Bad Name for a Good Construct," in Machlup, *Methodology*, pp. 211-221.

pacity to interpret experiences of certain kinds, greater flexibility in judging the influence of certain pieces of information (normally judged only by professional economists), and greater discernment in balancing probabilities of pecuniary gains and losses with the pains and pleasures of exposure to risk and uncertainty. Neither a change in method nor a change in methodology[19] is involved when the ideal type best suited for the understanding of particular problems is programmed in a more complex way than is required for decision-makers in simpler situations.

Preference for economic theory with emphasis on the intervention of human minds does not imply downright rejection of all "economics without minds." Since the operations of the mind are not operationally defined, and hence not measurable, economists engaged in quantitative empirical research connect their recorded numerical data by means of statistical analyses of covariance (correlation, regression). They may find regularities between rainfall and grain futures or between publications of trade statistics and foreign-exchange rates. Correlations of this sort involve suppositions of objective relationships without the aid of the ideal types of mental reflections that I want for explaining the connections to my satisfaction. I look to the imaginary grain speculator who associates the reported rainfall with crop expectations and future grain prices, and to the imaginary foreign-exchange speculator who associates the press release of the trade statisticians with (possibly naive or downright wrong) responses of people in the market.

Explanations of Observations, and Tests of Constructions

We are, at last, ready to enter the Middle Kingdom, the domain of application, situated between the two outer domains of observation and construction. Its population of terms and concepts is mixed, desegregated, composed of logical inmigrants from the segregated outer domains. Its population of propositions is characterized by a commitment to both realism and relevance, realism represented by empirical data of observation, and relevance by correspondence to theoretically interrelated abstract constructs of the analyst's mind.[20]

---

[19] I admit my intention to "rub it in": methodology is *not* talk about method either in research or any other activity (like accounting or statistics), as naive Mme. Malaprop believes in her semi-educated mind. Those interested may consult my essay "What is Meant by Methodology," in Machlup, *Methodology*, pp. 5-62.

[20] The tripartition of scientific work (where "scientific" is understood in the non-parochial sense of any systematic knowledge acquired by sustained studious effort)

A quick rehearsal of the topology of the three domains may be helpful before we start on a closer exploration of the Middle Kingdom.

The Schema of the Three Domains

The schematic arrangement shown below will best serve for quick orientation, even if the formulation is somewhat superficial. After all, our purpose here is not to present an outline of scientific methodology, but only to provide guidelines for distinguishing empirical, theoretical, and applied inquiries.

Taking the emphasized words from the description of the Middle Kingdom, one may characterize it as the "juncture of empirical-operational concepts and abstract-theoretical constructs" in "explanations and predictions" of concrete observations and in "illustrations and tests" of abstract constructions. This dichotomy within the domain of application will give us headaches as soon as we proceed to examine actual samples of applied research and analysis. At first glance, however, it seems easy to comprehend: explanations (or predictions) of concrete observations on the one hand, and tests (or illustrations) of abstract constructions, on the other.

The Instrument and the Objective

The essence of the dichotomy in applied studies is the reversal of functions: in explanations of concrete empirical observations, theory is the instrument needed to interpret specific data; in tests of theoretical constructions, empirical data serve as instruments for judging the verisimilitude of the abstract theory. In many instances it is not

---

has a long history. In 1620 Francis Bacon used the analogy of the ant, the spider, and the bee to characterize the work of the collector of masses of empirical facts, the fine-spun cobwebs of the abstract theorist, and the "middle course," the fruitful transformations of materials accomplished by the applied investigator:

"Those who have handled sciences have been either Empirics or Dogmatists. The Empirics are like the ant, they only collect and use; the reasoners resemble spiders, who make cobwebs out of their own substance. But the bee takes a middle course: it gathers its material from the flowers of the garden and of the field, but transforms and digests it by a power of its own. Not unlike this is the true business of philosophy; for it neither relies solely or chiefly on the powers of the mind, nor does it take the matter which it gathers from natural history and mechanical experiments and lay it up in the memory whole, as it finds it, but lays it up in the understanding altered and digested. Therefore from a closer and purer league between these two faculties, the experimental and the rational (such as has never yet been made), much may be hoped." Francis Bacon, The Novum Organum, § 95. I used for the first sentence the translation by G. W. Kitchin (Oxford: University Press, 1855, p. 78) and for the rest of the paragraph the translation by Fulton H. Anderson (Indianapolis: Bobbs-Merrill, 19..), p. 93. — I am indebted to Mark Perlman for calling my attention to this paragraph in Bacon's work.

Domain of Observation	*Domain of Application*	*Domain of Construction*
Propositions containing only *empirical-operational* concepts, i.e., terms defined by physical, statistical, and other observational operations, designed to *obtain and arrange empirical data* on the subject under observation.	*Juncture of empirical-operational concepts and abstract-theoretical constructs in propositions using the former as proxies for or counterparts of the latter.*	Propositions containing only *abstract-theoretical constructs,* i.e., terms defined by abstract properties of elements usable in syllogistic inferences, designed to obtain the logical implications of definitions, postulates and assumptions.
Comparisons of sets of data establishing regularities, especially covariances among them.	Explanations of the historical past—concrete events or changes observed and recorded at particular times and places.	*Logical interrelationships* among constructs arranged in abstract (verbal, algebraic, or geometric) models for the demonstration of conclusions inferred from definitions, axioms, and theorems.
	Predictions of the future—concrete constellation of observables at specified times and places.	
	Illustrations and Tests of the applicability or generality of a theoretical system by finding empirical counterparts of the ideal constructs and substituting the former for the abstract terms in the theoretical system.	

difficult to decide on the objectives of an investigation; indeed, in best investigative practice the author states at the beginning of his report what he attempts to accomplish. Alas, not every author follows best practice, and this may keep us guessing. We shall try to examine a few types of applied research where the judgment is relatively simple.

Historical studies are clear instances where recourse to theory is only instrumental to establishing the relevance of recorded events or conditions by finding that they were likely causes of other recorded events or developments. Theory in these instances serves the interpretation of the reports of concrete happenings in particular places at particular times. Needless to say, "theory" in this context is not confined to constructions formed in one narrowly circumscribed field of study, since several specialties in a variety of different disciplines may have to be brought to bear on the explanation of any concrete set of observations.

The same is true when an explanation is sought for a specific, concrete event—an accident, a violent death, an explosion, a conflagration, a riot—not as a part of history in the sense of a general narrative of a people in a stated period, but a single case the causes of which are of interest to inquisitive individuals, groups, or the government. For the investigation of any such case, theories from several sciences—natural, social, and cultural—may be required. The interest in the explanation of the "case" is not connected with any desire to test or illustrate the theories applied; the theories are accepted with confidence or with reservations, but if their standing or applicability is questioned, it is not done in order to amend the theoretical system of which they are a part but only to weaken or disconfirm the judgment of the particular case in question.

Case studies can be of an entirely different cast, namely, where the interest of the investigator lies not in the individual cases selected for study but instead in probing the theory or theories applied. The sample of cases is chosen chiefly for the light they can shed on the applicability or generality of a theory or hypothesis subjected to testing. Whereas each of the cases occurred at a particular time and place, these criteria of concreteness serve only to establish the empirical character of the evidence; but the significance of the inquiry lies in probing the theory as a general proposition about causal relationships in *all* cases of the specified type under specified conditions. The difference between a case study undertaken to examine, judge, or decide a case, and a case study designed to illustrate or test a theory can easily be exemplified. As an example of the former, consider an antitrust case argued before the courts, where the economic theory of competition, monopoly, and collusive oligopoly, particularly of the effects on prices and outputs, on newcomers' entry, extent of the market, or differences in product quality are of decisive importance. As an example of a test of theory, consider a case study involving several firms operating under similar conditions and sharing in common the characteristics, properties, and attributes specified in the theoretical construction, where the observed results are compared with one another and with the conclusions logically inferred in the theoretical system, with a view to declaring these conclusions confirmed or contradicted, depending on whether or not the observed outcomes are or are not consistent with the ideal-typical results inferred.

Measurements

Things are not that easy when we want to consider the methodological status of measurements. The empirical basis of measurement is beyond question: the raw data are always taken from records of observation. Questions arise, however, when raw data have to be processed, adjusted, or otherwise manipulated before they make sense in connection with other data, other empirical concepts, or underlying theoretical constructs; or when there are no unique "natural" units of measurement (such as "persons" in a census of population) but, instead, several options among different arbitrary units of measurement (for example, output measured by weight, length, square measure, cubic volume, labor contents, energy equivalent, money cost, money sales revenue, etc.); or when no unambiguously suitable empirical proxy exists for the ideally quantified theoretical construct (for example, net investment, human capital, total welfare, total wealth, etc.).

In all instances in which estimation or measurement is closely linked to or dependent on abstract constructs and on propositions that are parts of theoretical systems, research and analysis designed to produce such estimates or measurements will have to be assigned to the domain of application. This decision seems to contradict the resolution that operational definitions—and these are prerequisites for all measurements—be regarded as characteristic for the concepts in the domain of observation. To the extent, however, that the operational definitions are not only suggested by rules of correspondence with pertinent abstract-theoretical constructs but actually derived from propositions belonging to the domain of construction, research designed to produce the quantifications must clearly fall into the domain of application.

No one, for example, could possibly start estimating statistical series for annual gross and net investment in human capital and for totals of the nation's stock of human capital had he not been thoroughly informed by the pure theory of human capital. Readers who have the patience to peruse the pertinent chapters in the next part of this volume will accept this comment without objection or qualification. There are no records of data, indeed, there are no observables that could furnish an empirical basis for the estimates in question. The empirical researcher on the required quantifications has to go back to statistical data on personal earnings of workers with different educational and work experiences and then, with much ingenuity and speculative assumptions (including counterfactual ones), manipulate these data so drastically that the resulting figures can hardly still be called "givens." The figures obtained from the calculations and computations made with original data are as much the results of theoretical construction as of empirical observation. Hence, they belong in the domain of application. Whether, within that domain, the derived estimates are more appropriately seen as explanations of observations or as tests of theory is open to question. They do not fit well into either of these two boxes, which may indicate that the proposed schema is unsatisfactory. Perhaps, though, one can justify their assignment to the second category of applied inquiry if the word "test" of theory is bracketed and "illustration" of theory is accepted as a proper description of the task.

Testing versus Illustrating

The suggestion that "testing" is a less appropriate, and "illustrating" a more appropriate, description of what a researcher does to theories when he wants to find out how well these abstract constructions perform in connection with records of observation has a much wider application than has been intimated. The philosophy of science has, over the last eighty years, exhibited a consistent and continuing trend of diminishing perfectionism (or attenuating pretension) in methodological requirements for scientific propositions.

At the beginning of the twentieth century the ambition was to prove the "truth" of every proposition by means of "inductive generalization" of the findings of sense perception. This grand illusion was replaced by the less demanding requirement of "verification" by means of empirical protocol statements. Under criticism, this requirement was watered down and "confirmation" was found to be sufficient. Even confirmation was later seen to be impossible, and therefore deemed presumptuous to demand, since empirical findings consistent with the theory could at best disconfirm or "falsify" the theory but never confirm it. Thus testing the "verisimilitude" of the theory was all that one could ask for; such testing would lead either to (temporary) rejection of the theory, or to an admission that it deserved further testing. Only a "pass or fail" option remained open, and a grade of "pass" indicated no more than (temporary) survival until the next trial. These trials, however, are not always so rigorous as to deserve designation as "tests." They are often no more than illustrations by selected "cases" or by experiments with inadequate controls. When empirical findings are found to be inconsistent with conclusions derived from the theoretical system, the disappointing tests are usually thrown out as unsatisfactory and insignificant. The rejection of empirical findings inconsistent with the more trusted theoretical conclusion is usually done for good reasons; successful theoretical systems have great resistance to attempted subversion by supposedly contradictory findings in empirical "tests."[21]

The point of all this is that so-called "tests" of theories are ordinarily not real tests; they are not decisive for rejection or continued acceptance of the theories in question. The same empirical data are consistent with several alternative theories and hence cannot confirm any of the constructions rivaling one another; and in those instances in which the data do contradict a widely accepted theory, the data or the techniques employed in their adjustment and arrangement are often found faulty or made compatible with the (presumably tested) theory by the addition of auxiliary hypotheses, which plausibly explain what first appeared as an incompatibility or paradox. I do not expect that researchers will soon stop giving their (often misspecified) regression equations (with admittedly poor data) the pretentious designations of "tests" of theories; but I would feel better if they more modestly called them "illustrations."

---

[21] This paragraph attempted to provide in capsule form the story of the development of methodological thought from 1900 to the present. The list of authors of the philosophical literature known for important pronouncements on scientific truth, verification, confirmation, corroboration, nonfalsification, verisimilitude, consistency, correspondence, resistance to contradiction, and survival until further notice includes many names; a few may be mentioned here: Karl Pearson, Wilhelm Windelband, Josiah Royce, Henry Poincaré, William Pepperell Montague, Albert Einstein, Percy W. Bridgman, Alfred North Whitehead, Morris Cohen, Hans Reichenbach, Rudolf Carnap, Ludwig Wittgenstein, Alfred J. Ayer, Philipp Frank, Felix Kaufmann, Henry Margenau, Alexander Tarski, Karl Popper, Filmer S. C. Northrup, Herbert Feigl, Richard Braithwaite, Hermann Weyl, Ernest Nagel, Carl Hempel, Michael Polanyi. (For precise references and some excerpts see Machlup, *Methodology*.) It is surely not necessary that everybody who discusses methodological problems is familiar with the writings of all these men or of even five or six of them; but what is astounding is that so many present-day writers in the natural and social sciences have never read beyond Pearson (1900), Bridgman (1927), and the early Carnap (1928).

Distribution of Research Among the Three Domains

The explorations of the three domains of disciplined inquiry have been conducted with a view to formulating the arguments and conclusions in a most general way, applicable to all sciences, natural, social, and cultural. In choosing examples, however, I have, understandably, favored the field of economics, and within this discipline, the economics of knowledge and information. The questions raised in this section will all relate to economics and the special field selected for study.

How much of the economist's work is empirical research, and how much is theoretical analysis, and how much is applied inquiry? This question calls for counting and measuring and thus presupposes agreement on operational definitions of the three types of scientific effort. In a more general, philosophical discourse, we can go a great distance before stating the operations that can be used to distinguish the three types. But for a count one needs to single out characteristic features of the arguments contained in the articles. These features should clearly separate the two pure types—theoretical and empirical—from the mixed type that blends theoretical and empirical work. The sorters, or census takers, need to have the operations specified before they can perform their task.

Operational Definitions Needed for the Count

Thus, before embarking on an investigation of the contents of leading journals in economics to ascertain the relative frequencies of "purely empirical," "purely theoretical," and "applied" articles, I had to develop operational definitions for the three types. This proved to be a task far more difficult than I had expected. The "operations" proposed to the assayers had to be revised repeatedly in the course of their work; whenever they had serious problems of deciding how to characterize a borderline case, the question of an appropriate redefinition was raised. I shall report on the development of my operational definitions in the appendix to this chapter.

The Actual Count

The appendix will also report on the findings of the examination of the contents of five volumes of each of two journals, the *American Economic Review* and the *Journal of Political Economy*. The selected years were 1960, 1965, 1970, 1975, and 1980. The task was to find the relative shares of the three types of articles in all fields of economics and in the special field, "knowledge and information," in particular.

The Infrequency of Purely Empirical Research

One finding of this project of sorting and counting did surprise me: the infrequency of purely empirical research. While there has been plenty of "theory without data," there was only a negligible amount of publishing on "data without theory."[22] Since empirical research is indispensable and division of labor is more efficient, one should expect that a good many economists engage in the activities that make up the bulk of empirical work—interrogating, searching documents, computing coefficients of covariation, and so forth. Why then the infrequency of published articles reporting on strictly empirical findings?

Let me suggest a few "explanatory hypotheses." (1) The two journals examined (*AER* and *JPE*) are not representative of the entire journal literature. Their editors may deliberately reject manuscripts presenting data without theory. (2) The period 1960 to 1980 is different from earlier times, when many economists were suspicious, if not contemptuous, of theoretical speculation; a survey covering a longer period, going back to the 1920s, may show many more-strictly-empirical articles. (3) The distinction between empirical research and applied inquiry where recorded data are combined with theoretical constructions is not valid and, consequently, a category of reports on data without theory is virtually a null class. (4) The operational criteria that I formulated for my research assistants were too strong, so that almost all empirical articles were put into the category of applied inquiry. (5) The steady advance of the econometric research program, now dominating all graduate instruction in economics, proclaiming firm links among theory, statistics, and mathematics, has made data collection and measurement without explicit theory disreputable. (6) Strictly empirical research is being done, but it is largely assigned to graduate students, research assistants, and technicians, who do not often produce articles for publication. The authors of articles are using the empirical research done by others and publish the findings together with the theoretical arguments they are supposed to support.

There is something to be said in favor of every one of these hypotheses; they are not mutually exclusive, indeed they are partly overlapping. I leave it to the readers to make up their own minds.

---

[22] That the choice of data always *implies* theory, or at least general notions about causal or quasi-causal relationships, has been said several times in this chapter. The phrase "data without theory" is intended to refer to empirical research where the theoretical foundations are not shown and where the data are not doctored to conform to preconceived theoretical constructs.

Contents of Economic Journals:
Relative Shares of Empirical, Theoretical, and Applied Work

Brief comments on the distribution of published articles among those characterized as empirical, theoretical, and applied were offered in the last section of Chapter 7. This appendix is given to a report on the development of operational definitions and on some findings of numerical counts made in an examination of the contents of two major economic journals.

Operational Definitions of Empirical and Applied Research

Having found, in the first sections of Chapter 7, that obtaining and using empirical data, usually in the form of sets of numbers recorded in tabular form, is the essence of empirical research in economics, we can reasonably propose that the first operation is to see whether the paper, article, or chapter in question displays tabular material. If it does, the second operation is to see whether the numbers exhibited in the tables represent unadulterated records of observation, interrogation, or experimentation, either undertaken by the authors themselves—producing primary data—or taken from previously existing records. In the latter case the publication becomes a secondary source of data but would still qualify as empirical research if it is not disqualified for other reasons. One of the reasons for disqualification would be the admission that the sets of numbers were only "imaginary data," as for example numbers assumed for purposes of illustration, simulation, or exercise. A sorter would remain in doubt in instances where the sets of numbers shown in the publication were results of manipulation or computation rather than reproductions of original records of observation, interrogation, or experimentation.

We are often presented with series of numerical estimates or measurements of nonobservables; such numbers evidently are concoctions of both theoretical construction and empirical observation—no longer data given to the analyst from genuine ("protocol") records. This kind of work would be a blend of empirical and theoretical effort. It is difficult to give the assayer of the exact nature of the inquiry precise instructions regarding the operations that can establish the methodological status of the work in question. One operation ought to be designed to seek out the source of the original data, another operation to assess the degree to which these "given" data were adjusted, manipulated, or transformed in producing the sets or series of computed numbers. Footnote references are not likely to supply adequate clues; only a closer reading of the research report will tell about the speculative ingredients of the research. No doubt, the inquiry in question will have to be characterized as belonging to the middle domain of application.

Not all empirical research, or empirical inputs to applied inquiry, can be spotted by displays of rows or columns of numerical data. After all, not all empirical facts are quantifiable. Suitable operations to establish the empirical nature of textual material include checking the references, either in footnotes or in the body of the report, to dated occurrences, situations, or changes in conditions specified by time and place. In such studies with nonnumerical data it may be quite difficult to find the dividing line between empirical research and applied inquiry informed by theory in essential respects. Superficially one may suggest that the conventional differentiation between chronological and historical accounts is revealing in this respect. Chronology produces or reproduces genuinely empirical data, but historical narratives presuppose theoretical constructions to determine the causal relationships among the recorded events and, hence, their relevance as history. However, not only is theory called upon to inform history, but history reciprocates for this favor by serving as evidence for the applicability of theory. Both these kinds of scholarly cooperation between empirical and theoretical efforts characterize the inquiry as belonging to the middle domain of application.

Twice in this chapter I suggested that the avowed intentions or objectives of the investigator could tell the sorter what he needs to know about the methodological status of the project. This suggestion is practically operational only when the investigator explicitly declares his intentions; if he does not, the suggestion is not really operational, because it would not be practicable for the sorter to ask all authors about what they intended to show—events, theories, explanations, tests, or whatever. Thus, we must expect that a good many publications will resist our efforts to sort and count them correctly.

Operational Definition of Abstract-Theoretical Analysis

Is there an operational definition of abstract-theoretical analysis? Can the absence of all operational criteria of empirical and applied research serve as an effective "litmus paper" for the sorting? To some extent perhaps, but the classification of a nonempirical paper as a theoretical one would be acceptable only if no other types of paper, article, or essay were ever published—which is surely not true. Just think of surveys and reviews, memoirs, biographies and bibliographies, normative and evaluative economics, appraisals and recommendations of economic policy, papers on research methods, such as statistical and econometric techniques, essays on methodology and epistemology, reports on teaching methods, general statements on comparative economic systems, business administration, marketing, accounting, questions of legal or other institutional developments, and several other topics covered in some economic journals in articles that present neither empirical nor applied research nor abstract-theoretical analysis. Hence, the absence of any operational criteria of empirical or applied research is not a sufficient reason for characterizing the product in question as theoretical analysis. We have to look for the presence of positive criteria.

The acid test, I submit, lies in the presence of chains of arguments in the vein of logical derivations from nominal definitions, axioms and postulates, theorems, supplementary assumptions, and corollaries, to abstract-theoretical conclusions, where all terms connote mental constructs, rather than operational concepts. Operational proxies for the mental constructs may or may not exist, but in either case they are no part of an abstract-theoretical analysis. The chain of arguments in the analysis may be presented in algebraic, geometric, or purely verbal form, or in a mixture of such languages. The sequence of steps in the deductive chain need not always be explicitly described; indeed, some theorists take pleasure in showing their mental prowess by skipping a step or two (thereby keeping their readers reverently hobbling behind). Where the analysis is presented in mathematical form with numbered equations, designated as definitions, lemmas, propositions, corollaries, and conclusions, the classifier will have little trouble identifying the piece as theoretical.

Many economic theorists, though confining themselves to theoretical analysis, like to help the reader with suggestions for applied inquiries and with references to empirical research pertinent to the analysis in question. They may also suggest operational proxies or counterparts of the mental constructs used in the analysis. Such hints and heuristic aids need not change the methodological status of the report so much as to remove it from the domain of construction. As long as the argument remains theoretical, and empirical data, numerical or textual, remain in the role of "memorandum items" or advisory comments, the report need not be reassigned to the domain of application.

The Contents of Journals

The effort of assaying the contents of economic journals for the ratios of empirical, theoretical, and applied inquiries has not yielded any remarkable findings; it did confirm, however, my misgivings regarding the difficulty of unambigious judgments about the character of treatment in particular articles. I should therefore warn against taking my report on numerical shares, trends, and fluctuations too seriously. I am afraid a replication of the assaying by others may, because of different judgments, lead to divergent findings. Since I found the work not sufficiently encouraging, I stopped after having examined five volumes each, published between 1960 and 1980, of the two most widely cited American economic journals, the *American Economic Review* (AER) and the *Journal of Political Economy* (JPE). This is surely not a representative sample of the journal literature, but it is interesting to know the kind of article that was printed in these two strictly refereed outlets of current economic research.[1]

I was primarily interested in studies on the economics of information and knowledge, but one of the questions was whether in this specialty the mixture of empirical, theoretical, and applied work was different from that found in other articles. In order to make this comparison the assayers had to compile numbers that yielded a by-product: the share of articles explicitly linked to knowledge and/or information (K and I).

Classification by Subject Matter:
K and I versus Other Subjects

Even this limited, preliminary task proved on two grounds to be problematic: First, where the reference to knowledge or information, though explicit, is not further elaborated and cannot be recognized as being essential to the argument, the assayers may have decided against counting the article as falling into the economics of knowledge and information. Second, before one can show the share of the total, one has to agree on how many items published in the journal should be excluded from the count; as I had decided earlier, we excluded items with regard to which the question of whether the treatment was theoretical, applied, or empirical made little sense, such as articles on history of thought, memorials, review articles, survey articles, articles on method, and articles on methodology; we

---

[1] I am indebted to Mary Taylor Huber and Jalaleddin Jalali for the judging, sorting, counting, and calculating required for this piece of applied research. They assessed approximately 500 articles.

TABLE 7.1

Shares of Articles on Knowledge or Information Published in the 1960, 1965, 1970, 1975, and 1980 Volumes of the *American Economic Review* and the *Journal of Political Economy*, in Per Cent of the Total

Journal	1960	1965	1970	1975	1980
American Economic Review	31	47	57	54	58
Journal of Political Economy	43	49	32	58	57

also excluded papers from conference proceedings; finally, we decided to exclude most miscellaneous pieces marked in the tables of contents as "shorter papers" or "communications" or downgraded by smaller print. These exclusions left a margin of discretion and caused substantial variations (leading to divergent counts) in the numbers of items per volume sorted by subject and treatment.[2]

With these qualifications in mind, we may proceed to the findings about the relative shares of articles classified as belonging to the economics of knowledge and information (K and I). The volumes chosen for examination were those for the years 1960, 1965, 1970, 1975, and 1980. Table 7.1 presents the findings. We can see a sharp increase in the share of K and I articles—those with explicit and significant links to knowledge and information—in the *AER* from 1960 to 1970—from 31 to 47 and to 57 per cent—with a subsequent leveling-off—to 54 and 58 per cent.[3] We had expected such an increase and were therefore surprised by the rather different showing for the *Journal of Political Economy* (*JPE*). The beginning and end of the series exhibit a large increase from 43 per cent in 1960 to 57 per cent in 1980, but the first three figures give the appearance of a downward trend. How can we explain the difference between the two journals? The 1960 shares, so much higher in the *JPE* than in the *AER*—42:31—seem to reflect the particular research interests of the economists at the University of Chicago who edit the *JPE*. They include George Stigler and Theodore Schultz, the one pioneering in the economics of search, the other in the economics of education,

---

[2] For example, in the *AER* of 1965 only 20 articles remained for our consideration, against 52 articles in 1975. Since our findings will be reported in percentages, changes in the sample size remain concealed.

[3] The upward trend was more pronounced and more persistent in the count by Jalali, showing the five consecutive percentages in the *AER* as 21, 47, 53, 54, 63. I am using Huber's series, because they were based on a careful review of Jalali's earlier findings.

and both exerting strong influences on fellow researchers.[4] That the shares allotted to writings in these areas were actually reduced in the *JPE* in 1965 and 1970 may be merely a matter of accidental or deliberate "bunching" of manuscripts under editorial consideration, but I dare suggest a possible hypothesis: other journals may have been rapidly increasing their interest in the expanding subject area, just as the *AER* did, and this wider distribution of currently produced articles over more journals may have cut into the share published by the *JPE*. I have not attempted to test this hypothesis. In any case, the economics of knowledge and information was again strongly represented in the 1975 and 1980 volumes of the *JPE*. The noteworthy finding is that in 1980 the share of articles in this special field was more than one-half of the total: 57 per cent in the *JPE*, and 58 per cent in the *AER*. As a matter of fact, the percentage shares of "knowledge and information" were very close in the two journals in three of the five years: 1965, 49:47; 1975, 58:54; and 1980, 57:58 per cent (with the figure for the *JPE* placed first).

Classification by Mode of Treatment: Theoretical versus Applied and Empirical

Turning now to the findings about the modes of treatment of the subjects studied, I must first report that the judging of the proper methodological category to which an article should be assigned proved to be unexpectedly more difficult between empirical and applied pieces than between any of these and theoretical ones. The difficulties can be sized up by the probers' expressed doubts and misgivings, but more visibly by the disagreements in their decisions. The probers had little or no trouble in tagging an article as a piece of theoretical analysis, but they had a hard time making distinctions between reports on empirical research and applied inquiries. The two assayers disagreed on almost one-third of the articles that were empirical or applied.[5] The criteria that distinguish the two kinds of study are evidently too subtle for operational purposes. Such questions as to what extent prior theoretical construction had effectively "informed" the choice of empirical data and to what extent raw data had to be modified and transformed to make them into suitable proxies of the pure constructs employed in analytical arguments are difficult to answer in a cursory inspection of the articles probed. These difficulties account for the precariousness of some of the findings—unless

---

[4] These interests started before 1960. We checked the shares for 1955, and found them to be 47 per cent at the *JPE* against 30 per cent at the *AER*.

[5] Jalali had many more articles in the empirical category than in the applied; Huber marked only very few as empirical.

we are satisfied with a binary classification, theoretical analysis, on the one hand, empirical or applied research, on the other.[6]

Using this binary classification for all subjects treated in the *AER* and *JPE* in the selected five years, I reproduce in Table 7.2 the summary of Huber's findings. The share of theoretical analysis is relatively high throughout: it varies from a low of 29 per cent (in the *AER* of 1960) to a high of 50 per cent (in the *JPE* in 1975). Five of the ten percentages are above 45 per cent. Looking at the annual pairs of figures, we find that they are not very different for the two journals, though the share of theory in the *JPE* exceeds that in the *AER* in four of the five years examined. In both journals, however, the share of theory seems to increase, though not monotonically. Both series suggest an upward trend from 1960 to 1975, with a fall of the theory share in 1980 to a level still far above that of 1960. Having merged empirical and applied research into one category, we need not discuss the percentages shown in the first column: they are the complements of the shares of theory in the total.

Comparison of Modes of Treatment of K and I and Other Subjects

We now come to our main task: the classification of the articles in the special field of the economics of knowledge and information (K and I) by mode of treatment—theoretical, applied, empirical—and the comparison of the distributions with articles on other subjects in economics.

Mindful of the customary precept that before starting an inquiry the investigator should formulate the hypotheses he intends to test, I feel compelled to state my conviction that curiosity can be expressed in the form of any number of contradictory hypotheses. I might hypothesize, for example, that the share of theoretical articles

[6] To illustrate the task of classifying articles by methodological mode of treatment employed, I present three examples from the 1980 volume of the *AER*: John S. Chipman and James C. Moore, "Compensating Variation, Consumer's Surplus, and Welfare," pp. 933-949; Edwin Mansfield, "Basic Research and Productivity Increase in Manufacturing," pp. 863-873; and Robert W. Fogel and Stanley L. Engerman, "Explaining the Relative Efficiency of Slave Agriculture in the Antebellum South: Reply," pp. 672-690. There is not the slightest doubt about the Chipman and Moore article being purely theoretical analysis. That Mansfield's as well as Fogel and Engerman's articles were characterized (by Huber) as applied inquiries, although both make substantial use of not drastically doctored empirical data, has my full endorsement. Not a single article in the 1980 volume is empirical research without firm theoretical foundation. Huber judged one article in the 1960 volume of the *AER* as a report on empirical research; Norman M. Kaplan and Richard H. Moorsteen, "An Index of Soviet Industrial Output," pp. 295-318. Even this article could be regarded as applied inquiry inasmuch as it presupposes a number of preconceived theoretical constructs; but the constructs are not, in the particular inquiry, related to a hypothetico-deductive system.

TABLE 7.2

Modes of Treatment of Subjects Studied in the 1960, 1965, 1970, 1975, and 1980 Volumes of the *American Economic Review* and the *Journal of Political Economy*, in Per Cent of the Total

Volume	Journal	Empirical or Applied	Theoretical
1960	AER	71	29
	JPE	69	31
1965	AER	58	42
	JPE	67	33
1970	AER	53	47
	JPE	51	49
1975	AER	53	47
	JPE	50	50
1980	AER	64	36
	JPE	54	46

in the K and I area exceeds that for other economic subjects and has been increasing in the last twenty years. But I might just as well hypothesize the contrary, and all these and similar hypotheses would require the same kind of research to test them. Frankly, I had no clear suspicions of the state of affairs in K and I research. As a matter of fact, I presumed that different topics within the economics of K and I would invite different modes of inquiry. Certain problems in the economics of education or in the economics of research and development may at the present stage of knowledge have greater need for observational data, whereas inquiries or problems in the economics of job search, quality competition, and price expectations may not yet be saturated with theoretical analysis. Thus, a hypothesis about the field of K and I economics as a whole may not be very meaningful. If some problems require more factual information whereas others need more urgently a conceptual cleaning job and innovative formation of mental constructs, the methodological composition of K and I economics as a whole will depend on just what is being investigated. Understanding these conditional requirements does not imply that one is barred from asking about the present state and recent development of the field.

Although I do not entertain any clear hypotheses regarding the shares of theoretical, applied, and empirical work in modern economics of K and I, I can understand that some of my fellow economists did formulate hypotheses of this kind. Some, for example, declared that the economics of search has been too theoretical up to now and is in dire need of experimental testing.[7]

Relative shares of the three modes of treatment in articles on the economics of K and I were computed by Huber and are shown in Table 7.3. Its arrangement is a little complicated, because I wanted it to allow several comparisons at once. Besides the comparisons of the three modes, the table offers comparisons between K and I and other subjects, in two different journals, and for five different years.

Let us first look at the share of "theory without data" in the K and I field compared with the share in articles on other subjects. In the ten comparisons (two journals, five years, hence ten annual volumes) we find the share of theory in five observations larger and in the other five observations smaller in K and I than in other subjects. Comparing the two journals, we find the share of theoretical articles in four years larger and in one year smaller in the AER than in the JPE. We realize that the first comparison shows no systematic difference or bias and that the second comparison suffers from a failure to weight each share for the different numbers of articles contained in different volumes. A separate test, in which the contents of all five annual volumes were combined, yielded the opposite result: the share of theoretical articles on K and I was smaller in the five annual volumes of the AER (39 per cent) than in the five volumes of the JPE (47 per cent). Looking now for any trend over time, we are equally frustrated: the time series of the percentage of theoretical articles shows for the AER a zigzag movement (60, 29, 50, 40, 52) and for the JPE a rise until 1975 followed by a decline (17, 23, 47, 52, 42).

Why take time and space to exhibit inconclusive sets of data? First, because blind alleys should be marked lest several other investigators embark on the same approach and waste more time than it takes to read about the unsuccessful first attempt. Second, it is not completely useless to learn that economists studying K and I have, by and large, shown just about the same propensities to speculate and construct, to observe and record, and to combine records with constructions as they have shown in dealing with other subjects.

[7] "The literature surrounding the topic of optimal economic search . . . is loaded with a great variety of theoretical results and yet it is strikingly devoid of any real empirical verification. As a result, the abstract world of the theorists is left intact and unchallenged. In essence an entire theoretical edifice has been constructed describing the way people search without any empirical testing as to whether or not people actually do search that way." Andrew Schotter and Yale M. Braunstein, "Economic Search: An Experimental Study," Economic Inquiry, Vol. 19 (January 1981), p. 2.

TABLE 7.3

Modes of Treatment of Articles on Knowledge and Information and on All Other Subjects in the 1960, 1965, 1970, 1975, and 1980 Volumes of the American Economic Review and the Journal of Political Economy in Per Cent of the Total

Volume	Journal	Subject Treated	Empirical	Applied	Theoretical
1960	AER	Knowledge & Information	0	40	60
		Other Subjects	9	73	18
	JPE	Knowledge & Information	0	83	17
		Other Subjects	12	50	38
1965	AER	Knowledge & Information	—	71	29
		Other Subjects	—	63	37
	JPE	Knowledge & Information	9	68	23
		Other Subjects	4	35	61
1970	AER	Knowledge & Information	—	50	50
		Other Subjects	—	52	48
	JPE	Knowledge & Information	—	53	47
		Other Subjects	—	52	48
1975	AER	Knowledge & Information	4	56	40
		Other Subjects	—	38	62
	JPE	Knowledge & Information	—	48	52
		Other Subjects	—	61	39
1980	AER	Knowledge & Information	—	48	52
		Other Subjects	—	62	38
	JPE	Knowledge & Information	—	58	42
		Other Subjects	—	72	28

CHAPTER 8

Economic Agents, Equilibria, and Expectations

THE IDEAL TYPE "economic man" has served economic theory in the analysis of many *general* problems. For the analysis of *special* problems, however, economic man has to specialize: the all-around "utility maximizer" has to be transformed, for example, into a sophisticated corporate manager considering his alternatives in raising capital funds for the company; or into a job seeker considering his options in different locations and different occupations, including that of collecting unemployment benefits; or an inventor considering his chances of forming his own firm to exploit his idea, either patented or in secrecy, or selling it to others for ready money or for one of several different forms of participation in the expected profits from a temporary monopoly. A long list of specialized economic agents will be offered presently to indicate the virtually unlimited agenda for an economist inquiring into the process of "informed" decision-making.[1]

Economic Agents

It goes without saying that different kinds of information may be relevant for different types of economic agents and for their expectations, choices, decisions, and actions. But what do we mean by "types" of economic agents?

Real Persons or Ideal Types

Nonspecialized "economic man" is an ideal type; he has always been completely unreal. He has never been thought of—by those who created him—as anything but a heuristic fiction, an ideal type in the domain of theoretical construction.[2] When we begin to "spe-

---

[1] In the literature we find "economic actor" and "economic agent" used interchangeably; the latter seems to be more fashionable these days.

[2] For references to the position of John Stuart Mill on the fictitious nature of what later was called economic man, see Volume I of the present work, *Knowledge and Knowledge Production*, pp. 86-87; also my book on *Methodology of Economics and Other Social Sciences* (New York: Academic Press, 1978), pp. 270-271, and 287-289.

cialize" economic man, to focus, for example, on the consumer or the worker, we are still confined to the domain of idealized construction. With increasing specificity (and perhaps reduced anonymity) of the type, we may find it possible to identify suitable empirical counterparts for the theoretical constructs. Thus, when we model the process of decision-making by landlords and tenants in residential housing, we can identify living persons playing these roles in real life. That we have such economic agents in the empirical domain, that we can find them by appropriate operational definitions, and that we can interrogate them and inspect some of their records does not make us abandon the use of the corresponding ideal types. Indeed, for purposes of theorizing, of deriving interesting conclusions from agreed definitions, postulates, and assumptions, we can use *only* the ideal types. But for purposes of testing, of showing the relevance of the theoretical conclusions, we can now resort to data obtained from or about real persons in real life.

There is a purpose in stressing the difference between the ideal type of an economic agent and the real person in the corresponding role in the real world. We assume, for example, that the ideal type of a holder of cash balances watches what goes on in the money market, bond market, some commodities markets, and so forth and will not indifferently and insensibly pass up any opportunities for lowering the cost of being liquid; many money holders in real life, however, do not care, or even notice, how much they lose by their indolence, ignorance, or laziness. Similarly, for the ideal-typical buyer of insurance we make assumptions about the mathematical expectations of the risk against which he considers buying insurance, about his aversion to bearing these risks, and about the comparative cost of alternative forms of insurance—assumptions that only few insurance buyers in the real world approach very closely. The point is that the theoretical analyst can use his abstract constructs in a logical chain of inferences leading to definite conclusions. From the operational concepts of money holders, insurance buyers, or any other economic agents, nothing follows logically; but if a sufficient number of the real-world agents act in ways sufficiently similar to the ways assumed for the ideal types, the theoretical conclusions arrived at in the domain of construction will be applicable to and comparable with the empirical data from the domain of observation.[3]

Classification of types of economic agents may be by most general or by specified economic functions or occupations. Neoclassical mi-

[3] For a more detailed exposition of these questions, see my essay on "The Problem of Verification in Economics," *Southern Economic Journal*, Vol. 22 (July 1955), pp. 1-21; reproduced in my *Methodology*, Chap. 5, pp. 137-157.

croeconomic theory on a general level distinguishes only two major types: *households* and *firms*. The former are divided into consumers (buyers of goods and services) and factors (sellers of productive services), with the understanding that most (adult) real people are both consumers of goods and services and sellers of productive services. To these types of "individual" decisionmakers are added "groups" of decisionmakers: *industries* as groups of competing firms, and *markets* of groups of potential buyers (demand) and potential sellers (supply). The difference between the "micro-units"—households and firms—and the "group models"—industries and markets—is categorical in that the former are idealized as single decisionmakers whereas the latter are regarded as models of interactive systems composed of at least two, but usually several or many, decisionmakers. The industry is composed of firms, each of which is affected or influenced by the actions of the other members of the group and, in turn, affects or influences the others by its own actions and reactions. The market is composed of firms and households (as potential buyers of consumer goods and potential suppliers of productive services) or of firms only (as potential suppliers or buyers of intermediate products).

On some level of analysis another type of decisionmaker can be included: the *government* imposing prohibitions, controls, and regulations, tariffs and other constraints on imports; levying taxes; granting subsidies and other bonuses; providing public facilities; and purchasing goods and services. There is little to be gained, however, by treating government as an economic decisionmaker on a level with households and firms, or on a level with markets and industries. It makes sense to model a firm producing a good, G_1, and offering it for sale; but it hardly makes any sense to "model" a government imposing a restriction, R_1, especially as long as we are unable to formulate any general assumptions regarding the preferences, the fundamental objective, and the income of the government. Only on a rather different level of analysis can it be of heuristic value to include the government in the theoretical system, as taking not only actions regarded as independent variables affecting households and firms, but also actions considered dependent variables reacting to the actions of households and firms, or to the consequences of their actions.

Special Economic Agents

On the highest level of abstraction, with households and firms both as micro-units and as members of interactive groups, the types and models are unspecified as to the goods and services they produce, supply, and sell, or buy, demand, and consume. The models of interactive systems may thus be entirely formal and general: statements of axioms and theorems about completely anonymous agents without any hints as to where—or where not—in the world empirical counterparts might be recognized. As we proceed to more "specific" economic agents, the field of economics becomes far more variegated; as we add increasing numbers of details, the models—though always idealized—assume more and more the character of images: they look more realistic and one may even be persuaded to recognize certain phenomena or sequences of events in the real world as their empirical counterparts. No exhaustive list of economic agents can possibly be presented here, but it may be useful to furnish a list of those economic agents that have received much attention in the literature, old and new.

At the proposed level of specificity in the descriptions of the functions of the economic agents, the economist is no longer confined to the domain of construction. He will now be able to go to the domain of observation and look for empirical counterparts of most of the ideal types on the list. He may succeed in formulating operational definitions for each agent, but he must expect that no real person will fit only one set of specifications. If, for example, the list of constructs contains six types of consumers buying goods or services with different properties or through different channels, every adult real-life person, not in hospital or prison, will qualify for all six types of consumer. He will probably qualify also as an empirical representative of dozens of other types of economic agent, for he will most likely be a taxpayer, a worker, a homeowner or a tenant, a holder of money and other financial assets, and so forth. This multiplicity of roles played by each person causes no trouble in empirical research since the interrogator, investigator, or observer can concentrate his inquiry on the economic function selected for study. Thus, we may interpret each entry on the list as *ideal type* or as *real person* in a specified role. As a matter of fact, both theoretical and empirical studies have been published about almost all of the economic agents listed.

LIST OF SPECIAL ECONOMIC AGENTS
ACTING ON OR REACTING TO NEW INFORMATION

Consumers: buyers of consumables in general; buyers of nondurable goods and services; buyers of durable goods; buyers of branded goods; buyers of goods with quality guarantees; members of cooperatives

Savers, dissavers

Taxpayers, tax avoiders, tax averters

Students, dropouts, trainees

Workers: unskilled; skilled; technical, professional; unemployed, moonlighters, welfare recipients; job seekers, employed or unemployed; in growth jobs

Trade union: members; managers; nonmembers; strikers, subsidized or nonsubsidized

Self-employed professionals

Professional associations: members; managers; nonmembers

Owners: of exhaustible resources; of nonreproducible goods

Landowners and tenants, agricultural

Residential housing: landlords, tenants; single homeowners; condominium owners; mortgagor

Asset holders: real property; equity, shares in business firms; securities, bonds, stocks, warrants; money assets, liquid claims, cash; portfolio management

Hoarders, dishoarders: of cash balances (demand for money to hold); of precious metals

Banks: suppliers of loans and deposit money; financial intermediaries

Brokers, jobbers, market makers

Capitalists, lenders, borrowers

Investors: in productive facilities; in inventories; in research and development; in human resources

Disinvestors: liquidating through nonreplacement; reducing inventories

Entrepreneurs, innovators, risk takers, bearers of uncertainty

Employers: of firm-specific labor; of substitutable labor; selecting personnel, hiring, firing

Business managers: seeking money profits; seeking prestige; seeking personal gains; promoting national interest; taking it easy

Corporate finance officers: considering bond issues; considering stock issues; considering dividend policy

Inventors, patentees, licensees, holders of secret know-how

Insurers, insurance buyers, risk averters

Arbitrageurs, speculators, hedgers, gamblers

Producers: of single products; of joint and otherwise related products; of standardized products; of differentiated products

Traders: of staple commodities; of nonreproducible assets (e.g., art dealers)

Sellers: in auction sales; in atomistic competition; in monopolistic competition (differentiated polypoly); in oligopolistic compe-

tition, uncoordinated or coordinated; in monopoly positions exposed to newcomers' competition; in monopoly positions protected against entry; engaged in discriminatory pricing; engaged
in quality competition; offering guarantees; advertising
Sellers' coalitions: price cartels, concerted actions, pricing schemes;
quota cartels and selling syndicates; trade associations, members, outsiders
Government, executive branch: departments; top echelon, commis-
sars; magistrates; bureaucrats, civil servants

Legislatures: members; candidates for election; party leadership
Regulatory agencies, price controllers, planning commissions
Fiscal authorities: treasury, budget office; tax and revenue depart-
ments; debt management
Monetary authorities: central bankers; banking regulators

Information Relevant for Special Economic Agents

Some "*pure and general*" economic theory of information can be
formulated regarding new information, uncertainty, and optimal decision-making; however, economic analysis and research become
much more interesting when they focus on *special* economic agents,
idealized or real. Of course, information relevant for different economic agents differs in contents, form, and many other respects. A
few examples will suffice to illustrate this statement.

Consumers of household goods will be affected by information
about changes in price and quality of articles on their usual shopping
list and of possible substitutes. Special problems exist with regard
to branded goods and guarantees offered by the sellers. These problems are particularly interesting in the case of durable goods like
automobiles, refrigerators, washing machines, and so forth, which
are purchased by a household only occasionally, say, once every
three, or even ten or more, years.

Personal savers—individuals and households—may respond to information pertinent to their future incomes, old-age pensions, future
family obligations and contingencies, tax obligations in the immediate or distant future, and also information pertinent to the prospective yield of the funds saved and loaned out or invested in
earning assets. (Savers in different circumstances react differently to
higher yields, some saving more, some less, and some the same.)

Investors in productive facilities will be influenced by information
about matters of great variety: technological advances, changes in
supply of materials essential to the particular industry, develop-

ments on the labor front liable to change the cost of labor, changes in taxes, tax credits for investment, accelerated depreciation allowances, indications of increasing demand for the product, increasing competition from substitute products, and so on.

Information about attractive job opportunities, perhaps even definite job offers, may well make a skilled worker quit his old job and move to a more tempting one, considering, of course, the cost of relocating and the pain of giving up close associations with friends and loved places. Information about the length during which a jobless worker can draw unemployment benefits and about places and occupations in which he might find employment at perhaps less than tempting wages, may be important factors in his decision to apply for these jobs or rather to wait until something better turns up.

Holders of money assets, such as check deposits in commercial banks, may receive information causing them to switch into other kinds of liquid assets or into less liquid assets; the pertinent information is about comparative yields, conditions for withdrawal, and so forth. Information about rapidly rising prices of goods and services and about governmental policies conducive to continuing price inflation may influence money holders to switch funds into foreign currencies that have better promise of preserving their purchasing power, or to spend more for current purchases of goods and services.

In all these examples the influence of information on decision-making was made explicit in order to emphasize that additions to, or revisions of, existing knowledge ordinarily play a role in people's actions. What people have known for a long time will rarely induce them to change their conduct. New information, however, if relevant to the economic agent's activities, will induce them to consider the pros and cons of a change. This formulation exhibits the sequence from information via decision to action and prepares it for incorporation in the economists' basic concepts and models of equilibrium.

EQUILIBRIUM

The economic theory of knowledge and information has employed the notion of equilibrium, explicitly or implicitly, on various levels of analysis: (1) equilibrium of the decision-making unit called "household," (2) equilibrium of the decision-making unit called "firm," (3) equilibrium of the "industry," an open-ended group of firms, (4) equilibrium of the "market," involving two groups of decisionmakers, supply and demand, (5) "general" equilibrium of the entire economy, comprising decisionmakers on all levels and in all sectors, (6) equilibrium of "aggregate" economic magnitudes composed of heterogeneous things but involving all income recipients and all spending units in the economy, (7) equilibrium of "asset portfolios," and (8) equilibrium of "expectations" by economic agents, chiefly with regard to prices and quantities, initially incompatible but gradually converging through consecutive revisions in a process of learning. All these uses of the concept or, perhaps more correctly, all these concepts, have to be understood if the theories employing them are to be comprehended. Having just looked at a sample of the population of special economic agents—decisionmakers on specific matters—we should now deal with the use of the notion of equilibrium in the analysis of decision-making.

Equilibration Takes Time

Upon receiving new information, a decisionmaker may find that he can improve his position, or avoid its deterioration, by taking certain actions. In the economists' jargon, the receipt of new information is "disequilibrating." Taking the appropriate actions is then seen as "equilibrating," though the possibility of simultaneous and subsequent actions and reactions by others will often frustrate the initial expectations of the decisionmaker; he may then deem it advisable to take further actions, or to change his conduct in several respects. "Equilibration" may thus turn out to be a rather long sequence of steps, an extended process during which the situation is likely to change, not just once but several times. What looked at the outset like *the* equilibrium position may have become obsolete after a short time. Some critics question the use of "equilibrium theory" on the ground that equilibrium will hardly ever be reached. They fail to understand that every decision and action is taken with a view to what appears to be the "optimal" position *at the time*; the analyst can then explain (and, with some luck, predict) the directions of change effected by the continual pursuit of a continually moving equilibrium.

The equilibrium theorist does not believe that there exists "really" a position that is the best (or the least bad) of all possible positions. Indeed, if the theorist has given adequate attention to methodological analysis, he will be prepared to deny the existence of equilibrium as an *objectively identifiable* position; he may go further and question the likelihood that *any* position attained "at present" will be *subjectively recognized* as one of "equilibrium attained" or "equilibrium regained." Equilibrium, as a rule, lies in the future; moreover, it keeps changing all the time. New events and new information continually suggest new adjustments, and the ongoing "equilibrating" adjustments made by other agents continually change the picture. Perhaps we may say that equilibrium is a Fata Morgana, a mirage that lures people on its track and thus determines the direction in which they are going.

Equilibrium is a mental aid in our analysis of decision-making, an indispensable analytic device; it should not be hypostatized into anything observable, or into anything more than a mere vision in somebody's mind, presumably in the mind of a decisionmaker, but surely in the mind of an *outsider* who analyzes the essentials of decision-making and of processes of adjustments to specified changes.

Equilibrium of the Household

Illustrations may be helpful to some readers. The most popular examples are taken from the culinary sector of the householder's world; for example, a higher price tag for beef may make the family initially eat more chicken and less beef but later readjust to some extent when mass switching in the same direction raises the price of chicken and moderates the rise of beef prices. For an example that shows much better the futurity of equilibrium, we may point to the adjustments following an increase in the price of electric heat: it may involve installation of a heating system based on oil or natural gas, with time-consuming searches for the best solutions, affected by subsequent increases in the prices of these fuels, of the required equipment and its installation, and of the cost of the funds to be invested. The time lags in the decision process, in the execution of the decision (signing the contract), and in the eventual accomplishment of the substitution induced by the initial disequilibrating information may be considerable. At no moment, during the period of equilibration, is the household "in equilibrium": the ratio of electricity to oil (or gas) consumption is different from that which the household, or any outsider, would regard as optimal at the "given" price ratio.

The constructs "optimality," "maximization of utility," and "equilibrium of the household" are logical correlatives in the pure theory of the household. Most teachers of microeconomic theory use algebraic and geometric forms of exposition to teach how marginal cost, marginal utility, or marginal rates of substitution (along indifference curves) interact to establish an "optimum position" in acquiring consumables and in offering productive services. All the functions or curves employed in such analyses embody the expectations of the idealized householder. Any new information reaching the householder can at any time change one or all the functions or curves that depict his circumstances and opportunities.

As a rule, the prices of the consumables and of the productive services are treated as independent variables in the system; and the simplest case of "new" information is a price change. It is simplest because it need not involve any alterations of the curves but only of points on, or slopes of, "given" curves. Thus, the student can "read off" the quantities demanded or offered, respectively, from the graphs that depict the preferences and opportunities of the household; and each of the quantities is understood to be optimal under the circumstances. For situations in which a householder cannot affect prices by buying more or less of the consumables or by selling more or less of his services, theory furnishes individual demand curves (showing the quantities demanded at various given prices) and individual supply curves (showing the quantities supplied at various given prices). Any such curve is the locus of "equilibrium quantities" demanded or offered by the imaginary household analyzed.

This kind of analysis is too elementary to attract the attention of modern theorists of knowledge and information; only more complicated cases are treated in present-day literature. The complications include such elements as quality differences and guarantees, special risks or serious uncertainty, misinformation and deception, to mention only a few examples.

Equilibrium of the Firm

What has been said about the theory of the household holds true also for the theory of the firm: equilibrium is the hypothetical end point of a process of adjustment to a given change. Of course, there is the construct of "instantaneous equilibrium" of firms selling out of inventories or buying for inventory, or of firms buying and selling contracts for future delivery; but for many of the most important problems the constructs of short-term, medium long-term, and long-term equilibrium are more relevant.[4] Thus, in the analysis of changes affecting manufacturing firms, adjustments over longer periods have to be considered, because in manufacturing, the existence of fixed

[4] It may make a difference if one insists on seeing the disequilibrating change to be a matter of public record (such as a news item in the papers), or if one prefers to "date" it only as of the day the firm receives information about, or becomes aware of, the change. The difference lies in the possibility of delay in becoming aware of the objectively ascertained event or change. In most instances, delays in becoming aware are most unlikely: firms quickly notice if they have to pay higher wages or higher prices of material. In cases of new technological opportunities delayed awareness is more probable.

equipment often delays the substitutions among alternative factors or alternative products suggested by changes in conditions.

An automobile manufacturer, for example, may take years to adjust to a change in demand, say, to a switch from large cars to small. A steel producer may for many years defer adopting a more cost-efficient technique and, when at last he has made the decision, it may take another several years until the new equipment is in place. The first part of the delay, the deferment of the decision to adopt the better technique, is better not regarded as a period of disequilibrium (at least not in the short run) because sound calculation may show that the continued use of the old equipment is still optimal. This is so because bygones are bygones, and sunk costs need not cause any user costs whereas new equipment requires additional investment outlays. Thus, the marginal cost of producing with the old equipment includes no part of the past investment outlay; the long-run marginal cost of producing with new equipment would be higher because it would include some portion of the new investment cost. Only when the marginal cost of producing with the old equipment rises (as costs of repair increase, waste of material or energy becomes heavier, or the proportion of defective or lower-quality output increases) and eventually approaches or reaches the prospective marginal cost of producing with new equipment, will the firm find that it would do better scrapping the old plant and getting the new one. Hence, only with the determination that "the time has come" does the disequilibrium commence. It remains true, however, that by the time the firm can start producing with the advanced technology, many things will have happened and new adjustments will be under way.[5]

Dynamic Process Analysis and Comparative Statics

The repeated references to time intervals and periods, to sequences and processes of adjustment, may give the impression that static and dynamic theory are being confused. Is period analysis not the business of economic dynamics? Are time and changes over time not disregarded or assumed away in economic statics? Although this is quite so, and "comparative statics" furnishes no description of the process that leads from one equilibrium position to another—from

---

[5] Not all adjustments take that long in reality. Some substitutions among factors can be accomplished within a few days. In production processes where the ratios between factor prices are subject to fluctuation, firms may have made arrangements for rapid switches. They may, for example, have methods of economizing on materials when they are expensive, but economizing on labor when the materials are cheap. Of course, elasticities of substitution are always higher in the long run than in the short.

an initial equilibrium disturbed by an exogenous change to a new equilibrium position compatible with the changed conditions—it is nevertheless the very purpose of comparative statics to show the end-results of processes induced by exogenous changes.

Most analysts understand that both equilibria, the one *before* the disturbing change (the new information) and that *after* the consequent changes (the adjustments), serve merely to explain directions of movements of dependent variables, even if static theory does not deal with the intermediate positions between initial and ultimate equilibria and with the time intervals inherent in any such process. On the other hand, some time dimensions can be introduced into static analysis by including (or excluding) certain assumptions in (or from) the explicit set. Thus, the theorist assumes given and unchanged "fixed production facilities" (plant and equipment) for short-run-equilibrium analysis, but variable production facilities for long-run-equilibrium analysis. By means of this distinction an important time element is admitted into microstatics, though it is not clock time but only a sort of implicit fictitious time that is involved. Intermediate between the short run and the long run, as defined above, are several possible periods implied in different assumptions of just what parts of the firm's production facilities the analyst allows to be adjusted (for example, small appliances, large machines, floor space, power plant).

Decisions made by a producing firm relate to choices of the products to make, how to make them, how much of each, in what quality, at what prices to offer them for sale, with what guarantees (if any), with what selling effort (sales staff, advertising, etc.), and so forth. Decisions about how to make the products, and how much to make, imply some of the choices about what materials and productive services, and how much of each, to acquire, but many other choices regarding, for example, inventory policy, wage and employment policy, hiring, retirement, pension funds, and so forth are connected with inputs required in the firm's production program. Special mention ought to be made of the firm's decisions regarding its capital funds, decisions implying stock issues, bond issues, short-term borrowing, dividend policies, and more. We should not forget decisions that relate in more than one respect to "knowledge and information," namely, research and development, technological innovation, inventions, patenting, licensing, litigating, and so on. Decisions about tax matters, insurance contracts, management development, internal information systems, and many other problems may round out a list that surely is still very incomplete.

Economic theorists have given much attention, more than to any other portions of the spectrum of decision-making, to the firm's decisions about inputs, outputs, and prices. Indeed, inputs, outputs, and prices are the main subjects of the theory of the firm and usually occupy the largest portion of the teaching of elementary and intermediate microeconomic theory. This allocation of teaching time, though fully justified by the general importance of prices and production in economic affairs, has probably been influenced by the teachers' fascination with the geometric and algebraic models that were developed for presentation of the quantitative relationships between some (assumed) curves or functions. This instrumentarium of models includes curves for expected demand (or average revenue) for the firm's products (sales-expectations curves); marginal revenue; variable, fixed, and total cost; marginal cost; total, average, and marginal productivity of the firm's inputs; expected supply (or average cost) of the firm's inputs (factor-cost-expectations curves); and finally (or more correctly, primarily[6]), physical-production functions (technological input-output relations). In teaching the formal relationships to beginning students, the shapes and positions of these curves are supposed to be "given," that is, "known" to both the decision-maker and the economist-observer. This supposition helps perhaps some students but is surely confusing to most. In the analysis of economic decisions and actions we are interested mainly in the effects of shifts of some curves, with other curves staying put, and, as a rule, neither the shape nor the position of the curves matters. It follows that, as long as our concern is only with directions of change, it does not seriously matter how incomplete and how uncertain the knowledge of the conditions depicted by these curves really is. This reminder cannot be repeated too often.

The analysis of the equilibrium of the firm is not limited by the market position of the firm as buyer of inputs and/or seller of outputs. The analysis readily accommodates monopoly and monopolistic positions as well as purely competitive ones. If the firm as a seller of its products is a price taker, the theory is, of course, much simplified and the roles of information and uncertainty are minimized. The analyst can in this case construct the firm's supply curve as a function of market prices; this is not possible if the firm is in a monopolistic position, where marginal revenue differs from selling price. The most complicated case is that of the firm in a position of oligopoly, where any new information may induce changes that are not determinate without far more knowledge of expectations, propensities, and at-

---

[6] Physical-production functions are "primary" knowledge (or expectations) because they have to be known before the probable production costs of the output and the probable productivities of the inputs can be calculated.

titudes of the decisionmakers than is commonly available. Some of these problems were briefly discussed in Chapter 3 under the heading "Sellers' Uncertainty."

Equilibrium of the Industry

The group equilibrium called "equilibrium of the industry" refers to either an open-ended or a closed group of firms producing the same product. (In exceptional instances the use of the same major input, rather than the product, characterizes the firms in the group, for example, in the steel-processing industry.) The definition of the equilibrium of the industry takes as its criterion the determinateness of the group's total output: at given prices and with all other relevant conditions unchanged, total output will remain unchanged. The group's output will be unchanged if no firm in the group has any desire or ability to change its output and no new firms enter the industry. Alternatively, the group's output can remain unchanged also if changes of output in some firms are offset by equal and opposite changes by other firms in, or joining or leaving, the group. The second of these industry equilibria is not easy to model in a way that leads to widely applicable conclusions. It is far easier to imagine a group equilibrium that implies equilibria of all firms that comprise the industry. This has, in fact, been the concept generally employed in analyses of the effects exogenous changes—new information—will have upon the industry's prices and production. The conclusions of these analyses are usually summarized in the "industry-supply curve"—though this presupposes the strong assumption of atomistic competition.[7]

The industry-supply curve is sometimes used without adequate consideration of the serious limitations of its validity. Its purpose, ordinarily, is to show the effects of (exogenous) changes in demand upon price and output of the product in question, with the industry-supply curve given and unchanged. This limitation alone disqualifies the model from use in the analysis of many problems connected with information. Those who have written on the economics of information have, in general, avoided explicit use of industry equilibrium, but many have allowed it to reenter as a full-fledged member of the groups—potential buyers and sellers—combined in the concept of

[7] An industry-supply curve shows the quantities of a (standardized) product that will be supplied at various prices. The idea that output is a function of price implies that the firms are "price takers and quantity adjusters," which in turn presupposes that no single firm believes it could affect price by increasing or reducing its own output. Such belief may be founded on the assumption that the industry consists of many atomistically small firms.

market equilibrium. In a good many studies the market-supply curve that intersects with a market-demand curve is another manifestation of the industry-supply curve, although the assumptions that would legitimize it are inconsistent with conditions implied in the scenarios under examination.

Even in scenarios for which the industry-supply curve would be admissible as consistent with all other implied conditions, the problem of the various adjustment periods can be troublesome. What was said above in connection with the equilibrium of the firm holds, with even more complications, for the equilibrium of the industry: adjustment of output to changes in price is a function of time. Not one determinate quantity is produced (and offered for sale) at a given price, but, rather, a large variety of quantities, depending on the length of time allowed, as more material and energy are used, more workers hired, more machines installed, more plants constructed, and so on. In terms of calendar time, there are no clues to the determination of output as a function of price and time; in terms of categorical time, three or four functions can be distinguished for defined categories of degrees of adaptation of productive capacity. Price will hardly stay put while these adjustments are in progress. If a change in demand is the disequilibrating factor, the signal reaches the producers in the form of a changed market price and the early "short-run" adjustments are likely to affect that price long before the output from medium-long and long-run adjustments becomes available. Prices and outputs will vary throughout the various adjustment periods. The mental construct "equilibrium" is part of an explanation of the direction of a movement, but it denotes a position that may never be reached. At every moment on the way towards an (imaginary) "ultimate" equilibrium, the position reached is, by the logic of the definition, one of disequilibrium, that is, a position not sustainable for any substantial length of time.[8]

---

[8] To say this is not to criticize "equilibrium economics." Of course, if some interpret the concept "equilibrium" as a description of a position actually existing in the real world, then one can only join the critics in condemning such naiveté as utter nonsense. But interpreted as an imaginary end-point of an imaginary sequence of changes regarded as "adjustments," equilibrium is an indispensable aid to economic reasoning. In a similar vein, Knight wrote that "The system never really is in equilibrium . . . at any point; but its tendency toward such a state is the main feature to be made clear in a scientific description of it." Frank H. Knight, "Statics and Dynamics," in *Ethics of Competition and Other Essays* (New York: Harper, 1935), p. 170; reprinted in Knight, *On the History and Method of Economics* (Chicago: University of Chicago Press, 1956), p. 187. The paper was first published as "Statik und Dynamik—Zur Frage der mechanischen Analogie in den Wirtschaftswissenschaften," *Zeitschrift für Nationalökonomie*, Vol. 2 (1930), pp. 1-26.

Equilibrium of the Market

Having examined the equilibria of the household, the firm, and the industry, and having found all of them to be ingenious figments of the theorist's imagination—heuristic fictions, helpful in the explanation of directions of change but not in the explanation of any observable situation at any moment of time—an ultraempiricist might set his last hope in the "reality" of the equilibrium of the market. Alas, despite the thousands of times that we have been told about the "equilibrium price" being determined in a market that supposedly "clears" completely, that is, without any unsold quantities supplied at that price and without any unsatisfied effective demand by would-be buyers prepared to pay that price, the student's hope that market equilibria exist not only in the theorist's mind but also in observable reality is illusionary too. If, in the view of some, the conceptual distance between mental construction and recorded observation is a little shorter in the case of the presumably "equilibrated" market than in the equilibria discussed in the previous sections, the reason may be that market equilibrium is usually conceived as reflecting the *immediate* responses of potential sellers and potential buyers (who find the quoted price either acceptable or unacceptable). Nothing, so some have reasoned, is likely to happen (between the opening of the market and the "clearing" of the market) that would change the "situation"—that is, the reservation prices of the market participants—before the equilibrium price is established. This particular equilibrium, it may seem, does not lie in the future but is "right there" or "just around the corner."

There is something to this idea that the dispositions, propensities, and expectations of the market participants are unlikely to change in the course of a few hours and that the curves that depict the initial preparedness to sell or to buy remain unchanged during the process by which the market approaches and reaches its (presumed) equilibrium. But even this is by no means certain, since the movements of prices tentatively bid and offered may affect expectations and thus change the "reservation prices" that the agents had in mind before the market opened on the particular day. In any case, the methodological gulf between mental construction and observed record remains. The supposition that the price actually paid by the buyers to the sellers is the "equilibrium price" may appear plausible, if not "self-evident." This is only because of the (supposedly unquestionable) hypothesis that would-be sellers with unsold quantities of the commodity in question would have "driven down" the price, and that would-be sellers whose demand was not fully satisfied would have "bid up" the price. Yet, we may ask, where are the "records of observation" that prove this actually to have happened before the market closed? Who has interrogated all actual and potential parties to ascertain whether all of them really obtained all that they wanted to buy, or really disposed of all that they wanted to sell at the closing price?

Few markets have "price criers" or auctioneers, and still fewer have market makers who note all bids and offers before they "determine" the market-clearing price. The *tâtonnement*, or groping towards equilibrium prices, which Walras described for the fictitious "static state," does not result in equilibrium prices in real markets under changing conditions.[9] Neither has any real market the system of "recontracting" that Edgeworth invented as a fictitious technique of reaching an equilibrium price without having to go through a long sequence of trades at disequilibrium prices. As a matter of fact, it was Edgeworth who said that all actual trading in the market invariably takes place at disequilibrium prices, though the sequence of these prices may be explained as a gradual convergence towards an imaginary equilibrium position.[10] In order to reduce the conceptual gap between theoretical construction and empirical observation, Hicks proposed the notion of a "temporary equilibrium" at the close of the market day followed by a "week" without further price setting, but with the understanding that the closing price may not be sustainable, so that the market next "week" may begin with a different opening price.[11] Devices of this sort are needed for the construction of internally consistent models, but they should not mislead econometricians into treating observed prices as equilibrium prices.[12]

---

[9] In the "dynamic state" the "continuous market . . . is perpetually tending towards equilibrium without ever actually attaining it," because while the *tâtonnement* is going on "all the basic data" keep changing. Léon Walras, *Elements of Pure Economics* [1st French ed. 1874], translated by William Jaffé (Homewood, Ill.: Irwin, 1954), p. 380.

[10] Francis Ysidro Edgeworth, *Mathematical Psychics* (London: Kegan Paul, 1881), Part II. In a later paper Edgeworth made the following statement on the determinateness of equilibrium: "The use of a curve . . . to represent the amounts of a commodity offered, or demanded, at any particular price, . . . does not indeed determine what price will rule in any market. But it assists us in conjecturing the direction and general character of the effect which changes in the condition or requirements of the parties will produce." Francis Y. Edgeworth, *Papers Relating to Political Economy* (London: Royal Economic Society, 1924), Vol. II, p. 275. [From the Presidential Address delivered to Section F of the British Association in 1889.]

[11] John R. Hicks, *Value and Capital* (Oxford: Clarendon, 1939), pp. 122-129. Hicks discusses the implications of "false" prices, "very different from equilibrium prices" (p. 129). Hicks held that his device of the "week" enabled him "to treat a process of change as consisting of a series of temporary equilibria" (p. 127).

[12] In organized commodity markets—for metals, grains, etc.—and in stock ex-

The theorist's assumption that during the market "day" (standing for any short interval of time) fundamental conditions and dispositions remain unchanged, so that prices can approach their "equilibrium levels," serves purposes of coherent reasoning; it should not, however, be mistaken for a descriptively true condition, one that is representative of empirical reality. Most economists have learned to emphasize that "news"—information about unexpected events or emerging changes—may fundamentally alter prior expectations held by market participants. As such "news" can reach people any time during any day, it is clear that the theoretical day (during which nothing changes drastically) and the real day (during which new information is received) are different notions. During a real day a great deal of news may turn up, and some of it may induce people to revise their expectations in most essential respects. The effects of the revised expectations may take a long time—several days, weeks, or months—to work themselves out, with the result that the approach to an "equilibrium" may last so long that the theoretical device of the market day and the fixed-price week may lose much of its applicability. Even the best models will sometimes become useless for the explanation of empirical reality, that is, of the recorded data of observation.

General Equilibrium of the Whole Economy

Despite all the reasons militating against regarding equilibrium of the market as a good description of what can be observed in the real world and against taking the actual prices at which goods, services, and assets are sold and bought as equilibrium prices determined by "given" market forces, many economists are willing to overlook the difference between heuristic fiction and observable reality. In other words, they are prepared to concede the real-world likeness of the "partial equilibrium" of single markets for particular commodities. Few economists, however, extend this "tolerance" (or credulity) to the notion of "general equilibrium," a state of simultaneous equilibrium of all interdependent markets, industries, firms, and house-

---

changes, prices change within hours, indeed, from minute to minute. Neither the opening prices nor the closing prices, nor any midday prices, can be singled out as representing a counterpart of the theorist's equilibrium price. If markets were continuously in operation, day and night, it might be less tempting for statisticians to take the quotations at 3 or 4 o'clock p.m. as representing the equilibrium. They would probably appoint the arithmetic mean for the day to the rank of "equilibrium price," even if the price at midnight differed most drastically from that at the beginning of the day. I do not deny that such averages may still be useful as variables in some economically meaningful equations, but they are far from what the economic theorist means when he speaks of an equilibrium of the market.

holds. Most economists regard such a state as pure fiction, helpful though it may be in explaining much that is going on in the real world. Yet even "general" equilibrium is sometimes given the status of a "real thing," if only for specified purposes.[13]

We should guard against a possible misunderstanding. The words "general equilibrium of the whole economy" may suggest a highly complex model, a system composed of millions of households, hundreds of thousands of firms, thousands (or millions) of different commodities, and thousands of different factors of production. The thought of all these households and firms being simultaneously in equilibrium—having successfully groped towards positions of maximum utility and maximum profit at such sets of product prices and factor prices as are consistent with the households' preference functions, the firms' production functions, and everybody's resource endowment—is terrifying to most students of economics. The terror is much abated and sometimes dispelled when the student is told that he need not deal with vast numbers of products and factors but may reduce the scale of his model to just two or three commodities and two or three factors. Indeed, since even a partial equilibrium of a single market presupposes the existence of at least two commodities (for otherwise the concept of price makes little sense), "partial equilibrium analysis is to be regarded as a special case of general equilibrium analysis."[14]

The fact that a general-equilibrium model can be stripped down to two products and two factors does not mean that its analysis becomes simple. The difference is chiefly a matter of didactics: interactions seem easier to envisage if fewer interrelated entities are involved, and graphical representations (diagrams) in two-dimensional space may serve as welcome visual aids. In any case, the process of "equilibration" seems to be more easily comprehended if it does not operate through large numbers of interrelated variables. The fundamental problems of general-equilibrium analysis remain the same regardless of the absolute number of variables included in the model. They are usually discussed under the rubrics "existence" of equilibrium, "uniqueness" of equilibrium, and "stability" of equilibrium. For the purposes of these chapters—to acquaint the nonspecialist with some of the highlights of the economics of information—

[13] "Since the economy is in instantaneous equilibrium at all times, condition . . . holds at all times." Such statements (the quoted one is from a paper by William H. Branson at a Conference of the Federal Reserve Bank of Boston in June 1974) serve only as steps in a technical argument; they are not meant to be factual assertions.

[14] Kenneth J. Arrow, "Economic Equilibrium," *International Encyclopedia of the Social Sciences*, Vol. 4, p. 386.

it is not necessary to engage in an attempt to supply a generally intelligible exposition of the issues alluded to in these somewhat mysterious propositions.[15]

Aggregative Equilibrium

The concepts of equilibrium discussed in the preceding pages—the equilibria of the household, the firm, the industry, the market, and the general equilibrium of the whole economy—involve single decisionmakers or groups of decisionmakers concerned with the acquisition, production, or sale of specified goods, services, or assets at specified prices. The focus is different in the case of aggregative equilibrium, often called "macroeconomic" equilibrium. Although some analysts insist on examining the microeconomic foundations of macroeconomic models, individual decisionmakers are not given any active roles to play in the equilibrium among economic aggregates. Moreover, these aggregates are global magnitudes composed of heterogeneous things, or rather their money equivalents (or sometimes, labor-hour equivalents), in utter disregard of their real composition and of the prices of the things that compose them. The major aggregates or global magnitudes in these models are total consumption expenditures, total investment outlays, total government expenditures for goods and services, total tax revenues, total receipts for exports, total outlays for imports, total net national income, and total saving. The only price variable always present in such models is the rate of interest—because some of the aggregates (such as investment or saving) may be functions of the rate of interest—and possibly an index of price changes, to "deflate" some aggregates, such as total income, for general price inflation. In addition, the index of wage rates may come into the picture, indicating the relation between income and employment.

---

[15] Some readers, perhaps, may like to be warned against possible misconceptions regarding the quoted terms. "Existence" of competitive equilibrium does not mean "real" existence in the empirical world; instead, it means potential existence in the imaginary, idealized world, that is, in the fictitious (mental, algebraic) model constructed by the pure theorist. "Uniqueness" of the equilibrium does not mean "historical" uniqueness, that is, distinguished by special features making the situation different from situations at other times or places; instead, it means that only one particular set of prices and quantities satisfies the assumptions specified, that is, any other set of prices or quantities would be incompatible with the stated assumptions. "Stability" of the equilibrium does not mean that any observed magnitudes vary but slightly over time; instead, it means that, provided the specified assumptions remain unchanged, any deviations of any magnitude from its equilibrium value must, by logical necessity, lead to a process of (imaginary) responses and reactions that bring about or restore the unique equilibrium with all its determinate magnitudes.

Certain kinds of information and expectations may be significant in the operation of these models, or at least for their microeconomic foundations. For example, information about changes in interest rates or in tax rates may affect the propensities to consume, save, and invest; information about government budget deficits and monetary policy may change expectation of nominal and real income and affect decisions about consumption and investment.

Asset-Portfolio Equilibrium

That a discussion of asset-portfolio equilibrium is being placed after discussions of general equilibrium and aggregative equilibrium calls for an explanation. One would think that portfolio selections by individual asset holders affect the equilibria of asset markets and, hence, the general equilibrium of the entire economy as well as the aggregative equilibrium of macroeconomic magnitudes. Thus, portfolio equilibrium of the individual asset holder would seem to belong with the equilibria of the household and the firm. On the other hand, portfolio equilibrium can also be regarded as a group equilibrium, namely, the aggregation of the asset preferences of all asset holders combined. This aggregation would, so to speak, yield the "community indifference curves," showing the elasticities of substitution among the various assets in the people's portfolios.

In one respect, asset-portfolio equilibrium—for individuals, large groups, or the entire "community"—differs from all equilibria discussed so far in this chapter: it constitutes a stock equilibrium, in contrast with the six other equilibria, all of which are flow equilibria. Quantities consumed, produced, supplied, and demanded per *period* of time are featured in the equilibria of the household, the firm, the industry, the market, and in general equilibrium. Similarly, money sums earned, spent, saved, and invested per *period* of time are featured in aggregative equilibrium. Now we are to deal with a different category of equilibrium, one that features amounts of various assets held, or rather demanded for holding, at a *moment* of time. This difference alone justifies the place assigned to asset-portfolio equilibrium in the order of our agenda.[16]

The relationship between stock demand and flow demand should be clearly understood; an increase in the demand to *hold* a particular good or asset may lead to an increase in the demand to *acquire* it; once acquired, the good or asset will be held in stock, with the flow demand returning to zero. In other words, only *changes* in the stock

[16] For earlier references to asset-portfolio theory and models for capital-assets pricing, see above, Chapter 4, especially footnotes 47 and 54 and the last subsection.

demand, or in the stock available, will induce flows. If an increase in stock demand is exactly the same for all holders, in the sense that all of them raise the valuation of a particular asset by the same proportion relative to all other assets, and if the total quantities of all assets remain unchanged, no flow among asset holders will take place; the distribution of the total stock among holders remains unchanged. Only *unequal* increases in stock demand lead to exchanges of assets. If some want to hold more of a given asset, they will be prepared to offer other assets at a lower exchange ratio and they can acquire the preferred asset from those who, at the new price ratio, are willing to part with it.

The device of an aggregative asset-preference model suffers from a serious defect: a change in relative rates of substitution, indicative of a higher stock demand for some assets and a lower stock demand for other assets (perhaps money), may or may not induce actual exchanges of assets. It will induce asset switches only if the higher valuation of the asset in question is not generally shared by all holders. Similarly, it is conceivable that substantial but opposite changes in individual preferences for particular assets offset one another so that aggregate asset preferences remain unchanged—with large amounts of assets changing hands. In other words, flow demand and flow supply in the asset markets may change substantially without aggregate portfolio preferences having changed. Considerations like these should put us on guard concerning the use of models of aggregate asset selection. We should at least check our conclusions by dividing the asset-holding community into subgroups of those whose preferences have changed and those who have maintained their tastes and expectations.

The theory of optimal portfolio selection was first formulated as an advisory instrument for individual asset holders (households, business firms, nonprofit organizations) to enable them to make the best possible selections of securities with regard to return (including appreciation) and risk, taking account of the holder's risk aversion. Harry Markovitz was the inventor of the formula for the optimum in form of an efficiently diversified portfolio containing a mix of assets with different probabilities of return and risk. Risk was measured by variance from the mean; the "algorithms" allowed users to calculate "efficient portfolios" on the basis of estimates of means, variances, and covariances of returns on available securities.[17] To

[17] Harry M. Markovitz, "Portfolio Selection," *Journal of Finance*, Vol. 7 (March 1952), pp. 77-91; also *Portfolio Selection: Efficient Diversification of Investment* (New York: Wiley, 1959).

repeat, the efficiency of the selected portfolio is always relative to the holder's aversion to risk-bearing.

James Tobin transformed the advisory or "normative" theory of portfolio decision into a "positive" one: instead of saying how investors ought to act in order to get maximum returns without greater risk than they care to bear, he assumed that rational people do in fact act that way, and he deduced what this assumption implied for macroeconomic theory. In his own words, his main concern "is the implications for economic theory . . . that can be derived from assuming that investors do in fact follow such rules," whereas "Markovitz's main interest is prescription of rules of rational behavior for investors."[18] The essence of Tobin's idea is to apply "mean-variance analysis to the choice between safe liquid assets, on the one hand, and risky assets or portfolios, on the other. . . . An implication of mean-variance analysis is that assets are generally imperfect substitutes for one another . . ."; and imperfect substitutability may have significant "consequences for financial markets and for the economy at large."[19] These consequences include, as the citation by the Nobel Prize Committee pointed out, effects on "expenditure decisions, employment, production, and prices."

The assumption that asset holders try to optimize their portfolios in accordance with expected utilities from expected returns, and with expected disutilities from estimated risks, becomes an efficient tool of macroeconomic analysis only if we can assume that the directions of change in the pertinent variables due to external (exogenous) events or changes can be known to the analyst and that the relative magnitudes of such reactions remain reasonably stable over time. If the macroeconomic analyst were to go further, if he were to claim that asset-portfolio models can be serviceable in quantitative predictions, a further assumption would be needed: that any observed positions—the quantities and proportions in which assets are being held, and the recorded price relatives among different assets—can reasonably be interpreted as asset-portfolio equilibria.

In connection with previously discussed concepts of equilibria, I have objected to the fallacy of misplaced concreteness and, in particular, to the confusion of observed positions with equilibrium positions. Thus I can hardly be expected to be more hospitable to the idea of instantaneous equilibration of asset mixes *actually held* to the mixes *deemed most attractive*. Although I am prepared to take

[18] James Tobin, "Liquidity Preference as Behavior Towards Risk," *Review of Economic Studies*, Vol. 25 (February 1958), pp. 65-86, esp. p. 85, n. 1.

[19] James Tobin, Letters, "Portfolio Theory," *Science*, Vol. 214 (27 December 1981), p. 974.

consumer preferences for edibles and wearables as remaining stable enough to allow short- and medium-run explanations of price-and-income effects to be deduced, I am not prepared to accept such stability for asset preferences. My tastes for spinach and chocolate candies, or the expected utility associated with purchases of these goods, are far more firmly settled than my tastes for corporate stocks in the Dow-Jones package of industrial shares, for treasury notes, Eurobonds, domestic money-market funds, and commercial paper in foreign currencies. Although I can without excessive doubt rely on adjustments (equilibration with unchanged preference maps) of consumer purchases to changed prices of competing and complementary goods, I have serious doubts about analogous adjustments of asset portfolios to changed prices of different financial assets on the basis of "given" asset preference maps. These doubts are due to my strong suspicion that the expected utilities derived from many capital assets are seriously affected by movements of asset prices. Movements along given demand curves, or given indifference curves, are methodologically sound where consumers' expected utilities are given and unchanged; if, however, changes in relative prices shift and toss these curves faster than an adjustment with "given" curves can get under way, the procedure becomes highly questionable.

The notion of an asset-portfolio equilibrium may be helpful as long as it is not taken too seriously in the explanation, let alone prediction, of concrete developments at specified times and places. If econometricians are so naive as to take observed asset positions and recorded asset prices as representations of asset-portfolio equilibrium, intellectual mischief is almost unavoidable. The realization of the fact that adjustments to changes—to new information—may be slow and delayed should be enough to exclude this fallacy of misplaced concreteness.[20]

---

[20] Since James Tobin is being credited with the formulation and development of asset-portfolio theory, fairness requires that this note show he should not be blamed for the widespread misuse of the theory. Here are some of Tobin's warnings: ". . . Observations . . . during periods . . . when agents with expectations correct at least in sign were slow to act are not good data from which to infer the subjective probability distribution and risk preferences underlying portfolio choice. Likewise, sluggish and smooth adjustment to news casts doubt on theories that require prices to jump to that singular expectations fulfillment path that leads to equilibrium." Also: "The major alternatives to models of financial and asset markets that assume rational expectations and efficient use of information are models that assume slow adjustment periods and disequilibrium. Disequilibrium need not mean that markets are failing to clear, though it may take that form. It may be simply that portfolio investors are off their desired portfolios." James Tobin, "The State of Exchange Rate Theory: Some Skeptical Observations," in Richard N. Cooper; Peter B. Kenen; et. al., eds., The International Monetary System Under Flexible Exchange Rates, Global, Regional, and National (Cambridge, Mass.: Ballinger, 1982), p. 125.

Equilibrium of Expectations

If economic agents' expectations of future events or of the future consequences of present actions differ, their plans and courses of action are liable to be incompatible with one another. Some or all of the agents concerned must sooner or later find this out. Disappointed or pleasantly surprised, they will be forced or induced to revise their expectations and plans. The state of mutual compatibility of all plans and courses of action pursued by all economic agents is called "equilibrium of expectations." As long as this state is not reached, the sequence of surprises and revisions of expectations must continue. The equilibration in question may be regarded as a process of compulsory learning.

The process of equilibration of expectations is, of course, nothing separate from the working of other models of group equilibrium. It is part of the "mechanism" at work in the processes (supposedly) leading to the equilibrium of the industry, the equilibrium of the market, and the general equilibrium of the economy as a whole; and also in the microfoundations of aggregative equilibrium. Only because the theorist wants to place special emphasis on particular aspects of the adjustment processes does he single out the theme of the "converging expectations" for examination in greater detail.

In my *Economics of Sellers' Competition*, I placed much emphasis on "induced revisions of subjective expectations," induced by the inevitable learning experience of the market participants. The point is that expectations are ordinarily formed, not by "wild and unpredictable imaginations," but by intelligent consideration and reconsideration of observed changes.[21] My analysis of a "Model Sequence of Price Adjustment," in which I "described" the consecutive induced revisions of expectations in a process of equilibration of an

[21] The quoted words are from a section under a subheading "Objective Changes and Subjective Expectations"; they were included in the following lines:

If sales expectations changed without any rhyme or reason and if the revisions of expectations, which become necessary whenever sellers find their past expectations disappointed, were without any recognizable relationship to changes in the objective data, then economic equilibrium analysis would indeed be of little use. We should never be able to state the probable consequences of certain changes in consumers' demand or certain changes in production technique, because everything would depend on the wild and unpredictable imaginations of the sellers. If we can, however, assume that the revision of sales expectations will, by and large, proceed in an orderly fashion and according to intelligible principles . . . then the general equilibrium theorist need not give up. . . .

Fritz Machlup, *The Economics of Sellers' Competition* (Baltimore: Johns Hopkins University Press, 1952), pp. 206-207.

industry (after a disturbance of the group equilibrium by increased demand for its product), was preceded by this statement:

> The real problem within the scope of a theory of competition is the adjustment of subjective price expectations to such changes of market price as are expected by the economist to result from certain changes in market demand or cost conditions and from the subsequent entries (or exits) of firms into (or from) the industry. In other words, the relevant problem at this point is the adjustment of subjective price expectations as a part of the whole process of adaptation which is supposed to lead eventually to the equilibrium of the industry, that is, to the above-mentioned "group equilibrium."[22]

I have reproduced this paragraph chiefly for its allusion to the imaginary firms' subjective expectations gradually adapting to such changes as are *expected by the economist* as resulting from changes in market or cost conditions. This idea of economic *agents'* expectations adjusting in conformance with the economic *theorist's* expectations plays a role in what has come to be called (infelicitously) the "rational expectations" hypothesis.

In view of the close conceptual connection between information and expectations, it is appropriate to devote an extensive portion of this chapter to the discussion of economic expectations.

EXPECTATIONS

The literature on economic expectations goes back many decades, and even centuries; but some of the contributions to it during the last generation are especially noteworthy because they were written by a specialist who is one of the few masters of English prose style. I refer to George L. S. Shackle, who has given us not only several fine papers but no fewer than seven books on the subject, all eminently readable.[23]

---

[22] Ibid., p. 280.

[23] George L. S. Shackle, *Expectations, Investment and Income* (London: Oxford University Press, 1938; 2d ed., Oxford: Clarendon, 1968); *Expectations in Economics* (Cambridge: At the University Press, 1949; 2d ed., 1952); *Uncertainty in Economics and Other Reflections* (Cambridge: At the University Press, 1955); *Time in Economics* (Amsterdam: North-Holland, 1958); *Decision, Order and Time in Human Affairs* (Cambridge: At the University Press, 1961); *Expectation, Enterprise and Profit* (London: Allen & Unwin, 1970); *Imagination and the Nature of Choice* (Edinburgh: University of Edinburgh Press, 1979). For a short statement see his article "Economic

After the earlier presentation in this chapter of a long list of economic agents, each of them with different interests, it should be clear
that the analysis of economic expectations cannot reasonably be confined to *business* expectations. Consumers' expectations, savers' ex-
pectations, workers' expectations, trade-union managers' expecta-
tions, shareholders' expectations, insurers' expectations, to mention
only a few of the "expecting" agents, are in many aspects differently
constituted. The most frequently analyzed economic expectations,
however, are those of businessmen faced with choices of alternative
and mutually exclusive decisions. The formation and revision of
business expectations is the most-favored theme in the economics
of expectations.

Statistical and Subjective Probability and Possibility of Surprise

Economists with a strongly numerical-empirical bent have placed
the greatest weight on *statistical* probability, based on frequencies
of occurrence that are assumed to be of enduring significance. Economists inclined towards methodological subjectivism have emphasized the businessmen's intuitive judgment, formalized in distributions of *subjective* probability. To be sure, some elements in the
businessmen's "intuitive" conjectures are derived from experience,
their own as well as those of others, including some expressed in
statistical time series. The catagorical difference between statistical
and subjective probability lies in the fact that the former refers only
to one given type of occurrence or to outcomes of one given type of
action repeated or replicated any number of times. (The same action
repeated many times will yield a specified outcome with a particular
frequency.) However, the probability of a unique event, the outcome
of a decision never made before and perhaps never to be made again,
is of a very different kind. Where the situation changes rapidly, where
conditions in many markets are apt to change, the "probability" of
outcomes of particular actions is a subjective, not a mathematical
expectation.

Besides the notion of subjective probability there is, according to
Shackle, the notion of potential surprise, the possibility that an outcome may emerge that was initially regarded as impossible or almost
impossible. Shackle distinguishes "distributional" and "nondistributional" uncertainty. If a list of *all* possible outcomes is made, each
of these outcomes can be assigned some chance of being realized; if
the list is really complete (exhaustive), its combined probability is

Expectations," *International Encyclopedia of the Social Sciences*, Vol. 4, pp. 389-
395.

1, that is, there is absolute *certainty* that one of all possible outcomes will materialize; this combined certainty is then distributed among the listed possibilities, each getting a fraction of 1. If the list of possibilities is incomplete, it allows that an unexpected outcome emerges, to the "surprise" of the economic agent. This is the meaning of "nondistributional" uncertainty. Both kinds of uncertainty are inescapable features of all business expectations.

Perhaps I may offer a few literal quotations from Shackle's exposition: "Uncertainty of expectation is not a contingent, curable disability from which human beings will some day be rescued by the advance of science. . . . Consciousness is the continual apprehension of subjectively new things, circumstances, and conjectures that were hitherto not known to exist or to be imminent. To know the future would destroy the possibility of this stream of continually fresh perceptions. . . . Uncertainty is the price of hope, for only by exposing ourselves to possible loss can we expose ourselves to possible gain."[24]

Economic Man and Rational Expectations

If one does not know the special connotations grafted on the notion of rational expectations by some imaginative cultivators of sophisticated conceptualization, one may think that it hardly needs saying that economic man, the rational maximizer of utility, makes his decisions *always* on the basis of rational expectations.[25] He knows what he wants, he knows what means are required to attain the various ends, and he knows what means are at his disposal to be rationally allocated among these ends. If he is in business, he knows how he can rationally adjust to new information, how he can rationally ob-

---

[24] Shackle, "Economic Expectations," *International Encyclopedia*, p. 394.

[25] I am using the term "rational" expectations under protest. As I said elsewhere— for example, in footnote 16 of Chapter 2—rational and correct are quite different things. Economists who had read Max Weber—and every educated economist was supposed to have done so—have agreed that rationality meant consistency with one's preconceptions and prejudgments, right or wrong. (American Indians were perfectly rational if they, on the basis of their beliefs, performed a rain dance when they wanted rain, and they entertained rational expectations when they expected their rites to have the desired effect.) John Muth may be charged with an infraction of terminological discipline when he misused the term "rational" to denote "correct" expectations (or expectations in conformance with those of some economic theorists of the neoclassical school). See John F. Muth, "Rational Expectations and the Theory of Price Movements." *Econometrica*, Vol. 29 (July 1961), pp. 315-335. Muth's misappropriation of an accepted word of art was then approved and imitated by Robert E. Lucas, Robert J. Barro, Thomas J. Sargent, and dozens of others. Battling against the continued use of the misnomer would be fighting a hopeless cause. I feel compelled to record my protest, but I have to join the perpetrators of the terminological malpractice if I want my discussion of their hypotheses to be understood.

tain better information, how he can rationally balance the cost of additional information with expected benefits to be derived from it, and how he can rationally balance expected risks with his aversion to being exposed to risk. Such a rational man's expectations cannot help being rational in terms of his own tastes and insights. If no more is demanded of his capabilities, one cannot reasonably question that economic man is programmed to have always rational expectations, which, of course, implies that he may have to revise his expectations continuously as new information is obtained.[26]

More ambitious "requirements" are stipulated for what Stanley Fischer calls the "strong form" of rational expectations. The added postulate is "that individuals' subjective probability distributions are the same as those implied by the models in which they are presumed to be the agents."[27] Or, in the words of Herschel Grossman, the added (and rather strong) assumption is "that the information that is potentially relevant for private agents includes both knowledge of the specification of the structure of the economy itself and knowledge of the past and current data that this structure identifies as consequential."[28] Even those of us who allow the theorist to construct his ideal types any way he likes may object: economic man ought not to be endowed with superhuman abilities, at least not if we want him to serve, in applied economics, as a heuristic instrument for explaining observable reality. What the strong postulate of rational expectations implies is the efficient working of feedback loops among private economic agents, governmental agencies, and economic theorists who miraculously agree on all diagnoses of the economic state of affairs and on all prognoses of developments induced by actions of private economic agents and public agencies.

Going behind the professional jargon used in the preceding paragraph, we may try to explain what is superhuman and miraculous

[26] The rational-expectations postulate—"that private economic agents gather and use information efficiently"—"treats informational activities the same as any other activity that economic man undertakes. In this context, efficiency means that the amount of resources private agents devote to gathering and using information is such that the marginal alternative cost of these resources equals the marginal benefit from the information." Herschel I. Grossman, "Rational Expectations, Business Cycles, and Government Behavior," in Stanley Fischer, ed., *Rational Expectations and Economic Policy* (Chicago: University of Chicago Press, 1980), p. 10. — Stanley Fischer calls this postulate "the weak form" of rational expectations, namely, "that individuals form expectations optimally on the basis of the information available to them and the cost of using that information." Fischer holds that this "has become and will remain the leading theory of expectations." See his essay, "On Activist Monetary Policy with Rational Expectations," in the same volume, p. 212.

[27] Fischer, *Rational Expectations*, p. 212.

[28] Grossman, "Rational Expectations," p. 10.

in the assumptions inherent in the strong form of the postulate. In applications of the postulate of rational expectations to the analysis of the effectiveness of monetary and fiscal policies, the analysts treat the actions of the public authorities, not as independent variables, but as endogenous variables dependent on information about real output and employment (or, alternatively, about interest rates and changes in price indices). These determinants of policy are the results of the actions of masses of private economic agents; but the reactions of the authorities will now join the flow of information reaching the private agents, who will "rationally" revise their expectations and, consequently, their own decisions and economic conduct. Will the rational revision of expectations not, however, be based on the "probable consequences" attributed to the public policy, and will the attribution of consequences of public policies not vary according to the theories, naive or sophisticated, held by the agents? Since few economists agree about the consequences of any macroeconomic policy mix adopted by the authorities, how can one reasonably assume that the private agents, however well informed, entertain predictable expectations?

The methodological device of endowing an ideal type of any person (economic agent) with capabilities few real persons can possess is defensible, and indeed appropriate, as long as the construct in question is helpful (or, in the words of Karl Popper, has "proved its mettle") and is not self-contradictory. A purely fictitious construct can serve in "as if" explanations of a large class of recorded observations; that is to say, a sufficient number of real-world people act *as if* they were constituted like the unrealistic ideal type. If an ideal type, however, is inconceivable, because some of its essential properties contradict one another, then its use will be judged to be ill conceived. I am leveling this charge against the ideal type of an economic agent who forms "rational" expectations on the basis of economic interpretations of data on the presumption that these data will induce or will have induced government behavior that will produce determinate economic results. Even if one admitted the "possibility" that all private and public economic agents shared the same economic theory and had in their respective minds the very same "model," connecting all its variables in an identical "structure"—an assumption so fantastic as to be admitted only for the sake of the argument—one could not reasonably go so far as to assume that all agents would also learn to know the numerical "parameters" for the variables.[29]

[29] The strong hypothesis of "rational expectation" can be divided into four or five

All this still sounds excessively convoluted, and some readers may appreciate a brief sketch of the particular use of the strong postulate of rational expectations.

Anticipated and Unanticipated Monetary Policy

The thesis for the support of which the strong postulate of rational expectations has been used is, roughly stated, that *anticipated* monetary policy has no real effects. "Real effects," in this statement, means effects upon physical output and employment. "Monetary policy" means any mix of monetary and fiscal policy that cannot dispense with appropriate (complementary) changes in the supply of money. The stress on "money supply" is merely incidental to the fact that most representatives of this way of reasoning are monetarists; instead of money supply, the thesis could be formulated in terms of total spending or effective demand. "Anticipated" means predictable on the basis of available information and accepted interpretation. The thesis as a whole relates to the short run. (That real output in the *long* run is independent of a one-time increase in the quantity of money is probably one of the least disputed propositions in economics.) At issue is whether an increase in spending is likely to produce a higher level of real output and employment in the *short* or *medium* run, say, over a period of two to five years.

The issue arose when, in the late 1960s and the 1970s, the Keynesian recipe for creating employment through increased deficit spending failed to work, when confident forecasts of rates of real output, employment, and price indexes proved wrong, and when the presumed trade-off between price inflation and unemployment (in line with the Phillips Curve) was seen to be an illusion; in other words, when increases in spending resulted chiefly (or only) in price infla-

---

separate assumptions: the sameness of past experiences, the sameness of models in the minds of the agents and in the writings of the theorists, the sameness of the structures of these models, the sameness of new information reaching all agents, the sameness of the numerical parameters assigned to the variables included in the models. The attitudes of adherents and critics of the "rational expectations" hypothesis to these assumptions range from full acceptance via partial acceptance to modified or absolute rejection. To some extent these differences depend on whether the hypothesis allows a process of Bayesian *learning over time* or insists on the likelihood that "rational expectations move directly to the equilibrium value of the model without specifying an adequate process to produce the result." See Richard M. Cyert and Morris H. DeGroot, "Rational Expectations and Bayesian Analysis," *Journal of Political Economy*, Vol. 82 (January-February 1974), p. 523. These authors stress the learning process: ". . . even if all firms do not initially have the same priors, the feedback from the market will tend to modify the priors to the extent that similarity becomes a reasonable assumption at some point. Thus, we will postulate the same prior probability distributions for the decision makers in our models" (p. 522).

tion and hardly (or not at all) in reductions of unemployment. These disappointments had to be explained, and one of the explanations was that monetary expansion had succeeded in inducing more production only so long as that expansion was not generally expected; anticipated money creation would pull up prices but not real output. The most plausible argument was in terms of the "shift of the Phillips Curve." If the authorities were willing to tolerate a higher rate of price inflation in order to ensure a lower level of unemployment (and a higher rate of real output), such movements *along* the trade-off curve would in due course lead to expectations of continuing price inflation at the higher rate, and these expectations would *shift* the entire curve to the right. This shift would be such that the now tolerated high rate of demand inflation and price inflation would not buy a higher employment level, but only the "natural rate of unemployment," determined by the structure of the economy, such as given technological conditions, given relative prices, and, especially, given relations between the prices of labor and the prices of products (that is, real wage rates). Hence, according to this theory, attempts to use monetary expansion systematically to reduce unemployment rates below the "natural rate" are doomed to fail. Only if *actual* monetary expansion exceeds the *anticipated* rate can employment be temporarily increased; as soon as expectations catch up with the actual rate of monetary expansion, the economy will be back at the undesirably high level of unemployment but at the elevated rate of price inflation.[30]

Economists have long been acquainted with the phrase "neutrality of money." It is an ambiguous phrase. Some have understood it to mean that money is merely a veil over the real economic structure but will not change it. Others have understood it as a precept, an objective of sound monetary policy, to control the quantity of money in such a way that it will not distort the real structure of the economy. In the second sense of neutrality, it has been taken for granted that money circulation, by being expanded or contracted, or by being expanded too quickly or too slowly, can easily be nonneutral, causing real output to change in a nonsustainable way. Such changes can be in *magnitude* or *composition* of total output, or both. Theories of nonneutral monetary policies that cause industrial fluctuations (busi-

---

[30] This refutation of the theory of the trade-off between price inflation and unemployment goes back to Milton Friedman's writings. See, for example, his Presidential Address before the American Economic Association, "The Role of Monetary Policy," *American Economic Review*, Vol. 58 (March 1968), pp. 1-17. — My interpretation of the "natural rate of unemployment" differs from that of many authors; they would not include real wage rates and relative prices among the determinants.

ness cycles) by inducing unsustainable changes in the *structure* of production have explained the distortions as results of wrong signals, given to economic agents by market prices and market rates of interest. In particular, deviations of market rates of interest from "natural rates of interest" are attributed to destabilizing monetary policies.[31]

There are similarities as well as differences between these "old" monetary theories of the business cycle and the "new" theories of unanticipated changes in the rate of money creation. They are similar chiefly in their contention that presumably stabilizing monetary policy is in fact often destabilizing. Hayek, for example, held that a policy of increasing the money stock for the purpose of stabilizing the price level in an economy supplying increasing amounts of output would, if the new money were injected through commerical bank lending, result in an unsustainably high rate of investment expenditures: it would end in a retrenchment, associated with capital losses and unemployment.[32] Several of our contemporary monetarists hold that a policy of increasing the rate of money creation for the purpose of raising and stabilizing the rate of employment would be partly unsuccessful and partly destabilizing. To the extent that the increase would be expected, it would not succeed in raising output and employment but would only raise prices; to the extent that the increase in money creation would be unanticipated, that is, in excess of the expected increase, it would lead to a temporary increase in output and employment, both these magnitudes returning to the previous level when expectations catch up with the actual monetary expansion. Both theories, Hayek's and that of the modern monetarists, attribute the destabilizing nonneutrality of money creation to systematic error, misinformation, false cues. Hayek points to unnaturally low rates of interest and correspondingly high demand prices of durable assets, caused by the excessive supply of bank credit. Modern monetarists point to the "forecast error" due to the unanticipated boost to the rate of money creation and/or unexpected rise of the price index.[33] (The increase in employment due to this "error" is, for advocates of expansionary macroeconomic policies, not de-

---

[31] The major authors of business-cycle theories based on nonneutral monetary expansion were Knut Wicksell, Ludwig von Mises, and Friedrich A. Hayek. — The similarity was noted by several recent writers. See, for example, Brian Kaplan, "Rational Expectations and Economic Thought," *Journal of Economic Literature*, Vol. 17 (December 1979), pp. 1422-1441.

[32] Friedrich A. Hayek, *Prices and Production* (London: Routledge, 1931; 2d and rev. ed., 1935). Also *Monetary Theory and the Trade Cycle* (London: Jonathan Cape, 1933).

[33] Fischer, *Rational Expectations*, p. 220.

plorable but desirable; they do not accept the judgment that the higher employment rate is not sustainable.)

Although the theory of rational expectations was first used in an explanation of microeconomic adjustment, its major "application" nowadays is in discussions of monetary policy. Monetarists employ the theory to prove that demand management is not the cure for unemployment that it was purported to be during the decades when Keynesian policy prescriptions dominated macroeconomic theory and political discussions. That monetary expansion is impotent as a means of inducing "real" economic expansion if people have learned that it will be used whenever the rate of employment is regarded as too low, can be understood without the "rigorous" argument of "rational expectations." It is not necessary that everybody has learned what to expect from increased money supply and increased effective demand; it is enough if the largest industrialists and labor leaders have learned that the consistent use of the policy rule "full employment through more spending" is apt to lead to rising prices and rising wages. To be sure, inflationary expectations play an essential role in making official spending policies ineffective in promoting employment; but for this insight the hypothesis of "rational expectations," based on everybody using all available information and interpreting it in conformance with "the" correct economic model is not needed. Indeed, "the fundamental simplicity of the ideas involved has become obscured by overly rigorous development."[34]

If someone wonders why I have discussed problems of monetary policy, business cycles, and unemployment in a work exploring knowledge, its creation, distribution, and economic significance, he deserves an answer. The point is that economic theories in which knowledge and information seem to have played no explicit role have been reconsidered and, in exploring the problems more in depth, analysts have found that some special assumptions regarding information and expectations have become of strategic importance. In the process, the issues in question have been claimed by the new specialty, the economics of information.

[34] Rodney Maddock and Michael Carter, "A Child's Guide to Rational Expectations," *Journal of Economic Literature*, Vol. 20 (March 1982), p. 49. This article shows (on p. 48) in a brief footnote the (supposed) progress from "adaptive expectations," where "people just simply adapted to past errors," to "rational distributed-lag expectations," based on "the very best econometrically predicted estimates of prices derived from analysis of all past price information," and finally to "rational expectations" with all their "overly rigorous develpments" [of unnecessary assumptions and intricate arguments].

Irrational Implications of Rational Expectations

The flood of papers, articles, and essays about rational expectations in the last few years has been extraordinary. It imposes on me the duty to offer further explanatory and critical observations and some comments in slightly varied reiteration on this fashionable subject. Although I expect that it will be out of fashion before long, the problems it involves are of sufficient interest to merit exploration, even if I eschew the sophisticated exposition preferred by most protagonists and critics.[35]

[35] In order to give a taste of what present-day members of the growing club of expectation theorists are propounding, I select one of the papers produced in 1979. It carries the title "Feedback and the Use of Current Information: The Use of General Linear Policy Rules in Rational Expectations Models" and was authored by Willem H. Buiter (then at Princeton, now at the London School of Economics). In the first equation, presented on page 2, the terms included denote 1) a vector of endogenous (or state) variables, 2) a vector of policy instruments, 3) a vector of "i.i.d. random disturbances with a zero mean vector and contemporaneous variance-covariance matrix," and 4) "the rational expectation of t as of $t-1$," defined by an equation containing "the information set, common to the public and private sectors, available at the beginning of period $t-1$" and "the mathematical expectation operator." (For the benefit of "ignorant idiotic deprecators" of acronyms let it be stated that i.i.d. does not stand for "idyllic ideopathically deployed" but for "independent identically distributed.") The second equation specifies policy behavior, with terms such as a "current response component," a "feedback component," and a "non-stochastic open loop component" of the policy rule. This specification of only 2 out of the 42 equations (many of them shown in several variants and with subequations defining the variables) characterizes the author's rigorous argument, conducted with skill and elegance. It leads the author to the following conclusions (on p. 20 of the Working Paper):

> The scope for policy in the four models given by equations (1)-(1‴) can be summarized as follows. The conditional and unconditional means of the state vector z, whether single-period or asymptotic, will depend on the three non-stochastic policy components, G^0, G^1 and $\bar{x}_t$. Through its dependence on Σ_e, the conditional mean will also depend on the stochastic component of policy. The asymptotic variance will depend on all four policy components. The unconditional single-period variance will depend on the current response component and the stochastic component, but not on the feedback component, except in the case of model (1') which incorporates several lagged forecasts of the current value of z.
>
> If variability of z_t, whether anticipated or unanticipated, is of concern to the policymaker, the unconditional variance is the appropriate focus of policy concern. If uncertainty about z_t, i.e. unanticipated variability of z_t is what matters, the conditional variance is the appropriate object of policy design. In Poole's and Boyer's models the single-period conditional variance of output is independent of the current response component of policy. The design of optimal linear policy rules in stochastic dynamic rational expectations models along the lines sketched here, has applications in virtually all areas of macroeconomics stabilization policy.

My purpose in offering these quotations is not derisive, but only to show the nonspecialist how difficult it is to present these ideas in plain English.

The "weak" assumption of the formation of "rational" expectations is quite reasonable: a rational (and alert) decisionmaker will consider all information that he can get without undue cost provided that he believes it, or believes that many others (say, competitors in selling or buying) believe it, and provided further that according to his lights he regards it as relevant. "His lights" may, of course, change over time, as he learns from experience, his own and other persons'. The "strong" assumption of the formation of "rational" expectations is far more complex and, in fact, self-contradictory. It is assumed that the rational expectation-reviser will consider all "information" (including the most ancient and outdated) that is "available," will interpret this information the same way as all other agents on the basis of the same theories of interactive and reactive responses on the part of his contemporaries, including governments and other policy-making authorities, and will eventually (perhaps very soon, indeed, possibly without delay) arrive at the same conclusion as everyone else, a conclusion not surprisingly designated as the "rational-expectations equilibrium."

Members of this school or movement and their still unconvinced fellow analysts speculate about the "existence," the "uniqueness," and the "stability" of this equilibrium; about the path towards it, which means the process of gradual "convergence" of initially divergent expectations; about the "structure of the functions" that specify the rational-expectations equilibrium; and about the "parameters of the variables" in the relevant equations.[36] Among the most serious

---

[36] I acknowledge the help received from reading many essays and papers. Among them are the papers presented at the Seminar on Rational Expectations, held by the American Enterprise Institute on February 1, 1980, in Washington and published in the *Journal of Money, Credit, and Banking*, Vol. 12 (November 1980, Part 2), especially the papers by Robert E. Lucas, Jr., "Methods and Problems in Business Cycle Theory," pp. 696-715; William Fellner, "The Valid Core of Rationality Hypotheses in the Theory of Expectations," pp. 763-787; Arthur M. Okun, "Rational Expectations-with-Misperceptions As a Theory of the Business Cycle," pp. 817-825; and Gottfried Haberler, "Critical Notes on Rational Expectations," pp. 833-836. Further enlightenment was provided to me by the papers prepared for the Conference on Expectation Formation and Economic Disequilibrium, held at New York University on December 4, 1981, especially the following: Roman Frydman, "Individual Rationality, Decentralization, and the Rational Expectations Hypothesis"; Robert M. Townsend, "Equilibrium Theory with Disparate Expectations: Issues and Methods"; Alan Kirman, "On Mistaken Beliefs and Resultant Equilibria"; Margaret Bray, "Convergence to Rational Expectations Equilibrium"; and Edmund S. Phelps, "The Trouble with 'Rational Expectations' and the Problem of Inflation Stabilization."

In an unpublished paper, Margaret Bray and David M. Kreps, "Rational Learning and Rational Expectations" (Research Paper No. 616, Graduate School of Business, Stanford University, 1981) held that only "irrational learning" will lead to diverging

and most questionable issues, in my opinion, are first, the "infinite regress" in taking account of other decisionmakers' and policymakers' reactions to any moves made as a result of the successive revisions of expectations; second, the assumption that everybody, civilian or official, interprets all available information on the basis of one and the same model or theory; and third, the further assumption that everybody assigns the same parameters to the variables included in that model or theory, although these parameters are unknowable since they will emerge only as an end-result of ongoing interactive processes. The infinite regress in an endless chain of responses and adaptations, though rather unbelievable in a "model" of understandable human behavior, is not fatal to the theory if it is assumed that the magnitude of consecutive revisions of expectations decreases rapidly and becomes insignificant after a while. It would be an asymptotic approach to "equilibrium." The commonality of the relevant economic theories held by all persons involved—buyers and sellers, lenders and borrowers, employers and workers, cabinet members and opposition leaders, finance ministers and bank governors, Keynesian demand managers and Friedmanite monetarists, Marxian socialists and Hayekian libertarians—is an assumption unacceptable even as a heuristic fiction. The common knowledge of unknowable parameters, to be established only as an outcome, not as an input in the formation of expectation, is a logical impossibility.

The cited examples of irreconcilable contrasts among theories entertained by different schools of thought may seem too absurd, making a caricature of the postulated commonality of the theories basic to the "rational" interpretation of information in the light of a "commonly accepted" model of reasoning. Yet a set of two brief propositions essential to the formation of expectations regarding the effects of public-policy actions can make it clear that the assumption of generally shared models of economic processes is untenable even as a tentative hypothesis. I choose these propositions from monetary theory, because it is chiefly the area of monetary policy and monetary developments in which the rational-expectations hypothesis is applied.

Proposition A: An increase in the (basic) money supply, or in the rate of increase of the (basic) money supply, will lead to, or be associated with, a *decline* in the short-term rate of interest.

and "incorrect" beliefs, whereas "rational learning must entail convergence of beliefs" and this convergence will be "to correct beliefs . . . if the model is sufficiently regular" (p. 2). The use of the verb "must" indicates the tautological character of the exercise. My point is that this kind of "rational learning" cannot exist and should be "assumed" only in attempts to demonstrate the inherent contradictions.

Counterproposition A': An increase in the (basic) money supply, or
in the rate of increase of the (basic) money supply, will lead to,
or be associated with a *rise* in the short-term rate of interest.

Proposition B: A rise in the short-term rate of interest will lead to a
decline of commodity prices.

Counterproposition B': A rise in the short-term rate of interest will
lead to a *rise* of commodity prices.

If two hundred years of statistical observation and theoretical argumentation have not led to a consensus among the specialists regarding these relatively simple causal or functional relationships,
how can one reasonably assume that all (or most) economic agents,
public or private, will arrive at identical "rational" expectations of
the effects of monetary policy?

There is an alternative version of the strong hypothesis of uniform
rational expectations, a version that does not hold that the model of
the convergence of expectations is descriptive of typical human reasoning and acting, but holds merely that the hypothesis has only
predictive, not explanatory value. That is to say, the whole apparatus
of a "rational-expectations equilibrium" is only an "as if" instrument
of predictive macroeconomics. Protagonists of the school are not in
agreement on this point. But even if they were modest enough to
agree that the hypothesis cannot serve explanatory purposes but is
still usable as a tool of prediction, helpful to authorities in charge
of managing real demand, output, and employment, I see no good
reason to rely on it. It is true, of course, that people ordinarily learn
from experience; but we do not know how quickly they learn and
just what they learn. In some countries it took decades until people
learned to adjust to continuing price inflation; in other countries it
took them only a few years to catch on; and in a few countries people
have become so sensitized to the threat of monetary expansion that
they anticipate the feared effects, transforming thereby a possible lag
into a decisive lead. The advice to rely on statistical averages (reaching as far back as our time series allow) seems rather naive and cannot
possibly be helpful in arriving at short-run predictions of changes
in nominal or real terms. As a matter of fact, such averages could
never lead to a "rational-expectations equilibrium."[37]

[37] Roman Frydman, "Individual Rationality, Decentralization, and the Rational Expectations Hypothesis," Research Paper, Department of Economics, New York University (November 1981).

CHAPTER 9

The Expanding Specialty:
Surveys and Classifications

Six of the preceding chapters have been given to the task of telling the reader about the variety of subjects discussed under the heading "Economics of Information and Knowledge." One may say, without undue exaggeration, that all areas of economics—micro- and macroeconomic theory, monetary theory, international trade and finance, and every one of the applied fields—are being reformulated with special emphasis on knowledge gaps, uncertainty, new information, and changing expectations.

From this point of view the fast growth of the literature on the economics of information and knowledge does not seem surprising. If all chapters of books and all articles ever published in economics are to be rewritten with special emphasis on information and associated key concepts, and with allowance for different methodological bents and semantic tastes, thousands of economists can be kept busy for decades. Moreover, the search for topics for doctoral dissertations is made easy, as the opportunities for building new models with different assumptions about just what is unknown, dimly known, vaguely perceived, misperceived, slowly comprehended, quickly diffused, learned at great cost or with great ease, and so on seem limitless. No wonder that the new "specialty" is flourishing.

The present chapter will be devoted chiefly to two tasks: to describe the expansion of the literature on the subject and to report on available surveys and classifications.

The Expanding Specialty

It was for good reasons that I gave to the first chapter in this part the title "Old Roots and New Growth." I was able to show there that several of the most important problems in the economics of information and knowledge were thoroughly examined by economists of earlier times, some of these problems even more than two centuries ago. Instead of sending the reader back to the first chapters to refresh his memory, I offer a brief review.

A Sample of Old Roots

The oldest contributor cited in my survey of old roots was Daniel Bernouilli, who in 1738 wrote about games of chance and the expected utility of possible and probable gains from them. The most prolific contributor from the eighteenth century was surely Adam Smith, whose inquiry of 1776 offered a wealth of ideas about risk and risk bearing, invention, experimentation, and education, acquisition of how-to knowledge embodied in human capital, and other themes basic to the economics of information and knowledge.

I cited three writers of the first half of the nineteenth century: Johann Heinrich von Thünen, whose work in 1826 proposed the important distinction between insurable and noninsurable risk; Théodore Barrois, who in 1834 wrote about the applications of probability theory in accident insurance; and Antoine-Augustin Cournot, who was credited for two different achievements, first for his theory of duopolistic and oligopolistic competition (1838), and then for his work on probability (1843), the prototype of statistical decision theory.

In Chapter 6 I reported on a special topic with an unusually rich "early" literature: the social benefits and costs of patents as incentives for inventive activity. From the one hundred years between 1750 and 1850, at least ten contributions are worth citing: three in English—by Adam Smith (1776), Jeremy Bentham (1785), and John Stuart Mill (1848); four in German—by Johann Heinrich G. von Justi (1758), Ludwig Heinrich Jakob (1809), Johann Friedrich Lotz (1822), and Karl Heinrich Rau (1844); and three in French—by Jean Baptiste Say (1803), Simonde de Sismondi (1819), and Pierre-Joseph Proudhon (1846). All these statements on the economics of patents of invention were published before the "Patent Controversy" of the nineteenth century gathered momentum and produced an avalanche of articles and pamphlets between 1850 and 1875.

With the acceleration of the production of economic analyses of the patent monopoly, it would no longer be suitable to report on the most notable publications of a century or half-century. The third quarter of the nineteenth century saw so many contributions to the economics of patent protection that it is difficult to select the most noteworthy. (I would give first prize to Albert E. F. Schäffle, 1867.) On other topics in the economics of information and knowledge, Jean Courcelle-Seneuil (1852) and Hans Karl Emil von Mangoldt (1855) should be mentioned for recognizing the relationship between uncertainty, entrepreneurial venturesomeness, and profits of enterprise. George Joachim Goschen (1861) deserves to be cited for his book on the working of the forward exchange market. The economist who placed the heaviest emphasis on the role of ignorance and uncertain knowledge, of errors and vague expectations, was Carl Menger (1871), the founder of Austrian economics. Methodological subjectivism, the most essential tenet of the Austrian school, implies rejection of the notions of "true" and "certain" knowledge on the part of the economic decisionmaker.

The flow of output after 1871 became too rapid to allow for a condensed account here. Despite the growth of literature, however, it was another eighty years or so before the pertinent writings were recognized as sufficiently "special" to merit the status of belonging to a specialty.[1]

Emergence of the Specialty

If some of the fundamental conceptions of the economics of information and knowledge were well established by the end of the nineteenth century, why did it take until the 1950s or 1960s for the special field to be recognized? And, by the way, on what evidence can it be asserted that the field was not so recognized for such a long time? Let us try to answer the second question first.

What would be admissible evidence for the de facto recognition of a specialty within a discipline? I propose the following tests: (1) Most of the key words employed in the specialty appear in the subject indexes of comprehensive textbooks and histories of thought in the discipline. (2) Many of the key words of the specialty appear in ever greater numbers of instances in the titles of articles and books and in the subject designations of colloquia and conferences. (3) Survey articles are published to summarize the contents of publications in the special field. (4) The classification of the discipline is extended to provide a special heading under which publications in the special field can be brought together. (5) Within the new subject class the writings in the special field are subclassified as the number and variety of publications increases at a rapid rate. (6) University departments offer courses and seminars designed to teach the new specialty, first to graduate students, later also to undergraduates. (7)

---

[1] The new specialty, or even "new discipline," has also been recognized by authors outside the field of economics. In a methodological treatise on systems theory, Richard Mattessich coined for the economics of information and knowledge the term "epistemo-economics," and held that it "offers fascinating problems of basic research, above all it promises to reveal a close relationship between epistemology and economics on a completely new plane." Richard Mattessich, *Instrumental Reasoning and Systems Methodology* (Dordrecht: Reidel, 1978), pp. 224-225.

Books of readings and volumes of conference proceedings focusing on the new specialty, or on some of its subspecialties, are published.

It can be shown that on all these grounds the economics of information and knowledge became a recognized specialty of economics in about 1960. I have not attempted rigorous tests on all mentioned scores, but the evidence seems conclusive.

Subject Indexes, Titles of Journal Articles, Literature Surveys

The first test calls for an examination of the subject indexes of comprehensive textbooks or books on the history of thought. I chose to start with Joseph Schumpeter's encyclopaedic *History of Economic Analysis*, published in 1954. The index, prepared by Robert Kuenne, a highly competent economist, did not include, in its thirty crowded pages, any entries for knowledge, information, ignorance, certainty, uncertainty, future or futures, gambling, or insurance. All these subjects were actually treated in the text, but the indexer evidently assumed that readers would not look for them in the subject index.[2] In contrast, we can find that texts published about twenty years later do have entries for several of these and other cognate subjects in their indexes. Thus, the index of the textbook by Basil Moore, published in 1973, includes entries for decision-making, expectations, futures markets, human capital, innovation, insurance, research, speculation, and uncertainty.[3] The index of the textbook by Baumol and Blinder, published in 1979, shows brain drain, decision-making, education, expected rate of inflation, forecasting, human capital, innovation, invention, speculation, and technology.[4] The most telling comparisons are between early and later editions of Paul Samuelson's text, *Economics*.[5] The first edition was published in 1955, the eleventh twenty-five years later. Both editions

[2] Joseph A. Schumpeter, *History of Economic Analysis* (New York: Oxford University Press, 1954), pp. 1231-1260. The index has entries for "expectations" (referring only to Thornton and John Stuart Mill), for "speculation" (referring only to a passage about a Dutch writer by the name of Dirck Graswinckel), for "risks" (referring to Daniel Bernouilli, Cantillon, Thünen, Hawley, and Knight), and for "probability" (referring to Halley, Daniel and Jacques Bernouilli, Gauss, Quetelet, Edgeworth, Cournot, and Poisson).

[3] Basil J. Moore, *An Introduction to Modern Economic Theory* (New York: Free Press, 1973).

[4] William J. Baumol and Alan S. Blinder, *Economics: Principles and Policy* (New York: Harcourt Brace Jovanovich, 1979). I suspect that the index for this book was not prepared by the authors themselves; it omits subjects that not only are treated in the text but—as in the case of "imperfect information"—appear even in the titles of sections and in the table of contents.

[5] Paul A. Samuelson, *Economics* (New York: McGraw-Hill, 1st ed., 1955; 11th ed., 1980).

carried in the index entries for advertising, education, gambling, insurance, and speculation, but several entries for subjects recognized as constituents of the economics of information and knowledge, missing in the 1955 volume, were present in the 1980 edition: for example, brain drain, decision-making, forecasting, game theory, hedging, innovation, invention, investment planning, public goods, research, risk, technology transfer, and uncertainty. The first test may thus be declared to have been passed satisfactorily.

The second test was easy. A look at the tables of contents of the leading journals in economics shows that beginning around 1960 the key words listed above appear in ever-increasing numbers in the titles of articles published. An actual count of such titles in the *Journal of Political Economy* (*JPE*) and the *American Economic Review* (*AER*) confirmed this statement beyond doubt. Going beyond titles and including the initial paragraphs of the articles in the test for the appearance of the key words, more than 40 per cent of all articles published in the *JPE* in 1960 and 1965 were identified as belonging to the special field. As to titles of books, no systematic count was made, but it is sufficiently evident that the publishers' lists have become heavily slanted towards titles on information, uncertainty, expectations, and decisions.

The third test also was positive. At least four survey articles on the "economics of information" appeared in 1973 and 1974, reporting chiefly on items published since 1960. I shall come back to these surveys, because they deserve more detailed comments about their organization, findings, and judgments. At this point it suffices to state that one of the surveys covers as many as 144 items published between 1961 and 1973.

Classifications, Subclassifications, and University Courses

For the fourth test I turned to the classification system of the American Economic Association. The basic structure of this classification is the same for books, articles, and abstracts, and for the quarterly index in the *Journal of Economic Literature* (*JEL*) and the annual *Index of Economic Articles in Journals and Collective Volumes*. It consists of ten major subject categories, divided into forty-six subcategories. Books, usually wider in scope than articles, are classified into these forty-six groups, but a much more detailed classification is provided for articles, essays, and abstracts: approximately 170 three-digit classes in the quarterly issues of *JEL*, and almost 300 four-digit subclasses in the annual *Index*. "Human Capital" was added in March 1970 (as Class 850 in the category "Manpower, Labor, Productivity") and "Economics of Uncertainty and Information" was added in June 1976 as a sixth subclass (026) of the subcategory "General Economic Theory."[6]

Another piece of evidence in the fourth test is the set of cross-references in the *Social Sciences Index*, an index for publications from only 1974 on (hence after the economics of information had become a specialty).[7] The classification scheme features a heading "Information theory in economics"; at the end of the list of titles, the reader is invited to "see Uncertainty (econ.)"; from there he is sent to "Risk (econ.)"; thence to "Profit"; and in some volumes to "Speculation," "Arbitrage," "Investments," "Securities," "Stock exchange," and still more recently to "Search theory (employment)," "Search theory (consumption)," and "Expectations (economic)." The number of entries has increased steadily. For the year 1979-1980 the index listed under the three headings "Information theory in economics," "Uncertainty—economics" and "Search theory—employment," a total of 114 titles.[8] The point to note, however, in this context is that a classification system for the social sciences provides that many subdivisions of the literature on the economics of information.

The fifth test, the development of subclassifications within the new specialty, has been passed twice: once, when the survey articles mentioned above arranged the surveyed literature into subject-matter groups; and again, when a special bibliography for *The Economics of Information* was commissioned by a governmental agency. This classified bibliography, in its first edition, published in 1971, contained 329 items; the second edition, published in 1972, had 488 entries.[9] Because of multiple listings of titles in some of the sub-

---

[6] *Journal of Economic Literature*, Vol. 8 (March 1970), p. 189, and Vol. 14 (June 1976), p. 637. In the issue of March 1976, articles on such things as rational expectations, accuracy of information, effects of ignorance of prices upon market equilibrium, were listed under "022 Microeconomic Theory." In the June 1976 issue, 19 articles were listed under the new heading, "026 Economics of Uncertainty and Information" (pp. 748-749).

[7] *The Social Sciences Index*, edited by Joseph Bloomfield (New York: Wilson, 1975 and annually), Vol. 1, 1974-1975.

[8] Besides the 114 items under these three headings, Vol. 6, for 1979-1980, lists 61 titles under "Risk" and 63 titles under "Expectations."

[9] Harold Anker Olson, *The Economics of Information: Bibliography and Commentary on the Literature*, 2d ed., 1972. ED 076214. The 1971 edition of the publication was prepared pursuant to a contract with the Office of Education, U.S. Department of Health, Education, and Welfare. The bibliography contained an extraordinarily large number of publications on economic aspects of library science, which may be due to the fact that the bibliographer was affiliated with a school of library and information science. The compilation is biased in favor of books; several pertinent periodicals were not covered at all.

classes and because of the inclusion of excessively general publications, I eliminated 87 entries and thereby reduced the bibliography to 401 items. A breakdown by year of publication shows an increase from one single entry each in 1956 and 1958 to 100 entries in 1970.

Evidence for the sixth test is provided by the catalogues of course offerings by university departments of economics. Several major universities offer courses in the new specialty. I shall quote from the catalogue of Harvard University, 1979-1980, and add to the course titles some words from the course descriptions where they are particularly indicative of the contents: "Ec. 1553, *Markets and Market Structure*" (includes ". . . consumer information, welfare problems, and the effects of regulation. . . ."); "Ec. 2131, *Uncertainty and Information*"; "Ec. 2152, *Social Choices, Incentives, and Game Theory*" (includes "incentives for pooling private information"); "Ec. 2153, *The Theory of Central Planning and the Command Economy*" (includes "the design of appropriate resource allocation, information, and control mechanisms"); "Ec. 2190, *Seminar on Public and Organizational Decision Making*" (". . . emphasizes problems relating to incomplete information, structured communications. . . ."); "Ec. 2611, *Market Failure, Control, and Regulation*" (includes "market failure due to . . . impacted information. . . ."); "Ec. 2810a, *Labor Market Analysis*" (includes "human capital and investment in job skills. . . ."); "Ec. 2830, *Testing, Sorting, and the Distribution of Income*" (includes "minimum competency testing for high school graduates . . . selecting individuals for jobs . . . criteria for admissions standards, processes or insurance rating . . ."). If equivalents of any of these courses were given before the 1960s—perhaps something similar to Labor Market Analysis—contents and emphases were surely different, without the "modern" attention to search, information, job skills, and human capital.

Books of Readings and Conference Proceedings

On the seventh and last of the proposed tests—books of readings and volumes of proceedings—positive evidence is overwhelming, so much so that I can, in view of limits of space and of readers' patience, present only a small fraction of the long list of titles. An annual meeting of the American Economic Association, in December 1965, was devoted to the theme "Knowledge Production and Innovation"; the program was organized into 16 sessions with 46 papers and 43 discussion papers, all reproduced in the volume of proceedings.[10] A

---

[10] Seventy-Eighth Annual Meeting of American Economic Association, December 1965, "Knowledge Production and Innovation," *American Economic Review*, Vol. 56, Papers and Proceedings (May 1966), pp. 1-600. — The program was arranged by Fritz Machlup.

conference held by the International Economic Association in 1963 concentrated on the economics of education. Twenty-four papers and a summary record of the discussions were published in 1966 in the volume of proceedings.[11] In 1968 UNESCO published a volume of *Readings in the Economics of Education*.[12] It contained 66 papers, essays, and abstracts from books originally published between 1826 and 1967. In 1968 and 1969 Mark Blaug's two volumes of readings in the same subspecialty appeared.[13] They included 37 selections of articles first published between 1959 and 1968. As mentioned before, a general anthology on the *Economics of Information and Knowledge* was published in 1971, with 18 articles originally published between 1961 and 1970, selected by Donald Lamberton.[14]

This was only the beginning. Examination of the titles of collective volumes the contents of which were included in the annual *Index of Economic Articles* shows that from 1970 to 1976 between fifty and seventy books of readings and volumes of proceedings appeared in the various subspecialties of the economics of information and knowledge.[15]

The Lag in the Recognition of the Special Field

The first question raised at the beginning of this subsection is still to be answered: why did it take so long for the specialty to be recognized? If the old roots were so strong as I have indicated, why should it take some eighty years for the new growth to develop and to become so lush and exuberant as to burst the confinement of the traditional fields and be granted the status and independence of a specialty? The answer is simply that most classifiers are reluctant to depart from traditional schemes. One reason for this reluctance may be the classifiers' wish to have a uniform scheme usable for clas-

---

[11] Edward Austin G. Robinson and John E. Vaizey, eds., *The Economics of Education*. Proceedings of a conference held by the International Economic Association (London: Macmillan, 1966).

[12] Mary Jean Bowman, Michel Debeuvais, V. E. Komarov, and John Vaizey, eds., *Readings in the Economics of Education* (Paris: UNESCO, 1968).

[13] Mark Blaug, ed., *Economics of Education 1: Selected Readings* (Harmondsworth: Penguin, 1968); *Economics of Education 2: Selected Readings* (Harmondsworth: Penguin, 1969).

[14] Donald M. Lamberton, ed., *Economics of Information and Knowledge: Selected Readings* (Harmondsworth: Penguin, 1971).

[15] I counted 11 titles containing the words "decisions" or "decision-making," 10 titles with the words "technology" or "technological," 7 titles with the words "education" or "educational," 5 titles about "manpower" (forecasting, planning, movements), and a few titles each with the key words "uncertainty," "expectations," "games" (or "gaming"), "security (or portfolio) analysis," "human capital" or "human resources," "planning," and last but not least, "management."

sifying articles, books, and authors. Articles can usually be assigned to very narrow specialties, whereas books, dealing with broader aspects, cannot; and authors, interested in a variety of subjects, may firmly resist being labeled as narrow specialists. Thus, an economist writing on monetary theory and emphasizing in his reasoning such factors as uncertainty and expectations will still prefer to be called a specialist in macroeconomics or in monetary economics rather than a specialist in the economics of information. Similarly, a labor economist will still want to be known as a specialist in labor economics even if his work is chiefly in the economics of job search, skill screening, and human capital. Of course, finer subdivision can be provided for the classification of articles; but even there the classifiers will modify existing arrangements only when they become manifestly obsolete, for example, when once densely populated subject classes or subclasses become almost empty, or others become so overcrowded that they are unhelpful to the user.[16]

The Growth of the Literature

I have made some attempts at estimating the rate at which the literature in our new specialty has been growing. The best sources of data for such estimates are the annual *Index of Economic Articles in Journals and Collective Volumes* and the quarterly "Subject Index of Articles," in the *Journal of Economic Literature (JEL)*.[17] I did not expect to come up with precise numbers, but I hoped to ascertain a rough order of magnitude of the growth of the new specialty.

I first tried to establish the number of articles listed in the *Index* for 1970 and "belonging" in the specialty surveyed here.[18] For most

[16] I am speaking from experience. I was an almost perennial member of consecutive classification committees of the American Economic Association from the early 1940s to the middle 1960s and participated in the deliberations and decisions leading to the consecutive classification schemes and their modifications during that period. See the "Reports of the Secretary" in various volumes of Papers and Proceedings; also the "Report of the Committee on Classifications," in *American Economic Review*, Vol. 38, Papers and Proceedings, (May 1948), pp. 570-572.

[17] The former is based on a four-digit classification; the latter on a three-digit classification. The annual index has appeared with a time lag of between three and six years, whereas the quarterly index is current. Essays in collective volumes are listed only in the annual, not in the quarterly index. Both indexes allow multiple listings in several subcategories, but the finer breakdown of subject matter in the four-digit scheme invites more frequent listing of articles that are not extraordinarily narrow. Some of these differences make it difficult to use the two bibliographic services for the intertemporal comparisons needed for accurate estimates of growth.

[18] Mark Perlman et al., eds., *Index of Economic Articles in Journals and Collective Volumes*, Vol. XII, 1970 (Nashville, Tenn.: American Economic Association, 1976). — This index excludes books, but it covers over 200 journals and, for 1970, 153

items I could rely on the designations of the categories and subcategories in which the entries were collected, but I scanned also the entries in many other subject classes.[19] Having come up with 1,430 entries, the question was how to omit multiple counting. The editors of the *Index* estimated that "slightly over half of the articles are classified in more than one subcategory."[20] Alas, they had no estimate of the average number of listings per article.[21] If we assume that the articles on the subject pertinent to this growing field were entered, on the average, in three subclasses, we may conclude that in 1970 approximately 475 articles on the economics of information and knowledge were published in the journals and volumes covered by the index.[22]

In order to arrive at an estimate of the rate at which this literature has been growing, one may go back to 1960 or forward to the present (1978). Unfortunately, the *Index* for 1960, or for any of the years around 1960, did not cover many of the sources that were covered in 1970. It would have taken too much time and effort to reduce the coverage of the 1970 *Index* to that of the earlier ones, as would be

---

collective volumes (including books of readings) and 79 government documents. It lists articles (that appeared either in English or with English summaries), essays, conference papers, testimonies, notes, communications, comments, replies, and rejoinders. The items are entered under one or more of the almost 300 subject subclasses.

[19] I found entries relevant to the economics of knowledge and information in as many as 100 subclasses. From one subclass, Human Capital, I accepted all 120 items. Many of them were also among the 116 entries under Economics of Education. I found 65 relevant items under Business and Public Administration, 60 under Managerial Economics, 49 under Organization and Decision Theory, 61 under Insurance, 58 under Manpower Training and Development, 53 under Marketing and Advertising, 39 under Portfolio Selection, and another 39 under Economic Planning Theory and Policy. Altogether 1,430 entries qualified as writings on the economics of knowledge and information. — Perhaps I should explain how I selected the items that I regard as eligible for a bibliography on the economics of knowledge and information. I assumed that the titles of the articles appropriately conveyed their major concern, and I chose key words that would indicate it. Among these key words were knowledge, ignorance, information, uncertainty, expectations, forecasting, prediction, decision and game theory, gambling, speculation, hedging, risk, insurance, futures, forward market, research, invention, innovation, technology transfer, education, brain drain, human capital, advertising, telecommunication, public goods, investment planning, portfolio selection, search theory, screening and signaling, market prices as guides to action, market socialism, planning techniques. One ought to bear in mind that the choice of words in the titles of articles is influenced by fashion and that the key word technique may therefore lead to misleading measures of the growth of the literature.

[20] Perlman et al., *Index*, p. xii.

[21] Perlman knew only that in one exceptional instance an article was listed in seven places. Information by letter, 5 August 1979.

[22] Thus, more articles were listed in the index for the single year 1970 than Olsen's bibliography listed for a ten-year period. See footnote 9 above.

necessary for a meaningful comparison. The *Index* for 1978 will take a few years to appear. (The latest available at the time of my writing is for 1974—and for 1977 now, as this book goes to the printer.) In lieu of the annual *Index*, I consulted the quarterly "Subject Index of Articles" in the *JEL*, which covers the same journals, though it does not include papers, essays, or chapters in collective works.

My labors, though rather painstaking, did not yield estimates sufficiently reliable to be accepted as more than "impressions of rapid growth."[23] I am inclined to propose 700 as the figure for a reasonable approximation of the annual flow of journal articles in 1978. The estimate of 475 items published in 1970 included many pieces in collective volumes and government documents, whereas such pieces were not included among the 700 items in 1978. Thus, if contributions to, or reproductions in, collective volumes were deducted from the estimate for 1970 or added to the estimate for 1978, the increase in the flow of publications in the specialty would be even more impressive.

SURVEYS, BIBLIOGRAPHIES, AND CLASSIFICATIONS

As mentioned before, the early 1970s brought us the appearance of the first survey articles on the literature of the economics of information and knowledge. Usually, such survey articles arrange the literature according to a classification scheme newly developed by the author or adapted from an existing model. Other classification schemes become available as special bibliographies are published or distributed by instructors of courses on the new specialty. Finally, there are bibliographies on subspecialties published as appendices of monographic publications on a particular topic.

[23] I went through all entries in the subject index of the two latest issues of the *JEL*, for June and September 1978, and counted the items that would belong in a bibliography of the economics of knowledge and information. *Journal of Economic Literature*, Vol. 16 (June 1978), pp. 751-832; and Vol. 16 (September 1978), pp. 1193-1277. (Not satisfied with a mere estimate of average multiple listings, I went to the effort of eliminating all double and triple counting.) In the June 1978 issue I counted 188 articles, of which 33 were in Economics of Uncertainty and Information, 10 on Human Capital, and 145 distributed among many other subclasses. In the September issue I counted 157 articles, of which 27 were in Economics of Uncertainty and Information, 20 on Human Capital, and 110 distributed among other subclasses. Taking the two issues together, one may say that in half a year 345 journal articles were published on the economics of knowledge and information. This corresponds to an annual flow of almost 700 articles.

Classifying the New Specialty

Classification of scientific disciplines is always difficult, but when an area of inquiry is in a stage of fast development it may be virtually impossible to arrive at a satisfactory classification. What looks halfway appropriate at one time may, within a few years, be hopelessly inadequate. With regard to the economics of knowledge and information, two approaches to an acceptable classification have seemed relatively safe and viable: (1) to use one of the traditional or conventional outlines of the principles of economics and show how possession of knowledge and access to information impinge on the problems analyzed; and (2) to use an arrangement of the knowledge industries such as that proposed in my 1962 book, ranging from Education and R and D to the Mass Media of Communication, Information Machines, and Information Services. Each of these approaches has been used in surveys of the field, and at least one writer combined both in his survey.

Three Major Classes

It was in Michael Cooper's survey that the two approaches were combined.[24] He divided the "Micro-Economics of Information" into three major classes: (1) "Information Producers," subdivided according to the chapter titles of my 1962 book; (2) "Resources and Constraints on Information Services," subdivided into Funding, Taxation, Regulation, Patent and Copyright Systems; and (3) "Resource Allocation," subdivided into Information as a Commodity, Welfare Economics and Cost-Benefit Analysis, Demand Analysis, Cost-Effectiveness Analysis, Cost Analysis, and Operations-Research Models. Cooper's survey covers 144 items, all published between 1961 and 1973, most of them—127 items—between 1971 and 1973.

Six Headings

The 175 titles listed under "Further Reading" in Lamberton's *Economics of Information and Knowledge* were not classified,[25] but the eighteen reproduced selections were arranged under six headings that looked like a sensible classification: "General," "Economic Organization," "Information and Efficiency," "Information Policy," "Institutional Aspects," and "Business Planning." These headings are sufficiently broad to accommodate many of the subjects that other

[24] Michael D. Cooper, "The Economics of Information," in Carlos Cuadra, ed., *Annual Review of Information Sciences and Technology*, Vol. 8 (Washington, D.C.: American Society for Information Science, 1973), pp. 5-40.

[25] Lamberton, *Economics of Information*, pp. 366-376.

classifiers have offered as separate classes or categories. Of course, the coverage is selective and omits large parts of the field.

Fourteen Categories

In an ambitious, but unwieldy, classification of the literature on the economics of information, Harold Olson distinguished fourteen categories.[26] (1) Economics: Overview; Theory. (2) Economics: Industry Analysis; Production Function; Manpower. (3) Economics: Public Sector; Public Goods; Welfare; Benefit-Cost; Non-Market Decision-Making; Economic Organization. (4) Economics: Operations Analysis; Operations Research; Capital Budget Theory; Management Economics; Systems Analysis; Marketing; Cost Estimation. (5) Economics and Allied Sciences: Sector Studies Closely Related to Information Activity. (6) Economics and Allied Sciences: Innovation; The Entrepreneur; Incentives. (7) Economics and Allied Sciences: Policy Analysis; Planning. (8) Economics and Allied Sciences: Forecasting and Performance Indicators; Knowledge Utilization; Technology Assessment. (9) Economics and Allied Sciences: Sociology of Knowledge; Sociological Analyis; History; Organization Theory; Social Psychology. (10) Information: Overview; Documentation; Administration; Information Science and Library Research; National System-Industry-Policy Studies; Copyright. (11) Information: Surveys; User Studies. (12) Information: System Evaluation Analysis; General Management Studies. (13) Information: System Development; Planning; Automation. (14) Information: System Operations; Operational Analysis.

The fourteen categories fall into three major groups, indicated by the lead words: A. Economics (numbers 1 to 4), B. Economics and Allied Sciences (numbers 5 to 9), and C. Information (numbers 10 to 14). The subtitles in each category are so detailed that it must be difficult to decide how to classify particular items (for example, "operations analysis" in number 4 and "operational analysis" in number 14); as a matter of fact, several publications in Olson's bibliography had to be entered in two or three categories.[27]

---

[26] Harold Anker Olson, *The Economics of Information: Bibliography*. See footnote 9 above.

[27] Olson recognized these difficulties in the enlarged 1972 version of his bibliography: he abandoned his scheme for all new entries (which he selected from "nearly 500 items . . . which pertain to the economics of information") and grouped them into only two broad classes: "Economics Literature" and "Information Literature." (Assignments to either of these two groups evidently caused few or no difficulties, although the compiler observed in his preface that "the communications gap between the information community and the economics community appears to have narrowed during the year.") As a result of the collapse of the classification we now see publi-

Surveys with Special Emphases

Two survey articles, published in 1973 and 1974, made no attempt to classify the literature, because they were focused sharply on a subspecialty within the new specialty: on analyses of the effects of imperfections and asymmetries of information upon the performance of markets and the formation of market prices. Michael Rothschild[28] examined 45 articles published between 1956 and 1973, Michael Spence[29] reviewed 66 articles published between 1959 and 1974. Most of the sources surveyed had originated after 1970.

Rothschild's survey emphasized problems of adjustment towards an equilibrium price, or equilibrium distribution of prices, with incomplete or different information available to the market parties. Spence's survey concentrated on the literature about "information gaps," "informational asymmetries," and institutional conditions encouraging underproduction of knowledge, that is, analyses of situations that tend to result in "market failure." (By market failure most economists refer to conditions under which the free market is likely to generate prices inviting a less than optimal allocation of resources.) A small point may be made with reference to these two surveys. Rothschild chose for his survey article a title that indicated the special emphasis on the role of information in market performance. Spence, on the other hand, called his article "An Economist's View of Information," which might suggest to the reader that *all* economics of information is covered in the survey. Thus, the untutored reader might be led to believe that the effects of information on market prices are virtually all that matter to the economist. The economics of information and knowledge includes many topics besides the areas viewed and reviewed in this supposedly general survey.

Another survey article, published in two parts in 1976, concentrated on the literature on the economics of job search.[30] "Search

---

cations on broadcasting, journal publishing, library operations, research management, operations research, telephone service, university administration, medical information, school finance, advertising, the impact of computer technology, newspapers, marketing research, business decision-making, governmental central planning, and many other subjects, all thrown together in one unclassified bibliography.

[28] Michael Rothschild, "Models of Market Organization with Imperfect Information: A Survey," *Journal of Political Economy*, Vol. 81 (November-December 1973), pp. 1283-1308.

[29] A. Michael Spence, "An Economist's View of Information," in Carlos Cuadra, ed., *Annual Review of Information Science and Technology*, Vol. 9 (Washington, D.C.: American Society for Information Science, 1974), pp. 57-78.

[30] Steven A. Lippman and John J. McCall, "The Economics of Job Search: A Survey. Part I, Optimal Job Search Policies," *Economic Inquiry*, Vol. 14 (June 1976), pp. 155-189; and "The Economics of Job Search: A Survey. Part II, Empirical and Policy Implications of Job Search," *Economic Inquiry*, Vol. 14 (September 1976), pp. 347-368.

theory" had been put on the map in 1961 and 1962 by George Stigler in two seminal articles, one analyzing the demand for information—search—in general, the other applying search theory to the analysis of the labor market.[31] The theory of job search developed into an intensively cultivated subspecialty of the economics of information. The survey article provided a bibliography of 122 entries or, adjusted for duplications, 102 titles, of which 80 had been published between 1971 and 1976.

Not all special topics in the economics of information and knowledge are of recent vintage; indeed, the first section of this chapter told of several "old roots." One of the "old topics" mentioned there was the economics of patent protection and inventive activity. A survey, done by me and published in 1958, included 174 items.[32] Of these, 64 were published between 1750 and 1900, another 86 between 1901 and 1950, and only 24 in or after 1951. More recent bibliographies on the economics of patents as incentives for innovative technological research and development and for disclosure of the inventions show that research in this branch of the economics of knowledge and information continues, but not at a rate accelerating faster than the increase in the population of economists. A volume by Christopher Taylor and Aubrey Silberston,[33] published in 1973, does not permit of a bibliometric analysis, because its "Selected Bibliography" contains only 35 titles, the earliest going back to 1947. This bibliography contains only 3 titles published before 1951, 12 titles published between 1951 and 1965, and 20 titles published between 1966 and 1971. It surely would not be reasonable to conclude from these figures that there has been an increase in the rate at which the economics of patent protection has grown.

Neither can such a conclusion be drawn from an annotated bibliography made available in 1976 as Volume 3 of a report prepared for the National Science Foundation.[34] A total of 162 items, published

[31] George J. Stigler, "The Economics of Information," *Journal of Political Economy*, Vol. 69 (1961), pp. 213-225, and "Information in the Labor Market," *Journal of Political Economy*, Vol. 70 (October 1962), pp. 94-104.

[32] Fritz Machlup, *An Economic Review of the Patent System*. Study of the Subcommittee on Patents, Trademarks, and Copyrights of the Committee on the Judiciary, U.S. Senate (Washington, D.C.: Government Printing Office, 1958), bibliography on pp. 81-86.

[33] Christopher T. Taylor and Z. Aubrey Silbertson, *The Economic Impact of the Patent System* (Cambridge: At the University Press, 1973). The bibliography is on pp. 403-404.

[34] John Driffill, Carole Kitti, Mary Summerfield, and Charles L. Trozzo, *The Effects of Patents and Antitrust Laws, Regulations, and Practices on Innovation*, Vol. 3, *Annotated Bibliography* (Arlington, Va.: Institute for Defense Analysis, February 1976. Reproduced by the National Technical Information Service, U.S. Department of Commerce, PB 252 862).

between 1934 and 1974, were chosen for inclusion. The criteria for their selection were not stated, but the selected items are relevant and the annotations are exceptionally good. Twelve years of the period covered are represented by only one or two titles each; the years with record crops in publications on the special subject were 1962 with 24 titles, 1966 with 15, and 1969 with 13. The selection is heavily concentrated on particular authors: twelve authors produced 70 of the 162 listed pieces. Thus, no inferences on either fast or slow growth of the literature on this subspecialty would be warranted.

The Theory of Games

The theory of games of strategy, based on theories of probability and expected utility, and applied to economic decision-making has had both a long and dignified history and a most spectacular rate of growth in recent years. We recall that the pertinent literature goes back to 1738, to a work by Daniel Bernouilli.[35] Important contributions were made in the nineteenth century and in the first third of the twentieth century.[36] The most fundamental work, first published in 1944, and in a second edition in 1947, was by John von Neumann and Oskar Morgenstern.[37] Response to this work was not immediate but, after a few years, reached almost flood dimensions, especially if mathematical media are included in the survey. Martin Shubik estimated that "six thousand books and articles" were published on the theory of games.[38]

In the bibliography to a chapter prepared for a forthcoming volume, Martin Shubik arranged his references in a classificatory scheme following the organizational scheme of his text. General works were followed by titles grouped under twenty-five headings, twelve of which concerned economics: Duopoly; Oligopoly; Bilateral Monop-

---

[35] Daniel Bernouilli, "Specimen theoriae novae de mensura sortis," in *Commentarii academiae scientiarum imperialis Petropolitanae* (St. Petersburg, 1738). German translation by Alfred Pringsheim, *Die Grundlage der modernen Wertlehre: Daniel Bernouilli, Versuch einer neuen Theorie der Wertbestimmung von Glücksfällen* (Leipzig: Duncker & Humblot, 1896).

[36] Antoine Augustin Cournot, *Exposition de la théorie des chances et des probabilités* (Paris: Hachette, 1843); John von Neumann, "Zur Theorie der Gesellschaftspiele," *Mathematische Annalen*, Vol. 100 (1928), pp. 295-320; Karl Menger, "Das Unsicherheitsmoment in der Wertlehre," *Zeitschrift für Nationalökonomie*, Vol. 5 (1934), pp. 459-485.

[37] John von Neumann and Oskar Morgenstern, *Theory of Games and Economic Behavior* (Princeton: Princeton University Press, 1944; 2d ed., 1947).

[38] Martin Shubik, "Morgenstern, Oskar," *International Encyclopedia of the Social Sciences*, Vol. 18 (New York: Free Press, 1979), p. 543.

oly and Bargaining; Gaming; Auctions and Bidding; The Core; Value; The Bargaining Set (with a subcategory, The Nucleolus); Solutions, Market Games and the Price System; Public Goods, Externalities and Welfare Economics; Money and Financial Institutions; Macro and Other Topics. The remaining thirteen headings concerning the applications of game theory in other fields were: Game Theory and Political Science: Voting and Group Preference, Strategic Choice; Coalitions and Bargaining: Logrolling; Coalitions Other than Logrolling; Bargaining; Power; Gaming Associated with Political Science; Game Theory, Gaming and Social Psychology; Game Theory and Operations Research; Military Applications (with seventy-six titles, the largest section); Nonmilitary Operations Research; Sociology and Anthropology; Biology and Zoology; Other Applications.[39]

A survey article about the economic literature on the theory of games was published in 1980 by Andrew Schotter and Gerhard Schwödiauer.[40] The bibliography focuses on the economics of duopoly and oligopoly, general-equilibrium problems, bargaining, pricing of public goods, design for allocating procedures and planning mechanisms in informationally decentralized economies, and institutional arrangements. The list contains 278 entries.[41]

[39] Martin Shubik, "On the Applications of Game Theory," Chap. 13 of a forthcoming book (I am indebted to Shubik for making the manuscript available to me.)

[40] Andrew Schotter and Gerhard Schwödiauer, "Economics and the Theory of Games: A Survey," *Journal of Economic Literature*, Vol. 18 (June 1980), pp. 479-527; bibliography, pp. 519-527.

[41] A bibliometric test shows that such title counting can be quite misleading. In the *Index of Economic Journals* game-theoretical studies are entered chiefly in three subject subclasses: Organization and Decision Theory (Code 5110), Price and Market Theory of Firm and Industry in Noncompetitive Relations (Code 0226), and Social Choice (Code 0250). Game-theoretical articles entered in these subclasses numbered 9 in 1974, 10 in 1975, and 2 in 1976. The bibliography by Schotter and Schwödiauer lists 18 items published in 1974, 15 in 1975, and 16 in 1976. The discrepancies are too large for comfort, but can be explained as unavoidable outcomes of our indexing techniques. Take, for example, the article by Dermot Gately, "Sharing the Gains from Customs Unions among Less Developed Countries: A Game-Theoretic Approach," *Journal of Development Economics*, Vol. 1 (December 1974), pp. 213-233. Specialists in international trade and subspecialists in customs unions would like to find this title under (Code 4113) Theory of Protection or (4114) Theory of International Trade and Development or (4232) Theory of Economic Integration; specialists in development economics would probably be satisfied to find the title in 4232; but specialists in game theory may look for it—and are directed by the "Topical Guide to Classification Schedule" to look for it—under the heading (0250) Social Choice. Game theory, however, is not the subject matter of the article but only the method of analysis employed. Thus, it would be unreasonable to expect to find the article under Social Choice; yet, a bibliographer of the literature on game theory would want the item shown also in his list.

The Theory of Human Capital

Among the subspecialties of the economics of information and knowledge that were covered by survey articles is the theory of human capital. This is one of the themes that had its roots in a distant past but its growth only in the last two decades. In the first chapter and in the recapitulation in the present chapter I failed to pay sufficient attention to the precursors of the theory of human capital; I may now make up for this neglect.

Probably the first estimate of the stock of human capital was made around 1676 in Sir William Petty's *Political Arithmetick*.[42] Petty did not, however, use his estimate in support of any substantive hypotheses or in connection with any theoretical model for the derivation of causal connections. About two hundred years later, similar estimates were made, one by the German statistician Ernst Engel, the other by the English economist Joseph S. Nicholson. Engel, however, was chiefly concerned with the cost of food invested in the growing child.[43] Nicholson, on the other hand, looked to the cost of education as the major investment in human productivity. Assessing the human capital accumulated in the people of the United Kingdom, he estimated that the total value of the country's "living capital" was more than five times the stock of "dead" (physical) capital.[44] Nicholson had derived his notions from Adam Smith, who was most explicit

[42] Sir William Petty (1623-1687). His *Political Arithmetick* was written in or around 1670 and "first published surreptitiously in 1683 as 'England's Guide to Industry.' . . . The first authorized edition was published posthumously in 1690 by Petty's son." (See Phyllis Deane, "Petty, William," *International Encyclopedia of the Social Sciences*, Vol. 12, p. 67.) It is reprinted in Charles H. Hull, ed., *The Economic Writings of Sir William Petty* (Cambridge: At the University Press, 1899; New York: Kelley, 1963), Vol. I, pp. 233-313.

[43] Ernst Engel, *Der Kostenwerth des Menschen* [Vol. I of a planned series on *Der Werth des Menschen*] (Berlin: L. Simion, 1883).

[44] Joseph S. Nicholson, "The Living Capital of the United Kingdom," *Economic Journal*, Vol. 1 (March 1891), pp. 95-107. Nicholson did not pretend that he was breaking new ground. Indeed, he began his article with these sentences:

> Almost all systematic writers on Political Economy have discussed the question whether or not the skill of the artisan . . . , and other intangible elements of the social fabric should be included in the wealth of the individual or the nation. Adam Smith boldly places under "fixed capital" the acquired and useful abilities of all the inhabitants or members of the society on the grounds: *first*, that the acquisition of such talents "by the maintenance of the acquirer during his education, study or apprenticeship always costs a real expense, which is a capital fixed and realized as it were in his person"; and, *secondly*, because the improved dexterity of a workman may be considered in the same light as a machine or instrument of trade "which facilitates and abridges labour, and which, though it costs a certain expense, repays that expense with a profit.

on the subject.[45] Alfred Marshall can also be cited for his clear vision of these ideas.[46]

In the first half of the twentieth century Raymond Walsh sketched the history of the idea of human capital in an article,[47] and Milton Friedman and Simon Kuznets undertook an elaborate empirical test of the thesis that investment in scarce skills pays off.[48] Thus, the theory of human capital had been in the economic and statistical literature for almost three hundred years before it really "took off," chiefly under the influence of Theodore Schultz,[49] Gary Becker,[50] and Jacob Mincer.[51]

It was not a gradual increase in publications after 1960, it was as if floodgates had been opened. The new subspecialty of economics—especially if studies in the economics of education and the formation of human capital are combined in the count—became immediately the most widely researched single topic in the field.

It is not surprising in these circumstances that surveys as well as special bibliographies were soon forthcoming. A history of thought on human capital appeared in 1968, authored by Bernard Kiker.[52] But the most persevering and scholarly bibliographer of this special literature has been Mark Blaug. His annotated bibliography of the economics of education contained in its first edition, in 1966, no fewer than 800 items; in the second edition (1970), 1,350 items; in the third

[45] Adam Smith, *An Inquiry into the Nature and Causes of the Wealth of Nations* (London: 1st ed., 1776; London: Routledge, 1903), pp. 78-79. See the preceding footnote for Smith's sentences quoted by Nicholson.

[46] Alfred Marshall, *Principles of Economics* (London: Macmillan, 1st ed., 1890; 8th ed., 1920), Book VI, Chap. IV, §§2, 3, and 4 (pp. 560-566), Chapter XI, §1 (pp. 660-661) and Chapter XII, §9 (pp. 681-684). Marshall distinguished "material" and "personal" capital, and discussed the investment in personal capital, chiefly by parents paying and caring for the education of their children.

[47] John Raymond Walsh, "Capital Concept Applied to Man," *Quarterly Journal of Economics*, Vol. 49 (February 1935), pp. 255-285.

[48] Milton Friedman and Simon Kuznets, *Income from Independent Professional Practice* (New York: National Bureau of Economic Research, 1945).

[49] Theodore W. Schultz, "Capital Formation by Education," *Journal of Political Economy*, Vol. 68 (November-December 1960), pp. 571-583; "Investment in Human Capital," *American Economic Review*, Vol. 51 (March 1961), pp. 1-17.

[50] Gary S. Becker, "Investment in Human Capital: A Theoretical Analysis." *Journal of Political Economy*, Vol. 70 (Suppl. October 1962), pp. 9-49; *Human Capital* (New York: Columbia University Press, 1964).

[51] Jacob Mincer, "Investment in Human Capital and Personal Income Distribution," *Journal of Political Economy*, Vol. 66 (August 1958), pp. 281-302; "On-the-Job Training: Costs, Returns, and Some Implications," *Journal of Political Economy*, Vol. 70 (Suppl. October 1962), pp. 50-79.

[52] Bernard F. Kiker, *Human Capital: In Retrospect* (Columbia: University of South Carolina, Bureau of Business and Economic Research, 1968).

edition (1976), about 2,000 items.[53] Two survey articles on the theory of human capital were published in 1976 and 1977, one by Blaug, the other by Sherwin Rosen, both emphasizing the empirical status of the theory.[54] In his article Blaug observed that "the flood of literature in the field . . . seems . . . to be increasing . . . at an increasing rate."[55] One may wonder whether the stock of human capital accumulated by Western societies and valued according to the expected flow of return is growing as fast as the literature about it.

Comprehensive Classifications

In my survey of surveys and bibliographies I have in the preceding section dealt with subspecialties but may now return to more comprehensive treatments of the literature. One of the most astute surveyors and classifiers of this literature is Jack Hirshleifer, who has produced at least three papers designed to help us see "where we are in the theory of information"—or rather, in the economics of information.[56] The first of these papers, published in 1973, reported on "the economics of information . . . blooming with striking and novel ideas in the intellectual realm."[57] In this survey Hirshleifer presents two separate classifications, one for the subjects he covered in the survey, another for the subjects he omitted. He proposed three subject groups for the topics he covered, that is, essentially, the "microeconomics of information": I. "Information-Involved Modes

---

[53] Mark Blaug, *The Economics of Education: An Annotated Bibliography*, 3d ed. (Oxford, Pergamon, 1976). — Two earlier bibliographies in this area should be mentioned: a book by Kenneth A. Feldman and Theodore M. Newcomb, *The Impact of College on Students* (San Francisco: Jossey-Bass, 1969), contained approximately 1,450 references, and the textbook by Elchanan Cohn, *The Economics of Education* (Cambridge, Mass.: Ballinger, rev. ed., 1979), contained a bibliography with approximately 1,900 entries. These lists, however, were neither classified nor chronological.

[54] Mark Blaug, "The Empirical Status of Human Capital Theory: A Slightly Jaundiced Survey," *Journal of Economic Literature*, Vol. 14 (September 1976), pp. 827-855; Sherwin Rosen, "Human Capital: A Survey of Empirical Research," in Ronald C. Ehrenberg, ed., *Research in Labor Economics: An Annual Compilation of Research*, Vol. 1 (Greenwich, Conn.: Jai Press, 1977), pp. 3-39.

[55] Blaug, "The Empirical Status," p. 827.

[56] Economists had better avoid speaking of "theory of information" when they talk about economic theory. "Theory of information," or rather "information theory" is the name of a discipline that embodies the "mathematical theory of communication" (developed by Claude Shannon in 1948) and possibly a few other theories such as the theories of semantic information, coding theories, etc., but is quite unrelated to the role of information in the economy or in economics. These distinctions will be addressed in Volume IV, *The Disciplines of Information*.

[57] Jack Hirshleifer, "Where Are We in the Theory of Information?" *American Economic Review*, Papers and Proceedings, Vol. 63 (May 1973), pp. 31-39. The quoted phrase occurs in the first sentence of the article.

of Behavior, and Categories of Information." II. "Technological Information: The Underinvestment Issue." III. "Market Information." Each of these groups is subdivided. The "modes of behavior," distinguished in the first group, are either those of "possessors of knowledge" or of "seekers of knowledge." The possessors may (1) use their knowledge for their own purposes, that is, for their own decisions or activities, (2) sell it, or (3) disseminate it free of charge; the seekers of knowledge may (1) generate the knowledge by their own research, (2) purchase it, or (3) obtain it through monitoring (including spying). A fourth possibility is misinformation and deception, which may induce the recipient to "evaluate" and the transmitter to "authenticate" the messages conveyed. What Hirshleifer classified here so meticulously, however, was not actual but merely potential literature. Only when he proceeded to distinguish, still within the first group, possibly "economically significant attributes" of knowledge— dividing them into "certainty," "diffusion," "applicability," "environmental versus behavioral" reference, and "relevance to decisionmaking"—did he deal with problems that had actually been raised and discussed in the literature.

In the second group, "Technological Information: The Underinvestment Issue," Hirshleifer discussed (A) the problems of technical invention and of the patent system (which provides temporary monopolies as incentives to avoid underinvestment in inventive and developmental activities); (B) the problems of seeking and using "knowledge of particular circumstances of time and place,"[58] and the problems of disclosing the results of securities analysis by insiders who may engage in speculative trading in the corporation's own stock;[59] and (C) the problems of transferability of knowledge, with the possibility of overproduction of information under (imaginary) conditions of "perfect transferability" and the problems of "authenticity" and sellers' guarantees.

The third group, "Market Information," was subdivided into (A) information about price, (B) information about quality or brand, and (C) market-information processes and social efficiency.

The enumeration of the types of subjects that Hirshleifer omitted in his 1973 survey—not because he regarded them as less important but only because of constraints of time and space—may serve as a

---

[58] Friedrich A. Hayek, "The Use of Knowledge in Society," *American Economic Review*, Vol. 35 (September 1945), pp. 519-530.

[59] Eugene F. Fama and Arthur B. Laffer, "Information and Capital Markets," *Journal of Business*, Vol. 44 (July 1971), pp. 289-298.

supplementary classification.[60] (1) Knowledge implicitly or explicitly assumed as given in the theory of the firm with its demand functions (selling opportunities), cost functions (production possibilities), oligopolistic conjectures (rivals' reactions), etc.; (2) Knowledge explicitly assumed in bargaining and game theory; (3) Knowledge (expectations) implicit or explicit in macroeconomic theory, including positions of Keynesian equilibrium and disequilibrium; (4) Knowledge (expectations) of unemployed workers in search of better jobs than those immediately available; (5) Knowledge and uncertainty regarding future incomes and needs, leading to a demand for money to hold as liquid transactions-and-contingency balances; (6) Knowledge and uncertainty regarding future appreciation or depreciation of assets (portfolios), leading to a demand for money to hold as liquid speculative balances; (7) Knowledge emerging and changing, and giving rise to adaptive expectations and successive learning; (8) Knowledge transmitted among management and staff personnel of organizations in ways conducive to efficient decision-making.

Sometimes it is not easy to know whether an author surveying the literature really meant to undertake a comprehensive classification or only to offer a selection of topics or papers he found interesting to discuss. Yet, "comprehensive" does not necessarily mean "complete." One might expect Hirshleifer's classification to be complete, since he offered one arrangement for the literature he covered and another for the literature he omitted—and logic does not allow a third class. One should not be surprised, however, to find that certain subjects discussed in the literature and meriting inclusion cannot be fitted into the slots provided.

An Expository Survey

Hirshleifer offered another list in "An Expository Survey" presented in 1976 in a paper written jointly with John Riley.[61] The authors did not, however, aim at an exhaustive classification but intended only to give a selective survey of applications of the "new theory of information" in economics. Only five kinds of analysis

---

[60] I am taking considerable liberties in paraphrasing Hirshleifer's formulations in the hope of making his propositions more lucid and more euphoneous. Moreover, I consistently substitute "knowledge" for "information." Only in Nos. 3, 7, and 8 are *flows* of knowledge, and hence processes of informing, involved.

[61] Jack Hirshleifer and John G. Riley, "The New Economics of Information," Discussion Paper No. 14 (University of California at Los Angeles, July 1976). This paper was presented at the annual meeting of the American Economic Association, held in August 1976 in Atlantic City.

were included: (1) optimization of decisions regarding the receipt and use of knowledge; (2) influence of expectations regarding the receipt of costless information; (3) effects of inequality of stocks or flows of knowledge available to sellers and buyers of goods and services; (4) private and social benefits and costs of research-and-development activities; and (5) the efficiency of existing markets in generating prices that give the right signals for producers, consumers, sellers, and buyers to act in conformance with the principle of optimum allocation of resources. It is clear that this is merely a small selection of important topics in the economics of knowledge.

The most ambitious survey, prepared by the same two authors in 1979, was designed to take account of the "recent explosive progress in the economics of uncertainty" and of the "theoretical developments that have brought about this intellectual revolution."[62] In this paper Hirshleifer and Riley go beyond a survey of the literature: they "go somewhat more deeply into selected applications in order to convey some impression of the potential richness and power of the theory."[63] I shall confine myself, however, to the author's classification system.

The authors of the survey see a fundamental dichotomy in the field: Part I includes the economics of uncertainty and Part II, the economics of information. "The two categories correspond to what might be called passive versus active responses to our limitations of knowledge. In Part I individuals may be said to *adapt* to the fact of uncertainty; in Part II they are allowed also to *overcome* uncertainty by engaging in informational activities."[64] Informational activities are said to be "non-terminal in that the final decision is deferred while awaiting or actively seeking new evidence which will, it is anticipated, reduce uncertainty."[65]

The survey article has 150 bibliographical references to books, articles, papers in collective volumes, dissertations, and unpublished manuscripts; 5 references are to publications before 1940, 20 to publications from 1941 through 1960, and 125 to pieces published or written in the period 1961 to 1978. Here is the outline of the survey; the key words and phrases within parentheses are, except for a few paraphrases, literally quoted from Hirshleifer and Riley.

[62] Jack Hirshleifer and John G. Riley, "The Analytics of Uncertainty and Information—An Expository Survey," *Journal of Economic Literature*, Vol. 17 (December 1979), pp. 1375-1421. The quoted clauses are from pp. 1375 and 1376.

[63] Ibid., p. 1376.

[64] Ibid., p. 1377.

[65] Ibid., p. 1378.

1   THE ECONOMICS OF UNCERTAINTY

1.1   *Decision Under Uncertainty*

1.1.1   The Menu of Acts (terminal distinguished from non-terminal or informational)

1.1.2   The Probability Function (subjective probability; uncertainty versus risk; confidence)

1.1.3   The Consequence Function (interactions of acts and states; probabilistic consequences)

1.1.4   The Utility Function and the Expected-Utility Rule (rational choice; cardinal preference scales)

1.1.5   Risk-Aversion and the Risk-Bearing Optimum of the Individual (gambling; fair odds)

1.2   *Market Equilibrium under Uncertainty*

1.2.1   Risk-Sharing (share cropping; contract curves)

1.2.2   Insurance (social risk; state independent utilities; adverse selection and moral hazard)

1.2.3   Complete and Incomplete Market Regimes, the Stockmarket Economy, and Optimal Production Decisions

1.2.4   Other Applications (optimal contracts; corporate finance; optimal behavior regarding accidents; the value of life; the discount rate for public investment)

2   THE ECONOMICS OF INFORMATION

2.1   *Informational Decision-Making*

2.1.1   Acquisition of Information (prior confidence and value of information; informativeness of messages)

2.1.2   Other Informational Activities (disseminating; pushing; publishing; evaluating; authenticating; monitoring)

2.1.3   Emergent Information and the Value of Flexibility (waiting for emergent information; flexible choices)

2.2   *Public Information and Market Equilibrium*

2.2.1   Equilibrium in Complete versus Incomplete Market Regimes (absence of prior-round markets; numeraire-contingent markets; futures markets)

2.2.2   Speculation (uncertainty of future spot prices; hedging; price risks and quantity risks)

2.3   *The Economics of Research and Invention*
       (conflict between efficient use of information and sufficient motivation for its production; under and overinvestment in inventive activity; fugitive or

One may note the symmetry between the two categories in the economics of uncertainty and the first two categories in the economics of information: both distinguish between decision-making and market equilibrium (that is, between models of individual conduct and models of hypothetical end results of actions, reactions, and interactions of all agents involved). Symmetry and internal consistency are not so well served by the other three categories in the economics of information; but slots have to be provided for problems that cannot be sorted or forced into elegant patterns. The scheme proposed by Hirshleifer and Riley is better suited for a systematic presentation of the economic theory of uncertainty and information than for a sorting of the literature. I suppose that the authors intended their scheme only as an outline for their analysis and discussion. For example, subsection 1.1.1, "The Menu of Acts," is the place chosen for explaining the distinction between "terminal" and "nonterminal" actions, not a slot in which to collect any titles of publications. Similarly, subsection 1.1.3, "The Consequence Function," offers expository arguments but cites no literature. In several subsections the authors show novel ways to present problems and suggest solutions but give only a few references to other writers who have contributed to the issues in question. I conclude that the scheme was devised to organize the exposition of the theoretical problematic, not to catalogue existing literature.

An Outline for an Economic Analysis of Information

One of the most prolific and original writers on the economics of information, Joseph Stiglitz, is now in the process of completing a volume tentatively called *Information and Economic Analysis*. The table of contents runs at present to eight parts organized in 31 chapters. It is interesting to see this rough outline, because it does suggest the following classification scheme: A. The Theory of Screening; B. The Theory of Self-Selection; C. The Theory of Moral Hazard; D. Prices, Information, and Incentives; E. Search and Imperfect Information in Product Markets; F. Applications of the General Theory (including the issues of discrimination, and implications of imperfect information for labor markets and capital markets).

This outline may be helpful in any attempt to construct a more comprehensive classification system. This holds for Stiglitz's volume as well as for Hirshleifer's and Riley's expository survey. That any classification, however, can remain workable for only a short time should be clear to anybody who realizes that the literature is growing at an enormous rate and that the emphasis on particular issues or topics is changing fast. We therefore should look, at least for a moment, into the general criteria that may guide us in classifying the stock and flow of the literature.

Choice of General Criteria

Early in this chapter I discussed the conditions for deciding when a subject treated in the literature should be recognized under a new heading as a new subspecialty, or a new group or subgroup in a classification. The usual and quite reasonable criterion of classification has been the relative volume of the flow of new articles: when the number of new articles about a particular subject becomes rather large and seems to go on increasing, the class is subdivided into specialties or subspecialties. The rationale of this process of branching and twigging is twofold: On the one hand, there are the narrower specialists who need new outlets for their output and promote the establishment of new journals serving their specialty; on the other hand, there are the newcomers to the field who will no longer be overwhelmed by the size of the literature they are compelled to absorb if the field is split into manageable subfields. Thus the subfields become recognized specialties or subspecialties.

A new approach to the identification of specialties that are about to become autonomous is the establishment of boundaries by means of citation analysis. The analyst finds clusters of articles and books linked either by cocitation or by bibliographic coupling. "In co-citation, earlier documents become linked because they are later cited together; in bibliographic coupling, later documents become linked because they cite the same earlier documents."[66] Either of these approaches can easily verify, first, the development of an economics of knowledge and information and, later, the development of such subspecialties as the theory of decision-making, the theory of human capital, the theory of search, and the theory of the growth of the knowledge industries. The authors cited would surely include the economists Jacob Marschak, Theodore W. Schultz, Gary Becker, Jacob Mincer, George Stigler, Kenneth Boulding, and perhaps Fritz Machlup, to mention only those of the 1960 to 1965 vintages. I am not embarking on an actual citation count, because it would be too time consuming.[67]

The size of the flow of articles cannot, however, be accepted as the ultimate criterion for a bibliographic classification. A systematic treatment of the phenomena in a universe of discourse may call for separate subclasses even if the literature has been unbalanced, showering one application of the same theoretical principle with scores of contributions while giving only scant attention to another. Think, for example, of the labor market and the capital market as two subjects inviting inquiries into the significance of incomplete information available to the parties in question. If there were ten times as many articles on the labor market as on the capital market, this would not justify disallowing a rubric for publications about the role of imperfect knowledge in the market for capital. Conceivably there may be null classes if systematic treatment calls for them for the sake of consistency; chances are that they may be filled later, unless the conceptual framework of the discipline is radically altered.

Theoretically Sound But Easy to Find

The principle just advanced should not, however, be accorded exclusive allegiance, for it may be in conflict with the pragmatic rule that a bibliographic classification be serviceable. After all, the majority of those to be served are incompletely informed. Theoretical soundness of the classification is surely desirable, but compromises may be advisable. Some highly intelligent distinctions, fitting perfectly into the conceptual framework of the theorist, may be unknown and even unintelligible to the user of the bibliography. He would be served better by categories and designations with which he is fa-

[66] Eugene Garfield, Morton V. Malin, and Henry Small, "Citation Data as Science Indicators," in Yehuda Elkana, Joshua Lederberg, Robert K. Merton, Arnold Thackrey, and Harriet Zuckerman, eds., *Toward a Metric of Science: The Advent of Science Indicators* (New York: Wiley, 1978), p. 185.

[67] The *Social Science Citation Index* has appeared only since 1973.

miliar. After all, he wants to find what he seeks quickly and with a minimum of effort.

A few concrete examples may clarify the problem of unconventional and unexpected designations of headings that may be unhelpful to novices in the field: "asymmetrical information," "noisy monopolists," "informational externalities," "contingent markets," and "linear guarantees." All of these terms are perhaps—despite the lack of euphony or grace—acceptable in the contexts in which they are used, but ambiguous out of context. They may serve expository purposes in the articles for which they were coined, but they are not self-explanatory expressions. Their appearance in a subject index may arouse a reader's curiosity, but they will not help a searcher to find easily what he is looking for.

Special Bibliographies versus Intellectual Histories

A serious problem of special bibliographies, of lists of the monographs and articles focusing on some special issue—such as the economics of information and knowledge—lies in the fact that the particular issue or subject may have been covered in general treatises together with dozens or hundreds of other issues. Some of the treatises may have anticipated the discoveries supposedly made by the new specialists; they may have provided a more balanced treatment of the particular issue, precisely by discussing it in broader context together with other aspects of economic activity. Should then the special bibliography include these comprehensive volumes and give the "chapter and verse" where the discussions or allusions can be found?

An affirmative answer to this question would impose on the bibliographer a responsibility that only the historian of ideas can appropriately assume. In effect, then, the question has to be answered in the negative, although this negative answer results in bibliographies that give a distorted picture of intellectual history. The early general works, which may be not only occasional and casual precursors but actually the originators and first expositors of the issues in question, are ordinarily omitted in the bibliography, whereas the monographic elaborations and narrowly focused articles are featured prominently. If a history of the literature were inferred from a special bibliography, it would look more recent and more modern than it should, in that it omits the prehistory of the specialty.

Perhaps one ought to distinguish between two kinds of omissions in special bibliographies: not only are many of the special issues discussed in more comprehensive treatises left out by the compiler of the special bibliography, but also a particular emphasis, or methodological principle, that pervades the treatise but is not advertised in subtitles or chapter titles may escape the bibliographer's attention. To illustrate the distinction, I may refer once more to Adam Smith's treatment of schooling and training as formation of human capital, an idea he presented in a few pages of the *Wealth of Nations*, a large book offering many hundreds of ideas that later became the subject of specialists' investigations.[68] As an example of the second type— the general emphasis of a comprehensive treatise—I may refer to Carl Menger's *Principles of Economics*.[69] This work, published in 1871, might well have been given a subtitle containing the words "knowledge, uncertainty, and subjective value," for these notions pervade the exposition and are essential to the argument presented. In the absence of such a subtitle, however, bibliographers of the economics of information and knowledge have overlooked this important contribution to the field.[70]

The role of experience, information, expectations, and uncertainty in the determination of the demand for cash balances had been analyzed long before a special literature on these matters came into existence. The earlier analyses, however, were part of general monetary theory, included in comprehensive treatises. Thus, although Ludwig von Mises[71] and Alfred Marshall[72] had presented theories of the pertinent relationships, their expositions have not been included in most special bibliographies.[73]

[68] Adam Smith (1776), see footnote 45, above in this chapter.

[69] Carl Menger, *Grundsätze der Volkswirtschaftslehre* (Vienna: Braumüller, 1871). English translation, *Principles of Economics* (Glencoe, Ill.: Free Press, 1950).

[70] According to Erich Streissler, this "great book ... is, above all, basically an *information theory*, economic theory under uncertainty. . . ." Erich Streissler, "Menger's Theories of Money and Uncertainty: A Modern Interpretation," in John R. Hicks and Wilhelm Weber, eds., *Carl Menger and the Austrian School of Economics* (Oxford: Clarendon, 1973), p. 161. (Italics in the original.) — In a more recent article Israel Kirzner pointed to "Menger's recognition of the importance of knowledge, of error, and of uncertainty, in the economic process," and furnished ample documentation of Menger's "constant stress on problems of information." Israel Kirzner, "The Entrepreneurial Role in Menger's System," *Atlantic Economic Journal*, Volume 6 (September 1978), p. 32.

[71] Ludwig von Mises, *Theorie des Geldes und der Umlaufsmittel* (Munich and Leipzig: Duncker & Humblot, 1912; 2d ed. 1924). English translation *The Theory of Money and Credit* (London: Jonathan Cape, 1934; new ed., New Haven: Yale University Press, 1953).

[72] Alfred Marshall, *Money, Credit, and Commerce* (London: Macmillan, 1924).

[73] Lionel Robbins recognized these contributions to the theories of the value of money within the theory of uncertainty and subjective valuation: "Professor von Mises shares with Marshall and one or two others the merit of having assimilated the treatment of this theory [the theory of the value of money] to the general categories of the pure theory of value; and his emphasis in the course of this assimilation on

Our conclusions should be obvious: special bibliographies may be helpful to the historian of ideas but cannot substitute for intellectual history. Indeed, the historian's primary task is to search for the origins of particular ideas in general works and even in obscure places, not just in sources that advertise their contents and concerns in their titles.

---

the relation between uncertainty and the size of the cash holding and the dependence of certain monetary phenomena on the absence of foresight, anticipates much that has proved most fruitful in more recent speculation in these matters." Lionel Robbins, "Introduction to Ludwig von Mises" in Mises, *The Theory of Money and Credit.*

CHAPTER 10

A New Classification

I SHALL NOW PROPOSE my own classification of the literature on the economics of knowledge and information. I cannot, after all that I have said, expect that my attempt will satisfy all specialists in the field or even be workable for years to come. The flow of writing in some subspecialties may dry up before long, and new subspecialties will attract the interest of researchers. For the time being, however, the following scheme may be serviceable.

SEVENTEEN SUBJECT GROUPS

The scheme consists of 17 subject groups divided into 115 subgroups. To facilitate an all-encompassing overview I shall first present the 17 main headings.

1. The Economics of Knowledge and Information: General
2. Production and Distribution of Knowledge: Knowledge Industries, Information Services, Information Machines
3. Ignorance, Chance, Risk, and Uncertainty as Factors in the Explanation of Individual Choices and Particular Economic Institutions and Phenomena
4. Uncertainty, Risk-Aversion, Venture Spirit, Innovativeness, and Alertness as Factors in the Explanation of Entrepreneurship and Profit
5. New Knowledge (Invention, Discovery) and Its Application (Innovation, Imitation) as Factors in Economic Growth
6. The Transfer of Technology and Know-How
7. Economic Forecasting
8. Cost and Value, Private or Social, of Information and Alternative Information Systems
9. Decision Theory and Game Theory
10. Decision-Making by Consumers with Incomplete and Uncertain Knowledge
11. Decision-Making by Workers and Job Seekers with Incomplete and Uncertain Knowledge

12. Decision-Making by Private Firms, in Various Market Positions, with Incomplete and Uncertain Knowledge
13. Policy-Making by Governments and Public Agencies with Incomplete and Uncertain Knowledge
14. The Formation and Revision of Expectations and Their Role in Economic Dynamics
15. The Role of Information, Knowledge, Expectations, Risks, and Uncertainty in the Functioning of Markets and the Formation of Prices
16. Prices as Information System for Resource Allocation and Product Distribution in Market Economies and Planned Economies; National Programming and Planning
17. Human Capital: The Accumulation of Knowledge and Skills

Most of the critical comments received from those on whom I have tried out this scheme related to the order of the subject groups. Some wanted Human Capital to follow Group 2; some wanted Groups 3 and 4 moved down after Group 8; and so forth. Although the proposed arrangement could no doubt be improved, no arrangement would suit every taste or preconception, and there is no purpose to proving that the particular order chosen is better than any possible alternatives.

The next step is to present the classification together with the subgroups and with some explanatory comments.

1. The Economics of Knowledge and Information: General

1.1 General; 1.2 Collective Works and Anthologies; 1.3 Surveys, Bibliographies, Classifications.

Group 1, the "general" category, may accommodate publications that are regarded as either *fundamental* to the economics of knowledge and information or so *wide* in scope that the book or article in question defies attempts to assign it to some specific subject group.

A piece of writing may be called fundamental if, for example, it outlines or treats of the conceptual framework designed for the whole area of inquiry. It may be called too wide for a more narrowly delineated subject group if it straddles several of those provided in the classification scheme. Many publications could with equal justification be listed under two or three subject groups; in this case, they may be assigned to one group and can still be found without undue effort. But a book or article that straddles many subject groups could easily be lost to a searcher if it were placed, more or less arbitrarily, in one niche into which it would fit no better than in several others. The searcher's convenience is served better by having the multifaceted piece located in the general lobby of the edifice.

The group "General" is divided into three subgroups: 1.1 General, 1.2 Collective Works and Anthologies, and 1.3 Surveys, Bibliographies, Classifications. Under 1.1 one may place discussions of such fundamental distinctions as between knowledge as a stock and information as a flow, between knowledge as a state of knowing and information as a process designed to produce such a state, between knowledge as things known of enduring validity and relevance and information as messages transmitted or received about some things of only temporary or even ephemeral relevance, or between learning to "know what" and learning to "know how." Also under 1.1 one may wish to find writings on the general implications of the cost of obtaining desired information or of increases in the demand for information when the discussion is not linked to more specific issues of applied economics. (For example, one should look for writings on technological inventions, secret or patented, under 5.2 or 5.7, and for writings on special aspects of public goods under 13.5 or 16.2. For applied "search theory" one should look under 10.2, 11.3, or 12.6, depending on who searches—consumers, job seekers, or business firms.)

No explanations are needed for 1.2 Collective Works and Anthologies and 1.3 Surveys, Bibliographies, Classifications.

2. Production and Distribution of Knowledge: Knowledge Industries, Information Services, Information Machines

2.1 General; 2.2 Education; 2.3 Research and Development; 2.4 Print Media of Communication; 2.5 Electronic Mass Media of Communication; 2.6 Addressed Telecommunication; 2.7 Artistic Creation and Communication: Theater, Music, Dance, Cinema, Museums, and Art Galleries; 2.8 Libraries; 2.9 Science Information Services; 2.10 Technological Information Services; 2.11 Medical and Health Information Services; 2.12 Other Professional Information Services; 2.13 Financial Information Services; 2.14 Business Information Services and Management; 2.15 Government Information Services; 2.16 Advertising and Public Relations; 2.17 Information Machines and Equipment.

This group contains publications on the economic aspects of activities designed to generate or disseminate knowledge, or to produce machines or other facilities for processing information. General or comprehensive discussions of this broad area will come under 2.1.

Subgroup 2.2 is for Education, the largest of the knowledge industries. Since education at all levels can be regarded as investment in
human skills and capabilities resulting in future benefits, pecuniary
or psychic, it is often treated as a formation of human capital. When
analyses emphasize this aspect of the economics of education, they
should be classified in Group 17 Human Capital, particularly under
17.3 Differential Flows of Earnings and Their Sources; 17.4 Rates of
Return to Schooling; and 17.8 Public Policies for Education, Training
and Manpower. Many titles could with equal justification be listed
either in Group 17 or in 2.2. Where the investment aspects are not
paramount, Subgroup 2.2 is the preferred placement: for example,
studies on the cost-effectiveness of schooling, the comparative effi-
ciencies of alternative allocations of resources, the financing of education, subsidies, student loans, tuition, teachers' salaries, other
costs of schooling, public and private, and so forth, belong in 2.2.

Writings on the economics of research and development should
be listed under 2.3, except where their focus is on invention and
innovation or on the incentives governments have instituted for the
promotion of these activities. Where the emphasis is on these aspects,
the publications in question should go into Group 5 New Knowledge,
which provides also a slot for writings on technology and economic
welfare and growth. Sometimes research is regarded as another method
of accumulating human capital, and publications stressing this aspect would qualify for Group 17. Even if they were placed there,
there would remain enough for 2.2. Indeed, this subgroup of Knowledge Production is well filled.

Subgroup 2.4 accommodates publications on the economics of the
print media of communication. Economists have not until lately been
very active in this area; now, in connection with revisions of the
copyright law and with apprehensions concerning the viability of
scientific and scholarly publishing, the flow of publications has considerably widened. The print media comprise books, journals, magazines of various types, and a large variety of serials, including newsletters, newspapers, indexing and abstracting services, reports and
other printed materials, such as superseding catalogues and direc-
tories. Studies of the economics of copyright will be more appropriately placed under 5.7, together with the literature on patents and
other incentives for the production of new knowledge.

The electronic mass media of communication are chiefly radio and
television broadcasting. Some of the relevant economic literature,
listed under 2.5, raise fundamental questions of natural monopolies,
operated or franchised by government, because of the scarcity of
frequencies (wave lengths) within the technologically exploitable

bands. Several other problems of economic organization—local or regional stations versus national networks, commercial advertising versus pay television without commercials, to mention only two examples—have been widely discussed in publications belonging to this subgroup.

The economics of addressed communication, chiefly telegraph, telephone, and postal service, is the subject of the literature assembled under 2.6. It is concerned with issues like natural versus artificial monopoly, public versus private ownership and operation, principles of regulation, cost conditions with possible economies of scale over certain ranges of output, differences in the rates of expansions of demand, and actual and expected changes in technology.

Subgroup 2.7 provides the bibliographic home for literature on the economics of artistic creation and communication: theater, music, dance, cinema, museums and art galleries. A finer breakdown of this subgroup might be preferable, but it would have caused problems in classifying works that treat of all the arts, the fine arts together with the performing arts, for example, in connection with the justification of government subsidies.

The literature on economic problems of libraries is sufficiently large to warrant a separate subgroup, 2.8. Because of the large flow of writing on various information services, a single subgroup could not accommodate publications on all specialized information sources. Thus, the various sources were given separate slots: 2.9 Science Information Services; 2.10 Technological Information Services; 2.11 Medical and Health Information Services; 2.12 Other Professional Information Services (chiefly for or by lawyers and accountants); 2.13 Financial Information Services (including banking, securities, insurance); 2.14 Business Information Services and Management; and 2.15 Government Information Services. This breakdown corresponds fairly closely to the one I used in my 1962 work and plan to use in the later volumes of the present work.

That the economics of advertising and public relations needs a separate subgroup, 2.16, will hardly be questioned: the flow of literature on this topic has been and continues to be wide and rapid. The last subgroup, 2.17, is given to information machines and equipment, a subject that, with the rapid development of computer technology, has attracted increasing attention from economic researchers.

3. Ignorance, Chance, Risk, and Uncertainty as Factors in the Explanation of Individual Choices and Particular Economic Institutions and Phenomena

3.1 General; 3.2 Uncertainty and Time Preference; 3.3 Money and Liquidity; 3.4 Insurance; 3.5 Gambling; 3.6 Hedging and Speculation; 3.7 Guarantees.

Even a bibliography confined to old literature on the subjects served by this group would be quite voluminous; but the additions by more recent writers have much expanded it. The writings in question attribute the existence of particular choices, institutions, or phenomena in our society to the unquestioned fact that all knowledge on which actions are based is incomplete and uncertain. Knowledge of the future can only be expectation; and action designed to affect future states or events can only be based on presumption of knowledge.

The case of insurance may serve as our example: people want insurance, and are willing to pay for it, because they seek protection for themselves or other beneficiaries against the risk of damages such as loss of income, loss of valuables, or contingent expenditures through death, accidents, illness, fire, hailstorm, theft, and so on. This protection through indemnification is offered at a price that reflects the statistical probability, calculated from frequencies of occurrence in the past, of such damages arising for members of a large group of persons, real or legal. No individual can know whether and when he will suffer such damages, or when he will die, but for large groups the probabilities can be estimated. Thus the institution of insurance exists because the probabilities for large groups can within limits be calculated. If each individual could know with certainty what damages he was to suffer at what time and what damages he was to be spared, he would seek insurance only against the former and none against the latter. Obversely, if the insurer could know with certainty which individuals were to suffer damages at what time, he would offer insurance only at prices equal to the present value of the full damage, and nobody would be attracted to purchase such insurance.

It follows that only the impossibility of foreknowledge of particular events, of the time of their occurrence, and of the magnitude of the damages involved, can account for insurance contracts being supplied and demanded. The economic analysis of these problems has recently become more involved by the introduction of special conditions such as inequalities in the distribution of knowledge—one party being better informed than the other—and the possibility of manipulating the hazards (accidents, sickness, fire). The literature on the economics of insurance is accommodated under Subgroup 3.4, but alternative places are at the bibliographer's disposal. Analyses of decision-making by consumers with regard to buying insurance may be entered under 10.5; studies of the influence of unemployment insurance upon the incidence and duration of search-unemployment may be under 11.5; and writings on the role of information, expectations, and uncertainty in the functioning of the

insurance market may be under 15.7. The availability of these multiple choices encumbers both the bibliographer's and the searcher's
tasks but is a concession to a more methodical division of the field
in accordance with accepted principles of economic analysis.

For three other subgroups in this category the basic notion, that
certain institutions or practices in our society could not exist if the
future were known with precision and certainty, is almost equally
obvious. Surely there could be no "Gambling," since the chances of
winning or losing bets on uncertain outcomes, and the fun (for some
people) of taking such chances, are heart and soul of this activity.
Subgroup 3.5 is created to list the pertinent literature, though there
will be also alternative rubrics, such as in Group 14 Expectations or
in Subgroup 15.5 Stock Markets. Subgroup 3.6 is for writings on
hedging and speculation, activities that evidently exist only because
knowledge of future changes in prices is uncertain. Subgroup 15.9
Futures Markets provides an alternative. The unpredictable probability of a particular piece of a manufactured product turning out to
be defective, the buyers' desire to reduce the risk of getting stuck
with a "lemon," and the seller's desire to keep the loyalty of his
customers, explain the widespread use of producers' guarantees to
replace defective products or parts. Writings on the economics of
guarantees find their place in Subgroup 3.7, if they are not placed
in 15.2 Product Markets.

Classifiers' decisions are less obvious in the case of the existence
of money. There is no doubt that the size of the demand for liquid
cash balances is a function of uncertainty: households and firms want
to be prepared to meet contingencies, such as possible gaps in the
future flow of income, possible needs for repairs, medicines, or medical services, possible increases in prices of goods regularly purchased, emerging opportunities to buy goods or assets at bargain
prices, and so forth. The greater the probability of many such surprises, the greater the expectations of unexpected events or changes,
the larger will be the liquidity preference, the demand for money to
hold. Some writers on money, however, go much further and contend
that "in a world of certainty there is no need for the physical existence of markets or for money."[1] This is probably an overstatement.
Direct exchange, or barter, is inefficient; to engage in indirect exchange, that is, selling to a customer who is not at the same time a
source of supply of the goods and services the seller wants to acquire,
is greatly facilitated by a general medium of exchange, money, even

[1] Charles A. E. Goodhart, *Money, Information and Uncertainty* (London: Macmillan,
1975), p. 5.

if there is no uncertainty about the things wanted, about their suppliers, and about their prices. This is not the place, however, to argue the merits (or truth values) of particular propositions. It suffices to recognize that a fundamental association exists between the theory of money and the economics of knowledge and information. Writings on this theme are under 3.3.

4. Uncertainty, Risk-Aversion, Venture Spirit, Innovativeness, and Alertness as Factors in the Explanation of Entrepreneurship and Profit

4.1 General; 4.2 Uncertainty Bearing, Entrepreneurship, and Profit; 4.3 Innovation, Entrepreneurship, and Profit; 4.4 Alertness, Entrepreneurship, and Profit.

This group is in one respect significantly different from most of the other groups in this classification: some of the important literature on this subject is more than sixty years old, and there have been few additions in recent years. The two chief exponents of the theories concerned were Joseph Schumpeter (1911) and Frank Knight (1923). According to Schumpeter, the entrepreneur makes profits because he is an innovator and it takes time for the profits to be eroded by competition from imitators. According to Knight, some entrepreneurs make profits, whereas other lose, because they are willing or eager to bear the uncertainties associated with buying productive services to produce and sell products. Subgroup 4.2 is designed to contain publications by Knight, his precursors, followers, and critics: Subgroup 4.3, publications by Schumpeter and his followers and critics.

Knight's theory has the venturesome entrepreneur expose himself to uncertainties shunned by other producers; Schumpeter's theory has the venturesome entrepreneur do novel things while other producers stick to old ways that have proved relatively safe. Thus, novel knowledge and uncertain knowledge are at the core of these theories. The rare additions to this set of theories come from Neo-Austrian economists, such as Israel Kirzner (1979), who see in alertness and speedy response to emerging knowledge the characteristics of entrepreneurship and the source of profit. Subgroup 4.4 is designed to exhibit these contributions to the literature.

5. New Knowledge (Invention, Discovery) and Its Application (Innovation, Imitation) as Factors in Economic Growth

5.1 General; 5.2 Inventive Activity; 5.3 Innovative Activity; 5.4 Competitive Imitation; 5.5 Learning by Doing; 5.6 Obsolescence of

Knowledge and Skills; 5.7 Patents, Copyrights, and Other Incentives to Create Knowledge; 5.8 Technology and Economic Welfare and Growth.

This group is related to parts of Group 4 in that it also features "new knowledge"; it is not confined, however, to innovation or the venturesome use of emerging knowledge but comprises search activities, invention, and discovery. Publications on the economic aspects of inventive activities are assigned to Subgroup 5.2. Schumpeter's strict differentiation of invention, innovation, and imitation has been generally accepted by economists, and the separation of the respective discussions in different subgroups will probably be approved without dissent. In Subgroup 5.4 Competitive Imitation, one will look for studies on the question of the "optimal" lag of imitation behind innovation, optimal from the point of view of a society materially interested in both generation and utilization of new technology. The expectation of early imitation may reduce the rate of innovation, but delayed imitation implies a reduced rate of utilization.

Subgroup 5.5 Learning by Doing will accommodate writings on a topic initiated by Kenneth Arrow (1962). Learning by doing as a way of acquiring new knowledge is sufficiently different from inventive, innovative, and imitative activities to merit a special place in the classification.

New technological knowledge often reduces and sometimes eliminates the utilization of old knowledge; the competition from the new may make the old obsolete or at least obsolescent. The economic problems implied in this process have often been alluded to but rarely treated in systematic analyses. Any existing or forthcoming literature can be listed in Subgroup 5.6 Obsolescence of Knowledge and Skills.

One of the most crowded subgroups is 5.7 Patents, Copyrights, and Other Incentives to Create Knowledge. One reason why this subgroup is so densely populated is that it combines the literatures on patents of invention and on copyrights for published materials. They are combined because too many economic titles—books and articles—include *both* these instruments for promoting the creation of new knowledge—technological, literary, artistic—through promises of grants of temporary monopoly rights. (Establishing separate subgroups for writings on patents and for writings on copyrights would require a third subgroup for writings that treat of both types of exclusive rights.) Another reason for the size of the literature is that the subject is relatively old and that a heated controversy in the

nineteenth century on the economic justification—benefits and costs—
of the patent system gave rise to a rapid flow of books, pamphlets,
and articles arguing the economic case for maintaining or abolishing
the system or for replacing it by other incentives, such as prizes and
subsidies. In recent times it has been chiefly the existence of specialized societies and of journals dedicated to these subjects that
have given a steady impetus to the production of publishable work
on patent and copyright protection, though most of the contributions
have been about the statutes and their amendments, about legal and
administrative procedures, and about court decisions. But even the
economics of exclusive monopoly rights through patents and copyrights would be an overpopulated area of specialization if all economic reasoning and pleading by lawyers, engineers, and vested
interests were admitted into the bibliography without any sifting,
that is, without eliminating writings below a reasonable minimum
standard.

Another subgroup, 5.8 Technology and Economic Welfare and
Growth, provides an appropriate address for the rapidly growing
literature on the economic effects of increased generation and utilization of technological knowledge. To indicate the type of studies
under this heading one may point to analyses of advances in productivity and of the "unexplained residual" in the annual increases
in gross national product.

6. The Transfer of Technology and Know-How

6.1 General; 6.2 Among Firms and Industries; 6.3 Among Countries.

The innovating and imitating activities dealt with in the writings
corralled in Group 5 are related largely to technological knowledge.
The transfer of such knowledge has received growing recognition as
a subject of economic study, so that its literature deserves a separate
group in the classification. Transfer is understood here in a wide
sense: it is not confined to intentional dissemination of knowledge
but includes obtaining the essential knowledge against the will of
the innovator, be it through devious means or through technical
analysis and imitation of his product.

If technology and know-how are not to constitute a superfluous
pleonasm, just what is the difference between the two terms? Technology may be defined as the science of the technical, practical,
industrial arts, which presents in literary and often also pictorial
form descriptions of materials and processes for combining and fab-
ricating them. Technical know-how, in contradistinction, cannot be

transferred by means of verbal or pictorial description but requires interaction between those who know how to do something and those who want to learn it. This distinction, though not honored by all who use the pair of terms in their writings, can be significant in an analysis of the economic arrangements instrumental in the transfer of the knowledge in question.

Distinctions are made also for transfers to other firms in the same industry, to other industries, and to other countries. Writings on interfirm and interindustry transfers of knowledge are assigned to Subgroup 6.2; writings on international transfers, to Subgroup 6.3. In recent years the interest has been greatest in inquiries about the economic conditions and arrangements fostering transfer of technology to developing countries.

7. Economic Forecasting

7.1 General; 7.2 Forecasting Trends and Fluctuations; 7.3 Projections, Predictions, and Economic Indicators; 7.4 Predicting Stock-Market Prices; 7.5 Forecasting National Aggregates (Output, Employment, Saving, Investment, Price Level); 7.6 Forecasting Prices, Profits, and Interest Rates; 7.7 Forecasting Technological Change.

The literature on economic forecasting is in a class by itself, in that it is more on economic knowledge than on the economics of knowledge; that is, it is not on the roles of knowledge, expectations, and information activities in various microeconomic or macroeconomic theories, but rather on methods of estimating, and on actual estimates of, the magnitudes of economic variables at specified future dates or periods. It would be quite understandable if some economists preferred to exclude publications on economic forecasting from a bibliography on the economics of knowledge and information. On the other hand, forecasts by economic agents and "rational expectations" based on public information and official forecasts are among the determinants of economic actions by individual households, firms, and government agencies, including fiscal and monetary authorities. Thus, it would be somewhat unreasonable or intolerant to insist on excluding the forecasting literature from the bibliography. (Those who deplore its inclusion may skip it.)

The subgroups proposed for this group reflect the unstructured character of the literature. The distinction between trends and fluctuations has long been of great interest to the profession, whereas the distinction between projections and predictions has been emphasized in more recent writings. The literature on economic indicators is more than fifty years old but seems to be in no danger of drying up. Subgroups 7.2 Forecasting Trends and Fluctuations and 7.3 Projections, Predictions, and Economic Indicators should accommodate the pertinent writings.

Writings on stock-market predictions, in Subgroup 7.4, are of various kinds: theoretical discussions of the predictability of share prices, empirical evaluations of past forecasts, current attempts to forecast future stock-price movements, and theoretical arguments about the implications of stock-price forecasts for forecasting other economic developments.

Subgroup 7.5 Forecasting National Aggregates would almost be a null class if only writings before 1930 were to be classified. The art of measuring national aggregates had to be developed before economists could proceed to forecasting them; remember that econometrics, the term and the instrumentarium, was officially introduced only in 1930, and that Kuznets's pathbreaking work on *National Income and Its Composition* was published only in 1941. The technique of measuring does not imply knowledge of the technique of forecasting. Indeed, to know which quantities are to be ascertained and added together does not mean that one knows the forces that influence their changes over time. In any case, by now, forecasting the major items in the national income accounts has become one of the most popular games in the profession.

Subgroup 7.6 Forecasting Prices, Profits, and Interest Rates is proposed chiefly for writings stressing more microeconomic than macroeconomic magnitudes and relationships, though a classifier of literature cannot be more strict in drawing lines than the writers who produce it. The forecasting of changes in price *levels* is so closely linked with the aggregative forecasting game, separating nominal and real GNP growth, that attempts of foretelling the rates of price inflation belong more properly in 7.5 than 7.6. But the tastes of averagers and aggregators are not uniform, and one should not force their articles into Procrustean beds.

A separate slot has to be created for a more specialized topic: Subgroup 7.7 Forecasting Technological Change. There may be some overlap with Group 5, concerned chiefly with new technological knowledge. A theory of induced invention or induced innovation may well extend into attempts to apply it to forecasting future technological change.

8. Cost and Value, Private or Social, of Information and Alternative Information Systems

8.1 General; 8.2 Cost and Value of Greater Accuracy of Information.

The provision of a separate group for this topic may be considered strange in view of the fact that both cost and value are core variables in decision theory—Group 9—and that the literature on decision-making by consumers, workers, private firms, and public agencies seems amply provided for in Groups 10, 11, 12, and 13, respectively. Why then an extra slot for the cost and value of alternative information systems? The justification lies in the fact that alternative information systems are sometimes evaluated independently from the considerations of any decision-maker and from the usual determinants stressed in decision theory. The problem of externalities, for example, is of significance even if neither a firm nor a government is called upon to take action optimizing the system by taking account of, say, economies of scale or of the impossibility of excluding "free riders."

The problem of the optimal allocation of subventions with a budget constraint is related to governmental policy-making, hence to inquiries falling into Group 13, especially Subgroups 13.3, 13.5, 13.6, and 13.7; but some searchers may find the literature they seek much more quickly if it is assembled in Group 8.

9. Decision Theory and Game Theory

9.1 General; 9.2 Statistical Decision Theory; 9.3 Theory of Games; 9.4 Game Theory of Oligopolistic Competitions; 9.5 Group Decision-Making and Bargaining.

No explanation is needed for setting up this group; it is obvious that decision and game theories assume, once they are beyond expositional, didactic preliminaries, that the decision-makers have only incomplete and uncertain knowledge of the things that determine the outcomes of their possible actions.

There will surely be no quarrel about the separation of "Statistical Decision Theory" and "Game Theory" in Subgroups 9.2 and 9.3, respectively. Two other subgroups are proposed for writings on special or applied theory: Subgroup 9.4 Game Theory of Oligopolistic Competition and 9.5 Group Decision-Making and Bargaining. By and large, the great expectations entertained thirty years ago regarding the empirical and predictive fertility of game theory have not been realized. Even in its supposed applications to specific oligopolistic situations, the theory has remained rather formal. Although game theory has helped our general understanding of the decision process, it has not yielded any results that would not have been obtainable from more primitive methods of analysis. These observations may perhaps explain why Subgroup 9.4 has not been filled up to the point of explosion, that is, to an extent that would force a classifier to split it into several subgroups.

10. Decision-Making by Consumers with Incomplete and Uncertain Knowledge

10.1 General; 10.2 Search Effort; 10.3 Learning from Experience; 10.4 Legal Protection of Consumer against Risk; 10.5 Buying Insurance; 10.6 Saving and Asset Holding.

This group is reserved for the literature on consumers' decisions. Subgroup 10.1 accommodates general contributions that transcend the scope of any of the other five subgroups; for example, writing on utility and indifference curves, ordinal versus cardinal utility, substitutability and complementarity, revealed preference, coping with uncertainty, etc. Deliberate search efforts by consumers looking for the best buy, or for a satisfactory purchase, are distinguished from the consumers' learning by experience; writings on search efforts are assigned to 10.2, and on learning without search to 10.3.

Studies of the problem of legal protection of the consumer against buyers' risks, such as the risk of "getting stuck with a lemon," are assembled under 10.4, but there could be multiple listings of publications that emphasize, respectively, the institution of sellers' guarantees under 3.6, and the sellers' policies of advertising, truthful (12.7) or deceptive (12.8). Multiple listings may also be unavoidable for some writings on buying insurance: if they discuss insurance as an economic institution, 3.3 is the most appropriate subgroup; if they analyze the choices that underlie the consumers' decisions, 10.5 is the right slot; and if they focus on insurance markets, on supply as well as demand, 15.7 is the best place.

Of consumers' choices the most difficult to analyze is the decision by the consumer not to consume all his income but to save some of it. Subgroup 10.6 is provided for the literature on saving and asset holding; it will accommodate writings on the microeconomic foundations of macroeconomic consumption functions and saving propensities as well as writings on important aspects of portfolio theory. Alternative subject groups inviting the same or similar writings are 14.6 for aggregate investment and consumption, and 15.5 for stock markets and asset portfolios.

11. Decision-Making by Workers and Job Seekers with Incomplete and Uncertain Knowledge

11.1 General; 11.2 Mobility, Geographic and Occupational; 11.3 Employment Exchanges; 11.4 Wage and Job Search; 11.5 Search-Unemployment; 11.6 Work Effort, Quality, and Earnings; 11.7 Job Training and Work Experience; 11.8 Bargaining, Strikes, and Settlements.

The supply of labor can be derived from the theory of the household, together with the demand for consumer goods, services, and leisure. However, the literature on the economics of labor, even of that part of it that focuses on information and uncertainty, is so rich that it seems preferable to provide a separate group for writings about workers' and job seekers' decisions.

The influence of information about alternative job opportunities is especially strong in the determination of employees' mobility: their willingness to move to other places and into other occupations depends largely on what they learn about the chances of finding a better job—or any job. Writings on labor mobility will be placed in Subgroup 11.2. Among the institutions designed to increase labor mobility, loan programs to finance moving expenses are important, but more fundamental are employment exchanges, since they affect directly the informational basis of mobility. Subgroup 11.3 will accommodate publications on this subject.

The largest number of publications in the last fifteen years has been on "Wage and Job Search," Subgroup 11.4. The more optimistic the job seekers' expectations regarding high pay and good working conditions, the longer will they wait for a job they find acceptable: hence, the phenomenon of "search-unemployment," and the writings about it in 11.5. The effort that individual workers are willing to expend in their potential employment, their regularity and attachment to the job (or low propensity to be absent or to quit), and the quality and accuracy of their work, are not easily judged by the would-be employer; and the job seekers' self-evaluations of their attitudes and capabilities are highly uncertain sources of information. Self-selection for jobs with high or low rates of pay, and credentials, including so-called educational attainment, may have to take the place of testing by the employer. Studies of these problems are under 11.6 Work Effort, Quality, and Earnings. The role of job training and work experience in the screening of applicants, and the role of earnings expectations of workers in deciding whether to keep their old jobs or seek better ones, are under 11.7.

Finally, Subgroup 11.8 Bargaining, Strikes, and Settlements is to accommodate the rich literature on these aspects of labor relations, which depend so markedly on well or poorly informed expectations. That the bargaining part of this literature overlaps with Subgroup 9.5, and several other themes overlap with Subgroup 15.3 Labor Markets, is probably obvious.

12. Decision-Making by Private Firms, in Various Market Positions, with Incomplete and Uncertain Knowledge

12.1 General; 12.2 Market Positions (Pure Competition, Entry, Oligopoly, Monopoly); 12.3 Operations Research and Activities Analysis; 12.4 Investment, Capital, Dividends; 12.5 Organization and Expansion; 12.6 Job, Wage, and Price Discrimination; 12.7 Advertising, Signaling, and Screening; 12.8 Deception and Fraud.

Subgroups are provided for publications on various aspects of decision-making by private firms. Comprehensive or fundamental discourses go into 12.1; writings dealing predominantly with market positions of various types and degrees of competition, into 12.2; and those dealing with operations research or activity analysis associated with the decision-making process, 12.3. Many of the contributions to 12.2 treat of the decisionmaker's conjectures regarding the attitudes of their customers, suppliers, employees, or competitors, and probable reactions to potential changes in price, product quality, working conditions, and so forth. Decisions about investment, borrowing, stock issues, and dividends are the subjects of writings assigned to 12.4. Where the treatment goes beyond financial considerations or is focused on problems of the firm's organization, coordination, or expansion, the writings are shown under 12.5.

Subgroup 12.6 is for publications on discrimination, no matter whether it concerns price differentials for products sold in different markets or to different kinds of buyers, wage differentials for labor of workers of different race, sex, creed, or ethnic origin, or job discrimination through exclusion, or virtual exclusion, of particular groups of workers. Research on these issues has been intensified in recent years, not only because of political pressures and legislative actions but also because novel hypotheses have been advanced to explain the firms' decisions under the influence of conjectures regarding mass reactions to their practices.

Under 12.7 titles on advertising, signaling, and screening will be assembled, though they sometimes overlap with titles under 12.6. Screening devices include rules of thumb that are followed by a firm to avoid the high cost of individual testing and sorting (of labor or materials). Rules for the screening of labor may relate to past work experience or to educational records or certification, or to even broader "signals" such as race, sex, or personal appearance. Signaling has been defined as "the differentiating activities, as they pertain to information."[2] Perhaps "implied information" would convey the meaning of the term; it includes ostentatious as well as ordinary actions, offers, or indications of preparedness to accept certain terms, or, alternatively, information implicit in past achievements (for example, graduation from high school), past affiliations and associa-

---

[2] Michael Spence, "Symposium: The Economics of Information," *Quarterly Journal of Economics*, Vol. 90 (November 1976), p. 592.

tions, or even origin or descent. Advertising, in a narrower sense, is intentional information through words or pictures. Studies of advertising, and also of signaling, may overlap with those on deception, in 12.8.

13. Policy-Making by Governments and Public Agencies with Incomplete and Uncertain Knowledge

13.1 General; 13.2 Tax Policies; 13.3 Macropolicies: Stabilization, Budgeting, Fiscal and Monetary Measures, Employment and Inflation Policies; 13.4 Micropolicies: Conservation, Regulation, Direct Controls; 13.5 Public Investment, Subsidies, and Public Goods; 13.6 Benefits-and-Cost Analysis; 13.7 Research Policies; 13.8 Development Policies, National and Regional.

This group of writings on policy-making by governments and public agencies is the logical sequel to the preceding three groups on decision-making by consumers, workers, and firms. After Subgroup 13.1, for general or comprehensive writings on the implications of incomplete and uncertain knowledge for governmental policy-making, the subsequent seven subgroups divide the literature according to customary areas of economic policy. The division follows current academic practice but is far from satisfactory; for example, in trying to draw a line between macro- and micropolicies. Since "Tax Policies" include both aspects, a separate subgroup, 13.2, is provided for writings about the bearing of information on public choices regarding taxation. For all subgroups, but especially for 13.3 and 13.4 on macro- and micropolicies, an overlap with Group 7 Economic Forecasting is evident. The linking of forecasting with budgeting and the development of macropolicies ought to answer any doubts: where policies presuppose forecasting, and forecasting is oriented towards the formulation of budget and macreconomic policies, the publications in question belong to Subgroup 13.3.

Subgroup 13.5 Public Investment, Subsidies, and Public Goods may vex classifiers in that a public-investment program may serve macroeconomic policy objectives. Yet, the choice of investment is a microeconomic problem; decisions on the total budget—on how much to spend and how to finance the outlays—are different from decisions on what to spend for, what productive facilities to build or what activities to promote. The facilities or activities in question are, more likely than not, designed to produce services in the nature of public goods, services that private enterprise finds unprofitable to provide, chiefly because it cannot capture the external benefits, perhaps because it cannot exclude free riders from sharing them without paying.

The connection with uncertain knowledge is especially noteworthy since the absence of market prices and of otherwise revealed preferences by the beneficiaries—who mistakenly believe that they are getting something for nothing—often makes the valuation of the public goods sheer guesswork. To find some basis, however speculative, for these guesses, economists have developed benefit-and-cost analysis; their writings on this theme are placed under 13.6.

Two other subgroups, 13.7 Research Policies and 13.8 Development Policies, invite commentaries. Governmental policies to carry out, sponsor, or subsidize research are in several respects connected with the realization that knowledge is incomplete and uncertain. The policy objective is to generate more knowledge, fill apparent gaps of knowledge, and reduce uncertainty in some fields of knowledge; the policy is developed with the aid of processes of information that seem reasonably reliable and efficient but are necessarily in the nature of trial and error; and decisions are made on the basis of judgments that cannot help being subjective even if they are reached by a consensus of qualified persons with ample research experience. The development policies treated in writings placed under 13.8 refer, not to the development of research findings—the *D* of *R and D*—but to the economic development of less-developed countries or regions. Our knowledge of the factors promoting or facilitating economic development and growth is fragmentary, woefully uncertain, and highly controversial; moreover, factual knowledge of the attitudes, hidden capabilities, and motivations of the people whose productivity is supposed to be raised, and of their likely reactions to the governmental measures designed to achieve that rise, is almost nonexistent. This explains why some of the writings on development policies concern themselves with the problems of incomplete and uncertain knowledge.

14. *The Formation and Revision of Expectations and Their Role in Economic Dynamics*

14.1 General: Expectations—Elastic, Adaptive, Rational; 14.2 Expectations of Changes in Prices and Sales; 14.3 Expectations of Changes in Interest Rates; 14.4 Expectations of Changes in Income, Individual or Aggregate, Temporary or Permanent; 14.5 Expectations of Changes in Wages, Price Levels, and Employment; 14.6 Expectations of Changes in Investment and Consumption; 14.7 Expectations of Changes in Foreign-Exchange Rates.

Uncertain foreknowledge of future events and developments, usually in the form of expectations, influences the decision-making of many economic agents—individuals, firms, trade associations, trade unions, financial intermediaries, central banks, and fiscal authorities. Publications on the formation and revision of these expectations are assembled in Group 14. The now customary distinction between adaptive expectations and rational expectations is given due recognition by providing Subgroup 14.1 for writings on these concepts and their roles in economic dynamics. The Hicksian considerations of different elasticities of expectations influenced by changes experienced in the immediate past—expecting no further change or a continuing change in the same direction at the same, or a higher or lower rate, or a reversal and return to the previous state—qualify as adaptive expectations.[3] So-called rational expectations rest less on the experiences of the economic agents themselves than on full publicity of all statistical information available in the community and on its "correct" interpretation.

Expectations by economic agents may relate to a variety of economic variables, and five subgroups invite the listings of titles on expectations, with respect to changes in prices, 14.2; interest rates, 14.3; income, 14.4; wages, price levels, and employment, 14.5; and investment and consumption, 14.6. Price expectations, under 14.2, refer to particular prices,[4] whereas expectations of price levels, under 14.5, refer to the purchasing power of money in its relation to wages and employment. Expectations of changes in interest rates, 14.3, are significant in connection with the demand for durable assets, especially securities, and their substitute, cash balances. That is to say, these expectations influence the "speculative" demand for money balances, an important part of liquidity preference. Income expectations, 14.4, may be those of individual consumers, and their decisions may be attributed to temporary or permanent changes in their expected incomes; alternatively, these expectations may be held by policymakers in government or in firms with regard to aggregate (national) income and the resulting effective demand for goods and services. Expectations of levels of investment and employment, 14.6, are, in most publications, viewed as macroeconomic variables. Expectations of changes in foreign-exchange rates will be accommodated in Subgroup 14.7, though 15.8 may be an obvious alternative.

---

[3] John R. Hicks, *Value and Capital* (Oxford: Clarendon, 1939), pp. 204-208. For the role of expectations in "economic dynamics" see pp. 124-127. For the role of speculation and futures markets, see pp. 135-140.

[4] For a "model sequence" of adaptive expectations of cost and price relationships by individual firms in the adjustment process of an industry with a large and increasing number of firms, see my book *The Economics of Sellers' Competition* (Baltimore: Johns Hopkins University Press, 1952), pp. 279-292.

15. The Role of Information, Knowledge, Expectations, Risks, and Uncertainty in the Functioning of Markets and the Formation of Prices

15.1 General (Models of Market Equilibrium); 15.2 Product Markets; 15.3 Labor Markets; 15.4 Capital Markets; 15.5 Stock Markets and Asset Portfolios; 15.6 Short-Term Credit Markets; 15.7 Insurance Markets and Health-Care Systems; 15.8 Foreign-Exchange Markets; 15.9 Futures Markets.

The previous six subject groups, from 9 (Decision Theory) to 14 (Expectations), were designed for studies of decisions and actions by individual economic agents, such as a consumer, a producer, or a worker, and also of groups of agents in the same category (hence not for studies of interactions of two groups on opposite sides of a market). Now, Group 15 is the place for studies of the market mechanism as it is affected by incomplete and uncertain knowledge and inefficient information processes. General models of market equilibrium may be included in 15.1, and another eight subgroups are to accommodate writings on various kinds of markets: markets for products, 15.2; labor, 15.3; capital funds, 15.4; securities, 15.5; short-term credit, 15.6; insurance, including health care, 15.7; foreign exchange, 15.8; and futures contracts, 15.9.

16. Prices as Information System for Resource Allocation and Product Distribution in Market Economies and Planned Economies; National Programming and Planning

16.1 General; 16.2 Market Failures and Public Goods; 16.3 Markets versus Central Plans; 16.4 Indicative Programming in Market Economies; 16.5 Plans and Plan Execution in Socialist Countries; 16.6 Market Socialism.

It is accepted that market prices can have an "informational function," in the sense that they may guide consumers, workers, producers, traders, and entrepreneurs in their decision to buy, choose jobs, produce, sell, rent, hire, lend, invest, and so forth. For at least sixty years economists have speculated whether market prices could be replaced in this function by some techniques of central planning or dirigist organization of the economy, with the outcome satisfying the goal of economic rationality or optimality with given or changing tastes and preferences. The literature on such problems has been general and specific, theoretical and empirical, politically neutral and ideological.

In Subgroup 16.1 general discourses and conceptual analyses may be assembled. Under 16.2 one may place discussions of instances in which market prices cannot give the "right" information (that is, guidance that leads to optimal allocation of resources) or where market prices do not exist, as in the case of public goods that are publicly distributed. Comparisons of the working of the market mechanism with that of central planning and direction will be put under 16.3. Attempts to blend central planning with private enterprise and free markets as, for example, through "indicative programming," will have their published blueprints, descriptions, or appraisals listed in 16.4. Under 16.5 studies of plans and plan execution in socialist economies will be listed; and 16.6 will collect entries for "market socialism," the system of collective or community property of the means of production operated by enterprises buying and selling in competitive markets.

Publications qualify for Group 16 only if they take cognizance of the fact that knowledge of economic relevance—including people's preferences, ambitions, skills, and their perceptions of relevant circumstances of time and place—is widely dispersed and not accessible to any authority in charge of planning.

17. Human Capital: The Accumulation of Knowledge and Skills

17.1 General; 17.2 Contributions to Productivity; 17.3 Differential Flows of Earnings and their Sources; 17.4 Rates of Return to Schooling; 17.5 Training on the Job: Investment and Earnings; 17.6 Individual Decisions and Labor-Market Phenomena; 17.7 The Stock of Human Capital; 17.8 Public Policies for Education, Training, and Manpower.

The subject of this group was mentioned above in connection with the literature on education, in Subgroup 2.2, and on research and development, in 2.3. The likelihood of overlap is great, and multiple listing would seem appropriate for many entries. Whenever education or research is examined from the point of view of (private or social) investment, returns, and associated differentials in the productivity or earnings of labor, the aspect of human capital becomes relevant.

Because of the enormous growth of the literature on human capital its classification into many subgroups will aid the searcher, even if such subdivision increases the need for multiple listing. Subgroup 17.1 is for general, conceptual, and doctrinal writings and for surveys of the subject. Subgroup 17.2 is for discussion of the contributions that the services of human capital have made to the increase of the national product over the years. In Subgroup 17.3 are investigations of the differential flows of earnings and their sources—native ability, drive and diligence, inherited wealth, acquired skills and knowledge, and mere certification of years spent in school. Studies of the rates of return to schooling and job training are to be listed under 17.4 and 17.5, respectively.

Writings on individuals' considerations of expected returns in their decision-making as they reflect on their alternative educational and career choices, will go into Subgroup 17.6, together with studies of the consequent actions and the resulting labor-market phenomena. Subgroup 17.7 is designed to collect studies of the stock of human capital, that is, society's past investment in the knowledge and skills of its members, embodied in the present labor force or entire population. Finally, Subgroup 17.8 is to contain writings on public policies for education, training, and manpower, if they are treated within the conceptual framework of the theories of human capital and comparative returns to investment.

CHAPTER 11

A SAMPLE BIBLIOGRAPHY

THIS CHAPTER provides a sample bibliography of the economics of knowledge and information, containing more than a thousand titles of books and articles. A bibliography approaching complete coverage of the subject would probably contain at least twenty thousand titles. Thus, my sample is at best 5 per cent of the total. No claim can be made that the sample is representative of the total; I have made no attempt to construct a scientific random sample. I have selected relevant titles from the *Index of Economic Articles*, Volumes 11-16 (1969-1974), the *Journal of Economic Literature*, Volume 13-16 (1975-1978), and lists of references appended to books and articles on relevant subjects. In addition I allowed my memory to supply titles that I judged to be of special importance, and included them after appropriate bibliographic checks. Finally I added some more recent publications that attracted my attention.

Filling the Boxes

I have followed the classification scheme described in the preceding chapter. Where the indexes and lists of references failed to supply pertinent items to enter into subgroups provided by my classification, I searched for eligible titles to fill empty boxes. Some subgroups soon became so overcrowded that I had to use restraint in admitting more candidates for inclusion; other subgroups have remained sparsely populated despite diligent search. In one instance a subgroup was almost empty until I found a monograph that oversupplied me with references to highly suitable titles. I mention these details in order to make it quite clear that the distribution of the titles among the groups and subgroups of this bibliography cannot in any sense be regarded as representative of the literature.

One might think that inclusion of a book or article in the sample bibliography would justify a presumption that the selected publication is important or worth reading. This is not so; many of the entries were selected from the indexes or reference lists without examination of their value as scientific communications, didactic commentaries, or informative reports. Only in exceptional instances, where the selection was guided by my memory instead of the bibliographic services, did my judgment of the significance of the item play the determining role. This refers especially to older literature; when I knew that a particular subject had been treated in the early decades of this century, or in the eighteenth or nineteenth century, I tried to include some of these seminal or otherwise important publications in the bibliography.

This more or less haphazard method of selection resulted in a nonrepresentative distribution of the included items over chronological time. The frequency distributions among vintage years may be quite atypical; if, for some particular subject groups or subgroups, they happen to be typical, this can only be due to a lucky chance.

Arranging the Entries

The titles are arranged by the subject subgroups to which they were assigned, or for which they were chosen, and within each subgroup they are ordered chronologically.

Alphabetic ordering of entries in a special bibliography would make no sense. Only where the user of a bibliography knows what he is looking for—knows the authors for whose publications he needs more complete bibliographic details—is alphabetic ordering of the authors, and sometimes also of the titles, a helpful convention. Where a bibliography is designed to serve readers who want to be directed to literature on particular subjects, alphabetization is meaningless. Chronological ordering within each subgroup is desirable because it affords the user of the bibliography an opportunity to get without special effort a feeling for the historical development of the field or area over the years. With regard to journal articles, chronological listing should be not only by year of publication but, if possible, by the month or season in which the issue of the journal in question was published; and, within the same issue, the order should be according to page numbers. This rule may appear pedantic until one realizes that an author may have a rejoinder to a reply to his article published in the same issue of the journal. Clearly, reply and rejoinder should not be listed ahead of the article, even if their titles happen to begin with letters that in the alphabet precede the first letter of the title of the article.[1]

A word should be said about cross-referencing. Most publications are eligible for listing under several headings and it is often quite arbitrary to place a particular title into only one of the several groups

---

[1] These arguments for chronological and against alphabetical ordering apply also to bibliographies of the writings of particular authors. The propensity to alphabetize ought to be resisted where other types of ordering are more helpful.

or subgroups in which it properly "belongs." A bibliography becomes much more useful if it supplies generous cross-references; but it also becomes more expensive. Some indexers set a maximum of three listings for any one article, simply to strike a reasonable balance between the readers' benefits and the editors' and publishers' costs. In my sample bibliography, each publication appears only once. This makes its assignment to a subgroup even more arbitrary; but since the purpose of the exercise is chiefly to test whether the classification is serviceable, the limitation is probably justified—and forgivable even if its justification is questioned. General observations about possible cross-referencing were included in the description of the classificaton supplied in the preceding chapter.

THE BIBLIOGRAPHY

1. The Economics of Knowledge and Information: General

1.1 General

Hayek, Friedrich A., "Economics and Knowledge," *Economica*, N.S., Vol. 4 (February 1937), pp. 33-54.

Boulding, Kenneth E., *The Image: Knowledge in Life and Society* (Ann Arbor: The University of Michigan Press, 1956; 2d ed., 1961).

Stigler, George J., "The Economics of Information," *Journal of Political Economy*, Vol. 69 (May-June 1961), pp. 213-225.

Boulding, Kenneth E., "The Economics of Knowledge and the Knowledge of Economics," *American Economic Review*, Vol. 56 (May 1966), pp. 1-13.

Chorafas, Dimitrius N., *The Knowledge Revolution: An Analysis of the International Brain Market* (New York: McGraw-Hill, 1968).

Marschak, Jacob, "Economics of Inquiring, Communicating, Deciding," *American Economic Review*, Vol. 58 (Suppl. May 1968), pp. 1-18.

Olson, Mancur, "Information as a Public Good," in Robert S. Taylor, ed., *Economics of Information Dissemination: A Symposium* (Syracuse: School of Library Science, Syracuse University, 1973), pp. 7-14.

Arrow, Kenneth J., *Information and Economic Behavior* (Stockholm: Almqvist & Wiksell, 1974).

Arrow, Kenneth J., "Limited Knowledge and Economic Analysis." *American Economic Review*, Vol. 64 (March 1974), pp. 1-10.

Marschak, Jacob, *Economic Information, Decision, and Prediction, Selected Essays*, 3 vols. (Dordrecht: Reidel, 1974).

Machlup, Fritz, *Knowledge: Its Creation, Distribution, and Economic Significance*, Vol. 1: *Knowledge and Knowledge Production* (Princeton: Princeton University Press, 1980).

1.2   *Collective Works and Anthologies*

Seventy-Eighth Annual Meeting of the American Economic Association ["Knowledge Production and Innovation"], *American Economic Review*, Papers and Proceedings, Vol. 56 (Suppl. May 1966).

Kochen, Manfred, ed., *The Growth of Knowledge: Readings on Organization and Retrieval of Information* (New York: Wiley, 1967).

Lamberton, Donald M., ed., *The Economics of Information and Knowledge* (Harmondsworth: Penguin, 1971).

Diamond, Peter, and Rothschild, Michael, *Uncertainty in Ecomomics: Readings and Exercises* (New York: Academic Press, 1978).

1.3   *Surveys, Bibliographies, Classifications*

Havelock, Ronald G. et al., *Bibliography on Knowledge Utilization and Dissemination* (Ann Arbor: Institute for Social Research, University of Michigan, rev. ed. 1972).

Olson, Harold Anker, *The Economics of Information: Bibliography and Commentary on the Literature* (College Park, Md.: School of Library and Information Services, for the U.S. Department of Health, Education, and Welfare, ERIC No. ED 076214; 2d ed., 1972).

Cooper, Michael D., "The Economics of Information," in Carlos Cuadra, ed., *Annual Review of Information Sciences and Technology*, Vol. 8 (Washington, D.C.: American Society for Information Science, 1973), pp. 5-40.

Hirshleifer, Jack, "Where Are We in the Theory of Information?" *American Economic Review*, Papers and Proceedings, Vol. 63 (Suppl. May 1973), pp. 31-39.

Rothschild, Michael, "Models of Market Organization with Imperfect Information: A Survey," *Journal of Political Economy*, Vol. 81 (November-December 1973), pp. 1283-1308.

Spence, Michael A., "An Economist's View of Information," in Carlos Cuadra, ed., *Annual Review of Information Science and Technology*, Vol. 9 (Washington, D.C.: American Society for Information Science, 1974), pp. 57-78.

Hirshleifer, Jack, and Riley, John G., "The New Economics of Information," Discussion Paper No. 14 (University of California at Los Angeles: July 1976).

Hirshleifer, Jack, and Riley, John G., "The Analytics of Uncertainty and Information—An Expository Survey," *Journal of Economic Literature*, Vol. 17 (December 1979), pp. 1375-1421.

2. PRODUCTION AND DISTRIBUTION OF KNOWLEDGE: KNOWLEDGE
    INDUSTRIES, INFORMATION SERVICES, INFORMATION MACHINES

2.1   *General*

Machlup, Fritz, *The Production and Distribution of Knowledge in the United
    States* (Princeton: Princeton University Press, 1962).
Boulding, Kenneth E., "The Knowledge Industry," *Challenge* (May 1963),
    pp. 36-38.
Burck, Gilbert, "Knowledge: The Biggest Growth Industry of Them All,"
    Fortune (November 1964), pp. 128-132, 267-268, 270.
Porat, Marc Uri, *The Information Economy*, Report Series in 9 vols. [each
    of which has its own subtitle] (Washington, D.C.: U.S. Department of
    Commerce, Office of Telecommunications, 1977).
Sterling, Christopher H. and Haight, Timothy R., *The Mass Media: Aspen
    Institute Guide to Communication Industry Trends* (New York: Praeger,
    1978).
Rubin, Michael Rogers, and Taylor, Elizabeth, "The U.S. Information Sector
    and GNP: An Input-Output Study," *Information Processing & Manage-
    ment*, Vol. 17 (No. 4, 1981), pp. 163-194.

2.2   *Education*

Mushkin, Selma J., ed., *Economics of Higher Education* (Washington, D.C.:
    U.S. Office of Education, 1962).
Bowen, William G., *Economic Aspects of Education: Three Essays* (Prince-
    ton: Industrial Relations Section, Princeton University, 1964).
Robinson, Edward Austin G., and Vaizey, John E., eds., *The Economics of
    Education*, Proceedings of a Conference of the International Economic
    Association (London: Macmillan, 1966).
Welch, Finis, "Measurement of the Quality of Schooling," *American Eco-
    nomic Review*, Vol. 56 (May 1966), pp. 379-392.
Blaug, Mark, ed., *Economics of Education: Selected Readings* (Har-
    mondsworth: Penguin, 1968).
Hartley, Harry J., *Educational Planning—Programming—Budgeting: A Sys-
    tems Approach* (Englewood Cliffs, N.J.: Prentice-Hall, 1968).
Cartter, Allan M., "The Economics of Higher Education," in Neil W. Cham-
    berlain, ed., *Contemporary Economic Issues* (Homewood, Ill.: Irwin,
    1969), pp. 145-184.
Hansen, W. Lee, and Weisbrod, Burton A., *Benefits, Costs, and Finance of
    Public Higher Education* (Chicago: Markham, 1969).
Feldman, Kenneth A., and Newcomb, Theodore M., *The Impact of College
    on Students* (San Francisco: Jossey-Bass, 1969).
Powel, John H., and Lamson, Robert D., *An Annotated Bibliography of Lit-
    erature Relating to the Costs and Benefits of Graduate Education* (Wash-
    ington, D.C.: Council of Graduate Schools, 1972).
Layard, Richard, "Economic Theories of Educational Planning," in Maurice

Peston and Bernard Corry, eds., *Essays in Honour of Lord Robbins* (London: Weidenfeld & Nicolson, 1972).

Bailey, Duncan, and Schotta, Charles, "Private and Social Rates of Return to Education of Academicians," *American Economic Review*, Vol. 62 (March 1972), pp. 19-31.

Nerlove, Marc, "On Tuition and Costs of Higher Education: Prologomena to a Conceptual Framework," *Journal of Political Economy*, Vol. 80 (May-June 1972, Part 2), pp. S178-S218).

Solmon, Lewis C., and Taubman, Paul J., eds., *Does College Matter? Some Evidence on the Impacts of Higher Education* (New York: Academic Press, 1973).

Arrow, Kenneth J., "Higher Education as a Filter," *Journal of Public Economics*, Vol. 2 (July 1973), pp. 193-216.

Lumsden, Keith G., ed., *Efficiency in Universities: The LaPaz Papers* (Amsterdam: Elsevier Scientific, 1974).

Stiglitz, Joseph E., "The Demand for Education in Public and Private School Systems," *Journal of Public Economics*, Vol. 3 (November 1974), pp. 349-385.

Gramlich, Edward M., and Koshel, Patricia P., *Educational Performance Contracting: An Evaluation of an Experiment* (Washington, D.C.: Brookings Institution, 1975).

Rivlin, Alice M., and Timpane, P. Michael, eds., *Planned Variation in Education: Should We Give Up or Try Harder?* (Washington, D.C.: Brookings Institution, 1975).

Stiglitz, Joseph E., "The Theory of Screening, Education, and the Distribution of Income," *American Economic Review*, Vol. 65 (June 1975), pp. 283-300.

Kagann, Stephen, "The Foregone Earnings of High School, College and University Students," *Eastern Economic Journal*, Vol. 2 (October 1975), pp. 331-341.

Riley, John G., "Testing the Educational Screening Hypothesis," *Journal of Political Economy*, Vol. 87 (September-October 1979, Part 2), pp. S227-S252.

Cohn, Elchanan, *The Economics of Education* (Cambridge, Mass.: Ballinger, rev. ed., 1979).

2.3   Research and Development

Nelson, Richard R., "The Simple Economics of Basic Scientific Research," *Journal of Political Economy*, Vol. 67 (May-June 1959), pp. 297-306.

Hamberg, Daniel, *R & D: Essays on the Economics of Research and Development* (New York: Random House, 1966).

Tullock, Gordon, *The Organization of Inquiry* (Durham, N.C.: Duke University Press, 1966).

Marschak, Thomas; Glennan, Thomas K., Jr.; and Summers, Robert, *Strategy for R and D: Studies in the Microeconomics of Development* (New York: Springer-Verlag, 1967).

Scherer, Frederic M., "Research and Development Allocation under Rivalry," *Quarterly Journal of Economics*, Vol. 81 (August 1967), pp. 359-394.

Comanor, William S., "Market Structure, Product Differentiation, and Industrial Research," *Quarterly Journal of Economics*, Vol. 81 (November 1967), pp. 639-657.

Grabowski, Henry G., "The Determinants of Industrial Research and Development," *Journal of Political Economy*, Vol. 76 (March-April 1968), pp. 292-306.

Castro, Barry, "The Scientific Opportunities Foregone Because of More Readily Available Federal Support for Research in Experimental than Theoretical Physics," *Journal of Political Economy*, Vol. 76 (July-August 1968), pp. 601-614.

Allison, David, ed., *The R and D Game: Technical Man, Technical Managers, and Research Productivity* (Cambridge, Mass.: MIT Press, 1969).

Mansfield, Edwin, "Industrial Research and Development: Characteristics, Costs, and Diffusion of Results," *American Economic Review*, Vol. 59 (Suppl. May 1969), pp. 65-71.

Weisbrod, Burton A. "Costs and Benefits of Medical Research: A Case Study of Poliomyelitis," *Journal of Political Economy*, Vol. 79 (May-June 1971), pp. 527-544.

2.4 Print Media of Communication

Unwin, Sir Stanley, *The Truth about Publishing* (Boston: Houghton Mifflin, 1927: 6th ed., London: Allen & Unwin, 1950).

Markham, Jesse W. et al., *An Economic Media Study of Book Publishing* (New York: American Textbook Publishers, 1966).

Horvitz, Paul M., "The Pricing of Textbooks and the Remuneration of Authors," *American Economic Review*, Vol. 56 (Suppl. May 1966), pp. 412-420.

Meyer-Dohm, Peter, ed., *Das wissenschaftliche Buch* (Hamburg: Verlag für Buchmarkt-Forschung, 1969).

Bailey, Herbert S., Jr., *The Art and Science of Book Publishing* (New York: Harper & Row, 1970).

Berg, Sanford V., "An Economic Analysis of the Demand for Scientific Journals," *Journal of the American Society for Information Science*, Vol. 23 (January-February 1972), pp. 23-29.

Lovell, Michael C., "The Production of Economic Literature: An Interpretation," *Journal of Economic Literature*, Vol. 11 (March 1973), pp. 27-55.

Machlup, Fritz, "Publishing Scholarly Books and Journals: Is it Economically Viable?" *Journal of Political Economy*, Vol. 85 (February 1977), pp. 217-225.

Machlup, Fritz, and Leeson, Kenneth, *Information through the Printed Word: The Dissemination of Scientific, Scholarly, and Intellectual Knowledge*, Vol. I: *Book Publishing*, Vol. II: *Journals* (New York: Praeger, 1978).

2.5   *Electronic Mass Media of Communication*

Coase, Ronald, "The Federal Communications Commission," *Journal of Law and Economics*, Vol. 2 (October 1959), pp. 1-40.

Steiner, Peter O., "Monopoly and Competition in Television: Some Policy Issues," *Manchester School of Economic and Social Studies*, Vol. 29 (May 1961), pp. 107-131.

Minasian, Jora R., "Television Pricing and the Theory of Public Goods," *Journal of Law and Economics*, Vol. 7 (October 1964), pp. 71-80.

Samuelson, Paul A., "Public Goods and Subscription TV: Correction of the Record," *Journal of Law and Economics*, Vol. 7 (October 1964), pp. 81-83.

Harwood, Kenneth, "Broadcasting and the Theory of the Firm," *Law and Contemporary Problems*, Vol. 34 (Summer 1969), pp. 485-504.

Park, Rolla Edward, "The Growth of Cable TV and Its Probable Impact on Over-the-Air Broadcasting," *American Economic Review*, Vol. 61 (Suppl. May 1971), pp. 69-73.

Comanor, William S., and Mitchell, Bridger M., "Cable Television and the Impact of Regulation," *Bell Journal of Economics and Management Science*, Vol. 2 (Spring 1971), pp. 154-212.

McGowan, John J., and Peck, Merton J., "Television: Old Theories, Current Facts, and Future Policies, Discussion," *American Economic Review*, Vol. 61 (Suppl. May 1971), pp. 94-100.

Nelson, Boyd L., "Costs and Benefits of Regulating Communications," *American Economic Review*, Vol. 61 (Suppl. May 1971), pp. 218-225.

Crandall, Robert W., "The Economic Effect of Television-Network Program Ownership," *Journal of Law and Economics*, Vol. 14 (October 1971), pp. 385-412.

Comanor, William S., and Mitchell, Bridger M., "The Costs of Planning: The FCC and Cable Television," *Journal of Law and Economics*, Vol. 15 (April 1972), pp. 177-206.

Noll, Roger G.; Peck, Merton J.; and McGowan, John J., *Economic Aspects of Television Regulation* (Washington, D.C.: Brookings Institution, 1973).

Spence, Michael, and Owen, Bruce, "Television Programming, Monopolistic Competition, and Welfare," *Quarterly Journal of Economics*, Vol. 91 (February 1977), pp. 103-126.

2.6   *Addressed Telecommunication*

U.S. Congress, House, Federal Communications Commission, *Report on the Investigation of the Telephone Industry in the United States*, 76th Congress, 1st Session, Docket No. 340, 1939.

Sheahan, John, "Integration and Exclusion in the Telephone Equipment Industry," *Quarterly Journal of Economics*, Vol. 70 (May 1956), pp. 249-269.

Bowers, David A., and Lovejoy, Wallace F., "Disequilibrium and Increasing

Costs: A Study of Local Telephone Service," *Land Economics*, Vol. 41 (February 1965), pp. 31-40.

Senior, Ian, *The Postal Service: Competition or Monopoly?* (London: Institute of Economic Affairs, 1970).

Littlechild, Stephen C., "Peak-Load Pricing of Telephone Calls," *Bell Journal of Economics and Management Science*, Vol. 1 (Autumn 1970), pp. 191-210.

Irwin, Manley R., *The Telecommunication Industry: Integration vs. Competition* (New York: Praeger, 1971).

Trebing, Harry M., and Melody, William H., "Entry Conditions in Telecommunications," in Michael W. Klass and William G. Shepherd, eds., *Regulation and Entry: Energy, Communications, and Banking* (East Lansing: Graduate School of Business Administration, Michigan State University, 1976), pp. 93-116.

2.7 *Artistic Creation and Communication: Theater, Music, Dance, Cinema, Museums, and Art Galleries*

Rockefeller Panel Report, *The Performing Arts: Problems and Prospects* (New York: McGraw-Hill, 1965).

Toffler, Alvin, *The Culture Consumers: Art and Affluence in America* (Baltimore: Penguin, 1965).

Baumol, William J., and Bowen, William G., *Performing Arts: The Economic Dilemma* (New York: Twentieth Century Fund, 1966).

Moore, Thomas Gale, *The Economics of the American Theater* (Durham, N.C.: Duke University Press, 1968).

Novick, Julius, *Beyond Broadway: The Quest for Permanent Theatres* (New York: Hill & Wang, 1968).

Poggi, Jack, *Theater in America: The Impact of Economic Forces, 1870-1967* (Ithaca, N.Y.: Cornell University Press, 1968).

Peacock, Alan T., "Public Patronage and Music: An Economist's View," *Three Banks Review* (March 1968), pp. 1-19.

American Association of Museums, *America's Museums: The Belmont Report* (Washington, D.C., 1969).

Goldman, William, *The Season: A Candid Look at Broadway* (New York: Harcourt Brace Jovanovich, 1969).

Mark, Charles C., *A Study of Cultural Policy in the United States* (Paris: UNESCO Press, 1969).

Peacock, Alan T., "Welfare Economics and Public Subsidies to the Arts," *Manchester School of Economic and Social Studies*, Vol. 37 (December 1969), pp. 323-335.

Harris, John S., *Government Patronage of the Arts in Great Britain* (Chicago: University of Chicago Press, 1970).

National Endowment for the Arts, "The First Five Years: Fiscal 1966 Through Fiscal 1970," (Washington, D.C., 1970).

Taubman, Howard, "The Symphony Orchestra Abroad: A Report of A Study" (Vienna, Va.: The American Symphony Orchestra League, 1970).

Hewitt, Alan, "Like It Is, Man: Professional Theater Employment, 1961-68," *Performing Arts Review*, Vol. 1 (No. 4, 1970), pp. 623-667.

Lamson, Robert D., "Measured Productivity and Price Change: Some Empirical Evidence on Service Industry Bias, Motion Picture Theaters," *Journal of Political Economy*, Vol. 78 (March-April 1970), pp. 291-305.

Arian, Edward, *Bach, Beethoven and Bureaucracy: The Case of the Philadelphia Orchestra* (University: University of Alabama Press, 1971).

Fichandler, Zelda, "Theatres or Institutions," in *The American Theatre, 1969-1970*, edited by the International Theatre Institute of the United States (New York: Scribner, 1971), pp. 105-116.

Greenberger, Howard, *The Off-Broadway Experience* (Englewood Cliffs, N.J.: Prentice-Hall, 1971).

The Metropolitan Opera Association. "White Paper on the Metropolitan Opera" (1971).

Morley, Sheridan, ed., *Theatre 71* (London: Hutchinson, 1971).

National Endowment for the Arts, "Economic Aspects of the Performing Arts: A Portrait in Figures" (May 1971).

Hewitt, Alan, "Professional Theater Employment, 1970 Season," *Performing Arts Review*, Vol. 2 (No. 4, 1971).

Association of American Dance Companies, "The State of Dance in the United States: Parts I and II" (New York, 1972).

Dace, William, *Subsidies for the Theater: A Study of the Central European System of Financing Drama, Opera and Ballet: 1968-70* (Manhattan, Kansas: AG Press, 1972).

National Endowment for the Arts, "New Dimensions for the Arts: 1971-1972" (Washington, D.C., 1972).

New York City Cultural Council and New York State Council of the Arts, "Study of the New York Theater. Summary and Recommendations," Basic Report prepared by William J. Baumol, 1972.

Scitovsky, Tibor, "Arts in the Affluent Society: What's Wrong with the Arts is What's Wrong with Society," *The American Economic Review*, Vol. 62 (Suppl. May 1972), pp. 62-69.

Hewitt, Alan, "Professional Theater Employment: 1972 Season," *Performing Arts Review*, Vol. 3 (No. 4, 1972).

McKinzie, Richard D., *The New Deal for Artists* (Princeton: Princeton University Press, 1973).

The Ford Foundation, *The Finances of the Performing Arts*, Vol. 1: *A Survey of 166 Professional Resident Theaters, Opera, Symphonies, Ballets and Modern Dance Companies* (New York, 1974).

The Ford Foundation, *The Finances of the Performing Arts*, Vol. 2: *A Survey of the Characteristics and Attitudes of Audiences for Theater, Opera, Symphony and Ballet in Twelve U.S. Cities* (New York, 1974).

National Endowment for the Arts, *Museums U.S.A.: Art, History, Science and Others* (Washington, D.C.: U.S. Government Printing Office, 1974).

The Corporation for Public Broadcasting, "Public Broadcasting and Long Range Funding: Anatomy of a Bill"; "Public Broadcasting and Financing: Where the Money Comes From"; "Public Television," and "Annual Report: 1974" (Washington, D.C.).

Little, Stuart W., *After the Fact: Conflict and Consensus—A Report on the First American Congress of Theatre* (New York: Arno Press, 1975).

Greater Philadelphia Cultural Alliance, "An Introduction to the Economics of Philadelphia's Cultural Organizations" (Philadelphia, February 1975).

The National Committee for Symphony Orchestra Support, "Funding the Arts: An Economic, Educational, and Cultural Priority" (March 1975).

Andre, Carl et al., "The Role of the Artist in Today's Society," *The Art Journal*, Vol. 34 (No. 4, 1975), pp. 327-331.

Peacock, Alan T., "The 'Output' of the London Orchestras, 1966-75," *The Musical Times*, Vol. 117 (August 1976), pp. 641-644.

Anderson, Robert J.; Baumol, Hilda; et al., *The Condition and Needs of the Live Professional Theater in America*, Phase I Report, Vol. I: Executive Summary; Vol. II: Data Collection and Analysis; and 2 vols.: Exhibits (Princeton: Mathtech, Mathematica, 1978).

Netzer, Dick, *The Subsidized Muse: Public Support for the Arts in the United States* (Cambridge: At the University Press; and New York: Twentieth Century Fund, 1978).

2.8 Libraries

Baumol, William, *On the Economics of Library Operation* (Princeton: Mathematica, 1967).

Ellsworth, Ralph E., *The Economics of Book Storage in College and University Libraries* (Metuchen, N.J.: Scarecrow Press, 1969).

Raffel, Jeffrey A., and Shisko, Robert, *Systematic Analysis of University Libraries: An Application of Cost-Benefit Analysis to MIT Libraries* (Cambridge, Mass.: MIT Press, 1969).

Leimkuhler, Ferdinand F., and Cooper, Michael D., *Cost Accounting and Analysis for University Libraries* (Berkeley: Office of Planning and Analysis, University of California, 1970).

Goddard, Haynes C., "An Economic Analysis of Library Benefits," *Library Quarterly*, Vol. 41 (July 1971), pp. 244-255.

Baumol William J., and Marcus, Matityahu, *Economics of Academic Libraries* (Washington, D.C.: American Council on Education, 1973).

Gore, Daniel, ed., *Farewell to Alexandria: Solutions to Space, Growth, and Performance Problems of Libraries* (Westport, Conn.: Greenwood Press, 1976).

Smith, Stanley V., and Osso, Nicholas A., *Library Statistics of Colleges and Universities, Fall 1973* (Washington, D.C.: National Center for Education Statistics, U.S. Deptartment of Health, Education, and Welfare, 1976).

Fetterman, John J., "The High Costs of Information and Some Approaches to Its Acquisition," in Mark Perlman, ed., *The Organization and Retrieval of Economic Knowledge: Proceedings of a Conference Held by the International Ecomomic Association* (London: Macmillan, 1977), pp. 121-130.

Kilgour, Frederick G., "Economics of Computerized Library Networks," in Mark Perlman, ed., *The Organization and Retrieval of Economic Knowledge: Proceedings of a Conference Held by the International Economic Association* (London: Macmillan, 1977), pp. 181-189.

Machlup, Fritz, and Leeson, Kenneth, *Information Through the Printed Word: The Dissemination of Scientific, Scholarly, and Intellectual Knowledge,* Vol. III: *Libraries* (New York: Praeger, 1978).

2.9   Science Information Services

U.S. Congress, Senate, *Documentation, Indexing and Retrieval of Scientific Information,* 86th Congress, 2d Sess., Senate Document No. 113, 1960.

National Science Foundation, *Current Research and Development in Scientific Documentation,* No. 15 (Washington, D.C.: Office of Science Information Service, 1969).

U.S. Federal Council for Science and Technology, Committee on Scientific and Technical Information, *Progress in Scientific and Technical Communications,* 1969 Annual Report (Springfield, Va.: National Technical Information Service [PB193 386], 1969).

Committee on Scientific and Technical Communication, *Report of the Task Group on the Economics of Primary Publication* (Washington, D.C.: National Academy of Sciences, 1970).

Myatt, DeWitt O., and Jover, Susan I., *Compilation of Major Recommendations from Five Studies Relating to National Scientific and Technical Information Systems* (Springfield, Va.: National Technical Information Service, 1970).

Danilov, Victor J.; Herring, Conyers; and Hillman, Donald J., *Report of the Panel on Economics of the Science Information Council* (Washington, D.C.: National Technical Information Service, January 1973).

Anderla, J. Georges, *The Growth of Scientific and Technical Information: A Challenge.* Lecture and Seminar Proceedings (Washington, D.C.: National Science Foundation, Office of Science Information Service, January 1974).

U.S. Congress, Senate, Special Subcommittee on the National Science Foundation of the Committee on Labor and Public Welfare, *Federal Management of Scientific and Technical Information Activities: The Role of the National Science Foundation,* 94th Congress, 1st Sess., July 1975.

King Research Inc., *A Chart Book of Indicators of Scientific and Technical Communications* (Washington, D.C.: National Science Foundation, 1977).

Machlup, Fritz, and Leeson, Kenneth, *Information Through the Printed Word: The Dissemination of Scientific, Scholarly, and Intellectual Knowledge,* Vol. 4: *Books, Journals, and Bibliographic Services* (New York: Praeger, 1980).

2.10   Technological Information Services

Cetron, Marvin J., and Goldhar, Joel D., eds., *The Science of Managing Organized Technology* (New York: Gordon and Breach, 1971).

Wolfe, Jack N. et al., *The Economics of Technical Information Systems: A Study in Cost-Effectiveness*, 3 vols. (Edinburgh: University of Edinburgh, 1971).

2.11 *Medical and Health Information Services*

Coleman, James Samuel; Katz, Elihu; and Menzel, Herbert, *Medical Innovation. A Diffusion Study* (Indianapolis: Bobbs-Merrill, 1966).

Collen, Morris F., ed., *Proceedings of a Conference on Medical Information Systems* held in San Francisco, January 1970 (Washington, D.C.: U.S. Department of Health, Education, and Welfare, Public Health Service, 1970).

Dei Rossi, James A.; Heiser, Richard S.; and King, Naomi S., "A Cost Analysis of Minimum Distance TV Networking for Broadcasting Medical Information" (Santa Monica, Cal.: Rand Corporation, RM-6204-NLM, February 1970).

Dei Rossi, James A. et al., *A Telephone Access Biomedical Information Center* (Santa Monica, Cal.: Rand Corporation, April 1970).

Committee for Economic Development, *Building a National Health-Care System* (New York: Committee for Economic Development, 1973).

Russell, Louise B.; Bourque, Blair Bagwell; et al., *Federal Health Spending 1969-74* (Washington, D.C.: National Planning Association, 1974).

U.S. Department of Health, Education, and Welfare, Public Health Service, *Health: United States 1975* (Washington, D.C.: National Center for Health Statistics, 1975).

Maynard, Alan K., "An Economic Analysis of Medical Care in Western Europe," in Victor Halberstadt, and Anthony J. Culyer, eds., *Public Economics and Human Resources* (Paris: Editions Cujas, for International Institute of Public Finance, 1977), pp. 177-192.

2.12 *Other Professional Information Services*

Swoboda, Peter, "Comparison of Consolidated Financial Statements in the United States and West Germany," *International Journal of Accounting*, Vol. 1 (Spring 1966), pp. 9-24.

Weirich, Thomas R.; Avery, Clarence G.; and Anderson, Henry R., "International Accounting: Varying Definitions," *International Journal of Accounting*, Vol. 7 (Fall 1971), pp. 79-87.

Landes, William M., "An Economic Analysis of the Courts," *Journal of Law and Economics*, Vol. 14 (April 1971), pp. 61-107.

Hallauer, Robert Paul, "The Shreveport Experiment in Prepaid Legal Services," *Journal of Legal Studies*, Vol. 2 (January 1973), pp. 223-242.

Gould, John P., "The Economics of Legal Conflicts," *Journal of Legal Studies*, Vol. 2 (June 1973), pp. 279-300.

Posner, Richard A., "An Economic Approach to Legal Procedure and Judicial Administration," *Journal of Legal Studies*, Vol. 2 (June 1973), pp. 399-458.

Enthoven, Adolf J. H., "The Unity of Accountancy in an International Context," *International Journal of Accounting*, Vol. 9 (Fall 1973), pp. 113-133.

Ehrlich, Isaac, and Posner, Richard A., "An Economic Analysis of Legal Rulemaking," *Journal of Legal Studies*, Vol. 3 (January 1974), pp. 257-286.

Reder, Melvin W., "Citizen Rights and the Cost of Law Enforcement," *Journal of Legal Studies*, Vol. 3 (June 1974), pp. 435-455.

Schwartz, Warren F., and Tullock, Gordon, "The Costs of a Legal System," *Journal of Legal Studies*, Vol. 4 (January 1975), pp. 75-82.

Posner, Richard A., "The Economic Approach to Law," *Texas Law Review*, Vol. 53 (May 1975), pp. 757-782.

Vangermeersch, Richard, "An Improved Income Statement," *Management Accounting*, Vol. 58 (January 1977), pp. 29-33.

Hanson, Walter E., "Big Brother and the Big Eight," *Management Accounting*, Vol. 58 (April 1977), pp. 15-19.

Herzog, Raymond H., "The Numbers Game: What Industry Accountants Can Do For Society," *Management Accounting*, Vol. 58 (May 1977), pp. 17-19.

Moscove, Stephen A., "Accountants' Legal Liability," *Management Accounting*, Vol. 58 (May 1977), pp. 25-26, and 30.

Zolfo, Frank J., and Cooper, Barry N., "Considering the LIFO Election," *Management Accounting*, Vol. 58 (June 1977), pp. 41-43, and 51.

2.13   Financial Information Services

Ferber, Robert, "Short-Run Effects of Stock-Market Services of Stock Prices," *Journal of Finance*, Vol. 13 (March 1958), pp. 80-95.

Mastrapasqua, Frank, and Bolten, Steven, "A Note of Financial Analyst Evaluation," *Journal of Finance*, Vol. 28 (June 1973), pp. 707-712.

Emery, John T., "Efficient Capital Markets and the Information Content of Accounting Numbers," *Journal of Financial and Quantitative Analysis*, Vol. 9 (March 1974), pp. 139-149.

Melicher, Ronald W., and Rush, David F., "Systematic Risk, Financial Data, and Bond Rating Relationships in a Regulated Industry Environment," *Journal of Finance*, Vol. 29 (May 1974), pp. 537-544.

Albin, Peter S., "Information Exchange in Security Markets and the Assumption of 'Homogeneous Beliefs,' " *Journal of Finance*, Vol. 29 (September 1974), pp. 1217-1227.

2.14   Business Information Services and Management

McDonough, Adrian M., *Information Economics and Management Systems* (New York: McGraw-Hill, 1963).

Wilensky, Harold L., *Organization Intelligence: Knowledge and Policy in Government and Industry* (New York: Basic Books, 1967).

Blumenthal, Sherman C., *Management Information Systems: A Framework for Planning and Development* (Englewood Cliffs, N.J.: Prentice-Hall, 1969).

Goldschmidt, Yaagov, *Information for Management Decisions: A System for Economic Analysis and Accounting Procedures* (Ithaca, N.Y.: Cornell University Press, 1970).

Sanders, Donald H., *Computers and Management* (New York: McGraw-Hill, 1970).

House, William C., *The Impact of Information Technology on Management Operations* (Princeton: Auerbach, 1971).

2.15   *Government Information Services*

Lerner, Eugene M., and Moag, Joseph S., "Information Requirements for Regulatory Decisions," in Harry M. Trebing, and R. Hayden Howard, eds., *Rates of Return Under Regulation: New Directions and Perspectives* (East Lansing: Institute of Public Utilities, Michigan State University, 1969).

Basgall, E. J., "Information and Records Costs: An Interim Report," Office of Records Management, National Archives and Records Service, July 29, 1974.

Noll, Roger G., *Government Administrative Behavior and Private Sector Response: A Multidisciplinary Survey* (Pasadena: Division of the Humanities and Social Sciences, California Institute of Technology, revised October 1976).

Commission on Federal Paperwork, *Information Resources Management*, A Report of the Commission on Federal Paperwork (Washington, D.C.: September 1977).

Commission on Federal Paperwork, *Our Shadow Government: The Hidden Cost of Government Paperwork, Information and Communications Costs to the Taxpayer* (Washington, D.C.: Information Resources Management, Process Studies Division, October 1977).

Nutter, G. Warren, *Growth of Government in the West* (Washington, D.C.: American Enterprise Institute, 1978).

Weidenbaum, Murray L., and De Fina, Robert, *The Cost of Federal Regulation of Economic Activity* (Washington, D.C.: American Enterprise Institute, May 1978).

2.16   *Advertising and Public Relations*

Harris, Ralph, and Seldon, Arthur, *Advertising in Action* (London: Hutchinson, 1962).

Simon, Julian L., *Issues in the Economics of Advertising* (Urbana: University of Illinois Press, 1970).

Nelson, Phillip, "Information and Consumer Behavior," *Journal of Political Economy*, Vol. 82 (July-August 1970), pp. 311-329.

Landon, John H., "The Relation of Market Concentration to Advertising Rates: The Newspaper Industry," *Antitrust Bulletin*, Vol. 16 (Spring 1971), pp. 53-100.

Kirzner, Israel M., "Advertising," *The Freeman*, Vol. 22 (September 1972), pp. 515-528.

Brozen, Yale, ed., *Advertising and Society* (New York: New York University Press, 1974).

Nelson, Phillip, "Advertising as Information," *Journal of Political Economy*, Vol. 82 (July-August 1974), pp. 729-754.

Nelson, Phillip, "The Economic Consequences of Advertising," *Journal of Business*, Vol. 48 (April 1975), pp. 213-241.

Baird, Charles W., *Advertising by Professionals* (Los Angeles, Cal.: International Institute for Economic Research, 1977).

Stigler, George J., and Becker, Gary S., "De Gustibus Non Est Disputandum," *American Economic Review*, Vol. 67 (March 1977), pp. 76-90.

Ornstein, Stanley I., *Industrial Concentration and Advertising Intensity* (Washington, D.C.: American Enterprise Institute, 1977).

Tuerck, David G., ed., *Issues in Advertising: The Economics of Persuasion* (Washington, D.C.: American Enterprise Institute, 1978).

Worcester, Dean A., with Nesse, Ronald, *Welfare Gains from Advertising: The Problem of Regulation* (Washington, D.C.: American Enterprise Institute, 1978).

Ehrlich, Isaac, and Fisher, Lawrence, "The Derived Demand for Advertising: A Theoretical and Empirical Investigation," *American Economic Review*, Vol. 72 (June 1982), pp. 366-388.

2.17   Information Machines and Equipment

Chow, Gregory C., "Technological Change and the Demand for Computers," *American Economic Review*, Vol. 57 (December 1967), pp. 1117-1130.

Barr, James I., and Knight, Kenneth E., "Technological Change and Learning in the Computer Industry," *Management Science*, Vol. 14 (July 1968), pp. 661-681.

Gruenberger, Fred J., *Computers and Communication: Toward a Computer Utility* (Englewood Cliffs, N.J.: Prentice-Hall, 1969).

Sharpe, William F., *The Economics of Computers* (New York: Columbia University Press, 1969).

Bagdikian, Ben J., *The Information Machines: Their Impact on Men and Media* (New York: Harper & Row, 1971).

Braunstein, Yale M. et al., *Economics of Property Rights as Applied to Computer Software and Data Bases* (Springfield, Va.: National Technical Information Service, 1977).

Chow, Gregory C., "The Computer and Economics," *Proceedings of the American Philosophical Society*, Vol. 121 (October 1977), pp. 350-354.

3.   IGNORANCE, CHANCE, RISK, AND UNCERTAINTY AS FACTORS IN THE EXPLANATION OF INDIVIDUAL CHOICES AND PARTICULAR ECONOMIC INSTITUTIONS AND PHENOMENA

3.1   General

Smith, Adam, *An Inquiry into the Nature and Causes of the Wealth of Nations* (London: Strahan and Cadell, 1776).

Menger, Carl, *Grundsätze der Volkswirtschaftslehre* (Vienna: Braumüller, 1871).

Edgeworth, Francis Ysidro, *Metretike: Or the Method of Measuring Probability and Utility* (London: Temple, 1887).

Menger, Karl, "Das Unsicherheitsmoment in der Wertlehre: Betrachtungen im Anschluss an das sogenannte Petersburger Spiel," *Zeitschrift für Nationalökonomie*, Vol. 5 (1934), pp. 459-485.

Morgenstern, Oskar, "Vollkomme Voraussicht und wirtschaftliches Gleichgewicht," *Zeitschrift für Nationalökonomie,*" Vol. 6 (1935), pp. 196-208.

Fellner, William, "Distortion of Subjective Probabilities as a Reaction to Uncertainty," *Quarterly Journal of Economics*, Vol. 75 (November 1961), pp. 670-689.

Borch, Karl, *The Economics of Uncertainty* (Princeton: Princeton University Press, 1968).

Shackle, George L. S., *Epistemics and Economics: A Critique of Economic Doctrines* (Cambridge: At the University Press, 1972).

Balch, Michael; McFadden, D.; and Wu, S., eds., *Essays on Economic Behavior Under Uncertainty* (Amsterdam: North-Holland, 1974).

Coddington, Alan, "Creaking Semaphore and Beyond: A Consideration of Shackle's 'Epistemics and Economics,' " *British Journal for the Philosophy of Science*, Vol. 26 (June 1975), pp. 151-163.

Loasby, Brian J., *Choice, Complexity, and Ignorance* (Cambridge: At the University Press, 1976).

3.2 Uncertainty and Time Preference

Böhm-Bawerk, Eugen von, *Kapital and Kapitalzins*, Vol. 2: *Positive Theorie des Kapitals* (Jena: Gustav Fischer, 1889); English translation, *Capital and Interest*, Vol. 2: *Positive Theory of Capital* (South Holland, Ill.: Libertarian Press, 1959).

Fisher, Irving, *The Rate of Interest* (New York: Macmillan, 1907).

Levhari, David, and Srinivasan, Thirukodikaval T. N., "Optimal Savings under Uncertainty," *Review of Economic Studies*, Vol. 36 (April 1969), pp. 153-163.

Merton, Robert C., "Lifetime Portfolio Selection Under Uncertainty: The Continuous-Time Cast," *Review of Economics and Statistics*, Vol. 51 (August 1969), pp. 247-257.

Foldes, Lucien, "Optimal Saving and Risk in Continuous Time," *Review of Economic Studies*, Vol. 45 (February 1978), pp. 39-65.

Rossman, Michael, and Selden, Larry, "Time Preferences, Conditional Risk Preferences and Two-Period Cardinal Utility," *Journal of Economic Theory*, Vol. 19 (October 1978), pp. 64-83.

Selden, Larry, "An OCE Analysis of the Effect of Uncertainty on Saving under Risk Preference Independence," *Review of Economic Studies*, Vol. 46 (January 1979), pp. 73-82.

3.3 *Money and Liquidity*

Mises, Ludwig von, *Theorie des Geldes und der Umlaufsmittel* (Munich and Leipzig: Duncker & Humblot, 1912; 2d ed. 1924); English translation, *The Theory of Money and Credit* (London: Jonathan Cape, 1934; new ed., New Haven: Yale University Press, 1953).

Lachmann, Ludwig M., "Uncertainty and Liquidity Preference," *Economica*, N.S., Vol. 4 (August 1937), pp. 295-308.

Marschak, Jacob, "Role of Liquidity Under Complete and Incomplete Information," *American Economic Review*, Vol. 39 (Suppl. May 1949), pp. 182-195.

Tobin, James, "Liquidity Preference as Behavior Towards Risk," *Review of Economic Studies*, Vol. 25 (February 1958), pp. 65-86.

Streissler, Erich, "Menger's Theories of Money and Uncertainty: A Modern Interpretation," in John R. Hicks, and Wilhelm Weber, eds., *Carl Menger and the Austrian School of Economics* (Oxford: Clarendon Press 1973).

Goodhart, Charles A. E., *Money, Information, and Uncertainty* (London: Macmillan, 1975).

3.4 *Insurance*

Barrois, Théodore, *Essai sur l'application du calcul des probabilités aux assurances contre l'incendie* (Lille: Société royale des sciences de Lille, 1834).

Willett, Allan Herbert, *The Economic Theory of Risk and Insurance*, Columbia University Studies in Political Science, Vol. XIV, No. 2 (New York: Columbia University Press, 1901).

Smith, Vernon, "Optimal Insurance Coverage," *Journal of Political Economy*, Vol. 76 (January-February 1968), pp. 68-77.

Vickrey, William, "Automobile Accidents, Tort Law, Externalities, and Insurance: An Economist's Critique," *Law and Contemporary Problems*, Vol. 33 (Summer 1968), pp. 464-487.

Borch, Karl, *The Mathematical Theory of Insurance: An Annotated Selection of Papers on Insurance Published 1960-1972* (Lexington, Mass.: Heath, 1974).

Marshall, John M., "Insurance Theory: Reserves versus Mutuality," *Economic Inquiry*, Vol. 12 (December 1974), pp. 476-492.

3.5 *Gambling*

Bernouilli, Daniel, "Specimen Theoriae novae de mensura sortis," in *Commentarii academiae scientiarum imperialis Petropolitanae*, Vol. 5 (St. Petersburg: Imperial Academy of Sciences, 1738); English translation by Louise Sommers, "Exposition of a New Theory on the Measurement of Risk," *Econometrica*, Vol. 22 (January 1954), pp. 23-36.

Savage, Leonard J., and Dubins, Lester E., *How to Gamble If You Must: Inequalities for Stochastic Processes* (New York: McGraw-Hill, 1965).

Epstein, Richard A., *The Theory of Gambling and Statistical Logic* (New York: Academic Press, 1967).

Shapley, Lloyd S., "The St. Petersburg Paradox? A Con Game," *Journal of Economic Theory*, Vol. 14 (April 1977), pp. 439-442.

Danforth, John P., "Wealth and the Value of Generalized Lotteries," *Journal of Economic Theory*, Vol. 15 (June 1977), pp. 54-71.

Prakash, Prem, "On the Consistency of a Gambler with Time Preference," *Journal of Economic Theory*, Vol. 15 (June 1977), pp. 38-44.

Danforth, John P., "Wealth and the Value of Generalized Lotteries," *Journal of Economic Theory*, Vol. 15 (June 1977), pp. 54-71.

Gibbard, Allan, "Straightforwardness of Game Forms with Lotteries as Outcomes," *Econometrica*, Vol. 46 (May 1978), pp. 595-614.

3.6   Hedging and Speculation

Emery, Henry C., "Speculation on the Stock and Produce Exchanges of the United States," in *Studies in History, Economics, and Public Law*, Vol. 7 (New York: Columbia University, 1896), pp. 285-512.

Bachelier, Louis, *Théorie de la Spéculation* (Paris: Gauthiers-Villards, 1900).

Working, Holbrook, "Financial Results of Speculative Holding of Wheat," *Wheat Studies*, Vol. 7 (July 1931).

Williams, John Burr, "Speculation and the Carryover," *Quarterly Journal of Economics*, Vol. 50 (May 1936), pp. 436-455.

Kaldor, Nicholas, "Speculation and Economic Stability," *Review of Economic Studies*, Vol. 7 (October 1939), pp. 1-27.

Working, Holbrook, "Futures Trading and Hedging," *American Economic Review*, Vol. 43 (June 1953), pp. 314-343.

Baumol, William J., "Speculation, Profitability and Stability," *Review of Economics and Statistics*, Vol. 39 (August 1957), pp. 263-271.

Telser, Lester G., "A Theory of Speculation Relating Profitability and Stability," *Review of Economics and Statistics*, Vol. 41 (August 1959), pp. 295-301.

Johnson, Leland L., "The Theory of Hedging and Speculation in Commodity Futures," *Review of Economic Studies*, Vol. 27 (June 1960), pp. 139-151.

Cootner, Paul H., "Returns to Speculators: Telser versus Keynes," *Journal of Political Economy*, Vol. 68 (July-August 1960), pp. 397-404, 415-418.

Cootner, Paul H., "Speculation, Hedging, Arbitrage," *International Encyclopaedia of Social Sciences*, Vol. 15 (1968), pp. 117-121.

Ward, Ronald W., and Fletcher, Lehman B., "From Hedging to Pure Speculation: A Micro Model of Optimal Futures and Cash Market Positions," *American Journal of Agricultural Economics*, Vol. 53 (February 1971), pp. 71-78.

Hirshleifer, Jack, "Speculation and Equilibrium: Information, Risk, and Markets," *Quarterly Journal of Economics*, Vol. 89 (November 1975), pp. 519-542.

Salant, Stephen W., "Hirshleifer on Speculation," *Quarterly Journal of Economics*, Vol. 90 (November 1976), pp. 667-675.

Feiger, George, "What is Speculation?" *Quarterly Journal of Economics*, Vol. 90 (November 1976), pp. 677-687.

Hirshleifer, Jack, "Reply to Comments on 'Speculation and Equilibrium: Information, Risk, and Markets,' " *Quarterly Journal of Economics*, Vol. 90 (November 1976), pp. 689-696.

Hirshleifer, Jack, "The Theory of Speculation Under Alternative Regimes of Markets," *Journal of Finance*, Vol. 32 (September 1977), pp. 975-998.

Hart, Oliver D., "On the Profitability of Speculation," *Quarterly Journal of Economics*, Vol. 91 (Nov. 1977), pp. 579-597.

Miller, Ross M.; Plott, Charles R.; and Smith, Vernon L., "Intertemporal Competitive Equilibrium: An Empirical Study of Speculation," *Quarterly Journal of Economics*, Vol. 91 (November 1977), pp. 599-624.

3.7   Guarantees

McKean, Roland N., "Producer Liability: Trends and Implications," *University of Chicago Law Review*, Vol. 38 (Fall 1970), pp. 3-63.

Dorfman, Robert, "The Economics of Producer Liability: A Reaction to McKean," *University of Chicago Law Review*, Vol. 38 (Fall 1970), pp. 92-102.

Buchanan, James, "In Defense of *Caveat Emptor*," *University of Chicago Law Review*, Vol. 38 (Fall 1970), pp. 64-73.

Brown, John P., "Producer Liability: The Case of an Asset with Random Life," *American Economic Review*, Vol. 64 (March 1974), pp. 149-161.

Heal, Geoffrey, "Guarantees and Risk-Sharing," *Review of Economic Studies*, Vol. 44 (October 1977), pp. 549-560.

Spence, Michael, "Consumer Misperceptions, Product Failure, and Producer Liability," *Review of Economic Studies*, Vol. 44 (October 1977), pp. 561-572.

4.   UNCERTAINTY, RISK-AVERSION, VENTURE SPIRIT, INNOVATIVENESS, AND ALERTNESS AS FACTORS IN THE EXPLANATION OF ENTREPRENEURSHIP AND PROFIT

4.1   General

Thünen, Johann Heinrich von, *Der isolierte Staat*, 3d ed., 1842/1850, new impression edited by Waentig, Heinrich (Jena: Gustav Fischer, 1930), Vol. II, pp. 478-483; also edited by Braeuer, Walter, and Eberhard, E. A. Gerhardt (Darmstadt: Wissenschaftliche Buchgesellschaft, 1966), Part II, §7, pp. 83-89.

Courcelle-Seneuil, Jean, "Profit," in Charles Coquelin, ed., *Dictionnaire de l'économie politique* (Paris: Guillaumin, 1852).

Mangoldt, Hans Karl Emil von, *Die Lehre vom Unternehmergewinn* (Leipzig: Teubner, 1855).

Hawley, Frederick Barnard, *Enterprise and the Productive Process* (New York: Putnam, 1907).

Machlup, Fritz, "Competition, Pliopoly, and Profit," *Economica*, N.S., Vol. 9 (February and May 1942), pp. 1-23, 153-173.

Kalecki, Michael, *Theory of Economic Dynamics* (London: Allen & Unwin, 1954).

Kirzner, Israel M., "The Entrepreneurial Role in Menger's System," *Atlantic Economic Journal*, Vol. 6 (September 1978), pp. 31-45.

4.2   *Uncertainty-Bearing, Entrepreneurship, and Profit*

Carver, Thomas Nixon, "The Risk Theory of Profits," *Quarterly Journal of Economics*, Vol. 15 (May 1901), pp. 456-458.

Hawley, Frederick Barnard, "Reply to Final Objections to the Risk Theory of Profit," *Quarterly Journal of Economics*, Vol. 15 (August 1901), pp. 603-620.

Knight, Frank H., *Risk Uncertainty, and Profit* (Boston: Houghton Mifflin, 1921; reprinted London: London School of Economics, 1933).

Hardy, Charles O., *Risk and Risk-Bearing* (Chicago: University of Chicago Press, 1923).

Hicks, John R., "The Theory of Uncertainty and Profit," *Economica*, Vol. 2 (May 1931), pp. 170-189.

Weston, J. Fred, "A Generalized Uncertainty Theory of Profit," *American Economic Review*, Vol. 40 (March 1950), pp. 40-60.

Fellner, William J., "Profit as the Risk-Taker's Surplus: A Probabilistic Theory," *Review of Economics and Statistics*, Vol. 45 (May 1963), pp. 173-184.

4.3   *Innovation, Entrepreneurship, and Profit*

Schumpeter, Joseph A., *Die Theorie der wirtschaftlichen Entwicklung* (Leipzig: Duncker & Humblot, 1912), English translation by Redvers Opie, *The Theory of Economic Development* (Cambridge, Mass.: Harvard University Press, 1934).

Mueller, Dennis C., "Information, Mobility, and Profit," *Kyklos*, Vol. 29 (No. 3, 1976), pp. 419-448.

4.4   *Alertness, Entrepreneurship, and Profit*

Kirzner, Israel M., *Competition and Entrepreneurship* (Chicago: University of Chicago Press, 1973).

Kirzner, Israel M., *Perception, Opportunity, and Profit: Studies in the Theory of Entrepreneurship* (Chicago: University of Chicago Press, 1979).

5. New Knowledge (Invention, Discovery) and Its Application (Innovation, Imitation) as Factors in Economic Growth

5.1 *General*

Brozen, Yale, "Inventions, Innovation, and Imitation," *American Economic Review*, Vol. 41 (Suppl. May 1951), pp. 239-257.

Maclaurin, William Robert, "The Sequence from Invention to Innovation and Its Relation to Economic Growth," *Quarterly Journal of Economics*, Vol. 67 (February 1953), pp. 97-111.

Ames, Edward, "Research, Invention, Development and Innovation," *American Economic Review*, Vol. 51 (June 1961), pp. 370-381.

Schmookler, Jacob, *Invention and Economic Growth* (Cambridge, Mass.: Harvard University Press, 1966).

Mansfield, Edwin, *Industrial Research and Technological Innovation: An Econometric Analysis* (New York: Norton, 1968).

Nordhaus, William D., *Invention, Growth, and Welfare: A Theoretical Treatment of Technological Change* (Cambridge, Mass.: MIT Press, 1969).

Nordhaus, William D., "An Economic Theory of Technological Change," *American Economic Review*, Vol. 59 (Suppl. May 1969), pp. 18-28.

Fellner, William J., "Trends in the Activities Generating Technological Progress," *American Economic Review*, Vol. 60 (March 1970), pp. 1-29.

Mansfield, Edwin et al., *Research and Innovation in the Modern Corporation* (New York: Norton, 1971).

5.2 *Inventive Activity*

Merton, Robert K., "Fluctuations in the Rate of Industrial Invention," *Quarterly Journal of Economics*, Vol. 49 (May 1935), pp. 454-474.

Schmookler, Jacob, "The Level of Inventive Activity," *Review of Economics and Statistics*, Vol. 36 (May 1954), pp. 183-190.

Jewkes, John; Sawers, David; and Stillerman, Richard, *The Sources of Invention* (London: Macmillan, 1958).

Nelson, Richard R., "The Economics of Invention: A Survey of the Literature," *Journal of Business*, Vol. 32 (April 1959), pp. 101-127.

Machlup, Fritz, "The Supply of Inventors and Inventions," *Weltwirtschaftliches Archiv*, Vol. 85 (1960), pp. 210-254; reprinted in George Bitros, ed., *Selected Economic Writings of Fritz Machlup* (New York: New York University Press, 1976), pp. 439-483.

Nelson, Richard R., ed., National Bureau of Economic Research, *The Rate and Direction of Inventive Activity: Economic and Social Factors* (Princeton: Princeton University Press, 1962).

Kuznets, Simon, "Inventive Activity: Problems of Definition and Measurement," in National Bureau of Economic Research, *The Rate and Direction of Inventive Activity: Economic and Social Factors* (Princeton: Princeton University Press, 1962), pp. 19-51.

Scherer, Frederic M., "Firm Size, Market Structure, Opportunity and the

Output of Patented Inventions," *American Economic Review*, Vol. 55 (December 1965), pp. 1097-1125.

Ahmad, Syed, "On the Theory of Induced Invention," *Economic Journal*, Vol. 76 (June 1966), pp. 344-357.

Mueller, Dennis C., "Patents, Research and Development, and the Measurement of Inventive Activity," *Journal of Industrial Economics*, Vol. 15 (November 1966), pp. 26-37.

Baldwin, William L., and Childs, Gerald L., "The Fast Second and Rivalry in Research and Development," *Southern Economic Journal*, Vol. 36 (July 1969), pp. 18-24.

Hirshleifer, Jack, "The Private and Social Value of Information and the Reward to Inventive Activity," *American Economic Review*, Vol. 61 (September 1971), pp. 561-573.

5.3 *Innovative Activity*

Lange, Oskar, "A Note on Innovations," *Review of Economics and Statistics*, Vol. 25 (February 1943), pp. 19-25.

Carter, Charles F., and Williams, Bruce R., *Investment in Innovation* (London: Oxford University Press, 1958).

Samuelson, Paul A., "A Theory of Induced Innovation Along Kennedy-Weizsacker Lines," *Review of Economics and Statistics*, Vol. 47 (November 1965), pp. 343-356.

Johnston, Robert E., "Technical Progress and Innovation," *Oxford Economic Papers*, Vol. 18 (July 1966), pp. 158-176.

Barzel, Yoram, "Optimal Timing of Innovations," *Review of Economics and Statistics*, Vol. 50 (August 1968), pp. 348-355.

Havelock, Ronald G. et al., *Planning for Innovation Through Dissemination and Utilization of Knowledge* (Ann Arbor: Institute for Social Research, University of Michigan, 1969).

Encel, Solomon, "Science, Discovery, and Innovation: An Australian Case History," *International Social Science Journal*, Vol. 22 (No. 1, 1970), pp. 42-53.

Winter, Sidney, Jr., "Satisficing, Selection, and the Innovating Remnant," *Quarterly Journal of Economics*, Vol. 85 (May 1971), pp. 237-261.

Kamien, Morton I., and Schwartz, Nancy L., "Timing of Innovations Under Rivalry," *Econometrica*, Vol. 40 (January 1972), pp. 43-60.

Kamien, Morton I., and Schwartz, Nancy L., "Market Structure and Innovation: A Survey," *Journal of Economic Literature*, Vol. 13 (March 1975), pp. 1-37.

Binswanger, Hans P.; Ruttan, Vernon W.; et al., *Induced Innovation: Technology, Institutions, and Development* (Baltimore: Johns Hopkins University Press, 1978).

Dasgupta, Partha, and Stiglitz, Joseph, "Industrial Structure and the Nature of Innovative Activity," *Economic Journal*, Vol. 90 (June 1980), pp. 266-293.

5.4   *Competitive Imitation*

Machlup, Fritz, "The Optimum Lag of Imitation behind Innovation," in *Til Frederik Zeuthen* (Copenhagen: Nationalokonomisk Forening, 1958), pp. 239-256; reprinted in George Bitros, ed., *Selected Economic Writings of Fritz Machlup* (New York: New York University Press, 1976), pp. 485-502.

Vicas, Alex, "The Lag of Unrestricted Imitation Following Product Innovation," Ph.D. dissertation, Princeton University, 1966.

Scherer, Frederic M., "Nordhaus' Theory of Optimal Patent Life: A Geometric Reinterpretation," *American Economic Review*, Vol. 62 (June 1972), pp. 422-427.

Nordhaus, William D., "The Optimum Life of a Patent: Reply," *American Economic Review*, Vol. 62 (June 1972), pp. 428-431.

Kamien, Morton I., and Schwartz, Nancy L., "Patent Life and R and D Rivalry," *American Economic Review*, Vol. 64 (March 1974), pp. 183-187.

Baumol, William J., and Fischer, Dietrich, "Optimal Lags in a Schumpeterian Innovation Process," in Jacob S. Dreyer, ed., *Breadth and Depth in Economics: Fritz Machlup—The Man and His Ideas* (Lexington, Mass.: Heath, 1978), pp. 241-269.

Mansfield, Edwin; Schwartz, Mark; and Wagner, Samuel, "Imitation Costs and Patents: An Empirical Study," *Economic Journal*, Vol. 91 (December 1981), pp. 907-917.

5.5   *Learning by Doing*

Arrow, Kenneth J., "The Economic Implications of Learning by Doing," *Review of Economic Studies*, Vol. 29 (June 1962), pp. 155-173.

Fellner, William, "Specific Interpretation of Learning by Doing," *Journal of Economic Theory*, Vol. 1 (August 1969), pp. 119-140.

Weiss, Yoram, "Learning by Doing and Occupational Specialization," *Journal of Economic Theory*, Vol. 3 (June 1971), pp. 189-198.

Flueckiger, Gerald E., "Specialization, Learning by Doing and the Optimal Amount of Learning," *Economic Inquiry*, Vol. 14 (September 1976), pp. 389-409.

5.6   *Obsolescence of Knowledge and Skills*

Dubin, Samuel S., ed., *Professional Obsolescence* (Lexington, Mass.: Heath, 1971).

Rosen, Sherwin, "Measuring the Obsolescence of Knowledge," in Thomas R. Juster, ed., *Education, Income and Human Behavior* (New York: McGraw-Hill [Carnegie Commission and NBER], 1975), pp. 199-232.

5.7   *Patents, Copyrights, and Other Incentives to Create Knowledge*

Macfie, Robert Andrew, *The Patent Question Under Free Trade* (London: W. J. Johnson, 1864).

Schäffle, Albert E. F., *Die nationalökonomische Theorie der ausschliessenden Absatzverhältnisse, insbesondere des literarisch-artistischen Urheberrechtes, des Patent-, Muster- und Firmenschutzes nebst Beitragen zur Grundrentenlehre* (Tübingen: Laupp, 1867).

Vaughn, Floyd, L., *Economics of Our Patent System* (New York: Macmillan, 1925).

Plant, Arnold, "The Economic Theory Concerning Patents for Inventions," *Economica*, N.S., Vol. 1 (February 1934), pp. 30-51.

Plant, Arnold, "The Economic Aspects of Copyright in Books," *Economica*, N.S., Vol. 1 (May 1934), pp. 167-195.

Kahn, Alfred E., "Fundamental Deficiencies of the American Patent Law," *American Economic Review*, Vol. 30 (September 1940), pp. 475-491.

Polanyi, Michael, "Patent Reform," *Review of Economic Studies*, Vol. 11 (No. 2, 1944), pp. 61-76.

Fox, Harold G., *Monopolies and Patents* (Toronto: University of Toronto Press, 1947).

Plant, Arnold, "Patent and Copyright Reform," *The Three Banks Review* (September 1949), pp. 3-21.

Gilfillan, Seabury Colum, "The Root of Patents, or Squaring Patents by their Roots," *Journal of the Patent Office Society*, Vol. 31 (1949), pp. 611-623.

Machlup, Fritz, and Penrose, Edith, "The Patent Controversy in the Nineteenth Century," *Journal of Economic History*, Vol. 10 (May 1950), pp. 1-29.

Penrose, Edith Tilton, *The Economics of the International Patent System* (Baltimore: Johns Hopkins University Press, 1951).

Plant, Sir Arnold, *The New Commerce in Ideas and Intellectual Property* (London: University of London, Athlone Press, 1953).

Vaughn, Floyd L., *The United States Patent System* (Norman: University of Oklahoma Press, 1956).

Vernon, Raymond, *The International Patent System and Foreign Policy* (U.S. Congress, Senate, Committee on the Judiciary, Subcommittee on Patents, Trademarks, and Copyrights, Study No. 5, Washington, D.C., 1957).

Machlup, Fritz, *An Economic Review of the Patent System* (U.S. Congress, Senate, Committee on the Judiciary, Subcommittee on Patents, Trademarks, and Copyrights, Study No. 15, Washington, D.C., 1958).

Reichardt, Robert, *Die Schallplatte als kulturelles und ökonomisches Problem* (Zürich: Polygraphischer Verlag, 1962).

Phillips, Almarin, "Patents, Potential Competition, and Technical Progress," *American Economic Review*, Vol. 56 (May 1966), pp. 301-310.

McGee, John S., "Patent Exploitation: Some Economic and Legal Problems," *Journal of Law and Economics*, Vol. 9 (October 1966), pp. 135-162.

Marke, Julius J., *Copyright and Intellectual Property* (New York: Fund for the Advancement of Education, 1967).

Lightman, Joseph M., "Inventors' Cerificates and Industrial Property Rights," *IDEA*, Vol. 11 (Summer 1967), pp. 133-149.

Siegel, Irving H., "Changing Status of Sole Inventors: A Company Case Study," *IDEA*, Vol. 11 (Summer 1967), pp. 151-158.

Dale, Robert F., and Huntoon, James K., "A Cost-Benefit Study of the Domestic and International Patent Systems," *IDEA*, Vol. 11 (Autumn 1967), pp. 351-406.

Lightman, Joseph M.; Brufsky, Allen D.; and Bangs, Robert B., "Economic Aspects of Trademark Utilization," *IDEA*, Vol. 11 (Winter 1967-1968), pp. 472-499.

Harris, L. James, "Patents and Trade Secrets: Instruments of Positive Competition," *IDEA*, Vol. 12 (Spring 1968), pp. 631-641.

Machlup, Fritz, "Patents," *International Encyclopaedia of the Social Sciences*, Vol. 11 (1968), pp. 461-472.

Comanor, William S., and Scherer, Frederic M., "Patent Statistics as a Measure of Technical Change," *Journal of Political Economy*, Vol. 77 (May-June 1969), pp. 392-398.

Firestone, O. John, *Economic Implications of Patents* (Ottawa: University of Ottawa Press, 1971).

Prosi, Gerhard, *Ökonomische Theorie des Buches: Volkswirtschaftliche Aspekte des Urheber- und Verlegerschutzes* (Düsseldorf: Bertelsmann Universitätsverlag, 1971).

Taylor, Christopher T., and Silberston, Z. Aubrey, *The Economic Impact of the Patent System* (Cambridge: At the University Press, 1973).

Johnson, Harry G., *Aspects of Patents and Licenses as Stimuli to Innovation*. Bernhard-Harms Vorlesungen No. 7 (Kiel: Institut für Weltwirtschaft, Universität Kiel, 1976), pp. 25-36.

Cheung, Steven N. S., "Property Rights and Invention," and "The Right to Invent and the Right to an Invention," University of Washington, Institute of Economic Research, Reports No. 79-11 and 79-13, 1979.

Cheung, Steven N. S., "Property Rights in Trade Secrets," *Economic Inquiry*, Vol. 20 (January 1982), pp. 44-53.

5.8   Technology and Economic Welfare and Growth

Solow, Robert M., "Technical Change and the Aggregate Production Function," *Review of Economics and Statistics*, Vol. 39 (August 1957), pp. 312-320.

Griliches, Zvi, "Research Costs and Social Returns: Hybrid Corn and Related Innovations," *Journal of Political Economy*, Vol. 66 (September-October 1958), pp. 419-431.

Arrow, Kenneth J., "Economic Welfare and the Allocation of Resources for Invention," in Richard R. Nelson, ed., *The Rate and Direction of Inventive Activity: Economic and Social Factors*, Universities—NBER Conference (Princeton: Princeton University Press, 1962).

Encel, Solomon, and Inglis, A., "Patents, Inventions, and Economic Progress," *Economic Record*, Vol. 42 (December 1966), pp. 572-588.

Nelson, Richard R.; Peck, Merton J.; and Kalachek, Edward D., *Technology,*

Economic Growth, and Public Policy (Washington, D.C.: Brookings Institution, 1967).

Evenson, Robert, "The Contribution of Agricultural Research to Production," *Journal of Farm Economics*, Vol. 49 (December 1967), pp. 1415-1425.

Fellner, William, "Measures of Technological Progress in the Light of Recent Growth Theories," *American Economic Review*, Vol. 57 (December 1967), pp. 1073-1098.

Mansfield, Edwin; Rapoport, John; et al., "Social and Private Rates of Return Norton, 1968).

Williams, Bruce R., ed., *Science and Technology in Economic Growth*, Proceedings of a Conference Held by the International Economic Association at St. Anton, Austria (London: Macmillan, 1973).

Denison, Edward F., *Accounting for United States Economic Growth, 1929-1969* (Washington, D.C.: Brookings Institution, 1974).

Mansfield, Edwin; Rapoport, John; et al., "Social and Private Rates of Return from Industrial Innovation," *Quarterly Journal of Economics*, Vol. 91 (May 1977), pp. 221-240.

6. THE TRANSFER OF TECHNOLOGY AND KNOW-HOW

6.1 *General*

Carter, Charles F., and Williams, Bruce R., *Industry and Technical Progress: Factors Governing the Speed and Application of Science* (London: Oxford University Press, 1957).

Sovel, M. Terry, *Technology Transfer: A Selected Bibliography* (Denver: Denver Research Institute, University of Denver for the National Aeronautics and Space Administration, 1968).

Gruber, William H., and Marquis, Donald G., eds., *Factors in the Transfer of Technology* (Cambridge, Mass.: MIT Press, 1969).

Arrow, Kenneth J., "Classificatory Notes on the Production and Transmission of Technological Knowledge," *American Economic Review*, Vol. 52 (Suppl. May 1969), pp. 29-35.

Heller, H. S. et al., *Technology Transfer: A Selected Bibliography* (Denver: Denver Research Institute, University of Denver, 1971).

6.2 *Among Firms and Industries*

Isenson, Raymond S., "Project Hindsight: An Empirical Study of the Sources of Ideas Utilized in Operational Weapon Systems," in William Gruber and Donald C. Marquis, eds., *Factors in the Transfer of Technology* (Cambridge, Mass.: MIT Press, 1969), pp. 155-176.

Nasbeth, L., "The Diffusion of Innovations in Swedish Industry," in Bruce R. Williams, ed., *Science and Technology in Economic Growth* (London: Macmillan, 1973).

Nasbeth, L., and Ray, G. F., *The Diffusion of New Industrial Processes*, (Cambridge: At the University Press, 1974).

6.3   *Among Countries*

Svennilson, Ingvar, "Technical Assistance: The Transfer of Industrial Know-How to Non-Industrial Countries" in Kenneth Berill, ed., *Economic Development with Special Reference to East Asia* (New York: St. Martin's Press, 1964).
UNCTAD, "The Transfer of Technology," *Journal of World Trade Law*, Vol. 4 (September-October 1970), pp. 711.
Rosenberg, Nathan, "Economic Development and the Transfer of Technology," *Technology and Culture*, Vol. 11 (October 1970), pp. 550-575.
Pavitt, Keith, "The Multinational Enterprise and the Transfer of Technology," in John H. Dunning, ed., *The Multinational Enterprise* (London: Allen & Unwin, 1971).
Tilton, John E., *International Diffusion of Technology: The Case of Semi-Conductors* (Washington, D.C.: Brookings Institution, 1971).
Parpia, H.A.B., "Transfer and Adaptation of Western Methods in Agricultural Processing," *World Development*, Vol. 2 (February 1974), pp. 99-102.
Hoos, Ida R., "Systems Analysis as Technology Transfer," *Journal of Dynamic Systems, Measurement, and Control*, Vol. 96 (March 1974), pp. 1-5.
Carlson, Sune, "International Transmission of Information and the Business Firm," *Annals of the American Academy of Political and Social Science*, Vol. 412 (March 1974), pp. 55-63.
Nelson, Richard R., "Less Developed Countries—Technology Transfer and Adaptation: The Role of the Indigenous Science Community," *Economic Development and Cultural Change*, Vol. 23 (October 1974), pp. 61-77.
Mowlana, Hamid, "The Multinational Corporation and the Diffusion of Technology," in Abdul A. Said and L. R. Simmons, eds., *The New Sovereigns* (Englewood Cliffs, N.J.: Prentice-Hall, 1975).
Sarkar, P. L., "Transfer of Technology to Less Developed Countries: Indian Experience with Multinational Corporations," *Indian Economic Journal*, Vol. 26 (October-December 1978), pp. 131-152.
Walters, Ingo, and Gladwin, Thomas N., "Technology and Conflict in Multinational Corporation Operations," in *Multinationals in Conflict: Lessons in Conflict Management* (New York: Wiley, 1979).
Gustafson, Thane, *Selling Russians the Rope*, Report of the Rand Corporation, 1981.

7.   ECONOMIC FORECASTING

7.1   *General*

Morgenstern, Oskar, *Wirtschaftsprognose* (Vienna: Springer-Verlag, 1928).
Grunberg, Emile, and Modigliani, Franco, "The Predictability of Social Events,"

Journal of Political Economy, Vol. 62 (November-December 1954), pp. 465-478.

Kaminow, Ira, "How Well do Economists Forecast?" *Federal Reserve Bank Business Review of Philadelphia*, May 1971, pp. 9-19.

Butler, William F.; Kavesh, Robert A.; and Platt, Robert B., eds., *Methods and Techniques for Business Forecasting* (Englewood Cliffs, N.J.: Prentice-Hall, 1974).

7.2 *Forecasting Trends and Fluctuations*

Kondratieff, Nicholas Dmitrievich, "The Long Waves in Economic Life," trans. by Wolfgang F. Stolper, *Review of Economics and Statistics*, Vol. 17, Part 2 (November 1935), pp. 105-115.

Fand, David I., "The Monetary Theory of Nine Recent Quarterly Econometric Models of the United States: A Comment," *Journal of Money, Credit, and Banking*, Vol. 3 (May 1971), pp. 450-460.

Thompson, Howard E., and Tiao, George C., "Analysis of Telephone Data: A Case Study of Forecasting Seasonal Time Series," *The Bell Journal of Economics and Management Science*, Vol. 2 (Autumn 1971), pp. 515-541.

7.3 *Projections, Predictions, and Economic Indicators*

Persons, Warren M., "Construction of a Business Barometer Based upon Annual Data," *American Economic Review*, Vol. 6 (December 1916), pp. 739-769.

Persons, Warren M., "Indices of Business Conditions," *Review of Economic Statistics*, Vol. 1 (January 1919), pp. 5-107.

Bullock, Charles J.; Persons, Warren M.; and Crum, William L., "The Construction and Interpretation of the Harvard Index of Business Conditions," *Review of Economic Statistics*, Vol. 9 (April 1927), pp. 74-92.

Wiles, Peter J. D., ed., *The Prediction of Communist Economic Performance*, Soviet and East European Studies (London: Cambridge University Press, 1971).

Mitchell, Bridger M., "Estimation of Large Econometric Models by Principal Component and Instrumental Variable Methods," *Review of Economics and Statistics*, Vol. 53 (May 1971), pp. 140-146.

Emery, John T., "The Information Content of Daily Market Indicators," *Journal of Financial and Quantitative Analysis*, Vol. 8 (March 1973), pp. 183-190.

Howrey, E. Philip; Klein, Lawrence R.; and McCarthy, Michael D., "Notes on Testing the Predictive Performance of Econometric Models," *International Economic Review*, Vol. 15 (June 1974), pp. 366-383.

7.4 *Predicting Stock-Market Prices*

Cowles, Alfred, III, "Can Stock Market Forecasters Forecast?" *Econometrica*, Vol. 1 (July 1933), pp. 309-324.

Graham, Benjamin, and Dodd, David L., *Security Analysis* (New York: McGraw-Hill, 1934).

Osborne, F. M., "Periodic Structure in the Brownian Motion of Stock Prices," *Operations Research*, Vol. 10 (May-June 1962), pp. 345-379.

Cootner, Paul H., ed., *The Random Character of Stock Market Prices* (Cambridge, Mass.: MIT Press, 1964).

Granger, Clive W. J., and Morgenstern, Oskar, *Predictability of Stock Market Prices* (Lexington, Mass.: Lexington Books, Heath, 1970).

Levy, Robert A., The Predictive Significance of Five-Point Chart Patterns," *Journal of Business*, Vol. 44 (July 1971), pp. 316-322.

Malkiel, Burton G., *A Random Walk Down Wall Street* (New York: Norton, 1973).

Rosenberg, Barr, and McKibben, Walt, "The Prediction of Systematic and Specific Risk in Common Stocks," *Journal of Financial and Quantitative Analysis*, Vol. 8 (March 1973), pp. 317-333.

Winkler, Robert L., "Bayesian Models for Forecasting Future Security Prices," *Journal of Financial and Quantitative Analysis*, Vol. 8 (June 1973), pp. 387-405.

7.5 Forecasting National Aggregates (Output, Employment, Saving, Investment)

Warren, George Frederick, and Pearson, Frank Ashmore, "The Future of the General Price Level," *Journal of Farm Economics*, Vol. 14 (January 1932), pp. 23-46.

Spencer, Roger W., "Population, the Labor Force, and Potential Output: Implications of the St. Louis Model," *Federal Reserve Bank of St. Louis Review*, Vol. 53 (February 1971), pp. 15-23.

Bray, Jeremy, "Dynamic Equations for Economic Forecasting with the GDP—Unemployment Relation and the Growth of GDP in the United Kingdom as an Example," *Journal of the Royal Statistical Society*, Vol. 134 (No. 2, 1971), pp. 167-209.

Ivansen, T., "Problems in Forecasting the Monetary Savings of the Population," *Problems of Economics*, Vol. 17 (June 1974), pp. 65-75.

McNees, Stephen K., "How Accurate Are Economic Forecasts?" *New England Economic Review* (November-December 1974), pp. 2-19.

7.6 Forecasting Prices, Profits, and Interest Rates

Houthakker, Hendrik, "Can Speculators Forecast Prices?" *Review of Economics and Statistics*, Vol. 39 (May 1957), pp. 143-151.

Cragg, John G., and Malkiel, Burton G., "The Consensus and Accuracy of Some Predictions of the Growth of Corporate Earnings," *Journal of Finance*, Vol. 23 (March 1968), pp. 67-84.

Sandbulte, Arend J., "Sales and Revenue Forecasting," *Management Accounting*, Vol. 51 (December 1969), pp. 17-23.

Labys, Walter C., and Granger, Clive W. J., *Speculation, Hedging, and Commodity Price Forecasts* (Lexington, Mass.: Heath, 1970).

Bernstein, Peter L., "What Rate of Return Can You 'Reasonably' Expect," *Journal of Finance*, Vol. 28 (May 1973), pp. 273-282.

7.7   *Forecasting Technological Change*

Gilfillan, Seabury Colum, "The Prediction of Technological Change," *Review of Economics and Statistics*, Vol. 34 (November 1952), pp. 368-385.

Siegel, Irving H., "Technological Change and Long-Run Forecasting," *Journal of Business*, Vol. 26 (July 1953), pp. 141-156.

Bright, James R., ed., *Technological Forecasting for Industry and Government: Methods and Approaches* (Englewood Cliffs, N.J.: Prentice-Hall, 1968).

Arnfield, R. V., ed., *Technological Forecasting* (Edinburgh: Edinburgh University Press, 1969; and Chicago: Aldine, 1969).

Barrow, Roscoe L., and Manelli, Daniel J., "Communications Technology: A Forecast of Change," *Law and Contemporary Problems*, Vol. 34 (Spring and Summer 1969), pp. 205-243, 431-451.

Bright, James R., "Evaluating Signals of Technological Change," *Harvard Business Review*, Vol. 48 (January-February 1970), pp. 62-70.

8.   COST AND VALUE, PRIVATE OR SOCIAL, OF INFORMATION AND ALTERNATIVE INFORMATION SYSTEMS

8.1   *General*

Marschak, Jacob, "Remarks on the Economics of Information," in *Contributions to Scientific Research in Management* (Los Angeles: UCLA Graduate School of Business Administration, Study Center for Research, 1959), pp. 79-100.

Green, Paul E. et al., *Experiments on the Value of Information in Simulated Marketing Environments* (Boston: Allyn & Bacon, 1967).

Cohen, Burton J., *Cost-Effective Information Systems* (New York: American Management Association, 1971).

Baumol, William J. et al., *A Cost-Benefit Approach to Evaluation of Alternative Information Provision Procedures* (Princeton: Mathematica, 1971).

Marschak, Jacob, "Economics of Information Systems," *Journal of the American Statistical Association*, Vol. 66 (March 1971), pp. 192-219.

Marschak, Jacob, "Optional Systems for Information and Decision," in A. V. Balakrishnan, ed., *Techniques of Optimization* (New York: Academic Press, 1972), pp. 355-370.

Marschak, Jacob, "Value and Cost of Information Systems," in Eichhorn Wolfgang et al., *Production Theory: Proceedings of an International Seminar Held at the University of Karlsruhe, May-July 1973* (Berlin and New York: Springer-Verlag, 1974), pp. 335-358.

Wiio, Osmo A., "System Models of Information and Communication: Re-valuation of Some Basic Concepts of Communication," *Liiketaloudellinin Aikak*, Vol. 23 (No. 1, 1974), pp. 3-26.

Mount, Kenneth, and Reiter, Stanley, "The Informational Size of Message Spaces," *Journal of Economic Theory*, Vol. 8 (June 1974), pp. 161-192.

Marshall, John M., "Private Incentives and Public Information," *American Economic Review*, Vol. 64 (June 1974), pp. 373-390.

Reiter, Stanley, "The Knowledge Revealed by an Allocation Process and the Informational Size of the Message Space," *Journal of Economic Theory*, Vol. 8 (July 1974), pp. 389-396.

Eckstein, Otto, "National Economic Information Systems for Developed Economies," in Mark Perlman, ed., *The Organization and Retrieval of Economic Knowledge: Proceedings of a Conference Held by the International Economic Association* (London: Macmillan, 1977), pp. 67-79.

Ordover, Janusz A., and Willig, Robert D., "The Role of Information in Designing Social Policy Towards Externalities," *Journal of Public Economics*, Vol. 12 (December 1979), pp. 271-299.

8.2   Cost and Value of Greater Accuracy

Marschak, Jacob, "Towards an Economic Theory of Organization and Information," in Robert M. Thrall et al., eds., *Decision Processes* (New York: Wiley, 1954), pp. 187-220.

Hollingsworth, A. Thomas, "Perceptual Accuracy of the Informal Organization as a Determinant of the Effectiveness of Formal Leaders," *Journal of Economics and Business*, Vol. 27 (Fall 1974), pp. 75-78.

Bradford, David F., and Kelejian, Harry H., "The Value of Information for Crop Forecasting in a Market System: Some Theoretical Issues," *Review of Economic Studies*, Vol. 44 (October 1977), pp. 519-531.

9.   DECISION THEORY AND GAME THEORY

9.1   General

Arrow, Kenneth J., "Alternative Approaches to the Theory of Choice in Risk-Taking Situations," *Econometrica*, Vol. 19 (October 1951), pp. 404-437.

Blackwell, David, and Girshick, Meyer A., *Theory of Games and Statistical Decisions* (New York: Wiley, 1954).

Thrall, Robert M. et al., eds., *Decision Processes* (New York: Wiley, 1954).

Luce, Robert Duncan, and Raiffa, Howard, *Games and Decisions* (New York: Wiley, 1957).

Uzawa, Hirofumi, "Note of the Rational Selection of Decision Functions," *Econometrica*, Vol. 25 (January 1957), pp. 166-174.

Simon, Herbert A., "Theories of Decision-Making in Economics and Behavioral Science," *American Economic Review*, Vol. 49 (June 1959), pp. 253-283.

Shackle, George L. S., *Decision, Order, and Time* (Cambridge: At the University Press, 1961).

Raiffa, Howard, *Decision Analysis: Introductory Lectures on Choices Under Uncertainty* (Reading, Mass.: Addison-Wesley, 1968).

Lavalle, Irving H., "On Cash Equivalents and Information Evaluation in Decisions under Uncertainty," *Journal of the American Statistical Association*, Vol. 63 (March 1968), pp. 252-290.

Arrow, Kenneth J., *Essays in the Theory of Risk Bearing* (Chicago: Markham, 1971).

Menges, Gunther, *Economic Decision Making: Basic Concepts and Models* (London: Longman, 1974).

Churchman, Charles West; Auerbach, Leonard; and Sadan, Simcha, *Thinking for Decisions: Deductive Quantitative Methods* (Chicago: SRA, 1975).

9.2 Statistical Decision Theory

Cournot, Antoine-Augustin, *Exposition de la théorie des chances et des probabilités* (Paris: Hachette, 1843).

Wald, Abraham, *Statistical Decision Functions* (New York: Wiley, 1950).

Schlaifer, Robert, *Probability and Statistics for Business Decisions* (New York: McGraw-Hill, 1959).

Raiffa, Howard, and Schlaifer, Robert, *Applied Statistical Decision Theory* (Boston: Harvard University, Graduate School of Business Administration, 1961).

Champernowne, David G., *Uncertainty and Estimates in Economics* (San Francisco: Holden-Day, 1969).

Chance, William, *Statistical Methods for Decision Making* (Homewood, Ill.: Irwin, 1969).

DeGroot, Morris H., *Optimal Statistical Decisions* (New York: McGraw-Hill, 1970).

9.3 Theory of Games

Neumann, John von, and Morgenstern, Oskar, *Theory of Games and Economic Behavior* (Princeton: Princeton Univeristy Press, 1944; 2d ed., 1947).

Hurwicz, Leonid, "The Theory of Economic Behavior," *American Economic Review*, Vol. 35 (December 1945), pp. 909-925.

Marschak, Jacob, "Neumann's and Morgenstern's New Approach to Static Economics," *Journal of Political Economy*, Vol. 54 (March-April 1946), pp. 97-115.

Guilbaud, Georges T., "La Théorie des Jeux," *Economie Appliquée* (April-June, 1949); English translation by A. L. Minkes, "The Theory of Games," *International Economic Papers*, No. 1 (London: Macmillan, 1951), pp. 37-65.

Kaysen, Carl, "The Minimax Rule of the Theory of Games and the Choices of Strategies under Conditions of Uncertainty," *Metroeconomica*, Vol. 4 (April 1952), pp. 5-14.

Hurwicz, Leonid, "What Has Happened to the Theory of Games?" *American Economic Review*, Vol. 43 (Suppl. May 1953), pp. 398-405.

Kuhn, Harold, and Tucker, Albert W., "Theory of Games" *Encyclopaedia Britannica*, Vol. 10 (Chicago, 1956), pp. 5-10.

Davis, Otto A., and Whinston, Andrew, "Externalities, Welfare, and the Theory of Games," *Journal of Political Economy*, Vol. 70 (June 1962), pp. 241-262.

Schotter, Andrew, and Schwödiauer, Gerhard, "Economics and the Theory of Games: A Survey," *Journal of Economic Literature*, Vol. 18 (June 1980), pp. 479-527.

9.4   Game Theory of Oligopolistic Competition

Morgenstern, Oskar, "Oligopoly, Monopolistic Competition, and the Theory of Games," *American Economic Review*, Vol. 38 (Suppl. May 1948), pp. 10-18.

Mayberry, John P.; Nash, John F.; and Shubik, Martin, "A Comparison of Treatments of a Duopoly Situation," *Econometrica*, Vol. 21 (January 1953), pp. 141-154.

Shapley, Lloyd, "A Duopoly Model with Price Competition," (abstract) *Econometrica*, Vol. 25 (April 1957), pp. 354-356.

Shubik, Martin, "Edgeworth Market Games," *Annals of Mathematical Studies*, No. 40, *Contributions to the Theory of Games*, Vol. IV (Princeton: Princeton University Press, 1959), pp. 267-278.

Shubik, Martin, *Strategy and Market Structure* (New York: Wiley, 1959).

Shapley, Lloyd, and Shubik, Martin, "Price Strategy Oligopoly with Product Variation," *Kyklos*, Vol. 22 (1969), pp. 30-44.

Friedman, James, "A Non-cooperative Equilibrium for Supergames," *Review of Economic Studies*, Vol. 38 (January 1971), pp. 1-12.

Telser, Lester G., *Competition, Collusion, and Game Theory* (Chicago: Aldine-Atherton, 1972).

Shitovitz, Benjamin, "Oligopoly in Markets with a Continuum of Traders," *Econometrica*, Vol. 41 (May 1973), pp. 467-501.

Friedman, James, *Oligopoly and the Theory of Games* (Amsterdam: North-Holland, 1977).

Marschak, Thomas, and Selten, Reinhard, "Oligopolistic Economies as Games of Limited Information," *Zeitschrift für die gesamte Staatswissenschaft*, Vol. 133 (October 1977), pp. 385-410.

Marschak, Thomas, and Selten, Reinhard, "Restabilizing Responses, Inertia Supergames, and Oligopolistic Equilibria," *Quarterly Journal of Economics*, Vol. 92 (February 1978), pp. 71-93.

Rickard, John A., and Murry, Ian W., "The Dynamics of Some Duopoly Games Involving the Market Share and Nichol Strategies," *Journal of Economic Theory*, Vol. 17 (February 1978), pp. 51-65.

Levitan, Richard E., and Shubik, Martin, "Duopoly with Price and Quantity as Strategic Variables," *International Journal of Game Theory*, Vol. 7 (1978), pp. 1-11.

9.5   *Group Decision-Making and Bargaining*

Black, Duncan, "On the Rationale of Group Decision Making," *Journal of Political Economy*, Vol. 56 (January-February 1948), pp. 23-24.

Black, Duncan, "The Decisions of a Committee Using a Special Majority," *Econometrica*, Vol. 16 (July 1948), pp. 245-261.

Black, Duncan, "The Elasticity of Committee Decisions with an Altering Size of Majority," *Econometrica*, Vol. 16 (July 1948), pp. 262-270.

Nash, John F., "The Bargaining Problem," *Econometrica*, Vol. 18 (April 1950), pp. 155-162.

Harsanyi, John C., "Approaches to the Bargaining Problem Before and After the Theory of Games: A Critical Discussion of Zeuthen's Hicks' and Nash's Theories," *Econometrica*, Vol. 24 (April 1956), pp. 144-157.

Mack, Ruth P., *Planning on Uncertainty: Decision Making in Business and Government Administration* (New York: Wiley, 1971).

Marschak, Jacob, and Radner, Roy, *The Economic Theory of Teams* (Amsterdam: North-Holland, 1972).

10. Decision-Making by Consumers with Incomplete and Uncertain Knowledge

10.1   *General*

Friedman, Milton, and Savage, Leonard J., "The Utility Analysis of Choices Involving Risk," *Journal of Political Economy*, Vol. 56 (August 1948), pp. 279-304.

Marschak, Jacob, "Rational Behavior, Uncertain Prospects, and Measurable Utility," *Econometrica*, Vol. 18 (April 1950), pp. 111-141.

Friedman, Milton, *A Theory of the Consumption Function* (Princeton: Princeton University Press, NBER, 1957).

Borch, Karl, "Indifference Curves and Uncertainty," *Swedish Journal of Economics*, Vol. 70 (March 1968), pp. 19-24.

Ferber, Robert, "Consumer Economics: A Survey," *Journal of Economic Literature*, Vol. 11 (December 1973), pp. 1303-1342.

McCulloch, J. Huston, "The Austrian Theory of the Marginal Use and of Ordinal Marginal Utility," *Zeitschrift für Nationalökonomie*, Vol. 37 (1977), pp. 249-280.

Hanoch, Giora, "Risk Aversion and Consumer Preferences," *Econometrica*, Vol. 45 (March 1977), pp. 413-426.

Mitchell, Andrew, ed., *The Effect of Information on Consumer and Market Behavior* (Chicago: American Marketing Association, 1978).

Kreps, David M., and Porteus, Evan L., "Temporal Resolution of Uncertainty and Dynamic Choice Theory," *Econometrica*, Vol. 46 (January 1978), pp. 185-200.

Watkins, Thayer H., "A Property of Optimal Consumption Policies for Decision-Making under Uncertainty," *Southern Economic Journal*, Vol. 44 (April 1978), pp. 752-761.

10.2 *Search Effort*

Nelson, Phillip, "Information and Consumer Behavior," *Journal of Political Economy*, Vol. 78 (March-April 1970), pp. 311-329.

Masson, Robert Tempest, "Costs of Search and Racial Price Discrimination," *Western Economic Journal*, Vol. 11 (June 1973), pp. 167-186.

Rothschild, Michael, "Searching for the Lowest Price Where the Distribution of Prices Is Unknown," *Journal of Political Economy*, Vol. 82 (July-August 1974), pp. 689-711.

Kohn, Meir G., and Shavell, Steven, "The Theory of Search," *Journal of Economic Theory*, Vol. 9 (October 1974), pp. 93-123.

Axell, Bo, "Search Market Equilibrium," *Scandinavian Journal of Economics*, Vol. 79 (1977), pp. 20-40.

Landsberger, Michael, and Peled, Dan, "Duration of Offers, Price Structure and the Gain from Search," *Journal of Economic Theory*, Vol. 16 (October 1977), pp. 17-37.

Karni, Edi, and Schwartz, Aba, "Search Theory: The Case of Search With Uncertain Recall," *Journal of Economic Theory*, Vol. 16 (October 1977), pp. 38-52.

10.3 *Learning from Experience*

Nelson, Phillip, "Information and Consumer Behavior," *Journal of Political Economy*, Vol. 78 (March-April 1970), pp. 311-329.

Grossman, Sanford J.; Kihlstrom, Richard E.; and Mirman, Leonard J., "A Bayesian Approach to the Production of Information and Learning by Doing," *Review of Economic Studies*, Vol. 44 (October 1977), pp. 533-547.

10.4 *Legal Protection of Consumer Against Risk*

Murray, Barbara B., ed., *Consumerism: The Eternal Triangle, Business, Government, and Consumers* (Pacific Palisades, Cal.: Goodyear, 1973).

Oi, Walter Y., "The Economics of Product Safety," *Bell Journal of Economics and Management Science*, Vol. 4 (Spring 1973), pp. 3-28.

Peltzman, Sam, "An Evaluation of Consumer Protection Legislation: The 1962 Drug Amendments," *Journal of Political Economy*, Vol. 81 (September-October 1973), pp. 1049-1091.

Day, George S., and Brandt, William K., "Consumer Research and the Evaluation of Information Disclosure Requirements: The Case of Truth in

Lending," *Journal of Consumer Research*, Vol. 1 (June 1974), pp. 21-32.

Green, Mark J., "Appropriateness and Responsiveness: Can the Government Protect the Consumer?" *Journal of Economic Issues*, Vol. 8 (June 1974), pp. 309-328.

Goldberg, Victor P., "The Economics of Product Safety and Imperfect Information," *Bell Journal of Economics and Management Science*, Vol. 5 (Autumn 1974), pp. 683-688.

Spence, Michael, "Consumer Misperceptions, Product Failure and Producer Liability," *Review of Economic Studies*, Vol. 44 (October 1977), p. 561.

10.5 Buying Insurance

Yaari, Menahem E., "Uncertain Lifetime, Life Insurance, and the Theory of the Consumer," *Review of Economic Studies*, Vol. 32 (November 1965), pp. 137-150.

Spence, A. Michael, and Zeckhauser, Richard J., "Insurance, Information, and Individual Action," *American Economic Review*, Vol. 61 (Suppl. May 1971), pp. 380-387.

Ehrlich, Isaac, and Becker, Gary S., "Market Insurance, Self Insurance, and Self-Protection," *Journal of Political Economy*, Vol. 80 (July-August 1972), pp. 623-648.

Headen, Robert S., and Lee, J. Finley, "Life Insurance Demand and Household Portfolio Behavior," *Journal of Risk and Insurance*, Vol. 41 (December 1974), pp. 685-698.

Barro, Robert J., and Friedman, James W., "On Uncertain Lifetimes," *Journal of Political Economy*, Vol. 85 (July-August 1977), pp. 843-849.

Eden, Benjamin, "The Role of Insurance and Gambling in Allocating Risk Over Time," *Journal of Economic Theory*, Vol. 16 (December 1977), pp. 228-246.

10.6 Saving and Asset Holding

David, Paul A., and Scadding, John L., "Private Savings: Ultrarationality, Aggregation, and 'Denison's Law,'" *Journal of Political Economy*, Vol. 82 (March-April 1974), pp. 225-249.

Babeau, André, "Economies of Scale in Household's Cash Balances: A Series of Empirical Tests," *European Economic Review*, Vol. 5 (August 1974), pp. 87-101.

Munnell, Alicia H., "The Impact of Social Security on Personal Savings," *National Tax Journal*, Vol. 27 (December 1974), pp. 553-567.

Baranzini, Mauro, "The Effects of Interest Uncertainty in a Life-Cycle Model," *Schweizerische Zeitschrift für Volkswirtschaft und Statistik*, Vol. 113 (December 1977), pp. 407-423.

11. Decision-Making by Workers and Job Seekers with Incomplete and Uncertain Knowledge

11.1   General

Burton, John F., Jr. et al., *Readings in Labor Market Analysis* (New York: Holt, Rinehart & Winston, 1971).

Weiss, Yoram, "The Risk Element in Occupational and Educational Choices," *Journal of Political Economy*, Vol. 80 (November-December 1972), pp. 1203-1213.

Reynolds, Lloyd G.; Masters, Stanley H.; and Moser, Collette, eds., *Readings in Labor Economics and Labor Relations* (Englewood Cliffs, N.J.: Prentice-Hall, 1974).

11.2   Mobility, Geographic and Occupational

Burton, John F., Jr., and Parker, John E., "Interindustry Variations in Voluntary Labor Mobility," *Industrial and Labor Relations Review*, Vol. 22 (January 1969), pp. 199-216.

Gallaway, Lowell E., "Age and Labor Mobility Patterns," *Southern Economic Journal*, Vol. 36 (October 1969), pp. 171-180.

Johnson, David B., and Stern, James L., "Why and How Workers Shift from Blue-Collar to White-Collar Jobs," *Monthly Labor Review*, Vol. 92 (October 1969), pp. 7-13.

Rabianski, Joseph, "Real Earnings and Human Migration," *Journal of Human Resources*, Vol. 6 (Spring 1971), pp. 185-192.

Schwartz, Aba, "On Efficiency of Migration," *Journal of Human Resources*, Vol. 6 (Spring 1971), pp. 193-205.

Grossack, Irvin M., and Pfister, Richard L., "Estimating Patterns of Labor Mobility," *Journal of Human Resources*, Vol. 6 (Summer 1971), pp. 345-357.

Laber, Gene, and Chase, Richard X., "Interprovincial Migration in Canada as a Human Capital Decision," *Journal of Political Economy*, Vol. 79 (July-August 1971), pp. 795-804.

Vandercamp, John, "Migration Flows, Their Determinants, and the Effects on Return Migration," *Journal of Political Economy*, Vol. 79 (September-October 1971), pp. 1012-1031.

Todaro, Michael P., "Income Expectations, Rural-Urban Migration and Employment in Africa," *International Labour Review*, Vol. 104 (November 1971), pp. 387-413.

11.3   Employment Exchanges

Ullman, Joseph C., "Helping Workers Locate Jobs Following a Plant Shutdown," *Monthly Labor Review*, Vol. 92 (April 1969), pp. 35-40.

Davies, Gordon K., "Needed: a National Job-Matching Network," *Harvard Business Review*, Vol. 47 (September-October 1969), pp. 63-72.

Ruttenberg, Stanley H., and Gutchess, Jocelyn, *The Federal-State Employment Service* (Baltimore: Johns Hopkins University Press, 1970).

Ullman, Joseph C., and Huber, George P., "Are Job Banks Improving the Labor Market Information System?" *Industrial and Labor Relations Review*, Vol. 27 (January 1974), pp. 171-185.

11.4 Wage and Job Search

Stigler, George, J., "Information in the Labor Market," *Journal of Political Economy*, Vol. 70 (October 1962), pp. 94-104.

McCall, John, "Economics of Information and Job Search," *Quarterly Journal of Economics*, Vol. 84 (February 1970), pp. 113-126.

Whipple, David, "A Generalized Theory of Job Search," *Journal of Political Economy*, Vol. 81 (September-October 1973), pp. 1170-1188.

Lippman, Steven A., and McCall, John J., "The Economics of Job Search: A Survey, Part I, Optimal Job Search Policies," *Economic Inquiry*, Vol. 14 (June 1976), pp. 155-189.

Lippman, Steven A., and McCall, John J., "The Economics of Job Search: A Survey, Part II, Empirical and Policy Implications of Job Search," *Economic Inquiry*, Vol. 14 (September 1976), pp. 347-368.

McCafferty, Stephen, "A Theory of Semi-Permanent Wage Search," *Southern Economic Journal*, Vol. 45 (July 1978), pp. 46-61.

Schotter, Andrew, and Braunstein, Yale M., "Economic Search: An Experimental Study," *Economic Inquiry*, Vol. 19 (January 1981), pp. 1-25.

11.5 Search-Unemployment

Mortensen, Dale T., "Job Search, the Duration of Unemployment, and the Phillips Curve," *American Economic Review*, Vol. 60 (December 1970), pp. 847-862.

Gronau, Reuben, "Information and Fictional Unemployment," *American Economic Review*, Vol. 61 (June 1971), pp. 290-301.

Salop, Steven C., "Systematic Job Search and Unemployment," *Review of Economic Studies*, Vol. 40 (April 1973), pp. 191-201.

Lucas, Robert E., Jr., and Prescot, Edward C., "Equilibrium Search and Unemployment, *Journal of Economic Theory*, Vol. 7 (February 1974), pp. 188-209.

Barnes, William F., "Job Search Models, The Duration of Unemployment and Asking Wages: Some Empirical Evidence," *Journal of Human Resources*, Vol. 10 (No. 2, 1974), pp. 230-240.

Holen, Arlene, and Horowitz, Stanley A., "The Effect of Unemployment Insurance and Eligibility Enforcement on Unemployment," *Journal of Law and Economics*, Vol. 17 (October 1974), pp. 403-431.

Eaton, B. Curtis, and Neher, Philip A., "Unemployment, Underemployment and Optimal Job Search," *Journal of Political Economy*, Vol. 83 (March-April 1975), pp. 355-376.

Marston, Stephen T., "The Impact of Unemployment Insurance on Job Search," *Brookings Papers on Economic Activity*, Vol. 1 (1975), pp. 13-60.
Barron, John M., "Search in the Labor Market and the Duration of Unemployment: Some Empirical Evidence," *American Economic Review*, Vol. 65 (December 1975), pp. 934-942.

11.6   Work Effort, Quality, and Earnings

Greenwood, J. A., "Payment by Results Systems: A Case Study in Control at the Workplace with a National Piecework Price List," *British Journal of Industrial Relations*, Vol. 7 (November 1969), pp. 399-413.
Ehrenberg, Ronald G., "Absenteeism and the Overtime Decision," *American Economic Review*, Vol. 60 (June 1970), pp. 352-357.
Tuckman, Howard P., and Leahey, Jack, "What Is an Article Worth?" *Journal of Political Economy*, Vol. 83 (September-October 1975), pp. 951-967.
Spence, Michael, "Competition in Salaries, Credentials, and Signalling Prerequisites for Jobs," *Quarterly Journal of Economics*, Vol. 90 (February 1976), pp. 51-74.
Newbery, David M. G., "Risk Sharing, Sharecropping and Uncertain Labour Markets," *Review of Economic Studies*, Vol. 44 (October 1977), pp. 585-594.

11.7   Job Training and Work Experience

U.S. Department of Labor, Bureau of Apprenticeship and Training, *Apprenticeship Past and Present* (Washington, D.C., 1955).
Millar, James R., "On-the-Job Training and Wage Determination," Ph.D. dissertation, Carnegie-Mellon University, 1971.
Rosen, Sherwin, "Learning and Experience in the Labor Market," *Journal of Human Resources*, Vol. 7 (Summer 1972), pp. 326-342.
Rosen, Sherwin, "Learning by Experience as Joint Production," *Quarterly Journal of Economics*, Vol. 86 (August 1972), pp. 366-382.

11.8   Bargaining, Strikes, and Settlements

Walton, Richard E., and McKersie, Robert B., *A Behavioral Theory of Labor Negotiations* (New York: McGraw-Hill, 1965).
Cross, John G., "A Theory of the Bargaining Process," *American Economic Review*, Vol. 55 (March 1965), p. 67-94.
Ashenfelter, Orley, and Johnson, George E., "Bargaining Theory, Trade Unions, and Industrial Strike Activity," *American Economic Review*, Vol. 59 (March 1969), pp. 35-49.
Pencavel, John H., "An Investigation into Industrial Strike Activity in Britain," *Economica*, N.S., Vol. 37 (August 1970), pp. 239-256.
Kraus, A., and Melnik, Arie, "A Sequential Decision Model of Bargaining Theory," *Western Economic Journal*, Vol. 10 (December 1972), pp. 359-369.

Trifon, Raphael, and Landau, Moshe, "A Model of Wage Bargaining Involving Negotiations and Sanctions," *Management Science*, Vol. 20 (February 1974), pp. 960-970.

Comay, Yochanan; Melnik, Arie; and Subotnik, Abraham, "Bargaining, Yield Curves and Wage Settlements: An Empirical Analysis," *Journal of Political Economy*, Vol. 82 (March-April 1974), pp. 303-313.

12. Decision-Making by Private Firms, in Various Market Positions, with Incomplete and Uncertain Knowledge

12.1 *General*

Tintner, Gerhard, "The Theory of Choice under Subjective Risk and Uncertainty," *Econometrica*, Vol. 9 (July-October 1941), pp. 298-304.

Machlup, Fritz, "Marginal Analysis and Empirical Research," *American Economic Review*, Vol. 36 (September 1946), pp. 301-320.

Alchian, Armen A., "Uncertainty, Evolution, and Economic Theory," *Journal of Political Economy*, Vol. 58 (May-June 1950), pp. 211-221.

Machlup, Fritz, *The Economics of Sellers' Competition* (Baltimore: Johns Hopkins University Press, 1952).

March, James G., and Simon, Herbert A., *Organizations* (New York: Wiley, 1958).

Malmgren, Harald B., "Information, Expectations, and the Theory of the Firm," *Quarterly Journal of Economics*, Vol. 75 (August 1961), pp. 399-421.

Cyert, Richard M., and March, James A., *The Behavioral Theory of the Firm* (Englewood Cliffs, N.J.: Prentice-Hall, 1963).

Machlup, Fritz, "Theories of the Firm: Marginalist, Behavioral, Managerial," *American Economic Review*, Vol. 57 (March 1967), pp. 1-33.

Leland, Hayne, "The Theory of the Firm Facing Uncertain Demand," *American Economic Review*, Vol. 72 (June 1972), pp. 278-291.

Alchian, Armen, and Demsetz, Harold, "Production, Information Costs, and Economic Organization," *American Economic Review*, Vol. 62 (December 1972), pp. 777-795.

Stiglitz, Joseph E., "Incentives, Risk, and Information: Notes towards a Theory of Hierarchy," *Bell Journal of Economics*, Vol. 6 (Autumn 1975), pp. 552-579.

Blair, Roger D., and Heggestad, Arnold A., "The Impact of Uncertainty upon the Multiproduct Firm," *Southern Economic Journal*, Vol. 44 (July 1977), pp. 136-142.

Simon, Herbert, "From Substantive to Procedural Rationality," in Spiro J. Latsis, ed., *Method and Appraisal in Economics* (Cambridge: At the University Press, 1976), pp. 129-148.

12.2 Market Positions (Pure Competition, Entry, Oligopoly, Monopoly)

Cournot, Antoine-Augustin, *Recherches sur les principes mathématiques de la théorie des richesses* (Paris: Hachette, 1838). English translation by Nathaniel T. Bacon, *Researches into the Mathematical Principles of the Theory of Wealth* (New York: Macmillan, 1927).

Chamberlin, Edward H., *The Theory of Monopolistic Competition* (Cambridge, Mass.: Harvard University Press, 1931; 7th ed., 1956).

Machlup, Fritz, *The Basing-Point System* (Philadelphia: Blakiston, 1949).

Fellner, William, *Competition Among the Few* (New York: Knopf, 1949).

Scitovsky, Tibor, "Ignorance as a Source of Oligopoly Power," *American Economic Review*, Vol. 40 (March 1950), pp. 48-53.

Phelps, Edmund S., and Winter, Sidney G., Jr., "Optimal Price Policy Under Atomistic Competition," in Edmund S. Phelps et al., eds., *Microeconomic Foundations of Inflation and Employment Theory* (New York: Norton, 1970), pp. 309-337.

Fisher, Franklin M., "Quasi-Competitive Price Adjustment by Individual Firms: A Preliminary Paper," *Journal of Economic Theory*, Vol. 2 (June 1970), pp. 195-206.

Sandmo, Agnar, "On the Theory of the Competitive Firm under Price Uncertainty," *American Economic Review*, Vol. 61 (March 1971), pp. 65-73.

Salop, Steven, "Information and Monopolistic Competition," *American Economic Review*, Vol. 66 (Suppl. May 1976), pp. 240-245.

Hogatt, Austin C.; Friedman, James W.; and Gill, Shlomo, "Price Signaling in Experimental Oligopoly," *American Economic Review*, Vol. 66 (Suppl. May 1976), pp. 261-266.

Yohe, Gary W., "Single-Valued Control of a Cartel Under Uncertainty—A Multifirm Comparison of Prices and Quantities," *Bell Journal of Economics*, Vol. 8 (Spring 1977), pp. 97-111.

Lesourne, J., "Manager's Behavior and Perfect Competition," *Journal of Economic Theory*, Vol. 15 (June 1977), pp. 92-98.

Auster, Richard D., "Private Markets in Public Goods (or Qualities)," *Quarterly Journal of Economics*, Vol. 91 (August 1977), pp. 419-430.

Gates, D. J.; Rickard, John A.; and Wilson, D. J. "A Convergent Adjustment Process for Firms in Competition," *Econometrica*, Vol. 45 (September 1977), pp. 1349-1363.

Salop, Steven, "The Noisy Monopolist: Imperfect Information, Price Dispersion and Price Discrimination," *Review of Economic Studies*, Vol. 44 (October 1977), pp. 393-404.

12.3 Operations Research and Activities Analysis

Koopmans, Tjalling C., ed., *Activity Analysis of Production and Allocation* (New York: Wiley, 1951).

McCloskey, Joseph F., and Trefethen, Florence N., eds., *Operations Research for Management* (Baltimore: Johns Hopkins University Press, 1954).

Dorfman, Robert; Samuelson, Paul A.; and Solow, Robert M., *Linear Programming and Economic Analysis* (New York: McGraw-Hill, 1958).

Baumol, William J., "Activity Analysis in One Lesson," *American Economic Review*, Vol. 48 (December 1958), pp. 837-873.

Baumol, William J., *Economic Theory and Operations Analysis*, 2d ed. (Englewood Cliffs, N.J.: Prentice-Hall, 1965).

Ackoff, Russell L., *A Concept of Corporate Planning* (New York: Wiley, 1970).

12.4 *Investment, Capital, Dividends*

Hurwicz, Leonid, "Theory of the Firm and of Investment," *Econometrica*, Vol. 14 (April 1946), pp. 109-136.

Modigliani, Franco, and Miller, Merton, "The Cost of Capital, Corporation Finance, and the Theory of Investment," *American Economic Review*, Vol. 48 (June 1958), pp. 261-297.

Lintner, John, "Dividends, Earnings, Leverage, Stock Prices, and the Supply of Capital to Corporations," *Review of Economics and Statistics*, Vol. 44 (August 1962), pp. 243-269.

Baxter, Nevins D., and Cragg, John G., "Corporate Choice Among Long-Term Financing Instruments," *Review of Economic Statistics*, Vol. 52 (August 1970), pp. 225-235.

Krouse, Clement G., "On the Theory of Optimal Investment, Dividends, and Growth in the Firm," *American Economic Review*, Vol. 63 (June 1973), pp. 269-279.

Kamien, Morton I., and Schwartz, Nancy L., "Optimal Capital Accumulation and Durable Goods Production," *Zeitschrift für Nationalökonomie*, Vol. 37 (1977), pp. 25-43.

12.5 *Organization and Expansion*

Penrose, Edith, *The Theory of the Growth of the Firm* (Oxford: Blackwell, 1959).

Hawkins, Clark A., "Optimum Growth of the Regulated Firm," *Western Economic Journal*, Vol. 7 (June 1969), pp. 187-189.

Uzawa, Hirofumi, "Time Preference and the Penrose Effect in a Two-Class Model of Economic Growth," *Journal of Political Economy*, Vol. 77 (July-August 1969, Part II), pp. 628-652.

Mueller, Dennis C., "A Theory of Conglomerate Mergers," *Quarterly Journal of Economics*, Vol. 83 (November 1969), pp. 643-659.

Diwan, Romesh K., "About the Growth Path of Firms," *American Economic Review*, Vol 60 (March 1970), pp. 30-43.

Kast, Fremont E., and Rosenzweig, James E., *Organization and Management: A Systems Approach* (New York: McGraw-Hill, 1970).

Rubin, Paul H., "The Expansion of Firms," *Journal of Political Economy*, Vol. 81 (July-August 1973), pp. 936-949.

12.6 *Job, Wage, and Price Discrimination*

Machlup, Fritz, *The Political Economy of Monopoly* (Baltimore: Johns Hopkins University Press, 1952), pp. 135-168.

Becker, Gary S., *The Economics of Discrimination* (Chicago: University of Chicago Press, 1957).

Arrow, Kenneth J., "Models of Job Discrimination," in Anthony H. Pascal, ed., *Racial Discrimination in Economic Life* (Lexington, Mass.: Heath, 1972), pp. 83-102.

Salop, Steven, "Wage Differentials in a Dynamic Theory of the Firm," *Journal of Economic Theory*, Vol. 6 (August 1973), pp. 321-344.

Salop, Steven, and Stiglitz, Joseph, "Bargains and Ripoffs: A Model of Monopolistically Competitive Price Dispersion," *Review of Economic Studies*, Vol. 44 (October 1977), pp. 493-510.

12.7 *Advertising, Signaling, and Screening*

Dorfman, Robert, and Steiner, Peter O., "Optimal Advertising and Optimal Quality," *American Economic Review*, Vol. 44 (December 1954), pp. 826-836.

Nerlove, Marc, and Arrow, Kenneth J., "Optimal Advertising under Dynamic Conditions," *Economica*, Vol. 39 (May 1962), pp. 88-93.

Gabor, Andre, and Granger, Clive W. J., "Price as an Indicator of Quality," *Economica*, Vol. 33 (1966), pp. 43-70.

Spence, A. Michael, *Market Signaling: Information Transfer in Hiring and Related Processes* (Cambridge, Mass.: Harvard University Press, 1973).

Riley, John G., "Competitive Signalling," *Journal of Economic Theory*, Vol. 10 (April 1975), pp. 174-186.

Spence, A. Michael, "Competition in Salaries and Signaling as Prerequisites for Jobs," *Quarterly Journal of Economics*, Vol. 90 (February 1976), pp. 51-75.

Riley, John G., "Information, Screening, and Human Capital," *American Economic Review*, Vol. 66 (Suppl. May 1976), pp. 254-260.

Adams, William James, and Yellen, Janet L., "What Makes Advertising Profitable?" *Economic Journal*, Vol. 87 (September 1977), pp. 427-429.

Butters, Gerard R., "Equilibrium Distribution of Sales and Advertising Prices," *Review of Economic Studies*, Vol. 44 (October 1977), pp. 465-491.

Scheidell, John M., *Advertising, Prices, and Consumer Reaction: A Dynamic Analysis* (Washington, D.C.: American Enterprise Institute, 1978).

12.8 *Deception and Fraud*

Darby, Michael R., and Karni, Edi, "Free Competition and the Optimal Amount of Fraud," *Journal of Law and Economics*, Vol. 16 (April 1973), pp. 67-88.

Belth, Joseph M., "Deceptive Sales Practices in the Life Insurance Business," *Journal of Risk and Insurance*, Vol. 41 (June 1974), pp. 305-326.

13. Policy-Making by Governments and Public Agencies with Incomplete and Uncertain Knowledge

13.1 *General*

Kolm, Serge-Christophe, "The Optimal Production of Social Justice," in Julius Margolis and Henri Guitton, eds., *Public Economics*: Proceedings of a Conference Held [in Biarritz] by the International Economic Association (London: Macmillan, 1969), pp. 145-220.

Diamond, Peter A., and Mirrlees, James A., "Optimal Taxation and Public Production: I. Production Efficiency; II. Tax Rules," *American Economic Review*, Vol. 61 (March and June 1971), pp. 8-27, 261-278.

Feldman, Paul, "Efficiency, Distribution, and the Role of Government in a Market Economy," *Journal of Political Economy*, Vol. 79 (May-June 1971), pp. 508-526.

Pfaff, Martin, and Pfaff, Anita, "Grants Economics: An Evaluation of Government Policies," *Public Finance*, Vol. 26 (No. 2., 1971), pp. 275-303.

Stiglitz, Joseph E., and Dasgupta, Partha, "Differential Taxation, Public Goods, and Economic Efficiency," *Review of Economic Studies*, Vol. 38 (April 1971), pp. 151-174.

McFadden, Daniel, "The Revealed Preferences of a Government Bureaucracy: Theory," *Bell Journal of Economics*, Vol. 6 (Autumn 1975), pp. 401-416.

Hayek, Friedrich A. von, "The Pretence of Knowledge," Nobel Memorial Lecture, December 11, 1974, *Les Prix Nobel en 1974* (Stockholm: The Nobel Foundation, 1975), pp. 249-258.

13.2 *Tax Policies*

Pantaleone, Maffeo, "Contributo alla Teoria del riparto delle spese pubbliche," *Rassegna Italiana* (15 October 1883).

Sax, Emil, *Grundlegung der theoretischen Staatswissenschaft* (Vienna: Hölder, 1887).

Mazzola, Ugo, *I dati scientifici della finanza pubblica* (Rome: Loescher, 1890).

Lindahl, Erik, *Die Gerechtigkeit der Besteuerung* (Lund: Gleerup, 1919).

Sax, Emil, "Die Wertungstheorie der Steuer," *Zeitschrift für Volkswirtschaft und Sozialpolitik*, N.S., Vol. 4 (1924), pp. 191-240.

Musgrave, Richard A., and Peacock, Alan T., eds., *Classics in the Theory of Public Finance* (London: Macmillan, for the International Economic Association, 1958).

Mirrlees, James A., "An Exploration in the Theory of Optimum Income Taxation," *Review of Economic Studies*, Vol. 38 (April 1971), pp. 175-208.

Dornbusch, Rudiger, "Optimal Commodity and Trade Taxes," *Journal of Political Economy*, Vol. 79 (November-December 1971), pp. 1360-1368.

Weigard, Wolfgang, "The Optimum Tax Structure: A Comment," *Scandinavian Journal of Economics*, Vol. 78 (1976), pp. 103-108.

Helpman, Elhanan, and Sadka, Efraim, "Optimal Taxation of Full Income," *International Economic Review*, Vol. 19 (February 1978), pp. 247-251.

Yitzhaki, Shlomo, "A Note on Optimal Taxation and Administration Costs," *American Economic Review*, Vol. 69 (June 1979), pp. 475-480.

13.3 Macropolicies: Stabilization, Budgeting, Fiscal and Monetary Measures, Employment and Inflation Policies

Phelps, Edmund et al., eds., *Microeconomic Foundations of Employment and Inflation Theory* (New York: Norton, 1970).

Roskamp, Karl W., "Multiple Fiscal Policy Objectives and Optimal Budget: A Programming Approach," *Public Finance*, Vol. 26 (No. 2, 1971), pp. 361-374.

Hall, Robert E., "Prospects for Shifting the Phillips Curve Through Manpower Policy," *Brookings Papers on Economic Activity*, No. 3 (1971), pp. 659-701.

Parkin, Michael, and Sumner, Michael T., eds., *Incomes Policy and Inflation* (Manchester: Manchester University Press, 1972).

13.4 Micropolicies: Conservation, Regulation, Direct Controls

Brozen, Yale, "The Effect of Statutory Minimum Wage Increases on Teen-Age Employment," *Journal of Law and Economics*, Vol. 12 (April 1969), pp. 109-122.

Kneese, Allen V., "Environmental Pollution: Economics and Policy," *American Economic Review*, Vol. 61 (Suppl. May 1971), pp. 153-166.

Westfield, Fred M., "Methodology of Evaluating Economic Regulation," *American Economic Review*, Vol. 61 (Suppl. May 1971), pp. 211-217.

Cimini, Michael, "Government Intervention in Railroad Disputes," *Monthly Labor Review*, Vol. 94 (December 1971), pp. 27-34.

Fogel, Walter, and Lewin, David, "Wage Determination in the Public Sector," *Industrial and Labor Relations Review*, Vol. 27 (April 1974), pp. 410-431.

Annable, James E., Jr., "A Theory of Wage Determination in Public Employment," *Quarterly Review of Economics and Business*, Vol. 14 (Winter 1974), pp. 43-58.

Lave, Lester B., *The Strategy for Social Regulation: Decision Frameworks for Policy* (Washington, D.C.: Brookings Institution, 1981).

13.5 Public Investments, Subsidies, and Public Goods

Musgrave, Richard A., "The Voluntary Exchange Theory of Public Economy," *Quarterly Journal of Economics*, Vol. 53 (February 1939), pp. 213-237.

Bowen, Howard R., "The Interpretation of Voting in the Allocation of Economic Resources," *Quarterly Journal of Economics*, Vol. 38 (November 1943), pp. 27-48.

Bowen, Howard R., *Toward Social Economy* (New York: Rinehart, 1948), p. 177.

Samuelson, Paul A., "The Pure Theory of Public Expenditures, *Review of Economics and Statistics*, Vol. 36 (November 1954), pp. 387-389.

Samuelson, Paul A., "Diagrammatic Exposition of a Theory of Public Expenditure," *Review of Economics and Statistics*, Vol. 37 (November 1955), pp. 350-356.

Musgrave, Richard A., *The Theory of Public Finance* (New York: McGraw-Hill, 1959).

Kafoglis, Milton Z., *Welfare Economics and Subsidy Programs* (Gainesville: University of Florida Press, 1961).

Buchanan, James M., and Kafoglis, Milton Z., "A Note on Public Goods Supply," *American Economic Review*, Vol. 53 (June 1963), pp. 403-414.

Johansen, Leif, *Public Economics* (Amsterdam: North-Holland, 1965).

Kaizuka, Keimei, "Public Goods and Decentralization of Production," *Review of Economics and Statistics*, Vol. 47 (February 1965), pp. 118-120.

Buchanan, James M., *The Demand and Supply of Public Goods* (Chicago: Rand McNally, 1968).

Margolis, Julius, and Guitton, Henri, eds., *Public Economics*. Proceedings of a Conference held [at Biarritz] by the International Economic Association (London: Macmillan, 1969).

Arrow, Kenneth J., and Kurz, Mordecai, "Optimal Public Investment Policy and Controllability with Fixed Private Savings Ratio," *Journal of Economic Theory*, Vol. 1 (August 1969), pp. 141-177.

Head, John G., and Shoup, Carl S., "Public Goods, Private Goods and Ambiguous Goods," *Economic Journal*, Vol. 79 (September 1969), pp. 567-572.

Arrow, Kenneth J., and Lind, Robert C., "Uncertainty and the Evaluation of Public Investment Decisions," *American Economic Review*, Vol. 60 (June 1970), pp. 364-378.

Margolis, Julius, ed., *The Analysis of Public Output* (New York, National Bureau of Economic Research, 1970).

Shibata, Hirofumi, "A Bargaining Model of the Pure Theory of Public Expenditure," *Journal of Political Economy*, Vol. 79 (January-February 1971), pp. 1-29.

Bohm, Peter, "An Approach to the Problem of Estimating Demand for Public Goods," *Swedish Journal of Economics*, Vol. 73 (March 1971), pp. 55-66.

Musgrave, Richard A., "Provision for Social Goods in the Market System," *Public Finance*, Vol. 26 (No. 2, 1971), pp. 304-320.

Culyer, Anthony J., "Merit Goods and the Welfare Economics of Coercion," *Public Finance*, Vol. 26 (No. 4, 1971), pp. 546-572.

Bailey, Martin J., and Jensen, Michael C., "Risk and the Discount Rate for

Public Investment," in Michael C. Jensen, ed., *Studies in the Theory of Capital Markets* (New York: Praeger, 1972), pp. 269-293.

Mushkin, Selma, ed., *Public Prices for Public Products* (Washington, D.C.: Urban Institute, 1972).

Sandmo, Agnar, "Discount Rates for Public Investment Under Uncertainty," *International Economic Review*, Vol. 13 (June 1972), pp. 287-302.

Henry, Claude, "Investment Decisions under Uncertainty: The 'Irreversibility Effect,' " *American Economic Review*, Vol. 64 (December 1974), pp. 1006-1012.

Groves, Theodore, and Loeb, Martin, "Incentives and Public Inputs," *Journal of Public Economics*, Vol. 4 (August 1975), pp. 212-226.

Faulhaber, Gerald R., "Cross Subsidization: Pricing in Public Enterprises," *American Economic Review*, Vol. 65 (December 1976), pp. 966-977.

Mayshar, Joram, "Should Government Subsidize Risky Private Projects?" *American Economic Review*, Vol. 67 (March 1977), p. 20-28.

Harris, Milton, and Raviv, Artur, "Some Results on Incentive Contracts with Applications to Education and Employment, Health Insurance, and Law Enforcement," *American Economic Review*, Vol. 68 (March 1978), pp. 20-30.

Green, Jerry, and Laffont, Jean-Jacques, "An Incentive Compatible Planning Procedure for Public Good Production," *Scandinavian Journal of Economics*, Vol. 80 (1978), pp. 20-33.

Musgrave, Richard A., and Musgrave, Peggy B., *Public Finance in Theory and Practice*, 3d ed. (New York: McGraw-Hill, 1980).

Wiseman, Jack, "The Choice of Optimal Social Expenditures," in Karl W. Roskamp, ed., *Public Choice and Public Finance* (Paris: Editions Cujas, 1980), p. 252.

13.6   *Benefit-and-Cost Analysis*

Dorfman, Robert, ed., *Measuring Benefits of Government Investments* (Washington, D.C.: Brookings Institution, 1965).

Prest, Alan R., and Turvey, Ralph, "Cost-Benefit Analysis: A Survey," *Economic Journal*, Vol. 75 (December 1965), pp. 683-735.

Thurow, Lester C., and Rappaport, Carl, "Law Enforcement and Cost-Benefit Analysis," *Public Finance*, Vol. 24 (No. 1, 1969), pp. 48-68.

Baxter, Nevins D.; Howrey, E. Philip; and Penner, Rudolf G., "Unemployment and Cost-Benefit Analysis," *Public Finance*, Vol. 24 (No. 1, 1969), pp. 80-88.

Kwerel, Evan, "To Tell the Truth: Imperfect Information and Optimal Pollution Control," *Review of Economic Studies*, Vol. 44 (October 1977), pp. 595-601.

13.7   *Research Policies*

Price, Don K., *The Scientific Estate* (Cambridge, Mass.: Harvard-Belknap, 1965).

Wiesner, Jerome B., *Where Science and Politics Meet* (New York: McGraw-Hill, 1965).

Mansfield, Edwin, "The Economics of Science Policy: National Science Policy, Issues and Problems," *American Economic Review*, Vol. 56 (Suppl. May 1966), pp. 476-488.

Weinberg, Alvin M., *Reflections on Big Science* (Cambridge, Mass.: MIT Press, 1967).

Brooks, Harvey, *The Government of Science* (Cambridge, Mass.: MIT Press, 1968).

Brim, Orville G., Jr., *Knowledge Into Action: Improving the Nation's Use of the Social Sciences* (Washington, D.C.: National Science Foundation, National Science Board, 1969).

Lyons, Gene M., *The Uneasy Partnership* (New York: Russell Sage Foundation, 1969).

Reagan, Michael D., *Science and the Federal Patron* (New York: Oxford University Press, 1969).

Salomon, Jean-Jacques, *Science and Politics* (Cambridge, Mass.: MIT Press, 1973).

13.8   *Development Policies, National and Regional*

Hirsch, Werner Z., and Sonnenblum, Sidney, *Selecting Regional Information for Government Planning and Decision Making* (New York: Praeger, 1970).

14.   THE FORMATION AND REVISION OF EXPECTATIONS AND THEIR ROLE IN ECONOMIC DYNAMICS

14.1   *General: Expectations—Elastic, Adaptive, Rational*

Tinbergen, Jan, "The Notions of Horizon and Expectancy in Dynamic Economics," *Econometrica*, Vol. 1 (July 1933), pp. 247-264.

Hicks, John R., *Value and Capital* (Oxford: Clarendon, 1939).

Shackle, George L. S., *Expectation in Economics* (Cambridge: At the University Press, 1949).

Carter, Charles F., "Expectation in Economics," *Economic Journal*, Vol. 60 (March 1950), pp. 92-105.

Nerlove, Marc, "Adaptive Expectations and Cobweb Phenomena," *Quarterly Journal of Economics*, Vol. 73 (May 1958), pp. 227-240.

Muth, John F., "Rational Expectations and the Theory of Price Movements," *Econometrica*, Vol. 29 (July 1961), pp. 315-335.

Turnovsky, Stephen J., "A Bayesian Approach to the Theory of Expectations," *Journal of Economic Theory*, Vol. 1 (August 1969), pp. 220-227.

Lucas, Robert E., Jr., "Expectations and the Neutrality of Money," *Journal of Economic Theory*, Vol. 4 (April 1972), pp. 103-124.

Cyert, Richard M., and DeGroot, Morris H., "Rational Expectations and Baye-
    sian Analysis," *Journal of Political Economy*, Vol. 82 (January-February
    1974), pp. 521-536.
Sargent, Thomas J., and Wallace, Neil, *Rational Expectations and the Theory
    of Economic Policy* (Minneapolis: Research Department, Federal Re-
    serve Bank of Minneapolis, 1975).
Sargent, Thomas J., and Wallace, Neil, "Rational Expectations, the Optimal
    Monetary Instruments, and the Optimal Money Supply Rule," *Journal
    of Political Economy*, Vol. 83 (March-April 1975), pp. 241-254.
Barro, Robert J., and Fischer, Stanley, "Recent Developments in Monetary
    Theory," *Journal of Monetary Economics*, Vol. 2 (April 1976), pp. 133-
    167.
Fischer, Stanley, "Long-Term Contracts, Rational Expectations, and the Op-
    timal Money Supply Rule," *Journal of Political Economy*, Vol. 85 (Jan-
    uary-February 1977), pp. 191-205.
Phelps, Edmund S., and Taylor, John B., "Stabilizing Powers of Monetary
    Policy under Rational Expectations," *Journal of Political Economy*, Vol.
    85 (January-February 1977), pp. 163-190.
Kreps, David M., "A Note on 'Fulfilled Expectations' Equilibria," *Journal of
    Economic Theory*, Vol. 14 (February 1977), pp. 32-43.
Green, Jerry, "The Non-Existence of Informational Equilibria," *Review of
    Economic Studies*, Vol. 44 (October 1977), pp. 451-463.
Turnovsky, Stephen J., "Structural Expectations and the Effectiveness of
    Government Policy in a Short-Run Macroeconomic Model," *American
    Economic Review*, Vol. 67 (December 1977), pp. 851-866.
Kaplan, Brian, "Rational Expectations and Economic Thought," *Journal of
    Economic Literature*, Vol. 17 (December 1979), pp. 1422-1441.
Grossman, Herschel I., "Rational Expectations, Business Cycles, and Gov-
    ernment Behavior," in Stanley Fischer, ed., *Rational Expectations and
    Economic Policy* (Chicago: University of Chicago Press, 1980), pp. 5-
    22.
Fischer, Stanley, "On Activist Monetary Policy with Rational Expectations,"
    in Stanley Fischer, ed., *Rational Expectations and Economic Policy*
    (Chicago: University of Chicago Press, 1980), pp. 211-247.

14.2   *Expectations of Changes in Prices and Sales*

Fisher, Irving, *Appreciation and Interest* (New York: Macmillan, for the
    American Economic Assocation, 1896).
Machlup, Fritz, *The Economics of Sellers' Competition* (Baltimore: Johns
    Hopkins University Press, 1952), pp. 279-292.
Working, Holbrook, "A Theory of Anticipatory Prices," *American Economic
    Review*, Vol. 48 (Suppl. May 1958), pp. 188-199.
Zabel, Edward, "The Competitive Firm and Price Expectations," *Interna-
    tional Economic Review*, Vol. 10 (October 1969), pp. 467-478.

Laidler, David, "Expectations, Adjustment and the Dynamic Response of Income to Policy Changes," *Journal of Money, Credit and Banking*, Vol. 5 (Part I, February 1973), pp. 157-172.

Modigliani, Franco, and Shiller, Robert J., "Inflation, Rational Expectations and the Term Structure of Interest Rates," *Economica*, N.S., Vol. 40 (February 1973), pp. 12-43.

Sargent, Thomas J., "Rational Expectations, the Real Rate of Interest, and the National Rate of Unemployment," *Brookings Papers on Economic Activity*, No. 2 (1973), pp. 429-472.

Cebula, Richard J., "Deficit Spending, Expectations, and Fiscal Policy Effectiveness," *Public Finance*, Vol. 28 (Nos. 3-4, 1973), pp. 362-370.

Ando, Albert K. et al., "On the Role of Expectations of Price and Technological Change in an Investment Function," *International Economic Review*, Vol. 15 (June 1974), pp. 384-414.

Hahn, Frank H., "Exercises in Conjectural Equilibria," *Scandinavian Journal of Economics*, Vol. 79 (No. 2, 1977), pp. 210-226.

14.3   *Expectations of Changes in Interest Rates*

Keynes, John Maynard, "The 'Ex-Ante' Theory of the Rate of Interest," *Economic Journal*, Vol. 47 (December 1937), pp. 663-669.

Robertson, Dennis H., "Mr. Keynes and the Rate of Interest," in *Essays in Monetary Theory* (London: King, 1940), pp. 1-38.

Lutz, Friedrich A., "The Structure of Interest Rates," *Quarterly Journal of Economics*, Vol. 55 (November 1940), pp. 36-63.

Malkiel, Burton G., "Expectations, Bond Prices, and the Term Structure of Interest Rates," *Quarterly Journal of Economics*, Vol. 76 (May 1962), pp. 197-218.

Feldstein, Martin S., and Chamberlain, Gary, "Multi-Market Expectations and the Rate of Interest," *Journal of Money, Credit, and Banking*, Vol. 5 (November 1973), pp. 873-902.

14.4   *Expectations of Changes in Income, Individual or Aggregate, Temporary or Permanent*

Van Syckle, Calla, "Economic Expectations and Spending Plans of Consumers," *Review of Economics and Statistics*, Vol. 36 (November 1954), pp. 451-455.

Friedman, Milton, *A Theory of the Consumption Function* (Princeton: Princeton University Press, 1957).

Gibson, William F., "Price Expectations and Changes in Income," *Western Economic Journal*, Vol. 9 (June 1971), pp. 192-198.

Cebula, Richard J., "A Reconsideration of the Effects of Expected Income Changes," *Rivista Internazionale di Scienze Economiche Commerciali*, Vol. 21 (February 1974), pp. 192-195.

14.5   *Expectations of Changes in Wages, Price Levels, and Employment*

Leijonhufvud, Axel, *On Keynesian Economics and the Economics of Keynes* (New York: Oxford University Press, 1968).

Mortensen, Dale T., "A Theory of Wage and Employment Dynamics," in Edmund S. Phelps et al., eds., *Microeconomic Foundations of Inflation and Employment Theory* (New York: Norton, 1970), pp. 167-211.

Friedman, Milton, "Nobel Lecture: Inflation and Unemployment," *Journal of Political Economy*, Vol. 85 (May-June 1977), pp. 451-472.

Maccini, Louis J., "The Impact of Demand and Price Expectations on the Behavior of Prices," *American Economic Review*, Vol. 68 (March 1978), pp. 134-145.

Sweeney, Richard J., "Efficient Information Processing in Output Markets: Tests and Implications," *Economic Inquiry*, Vol. 16 (July 1978), pp. 313-331.

14.6   *Expectations of Changes in Investment and Consumption*

Solow, Robert M., *Capital Theory and Rate of Return* (Amsterdam: North-Holland, 1963).

Lucas, Robert E., Jr., and Rapping, Leonard A., "Real Wages, Employment, and Inflation," in Edmund S. Phelps et al., eds., *Microeconomic Foundations of Inflation and Employment Theory* (New York: Norton, 1970), pp. 257-305.

Poole, William, "Rational Expectations in the Macro-Model," in Arthur M. Okun, and George L. Perry, eds., *Brookings Papers on Economic Activity*, No. 2 (1976), pp. 463-505.

14.7   *Expectations of Changes in Foreign-Exchange Rates*

Dornbusch, Rudiger, "Exchange Rate Expectations and Monetary Policy," *Journal of International Economy*, Vol. 6 (August 1976), pp. 231-244.

Dornbusch, Rudiger, "Expectations and Exchange Rate Dynamics," *Journal of Political Economy*, Vol. 84 (December 1976), pp. 1161-1176.

Dornbusch, Rudiger, "Monetary Policy under Exchange Rate Flexibility," in *Managed Exchange-Rate Flexibility: The Recent Experience*, Federal Reserve Bank of Boston Conference Series, No. 20 (1978).

Flood, Robert P., "Exchange Rate Expectations in Dual Exchange Markets," *Journal of International Economics*, Vol. 8 (February 1978), pp. 65-77.

Ethier, Wilfred, "Expectations and the Asset-Market Approach to the Exchange Rate," *Journal of Monetary Economics*, Vol. 5 (April 1979), pp. 259-282.

15.   THE ROLE OF INFORMATION, KNOWLEDGE, EXPECTATIONS, RISKS, AND UNCERTAINTY IN THE FUNCTIONING OF MARKETS AND THE FORMATION OF PRICES

15.1   *General (Models of Market Equilibrium)*

Ożga, S. A., "Imperfect Markets Through Lack of Knowledge," *Quarterly Journal of Economics*, Vol. 74 (February 1960), pp. 29-52.

Arrow, Kenneth J., *Aspects of the Theory of Risk Bearing*, Yrjö Jahnssonin Lectures (Helsinki: Suomen Teknillinen Korkeakoulu, 1965).

Radner, Roy, "Competitive Equilibrium Under Uncertainty," *Econometrica*, Vol. 36 (January 1968), pp. 31-58.

Baron, David P., "Price Uncertainty, Utility, and Industry Equilibrium in Pure Competition," *International Economic Review*, Vol. 11 (October 1970), pp. 463-480.

Drèze, Jacques H., "Market Allocation under Uncertainty," *European Economic Review*, Vol. 71 (Winter 1970), pp. 133-165.

Stiglitz, Joseph E., and Diamond, Peter A., "Increases in Risk and in Risk Aversion," *Journal of Economic Theory*, Vol. 8 (July 1974), pp. 337-360.

Grossman, Sanford J., and Stiglitz, Joseph E., "Information and Competitive Price Systems," *American Economic Review*, Vol. 66 (Suppl. May 1976), pp. 246-253.

Spence, Michael, "Informational Aspects of Market Structure: An Introduction," *Quarterly Journal of Economics*, Vol. 90 (November 1976), pp. 591-599.

Stiglitz, Joseph E., "Symposium on Economics of Information: Introduction," *Review of Economic Studies*, Vol. 44 (October 1977), pp. 389-391.

Wilson, Robert, "A Bidding Model of Perfect Competition," *Review of Economic Studies*, Vol. 44 (October 1977), pp. 511-518

15.2   Products Markets

Akerlof, George A., "The Market for 'Lemons': Qualitative Uncertainty and the Market Mechanism," *Quarterly Journal of Economics*, Vol. 84 (August 1970), pp. 488-500.

Kihlstrom, Richard, "A General Theory of Demand for Information about Product Quality," *Journal of Economic Theory*, Vol. 8 (August 1974), pp. 413-439.

Heal, Geoffrey, "Do Bad Products Drive Out Good?" *Quarterly Journal of Economics*, Vol. 90 (August 1976), pp. 499-502.

Stiglitz, Joseph E., "Equilibrium in Product Markets with Imperfect Information," *American Economic Review*, Vol. 69 (Suppl. May 1979), pp. 339-345.

15.3   Labor Markets

Smith, Adam, *An Inquiry into the Nature and Causes of the Wealth of Nations* (London: 1776; Routledge, 1903), pp. 77-113.

Rees, Albert, "Information Networks in Labor Markets," *American Economic Review*, Vol. 56 (Suppl. May 1966), pp. 559-566.

Pascal, Anthony H., ed., *Racial Discrimination in Economic Life* (Lexington, Mass.: Heath, 1972).

Spence, A. Michael, "Job Market Signaling," *Quarterly Journal of Economics*, Vol. 87 (August 1973), pp. 355-374.

Baily, Martin Neil, "Wages and Employment under Uncertain Demand," *Review of Economic Studies*, Vol. 41 (January 1974), pp. 37-50.

Stiglitz, Joseph E., "Incentives and Risk-Sharing in Share Cropping," *Review of Economic Studies*, Vol. 41 (January 1974), pp. 219-255.

Salop, Joanne, and Salop, Steven, "Self-Selection and Turnover in the Labor Market," *Quarterly Journal of Economics*, Vol. 90 (November 1976), pp. 619-627.

Akerlof, George, "The Economics of Caste and of the Rat Race and Other Woeful Tales," *Quarterly Journal of Economics*, Vol. 90 (November 1976), pp. 600-617.

Pettengill, John S., *Labor Unions and the Inequality of Earned Income* (Amsterdam and New York: North-Holland, 1980).

15.4   Capital Markets

Mossin, Jan, "Equilibrium in a Capital Asset Market," *Econometrica*, Vol. 34 (October 1966), pp. 768-783.

Fama, Eugene F., "Efficient Capital Markets: A Review of Theory and Empirical Work," *Journal of Finance*, Vol. 25 (May 1970), pp. 383-417.

Fama, Eugene F., and Laffer, Arthur B., "Information and Capital Markets," *Journal of Business*, Vol. 44 (July 1971), pp. 289-298.

Jenson, Michael C., "Capital Markets: Theory and Evidence," *Bell Journal of Economics and Management Science*, Vol. 3 (Autumn 1972), pp. 357-398.

Gonedes, Nicholas J., "Information-Production and Capital Market Equilibrium," *Journal of Finance*, Vol. 30 (June 1975), pp. 841-864.

15.5   Stock Markets and Asset Portfolios

Markovitz, Harry M., *Portfolio Selection* (New York: Wiley, 1959).

Alexander, Sidney, "Price Movements in Speculative Markets: Trends or Random Walks?" *Industrial Management Review*, Vol. 2 (May 1961), pp. 7-26.

Chase, Samuel B., Jr., *Asset Prices in Economic Analysis* (Berkeley: University of California Press, 1963).

Arrow, Kenneth J., "The Role of Securities in the Optimal Allocation of Risk Bearing," *Review of Economic Studies*, Vol. 51 (April 1964), pp. 91-96.

Sharpe, William F., "Capital Asset Prices: A Theory of Market Equilibrium under Conditions of Risk," *Journal of Finance*, Vol. 19 (September 1964), pp. 425-442.

Lintner, John, "The Valuation of Risk Assets and the Selection of Risky Investments in Stock Portfolios and Capital Budgets," *Review of Economics and Statistics*, Vol. 47 (February 1965), pp. 13-37.

Sharpe, William F., "Risk Aversion in the Stock Market: Some Empirical Evidence," *Journal of Finance*, Vol. 20 (September 1965), pp. 416-422.

Manne, Henry G., *Insider Trading and the Stock Market* (New York: Free Press, 1966).

Brealy, Richard A., *An Introduction to Risk and Return from Common Stock* (Cambridge, Mass.: MIT Press, 1969).

Fama, Eugene F.; Fisher, Lawrence; et al., "The Adjustment of Stock Prices to New Information," *International Economic Review*, Vol. 10 (February 1969), pp. 1-21.

Jensen, Michael C., "Risk, the Pricing of Capital Assets, and the Evolution of Investment Portfolios," *Journal of Business*, Vol. 42 (April 1969), pp. 167-247.

Brainard, William, and Dolbear, F. Trenery, "Social Risk and Financial Markets," *American Economic Review*, Vol. 61 (Suppl. May 1971), pp. 360-370.

15.6 Short-Term Credit Markets

Hodgman, Donald R., "Credit Risk and Credit Rationing," *Quarterly Journal of Economics*, Vol. 74 (May 1960), pp. 258-278.

Chase, Samuel B., Jr., "Credit Risk and Credit Rationing: Comment," *Quarterly Journal of Economics*, Vol. 75 (May 1961), pp. 319-327.

Hodgman, Donald R., "Credit Risk and Credit Rationing: Reply," *Quarterly Journal of Economics*, Vol. 75 (May 1961), pp. 327-329.

Ryder, Harl E., Jr., "Credit Risk and Credit Rationing: Comment," *Quarterly Journal of Economics*, Vol. 76 (August 1962), pp. 471-479.

Miller, Merton H., "Credit Risk and Credit Rationing: Further Comment," *Quarterly Journal of Economics*, Vol. 76 (August 1962), pp. 480-488.

Hodgman, Donald R., "Credit Risk and Credit Rationing: Reply," *Quarterly Journal of Economics*, Vol. 76 (August 1962), pp. 488-493.

Stein, Jerome L., "International Short-Term Capital Movements," *American Economic Review*, Vol. 55 (March 1965), pp. 40-66.

Jaffee, Dwight M., *Credit Rationing and the Commercial Loan Market* (New York: Wiley, 1971).

Smith, Vernon L., "Default Risk, Scale, and the Homemade Leverage Theorem," *American Economic Review*, Vol. 62 (March 1972), pp. 66-76.

Smith, Vernon L., "A Theory and Test of Credit Rationing: Some Generalizations," *American Economic Review*, Vol. 62 (June 1972), pp. 477-483.

Fama, Eugene F., "Short-Term Interest Rates as Predictors of Inflation," *American Economic Review*, Vol. 65 (June 1975), pp. 269-282.

Jaffe, Dwight M., and Russell, Thomas, "Imperfect Information, Uncertainty, and Credit Rationing," *Quarterly Journal of Economics*, Vol. 90 (November 1976), pp. 651-666.

15.7 Insurance Markets and Health-Care Systems

Borch, Karl, "Equilibrium in a Reinsurance Market," *Econometrica*, Vol. 30 (July 1962), pp. 424-444.

Arrow, Kenneth J., "Uncertainty and the Welfare Economics of Medical

Care," *American Economic Review*, Vol. 53 (December 1963), pp. 941-973.

Kihlstrom, Richard E., and Pauly, Mark, "The Role of Insurance in the Allocation of Risk, " *American Economic Review*, Vol. 61 (Suppl. May 1971), pp. 171-179.

Pauly, Mark V., "Overinsurance and Public Provision of Insurance: The Roles of Moral Hazard and Adverse Selection," *Quarterly Journal of Economics*, Vol. 88 (February 1974), pp. 44-62.

Rothschild, Michael, and Stiglitz, Joseph E., "Equilibrium in Competitive Insurance Markets: The Economics of Markets with Imperfect Information," *Quarterly Journal of Economics*, Vol. 90 (November 1976), pp. 629-649.

Stiglitz, Joseph E., "Monopoly, Non-linear Pricing and Imperfect Information: The Insurance Market," *Review of Economic Studies*, Vol. 44 (October 1977), pp. 407-430.

Wilson, Charles A., "A Model of Insurance Markets with Incomplete Information," *Journal of Economic Theory*, Vol. 16 (December 1977), pp. 167-209.

15.8 *Foreign-Exchange Markets*

Goschen, George Joachim, *Theory of Foreign Exchanges* (London: E. Wilson, 1861).

Bagehot, Walter, *Lombard Street: A Description of the Money Market* (London: H. S. King, 1873).

Spraos, John, "The Theory of Forward Exchange and Recent Practice," *The Manchester School of Economics and Social Studies*, Vol. 21 (May 1953), pp. 87-117.

Tsiang, Sho-Chieh, "A Theory of Foreign-Exchange Speculation Under a Floating Exchange System," *Journal of Political Economy*, Vol. 66 (September-October 1958), pp. 399-418.

Tsiang, Sho-Chieh, "The Theory of Forward Exchange and Effects of Government Intervention on the Forward Market," *International Monetary Fund Staff Papers*, Vol. 7 (April 1959), pp. 75-106.

Stein, Jerome L., "The Simultaneous Determination of Spot and Future Prices," *American Economic Review*, Vol. 51 (December 1961), pp. 1012-1025.

Kenen, Peter B., "Trade, Speculation, and the Forward-Exchange Rate," in Robert E. Baldwin et al., eds., *Trade Growth, and the Balance of Payments*, Essays in Honor of Gottfried Haberler (Chicago: Rand McNally, 1965), pp. 163-169.

Grubel, Herbert G., *Forward Exchange, Speculation, and the International Flow of Capital* (Stanford: Stanford University Press, 1966).

Sohmen, Egon, *The Theory of Forward Exchange*, Studies in International Finance, No. 17 (Princeton: International Finance Section, Princeton University, 1966).

Feldstein, Martin, "Uncertainty and Forward Exchange Speculation," *Review of Economics and Statistics*, Vol. 50 (May 1968), pp. 182-192.

Machlup, Fritz, "The Forward Exchange Market: Misunderstandings Between Practitioners and Economists," in George N. Halm, ed., *Approaches to Greater Flexibility of Exchange Rates: The Burgenstock Papers* (Princeton: Princeton University Press, 1970), pp. 297-306.

Leland, Hayne E., "Optimal Forward Exchange Positions," *Journal of Political Economy*, Vol. 79 (March-April 1971), pp. 257-269.

Roper, Don E., "The Role of Expected Value Analysis for Speculative Decisions in the Forward Currency Market," *Quarterly Journal of Economics*, Vol. 89 (February 1975), pp. 157-169.

Frenkel, Jacob A., "Flexible Exchange Rates, Prices, and the Role of 'News': Lessons from the 1970s," *Journal of Political Economy*, Vol. 89 (July-August 1981), pp. 665-705.

15.9   Futures Markets

Keynes, John Maynard, *A Treatise on Money*, Vol. II (London: Macmillan, 1931), pp. 142-144.

Working, Holbrook, "New Concepts Concerning Futures Markets and Prices," *American Economic Review*, Vol. 52 (June 1962), pp. 431-459.

Schrock, Nicholas W., "The Theory of Asset Choice: Simultaneous Holding of Short and Long Positions in the Futures Market," *Journal of Political Economy*, Vol. 79 (March-April 1971), pp. 270-293.

Gumelson, Jerald A., and Farris, Paul L., "Use of Soybean Futures Markets by Large Processing Firms," *Agricultural Economics Research*, Vol. 25 (April 1973), pp. 27-40.

Kofi, Tetteh A., "A Framework for Comparing the Efficiency of Futures Markets," *American Journal of Agricultural Economics*, Vol. 55 (Part I, November 1973), pp. 584-594.

Grossman, Sanford J., "The Existence of Futures Markets, Noisy Rational Expectations, and Informational Externalities," *Review of Economic Studies*, Vol. 44 (July 1977), pp. 431-449.

Dubey, Pradeep, and Shubik, Martin, "Trade and Prices in a Closed Economy with Exogenous Uncertainty, Different Levels of Information, Money and Compound Future Markets," *Econometrica*, Vol. 45 (October 1977), pp. 1657-1680.

Danthine, Jean-Pierre, "Information, Future Prices and Stabilizing Speculation," *Journal of Economic Theory*, Vol. 17 (February 1978), pp. 79-98.

16.   PRICES AS INFORMATION SYSTEM FOR RESOURCE ALLOCATION AND PRODUCT DISTRIBUTION IN MARKET ECONOMIES AND PLANNED ECONOMIES; NATIONAL PROGRAMMING AND PLANNING

16.1   General

Mises, Ludwig von, *Die Gemeinwirtschaft* (Jena: Fischer, 1922; 2d ed., 1932); English translation: *Socialism* (London: Jonathan Cape, 1936; Indianapolis: Liberty Classics, 1979).

Taylor, Fred M., "The Guidance of Production in a Socialist State," *American Economic Review*, Vol. 19 (March 1929), pp. 1-8.

Roper, Willet Crosby, *The Problem of Pricing in a Socialist State* (Cambridge, Mass.: Harvard University Press, 1931).

Mises, Ludwig von, "Economic Calculation in the Socialist Commonwealth" (translated from German article of 1920), in Friedrich A. Hayek, ed., *Collectivist Economic Planning* (London: Routledge, 1935), pp. 87-130.

Hayek, Friedrich A., "The Use of Knowledge in Society," *American Economic Review*, Vol. 35 (September 1945), pp. 519-530; reprinted in Friedrich A. Hayek, *Individualism and Economic Order* (Chicago: University of Chicago Press, 1948), pp. 79-91.

Hurwicz, Leonid, "Optimality and Informational Efficiency in Resource Allocation Processes," in Kenneth J. Arrow; Samuel Karlin; and Patrick Suppes, eds., *Mathematical Methods in the Social Sciences, 1959* (Stanford: Stanford University Press, 1960), pp. 27-46.

Boulding, Kenneth E., "Reflections on Planning: The Value of Uncertainty," *Technology Review*, Vol. 77 (October-November 1974), p. 8.

Reiter, Stanley, "Information and Performance in the (New) Welfare Economics," *American Economic Review*, Vol. 67 (Suppl. May 1977), pp. 226-239.

Grossman, Sanford J., "A Characterization of the Optimality of Equilibrium in Incomplete Markets," *Journal of Economic Theory*, Vol. 15 (June 1977), pp. 1-15.

16.2 Market Failures and Public Goods

Pigou, Arthur Cecil, *The Economics of Welfare* (London: Macmillan, 1920; 4th ed., 1932).

Ellis, Howard S., and Fellner, William, "External Economies and Diseconomies," *American Economic Review*, Vol. 33 (September 1943), pp. 493-511.

Davis, Otto A., and Kamien, Morton I., "Externalities, Information and Alternative Collective Action," in *The Analysis and Evaluation of Public Expenditures: The PPB System*, Vol. I, Joint Economic Committee Print (Washington, D.C.: U.S. Congress, 1969), pp. 67-86.

Mishan, Ezra J., "The Relationship Between Joint Products, Collective Goods, and External Effects," *Journal of Political Economy*, Vol. 77 (May-June 1969), pp. 329-348.

Ayres, Robert U., and Kneese, Allen V., "Production, Consumption, and Externalities," *American Economic Review*, Vol. 59 (June 1969), pp. 282-297.

Mishan, Ezra J., "The Postwar Literature on Externalities: An Interpretative Essay," *Journal of Economic Literature*, Vol. 9 (March 1971), pp. 1-28.

Malinvaud, Edmond, "A Planning Approach to the Public-Good Problem," *Swedish Journal of Economics*, Vol. 73 (March 1971), pp. 96-112.

Drèze, Jacques H., and de la Vallée Poussin, Dominique, "A Tâtonnement Process for Public Goods," *Review of Economic Studies*, Vol. 38 (April 1971), pp. 133-150.

Baumol, William J., "On Taxation and the Control of Externalities," *American Economic Review*, Vol. 62 (March 1972), pp. 307-322.

Tideman, Nicolaus, "The Efficient Provision of Public Goods., in Selma J. Mushkin, ed., *Public Prices for Public Products* (Washington, D.C.: Urban Institute, 1972), p. 111.

Milleron, Jean-Claude, "Theory of Value with Public Goods: A Survey Article," *Journal of Economic Theory*, Vol. 5 (December 1972), pp. 419-477.

Head, John G., *Public Goods and Public Welfare* (Durham: Duke University Press, 1974).

Frey, Bruno S., "A Dynamic Theory of Public Goods," *Finanzarchiv*, Vol. 32 (1974), pp. 185-193.

Atkinson, Anthony B., and Stern, Nicholas H., "Pigou, Taxation, and Public Goods," *Review of Economic Studies*, Vol. 41 (January 1974), pp. 119-128.

Oakland, William H., "Public Goods, Perfect Competition, and Underproduction," *Journal of Political Economy*, Vol. 82 (September-October 1974), pp. 927-939.

Tideman, T. Nicolaus, and Tullock, Gordon, "A New and Superior Process for Making Social Choices," *Journal of Political Economy*, Vol. 84 (September-October 1976), pp. 1145-1159.

Groves, Theodore, and Ledyard, John, "Optimal Allocation of Public Goods: A Solution to the 'Free Rider' Problem," *Econometrica*, Vol. 45 (May 1977), pp. 783-809.

Groves, Theodore, and Ledyard, John O., "Some Limitations of Demand Revealing Processes," *Public Choice*, Vol. 29 (Suppl. Spring 1977), pp. 107-124.

Green, Jerry, and Laffont, Jean-Jacques, "On the Revelation of Preferences for Public Goods," *Journal of Public Economics*, Vol. 8 (August 1977), p. 80.

Riker, William H., "Is 'a New and Superior Process' Really Superior?" *Journal of Political Economy*, Vol. 87 (July-August 1979), pp. 875-890.

16.3 *Markets versus Central Plans*

Hayek, Friedrich A. von, ed., *Collectivist Economic Planning* (London: Routledge, 1935).

Meade, James Edward, *Planning and the Price Mechanism: The Liberal Socialist Solution* (London: Allen & Unwin, 1948).

Kaser, Michael, and Portes, Richard, eds., *Planning and Market Relations*, Proceedings of a Conference Held by the International Economic Association (London: Macmillan, 1971).

Eckstein, Alexander, ed., *Comparison of Economic Systems: Theoretical and Methodological Approaches* (Berkeley: University of California Press, 1971).

Bornstein, Morris, ed., *Plan and Market: Economic Reform in Eastern Europe* (New Haven: Yale University Press, 1973).

16.4   *Indicative Programming in Market Economies*

Hackett, John and Anne-Marie, *Economic Planning in France* (Cambridge, Mass.: Harvard University Press, 1963).

Wickham, Sylvain, "French Planning: Retrospect and Prospect," *Review of Economics and Statistics*, Vol. 45 (November 1963), pp. 335-347.

Lutz, Vera, *French Planning* (Washington, D.C.: American Enterprise Institute, 1965).

Albin, Peter S., "Uncertainty, Information Exchange and the Theory of Indicative Planning," *Economic Journal*, Vol. 81 (March 1971), pp. 61-90.

Balassa, Bela, "Planning and Programming in the European Common Market," *European Economic Review*, Vol. 4 (October 1973), pp. 217-233.

16.5   *Plans and Plan Execution in Socialist Countries*

Montias, John Michael, "Planning with Material Balances in Soviet-Type Economies," *American Economic Review*, Vol. 49 (December 1959), pp. 963-985.

Grossman, Gregory, ed., *Value and Plan: Economic Calculation and Organization in Eastern Europe* (Berkeley: University of California Press, 1960).

Montias, John Michael, *Central Planning in Poland* (New Haven: Yale University Press, 1962).

Bergson, Abram, and Kuznets, Simon, eds., *Economic Trends in the Soviet Union* (Cambridge, Mass.: Harvard University Press, 1963).

Bergson, Abram, *Economics of Soviet Planning* (New Haven: Yale University Press, 1964).

Bergson, Abram, *Planning and Productivity Under Soviet Socialism* (New York: Columbia University Press, for Carnegie-Mellon University, 1968).

Marglin, Stephen A., "Information in Price and Command Systems of Planning," in Julius Margolis and Henri Guitton, eds., *Public Economics*, Proceedings of a Conference Held [at Biarritz] by the International Economic Association (London: Macmillan, 1969), pp. 54-57.

Aganbegian, A. G., and Bagrinovsky, K. A., "Problem-Complexes in Optimal Planning," *Acta Oeconomica*, Vol. 10 (1973), pp. 21-27.

Manescu, Manea, "The Planned Economic-Social Development of Romania," *Revue Roumaine des Sciences Sociales, Série Sciences Economiques*, Vol. 17 (No. 1, 1973), pp. 13-33.

Chung, Pham, "A Note on the Optimal Product Mix in a Centrally Planned Economy," *Journal of Political Economy*, Vol. 81 (March-April 1973), pp. 427-434.

Fedorenko, Nikolay P., "On the Elaboration of a System of Optimal Functioning of the Socialist Economy," *Problems of Economics*, Vol. 15 (April 1973), pp. 3-27.

Friss, Istvan, "Practical Experiences of the Economic Reform in Hungary," *Eastern European Economics*, Vol. 11 (Spring 1973), pp. 3-26.

Kornai, Janos, and Martos, Bela, "Autonomous Control of the Economic System," *Econometrica*, Vol. 41 (May 1973), pp. 509-528.

Perkins, Dwight H., "Plans and their Implementation in the People's Republic of China," *American Economic Review*, Vol. 63 (Suppl. May 1973), pp. 224-231.

Granick, David, "A Management Model of East-European Centrally-Planned Economies," *European Economic Review*, Vol. 4 (June 1973), pp. 135-161.

16.6   *Market Socialism*

Dickinson, Henry D., "Price Formation in a Socialist Community," *Economic Journal*, Vol. 43 (June 1933), pp. 237-250.

Dobb, Maurice, "Economic Theory and the Problem of a Socialist Economy," *Economic Journal*, Vol. 43 (December 1933), pp. 588-598.

Lerner, Abba P., "Economic Theory and Socialist Economy," *Review of Economic Studies*, Vol. 2 (October 1934), pp. 51-61.

Lange, Oskar, "On the Economic Theory of Socialism," Parts I and II, *Review of Economic Studies*, Vol. 4 (October 1936 and February 1937), pp. 53-71, 123-142.

Lippincott, Benjamin E., ed., *On the Economic Theory of Socialism* (Minneapolis: University of Minnesota Press, 1938).

Lerner, Abba P., "Theory and Practice in Socialist Economies," *Review of Economic Studies*, Vol. 6 (October 1938), pp. 71-75.

Dickinson, Henry D., *Economics of Socialism* (London: Oxford University Press, 1939).

Hayek, Friedrich A., "Socialist Calculation: The Competitive Solution," *Economica*, N.S., Vol. 7 (May 1940), pp. 125-149.

Malinvaud, Edmond, and Bacharach, Michael O. L., eds., *Activity Analysis in the Theory of Growth and Planning*, Proceedings of a Conference Held [at Cambridge] by the International Economic Association (London: Macmillan, 1967).

Sik, Ota, *Plan and Market Under Socialism* (Prague: Academia, Publishing House of the Czechoslovak Academy of Science, 1967).

Ward, Benjamin N., *The Socialist Economy: A Study of the Organizational Alternatives* (New York: Random House, 1967), p. 25.

Dorn, James A., "Markets, True and False: The Case of Yugoslavia," *Journal of Libertarian Studies*, Vol. 2 (Fall 1978), pp. 243-268.

Lavoie, Don, "A Critique of the 'Standard' Account of the Socialist Calculation Debate," Ph.D. dissertation, New York University, 1981.

17.   HUMAN CAPITAL: THE ACCUMULATION OF KNOWLEDGE AND SKILLS

17.1   *General*

Engel, Ernst, *Der Werth des Menschen*, Part I, *Der Kostenwerth des Menschen* (Berlin: L. Simion, 1883).

Dublin, Louis I., and Lotka, Alfred J., *The Money Value of a Man* (New York: Ronald Press, 1930: 2d ed., 1946).

Schultz, Theodore W., "Capital Formation by Education," *Journal of Political Economy*, Vol. 68 (November-December 1960), pp. 571-583.

Schultz, Theodore W., "Investment in Human Capital," *American Economic Review*, Vol. 51 (March 1961), pp. 1-17.

Weisbrod, Burton A., "The Valuation of Human Capital," *Journal of Political Economy*, Vol. 69 (September-October 1961), pp. 425-436.

Becker, Gary, "Investment in Human Capital: A Theoretical Analysis," *Journal of Political Economy*, Vol. 70 (Suppl. October 1962), pp. 9-49.

Weisbrod, Burton A., "Education and Investment in Human Capital," *Journal of Political Economy*, Vol. 70 (September-October 1962, Part 2), pp. 106-123.

Bowman, Mary Jean, "Social Returns to Education," *International Social Science Journal* (UNESCO), Vol. 14 (No. 4, 1962), pp. 647-659.

Bowman, Mary Jean, "Human Capital: Concepts and Measures," in Selma Mushkin, ed., *The Economics of Higher Education* (Washington, D.C.: U.S. Office of Education, 1962), chap. 6, pp. 69-92.

Becker, Gary, *Human Capital* (New York: Columbia University Press, 1964; 2d ed., 1975).

Colberg, Marshall R., *Human Capital in Southern Development, 1939-1963* (Chapel Hill: University of North Carolina Press, 1965).

Kiker, Bernard F., *Human Capital: In Retrospect* (Columbia: University of South Carolina, Bureau of Business and Economic Research, 1968).

Cochrane, James L., and Kiker, Bernard F., "An Austrian Approach to the Theory of Investment in Human Beings," *Southern Economic Journal*, Vol. 36 (April 1970), pp. 385-389.

Hansen, W. Lee, ed., *Education, Income, and Human Capital*. Studies in Income and Wealth, No. 35 (New York: Columbia University Press, for National Bureau of Economic Research, 1970).

Ben-Porath, Yoram, "The Production of Human Capital Over Time," in W. Lee Hansen, ed., *Education, Income, and Human Capital*, Studies in Income and Wealth, Vol. 35 (New York: Columbia University Press for the National Bureau of Economic Research, 1970), pp. 129-147.

Machlup, Fritz, *Education and Economic Growth* (Lincoln: University of Nebraska Press, 1970; reprinted New York: New York University Press, 1975).

Schultz, Theodore W., *Investment in Human Capital: The Role of Education and Research* (New York: Free Press, 1971).

Parsons, Donald O., "The Cost of School Time, Foregone Earnings, and Human Capital Formation," *Journal of Political Economy*, Vol. 82 (March-April 1974, Part I), pp. 251-266.

Blaug, Mark, "The Empirical Status of Human Capital Theory: A Slightly Jaundiced Survey," *Journal of Economic Literature*, Vol. 14 (September 1976), pp. 827-855.

Razin, Assaf, "Lifetime Uncertainty, Human Capital and Physical Capital," *Economic Inquiry*, Vol. 14 (September 1976), pp. 439-448.

Blinder, Alan S., "On Dogmatism in Human Capital Theory," *Journal of Human Resources*, Vol. 11 (Winter 1976), pp. 8-22.

Stephan, Paula E., "Human Capital Production: Life-Cycle Production with Different Learning Technologies," *Economic Inquiry*, Vol. 14 (December 1976), pp. 539-557.

Rosen, Sherwin, "Human Capital: A Survey of Empirical Research," in Ronald G. Ehrenberg, ed., *Research in Labor Economics: An Annual Compilation of Research*, Vol. 1 (Greenwich, Conn.: Jai Press, 1977), pp. 3-39.

17.2   *Contributions to Productivity*

Griliches, Zvi, "Research Expenditures, Education, and the Aggregate Production Function for Agriculture," *American Economic Review*, Vol. 54 (December 1964), pp. 961-974.

Welch, Finis, "Education in Production," *Journal of Political Economy*, Vol. 78 (January-February 1970), pp. 35-59.

Hansen, W. Lee; Kellog, Allen C.; and Weisbrod, Burton A., "Economic Efficiency and the Distribution of Benefits from College Instruction," *American Economic Review*, Vol. 60 (Suppl. May 1970), pp. 335-340.

Gintis, Herbert, "Education, Technology, and the Characteristics of Worker Productivity," *American Economic Review*, Vol. 61 (Suppl. May 1971), pp. 266-279.

Wise, David A., "Academic Achievement and Job Performance," *American Economic Review*, Vol. 65 (June 1975), pp. 350-366.

Riley, John G., "Information, Screening and Human Capital," *American Economic Review*, Vol. 66 (Suppl. May 1976), pp. 254-260.

17.3   *Differential Flows of Earnings and Their Sources*

Friedman, Milton, and Kuznets, Simon, *Income from Independent Professional Practice* (Princeton: Princeton University Press, NBER, 1954).

Mincer, Jacob, "Investment in Human Capital and Personal Income Distribution," *Journal of Political Economy*, Vol. 66 (July-August 1958), pp. 281-302.

Houthakker, Hendrik S., "Education and Income," *Review of Economics and Statistics*, Vol. 41 (February 1959), pp. 24-27.

Miller, Herman P., "Annual and Lifetime Income in Relation to Education," *American Economic Review*, Vol. 50 (December 1960), pp. 962-986.

Becker, Gary S., and Chiswick, Barry R., "Education and the Distribution of Earnings," *American Economic Review*, Vol. 56 (Suppl. May 1966), pp. 358-369.

Wilkinson, Bruce W., "Present Values of Lifetime Earnings for Different Occupations," *Journal of Political Economy*, Vol. 74 (November-December 1966), pp. 556-572.

Hanoch, Giora, "An Economic Analysis of Earnings and Schooling," *Journal of Human Resources*, Vol. 2 (Summer 1967), pp. 310-319.

Ben-Porath, Yoram, "The Production of Human Capital and the Life Cycle of Earnings," *Journal of Political Economy*, Vol. 75 (July-August 1967), pp. 352-365.

Mincer, Jacob, "The Distribution of Labor Incomes: A Survey with Special Reference to the Human Capital Approach," *Journal of Economic Literature*, Vol. 8 (March 1970), pp. 1-26.

Hansen, W. Lee; Weisbrod, Burton A.; and Scanlon, William J., "Schooling and Earnings of Low Achievers," *American Economic Review*, Vol. 60 (June 1970), pp. 409-418.

Griliches, Zvi, and Mason, William M., "Education, Income, and Ability," *Journal of Political Economy*, Vol. 80 (May-June 1972, Part 2), pp. S74-S103.

Bowles, Samuel, "Schooling and Inequality from Generation to Generation," *Journal of Political Economy*, Vol. 80 (May-June 1972, Part 2), pp. S219-S251.

Chiswick, Barry R., "Schooling and Earnings of Low Achievers: Comment," *American Economic Review*, Vol. 62 (September 1972), pp. 752-754.

Masters, Stanley, and Ribich, Thomas, "Schooling and Earnings by Low Achievers: Comment," *American Economic Review*, Vol. 62 (September 1972), pp. 755-759.

Hansen, W. Lee; Weisbrod, Burton, A.; and Scanlon, William J., "Schooling and Earnings of Low Achievers: Reply," *American Economic Review*, Vol. 62 (September 1972), pp. 760-762.

Mincer, Jacob, *Schooling, Experience, and Earnings* (New York, Columbia University Press, NBER, 1974).

Layard, Richard, and Psacharopoulos, George, "The Screening Hypothesis and the Returns to Education," *Journal of Political Economy*, Vol. 82 (September-October 1974), pp. 985-998.

Marin, Alan, and Psacharopoulos, George, "Schooling and Income Distribution," *Review of Economics and Statistics*, Vol. 58 (August 1976), pp. 332-338.

Hirsch, Barry T., "Earnings Inequality Across Labor Markets: A Test of the Human Capital Model," *Southern Economic Journal*, Vol. 45 (July 1978), pp. 32-41.

17.4   Rates of Return to Schooling

Becker, Gary S., "Underinvestment in College Education?" *American Economic Review*, Vol. 50 (May 1960), pp. 346-354.

Hansen, W. Lee, "Total and Private Rates of Return to Investment in Schooling," *Journal of Political Economy*, Vol. 71 (March-April 1963), pp. 128-140.

Ashenfelter, Orley, and Mooney, J. D., "Some Evidence on the Private Returns of Graduate Education," *Southern Economic Journal*, Vol. 35 (January 1969), pp. 247-256.

Maxwell, Lynn, "Some Evidence on Negative Returns to Graduate Education," *Western Economic Journal*, Vol. 8 (June 1970), pp. 186-189.

Bailey, Duncan, and Schotta, Charles, "Private and Social Rates of Return to Education of Academicians," *American Economic Review*, Vol. 62 (March 1972), pp. 19-31.

Eckaus, Richard S., *Estimating the Returns to Education: A Disaggregated Approach* (Berkeley, Cal.: Carnegie Commission on Higher Education, 1973).

Johnson, George E., and Stafford, Frank, "Social Returns to Quantity and Quality of Schooling," *Journal of Human Resources*, Vol. 8 (Spring 1973), pp. 139-155.

Tomaske, John A., "Private and Social Rates of Return to Education of Academicians: Note," *American Economic Review*, Vol. 64 (March 1974), pp. 220-224.

Raymond, Richard, and Sesnowitz, Michael, "The Returns to Investment in Higher Education: Some New Evidence," *Journal of Human Resources*, Vol. 10 (Spring 1975), pp. 139-154.

Freeman, Richard B., "Overinvestment in College Training?" *Journal of Human Resources*, Vol. 10 (Summer 1975), pp. 287-311.

Link, Charles R., and Ratledge, Edward C., "Social Returns to Quantity and Quality of Education: A Further Statement," *Journal of Human Resources*, Vol. 10 (Winter 1975), pp. 78-89.

Griliches, Zvi, "Estimating Returns to Schooling: Some Econometric Problems," Presidential Address, Econometric Society (Toronto 1975).

Bowen, Howard R., *Investment in Learning: The Individual and Social Value of American Higher Education* (San Francisco: Jossey-Bass 1977).

17.5 Training on the Job: Investment and Earnings

Mincer, Jacob, "On-the-Job Training: Costs, Returns, and Some Implications," *Journal of Political Economy*, Vol. 70 (September-October 1962, Part 2), pp. 50-79.

Parsons, Donald O., "Specific Human Capital: An Application to Quit Rates and Layoff Rates," *Journal of Political Economy*, Vol. 80 (November-December 1972), pp. 1120-1143.

17.6 Individual Decisions and Labor-Market Phenomena

Levhari, David, and Weiss, Yoram, "The Effect of Risk on the Investment in Human Capital," *American Economic Review*, Vol. 64 (December 1974), pp. 950-963.

Blinder, Alan S., and Weiss, Yoram, "Human Capital and Labor Supply: A Synthesis," *Journal of Political Economy*, Vol. 84 (May-June 1976), pp. 449-472.

17.7 The Stock of Human Capital

Schultz, Theodore W., *The Economic Value of Education* (New York: Columbia University Press, 1963).

Wagner, Leonore U., "Problems in Estimating Research and Development Investment and Stock," *American Statistical Association, Proceedings of the Business and Economic Statistics Section* (1968), pp. 189-198.

Kendrick, John W., *The Formation and Stocks of Total Capital* (New York: National Bureau of Economic Research, 1976).

17.8   Public Policies for Education, Training, and Manpower

Weisbrod, Burton A., "Preventing High-School Dropouts," in Robert J. Dorfman, ed., *Measuring Benefits of Government Investment* (Washington, D.C.: Brookings Institution, 1965), pp. 117-149.

Ziderman, Adrian, "Costs and Benefits of Adult Retraining in the United Kingdom," *Economica*, N.S., Vol. 36 (November 1969), pp. 363-376.

Goldfarb, Robert S., "The Evaluation of Government Programs: The Case of New Haven's Manpower Training Activities," *Yale Economic Essays*, Vol. 9 (Fall 1969), pp. 59-104.

Doeringer, Peter, "Low Income Labor Markets and Urban Manpower Programs: A Critical Assessment," Joint Harvard-MIT report submitted to the Manpower Administration (reproduced by National Technical Information Service, 1969).

Commins, William, *Social Security Data: An Aid to Manpower Program Evaluation* (McLean, Va.: Planning Research Corporation, 1970).

Borus, Michael, ed., *Evaluating the Impact of Manpower Programs* (Lexington, Mass.: Heath, 1972).

U.S. Department of Labor, *Manpower Advice for Government* (Washington, D.C.: Manpower Administration, 1972).

Ashenfelter, Orley, "Estimating the Effect of Training Programs on Earnings," *Review of Economics and Statistics*, Vol. 60 (February 1978), pp. 47-57.

PART TWO

KNOWLEDGE AS
HUMAN CAPITAL

THE NOTION of "human capital" is quite old, at least three hundred years if we are willing to look for implied meanings. After all, ideas of shaping a tool for later use, of sowing now in order to reap later, and of *learning now to acquire know-how for later use* are such close analogues that it would be an insult to the intelligence of our precursors if we thought they had not seen the common element in these ideas. Learning now and earning later is the fundamental idea of forming human capital.

It is my aim to present rather complex problems in the simplest possible way, though I shall not be able to avoid some technical arguments. Still, I shall do without mathematical language, stick to English prose, and foreswear the use of strange acronyms, algebraic symbols, and telegram style.

CHAPTER 12

BASIC NOTIONS OF
CAPITAL THEORY

THE THEORY of capital is a highly complex area of economic analysis, and I must not assume that most readers are familiar with it. I shall therefore begin with a sketch of the relations between the flow of *real* investment and the accumulation of *real* capital, that is, physical capital goods. If some readers find this chapter forbidding, they may settle for a merely intuitive grasp of the ideas and not bother with excessively technical notions.

All theories of capital deal with four fundamental concepts: (1) valuable *stocks of resources*, durable but exhaustible or depreciating; (2) *investment*, or accumulation, additions to the stock of resources; (3) *flows of services*, or returns, earnings, incomes, benefits, and satisfactions attributable to the stock or to any particular investment; and (4) *rates of return*, or yields, relating the flow of services to the stock of resources or to any investment, any particular addition to the stock of resources.

Whereas stocks refer to a moment of time, investment and returns refer to periods of time. The calculation of rates of return presupposes that returns, investments, and stocks of resources are expressed in the same units; apart from rare exceptions, they are all expressed in terms of money. This does not mean, however, that resources and services that flow from them *are* money. In the case of tangible capital, the resources are physical goods; the services that they render may be intangible but nevertheless physical in some sense. Think, for example, of a hydroelectric plant with its turbines, generators, and other productive facilities, and of the current they generate, electric power having been transformed from water power. There is no way to relate numerically the kilowatt hours of electric energy to the cement foundations, steel casings, copper wires, and the many other physical things embodied in the physical plant and equipment. The services as well as the resources have to be converted into money values before rates of return can be calculated.

Investment is undertaken, as a rule, in expectation of additional incomes that it may generate. The *expected* rate of return to the additional investment has much to do with the propensity to invest, although it may not be easy to know just what to expect. Experience with *past* investment, and the returns yielded by it, may be important influences on the rates of *future* returns that *current* investment is expected to yield.

Let us first rehearse our understanding of the concept of real (tangible, physical) capital, before we extend the implied notions to human capital (embodied in and inseparable from individual persons).[1]

The Stock of Real Capital

I shall not propose a definition of capital or capital goods. Economists have quarreled about these definitions for centuries, and it would serve no good purpose to go into a fruitless semantic exercise. The major difficulty in agreeing on a definition is that capital is not an observable thing that can be described in terms of perceivable attributes or qualities. Capital, for most writers, is a source of future productive services; for some, the essential feature is that it owes its existence to a human decision—an investment decision; for others, the essential feature is that the particular resources, or the stream of benefits, will not last forever unless a conscious effort is made to "maintain" them, that is, to replace the parts considered to have been depleted, worn out, become obsolete, or depreciated for any other reason. Thus, certain physical goods are conceived of as capital, because they are "produced producers' goods"; or because they are "produced durable goods" used for future production and/or future consumption; or because they are "exhaustible" resources that have to be replaced by their provident owners.[2]

We are, of course, talking about goods to which people attach economic value. Not all physical things are valuable goods. Goods are valuable or "economic" only because they are relatively scarce. (Of course, what is not wanted by anybody is never scarce.) Physical things that are so plentiful that it would make no difference if fewer of them were available, have no value and thus are not goods. The

[1] A warning on ambiguous uses of the words "real" capital: The original distinction was between *money* capital—investible money funds—and real capital—capital goods (chiefly those used in the production of goods and services). Then came the distinction between *human* capital and real capital, as in the present context. Thirdly, there are those who use "real capital stocks" to mean investments accumulated at money values adjusted for changes in the price index, in contradistinction to *nominal* capital. You cannot trust economists to use words consistently.

[2] For informative discussions about concepts of capital see Irving Fisher, *The Nature of Capital and Income* (New York: Macmillan, 1930), pp. 2-12, 51-65, 90-98, and Friedrich A. Hayek, *The Pure Theory of Capital* (London: Macmillan, 1941), pp. 50-64.

same is true for *durable* objects that could be used for something: if they are available in abundance, they are not regarded as resources, because no services or benefits depend on the availability of any particular unit or any small quantity. Only if they are scarce, so that a reduction or an increase in their quantity would make a difference, are they regarded as resources.

Real capital goods, tangible resources capable of yielding services or benefits, are thus valuable by definition, but *how* valuable is a different question. A stock, or the total stock, of capital goods has economic value, but the *magnitude* of that value (in terms of any good, service, medium of exchange, or unit of account) remains to be determined. Let us discuss the question of the value of a collection of capital goods, a stock of real capital.

The Value of a Stock of Capital Goods

There are alternative ways to "determine" the value of the stock of real capital that exists at a moment in time, and that value may be different depending on the way chosen. In principle, two points of view may be contrasted: one may look either back into the past or forward into the future. The backward look focuses on the investments, the forward look on the returns. The backward look values the capital goods by their historical cost, the forward look values them by expected benefits.

This duality of perspectives may be of significance both for private holders of capital goods and for society at large. To what extent one or the other perspective may be significant depends on the purposes of the valuation. In other words, who wants to know and for what purpose, are essential questions. Yet, I shall defer them for discussion in a later chapter, simply because the very general—logical or mathematical—relationships should be set forth first. (I realize that the priority given to the more abstract discussion may present an obstacle to easy comprehension.)

The duality of perspectives corresponds to a duality regarding the rate of return, the ratio of a flow of returns to a stock of capital: one may take either the value of the capital stock as given and the rate of return as unknown or the rate of return as given and the value of the capital stock as unknown. In the first case, more in keeping with the backward look, the rate of return is calculated from the (historically) given value of the capital stock and the (presumably) given stream of returns expected to flow from the stock. In the second case, favored by the forward look, the rate of return is taken as given—by current market conditions or by long-run expectations of future market conditions (expectations that may be affected by experience, tra-

dition, or any other norm)—and is applied in calculating the unknown value of the capital stock by discounting the expected future
returns to their "present value."[3] The backward look is likely to yield
a multiplicity of ("internal") rates of return for different assemblages
of capital goods. The forward look implies forgetting the past outlays
and valuing the capital stock by applying a given discount rate to
the expected flow of returns. These excessively simplified formulations are subject to successive qualifications as we proceed.

One qualification had better be made right now, lest the experts
become impatient. The accumulation of past investment expenditures must not be thought of as a mere adding-up procedure; accrued
interest has to be *included*, and depreciation for wear and tear, for
obsolescence, or for other causes, has to be *deducted*. The charges
for cumulative interest are to be understood as added cost, since the
funds so invested would have earned interest (or profit) in alternative
investments. (Foregone earnings are costs in the sense of opportunities sacrificed for the sake of the investments actually undertaken.)
Deductions of depreciation may relate to two different facts: (1) Some
capital goods in the existing stock may have been used and may have
earned the user cost or appropriate depreciation allowances; they
have already rendered a portion of the services they were intended
to yield and, although they remain a source of services in the future,
the services already received may justify reducing the value of the
resources by the earned depreciation allowances. (2) Some capital
goods produced in the past, and either used or not used in the past,
may have depreciated even if they have not yet earned the appropriate
depreciation allowances; declaring them depreciated reflects a glance
into the future, namely, a conclusion that one cannot any longer
expect them to earn the returns that were expected when the investment decisions were made. Such a write-down of capital goods
below their costs corrects the findings attained from looking back by
taking account of findings from looking forward.

[3] Readers not familiar with the notion of discounting may be helped by the proposition that a promise of a million dollars next year is worth now only much less
than a million dollars. This has nothing to do with inflation of prices but is merely
a matter of the passage of time in a world in which it is preferable to have goods now
rather than later, even if there is no substantial uncertainty involved. The preference
for earlier possession may be due to people's impatience to enjoy the goods, or to an
opportunity of using them profitably.

The relation between discount and interest can be explained briefly: at an interest
rate of 10 per cent, $100 on January 1 are equivalent to $110 at the end of next
December. This means that the $110 next December have a present (discounted) value,
on January 1, of $100. Although the absolute amount of interest and discount is the
same, $10, it corresponds to a rate of interest of 10 per cent of $100, but to a rate of
discount of 9.09 per cent of $100.

Interest rates are involved in both ways of capital valuation: in the add-up-the-costs procedure, interest is compounded as an integral part of the accumulated investment, and in the discount-the-returns procedure, interest reduces future returns to their present values. Of course, these two interest rates are usually different from each other; only in the most extraordinary circumstances could they be the same. The rates at which investment outlays of the *past* are to be *magnified* to make them include the cost of funds and, hence, the total amount invested up to the present should reflect past conditions in the capital markets, that is, the supply of investible funds and the alternative opportunities to invest them at the time. The rates at which returns receivable in the *future* are to be "*minified*" to pare them down to the present value of future accruals should reflect *present* market conditions, that is, the supply of capital funds and investment opportunities at the present time.

The difference in interest rates relevant to the evaluation of capital stocks may be troublesome, but far less so than the more fundamental problem of capital formation, namely, the problem arising from structural changes in the economy between the time when investment decisions are made and the time when the goods and services they are designed to produce are ready to be marketed. Some or many of the past investments may have turned out to be bad investments and can no longer be expected to yield a stream of future incomes commensurate with what can be anticipated from "good" investments. If the accumulated stock of capital includes many poor investments, a calculation adding up the past outlays will result in a sum of "historical costs" (plus accrued interest) much higher than the amount obtained by capitalizing[4] the future incomes now expected from the existing capital stock. Expressed in other words, the present values that reflect the revised expectations now entertained regarding the flows of future incomes derived from the given stock of accumulated capital may fall seriously short of that capital stock valued on the basis of historical cost with all bad investments counted in.

Revaluations of Capital Stocks When Times Have Changed

The problem of changing the valuation of existing collections of capital goods when economic conditions have drastically changed

---

[4] The verb "to capitalize" is used in economics with several meanings; in the present context it means calculating the present value of a flow or stream of future receipts by discounting each single receipt expected, and adding up all these discounted values. Another meaning of the verb, not relevant in the present context but significant in private and social accounting, relates to the treatment of expenditures: to "capitalize an outlay" is to treat it as an addition to assets, not as a current expense to be subtracted from sales revenues to obtain the amount of profit.

has concerned several groups besides economists. Corporate managements, accountants, tax authorities, public-utility regulators, legislatures, and the courts have all engaged in economic theorizing about the best accommodations to the problem, though the quality of their theories has not always been on the highest levels of discernment. For example, the judiciary authorities in the United States have in cases of utility-rate regulation (say, for gas and electric power) tried to deal with matters of capital-stock valuation by enunciating a sequence of presumably fair and reasonable procedures. They recognized first that a valuation of an existing stock of capital goods on the basis of *historical costs* is unacceptable when prices have substantially changed and that these capital goods—plant and equipment—should instead be valued according to their *replacement costs*. Such an appraisal, however, would not be helpful if serious mistakes had been made in the original investment decisions or if technology had in the meantime changed substantially; in many instances it would not be prudent to replace these same or analogous capital goods at all. The theory of *prudent investment* has advanced a third notion: instead of valuing the given assemblage of capital goods either by their historical cost or by their replacement cost, one should value them by the cost of the most economical set of goods capable of producing the same output.

These notions may have relevance in a particular publicly regulated industry confined to the production of an essentially unchanged product; they would not be appropriate or relevant for industries producing changing combinations of changing products. The notion of valuation on the basis of prudent investment has no application in unregulated industries and, still less, in the economy as a whole, especially in times of large structural changes. In many instances it would not be economical to produce that output for which the investments originally were made. Past investments may have proved to be bad investments precisely because the originally intended product is no longer profitable to produce. Appropriate write-downs or write-offs of the malinvestments (investments that have proved to be failures) would then seem to be in order. However, such reductions in the valuation of the accumulated real capital in light of present expectations of future returns would amount to adopting the forward look. It would mean abandoning the backward look in conformance with the principle that bygones are forever bygones and that all values of capital goods and their services are determined by the future benefits they now are expected to yield.

This principle—"forget the past, except for experiences promising to be helpful for the future, and look to the future only"—may be the overriding rule in all economic theory; it certainly is decisive in rational economic reactions to environmental changes and in optimal decision-making, private as well as public. To be sure, the principle is often disregarded in actual fact, especially in public policy—in which protective measures are adopted to maintain the value of collections of capital goods assembled as a result of malinvestments—but the disregard is almost always at the cost of potential benefits, at the expense of better investments, higher returns, and rising incomes.

As a matter of fact, the valuation of existing capital goods is economically significant chiefly for considerations regarding their alternative uses for future production. These uses almost always involve cooperation with current and future productive services expected to accrue from natural and human resources and also from other capital goods, newly produced in the course of new capital formation, that is, new investments complementary with existing capital stocks. This way to evaluate stocks inherited from the past, without regard to their historical costs but with an exclusive view to their opportunity costs, is in keeping with the economic principle of using available means to attain a maximum of ends. To repeat for emphasis, the relevant cost of existing capital goods or collections of capital goods that enters into their valuation in *rational* economic calculations is their opportunity cost in forward-looking considerations, never their historical cost.[5]

Past Experiences Helpful in Decisions for the Future

Bygones are forever bygones, except for such experiences as may prove valid and helpful for the future. It may be worthwhile spec-

[5] This conclusion does not necessarily contradict the procedures adopted by statisticians of national wealth and total stocks of capital. For obtaining data on values of physical capital the statistician is limited to what he can get from the balance sheets of business firms, and this compels him to adopt the historical-cost approach, adjusted for past depreciation and, in exceptional cases, also for price changes. Anticipating my later discussion of valuations of the stock of human capital, I may report here that the majority of the few who have attempted to compile series of stocks of human capital have employed the historical-cost approach but were criticized on theoretical grounds for not using the present-value approach. Since data on returns on investment in human capital are not any more difficult to obtain than data on outlays and other costs, but are more relevant for considerations of economic policy, the forward looking present-value approach is to be preferred. See Mary Jean Bowman, "Postschool Learning and Human Resource Accounting," *Review of Income and Wealth*, Vol. 20 (December 1974), pp. 483-499; and John W. Graham and Roy H. Webb, "Stocks and Depreciation of Human Capital: New Evidence from a Present-Value Perspective," *Review of Income and Wealth*, Vol. 25 (June 1979), pp. 209-224. Some writers define human capital as "potential earnings" expected as return to investments embodied in individuals. Alan S. Blinder and Yoram Weiss, "Human Capital and Labor Supply: A Synthesis," *Journal of Political Economy*, Vol. 84 (May-June 1976), p. 450.

ulating about circumstances in which the outcome of past investment experiences can be of use to repeating investors, new investors, shareholders, legislators, voters, other observers, and also economic historians, and even economic theorists.

Officers of large corporations and government agencies are in charge of the largest investment decisions of the nation. Their judgment, prudence, wisdom, and foresight can be judged only from their past performance, from their "track record." They deserve to be kept in their positions of economic power if the rates of return on the past investments for which they have been responsible have been high; if the rates have been low or negative, it may be time to replace them. Legislators who have a record of protecting industries that earn inadequate rates of return but are kept alive by tariffs, subsidies, and restrictions on competition from cheaper or better products or services should be carefully watched for their inclination to favor special interest groups at the expense of the nation at large. Nations with relatively high rates of investment relative to their national income, but low rates of return and slow growth of productivity, should examine, and perhaps reconsider, their system of resource allocation. The causes and effects of declining rates of return to investment should be studied, especially if they are associated with a deceleration in the growth of labor productivity. In all these instances, and in many that might be added, the purposes of looking back at past investments and at disappointingly low rates of return are diagnostic. This concern with the past may be helpful in suggesting remedial changes in practices, policies, methods of decision-making, and selection of decisionmakers, for the sake of improvements in the management of the nation's resources.

A second reason for looking at past investments and the past growth of the nation's capital stock lies in our interest in historical-statistical research. The economic historian will want to study the accumulation of capital along with the growth of the population and of the employed labor force, and with the rate of technical progress and the growth in the national product. He may also wish to estimate the relative contributions that capital accumulation, additional employment, and technological and organizational innovations have made to the growth of output. Estimates of this sort imply computations of past rates of return to capital.

A third reason for calculating past rates of return, by relating returns that have accrued to investments made in the still more distant past, may be found in particular instances, or in certain sectors of the economy, in which conditions have not substantially changed and are not expected to change in the future. The assumption that no change has occurred in the past—although the investment itself must have changed conditions to some extent—and that no change will occur in the future—although any additional investments, made on the basis of a satisfactory experience in the past, should affect conditions in the future—seems somewhat simplistic. If a particular type of investment made long in the past has during the last ten years yielded a high rate of return, this experience tells very little about the likelihood that investments of the same type starting now will earn a similarly high rate of return beginning ten years from now. Inductive generalizations of this sort are too naive to be taken seriously. Years of high returns on early investments in facilities to produce, say, electronic tubes or transistors, soon gave place to years of meager returns, and even losses, on similar investments. Indeed, if the history of earnings on specific investments teaches us anything, it is that one may not count on the same investment outlets to remain promising for very long.

The notion of a capital stock consisting of capital goods accumulated through investments made over a long period needs to be clarified in several respects. How far back should one go in estimating and cumulating the past outlays? Should *all* investments be counted or should evident malinvestments be omitted? Should capital goods—buildings, machines, and so forth—be counted at their historical cost, no matter whether or not they are now being used? Should one perhaps adopt a rule to the effect that investment outlays for capital goods that have been scrapped be eliminated from the valuation of the present stock, whereas all capital goods still used in the production process be counted with the full value invested in them, plus cumulative interest, minus depreciation earned up to now? This rule, however, says nothing about the inclusion or exclusion of goods that still exist as physical objects but are not actually used in production. If these capital goods have not been scrapped but kept physically intact, this may be taken as an indication that their owner still thinks they may be of some use in the future; hence, they are still part of the existing capital stock, though an unemployed portion of the stock.

One cannot really expect that national-income accountants will take annual inventories of capital goods in use and out of use; a more practically operational rule for the valuation of the real capital stock of the nation is to rely on the financial statements and balance sheets of business firms, and to accept their book values of all capital assets.[6]

---

[6] It is convenient to assume a "closed economy," and thus avoid the problems of how to treat capital goods owned by foreigners and capital assets located abroad but owned by our nationals or residents.

The books of the firms probably show the assets valued at cost minus depreciation (though exclusive of cumulative interest). For capital goods owned by individuals (not corporations), the statisticians may in some instances have to resort to estimates of the asset values in purely imaginary balance sheets.

I have presented the backward-looking analysts of capital investments as rather rare and somewhat queer birds, who are not wholly familiar with the only sound way to treat the valuation of stocks, namely, as sources of future returns. I must admit, however, that both ways of looking have been customary among theorists as well as among practitioners. Incidentally, even the most intolerant theorist will admit that under one condition no forward look is possible and a historical rate of return to past investments is all that can be calculated: namely, if all capital goods that were included in the particular productive assemblage have finished their service lives and no capital stock from this undertaking is left. In this case, everything has been in the past, the investments, the interest charges, and the returns. Then one can look back—in anger or contentment—and calculate a rate of return without any glances into the future.

An Attempt at Graphical Elucidation

Some readers find graphical representation helpful for comprehension. For their benefit I propose the following exposition.

Assume that some time in the past a group of entrepreneurs began to invest in certain productive facilities and thus to accumulate capital goods. The capital stock has grown larger over time on two counts: capital goods have been added year after year in the course of an ongoing flow of investment, and cumulative interest charges have been made for the invested funds (either actual payments of interest for borrowed funds or opportunity costs of the funds withheld from alternative investments). For the sake of simplicity let us assume at first that the capital stock accumulated up to the present has not yet been used in production, has not yet yielded any returns, and has not yet been reduced in value through any allowances for depreciation. But it is now ready for productive use. Its present value, according to the backward view, is taken to be the sum of the actual investment outlays of the past and the interest on each outlay cumulated to the present. The left side of Figure 12.1 represents this record of the past. (Just as a further aid, or perhaps complication, an intermediate point, t-n, is shown in the graph in order to indicate the stock accumulated, not to the present, but only to a time somewhere during the process of building up the assemblage of capital goods.)

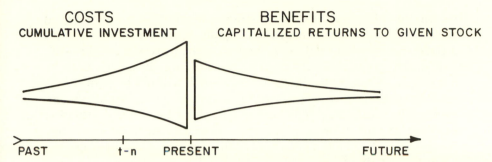

FIGURE 12.1   Accumulated stock of capital valued at cost including compound interest, and capitalized gradually vanishing returns to the given stock, assuming that expectations at present are less optimistic than those held in the past.

The right side of the figure represents the expectations of the future flow of gross returns on the capital—gross in the sense that depreciation is not deducted. Deducted are, however, the discounts (conceptually and arithmetically very similar to interest) for every future receipt (net revenue in excess of all noncapital costs, payments for labor, material, etc.). The discount on a receipt expected ten years from now is, of course, much greater than that on a receipt expected five years from now.[7] If the capital stock is not maintained through replacements, that is, through reinvestments of parts of the cash flow (or new funds), the returns will decline over time, as the capital goods wear out and become less serviceable. Thus, without any future net investments to increase the current stock of capital goods and without reinvestments to maintain it, the flow of returns attributable to the present stock must approach zero. The two factors, the gradual decline in expected returns and the discount on these future receipts, explain why the cone of future returns looks as it does in Figure 12.1.

The present value of the capital stock as derived from the expected flow of returns in the future is, in Figure 12.1, much smaller than the accumulation of investment outlays and interest charges of the past. Some of that difference could be the result of interest rates higher at present than they were in the past; large discounts reduce the present value of given future receipts drastically. On the other hand, much or all of the difference between the present value of estimated future returns and the total of cumulative investments of the past may be the result of changes in the prospects of future

---

[7] At an interest rate of 7 per cent, the discount on $100 to be received in 10 years is $49.20, giving $50.80 as the present value of the receipt; for $100 to be received in 5 years the discount is only $28.70 and its present value is $71.30.

returns. If things look less promising at present than they have in the past, the present value of the existing capital stock may show a substantial shortfall relative to the cumulative investment outlays.

The assumption underlying the right side of Figure 12.1, that the capital goods assembled in the present stock will not be maintained and, consequently, the flows of future returns will diminish and eventually vanish, is highly unrealistic. In reality, such a situation could arise only in a decaying and dying industry branch, where replacement does not pay, either because technological progress has made the existing equipment hopelessly obsolete or because demand has shifted away from the goods produceable with the available facilities. A graph depicting more normal situations, in which worn-out or obsolescent capital goods are replaced by new and improved ones, need not exhibit declining future returns to the present capital, and certainly would not show returns vanishing to zero. The discount factor would still reduce future returns to substantially lower present values, but the *undiscounted* amounts of the expected returns need not get smaller, and may even get larger. Larger capital returns in future years could be the consequence of favorable changes in the demand for the products, or of technological developments that make the available stock of capital goods compatible and complementary with additional investments.

Instead of trying to devise additional graphs depicting such conditions, it is probably more helpful to provide a verbal description of the options that may offer themselves to the user of an existing capital stock.

Various Options for Future Uses of Existing Capital Goods

The appraisal of a stock of capital goods is complicated by the fact that several options may exist for its use, and the returns expected from each course of action may differ in magnitude, time structure, probability distribution, risks, and uncertainty. Some of the alternatives under consideration may require major or minor alterations in the existing productive facilities, and some may call for sizable new investments. One of the options may be to use the assemblage of capital goods "as is," that is, without modification or improvement, without any supplemental investment. This option may promise reasonable returns in the future, but it may still be a relatively poor decision to accept this "conservative" option if some of the alternatives look much better. Surely the valuation of the existing capital stock will disregard all less satisfactory streams of expected returns; instead, it will take account only of superior prospects, even if this means that supplementary investments have to be made. In such a case, how will the present value of existing capital goods be calculated or, alternatively, how will the rate of return to capital valued by cumulation of past investments be calculated?[8]

If the more promising of the available options of using existing capital goods call for supplemental investments, these new investments have a prior "claim" upon future returns; and only after these claims have been met—after the new investments have paid for themselves—will the remainder of the future returns be attributed to the "old" capital goods, that is, the present stock. The "excess returns," if we may give this designation to the returns in excess of interest charges and depreciation allowances for the new capital assets, determine the value of the present capital stock (present, before it is improved and/or supplemented by the new investments). In "determining" the present value of this stock, the present interest or discount rates play, of course, a significant role.

Things would be relatively simple if just one of all available options appeared "optimal" (in that it would leave the largest excess returns for the existing capital stock after paying for interest and depreciation charges for the required supplemental investments). Unfortunately, rarely does one option appear the best; rather, it will depend on the rate of interest which of several alternatives is "optimal." In the contest of options, some will look better at low interest rates, others at high interest rates; and the excess returns attributable to the existing assemblage of capital goods will be different. In this jigsaw puzzle, the going rate of interest plays several roles at once. In the first place, the interest rate[9] will determine the "prior" claims reserved for the new funds and, hence, the size of the excess returns that can be expected to be left over and therefore attributed to the given assemblage of capital assets. The lower the interest cost of the new capital funds, the larger the excess returns. In addition, there will be a lower discount in reducing these excess returns to present values, so that the present value of the given capital will be larger

[8] Is it really necessary to inflict these intellectual hardships on readers who do not really care to be instructed in the theory of capital? They may only be vaguely interested in the basic notions, or perhaps just interested enough to comprehend what they ought to know about human capital. The complications introduced in the text above do have an application in the theory of human capital: one of the benefits expected from certain types of additional schooling is that it may offer a variety of options beyond the originally planned curriculum and career. The value of educational investment is to no small extent determined by opportunities implied in various "options" it provides for the future.

[9] More correctly: the internal interest rate, that is, the marginal cost of new funds obtainable for investment. This marginal cost to the seeker of funds is usually much higher than the market rate of interest for liquid funds in relatively riskless placements.

for both these reasons. On the other hand, at low interest rates, larger investment outlays with longer amortization periods (or periods over which they will "pay for themselves") will appear optimal; at high interest rates, smaller investment outlays with shorter pay-back periods will look more attractive.

No precise general statement can be made because not only the magnitude of the supplemental investments but also the time distribution of the required outlays and of the expected returns determine the comparative attractiveness of the alternatives at different interest rates. The combined returns (to the new and old capital) may be larger or smaller, because the excess returns (after meeting the interest and depreciation charges for the new capital) are the relevant magnitudes in the comparisons.

All these considerations are usually presented in algebraic form, but for our purposes there is no need to strive for degrees of precision and elegance that contribute little to a grasp of the essential ideas. All that we might wish to carry over from these preliminaries to a discussion of human capital are some very general observations. In the context of this section, the chief lesson is the interdependence among several strategic factors: the existence of options, the relativity of optimality, the role of interest or marginal cost of capital, the role of supplementary and complementary investments, and the discounting or capitalization of expected earnings. The most important point is that the value of an existing capital stock depends on a set of variables that are subject to change.

Different Questions Call for Different Concepts and Different Measures

My exposition of the "basic" notions of capital theory may have been influenced too much by the mainstream literature of our time. What is basic for the comprehension of current publications, especially of highly technical articles in the learned journals, need not be basic for understanding the broader questions pertinent to the issues involved. When we find that "stocks of capital" are important, and when we realize that stocks of heterogeneous things cannot be quantified and compared except in terms of homogeneous units, such as money values, we are easily led into technicalities about valuation and measurement before we know for what kinds of questions the resulting numbers are supposed to be relevant. Just why do economists want to measure the capital stock of a person, a group, a nation? What are the questions that can be answered only if we know how much capital has been accumulated or how much is its present value on the basis of either past investments or future returns?

It will not take much effort to see that different questions call for different concepts of capital and different measures of capital. The belief in the desirability of developing all-purpose concepts and all-purpose measures is firmly entrenched in the thinking of many students; we should shake this belief and show that we are better served with conceptual tools and operational measures adapted to the particular purposes in question. Let me illustrate this by posing three questions, each referring to a very special situation, and then showing that each will require special theoretical constructs and special empirical surrogates.

Question No. 1: Observing that the records of the national accounting system show almost continuous increases in gross national product and national income in real terms (that is, corrected for price changes), we may ask to what extent these changes can reasonably be attributed to increasing stocks of capital, and how large these stocks were ten years ago and how large they are at present.

Question No. 2: Taking note that an emergency requires that major efforts be made to utilize the nation's resources to the largest possible extent and to realize the full potential in gross product during the next two or three years, we may ask how much the available stock of capital is capable of contributing to the maximum increase in total production in the near future, even at the cost of the product of later years.

Question No. 3: Called upon to project potential growth of gross national product and national income for the next ten or fifteen years, we may ask how large the present stock of capital is and how much it can be expected to contribute to long-term growth of output.

Each of the three questions includes a query concerning the present stock of capital—but the relevant concepts are different. For the explanation of past developments we need information about annual net investments, that is, gross investments plus appreciation minus depreciation taking account of deterioration, obsolescence, withdrawals, and abandonment of equipment and installations, and about the degrees of utilization of the available capital. On the other hand, the present value of the stock, calculated through capitalization of expected future returns will not be relevant for Question No. 1.

For the estimate of the maximum product obtainable in the next few years, the relevant stock of capital is not dependent on its longevity—the length of the remaining service life—as long as it can hold up for the next two or three years. Neither the past history of its accumulation nor expectations of accretions or exhaustion in the more distant future will matter in the short run. The present value of the stock, essentially affected by anticipated rates of obsolescence, deterioration, and mortality, will be of no concern when only the production capacity in the near future is of interest.

For Question No. 3, however, for projections and forecasts of economic growth over longer periods, considerations omitted for the previous question are essential. The relevant concept will be of capital as a value of a stock seen as a source of future income, with the time horizon as distant as the perspective of the present rate of interest allows.[10]

Concluding Note

We are now equipped to approach the theory of human capital. We shall find that all issues reviewed, from the "two-view" problem to the problem of options for further improvements of a capital stock accumulated in the past, will have their applications in the theory of human capital. But first we shall need a better understanding of the concept of human capital.

[10] These reflections were inspired by comments of Theodore W. Schultz on "stock of education" and of Mary Jean Bowman on "effective current stock." Schultz, "Capital Formation by Education," *Journal of Political Economy*, Vol. 68 (November-December 1960), pp. 571-583; and "Investment in Human Capital," *American Economic Review*, Vol. 51 (March 1961), pp. 1-17; Bowman, "Human Capital: Concepts and Measures," in Selma Mushkin, ed., *The Economics of Higher Education* (Washington, D.C.: U.S. Office of Education, 1962), pp. 70-71 and 89-90.

CHAPTER 13

INVESTMENT IN HUMAN RESOURCES
AND PRODUCTIVE KNOWLEDGE

IN AN APPLICATION of capital theory to human resources, we need not immediately use all the conceptual tools exhibited in the preceding chapter. The tool most difficult to handle, the rate of returns to the capital stock and to new investment, can be left aside for a while. In this and the next few chapters, investment and returns will play the main roles, as magnitudes, not as ratios (such as per cent of capital per year). The difficulty with the concept of returns to investment or to capital becomes "compounded" by the calculation of "rates."

To comprehend the capital character of improved *human* resources, one may think of an analogy: the capital embodied in improved *land* resources. To the extent that natural resources, such as land, are received as free gifts of nature, with no replacement needed to maintain their productive capacity, they are not treated as capital from the point of view of society as a whole. *Improved* land, however, is something else: the improvements, whether they consist in greater fertility of the soil or in structures erected on it, are regarded as capital. An analogous statement holds for human resources: unimproved labor (rendering "pure" or "raw" labor services) is to be distinguished from improved labor, that is, labor made more productive by means of investments that raise its physical or mental capacity.[1] Such improvements constitute human capital.

Definitions and Distinctions

A definition of human capital as "increased productive capacity of persons" is at once too wide and too narrow. It is too wide in that it fails to distinguish between increases in capacity achieved through the use of material things (physical tools) or ideas (technology, organization) *separable* from the individuals whose work they make more efficient, and capacity increases that are *embodied* in the work-

---

[1] In both cases, the fertility of land and the capacity of humans, it may be impossible to ascertain *ex post* how much is due to "natural endowment" and how much to "improvements." Chapter 15 will address itself entirely to the question of "nature versus nurture."

ing individuals—in their minds, bodies, and presence—and cannot be separated from them. Only built-in, nonseparable investments count as human capital; productivity-increasing instruments are seen as tangible, real capital; and productivity-increasing nonembodied knowledge is regarded as nonmaterial nonhuman capital.

The definition is too narrow in that it confines the improvements, achieved through whatever is being done for human minds or bodies, to *productive* capacity. Some other kinds of improvement should also be included: increases in the individuals' earning capacity in cases in which increased earnings are not attributable to their producing larger or better outputs; increases in the individuals' discriminating capacity to make intelligent choices as consumers (have more foresight and avoid being cheated); and increases in people's capacity to enjoy life. In other words, one speaks of formation of human capital when investments (outlays or sacrifices) are made to transform the mental or physical equipment embodied in individual persons in ways that enable them (1) to produce more or better goods or services, (2) to earn higher pecuniary incomes, (3) to spend their incomes more intelligently, or (4) to get more pleasure out of life thanks to enhanced awareness and appreciation of some "finer things" appealing to more sensitized minds—"nonpecuniary satisfactions."

The differentiation between *producing*-capacity and *earning*-capacity is controversial. Some economists prefer to take pecuniary earnings as the sole index of productivity regardless of whether more or less is produced; others emphasize that what a firm pays to employees may depend, not on their real productivity, but on possibly misleading signals of their worth. (Such divergencies are analogous to those that may arise if a business firm judges the qualities of physical equipment on the basis of trademarks and trade names rather than by tests of actual performance. [See below, Chapter 18, "Productivity versus Credentials."]) The differentiation between workers' producing- and earning-capacity, on the one hand, and consumers' choosing- and enjoying-capacity, on the other, is fairly well recognized, but little has been done to quantify consumer satisfaction. Benefits accruing to consumers thanks to greater knowledge and acquired skills in choosing and checking what they buy can perhaps be measured by comparing, with proper allowance for differences in taste, the contents of the market baskets of people with different amounts of education spending the same amounts of money. Benefits from greater capacity to enjoy, so-called psychic income in the form of nonpecuniary satisfaction, cannot be estimated. Most economists recognize the significance of such satisfaction but would be disinclined to put a money value on human capital that yields only subjective utility (pleasure) without producing material goods or services.

As concrete examples of the four types of capacity, all of which can be created by investment in education, we may point to (1) the performance of a trained computer programmer, (2) the screening role of a college degree, (3) the consumer's intelligent budgeting, selecting, and shopping, and (4) the ability to enjoy Shakespeare's plays. Let me make the four examples more descriptive. (1) The increased productive capacity of the trained computer programmer, if adequately utilized, yields actual output, which may be counted as a part of the national product. (2) The increased earning capacity of the low-grade college graduate whose perfunctory "studies" have done little or nothing to make him more efficient, more industrious, or more conscientious, may be due merely to his credentials, the bachelor's degree, which serves employers as a screening device for selecting job seekers at small expense to themselves (although, from the point of view of the economy as a whole, cheaper screening techniques would be available). The screening hypothesis is often rejected. (See Chapter 18.) (3) The increased choosing-and-shopping capacity of consumers who have learned to read small print, comprehend directives, check weights and sums, and discern deferred consequences, allows them to get more out of their money incomes. (4) The increased capacity for enjoyment of persons who have learned to appreciate literature is likely to yield an enduring flow of satisfactions as they read and reread great books and listen to great plays.

The significance of human capital of the fourth type has been strongly affirmed by many economists. Milton Friedman gave it the name "human consumption capital," owned by the individual who invests "in his capacity to derive utility. For example, that is what he does when he takes piano lessons, or lessons in musical appreciation: he is building up his future capacity to derive utility."[2]

---

[2] Milton Friedman, *The Optimum Quantity of Money and Other Essays* (Chicago: Aldine, 1969), p. 48. Friedman assumes his typical individual to own "four kinds of capital assets: 1. Physical productive capital, 2. Human productive capital, 3. Physical consumption capital, 4. Human consumption capital." Let me suggest some examples to aid the understanding of Friedman's matrix:

Capital	Productive	Consumption
Physical	Sewing machine	TV set
Human	Computer know-how	Music appreciation

The reference to musical knowledge as "human consumption capital" has a long history. For example, Nicholson wrote in 1891: "The musical and artistic skill . . . 'fixed and embodied' in young ladies should be included in an estimate of living capital, just as much as their pianos and paint-boxes are included in the dead capital." Joseph S. Nicholson, "The Living Capital of the United Kingdom," *Economic Journal*, Vol. 1 (March 1891), p. 101.

Earlier generations of economists, who distinguished a narrower category of "capital" within a wider category of "wealth," would have denied the designation "capital" to a mere source of consumer benefits. In recent years, however, many economists have stopped insisting on the distinction.

That capital need not be a source of future *productive* services, like a machine, but may instead be a source of future *consumer* satisfaction, has been clearly realized with regard to physical (tangible, real) capital. As a matter of fact, physical "consumption capital" constitutes a large part of the nation's total stock of real capital; just think of all residential housing and other durable consumer goods. (To be sure, the conventional national-product accounts do not include furniture, automobiles, refrigerators, pianos, and other consumer durables among investment goods but treat them as goods consumed at the time of purchase. In economic theory, however, they are regarded as capital assets yielding flows of consumer services over the years.) Incidentally, intellectual, aesthetic, or emotional elements in the satisfactions derived from future flows of consumer services may be present in the consumer services yielded by physical capital assets as in those yielded by human capital. The beauty of one's well-designed house or apartment, may count as much as, and for some people even more than, the beauty of good poetry or classical music—all appreciated thanks to the improvements in human capacity to enjoy things appealing only to more "cultivated" tastes.

Investments That Improve Human Capacities

Acquisition of knowledge, both of the know-*how* and of the know-*what* type, has been the paradigmatic investment in human beings. But Gary Becker, who together with Theodore Schultz[3] should be credited with having brought the theory of human capital from the classical stage of largely analogical reasoning to the modern stage of rigorous logical, algebraic, and statistical analysis, showed that there are several ways to form human capital besides knowledge accumulation.[4] The list, conveniently arranged by Mark Blaug,[5] includes

[3] Theodore W. Schultz, "Capital Formation by Education," *Journal of Political Economy*, Vol. 68 (November-December 1960), pp. 571-583; "Investment in Human Capital," *American Economic Review*, Vol. 51 (March 1961), pp. 1-17; *The Economic Value of Education* (New York: Columbia University Press, 1963).

[4] Gary S. Becker, "Underinvestment in College Education?" *American Economic Review*, Vol 50 (May 1960), pp. 546-554; "Investment in Human Capital: A Theoretical Analysis," *Journal of Political Economy*, Vol. 70 (September-October, 1962, Part 2), pp. 9-49; *Human Capital: A Theoretical and Empirical Analysis with Special Reference to Education* (New York: National Bureau of Economic Research, 1964; 2d ed., 1974).

[5] Mark Blaug, "The Empirical Status of Human-Capital Theory: A Slightly Jaundiced

six types of investments in human capacities: health care, additional education, job search, information retrieval (chiefly about job opportunities), migration (to take advantage of better job opportunities), and in-service training (either on the job or with the job). Becker later extended the theory to the economics of the family, trying to explain marriage and family planning by rational considerations of additional net earnings over the lifetime of the head of the household. Finally, there have been attempts to apply the human-capital approach to investment in technological research and development.

These extensions of the theory raise bewildering conceptual problems, as we shall see when we talk about research and development and the resulting technological knowledge. It is preferable for now to stay with the six investment opportunities in the first list and ask what their common features are. First and foremost, many writers mention that the capital created by these investments is intangible. (A slightly frivolous qualification: the stronger muscles, developed through better nutrition, better health care, and better physical training may occasionally be touched and seen.) What matters, however, is not the invisibility or intangibility of the improvement but its *embodiment* in, and *inseparability* from, the human body, brain, and soul (whatever that may be). The inseparability from the human mind and body makes human capital salable only in a slave economy. This is probably the most important difference between physical and human capital. It has a highly significant corollary: since real capital goods can be sold in the market, and sales prices can be recorded, there may exist data reflecting the approximate valuations of the assets by buyers and sellers. (The value to the buyer probably was at least as high as the price he paid for the asset; and the value to the seller probably did not exceed the price he accepted for it.) The absence of market prices for human capital is one of the greatest obstacles to empirical tests of this segment of economic theory.

To be sure, we often have market prices for the *services* of human capital, usually in the form of "rentals." It has been said that statistical records are available for rentals paid for various kinds of human labor—wage rates—and that this suffices for observing empirical regularities and for carrying out empirical tests of propositions derived from the theory of human capital.[6] Yet, for tangible and salable cap-

---

Survey," *Journal of Economic Literature*, Vol. 14 (September 1976), pp. 827-855. The list is on p. 829.

[6] Sherwin Rosen, "Measuring the Obsolescence of Knowledge," in F. Thomas Juster, ed., *Education, Income, and Human Behavior* (New York: McGraw-Hill, 1975), p. 201. Rosen holds that "no real difficulty arises on that score, i.e., the absence of observable market valuation of human capital, for services of knowledge and skills

ital goods we have records of market prices for both assets and rentals. Automobiles can be bought or rented; computers are sold as well as leased; office space and residential housing is offered for sale or for rent. Thus, both kinds of data—asset prices and rental prices—are available for physical capital. For human capital, however, only rentals are determined in the market, and even these cannot be established with any degree of accuracy.

Having stated important differences between physical and human capital, I should hasten to reassure the reader that the previously listed types of investment in human beings do in most other respects constitute formation of capital with all traditional characteristics: the capital is durable and yet of limited service life; it calls for maintenance and replacement as does any other exhaustible or "wasting" resource; it may become obsolete before being depleted; and, as far as its subjective value is concerned, it can appreciate as well as depreciate depending on the supply of complementary factors and the demand for their joint products. Though its value may be appraised by the individual in whom it is embodied, it may also be appraised by others, including the policy-making members of society. Such appraisal, however, is arbitrary and subjective and rarely recorded in any written or printed statements of the type corporations issue regarding the stock of their real or financial capital. (The question of differences between private and social valuations will be examined in the next chapter.)

I must warn against inappropriate identifications. Let us keep two points in mind: (1) Not all production of knowledge represents formation of human capital; thus an increase in the stock of knowledge (recorded or in people's minds) is not necessarily an increase in human capital.[7] (2) Not all formation of human capital is creation of knowledge; there are forms of human capital that are not per se accumulation of knowledge, though still improvements of human performance and earning capacity.[8]

---

embodied in people are traded on well-developed rental markets—namely, labor markets—and rental values contain the same information as capital values." Rosen sees no difficulty in making "necessary assumptions" about "equivalent units of knowledge," although the equivalence is established by nothing but the rental prices paid. — The recognition of the availability of data on rental values goes back to Mary Jean Bowman, "Human Capital: Concepts and Measures," in Selma Mushkin, ed., The Economics of Higher Education (Washington, D.C.: U.S. Office of Education, 1962), p. 83: " . . . human capital is continuously for hire and its 'rent' is continually given a value in the market. Physical capital in the form of plant and equipment is not so regularly either rented or sold after its initial purchase by the user."

[7] For example, production of pastime knowledge published in daily papers or broadcast over television will hardly qualify as formation of human capital. See next section.

[8] For example, improvements of physical health or relocation of workers to places

*Investing in Knowledge versus Using Knowledge
in Making Investments*

The role of knowledge in the formation of human capital can be clarified by a distinction between investments *in* knowledge, and investments that *use* knowledge as a means of otherwise improving the performance and earning capacity of the individual. Thus investments in schooling, training, job search, and job-related information are *investments in knowledge*, enduring or ephemeral, but investments in health care and migration are not; they merely involve or presuppose *the use of knowledge*. The explanation of the difference may appear to be hair-splitting; I shall nevertheless attempt it.[9]

Investment in health care is not *in itself* an investment in knowledge but involves some acquisition of knowledge in the process, to the extent that health-care *information* and medical *advice* are necessary parts of any individual or collective health-care program. These pieces of information do not constitute capital formation; they are only intermediate products, instrumental services; the information is sought or demanded, not to create or increase human capacities to produce, earn, or enjoy, but to guide actions that constitute health care. Investments in health care *are* investments in human capital, but the "informational input" into the restoration and maintenance of people's health, although it may amount to half or more of the total expenditures for health care, is *current* production of knowledge rather than *investment* in knowledge. It would be an instance of double-counting if we were to treat the current production of knowledge for immediate use in the production of health care as also the creation of human capital, since it merely serves to allow "informed decisions" on the part of individuals, families, or communities concerned. Other inputs—besides the information services rendered by researchers, doctors, nurses, physical-education teachers, therapists, and the staffs of hospitals and other institutions—include salubrious foods, prescribed or recommended medicines, adequate and possibly time-consuming physical exercise, and other things that make up the package called health care. The intended output, the actual purpose of the investment, is personal health and the resulting capacity to perform, to earn, and to enjoy. To repeat, investment in personal health care, although a use of knowledge for investment in human capital, is not investment in knowledge, at least not in the sense that schooling, training, and job search are.

---

where they are more eagerly demanded represent formation of human capital but not production of knowledge. See next section.

[9] The argument is subtle and perhaps confusing; readers may skip it without loss of comprehension of the rest of the chapter.

Investment in migration is even less an investment in knowledge, because the cost of information that guides the decision to migrate is *separate* from the cost of moving persons and their belongings; it is allocated to "investment in information about job opportunities."[10] Transport costs, moving expenses, and other sacrifices and disutilities connected with relocation are the major items in the investment in migration. Migration is human capital in the sense that the bodily presence of the individuals at the places to which they have moved is *inseparable* from the persons and creates their capacity to earn the wages or salaries that attracted them and induced them to migrate.[11]

The cases of health care and migration have been discussed here only to show that the formation of human capital, though it may involve the use of knowledge, is not always tied to investment in knowledge. Such ties are intrinsic in the four most widely discussed forms of investment in human beings: schooling, job training, job search, and job-information retrieval. In the cases of schooling and job training, the knowledge acquired is chiefly of the enduring type; in the cases of job search and information about job opportunities, the knowledge acquired is of the transitory, ephemeral type. The knowledge conveyed by schooling and job training is partly of the "knowing-*how*" type and partly of the "knowing-*what*" type.[12]

The Strange Notion of Tangible Human Capital

The dichotomy, tangible (physical) capital versus human capital, has been regarded as inappropriate. John Kendrick proposed that we

[10] Becker, *Human Capital*, p. 32.

[11] The connections between human capital and migration of labor are manifold and not easily kept apart. In the text above we distinguished between investment in *information* about (perhaps distant) job opportunities and investment in *moving* individuals (perhaps with their families and belongings). Both these investments may constitute additions to the "stock" of human capital, though the former, the information, being of transitory value, is probably subject to rapid depreciation. Different from both, but also related to human migration, is the question of human-capital movements. Capital movements reduce the stock of capital in the region or country from which it is removed and increase the stock of capital in the receiving region or country. With regard to movements of labor, the valuation of the human capital embodied in the migrating workers may raise problems. Should, in the capital account, unskilled labor be given "book values" lower than those of skilled labor? Should perhaps only skilled labor be counted in the stock of capital? Marshall Colberg decided that for the purposes of his inquiry it would not be appropriate "to characterize the migration of poorly educated Negroes to the North as a capital movement." He treated as capital movement only the migration of better-educated workers. Marshall R. Colberg, *Human Capital in Southern Development 1939-1963* (Chapel Hill: University of North Carolina Press, 1965), p. 107.

[12] All these and other types of knowledge were described and discussed in Volume I, Chapters 2 and 3.

distinguish four categories: nonhuman tangible capital, nonhuman intangible capital, human tangible capital and human intangible capital.[13] "Nonhuman intangible capital," is exemplified by quality improvements of physical capital goods, for example, an improvement in the productive capacity of machinery as a result of new findings from research and development.[14] Other economic analysts have preferred to treat investments in R and D, or the inventions and discoveries derived from R and D, as human capital. One may argue, however, that what has been learned from research-and-development activities does not usually remain embodied in the minds of R and D personnel but can be readily duplicated in minds other than those of the particular individuals who have first absorbed the new knowledge. If this knowledge is recorded in print and easily accessible to many, Kendrick is justified in treating it as *nonhuman intangible* capital. Investments in R and D have then a separate home, or at least a separate box into which the statisticians concerned with national accounts may classify them.

There is less justification, if any, for accepting Kendrick's category of "human tangibles." He finds it "inconsistent to count the costs of educating a man as investment but not the cost of producing the physical being whose mind and reflexes are being educated and trained."[15] Kendrick proposes to count the "rearing cost" of the future worker—"the average variable cost of raising children to working age" (14 years)—as investment in human *tangible* capital, and

[13] John W. Kendrick, *The Formation and Stock of Total Capital* (New York: National Bureau of Economic Research, 1976), pp. 3, 4-17.

[14] Ibid., pp. 9-11. Note the difference between technological knowledge enabling us to use machines more efficiently and technological changes embodied in specific types of machines. The former is nonembodied knowledge, regarded as intangible capital, whereas the latter is embodied in physical capital. The term "embodied technological progress" was coined by Robert M. Solow, for his paper "Investment and Technical Progress" in Kenneth Arrow, S. Karlin, and Patrick Suppes, eds., *Mathematical Methods in the Social Sciences, 1959* (Stanford: Stanford University Press, 1960), pp. 90-91. Thus he wrote that "many if not most innovations need to be embodied in new kinds of durable equipment before they can be made effective" (p. 98). Solow used "disembodied technological progress" as the opposite. I prefer the adjective "nonembodied" and the noun "knowledge," but the idea of the pair of concepts was Solow's. His terms have been adopted by most writers on economic growth.

[15] Kendrick, *Formation*, p. 6. Kendrick thinks he is supported by Irving Fisher's statement that "The 'skill' of a mechanic is not wealth in addition to the man himself; it is the 'skilled mechanic' who should be put in the category of wealth." Irving Fisher, *The Nature of Capital and Income* (New York: Macmillan, 1930), p. 9. — In actual fact, Fisher warns against double-counting and does not support a separate accounting of the tangible body of the worker.

the subsequent cost of education, training, and health care, affecting the quality or productivity of labor, as investment in human *intangible* capital.[16]

The proposed separation of investment in human capital into a tangible and an intangible portion—tangible because it produces warm bodies up to fourteen years of age, and intangible afterwards because it improves their "skills and reflexes"—cannot reasonably be defended unless one wishes to make the grotesque assumption that children below working age are "consumer durables" produced to give joy and pleasure to their parents, not much different from toys, pets, and television sets. Perhaps one may see some inconsistency in our national accounts showing income originating in the production and maintenance of toys and television sets but not in the production and maintenance of children; but—except in a slave economy—one is on firm philosophical ground in making this differentiation. If we agree to change our national accounts to show the costs of schooling and training as intangible investments in human capital, we rely mainly on the argument that these investments are undertaken largely with a view to pecuniary returns accruing in later years. (And, certainly, these investments begin much earlier than at age 14.) The human capital thus created is clearly intangible and, what is more important, inseparable from the individuals in which it is embodied.

Perhaps the term "tangible" capital is misleading. The fact that a machine can be seen and touched with our hands (and its presence thus certified by two of our senses) does not make the machine a capital good. What we see and touch is a surface of steel, copper, plastic, or other material, but not capital. It is capital thanks only to its assumed capacity to produce future returns, and this capacity is not tangible; it is not even observable, since we can observe, at best, the machine's operation in producing something, but these products may not be valuable, or not sufficiently valuable to secure a positive net revenue including a net return to the investment. Thus, although capacity to perform valuable operations may be embodied in physical objects (machines) as well as in human beings (workers), the capacity itself is never tangible. The costs of creating, improving, or maintaining such capacity are investments (gross or net) either in capital goods or in human capital. The concept of human tangible capital is not acceptable for a society without slaves.

Kendrick's idea of measuring "the real gross stock of tangible human capital" by "the accumulated rearing costs" of children to age

[16] Kendrick, *Formation*, p. 8.

fourteen is not without precedent. Indeed, the history of the idea of human capital can be better understood if one distinguishes between two main strands of thought: one is centered on the notion that humans are not only producers and consumers of goods and services but also procreators of human life, and that family, community, and nation regard each human life as a part of its wealth; the other is centered on the notion that human capacity to produce and consume can be improved through prudent investment, particularly through acquisition of knowledge. Those interested in the economics of the "value of man" as a part of the nation's wealth have focused on the cost of raising children and on incomes earned throughout people's working lives, without regard to any particular investments to improve their capacities. Those interested in estimates of returns to these investments have focused only on the cost of improvements and the returns attributable to them. The two interests cannot easily be combined and served by the same methods of arranging the social accounts.

Once we understand that the stock of capital can be totaled either by accumulating the costs or by anticipating the benefits, and that there are many reasonable ways to decide what to allow or to disallow as costs or as benefits, we cannot be surprised that we have a choice of many different measurements or estimates of the stock of human capital. If some choices seem "preferable," they are preferable only for particular purposes. To mention here another of the many possible variants, the flow of benefits from the stock of human capital has been corrected for the personal consumption of the income earners, that is, the benefits are net of the consumption by the persons in which the investment had been embodied. Burton Weisbrod has regarded this procedure as appropriate for an attempt to find the capital value of a person for "society," where society is "defined to include the entire population except for the person being valued." Society might value each person by "any excess of his contribution to production over what he consumes from production—this difference being the amount by which everyone else benefits from his productivity."[17] Marshall Colberg has found the idea applicable to his inquiry about how much human capital a region would lose through emigration of members of its labor force. And he argued that the consumption expenditures of individuals who represent human capital may be regarded as analogous to the operating costs of machines that represent physical capital.[18] Deducting consumption from

[17] Burton A. Weisbrod, "The Valuation of Human Capital," *Journal of Political Economy*, Vol. 69 (October 1961), pp. 425-436.

[18] Colberg, *Human Capital*, p. 107.

income as cost of upkeep, or maintenance, of the productive capacity is most sensible where consumption requirements differ for persons who have invested in different improvements of their capacities. However, where differences in earnings are the chief benefit from additional investments in human capacities, deducting consumption from earnings makes little sense.

Three Categories of Knowledge Capital

For the analysis of various problems connected with knowledge production—for example, the problem of depreciation of knowledge stocks (treated in Chapter 19)—it will be advantageous to distinguish three sites of knowledge stocks and, corresponding to them, three categories of capital: (a) knowledge embodied in individual physical tools or machines specially built according to specifications developed in costly research and development, (b) knowledge embodied in individual persons, specially schooled and trained "knowledge carriers" and qualified workers with acquired skills, (c) nonembodied knowledge, created and disseminated at a cost but not inseparably embodied in any particular knowledge carriers or any particular products. The use of this nonembodied knowledge (for example, an invention of a new process of production) may, under legal or other social institutions (patents or other exclusive privileges), be reserved to privileged producers or vendors of goods or services, or it may be "in the public domain," accessible and freely available to anybody.

The three categories of capital that correspond to the three sites of knowledge are physical or material capital, human capital, and nonmaterial nonhuman capital. Neither material nor human capital need be associated with knowledge-producing activities and with investments in knowledge acquisition, though the most frequent forms of human capital do in fact relate to knowledge embodied in persons. Nonmaterial nonhuman capital, however, consists entirely of knowledge, embodied neither in persons nor in material things, and which is chiefly the result of research and development and therefore named, by several writers, "stocks of R and D." This is a recently invented concept; technological progress as a lever of productivity had been relegated to the residual of the production function, was then promoted to the rank of an independent variable with accumulated R and D expenditures as an empirical proxy, and has finally been elevated to the stately class of capital, neither physical nor human.

The easiest way to distinguish the three sites of knowledge and categories of capital is to trace the flows of benefits derived from their use. Knowledge embodied in machines and similar material goods improves the performance and value of these machines, and the returns to the investment come in the form of sales prices or rentals of the machines or differential rents included in the sales revenues of their products. Knowledge embodied in persons improves the performance of the knowledge carriers, and the returns to the investment come in the form of differentials in salaries and wages. Knowledge not embodied in persons or machines improves the performance of many or all productive factors, and the returns to the investment come either in the form of monopoly rents or, if the use of the knowledge is unrestricted, in the form of increased real incomes of consumers.

There will be several occasions in subsequent chapters to refer to nonmaterial nonhuman capital in the form of nonembodied knowledge produced by costly R and D activities.[19] However, since the rich literature on human capital demands primary attention, knowledge and skills embodied in persons will be the chief subject of our discussion.

Formation of Human Capital Through Education

Education, in a wide sense of the word, covers much more than formal schooling; it includes all sorts of teaching and learning, formal and informal, inside and outside schools. In Volume V of this work, education in the home, in the church, in the armed forces, on the job, and even self-education will be discussed in considerable detail. In the present examination of the concept of human capital and its use in economic analysis, I shall discuss only two types of investment—additional schooling and job training.[20]

The costs of additional schooling and job training are regarded as investments, as formation of human capital, because they may yield positive returns in future years. These returns are expected, with some degree of confidence, by those who bear the costs, that is, the investors. In the case of schooling, the investors may be national, state, and local governments (spending the taxpayers' money), private benefactors, families, and (if they are potential earners of incomes) the students themselves. In the case of job training, the investors may be, apart from instances of governmental subsidization, the employers or the workers themselves.

---

[19] The research activities resulting in nonembodied knowledge are not restricted to technological R and D but comprise scholarly research and production of literature.

[20] Although I would prefer to use the word "training" in connection with useful, practical knowledge and skills, and to reserve the work "education" for useless, nonpractical knowledge, I must not indulge in this semantic idiosyncrasy: I would risk being misunderstood because common usage is against me. Becker, for example, defines a school "as an institution specializing in the production of training" (p. 29); most writers use "education" and "schooling" as synonyms.

Where the expected returns consist in *nonpecuniary satisfactions* of the educated, their families and friends, or other members of the community, calculations of rates of return to the investment are entirely imaginary. Still, these purely cultural investments are not less important; much time, effort, and money go into the teaching of literature, fine arts, music, sports, and other highly worthwhile programs that will "pay" only in sensations of pleasure and intellectual and emotional gratification. Theoretical models may put money values on these yields, but statistical tests are out of the question. Where the expected returns consist of *money earnings*, empirical testing (estimates) through imaginative uses of statistical proxies is possible, and many examples as well as findings will be presented in subsequent chapters. Where the returns in the form of pecuniary earnings are derived from increased or improved *physical products*, one could conceive of empirical tests, but the practical difficulties seem overwhelming. Empirical research has therefore been confined to identifying differential money earnings of groups of people with differential schooling or job training.

Just how does education on all levels improve human capacity and increase the value of human resources in production? The essential contribution of education, no doubt, is the dissemination of knowledge of both the know-*how* and know-*what* types, that is, skills and cognitive knowledge. The contribution of education to productive efficiency has been divided into "worker effects," "allocative ability," and "innovative ability."[21] More detailed breakdowns of the sources of increases in productivity through abilities improved by education may be helpful. The "worker effect" is evidently the workers' ability to do a given task faster or better or both. Either their manual skills or their mental skills are improved by the training received: they have learned how to do things more efficiently with their hands and/or with their brains. "Allocative ability" refers to their ability to choose the most appropriate possible alternatives, an ability that presupposes judgment, cognitive knowledge, as well as know-how.[22] This ability to choose well may be exercised in a variety of functions—as practicing craftsman, foreman, supervisor, expediter, technician, engineer, consultant, researcher and, of course, manager, to mention only a small fraction of the "allocators" working in

[21] Finis Welch, "Education in Production," *Journal of Political Economy*, Vol. 78 (January-February 1970), p. 47.

[22] "If education enhances allocative ability in the sense of selecting the appropriate input bundles and of efficiently distributing inputs between competing uses, the return to this ability is part of the return to education." Ibid., p. 55.

industry.[23] The third of the stated effects of education enhancing productivity is "innovative ability." There can be no doubt about the importance of innovation to the growth of productivity and to the earnings of the innovators. The causal connection between schooling and innovative ability, however, is not conclusively established. It is clear, of course, that innovators must have a great deal of cognitive knowledge, much of it acquired by schooling and postschool training; but whether their educational experiences are to be credited for their innovative flair, originality, and courage is far from certain.

Knowledge is not the only thing taught and learned in school: adherence to moral values, loyalty, sociability, discipline, industry, perseverance, punctuality, reliability, adjustability, critical judgment, physical fitness, cleanliness, proper sexual behavior, and sometimes nationalistic and religious allegiances are among the objectives educationists and politicians recommend to, or impose upon, school authorities.[24] As far as I know, no assessment of school performance on these counts or their relative weights exists, whereas assessments of cognitive achievements have become routine in evaluations of the effectiveness of schools. In any case, it is not too far from the truth if we say that the transmission of knowledge is the prime objective of schools.

Job training is also primarily dissemination of knowledge. Is the ratio of "know *how*" to "know *what*" higher in job training than in schooling? The answer depends on whether the comparison is made with primary or with secondary school. Schools on the elementary level concentrate on reading, writing, and doing numbers; that is, they try to teach youngsters "*how*-to" knowledge, practical skills. On the secondary level, schools are supposed to teach more of the

---

[23] Some of the most significant empirical research on the contribution of schooling to productivity has been for agriculture, chiefly because its smaller product variety allows better comparisons. Zvi Griliches, "Research Expenditures, Education, and the Aggregate Agricultural Production Function," *American Economic Review*, Vol. 54 (December 1964), pp. 961-974, and Voav Kislev, "Estimating a Production Function from U.S. Census of Agriculture Data" (Ph.D. dissertation, University of Chicago, 1965). However, these researchers report contradictory findings, the former crediting schooling with a large contribution to agricultural productivity, the latter finding almost no such effect, although both used the same source of data. Finis Welch, "Education," pp. 45-46, explains the contradiction mainly by the fact that Kislev worked with county data and Griliches with state data, but only at the state level can one expect sufficient diversity of product to permit room for allocative choices.

[24] For an elaborate discussion of similar sets of values and goals, especially of college education, see Kenneth A. Feldman and Theodore M. Newcomb, *The Impact of College on Students* (San Francisco: Jossey-Bass, 1969).

"know-*that*" and "know-*what*" kinds. Job training is ordinarily more concerned with manual skills and other kinds of know-how; it may be general or specific training. The latter is for a particular job at a particular firm. General training is useful for the trainees' performance at other firms as well.

In-Service Training

The training provided by an employer may be of many kinds: in learning by doing, the trainee participates in actual production processes; in learning by watching, he works as helper or apprentice with an experienced worker until he acquires the required skill; the training may also be separate from actual work performance, taking the form of instruction, either at the premises of the firm or at a different location, perhaps in a vocational school or in evening classes at a college or university. In the latter case the expression "on-the-job training" no longer fits. The expression "in-service training" covers all these forms of knowledge transmission, no matter whether they are paid for by the employer or the employee.

Blaug distinguishes (a) costless on-the-job learning; (b) informal on-the-job training; (c) formal off-the-job but in-plant training; and (d) formal off-the-job out-of-plant training paid for by the employer. (Manpower-retraining programs are mentioned as similar to type d, though differently financed.) These distinctions, however, are less important from an economic point of view than the distinction between general and specific training. General training is an investment in the worker's capacity to perform and earn not just in his present employment but in many other jobs too; if he is free to quit and collect higher wages working for another employer, the firm that provides free training may lose money. Hence, even if firms "finance" general training of their employees, they can rationally afford to do so only if the cost of the training is shifted to the trainee. This shifting takes place through lower wages being paid to workers receiving these valuable learning experiences.

Matters are different in the case of specific training, an investment in the workers' capacity to perform in the job for which they are trained, in the firm that provides the training but not elsewhere. In this case, although the firm would lose if the trained employee were to quit, the worker too would lose, since what he has learned cannot improve his performance elsewhere. Thus, the risk of trained workers leaving their jobs is small and firms can afford to bear the cost of specific training.

In actual fact, most kinds of training are partly general, partly specific; it is most likely, therefore, that the cost of in-service training is shared between worker and employer, not in any explicit way, but in the implied form of the trainees' wages being somewhat lower (during the training period) than the wages of unskilled workers in the same locality and same occupation; the trainees' wages are likely to increase with work experience. In order to reduce the risk of losing its investment in its workers, a firm would offer "higher wages after training than could be received elsewhere. In effect, it would offer employees some of the return from training."[25] One may perhaps assume that "firms do not pay any of the completely general costs and only part of the completely specific costs."[26] If so, the firm's share of the training cost is larger the larger the specific component of the training; and is smaller the larger the general component. Since "quits" of trained workers are costly to firms, and "layoffs" are costly to workers, one may conclude that "quit and layoff rates are inversely related to the amount of specific training."[27] This is a theoretical conclusion deduced from abstract assumptions, but testable (however roughly) by empirical research.

Incremental Schooling

A young person reaching working age can either quit school and take a job or stay in school and pass up the chance of earning a wage income. If he expects that by staying in school for one or more years he will later have a chance of getting a better job (with higher pay, better prospects for advancement, more attractive working conditions), and if he, consequently, opts for incremental schooling, he is making an investment in himself. If he finds going to school to be neither pleasure nor pain, neither fun nor drudgery, his investment outlay is measured only by his foregone earnings (plus accruing interest).

Of course, the number of options is much greater than these four, even if we confine ourselves to the case of a person who may lawfully drop out of school. The following options are to be considered: (1) He can quit school and (a) take a job as an unskilled laborer at a wage that is not expected to increase substantially over the years; (b) take a job at less than the going wage but with an opportunity of in-service training and good prospects of higher and increasing wages after training; (c) stay unemployed. (2) He can stay in school full-time and (a) forego the earnings a full-time job would offer; (b) take a part-time job and thus forego only a part of the potential earnings offered by a full-time job. (3) He can continue in school part-time

---

[25] Becker, *Human Capital*, p. 22.
[26] Ibid., p. 23.
[27] Ibid., p. 24.

and (a) take a part-time job and thus sacrifice only a part of the earnings from full-time work; (b) take a full-time job as an unskilled laborer, working at the going wage, but with the expectation of a better job after completion of incremental schooling; (c) take a full-time job at less than the going wage but with in-service training and good prospects of advancements later.

This may not be an exhaustive list of options, but it is surely sufficient for purposes of our discussion here. The option of combining part-time school attendance and part-time employment—(3a)—is one that has proved attractive to many young people as well as to many educationists and social workers. The options involving double-time arrangements, either full-time school attendance combined with part-time employment—(2b)—or part-time school attendance with full-time employment—(3b) and (3c)—will present themselves only to exceptionally industrious and ambitious youths. Investment in self-improvement is inherent in options (1b), (2a) and (b) and (3a) through (c). The investments consist in earnings foregone either because of continued schooling or because of job training; in one case, however—(3b)—in which the student holds a full-time job, he sacrifices leisure time. The leisure foregone is valued at the time rate of pay he earns (though he valued his leisure a little lower, or he would not have exchanged it for the money earned). An individual with such diligence—combining full-time employment and part-time school attendance—might consider another alternative, namely, a second job, so-called "moonlighting." The earnings foregone by not moonlighting would be an alternative money measure of his investment in incremental schooling.

The choices among all these options involve considerations of costs (expenses and sacrifices) and future earnings. No one can really make these comparisons except on the basis of uncertain expectations formed on other people's experiences. Persons who have chosen one option will never really know how they would have fared had they chosen one of the alternatives. At best, they can know how others, who made the choice they did not make, have fared. These others, however, may be persons differing from them in tastes, personal endowments (innate and acquired), attitudes, energy, drive, and ambition. Indeed, the very fact that these others have made different choices attests to their different attributes. Hence, although some differences in lifetime earnings can be attributed to different years of schooling and training, differences in many other factors may be equally important, if not more so. Few serious researchers would deny this.

The Human-Capital Approach

Some of the best authorities on the theory of human capital have expressed rather enigmatic views about the use of the human-capital model in the explanation of earnings from work of different quality. We are told, for example, that "schooling and years of work experience are rather obvious determinants of wage rates and . . . (current) hours of work are an arithmetical factor in annual earnings. Their inclusion in earnings equations does not require analytical models such as human capital theory. . . ."[28] To be sure, not every equation is a model, and not every model comes in the form of an equation. However, equations with variables selected for their presumptive explanatory power can be regarded as models. The variables are not thrown together at random; they are selected on the basis of hypotheses or theories about their causal connections, or at least on the basis of a hunch—which is a modest kind of hypothesis or tentative theory. In this sense, an equation that is supposed to explain anything must either constitute or presuppose an analytical model.[29]

Of course, the model or theory that is designed to explain earnings of persons with different schooling and training need not always be a model or theory of *human capital*. If, however, "contributions of the human-capital model to the analyses of earnings" are "distinguished from ad hoc analyses with the same variables,"[30] the criterion for the distinction seems to be the "ad hoc." Perhaps "ad hoc" is meant to refer, not to a complete absence of theory, but only to the suspicion that the theory in question is not a part of a coherent theoretical system but merely an isolated, disconnected hypothesis, not integrated with other propositions applicable to a wide area of phenomena. Now, if schooling and training are selected as explanatory variables for wage rates and earnings, this does not look like a mere ad hoc choice but like a short-cut theory relating earning to learning. The hunch that more learning leads to more earning is a hypothesis not unrelated to a theoretical system of greater generality

[28] Jacob Mincer, "Human Capital and Earnings," in Douglas M. Windham, ed., *Economic Dimensions of Education* (Washington, D.C.: National Academy of Education, 1979), p. 14.

[29] For a fuller exposition of this view I may refer to many writers in economics as well as virtually all other fields of inquiry. From my own writings, relevant statements can be found in my *Political Economy of Monopoly* (Baltimore: John Hopkins University Press, 1952), for example, on p. 466; reprinted in my *Methodology of Economics and Other Social Sciences* (New York: Academic Press, 1978), p. 128. In the same volume, discussions on the relationship between theoretical constructs and empirical or operational concepts, and between theoretical propositions and empirical statements will be found in the articles on operationalism, pp. 159-203.

[30] Mincer, "Human Capital," p. 14.

and relatively wide applicability. The fact that learning usually precedes earning, and that, therefore, the learner has to wait for the beneficial results of his learning efforts, constitutes a natural link to capital theory. Not that a time lag *by itself* makes a mathematical equation or a verbal proposition a part of capital theory; but if there is a time interval between input and output, and account is taken of rates of interest, discount, or return, then we are definitely in capital theory. If the relevant input consists in an improvement of human capacity, we deal with the theory of human capital. Thus, the "human-capital model" is employed whenever improvements of human resources, deferred benefits, and rates of return are analyzed.

Decisions on investments in schooling are made by individuals and by governments. Individuals decide on grounds of expected private returns, governments on grounds of expected social returns; the two kinds of calculation differ. Private *investment* in schooling is ordinarily smaller than social investment (which includes all private investments plus additional public outlays), because a large part of the expenses of operating the schools is usually borne by the government or by philanthropic institutions (and therefore by taxpayers and benefactors, rather than by the students and their families). Private *returns*, however, may be larger or smaller than social returns, depending on various circumstances. These will be discussed in the next chapter.

CHAPTER 14

Private and Social Valuation

In the preceding chapter I spoke of private returns and social returns to private and social investments as though these concepts were generally accepted and fully understood. Yet, these are difficult concepts, involving fundamental methodological questions that ought to be examined more closely before we proceed with an analysis that relies heavily on the way they are answered. This is why I feel compelled to deal with private and social valuation.[1]

Who Estimates, Who Valuates?

Who actually estimates investment expenditures and differences in incomes? Who discounts future incomes or benefits, pecuniary and nonpecuniary, to determine their present values? And who compares these values with the costs potentially or actually incurred? Are economic analysts talking about individuals who are directly concerned or about the somewhat mysterious entity called society—or do they perhaps speak only for themselves? One often gets the impression that they speak with all these voices simultaneously, or rather in turn and in quick succession without divulging the identity of the one whose thought is supposedly being expressed. Thus, we are often left wondering about who estimates, valuates, calculates, and pronounces a verdict of "too little," "too much," or "just right."

There are several possible "appraisers" of the variables involved in human-capital theory: (1) individual investors, for example the young people who choose between continuing school or taking a job, or their parents or guardians who choose for them; (2) economists who "model" individual decision-making, hypothesizing certain patterns of ideal-typical thinking and acting, in attempts to explain observed statistical records, and perhaps also to predict future developments, such as changes in college enrollment, course election,

---

[1] A reader has queried me about the use of "valuating"—a key word in this chapter—instead of the simpler word "valuing" and the more customary "evaluating." I *value* something, usually without thinking of its money value. I *evaluate* something, judging its merit, its moral value. If I *valuate* something, I think of its market value or of its monetary, pecuniary equivalent. These shades of meaning are not supported by the dictionaries; they were impressed upon me by a professor of social psychology who objected to my use of evaluation when I was referring to a money equivalent.

and career choices; (3) governments—legislators, administrators, staff officers, advisors—making decisions about public education, about financial support, subsidies, and regulation of educational institutions, about compulsory school attendance, and so forth; and (4) economists and other social scientists who, as self-appointed spokesmen, counselors, and critics of society, "model" public or collective decision-making; they postulate the goal of optimization of social welfare on the basis of a presumably given social-welfare function or bliss function.[2]

What is the relation between the first two appraisers of returns to investment in human capital? Although it may not be easy to comprehend, it is not assumed that all real-life decisionmakers (No. 1) think and act just as the imaginary decisionmakers in the theorist's model (No. 2); this model may, nevertheless, yield insights, explanations, and even predictions. The merely fictitious (ideal-typical) individual is supposed to make optimal (perfectly rational) decisions based on reasonable expectations of outlays and sacrifices to be incurred currently and in the near future and of benefits to be obtained in a more distant future. Economic theorists have constructed this *homunculus oeconomicus* as an analytical tool, not as a likeness of any real human being.[3] For the inferences from constructed models to be applicable to recorded data of observation, and to "explain" them satisfactorily, it is not necessary that any single real-life person actually engages in the detailed numerical calculations of the hypothesized type; nor is it necessary that the majority of real people, let alone all of them, engages in rough, approximate calculations. If a sufficient number of them try to make reasonably well informed decisions, the observed outcome will tend to correspond roughly to the inferences from the rational model. This is not to deny that a few exceptional people in real life, students or their parents, do make

---

[2] In this role, the economist has appointed himself to the honorary office of "Inspector General of Society," charged with seeing to it that his contemporaries, making up society, do follow the proper path to the collective *summum bonum*. If this remark sounds unduly facetious, I apologize. I merely want to show that we are moving at an exalted level of esoteric value judgments.

[3] Writers not familiar with the literature have contended that theorists believe economic man to be "real." Yet, John Stuart Mill had exclaimed, "Not that any political economist was ever so absurd as to suppose mankind are really thus constituted." John Stuart Mill, *A System of Logic*, Vol. II (London: Parker, 1843), p. 571. — I have expounded the role of this heuristic fiction in two brief essays: "Homo Oeconomicus and His Class Mates" and "The Universal Bogey: Economic Man," first published in 1967 and 1972, respectively, and reproduced as Chapters 10 and 11 of my book *Methodology of Economics and Other Social Sciences* (New York: Academic Press, 1978), pp. 267-281 and 283-301.

calculations similar to the imaginary ones made by the fictitious decisionmakers; but this is irrelevant for the validity and applicability of the theory. The postulate of rationality has proved its heuristic value. It has been shown, for example, that students react rather quickly to reported changes in earnings foregone, in prospective job opportunities, and in differences in earnings from different vocational or professional work.[4]

The Voice of Society

Proceeding to the second pair of appraisers of (actual or potential) effects of investment in education, we should realize that the jump from private to social investment and from private to social returns involves serious methodological issues. There are very good reasons for rejecting the "point of view of society as a whole"; society neither thinks nor acts, although there are individuals and committees speaking and acting "on behalf of society" on the basis of more or less specious theories about the "general will" (volonté générale) and "social preferences." It would go too far beyond the scope of this chapter if I were to do more than indicate where the problem lies.

The tastes and preferences of the members of society differ, and there is no way to homogenize them or reduce them to a common hierarchy of goals. Attempts to construct social-welfare functions and "community indifference curves" have failed. And the idea that the standard voting procedures for the democratic group decisions that prevail in most advanced countries secure consistent social choices reflecting individual preferences has been shown to be illusory.[5] Not that all or most of those who have shown the weaknesses of the theoretical foundation of social decision-making have become archindividualist, anticollectivist, anti-interventionist, and antisocialist in their political philosophy. Some of them have; they have concluded that only in an authoritarian society is there a proper place for social values, whereas in a really free society social valuations and social choices are ruled out by definition.[6]

---

[4] Richard B. Freeman, The Labor-Market for College-Trained Manpower (Cambridge, Mass.: Harvard University Press, 1971). Freeman analyzed the demand for specialized fields of study and found that it was well explained by the earnings in different careers, as in the cases of engineers, accountants, chemists, and mathematicians. Of course, he observed the regular lags of the supply of graduates behind the observed salaries in the various fields. In the words of Mark Blaug, Freeman's results "constitute a striking confirmation of human-capital theory." Mark Blaug, "The Empirical Status of Human-Capital Theory: A Slightly Jaundiced Survey," Journal of Economic Literature, Vol. 14 (September 1976), p. 834.

[5] Kenneth J. Arrow, Social Choice and Individual Values (New York: Wiley, 1951).

[6] Friedrich A. Hayek, Law, Legislation and Liberty, Vol. 2, The Mirage of Social

The majority of economists, however, accept the notions of social welfare and of "economic welfare of society." Even the skeptics, if they want to take part in the discussion, cannot use their methodological and philosophical position as an excuse for wearing blinders; they must at least try to understand the theorizing based on these notions. Even if one rejects the ideology of social value judgments, one cannot reasonably dodge the task of dealing with the problems involved.

An essential methodological difference distinguishes the analysis of private investments and returns from that of social investments and returns. Models of the individual's rational decisions to invest in himself in view of his rational expectations of benefits accruing to himself in the future can serve in *explanations and predictions* of mass behavior. In contradistinction, models of social considerations of future social benefits to be derived from social investment in human capacities serve in *justifications and rationalizations* of political decisions. The *assumed* rationality of the private investor is a methodological device of positive economics; the *claimed* rationality of the political organs empowered to decide on social investment is a principle of evaluative or normative economics.

These distinctions are not ordinarily made when private and social benefits and costs are contrasted, the usual distinction being chiefly in terms of the items that are included or excluded. In the next sections I shall set forth and explain the major items in the conceptual framework within which the differences between private and social benefits and costs are usually discussed.[7]

Private and Social Benefits and Costs of Education

The benefits and costs of education—to use education as the paradigmatic investment in human beings—may be viewed as *private*, that is, those accruing to or incurred by the individual recipient of education (or his parents); or they may be *social*, that is, they may include, over and above the private benefits and costs, those accruing to or incurred by third persons and society at large.

Private costs are partly explicit—for example, money outlays for tuition fees or expenditures for books, stationery, and transportation—and partly implicit—chiefly the earnings foregone by older

Justice (Chicago: University of Chicago Press, 1976). Hayek argues chiefly against the notion of social justice, but he states that "the addition of the adjective 'social' makes them [various terms] capable of meaning almost anything one likes" (p. 79).

[7] The next two subsections are taken from my book *Education and Economic Growth* (Lincoln: University of Nebraska Press, 1970; reprinted New York: New York University Press, 1975), pp. 31-39.

students who could have taken jobs instead of going to school, but partly also leisure foregone while students at all ages exert themselves trying to absorb what they are supposed to learn. Add to these the psychic cost of disappointment, shattered self-confidence, and lasting alienation from intellectual society in the case of students who have been pressured into studying although they have had no craving for it. (My emphasis on nonpecuniary private costs of education is quite untraditional. The literature is almost silent on this.[8])

Social costs include, in addition to all private costs, the capital cost and operating expenses of public schools and universities, and the various subsidies, stipends, and grants from governments and from philanthropic individuals, corporations, and foundations, as well as some implicit costs of the government, for example, tax revenues foregone because of exemptions from real-property taxation or because of income taxes lost on the earnings students sacrificed by going to school. In addition there are nonpecuniary social costs connected with an oversupply of educated personnel trained for nothing.

The benefits from education are partly pecuniary and partly nonpecuniary. Private pecuniary benefits consist of the (after-tax) increments in earnings that are attributable to additional years of education. (The basic data required are the incomes earned by persons with different amounts and levels of education. If all other factors that may account for differences in earnings can be properly evaluated, one may obtain the differential earnings that can reasonably be attributed to different amounts and types of education.) Private nonpecuniary benefits consist of the various satisfactions that the student (or his family) derives, at the time, from his school attendance and, in later years, from the education received in the past. (Since appraisals of money equivalents of such psychic incomes would be entirely subjective on the part of the individuals and not ascertainable by any statistical-census taker, nonpecuniary benefits are, as a rule, omitted from estimates of returns on educational investment.)

Social benefits from education, as usually conceived, include, in addition to the private benefits, any benefits that accrue to third parties and to society at large. Third-party benefits and most of those to society cannot be estimated, however; only one factor, the contribution of education to technological progress, is sometimes assessed as an additional element in the social benefits of education.

[8] See, however, W. Lee Hansen and Burton A. Weisbrod, *Benefits, Costs, and Finance of Public Higher Education* (Chicago: Markham, 1969), pp. 36-40.

A line-by-line summary, enumerating four items of costs of education and four items of benefits from education may be helpful:

A. Explicit costs incurred by students or their families (money outlays)
B. Implicit costs incurred by students or their families (chiefly earnings foregone, net of potential taxes)
C. Explicit costs incurred by third parties or the public (money outlays)
D. Implicit costs incurred by third parties or the public (chiefly earnings or tax revenues foregone)
E. Pecuniary benefits accruing to the educated or their families (earnings, in money or in kind, after tax)
F. Nonpecuniary benefits accruing to the educated or their families (satisfactions, psychic incomes)
G. Pecuniary benefits accruing to third parties or the public (money incomes or tax revenues)
H. Nonpecuniary benefits accruing to third parties or the public (satisfactions, psychic incomes)

Items A and B together are the private costs; items A, B, C, and D together are the social costs.

Items E and F together are the private benefits; items E, F, G, and H together are the social benefits.

Private benefits minus private costs are private net benefits, or private net returns. Social benefits minus social costs are social net benefits, or social net returns. The rate of return is calculated by finding the rate of discount (capitalization) that equates the capitalized value (present value) of the stream of benefits with the capitalized value of the stream of costs.[9]

Differences in Private Incomes and National Product

The strategic item in any discussion of the returns on investment in education is E, the pecuniary benefits accruing to the educated.

---

[9] The customary exclusion of nonpecuniary (positive or negative) benefits is chiefly a matter of avoiding the arbitrary appraisals that would have to be made in the absence of information about the subjective valuations by all the individuals concerned. Even if one entertained the fiction that all individual valuations of satisfactions and dissatisfactions were becoming known to an imaginary analyst of benefits and costs, the analyst would have to exclude all dissatisfactions that are caused by envy of the fortunes of luckier persons and by pity for the misfortunes of unluckier ones, and exclude likewise all feelings of satisfaction about the good fortunes of friends and about the misfortunes of enemies. This remark serves merely as a safeguard against possible misunderstandings regarding the role of psychic incomes in benefit-and-cost analyses, for, if double-counting or cancellations of increases in the incomes of some persons or groups are to be avoided, psychic incomes must not include the joys and heartaches about the affluence or poverty of other people.

These benefits are understood as the additional lifetime earnings that can be attributed to additional education. The question is, additional to what? The answer at first seems simple: additional to something less, perhaps additional to the lower level of education at which a less eager student may have stopped. If education is regarded as an investment in one's earnings capacity, the relevant benefits may be additional to those earned at the level of education beyond which a rational person may consider continuing as a prudent investor in greater earning capacity. The rational college graduate who considers going to graduate school asks among other questions what additional income the average holder of a master's degree can expect to earn over and above the income of one who has a bachelor's degree, and what further income a Ph.D. holder can earn above the income of an average holder of an M.A. Rational high-school graduates compare the earnings of college graduates with those of people without college education, and high-school students who consider dropping out after their junior year will, if they are rational, ask how large the difference is between the earnings of a high-school graduate and the earnings of a person with only eleven years of schooling. In a similar way, the rational parents of children approaching school age will ask what difference it may make for their childrens' future incomes if they do or do not go to elementary school.

For private returns to educational investment, this simulation of rational considerations makes good sense. After deducting for all other contributing factors, the incremental earnings that can be confidently attributed to additional schooling may be seen as measures of the essential pecuniary benefits that should accrue to the rational investor in further schooling. There is a question, however, whether these same differentials in the earnings of the recipients of different amounts of education can be legitimately used for determining the social returns. It is conceivable that the incremental earnings of the group with more schooling neither represent additions to national product nor reflect the magnitude of such additions.[10] Assume a society in which all workers have had nine years of schooling; a certain percentage of the people now extend their education to twelve years. If, after they enter the labor force, they earn more than those with only nine years, the difference in incomes will measure the addition to the aggregate product only if the income of those with only nine years of schooling has not changed in the process. Perhaps, however, the availability of more highly qualified labor has raised

[10] Mary Jean Bowman, "Social Returns to Education," *International Social Science Journal* (UNESCO), Vol. 14 (1962), pp. 656-657.

the productivity of the less qualified; this will be the case if a large degree of complementarity exists between the two types of labor. That is to say, the cooperation of those with superior skills may increase the productive efficiency of the less skilled workers. In this case, the difference in the incomes of the two groups will understate the increase in national product that results from the added education. Perhaps, on the other hand, the opposite condition prevails and the two types of labor are essentially competitive. If so, the new supply of superior labor will reduce the demand for and consequently the income of less qualified labor; in this case, the income differential will overstate the contribution of added education to national product.

In an extreme case there may be a large income differential between the two groups without there being any addition to national product. Assume that the additional education makes its recipients no more efficient but nevertheless more desirable to employers.[11] Incomes of the less educated will decline as a result of the availability of the more favored and better-paid group. The private rate of return on the investment in additional education, then, may be high while the social rate is zero. Real national income is unchanged; only its distribution is altered.[12] The pay-off to those who have invested in three more years of education may be satisfactory, but from the point of view of society the additional cost of education may be sheer waste, at least as long as material product is taken as the sole criterion of social productivity.

The conceptual scheme of social benefits and costs is equipped to take account of all such divergences between social and private re-

[11] The employee with more schooling but no greater efficiency may be more desirable to the employer because (a) supervisors enjoy the company of more educated workers, (b) management gains prestige and greater consumer loyalty, (c) the personnel office takes school certificates as less expensive substitutes for its own tests and evaluations, and/or (d) the personnel office takes a certification of longer school attendance, or a college degree, as proof of the job seeker's perseverance and work morale. About the last two reasons, stressed by the theory of "signaling and screening," a little was said before and more will be said later; indeed, Chapter 18 will be devoted entirely to an analysis of "credentialism."

[12] If one considers the cost of unproductive schooling, inclusive of the earnings foregone, as negative items in a revised national-product account, one may even say that real national product is *reduced* as a result of that schooling. If the years of schooling and the years of work are taken as one (rather long) period, total product is certainly less than it would be if the persons in question had been gainfully employed instead of wasting time in school. The statement in the text above, to the effect that "real national income is unchanged," is correct only if the educational malinvestments are regarded as bygones, and only the subsequent years of gainful employment are counted.

turns. Item G of the list could reflect the divergences, for, in these instances, positive or negative pecuniary benefits accrue to third parties. As the group with additional schooling is absorbed into the economy and receives pecuniary benefits attributable to investment in its education, those with less education have their incomes increased or reduced, as the case may be. A major difficulty with the usual computations of social returns is that these third-party effects ("externalities") are not observable and cannot be estimated by means of any existing statistical techniques. Analysts of the returns to education have not shown serious concern about these problems.

Alternative Social Investment Opportunities

The political pressure for ever larger involvement of governments at all levels in educational programs has been strong and effective. In virtually all developed nations public expenditures for education have been increasing faster than the population and faster than national income. One may assume that governments have approved increasing allocations of funds for education because of widespread convictions that these expenditures are good investments.

At any particular moment, at least four alternatives offer themselves to governments prepared to expand total investment in the schooling of a population of a given size: first, the legal school-leaving age can be raised; second, through moral suasion, the percentage of students in secondary and tertiary education beyond the legal school-leaving age can be raised; third, the quality and cost of education at some or all levels or in some or all subject areas can be raised; and fourth, the distribution of students over different subject areas can be changed so that the percentage of students concentrating in more expensive subject areas (for example, physics, requiring costly equipment and laboratory space) is raised.

Whereas much statistical research has been done on investment in longer education, relatively little empirical work has been published on the third and fourth types of outlay. It has been too difficult to obtain reliable numerical information on the cost of quality improvements and on the cost differences between different subject areas.[13]

Do Wasteful Investments Create Capital?

Should every increase in the social cost of schooling be regarded as a social investment? Probably not. Educational efforts may be

---

[13] There are only a few studies on the cost-effectiveness of attempts to improve the quality of schooling by increasing expenditure per student. They will be reviewed in Volume V.

regarded as consumption, investment, waste, or drag. They are consumption to the extent that they give immediate satisfaction to the pupil or student (for example, the joy of learning) or to others (for example, mothers and neighbors enjoying some peaceful hours while the youngsters are at school). They are investment to the extent that they create either future nonpecuniary satisfaction (for example, the joy of reading and learned discourse) or future gains in productivity. They are waste to the extent that they contribute neither to pleasure nor to productivity. They are a handicap, or drag, to the extent that they make workers' preferences and opportunities of employment incompatible.[14]

Unproductive and Counterproductive Education

If an incremental educational effort of society creates neither nonpecuniary satisfactions in the future nor future gains in material productivity, there is only one cause for regarding it as investment: ignorance of the facts. An outlay, effort, or sacrifice will be called investment as long as the decisionmakers think that it will have positive returns. It may later prove to have been a malinvestment. Is a bad investment still an investment even if the investor is poorer for having made it? Evidently, this is an instance of hindsight being sharper than foresight. There may be instances, however, of conflicting "foresight," with optimists (or idealists) making the investment decisions despite warnings from pessimists (or realists). If the pessimists are right, the presumptive investments have not added to the stock of capital.

Whether incremental expenditures for education will contribute to productivity will depend on what is taught and how, to whom and at what levels, in what proportions and under what conditions. The same methods or school curricula that are highly productive in one country may be counterproductive in another. And, of course, many educational services—subjects taught and methods used—have no effect, either positive or negative, upon productivity and are not really designed for such a purpose.

It is not immediately clear why some educational efforts should have negative effects upon productivity. One or two examples, however, will show how education sometimes can be a hindrance instead of a help to economic efficiency. We have learned of the growth-retarding effects of primary education in chiefly agricultural societies

[14] Fritz Machlup, *The Production and Distribution of Knowledge in the United States* (Princeton: Princeton University Press, 1962), pp. 108-110, 115; and *Education and Economic Growth*, p. 5. Much of the contents of the next subsections comes from the latter book, pp. 21-30.

where the "educated" refuse to work in agriculture but cannot be absorbed into industry. Similarly, it has often been observed that secondary and higher education may lead to aversion to manual work while opportunities for nonmanual work are lacking. As Sir Arthur Lewis has said, "An education system may very easily produce more educated people than the economic system can currently absorb in the types of jobs or at the rates of pay which the educated expect. . . . In the long run the educated learn to expect different jobs and to accept lower rates of pay. But the long run may be very long, and the jobs accepted may gain very little from the education received.[15] The transition period may be of agonizing length and may be characterized by distressing unemployment, poverty, and frustration. To be sure, the uneducated members of the family who stay on the farm are by no means well off and the product of their labor may be meager, but those who have gone to school and away from home crowd the city slums, have no jobs, are miserable, and produce nothing except threats to political stability. In such circumstances education is a drag to economic development.

This is a very different story from the one some idealists tell about the great blessings that increased education bestows on a poor country. Alas, "the amount of education which 'pays for itself' in a poor country is limited."[16] "In most African territories less than 25 percent of children aged 6 to 14 are in school," and it would be too ambitious to aim at "a goal of 50 percent within ten years."[17] According to a 1968 press report, in Kano, one of the richest of the northern states of Nigeria, only about 50,000 children of a school-age population of 850,000, that is, 1 child out of every 17, or less than 6 per cent, attended primary school. In these circumstances it would be most unwise to expect a people in an early stage of development to engage in human-capital formation at a rapid rate and to derive large returns from it.

Social Justice and Social Waste

Instead of aiming at social justice by providing schooling for all, a poor country does much better by having only one-fifth or even fewer of its children go to primary school and by providing secondary

[15] W. Arthur Lewis, "Education and Economic Development," *Social and Economic Studies* (Jamaica), Vol. 10 (1961); reprinted in *International Social Science Journal*, Vol. 14 (1962) (hereafter cited as *ISSJ*); and in Mary Jean Bowman et al., eds., *Readings in the Economics of Education* (Paris: UNESCO, 1968) (hereafter cited as *Readings*). The quotation is from *ISSJ*, p. 686, and *Readings*, p. 136.

[16] Lewis, *ISSJ*, p. 686, *Readings*, p. 135.

[17] Lewis, *ISSJ*, p. 689; *Readings*, p. 138.

education for some of the more talented. To offer several additional years of schooling for fewer children seems to be the optimum educational plan for the poorest countries.

To aim for large enrollment ratios in the lower grades is especially wasteful if the drop-out rate is very high. There is adequate evidence for the judgment that only one or two years of schooling are completely worthless.[18] Yet, in Haiti in 1960 only one-sixth of those in first grade went to second grade, and only one-tenth to third grade. The situation is a little better in "semiadvanced" countries, to use the terminology of researchers of comparative educational development.[19] In Mexico and Venezuela, for example, 15 per cent of the children attending first grade stayed in school through the sixth grade; and in Chile 21 per cent completed sixth grade.[20] It is difficult to say whether and how the waste of abortive first years could be avoided.

Secondary and vocational education for the most teachable graduates of primary school has paid off very well for most developing countries. Secondary schools produce the persons who, with some brief additional training, become "technologists, secretaries, nurses, school teachers, bookkeepers, clerks, civil servants, agricultural assistants and supervisory workers" as well as those who make up "the middle and upper ranks of business."[21]

Higher education in very poor countries can be justified only on grounds other than contribution to economic growth: perhaps satisfaction of national pride or creation of a nucleus for cultural development. In some countries, such as Colombia, as many as one-half of the university graduates cannot find any jobs in which their education can be used.[22] Most of them emigrate, but in any case the large cost of their education may be wasted from the point of view of the nation.[23] Whether the difficulty lies with inadequate demand

---

[18] " . . . evidence concerning lapses into illiteracy strongly suggests that 2 or 3 years of schooling is almost total waste when schooling is not completed." Mary Jean Bowman, "Human Capital: Concepts and Measures," in Selma Mushkin, ed., The Economics of Higher Education (Washington, D.C.: Office of Education, 1962), pp. 82-83.

[19] Frederick Harbison and Charles A. Myers, Education, Manpower and Economic Growth (New York: McGraw-Hill, 1964), p. 110.

[20] Ibid.

[21] Lewis, ISSJ, p. 690; Readings, p. 138.

[22] Theodore Paul Schultz, Returns to Education in Bogota, Colombia (Santa Monica, Cal.: Rand Corp., 1968), pp. 37-40.

[23] Emigration reduces the loss if the alternative is domestic unemployment, or underemployment, of the educated. It is assumed that public subsidies make the social cost of higher education exceed the private cost. If the graduates stay at home, either unemployed or in jobs for which their education is useless, both the public and the

for top-level talent in an underdeveloped economy or whether the universities offer the wrong type of education, these poor countries could surely make more productive use of their scarce resources.[24]

This situation does not hold for all developing countries. Where the universities stress scientific and technical education and where the economies are sufficiently industrialized to absorb the university graduates, the case for institutions of higher education may be strong. However, in many of the developing countries the majority of university students are enrolled in humanistic studies, fine arts, and law—courses of study that are unlikely to contribute to increases in material productivity. In India—if the data of the late 1960s are still indicative of the situation—58 per cent of the students are in these materially unproductive fields. In Uruguay, only 6 per cent of the students are in scientific or technological departments. These countries may be contrasted with Czechoslovakia, where only 6 per cent of the university students study humanities, fine arts, and law, and 46 per cent are in scientific and technological fields.[25] Lest I be accused of gross materialism and anti-intellectualism, let me emphasize that nothing in my statements is intended to disparage the cultural value of literature and the fine arts; but I do question whether very poor countries can afford this kind of education while they have to stint on investments in human and physical capital with high rates of return.

Investments with Fast Pay-Off in Poor Countries

Even those types of school education that may, in fact, raise the productive capacity of their recipients have rather long pay-off periods, longer perhaps than very poor countries can afford. This may be true for most levels of formal schooling, but especially for elementary education, because several years must elapse before the pupil is old enough to become gainfully employed; and also for some forms of higher education, chiefly because its high cost (largely in

---

private portions of the social cost are wasted. However, if the graduates emigrate and find abroad opportunities to use what they have learned, their private benefits may exceed the total cost of their education.

[24] This conclusion is strongly supported by a recent study on India. Differential earnings yield much lower returns to college graduates than to primary-school leavers. This is so even though the bulk of the college graduates are employed in the public sector (and probably paid above their marginal private product), whereas the bulk of primary-school leavers are employed in the private sector. The conclusion, clearly, is that "higher education [in India] is overexpanded relative to primary education." Mark Blaug, Richard Layard, and Maureen Woodhall, The Causes of Graduate Unemployment in India (London: Allen Lane, Penguin, 1969), p. 241.

[25] Harbison and Myers, Education, p. 115.

the form of income foregone during the years of study) can be repaid only by many years of increased earnings by the graduate.

The one type of education that may pay for itself within a brief period is training on the job, particularly if it is provided by business firms, either in brief formal training programs or in informal "breaking-in" of new employees under the supervision of a foreman or an older worker as the newly hired "apprentices" perform their new tasks with increasing speed and accuracy.

Adult education, sponsored by public or civil agencies, may also pay off in relatively short periods. Although the return is probably lower and less certain for adult education than for training on the job, it may be much faster in coming than for primary-school education. After completion of evening classes, vocational training, agricultural-extension programs, and similar kinds of adult education, the upgraded adult may, often without delay, be fit for employment that makes use of the newly acquired skills. However, if programs of adult education are to succeed, it will be necessary to arouse popular enthusiasm for learning. Most people do not learn against their will; it takes a degree of commitment and passion for people to make the required effort. If a "mass movement" for adult education can be stirred up, the rate of return on this investment may be higher than that on other educational outlays.

CHAPTER 15

HUMAN CAPACITY, CREATED BY
NATURE AND NURTURE

IN THIS CHAPTER I attempt to explore issues not usually considered integral parts of the theory of human capital, yet definitely linked with the analysis of human resources and the creation and development of human ability to learn and capacity to perform.

One of the issues in question concerns the extent to which mental abilities can be attributed to genetic endowment rather than to improvements achieved through environmental influences, in particular, through conscious investment activities. More important, however, is the problem of gradual improvements in the individual's mental abilities and capacities over periods of time, chiefly as a result of positive learning experiences. Closely connected is the problem of measuring achievements and aptitudes through standardized tests.

I believe that, for the purposes of this analysis, the "regress to genes" is not necessary or really relevant, but I also believe that I should not shrink from a discussion of this issue. Although the central topics of this study are, of course, the growth and cultivation of mental capacity and the investment character of the accumulation of knowledge in individuals' minds, the question of the role of genetic endowment is too interesting to be disregarded.

Genetic Endowment and Conscious Improvement

In introducing the notion of investment in human capital, I made use of an analogy: existing land resources can be regarded partly as a free gift of nature and partly as the result of deliberate improvements. This analogy was supposed to help us understand that human resources, like land and other natural resources, could be regarded partly as inherited capacity and partly as consciously improved capacity. In actual fact, however, a clean separation between nature and nurture, or between natural endowment and purposive melioration, is difficult, perhaps impossible, in both cases. Who knows whether the fertility of the soil is not to some extent attributable to prudent investments undertaken by previous owners or cultivators? Who knows whether the land itself is not the result of costly landfills producing arable land from worthless swamps? Similarly, who knows what part of human capacity is due to genetic endowment and what part to conscious improvements through child care and education?

I meant it to be a merely rhetorical question when I asked "who knows." Actually, many psychologists, especially some of the founders of psychometrics, have been convinced that they do know. For what purposes do these metrophiles care to know the "nature/nurture ratio?" What depends on knowing the answer? Those who have worked hard to find the answer have usually linked it to questions of educational policy, social and economic policy, educational counseling, career guidance, personnel selection, and other pragmatic objectives; others have thought that intellectual curiosity was a sufficient reason for research on the genesis of the intellect. Finally, what bearing, if any, would a division of the "stock" of intelligence into an inherited and an acquired portion have upon the theory of human capital? Perhaps none at all. Nevertheless, that question has raised some problems related to the production of knowledge in human minds.

Intelligence, Inherited and Acquired

There was a time when most educational psychologists believed that native intelligence could be measured by standardized age-adapted tests yielding unchanging scores not affected by education, cultural background, or other environmental factors. Such theories of innate intelligence, measurable by standardized tests with scores translated into "intelligence quotients" (IQ, reflecting the ratio of "mental age" to chronological age) have been subject to heated controversies for almost eighty years. Not only the notion of inherited intelligence but also the very meaning of intelligence—innate as well as acquired— has been controversial.

Intelligence has been defined as "the ability to judge well, understand well, and reason well."[1] A far more pragmatic view makes intelligence "the aggregate or global capacity . . . to act purposively, to think rationally, and to deal effectively with the environment."[2] A consistent critic of abstract-theoretical concepts and apostle of operationalism declared that intelligence is "what intelligence tests measure."[3] A firm disbeliever in the existence of any "entity" that could be called "intelligence" proposed that we make it denote the

---

[1] Alfred Binet, "Nouvelles recherches sur la mésure du niveau intellectuel chez les enfants d'école," Année Psychologique, Vol. 17 (1911), pp. 145-201.

[2] David Wechsler, The Measurement and Appraisal of Adult Intelligence, 4th ed. (Baltimore: Williams & Wilkins, 1958), p. 7.

[3] Edwin G. Boring, "The Logic of the Normal Law of Error in Mental Measurement," American Journal of Psychology, Vol. 31 (1920), pp. 1-33.

unstructured "sum total of all the learning experiences [the individual] has uniquely had up to any moment of time."[4]

Many psychologists have concluded, on the basis of either theoretical conviction or empirical "factor analysis," that intelligence is a composite of two, seven, nine, twenty, or even more mental abilities or factors. Most influential, at least in the early period of intelligence measurements, was the idea that intelligence consisted of "a general factor, g," reflected in all tests, plus one or more "specific factors," unique to each test.[5] A strong suggestion that the g was of genetic origin was implicit for some, explicit for others. This theory was extended to "the theory of two g's": one "fluid general ability, g_f," the other "crystallized general ability, g_c."[6] "Tests of fluid ability have little relation to a well-stocked memory," they are "culture-fair," whereas tests of crystallized ability reflect "both the neurological integrative potential of the individual and his fortune in cultural experience."[7] Many more than two general abilities, however, had earlier been distilled by use of multiple-factor analysis, resulting in distinctions of seven—and later nine or more—"primary mental abilities."[8] In a process of partly factor-analytical and partly purely theoretical cell division, the number of elementary mental-ability factors has increased to no fewer than 120: a three-dimensional combination of five "mental operations" interacting with four "mental contents" and resulting in six mental "products," together (5 x 4 x 6 =) 120

[4] Alexander G. Wesman, "Intelligent Testing," *American Psychologist*, Vol. 23 (1968), p. 274.

[5] Charles E. Spearman, " 'General Intelligence' Objectively Determined and Measured," *American Journal of Psychology*, Vol. 15 (1904), pp. 201-293; also "The Theory of Two Factors," *Psychological Review*, Vol. 21 (1914), pp. 101-115; and *The Abilities of Man* (New York: Macmillan, 1927).

[6] Raymond B. Cattell, "A Culture-Free Intelligence Test," *Journal of Educational Psychology*, Vol. 31 (1940), pp. 161-179.

[7] Raymond B. Cattell, "Are I.Q. Tests Intelligent?" *Psychology Today* (March 1968), pp. 58, 59; reprinted in Lewis R. Aiken, Jr., ed., *Readings in Psychological and Educational Testing* (Boston: Allyn & Bacon, 1973), pp. 191, 193.

[8] Louis L. Thurstone, "Primary Mental Abilities," *Psychometric Monographs* No. 1 (Chicago: University of Chicago Press, 1938). The seven primary abilities were spatial visualization, perceptual ability, verbal comprehension, numerical ability, memory, word fluency, and reasoning. When he found that some of these mental abilities could be separated, the number of "primary" abilities increased to nine or more. Thus, reasoning was divided into inductive and deductive; spatial orientation was separated from spatial visualization; memory was divisible into visual, verbal, and numerical; etc. On the other hand, Thurstone found that all primary factors were positively correlated, so that a factor analysis of these correlations might reveal a "second-order factor" similar to Spearman's "general" intelligence. See Thurstone, "Psychological Implications of Factor Analysis," *American Psychologist*, Vol. 3 (1948), pp. 402-408.

"unique abilities," all of which "increase with experience."[9] These different abilities require, of course, "differential aptitude tests" if they are to be exhibited and "measured." Ingenious designers of special tests have produced large quantities of measuring "instruments" (as some friends of specialized jargon like to call them), but they have not yet furnished differential tests to measure all of the 120 "unique abilities."

Where does this short survey of a small fraction of the psychometric literature leave us with regard to the notion of a general intelligence determined largely by genetic factors? Writing in the same year, 1968, two psychologists recorded their contrary conclusions about the existence of a general intelligence. One of them declared that "the hierarchical type of model [which places g at the apex of the system] had to be discarded" and "there had to be a rejection of g itself."[10] The other declared that "neither g nor the IQ were invalidated" and "the general intelligence concept was strengthened, for the pyramids of primary factors provided a far more reliable base. . . ."[11]

Perhaps even farther apart in their conclusions are two psychologists writing in 1979. One of them holds that "we know that there is a genetic basis for the development of intelligence and that genetic factors are involved in individual differences of intelligence."[12] The other reports that he "reviewed the evidence on IQ heritability within whites, and concluded that a reasonable person ought not to reject the hypothesis that the heritability of IQ scores is zero."[13]

[9] Joy Paul Guilford, "Intelligence Has Three Facets," *Science*, Vol. 160 (1968), pp. 615-620; reprinted in Lewis R. Aiken, Jr., *Readings*, pp. 177-188.

[10] Ibid., *Science*, p. 617; in Aiken, *Readings*, p. 180.

[11] Cattell, "Are I.Q. Tests Intelligent?" p. 56; in Aiken, *Readings*, p. 190.

[12] Arthur R. Jensen, *Bias in Mental Testing* (New York: Free Press, 1980), p. 183. Following the suggestions in D. O. Hebb, *The Organization of Behavior: A Neuropsychological Theory* (New York: Wiley, 1949) and Philip E. Vernon, *Intelligence and Cultural Environment* (London: Methuen, 1969), Jensen distinguishes three concepts. Intelligence A refers to "the individual's genotype, that is, the complement of genes . . . that conditions the individual's intellectual development." Intelligence B, "the individual's phenotypic intelligence," is seen as the "product, at any given time in the individual's life span, of the genotype and all the environmental factors that have interacted with the genotype from the moment of conception. The phenotype is not a constant value like the genotype, but is altered by constitutional and experiential factors." Intelligence C is "the sample of 'intelligent' behavior that we can actually observe and measure at a given point in time" and thus "an imprecise estimate" of Intelligence B. "Each of [the] separate measurements is an instance of Intelligence C" and, although they vary, they show "substantial intercorrelations," which point to something they have in common, namely, Intelligence B. The scores on a particular test show Intelligence C. The other two, B and A, are "theoretical constructs."

[13] Leon J. Kamin, "Psychology as Social Science: The Jensen Affair, Ten Years

Some puzzles are posed by the discovery of national differences of average IQs between Japan and the United States, and of gradual increases in the mean IQ in one nation, Japan. "Evidence from 27 samples indicates that the mean IQ in Japan is higher than in the United States by around one-third to two-thirds of a standard deviation."[14] This amounts, in terms of the American Wechsler Intelligence Scale, to a mean disparity of 11 IQ points; that is, the mean Japanese IQ is approximately 111. For earlier ages the Japanese IQ is 112, for ages 15 and 16, it is 109 and 106, respectively, compared with 100 on the American scale. The disparities were smaller for cohorts born before 1944; the increase since then has been about 7 IQ points. One cannot reasonably asssume that a rise of this magnitude within one generation "could be accounted for by a change in the genetic structure of the population." Since "the increase in IQ was present among 6-year-olds," it cannot be explained by superior schooling and "must be attributed to effects taking place before the age of six. Improvements in health and nutrition may be involved as it has been shown that the birth weight of Japanese babies has increased over the middle decades of the century."[15] If this is the explanation of the *growth* of the disparity over the last thirty or forty years, it leaves the disparity *as such* unexplained. Candidates for explanations seem to be child care and discipline, and—genes.

Virtually all discussions of the relative roles of nature and nurture in the development of human intelligence are based on intelligence tests or, more generally, on tests of mental ability.[16] Although a more

---

After." Presidential Address, Eastern Psychological Association, Philadelphia, April 1979 (mimeographed). Kamin reviews recent studies of genetic and environmental explanations of similarities and variances in IQ scores of adopted and biological children and of monozygotic and dizygotic twins, and also of familial resemblances. He finds that none of the usable data are consistent with a finding of high heritability, whereas they would be consistent with zero heritability.

[14] Richard Lynn, "IQ in Japan and the United States Shows a Growing Disparity," *Nature*, Vol. 297 (May 1982), p. 222.

[15] Ibid., p. 223.

[16] A very different question of heritability was examined by "radical political economists." Instead of dealing with the unanswerable question of how much of mental ability, or intelligence, is inherited and how much of it is acquired, they inquired about (1) the relative roles of cognitive and affective personal characteristics in the determination of earnings and (2) about the relative significance of preschool intelligence and parental socioeconomic background in the determination of income and occupation. On the basis of regression and correlation analyses they concluded that cognitive characteristics and preschool intelligence were insignificant in comparison with school-acquired personality traits (such as conformance with the "dominant role-structure") and socioeconomic background variables. Herbert Gintis, "Education, Technology, and the Characteristics of Worker Productivity," *American Economic Review*, Vol. 61 (Suppl. May 1971), pp. 266-279; Samuel Bowles and Valerie I. Nelson, "The 'Inheritance of IQ' and the Intergenerational Reproduction of Economic Ine-

detailed exposition of educational testing has to be reserved for Volume V, we should familiarize ourselves at this juncture with the elements of ability tests.

Ability Tests

The most widely used intelligence tests are not sufficiently specialized to "measure" specific abilities, but it has become customary to distinguish memory tests, reasoning tests, and spatial-perception tests, either as separate instruments of or as parts of the same instrument. Memory tests and reasoning tests are often divided into verbal sections and numerical sections.

Many testing experts distinguish among three supposedly very different types of ability tests: aptitude tests, achievement tests, and intelligence tests. To be sure, the purposes of these three "types" of test may be different. Aptitude tests are supposed to predict the individual's preparedness to take certain academic courses, study a particular discipline, excel in a certain career, or undertake an assignment requiring the tested aptitude. Achievement tests are supposed to measure the successful learning of what has been taught in a course, department, or school. Intelligence tests are supposed to predict the capacity to acquire more learning over broad areas or to perform well in a variety of tasks demanding quick thinking, comprehension, and reasoning power.

These differences in purpose have led to some untenable distinc-

---

quality," *Review of Economics and Statistics*, Vol. 56 (February 1974), pp. 39-51.

Similar results concerning the relative insignificance of variables influenced by hereditary factors in the determination of income were reported by Griliches and Mason. Their findings "throw doubt on the asserted role of genetic forces in the determination of income. If AFQT (Armed Services Qualification Test) is a good measure of IQ and if IQ is largely inherited, then the direct contribution of heredity to current income is minute. Its indirect effect also is not very large." Zvi Griliches and William M. Mason, "Education, Income, and Ability," *Journal of Political Economy*, Vol. 80 (May-June 1972, Part 2), pp. S74, S103, esp. p. S99.

In a paper that purports to "use a version of the human capital model that is fairly general and not particularly rigorous," Paul Taubman, applying regression analysis to a sample of twins (the NAS-NRC sample), compared the coefficients of schooling when one does and does not "control for genetics and family environment." Without such control, the results are not much different from those obtained from census data. When controlled, however, "the coefficient of schooling declines by two-thirds"; other studies, where the data were controlled only for proxies for family environment, showed the coefficient for schooling reduced by only 12 per cent. Taubman concludes that "a large proportion of the variance in earnings at age 50 is accounted for by a combination of family environment and genetic endowments." Paul Taubman, "Earnings, Education, Genetics, and Environment," *Human Resources*, Vol. 11 (Fall 1976), pp. 447-461, esp. p. 459.

tions in definitions. Thus, according to some authorities achievement tests are designed to find out what the tested individual *has* learned, whereas aptitude and intelligence tests are designed to indicate what the individual *can* learn. In actual fact, all three types of test show at best what the individual *has* learned, even when the results, the test scores, are to be used as predictors of potential success in further learning.[17]

The widely advertised and highly approved demands for culture-free and culture-fair tests have been effectively debunked. No test can really be culture-free; trying to test knowledge, or learning "not affected by environment," has rightly been called "sheer nonsense." Attempts to make tests culture-fair serve no real purpose: by an achievement test we want to find out what the student has successfully learned; and by aptitude and intelligence tests we want to find how well the individual is prepared for further learning or for particular jobs. The latter aim involves a short-term prediction, which can only be less valid, and therefore less useful, if an attempt is made, "in fairness" to underprivileged candidates, to conceal that some of them lack an essential aptitude, say, the verbal aptitude needed in the study or job for which they are to be selected.[18] For long-term predictions of success neither aptitude nor achievement tests are suitable, since additional learning experiences could well improve the candidates' performances and raise their test scores before they begin further studies or employment.[19]

Tests of mental ability—achievement tests, aptitude tests, and intelligence tests—may be valid for some purposes, but invalid for others. The use of test scores to advise students on their short-term plans of study and career is unobjectionable, provided the advisor makes it clear that only *present* preparation is being judged and that any deficiencies might possibly be made up by more preparatory

[17] Alexander G. Wesman, "Intelligent Testing," *American Psychologist*, Vol. 23 (1968), pp. 267-274; reprinted in Aiken, *Readings*, pp. 203-215. A statement in the same vein may be quoted: ". . . what is regarded as achievement at the conclusion of one level of education or training could quite properly be regarded as a measure of aptitude for some advanced instruction." Jerome E. Doppelt and George F. Bennett, "Aptitudes, Measurement of," *The Encyclopedia of Education* (New York: Crowell Collier and Macmillan, 1971), Vol. 1, pp. 245-246.

[18] These tests "are not, nor are they intended to be, 'culture free.' Quite the reverse: they are culture bound. What they measure are the skills which are among the most important in our society for getting a good job and moving up to a better one, and for full participation in an increasingly technical world." James S. Coleman; Ernest Q. Campbell; et al., *Equality of Educational Opportunity* (Washington, D.C.: U.S. Department of Health, Education and Welfare, Office of Education, 1966), p. 20.

[19] Wesman, "Intelligent Testing."

study. To encourage high-school seniors whose tests show serious shortcomings in verbal aptitude to proceed immediately to college would be foolish; instead, the students should be advised first to bring their language skills to the level needed for success in post-secondary education.

Even staunch fighters against privilege, prejudice, and improper discrimination ought to accept as a reasonable practice the use of test scores by admissions officers of colleges and universities, even though the predictive value of the scores may sometimes be questionable. The damage to students admitted to courses of study in which they are likely to fail is far greater than the damage to those whose scores do not do justice to their real ability and who therefore are denied admission. The rejected can try again; they can show in a new test that they do have the ability to master the kind of learning that the educational testers believe to be required for the intended academic work.[20]

Use of educational testing to identify schools that fail to teach students what they need for further study or for gainful employment is among the proper functions of the administrators in a school system. Teachers and school principals long fought all attempts at school evaluation by standardized testing, but, after the national assessment project proved useful, comparative evaluations by uniform achievement tests became accepted practice in many school districts and states.[21]

In the discussion of comparative advantages of different teaching methods and alternative kinds of school administration, purely theoretical arguments, appealing to the educator's reason, may have great merit, but conclusive judgments should rest on empirical tests. If the objectives of educational programs are agreed upon, tests oriented towards these objectives can provide firmer ground for evaluating the comparative effectiveness of alternative techniques.

Having looked at a few examples of accepted uses of standardized tests of mental ability, we may ask whether these tests have a proper place in analyses of nature/nurture ratios. No general answer, of

[20] This is not to deny that some tests have an improper culture bias; thus, critical testing of tests is wholesome and essential. A certain kind of culture bias, however, is proper: if, for example, a very able immigrant does not know any English, the test scores ought to reflect this; there is nothing wrong in asking that the candidate learn the language before enrolling in courses taught in English.

[21] The National Assessment of Educational Progress was designed between 1964 and 1968 and executed between 1969 and 1972 for ten subject areas. Reports were published beginning in 1970. For a concise study see William Greenbaum et al., *Measuring Educational Progress: A Study of the National Assessment* (New York: McGraw-Hill, 1977).

course, is possible *in vacuo*; one has to see precisely what the particular psychometrician does with the test scores in trying to relate them to genetic and environmental factors. However, since all tests reflect acquired knowledge—of the knowing-*how* type (skills) and of the knowing-*what* type (memory of cognitive learning)—it is hard to believe that it is possible to sort out the influences of innate and of acquired abilities.

Mental Ability, Knowledge, and Intellectual Growth

Mental ability, intelligence, and knowledge, or knowledgeability, are surely closely related, and perhaps even synonyms for the same concept. If one writer holds that "the bits or modules which constitute intelligence may be information or may be skills,"[22] and if the skills in question are essentially mental ones, intelligence is defined as the sum of knowing *what* and knowing *how*. Alternatively, intelligence may be defined as ability to *acquire* knowledge (of both types). Going one step further, intelligence may include the ability to *retain* knowledge. Learning may be seen as consisting of both acquiring and retaining knowledge; and the ability to learn would then be the ability to acquire knowledge (how quickly?) and to retain it (for how long?). Yet, learning speeds and memory spans differ among individuals, and differ over time for the same individual.

Are fast learning and long retention considered substitutes in the rating of intelligence? If you can memorize a poem in one hour, whereas it takes me four hours, but I retain it for ten years (or perhaps for life), whereas you forget it within a year or a month, which of us has the greater ability to learn? Incidentally, memory can be trained: both the speed of memorizing and the duration of retention can be improved by exercise. There may be a special talent or gift of memorizing, but the ability to commit new learning to memory and to retrieve it upon demand can be trained and significantly strengthened. No technique has been developed, so far as I know, to separate and measure the respective contributions that genetic endowment and environmental melioration have made to the ability to learn and remember.

Intelligence, or any combination of mental abilities, can be measured or rated only by tests of *performance*, and on the basis of an underlying assumption that the subjects have performed to the best of their ability. This assumption is contradicted by the presumed existence of "underachievers." The performance consists, as a rule, of acts of retrieving from the memory pieces of knowledge acquired

---

[22] Wesman, "Intelligent Testing," in Aiken, *Readings*, p. 204.

in the more or less distant past (long-term memory) or only in the last few seconds (short-term memory), of acts of quick perception of images, realistic, ornamental, or geometric, of acts of arithmetic computation, of acts of selecting and combining words or figures that exhibit some logical relationships (congruence, similarity, contrariety), and other acts that cannot be successfully performed without particular aptitudes or abilities—except in rare instances of luck in guessing. Virtually all the abilities tested by these performances relate to knowledge of some sort, either knowing *what* or knowing *how*.

The abilities to perform these or similar tasks have been found to improve between ages 4 and 16. The raw scores on tests designed to measure "intelligence" showed, on the average, such regular rates of increase with age that early testing experts were persuaded that mental abilities improved at a roughly linear rate. They took the mean score for each age group as the norm for establishing the "mental age" of any individual and computed his/her IQ by the ratio of mental age to chronological age. They expected this IQ to remain constant throughout the youngster's mental development, which implies that they expected that, as a rule, all persons would grow mentally at the same rate, at least until age 16. If the rate of intellectual growth of any individual were faster in some years than that of the peer group, and slower in other years, his IQ would show wide fluctuations. Is it likely that mental growth is much more uniform than physical growth? It is well known that some boys are relatively short for their age during some years and then "shoot up" at an extraordinary rate; and some girls may be "underweight" for years and then suddenly start gaining weight rapidly. If "size quotients," "weight quotients," and "physical-strength quotients" are not likely to remain constant between ages 4 and 16, why should "intelligence quotients" exhibit such constancy? As a matter of fact, they do not.

Tests of intelligence share with tests of physical strength several features, especially (1) that there is no sure way to know whether the performance observed and measured (or rated) is actually the optimum or maximum of which the tested individual is capable, and (2) that the selection of tasks and the assignment of weights to the tasks performed are arbitrary. The selection of tasks for tests of intelligence has just been discussed; with regard to physical strength, one may wonder whether it is measured (rated) more reliably by weight lifting, discus throwing, hammer throwing, shot put, or any particular combination of these and other athletic tests. In both sets of tasks selected for tests of mental and physical abilities, the numerical scoring can be done with a high degree of objectivity once the distribution of weights is agreed upon. This is not so in the case of many other tests or contests of mental and physical abilities. Creativity, for example, is sometimes proposed for inclusion in tests of mental ability, but ratings of this quality can be judged only by referees exercising a considerable range of discretion. In several sports, such as diving, free-figure ice skating and dancing, scores given by members of juries (whose impartiality is sometimes doubtful) are averaged in order to arrive at the ratings of the contestants. These "measurements of ability" are somewhat akin to ratings in beauty contests, which really test the tastes of the jurors simultaneously with the contestants' ability to impress the jurors with their physical appearance. Concluding these somewhat frivolous observations about testing, I may submit that the question of the relative contributions of genetic endowment and deliberate melioration may be equally pertinent, or equally impertinent, with regard to physical strength and bodily beauty as with regard to mental ability.

Avoiding the Regress to Genes

My contention that the nature/nurture ratio is irrelevant to the problems I consider in this discussion needs an explanation. Let me resort to analogies. Physical strength is undoubtedly a function of genetic constitution and environmental conditioning. A great deal can be done through conscious improvement; ask the athletes, joggers, trainers, nutritionists, and body builders. No one questions, however, that the same physical training has different effects on persons with different genetic endowment, on persons strong or weak "by nature." An equal investment in building physical strength is likely to result in unequal improvements. An equal increase in physical capacity will call for unequal investments in the person's physical development.

The analogy of improvement of land through investment in tangible capital may be referred to once again. No one can doubt that the productivity and profitability of land use may have to be attributed to the natural quality of the land as well as to investments in its improvement. Equal investments in varied land, however, are likely to result in unequal productivity; equal productivity can be achieved only by unequal investments. These inequalities are well known and taken for granted.

If these "facts" regarding the combined effects of nature and nurture are unquestioned, indeed commonplace, why are they not assigned leading roles in the theory of capital formation? The answer is, simply, that the capital theorist need not, in an indefinite or infinite regress, go back to the creation of the earth, the emergence of Homo sapiens, the biological conception and later development of any particular persons, or, indeed, to any occurrences of the past. The theorist may, in most of his reasoning, begin at the present, with the existing stock of tangible and human resources at our disposal, and he need not ask what portion of this stock is due to nature and what portion is due to nurture. Starting with *given* capacities, he may simply compare the likely effects of improving those capacities beyond their present state with the likely effects of using them without attempts to improve them. What chiefly matters in capital theory, as in most parts of economic theory, is choosing among alternative courses of action for consideration at present; among the alternatives is the use of existing stocks of resources as they are or the building of additional capacity beyond that which exists. How much of what exists has been a gift of God's providence or a result of human providence may be of theological, biological, or historical interest, but it is not one of the concerns of the economic theorist.

The regress to genes in the theory of human capital is avoided by the device of analyzing investment in human capacity by period analysis, for example, by dividing the process of capacity development into school years or age intervals. There is no need to go back to a state of primordial intelligence or even of mental ability at birth. Investments in improving mental abilities during one or more years of preschool education, during four, five, or six years of primary school, and so forth, can be examined for progress, benefits, and costs without ever raising the question of original genetic endowment.[23] The individual's state of ability to perform at time t_1, the various influences that subsequently operate on his ability, and the state of ability to perform at time t_2 will be the (given and/or de-

---

[23] Even some early writers on intelligence tests denied that they were trying to measure innate mental ability. Thus, a statement made in 1922 said this: "We never measure inborn intelligence; we always measure acquired intelligence, but we infer, from differences in acquired intelligence, differences in native endowment when we compare individuals in a group who have had common experiences. . . ." Stephen S. Colvin, "Principles Underlying the Construction and Use of Intelligence Tests," in Guy M. Whipple, ed., *Intelligence Tests and Their Use*, 21st Yearbook of the National Society for the Study of Education, Part I, Chap. 2 (Bloomington, Ind.: Public School Publishing, 1922), p. 19. — The fallacy in this statement is the assumption that all individuals in the tested group have had "common experiences." They may have been exposed to the same (or similar) formal schooling, but their childhood experiences were probably very different. Their education in the home—their lives with father, mother, siblings, and playmates—may have affected their capacity to learn and their motivations and other attitudes so strongly that the supposedly "common experiences" at school could not have had equal effects on them, even if their innate endowments were equal.

pendent) variables in such an analysis of the formation of human capital.

To say that the regress to genes can be avoided in the theory of human capital if period analysis is used is not to promise that we need not ever come back to the notion of innate ability. In the chapters that follow, I shall several times be forced to return to the issue, particularly when I discuss views of writers who, in their explanations of earnings, do give a place to "general intelligence" or, more explicitly, to native ability.

Students with higher ability at the start of a learning period usually benefit more from the same exposure to schooling than their less able classmates. If improvements of ability are consistently higher for those already ahead at the start, it follows that the ability gap will widen from year to year. Hence, inequality in the distribution of ability increases with the duration of education. (Needless to say, if ability and learning capacity account also for earning capacity, the effect of equal exposure to longer schooling will be reflected in increasing inequality of earnings.) This "law" of increased inequality of ability due to increased schooling is counteracted to some extent by the quality of education: teaching is usually not geared to fast learners, who may be bored by underutilization of their learning capacity and may react by "tuning out." This boredom effect on the abler members of the class need not retard their learning so much as to equalize it with the progress of the less able; hence, the ability gap is still likely to keep widening if the duration of schooling is extended.

It would be wrong to conclude that the widening of the ability gap in the course of extended schooling could be avoided by denying more schooling to the least able students. For, if the least able had to leave school at an earlier stage, while the abler ones continued, the difference in ability at the time each left school might be even greater. This is because the modest improvement that additional schooling could have produced for the less able students would now be lost—unless it is replaced by training on the job. Training on the job may indeed be a superior alternative to continued schooling. Whether enforced continuation of schooling, without realistic hope for much, if any, additional learning, would constitute an investment with a positive rate of return is a question deserving much more attention than it has been receiving.

Growth and Cultivation of Mental Capacity

The device of measuring mental capacity of individuals at various intervals, and thus tracing its growth over time, should not mislead us into interpreting all implied increases in capacity as improvements due to purposive investment. After all, there is such a thing as natural growth or maturation without explicit cost. If the term "improvement" is given the same connotation in discussions of human resources as in discussions of land and other natural resources, it refers solely to expenditures of time, effort, or money for the sake of future returns, hence, to investment. Costless growth or maturation is then different from cultivation, or deliberate improvement, of mental capacity.

Investment in human resources, or formation of capital through improving the capacities of any human being, does not have to wait for the child's attendance in nursery school or kindergarten. It begins even before birth, with prenatal care, or long before that, with the education of the mother. The benefits accruing to children thanks to their mothers' education are undeniable, but one may nonetheless prefer to regard them as valuable byproducts rather than as expected and intended returns of investment deliberately undertaken to benefit one's progeny. If the analyst decides against going back that far, and thus against a carry-forward procedure in intergenerational cost accounting, he may still recognize human-capital formation in prenatal care and preschool nurture preceding the investments in school lessons and postschool learning. These four types of investment need not exhaust the possibilities—"investment opportunities in human-capital formation"—but they are the ones singled out for discussion in the literature of the field. The fact that in many communities prenatal and preschool investments are *parental* concerns, whereas postschool investment is largely *self*-improvement, and schooling draws on *combined* efforts of parents, students, and society, makes a difference in some respects, especially with regard to divergences between private and social rates of return; but there are enough common features to justify bringing them together under the common heading of investment in improvements of mental capacity.

Prenatal care has not yet attracted much empirical research in the context of human-capital analysis. This is largely explained by the fact that no data have been available to allow the application of regression analysis to estimating the effects of expenditures for prenatal care on the lifetime earnings of the beneficiaries. The increasingly frequent references to prenatal care in discussions of human capital have probably been prompted by the controversy about the role of genetic endowment. They have served to recall that the potential for mental development of the newly born is the "product," not solely of genes and other natural factors, but of joint contributions of nature and nurture; in particular, that not only the genes but also the social and economic conditions of the parents are responsible for the potential development of the mental capacity of the human being at age zero. No matter whether or not numerical data support the factual judgment, there is investment in unborn humans.

The role of preschool investment is less speculative in that we do have better empirical data on the expenditures of time, effort, and money for caring for babies and preschool infants.[24] In addition, we have a very large literature, produced by psychologists, educationists, social workers, sociologists, and others, on bringing up babies, on infant development, early-childhood education, day-care centers, nursery schools, headstart programs, effects of nutrition and play, and everything else that can be thought of as having an influence on the child's cognitive and emotional development. Empirical data on the benefits from preschool investment are not available; we have no quantitative estimates of the effects on ability, capacity, performance, or earnings. A fortiori, no calculations of rates of return on preschool investment have been undertaken.

The other two types of investment—formal schooling and postschool training and learning—are well researched. Empirical data on expenditures and on (estimated) benefits are available; and where both can be adequately converted into a series of dollar figures, calculations of rates of returns have become tempting. But there should be a solemn warning: expenditures and benefits are separated by a good many intervening variables, some of which are not quantifiable, not measurable, or not accessible, and are of unknown significance in the causal linkage. The next chapters are designed to report on explorations of these issues.

[24] See, for example, Arleen Leibowitz, "Home Investments in Children," *Journal of Political Economy*, Vol. 82 (March-April 1974, Part 2), pp. S111-S131; also Arleen Leibowitz, "Education and the Allocation of Women's Time," in F. Thomas Juster, ed., *Education, Income, and Human Behavior*. Prepared for the Carnegie Commission on Higher Education and the National Bureau of Economic Research (New York: McGraw-Hill, 1975), pp. 171-197.

CHAPTER 16

THE ROUTE FROM INVESTMENTS TO RETURNS

THE CAUSAL LINKAGE between educational investments and returns is by no means simple. There is no "through train" going, without intermediate stops, from investments to returns, even if some econometrically inclined travelers seem to sleep through the long trip and take notice only of the origin and the destination—the investments and the monetary returns. I propose that, for an adequate analysis of the causal linkage, the most likely *intervening variables* must be considered. The connections shown in the following schedule may look reasonable:

FROM	TO
1. endowment and investment	ability
2. ability and attitudes	capacity
3. capacity and its utilization	performance
4. performance at selling price times hours per year	earnings

This is only one of many ways to map the connections. One may prefer to make the route shorter or longer. It would be shortened if ability and capacity were regarded as only one potential, but I prefer to see them as two: something is added to ability before it becomes capacity. The additional something may be willpower, discipline, working intensity, or some other personal qualities essential for working capacity. The question may again be raised whether this additional element, or bundle of elements, is fixed by genetic endowment, say, innate energy, or whether (and if so, how much) it is affected by educational investment, for example, acquired diligence, perseverance, and discipline. These three personal faculties can surely be increased by schooling and training. (They can also be reduced by bad schooling, especially if the school climate favors loafing and violence.) I shall assume, throughout this analysis, that all factors involved, mental ability and the added package of ingredients that raise ability to capacity, can be improved.

If the extra ingredients of capacity are admitted into our causal chain, we obtain on the way from initial personal endowment to eventual earnings four intervening variables: (1) educational investment improving mental ability, (2) educational investment improving the extra elements that make for capacity, (3) the actual utilization of that capacity resulting in work performance, and (4) the number of hours of performance leading to earnings from work. This sequence is still quite primitive in that it omits several factors influencing the outcome either directly or indirectly through affecting the intervening variables. Before turning to these additional factors, I offer a few observations on the ability-capacity-performance triad.

Ability and Capacity

I have elsewhere distinguished eight components of the capacity to learn and perform tasks that demand cognitive aptitudes and moral attitudes of a higher order: (1) mathematical ability, (2) verbal ability, (3) alertness (also enterprising spirit, moral courage), (4) creativity (resourcefulness, imaginativeness, inventiveness), (5) interest (intellectual curiosity, inquiring mind), (6) ambition (drive, resolution), (7) diligence (industry, working intensity), (8) perseverance (enduring dedication, constancy).[1]

This list may be incomplete; it omits, for example, discipline, a very important component of capacity to learn and perform; discipline is not the same thing as either diligence or perseverance. On the other hand, some of the eight components may be regarded as overlapping. In a similar context I have, on another occasion, reduced my list to six items, chiefly by merging the first three under the heading "intelligence."[2] This is probably inappropriate in view of findings to the effect that the correlation between mathematical and verbal ability is sometimes quite slight and that neither of the two need be combined with alertness. I therefore prefer to split "intelligence" into the three components. (I would understand if even more components were proposed.) My separate listing of diligence and perseverance was criticized on the ground that these qualifications "are so closely related that we may consider them as one."[3] I submit that diligence and perseverance differ with respect to the

---

[1] Fritz Machlup, *Hochschulbildung für jedermann: Eine Auseinandersetzung mit einem Gleichheitsideal*, Basler wirtschaftswissenschaftliche Vorträge, No. 7 (Zürich: Schulthess Polygraphischer Verlag, 1973), p. 3.

[2] Fritz Machlup, "The Illusion of Higher Education," in Sidney Hook, Paul Kurtz, and Miro Todorovich, eds., *The Idea of a Modern University* (Buffalo: Prometheus, 1974), p. 8.

[3] Sidney Hook, "Democracy and Higher Education," in *The Idea of a Modern University*, p. 39.

time dimension: one may work diligently for weeks or months without necessarily persevering for years. Both are needed. The same critic objected to my merging of "interest" and "intellectual curiosity," because the latter "is only one way in which interest is expressed."[4] These quibbles, however, do not deny the essential distinction between factors that are integral parts of mental ability—perhaps the first three or four in my list—and others needed to supplement ability to constitute capacity. I propose to regard discipline, interest, ambition, diligence, and perseverance as the requisites to be conjoined with mental ability; without them, the capacity to learn and to perform may be small indeed.

The nine qualities are substitutes in some respects and complements in others. They are substitutes in the sense that deficiencies of some qualities may be compensated for by more generous helpings of others. This is evidently true for ability and diligence: lower intelligence can be made up for by more diligence, and vice versa. Some lazy geniuses have made important contributions; and many diligent and persevering mediocrities have done very well. Several of the nine qualities are complementary with one another, in the sense that their combined effect may be greater than the sum of the effects that each would have if the others were present in smaller amounts or were altogether missing.[5] If, for example, a high degree of intelligence (unaided by much diligence) can contribute to a person's capacity an amount c_1; and if a large dose of diligence (unaided by much intelligence) can contribute an amount c_2; the combination of that high degree of intelligence with that large dose of diligence can contribute more than c_1 plus c_2 to his capacity.

One of the nine qualities, creativity, may be very important for certain tasks, but not for others. These other tasks may, nevertheless, be highly regarded, perhaps because they require, for example, extraordinary degrees of mathematical ability, discipline, and perseverance.

Capacity and Performance

Neither mental ability nor mental capacity can be measured directly; tests can measure performance at a particular time and place only, and educators as well as psychologists are well aware that a person's test performance may fall short of his potential. The scores on performance tests may depend on several factors besides capacity:

[4] Ibid.

[5] Substitutability refers to trade-offs for a given result (product) whereas complementarity refers usually to an *increase* in product.

special motivations, energy and physical condition at the moment, concentration, endurance, and probably also special training in examination techniques. (Many educators have so deep a mistrust of standardized test scores on single examinations that they prefer to rely on sequences of nonstandardized tests over a year, with marks averaged into course grades and class rank,[6] although these may be strongly affected by the teachers' subjective impressions and by the composition of the class or entire student body being graded and ranked.) Since performance tests cannot really measure capacity, and since "ratings" of capacity are often much higher than actual test scores—think of the judgment that "this student performed far below his capacity"—one must ask by what criteria capacity is rated. No really satisfactory answers have been forthcoming. Potentials cannot be measured, but can at best be rated, and the criteria for such ratings are arbitrary and often excessively impressionistic.[7]

The impossibility of devising reliable measuring techniques for intervening variables will not upset any analyst versed in methodology. An intervening variable is, by definition, one that is inserted into a theoretical model to make the model more plausible as an elucidation of a causal chain with no missing links, even though no close operational counterpart or counterparts for these links can be found. Sometimes the analyst comes up with a proxy or surrogate for an empirical counterpart to a theoretical variable but, more often than not, the proxy is admitted only with a large dose of forbearance and for want of anything that would be more closely related to the nonobservable link. In brief, intervening variables are nonobservable but "reasonable" links in the causal chain. When I spoke of test performance I did not mean it to serve as an extra intervening variable; it is merely one of the devices people use to obtain scores that might roughly indicate capacity—which is the intervening variable in question. Next in line to capacity, as the subsequent intervening variable, would be job performance—not test performance. The dis-

[6] Taubman and Wales believe that class rank depends to a large extent on the students' docility and willingness to memorize and on their performance in physical education and on manual skills ("shop"), and thus does not reflect mental ability. Paul Taubman and Terence Wales, "Mental Ability and Higher Educational Attainment in the Twentieth Century," in F. Thomas Juster, ed., *Education, Income, and Human Behavior* (New York: McGraw-Hill, 1975), p. 53.

[7] My view—that potentials, such as ability and capacity, cannot be measured—is supported by Kenneth Arrow, who regards ability as "an unmeasured and unmeasurable variable. . . . There may be no way of ever achieving a direct measurement. . . ." Kenneth J. Arrow, "Higher Education as a Filter," *Journal of Public Economics*, Vol. 2 (July 1973), p. 215.

tinction between test performance and job performance is probably clear to everybody.

The move from capacity (as one intervening variable) to job performance (as the next one) involves "making use" of one's capacity in two different senses. Full utilization during a short period of time, and full utilization over the period of a year, are two very different things (we must refer back to the distinction between diligence and perseverance, but we are now no longer at the level of personal qualities but on the level of actual doing). To use one's capacity fully in the sense of maximum performance per unit of time is one thing; to use one's capacity for forty or sixty hours a week, for nine months rather than eleven months a year, is another. A time dimension in the second sense is undoubtedly an integral part of the concept of job performance, an "input" to be ascertained before we can come to the end of the line—observable earnings. The pecuniary equivalent of job performance presupposes a multiplication of performance per hour of work with the number of hours worked per year. To suggest this simple multiplication, however, is to oversimplify the problem. A few more comments will be needed to describe and explain the last leg of the journey, from job performance to earnings.

Performance and Earnings

No doubt, performance and compensation for performance are different things. This is most clearly seen in instances in which the performer produces a physical output. If the utilization of capacity leads to performance, and performance yields countable units of physical products, the performances of different persons producing different products can be compared only with the help of money prices and/or money wages. The need of a recourse to valuation in terms of money is even more obvious when performance yields essentially intangible services; even if the services are of the same type, the only way to compare performances may be by the money values the services have for users or employers. Hence, the two different factors, performance and compensation for performance, are rolled into one, even though we want to retain their conceptual independence in our scheme of thinking where job performance is only one of the intervening variables for which no operational counterpart is available.

To take annual earnings as determined simply by multiplying hourly "performance" by hours worked per year is to suppose, tacitly or explicitly, that every employee's hourly rate of compensation is uniquely determined by his performance. Many assumptions of varying degrees of fictitiousness are implied in that supposition. Any listing of the assumptions will include the following: absence of limitations or restrictions of competition in the labor markets as well as in product markets; absence of imperfections in the mobility of workers among occupations, regions, locations, industries, and firms; absence of nonpecuniary elements in employers' and employees' decisions, such as trade-offs between wage rates and working conditions, or any other choices between money earnings and merely psychic rewards; absence of overvaluation by employers of the significance of credentials, such as school diplomas and academic degrees; absence of investments by workers in themselves through learning on the job for the sake of compensations that promise to increase more rapidly than usual with years of experience; and the absence of luck in determining annual (or lifetime) earnings. Fortunately, some of the assumptions may be dropped, so that the theorist can speculate about how much they matter (or the empirical analyst can estimate unexplained residuals); some can perhaps be replaced by specific factors entered as additional variables in the causal connection between performance and earnings.

The difference between sustaining or dropping some of the most unrealistic assumptions may not be of strategic significance. For example, satisfactions, nonpecuniary psychic rewards, compensating for low money earnings, are perhaps not very important for many employed people, so that one need not worry about this deviation from conditions set for the idealized model when merely general economic relationships are to be explored. The assumption that academic credentials do not matter may be replaced by inserting the possession of credentials as a separate (dummy) variable affecting earnings. (A large literature deals with credentials as a factor in the determination of earnings; see Chapter 18.) Workers' investment in their own capacity—earnings foregone by accepting growth jobs with initially low rates of pay—has been found to be so important that postschool learning on the job has been classified as a special type of human-capital formation; it has, thus, become a part of the investment intended to raise capacity. Immobility of workers is especially difficult to deal with; one cannot reasonably assume it away, except provisionally, and one cannot easily replace the assumption of perfect mobility with the introduction of operationally identifiable factors inserted in the causal chain. Immobility may create chronic scarcities of particular performers, and chronic redundancies of others; thus, imperfect mobility may be responsible for long-lasting scarcities and redundancies. All these relative scarcities and redundancies account for valuations of performances (and hence variances in earnings) that are not explained by the abilities, capacities, and efforts of the persons employed in the respective activities. To explain the variances one would need, as additional independent variables, clearly specified changes in the demand for these activities, and manifest obstacles to such reallocations (transfers, migrations) as would achieve the adjustments of wage rates and thereby restore the ideal one-to-one relationship between performance and earnings.

What is the role of luck in the determination of earnings, or of differences in earnings, of different people? "Luck" is the term employed, in the production function of earnings, for the part of the variance that is not "explained" by the specified factors, or variables. If we formulate a production function that uses the quantity of schooling as the only explanatory variable, any part of the earnings that cannot be accounted for by that single variable (and a constant to which it is added) will be the unexplained residual; and some interpreters might be whimsical enough to call it "luck." Those who realize that mental ability or physical strength may have something to do with performance and earnings may be told that the distribution of ability and strength is a matter of luck. Those who insist that hard work may be an important factor in accounting for larger earnings may be answered that possessing a disposition to work hard is good luck—or perhaps tough luck, in the view of confirmed and dedicated loafers. Those who emphasize that parents' income and education may be highly influential in the determination of individual incomes may be rebutted by the assertion that it takes luck to be born into a rich family and to well-educated parents. It is practically impossible to name all the things that may be thought of as influencing differential earnings; if we include in the production function of earnings all factors that appear to be reasonably "explanatory," there will still remain an unexplained residual, an error term that deserves to be given the designation "luck."[8]

Various Influences on Ability, Capacity, Performance, and Earnings

In presenting the causal chain leading from initial endowment to earnings, I enumerated four variables: (1) educational investment (preschool, school, and postschool) improving ability, (2) educational investment improving the extra elements, such as discipline, diligence, and endurance, that are combined with ability to create

---

[8] " 'Luck' is another way of saying that myriads of factors influence peoples' lives, including what they earn." Mary Jean Bowman, "Through Education to Earnings? A Review," in *Proceedings of the National Academy of Education*, Vol. 3 (1976), p. 251. — See also the interesting discourse on luck in Christopher Jencks et al., *Inequality: A Reassessment of the Effect of Family and Schooling in America* (New York: Basic Books, 1972), pp. 227-228.

capacity, (3) the utilization of the (potential) capacity in actual performance, and (4) the number of hours of actual performance per year. I also mentioned the possibility of increasing both ability and capacity through costless learning from experience, from other people, from exposure to radio and television broadcasts, from reading, and so forth. We must not, however, assume without question that all these influences are always positive, even formal schooling. (In the next chapter, I shall report on the reduction in tested aptitudes of schoolboys in their first year of elementary school, and at various places I mention the possibility of damaging effects of compulsory schooling beyond age 15.) Negative influences from "bad company" (including, in exceptional cases, parents and siblings) and from too much watching of bad television programs are quite plausible, even if we have no statistical evidence for those effects.

The influences in question may work on all levels: they may affect ability, capacity, performance, and earnings, directly as well as indirectly. Thus, life with father—perhaps a strong personality, a rich man, well educated, and with good connections—may have much to do with the children's success, or failure. Their capacity may be determined partly by mental ability, and partly by diligence and perseverance acquired under the father's (or mother's) influence.[9] Their performance may be affected partly, indirectly, by their capacity, and partly, directly, by an acquired inclination (nay urge) implanted by father, to make full use of their capacity. Finally, their earnings may be determined partly, indirectly, by their job performance, and partly, directly, by the fine jobs they got thanks to father's connections. These are only some of the many parental influences affecting the earnings of sons and daughters. Some may be counterproductive influences: parental pressure or parental pecuniary indulgence may spoil or ruin the children's careers; they may become neurotic failures instead of successful performers and earners.

Careful analysis of direct and indirect influences is necessary for an understanding of the causal relationships involved. Only scientistic puritans will choose to disregard the tangled lines of causal interconnections on the ground that nonquantifiable and nonmeasurable entities and forces do not merit their attention. Of course, the absence of quantifiable variables makes the analysis largely speculative and some of the findings nontestable. Most researchers have selected a somewhat amorphous variable, supposed to comprise many

---

[9] The reference to father, instead of parent, is merely designed to carry on the allusion to the title of Clarence Shepard Day's famous humorous essays on "Life with Father," later made into a successful comedy.

of the diverse influences under the heading "parents' socioeconomic status" (SES). For this composite variable they have accepted empirical and quantifiable proxies, such as father's income (dollars), father's education (years of formal schooling, degrees), father's occupation (assigned points for rated prestige), mother's education, and so on. The composite SES variable has been admitted as a factor in a production function of earnings, with regression coefficients estimated along with those for other factors, such as the number of years of school attendance. Of course it is widely recognized that parental influence—moral pressure as well as affluence—may affect, among other things, also the quantity of schooling.

Closely related to the influence of SES upon schooling is the number of siblings. The dominant influence is probably the fact that a given parental income may not support extended schooling for too many children; hence, the more children the less schooling per child. (This will not hold true for very poor and for very rich families.) There is, however, an altogether different influence of the number of siblings upon ability, capacity, and performance: children learn from one another. Younger children profit from the learning experiences of their elder siblings, and the latter learn from teaching the younger. They all may mature faster thanks to the cross-stimulation and the consequent speeding up of cognitive and emotional learning; and the older children in large families learn much earlier to assume responsibilities, which may significantly affect their ability, capacity, and performance. These findings of casual experience are not supported, however, by regression analysis, which in the explanation of earnings has yielded negative signs for the variable "number of siblings." The negative relationship is evidently due to the financial effects of family size, partly on the quantity and quality of schooling that can be afforded, and partly on the different priorities that the budget constraints and other circumstances of a large family impose on the household. (It is not easy to study with an empty stomach or to concentrate on the intellectual development of the children when the main concern is to cope with life.)

A more detailed examination of the strands of influences lumped in SES may be dealt with under the heading of family influences.

Family Influences

In addition to genes, children may receive from their parents care, love, attention, stimulation, instruction, example, prodding, pushing, encouragement, various other environmental comforts (healthy food, cleanliness, domestic peace) and last, not least, money to afford learning experiences of high quality and for extended periods. Pa-

rental influences upon their children's ability, capacity, performance, and, eventually, earnings may also be rather indirect; for example, the existence of siblings and the kind of stimulation and
learning obtained from them may in essential respects be credited
(or charged) to the parents. If there is positive learning from television
watching, the parents may have a role in selecting programs and in
limiting the time spent before the television screen, apart from the
fact that the parents may have bought the equipment. If there is
learning from "pals," the parents' choice of neighborhood, and perhaps also some selectivity in choosing (or excluding) playmates for
the children, may have much to do with the positive or negative
effects of peer-group influences. If there is learning from private
tutors, music teachers, athletic clubs, and so forth, this again may
be the parents' doing, largely associated with their affluence. Finally,
whereas the parents' pushing a child to work harder and to persevere
may be important for developing capacity and improving performance, the parents' "pull" with influential acquaintances and friends
may largely determine the child's first job, and perhaps even promotion, and hence, earnings.

Few, if any, of the relationships just described can be established
by more than casual empiricism. To be sure, some factors in the lines
of influence can be estimated, counted, or measured, for example,
the number of siblings, the possession of television equipment, the
hours of television watching and the selection of educational programs, the employment of private tutors and music teachers, but all
these are only accessories to the real factors. The intermediate products to which the factors contribute—ability, capacity, and performance—cannot be measured at all, except indirectly by very imperfect
and unreliable proxies. Researchers, however, have tried to find
regression coefficients for all sorts of influences upon mental abilities
and earnings.[10]

[10] In the next chapter several models of "production functions" connecting various
"inputs" with earnings will be compared. For the benefit of the impatient, a few
examples may be presented here.

Otis Dudley Duncan selected six variables for inclusion in a model explaining
earnings and occupation of "white men 25 to 34 years old in the contemporary United
States." Three of these variables represented aspects of family background: number
of siblings, father's education, and father's occupation. These variables, together with
"early intelligence," influence the individuals' occupation and earnings both directly
and indirectly. The indirect influences are those operating through two dependent
variables, education and "later intelligence." A "path diagram" shows the directions
of influences and states the "path coefficients." It is interesting that some of the highest
coefficients come from outside the model, from unspecified factors. Otis Dudley Duncan, "Ability and Achievement," *Eugenics Quarterly*, Vol. 15 (March 1968), pp. 1-
11.

The apparent strength of family influences on the child's education, particularly on the quality and duration of formal schooling, raises problems for the estimation of the effect of schooling upon earnings. If earnings are regressed on family influences—say, parents' income, occupation, and education—as well as on the earner's own schooling, will not the estimate of the contribution of the earner's schooling be unduly reduced? If we had separate measurements of initial, intermediate, and final abilities and capacities, and were able to estimate the *direct* influences of family variables upon earnings (*after* having obtained a postschool performance measure), we might be able to see also the *indirect* paths from variables to earnings. The difficulty, however, with such a causal-sequence model is that the actual operation of family influence is very different—even quite apart from prenatal care—at different stages of the child's or youth's development.

Let us try to visualize how these family influences may work at different stages, always assuming a family of means sufficient to afford the time and money required for providing the strongest possible positive support for the growing individual's intellectual and emotional development. Family influence on the preschool child is exercised chiefly through play and talk to provide cognitive stimulation and emotional security, and to cultivate curiosity, responsiveness, interests, truthfulness, a sense of fairness, and so forth. Family influence on the child of primary-school age is exercised mainly through a show of interest in the child's progress at school, with some supervision of his homework, through discussions at the breakfast and dinner table, development of reading habits, civilized manners, and moral precepts, and, of course, through plenty of affective support. The youngster at the secondary-school level can gain

---

Ingemar Fägerlind, a Swedish author, charted a similar array of paths from father's education, socioeconomic status, and number of siblings to the preschool ability and to the schooling (duration and type) of a group of Swedish children who were 10 years old in 1938. These two dependent variables together affect postschool ability and earnings. Ingemar Fägerlind, *Formal Education and Adult Earnings* (Stockholm: Almqvist & Wiksell, 1975).

A study by William Sewell and Robert Hauser, using data collected for a 1957 cohort of high-school seniors in Wisconsin, undertook "to chart the complex process by which one's social origins influence one's capacities and achievements in education, occupational, and economic spheres." Among the independent variables were father's education, father's occupation, and parental income, determining, directly and indirectly, education and mental ability, which, in turn, determined occupations and annual earnings a few years after school. William H. Sewell and Robert M. Hauser, *Education, Occupation, and Earnings: Achievement in the Early Career* (New York: Academic Press, 1975). — This study and also Fägerlind's are carefully and lucidly reviewed by Mary Jean Bowman, *Proceedings of the National Academy of Education* (Washington, D.C., 1976), pp. 221-292.

most from family influence through a sharing of interests by parents and siblings in activities complementary with and supplementary to academic learning, through their sympathetic understanding of the youngster's academic, social, and personal problems, through involvement, perhaps with special tutors, in literature, music, fine arts, and the performing arts, through tactful involvement in the choice of companions and friends, and through the avoidance of unhealthy habits such as smoking, or use of drugs, partly by firm though well-explained constraints, but mainly by good example.

Family influences on the adolescent or young adult ordinarily become weaker, but where parents and siblings have gained the love and/or respect of the maturing person, the influence may remain quite strong. Students on the tertiary level and, later, investors in self-improvement through postschool and in-service training may still be motivated by the thought of their parents' approval of their decisions and may be aided by their actual advice and perhaps also financial support. What conclusion can the analyst draw when he realizes the constantly changing character of the operation of "family influence"? Can he be satisfied with regressing earnings on the socioeconomic status of the family? Perhaps this is all he can do if he is intent on obtaining quantitative findings. Models designed for numerical estimates cannot be so rich in content as models depicting causal relationships among nonquantitative variables and, hence, not yielding numerical estimates.

Cross-Influences and Recursive Dependences

Analysts who speak of interdependence between two variables, say, A and B, mean that the magnitude of A at the time t is influenced by the magnitude of B at the time $t - 1$, and influences the magnitude that B will reach at the time $t + 1$; similarly, the magnitude of B at the time t is influenced by the magnitude of A at the time $t - 1$, and influences the magnitude that A will reach at the time $t + 1$. Thus, A_t and B_t are, strictly speaking, independent of each other. A recursive system, or causal-chain model, with lagged variables may show the causal relationships in an unambiguous way.[11]

In a stream of contributions to the study of teaching and learning

[11] For methodological analyses of multirelational models, causal-chain models, and interdependent systems see Herman Wold, "A Generalization of Causal Chain Models," *Econometrica*, Vol. 28 (April 1960), pp. 443-463; also "Forecasting by the Chain Principle," in Murray Rosenblatt, *Time Series Analysis Symposium* (New York: Wiley, 1963), pp. 471-497; and "Toward a Verdict on Macroeconomic Simultaneous Equations," in *Semaine d'étude sur le rôle de l'analyse économétrique dans la formulation de plans de développement* (Rome: Pontificiae Academiae Scientiarum Scripta Varia, No. 28, 1965), pp. 115-185.

economics at various levels of schooling, researchers have focused on the relationship between achievement and attitude. One team of researchers reported that "as students learn more economics, they tend to like it more, and the more they like it, the more they learn."[12] This conclusion can surely be extended to virtually all academic subjects. Correlation analysis is sometimes employed to test the interdependence between achievement and attitude by measuring the learning of a subject by achievement tests, and the students' liking of it by their answers in questionnaires or interviews. A high correlation coefficient, however, does not prove the existence of a causal relation, let alone the direction of causation or the existence of a causal interdependence. A causal chain model on the other hand, showing how achievement tested at t_1 will influence attitude at t_2, and how attitude at t_1 will influence achievement at t_2, and similarly in subsequent points of time, can "confirm" the assertion of the cross-influences, or at least increase our confidence in it.

To elucidate the operation of cross-influences over time, let us construct a model with only four variables: achievement, attitude, family influence, and time and effort devoted to learning. Assuming that (1) achievement affects attitude, (2) attitude and family influence jointly determine time and effort devoted to learning, (3) time and effort devoted to learning act upon achievement as well as attitude, and (4) family influence affects attitude also directly, we obtain the model depicted in the following figure, in which all lines represent connections from causes (left) to effects (right). Empirical proxies can be found and recruited for the variables in this model, though some can be quantified only with considerable strain to our imagination. Achievement—the proxy, not the theoretical construct—is "measured" by test scores; attitude is rated by a scale applied to replies in questionnaires; time and effort can be estimated by reported hours of study adjusted by an intensity index still to be devised by ingenious psychologists; and family influence has to be represented by still-to-be-discovered proxies. The usual proxy, the socioeconomic status (SES) of the parents, is not really indicative of actual family influences on the student's input to the learning process. As I said before, positive family influences appropriate at various stages of the child's or student's education differ in form and substance, and the parents' income, education, and occupation are poor empirical proxies for their ability to exercise the influences likely to be effective at their youngsters' levels of education and maturation.

[12] David E. Ramsett, Jerry D. Johnson, and Curtis Adams, "Some Evidence of the Value of Instructors in Teaching Economic Principles," *Journal of Economic Education*, Vol. 5 (Fall 1973), p. 60.

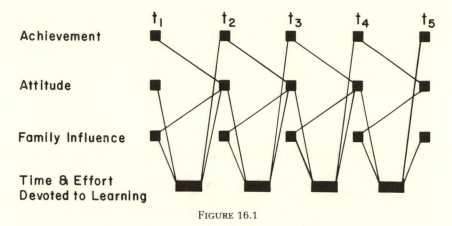

FIGURE 16.1

I have presented this model primarily to chart a possible process of complex interactions of possibly relevant factors over time. I have not myself attempted an empirical study of this sort, nor do I know whether it would be feasible and worthwhile. If this kind of study were to be undertaken, it should be made with unchanged cohorts of persons standardized by various criteria and observed from pre-school age to the end of their educational careers. The intervals between t_1, t_2, t_3, etc., could be as short as one year and should not be longer than three or four years. Achievement and attitude would be predetermined (given) only at the start but would be dependent variables thereafter. Family influence, an independent variable throughout, should be specified by particular activities or attitudes of parents (and siblings), not just by indexes of affluence and background. Some of the researchers who have regressed earnings on SES are satisfied to have proved that, as a rule, it is advantageous to have rich and well-educated parents. This has not been denied by any reasonable analyst of personal income distribution, but some of them, including me, would find it important if it could be shown exactly what kinds of family influence have contributed most to success in study and career.

Other Causal-Chain Models

In the causal-chain model shown in the preceding section, achievement and attitude were used as variables because many researchers have trusted the reliability of the chosen proxies for these links in the chain. I am not so sure that equally trustworthy proxies are available for ability and capacity. As a matter of fact, in models in which *mental ability* has been specified as an explanatory variable for performance or earnings, virtually the same kind of test scores cast in the role of operational proxy for achievement was made to stand in for mental ability. Intelligence tests and aptitude tests are not really different from achievement tests. I have preferred to split intelligence into mathematical ability, verbal ability, and alertness but have not examined what empirical referents could appropriately serve as proxies for these qualities. Test scores, it is agreed, cannot without reservation be accepted as measures of ability. However, as long as we cannot have anything better than test scores as empirical proxies for ability, we have to resign ourselves to what we can get.

Matters are even worse with regard to *capacity*. I have proposed discipline, interest, ambition, diligence, and perseverance as requisites to be conjoined with ability as components for capacity. Yet, I have not been able to come up with quantitative measures or proxies either for any of the parts or for the whole.

The absence of empirical counterparts of theoretical concepts should not prevent us from building abstract models elucidating suspected causal relationships among these concepts. For the sake of simplicity I confine myself to three variables: ability, discipline and ambition (standing also for interest, diligence, and perseverance), and learning experiences. I propose the following four relationships: (1) ability (at the beginning of the stage) affects learning, (2) discipline and ambition (at the beginning of the stage) affect learning, (3) additional learning experiences affect ability (reached at the end of the stage), and (4) learning experiences affect discipline and ambition. The causal-chain model is shown below, with all lines running from the left (causes) to the right (effects):

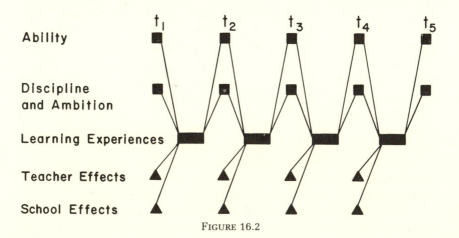

FIGURE 16.2

The model provides also for two exogenous influences upon learning experiences at each stage: teacher effects and school effects. Teacher effects, undoubtedly, depend on the qualities of the teachers, on their techniques, and on their dedication. School effects are attributable to the environmental qualities of the school, including its physical condition and location, its physical facilities and educational programs, but chiefly to its intellectual and moral atmosphere (friendliness versus violence, teams versus gangs, honesty versus cheating, healthful sports versus drug culture, etc.).

Why has capacity been omitted from this model as a separate intervening variable? Remembering that capacity is a composite of "ability" and "discipline and ambition" (and other attitudinal components), I realized that school experiences may have partly positive and partly negative effects upon abilities and attitudes. These separate influences might be overlooked if we were to show only the net contributions of learning experiences, or rather of "schooling" (teacher effects and school effects), upon capacity. Even the concepts "ability" and "discipline and ambition" should not be taken literally. We know that mathematical ability and verbal ability are not necessarily associated or correlated with each other, and hence we should understand that it may be difficult to express properly the results of a combination of excellent teaching of verbal skills and atrocious teaching of mathematical comprehension; if mathematical ability deteriorates while verbal ability improves, the net effect on a composite "ability" is doubtful. It is by no means unlikely that "school effects" (especially those connected with compulsory schooling) lead to a deterioration of some youngsters' discipline and ambition, at least at some stages in their educational careers.

The meaning of "learning experience" as a variable in the causal chain is arcane. In the earlier model I used a variable designated "time and effort devoted to learning," which was less ambiguous and more easily accoutered with an empirical proxy. Now I want the learning variable to include not only the student input but also the teacher input and the school input. The student input is, after the "initial" stage, determined by several dependent variables, especially ability, discipline, and ambition, all developed by a series of consecutive learning experiences; the teacher input and the school input, however, are seen as exogenous factors. In some studies of the learning process, researchers have identified sets of empirical data that they regarded as eligible proxies for the theoretical constructs of teacher input and school input in the production function of enhanced student capacity. I have seen very few studies, however, in which differences in the qualities of teaching were given much attention or weight.[13] Most of us know that we have learned a great deal from some exceptional teachers and hardly anything from others. Thus, casual empiricism—impressions—would make us think that teacher effects weigh heavily in the process. Yet, conclusive evidence is lacking, and a few studies have strongly suggested that teacher effects are not of significant magnitude.[14] One hypothesis posits that students, especially at higher levels, compensate for differences in the teachers' relative effectiveness by studying harder when the teacher is bad, and by skimping on reading for courses in which the good teacher makes everything perfectly clear.[15]

School Effects, Teacher Effects, and Learning Experiences

In discussing the teacher effects upon students' learning, I should not give the impression that these effects are the same for all kinds of students. The same "teacher inputs" may have large or small effects on students with different aptitudes or different attitudes; and

[13] The same complaint about the scarcity of studies of the effects of the quality of teaching is being made by Eric A. Hanushek, "Conceptual and Empirical Issues in the Estimation of Educational Production Functions," *Journal of Human Resources*, Vol. 14 (Summer 1979), p. 356. A brave and illuminating attempt to examine some elementary facts regarding teacher quality—not teaching quality—was made by Anita A. Summers and Barbara L. Wolfe, "Intradistrict Distribution of School Inputs to the Disadvantaged: Evidence for the Courts," *Journal of Human Resources*, Vol. 11 (Summer 1976), pp. 328-342. They found that, in conformance with the intention of school programs to compensate for disadvantages of poor, mainly black, children, "instructional salary cost per pupil" was higher in schools with more disadvantaged pupils, but that "the individual qualities of teachers" were lower, with "counter-compensatory" results (p. 338). The additional outlay was for smaller class size and other school inputs but not for better teachers; the teachers were less qualified, that is, less prepared, less experienced.

[14] One possible explanation of the finding that teacher effects are insignificant may be that the teacher's performance, technique, or choice of emphasis may be "optimal for some students" but "detrimental to the achievement of others," so that the positive effects on some students may be offset by roughly equal negative effects on others. W. Lee Hansen, Allen C. Kelley, and Burton A. Weisbrod, "Economic Efficiency and the Distribution of Benefits from College Instruction," *American Economic Review*, Vol. 60 (Suppl. May 1970), pp. 364-369, esp. pp. 366-367; also, Wilbert J. McKeachie, "Research on Teaching at the College and University Level," in Nathaniel L. Gage, ed., *Handbook of Research on Teaching* (Chicago: Rand McNally, 1963), p. 1157. These propositions apply equally to students on the secondary level.

[15] Fritz Machlup, "Poor Learning from Good Teachers," *Academe*, [Bulletin of the American Association of University Professors], Vol. 65 (October 1979), pp. 376-380. My hypothesis regarding students' highly selective allocation of time is supported by other inquiries." . . . the student is viewed as a utility maximizer making choices at the margin between allocating his time among the course in question, all other courses, and leisure. . . ." Allen C. Kelley, "The Student as a Utility Maximizer," *The Journal of Economic Education*, Vol. 6 (Spring 1975), p. 82.

the effects may be positive on some kinds of students, but negative on others.[16]

In the previous chapter I stated that, in general, schooling helps the abler students more than the less able. Although I qualified this statement then, I should qualify it now in greater detail. The statement is most likely to hold true if the selection of the materials taught and the teaching methods employed are in accord with the successively rising level of the students' intellectual achievements. However, if less able students fall behind and teachers (or school systems) slow down in order to avoid "losing" the stragglers, the abler students will be held back by their unsatisfactory learning experiences. Teaching is often pitched to the level of the students whose improvement is regarded as the most important. If the teaching is pitched to average abilities and average attitudes, it may harm both the ablest and the least able; the ablest may become bored and stop learning, and the least able may become resistant and intractable. One hopes that the percentage of students at the tails of the distribution curve may be small enough for an overwhelming majority to gain in the process. Where, however, the dispersion in the distribution of abilities and attitudes is very wide—which is particularly likely in groups beyond ages 14 or 15—the percentage of students in danger of being harmed by inappropriate learning experiences may be uncomfortably large.[17]

Several well-known research undertakings have come out with findings suggesting that school effects are relatively small.[18] The

---

[16] In an interesting study on schooling and earnings of "low achievers" (that is, the lower percentiles in an achievement test administered by the U.S. Air Force) the analysts made the point that attending school does not imply learning when the students' attitudes are adverse to learning. If school attendance is at the expense of training on the job, it may actually reduce the eventual earning power of the unwilling students. W. Lee Hansen, Burton A. Weisbrod, and William J. Scanlon, "Schooling and Earnings of Low Achievers," American Economic Review, Vol. 60 (June 1970), pp. 414 and 417. See also W. Lee Hansen, "Income Distribution Effects of Higher Education," American Economic Review, Vol. 60 (Suppl. May 1970), p. 339.

[17] If this statement is taken as an argument in support of "tracking," it will probably be unpopular with many readers. Tracking is opposed by most educationists because it may discourage slower learners.

[18] "The first finding is that the schools are remarkably similar in the way they relate to the achievement of their pupils when the socioeconomic background of the students is taken into account. It is known that socioeconomic factors bear a strong relation to academic achievement. When these factors are statistically controlled, however, it appears that differences between schools account for only a small fraction of differences in pupil achievement." James S. Coleman; Ernest Q. Campbell; et al., Equality of Educational Opportunity (Washington, D.C.: U.S. Department of Health, Education, and Welfare, Office of Education, 1966), p. 21. In this "Coleman Report," school effects are understood to include teacher effects. This merger is understandable because in

characteristics of schools examined in an attempt to identify the
sources of differences in average achievements—test scores of their
students—have been divided into four categories: physical facilities,
programs, student body, and teachers. Quantifiable indicators had
to be chosen for all these characteristics in order to "explain" findings of numerical variances; these indicators, of course, had to be
plausible counterparts of theoretical variables in a hypothetical relationship between qualities of schooling provided and of learning
achieved.

Indicators of the quality of physical facilities have included the
existence of a cafeteria, a gymnasium, an infirmary, a school library,
the number of books per student, the existence of physics, chemistry,
and language laboratories, the number of students in the classroom,
and so forth. The descriptions of educational programs have included
both academic courses and extracurricular activities (debating teams,
student newspapers), the provision of a college-preparatory curriculum and of an accelerated curriculum, regular intelligence testing,
remedial reading instruction, and so on. The quality of the student
body—conceivably a very significant influence on the individual's
intellectual progress—has been rated by such numerical criteria as
the numbers of classmates in whose homes an encyclopaedia was
available, of classmates whose mothers had completed high school,
of classmates enrolled in the college-preparatory curriculum, and of
classmates taking physics and foreign languages. Finally, the quality

---

a large survey it is not possible to go into all the details that would be needed for an
analysis of teacher effects alone. After all, most schools have too many teachers to
allow the empirical researcher to isolate the students' learning experiences derived
from different teachers.

Later researchers have been able to obtain data that allowed some of the crucial
disaggregations. Thus, Summers and Wolfe succeeded in identifying the teachers each
student in the Philadelphia School District had over a three-year period; all teachers
were rated according to their training—whether they had earned B.A. degrees from
good colleges or from colleges with lower standing—and the length of their teaching
experience. The personal characteristics and family backgrounds of all students were
also included as independent variables (sometimes interacting variables). With such
degrees of disaggregation, school effects and teachers effects, previously concealed
by noisy aggregated data, are uncovered. Anita A. Summers and Barbara L. Wolfe,
"Do Schools Make a Difference?" American Economic Review, Vol. 67 (September
1977), pp. 639-652. — One of their findings is particularly interesting: Confirming the
results obtained by other researchers (including Coleman, Hanushek, Murnane) the
regression coefficients show "teacher experience" to be unimportant, at least after the
first three years on the job; however, the poorest students, poor in achievement as
well as background, have gained most from inexperienced teachers. Summers and
Wolfe suggest that this positive teacher-effect may be attributed to the enthusiasm
and idealism of novice teachers, still filled with optimistic expectations regarding
their mission. (More on this study will be said in Chapter 17.)

of the teaching staff has been described numerically by the teachers' own schooling and the schooling of their mothers, the years of their teaching experience, their salaries, their ratings in vocabulary tests, their past movements (geographic changes of residence) and their mobility (preparedness to take a job elsewhere). One may doubt the relevance of some of the chosen indicators for judging the quality and effectiveness of the teaching services rendered and the learning experiences provided, but, by and large, researchers have shown much ingenuity in seeking empirical proxies for abstract (nonobservable) factors of possible (though never certain) significance for the outcome, that is, for "measured" improvements in the students' performance.[19]

Schoolmate Effects as Extensions of Family Influences

That the same school inputs, including teacher inputs, may have different effects on different students has been corroborated by a seemingly paradoxical, and heatedly debated, conclusion of the inquiry into *Equality of Educational Opportunity*. The inquiry's conclusion—that school does not matter much, if at all, and, thus, that differences in the quality of schooling cannot be found to be responsible for differences in students' achievements—was qualified as applying only to the student population as a whole and to the white majority of students, but not to minority students. It follows that, if a majority student from a good school and a minority student from a poor school trade places, the latter will benefit much more than the former will suffer in his prospects of getting a good education.[20] This conclusion has been used as a strong argument for "integration," in the sense of getting a better racial balance in the composition of the student bodies at public schools. The chief means was to be bus transportation of students to schools located at greater distance from the students' homes. (The argument was countered by the observation that many families objecting to such schemes would

[19] All examples of possible indicators were taken from the Coleman Report cited above. Later research, however, has treated some of the variables differently and has yielded quite different findings, depending in part on higher degrees of disaggregation, for example, regarding school-specific, classroom-specific, and student-specific factors. See the sources cited on preceding pages.

[20] "Thus, if a white pupil from a home that is strongly and effectively supportive of education is put in a school where most pupils do not come from such homes, his achievement will be little different than if he were in a school composed of others like himself. But if a minority pupil from a home without much educational strength is put with schoolmates with strong educational background, his achievement is likely to increase." Coleman Report, p. 22.

"opt out" by moving away from the school districts affected by such measures.)

The preceding discussion should have made it clear that it is misleading to combine into a single variable, called "school resources," the quality of the student body, physical school facilities, educational programs, and the background of the teachers. If it is true that minority students, or students from poorer homes, can benefit from being associated with majority students or, more correctly, with students with more fortunate "home resources" or family influences, it follows that any careful analysis requires separation of the "schoolmate and playmate effects" from other school effects. Since the schoolmate effects are due to associations with fellow students who have had the benefit of more fortunate family influences, they can be interpreted as being an "extension" of, or derived from, the schoolmates' family influences. In other words, family influences, which explain some of the differences in student achievement, might be credited not only for what they do for the children from well-endowed homes, but also for what they do for the schoolmates and playmates of these children. If these remote effects of family resources are substantial, they can actually reduce the differences in student achievements within the same school.

To the extent that the effects of family influences can be "measured" (estimated) by achievement-test scores regressed on some such proxy as the socioeconomic status (SES) of the parents, they will be visible in comparisons of students both within the same school and between different schools. The indirect effects of these family influences on the underprivileged classmates of the fortunate children of parents with high SES cannot be shown within the same school but only by comparing schools with student bodies of different "quality" (composition).[21]

The comparative effects of school and of family influences on students' achievement-test scores can best be seen after periods in which schools were closed. One study in New York City attempted to compare rates of progress during the school year and during the summer vacation. "In some cases children's scores actually drop over

---

[21] Coleman, in a book published in 1971, found that the data for verbal achievement of 12th grade students showed "the considerably greater strength of family variations than of school variations in determining student achievement, even though the tests are designed to measure exactly those things the schools are designed to teach. They show as well the importance of the community of other children in which the child finds himself, particularly among Negro students. The combined importance of family and student body resources is far larger than the importance of either school facilities or teacher resources." James S. Coleman, *Resources for Social Change: Race in the United States* (New York: Wiley, 1971), p. 45.

the summer."[22] The study concluded that "only half the achievement gap between black and white children in New York City was attributable to differential growth during the school year. The other half was explained by differential growth over the summer."[23] In general, "variations in what children learn in school depend largely on variations in what they bring to school, not on variations in what schools offer them."[24]

Causal Connections and Empirical Testing

Several times in these discussions I have indicated that some of the most important causal connections cannot be empirically tested, chiefly because the strategic variables cannot be measured, estimated, quantified, or even observed. Sticking slavishly to the dogma that "science is measurement," some researchers have attempted to find semiacceptable empirical proxies for nonobservables or, where this was clearly impossible, to substitute for strategic causal connections some peripheral or even trivial connections if only they can be tested by some coefficients of correlation, determination, or regression.

A researcher has recently summarized the "experience of empirical estimation of educational production functions to date." We look in vain, in that summary, for an empirical test of any connections that would include a variable representing a magnitude standing for human capital or anything closely related to it. This is not surprising, since the attempted estimates of stocks of human capital or accummulated knowledge—which surely are parts of a reasonable educational production function—cannot pass the strict requirements of rigorous "testmasters." Yet, can we be proud of the achievements of rigorous testing in this field of inquiry? Here is a list of the findings enumerated in the summary:

> First, variations in cognitive achievements are highly correlated with variations in home background variables. . . .
> However, . . . one may be unable to separate the effect of

[22] Christopher Jencks et al., *Inequality*, p. 87. — This finding was confirmed by Murnane: "During the summer months . . . math achievement declined by an amount approximately equal to half of the gain made during the school year." Richard J. Murnane, *The Impact of School Resources on the Learning of Inner City Children* (Cambridge, Mass.: Ballinger, 1975), p. 88.

[23] Jencks, *Inequality*, p. 87. To Jencks, "these findings imply that if all elementary schools were closed down, so that growing up became an endless summer, white middle-class children might still learn much of what they now learn."

[24] Ibid., p. 53. Jencks does not contend that the differences in what the children "bring to school" derive from "genetic inequality"; variations in family influences may be the chief factor.

the home learning environment from the effect of student
innate ability.

Second, there is no consistent relationship between cognitive achievement and class size.

Third, there is no consistent relationship between cognitive
achievement and various dimensions of teacher quality.

Fourth, there is no consistent relationship between cognitive achievement and teacher attitudes.

Fifth, student *time inputs* are important determinants of
cognitive achievement.

Sixth, student attitude variables include expected achievement, degree of interest, and self-estimate.[25]

The quoted surveyor of these findings admits that they are not
startling. He concludes, however, with this statement: "The only
relatively new addition is perhaps the observed importance of student time inputs in educational production, for which a substantial
amount of evidence has been accumulated over the past few years."[26]
I wonder who needed this evidence; and I am embarrassed when
time and money is spent to collect numerical evidence for something
so obvious, so well known, and never doubted by anybody since
Homo sapiens had his first learning experience. On the other hand,
"there is value in documenting the obvious, since the obvious is so
frequently untrue."[27]

Improvement of Capacity as Formation of Capital

We have come a long way in our discussion of improvements of
human capacity that merit the designation "formation of capital."
The flow of thought may have been straightforward at some places
and meandering at others but, by and large, it has been rather smooth.
Yet, we have come to some special topics that seem to have little
bearing on the main subject, accumulation of knowledge as investment in human capital. Have we perhaps lost our way?

I believe we have not deviated far from the main road. To be sure,
the controversy about busing students to more distant schools in
order to achieve racial integration looks like a rather extraneous
issue. Still, the connection with the central issue can hardly be overlooked if one sees in enforced integration of previously segregated

[25] Lawrence J. Lau, "Educational Production Functions," in Douglas M. Windham,
ed., *Economic Dimensions of Education* (Washington, D.C.: National Academy of
Education, 1979), pp. 41-43. (Emphasis in the original.)

[26] Ibid., p. 43.

[27] The quoted statement is from a letter from Mark Blaug, dated 1 September 1980,
taking me to task for my disrespect for empirical testing of presumably obvious propositions.

schools a step to improve the learning and earning capacity of large groups of people. Such an observation does not involve us in a political controversy; one need not side either with the advocates or with the opponents of government measures intended to help enforce racial integration; the point is merely to explain why the discussion has been pertinent in the context of this chapter.

Not all expenditures for education in general, or for public schooling in particular, are in themselves formation of human capital. Expenditures are regarded as investments only if they are expected to yield a positive return.[28] Hence, human capital is increased only by means of expenditures that promise to improve capacity to an extent sufficient for the additional gross returns to pay for the investment at its full opportunity cost, that is, to compensate for the alternatives that have to be foregone for the sake of the particular investment. In order to make sound judgments about performance-improving investments, it is necessary to understand the causal connections between abilities, attitudes, capacities, performances, and earnings. This chapter was written in the hope that it may contribute to that objective.

[28] A friendly reader advised me that the sentence about expenditures that may not qualify as investments needs elaboration: (a) Avoidance of damage, injury, or loss counts as positive return; hence expenditures for infirmaries, first-aid kits, fire extinguishers, burglar alarms, and other devices, installations, or operations to avert other probable dangers constitute investments. (b) Nothing in the real world is ever perfect and every large investment program includes some waste through inefficiency, negligence, stupidity, and perhaps even fraudulence; within limits such waste is par for the course and counts as a normal part of the cost of the investment. (c) Investment decisions are often group decisions, with the majority in the group convinced of the promise of satisfactory returns and outvoting or persuading those who may have hesitated or opposed the project; even if the pessimists eventually prove right, the investment was still undertaken in the honest expectation that it will bring returns. (d) It would, however, be wrong to conclude from the preceding propositions that any expenditures that its proponents *designate* as investments really *are* investments; when decisions are made to spend other people's money, the decisionmakers sometimes expect personal benefits for themselves (in the form of pecuniary emoluments or in glory, prestige, or political pay-off) while others (stockholders, taxpayers) have to bear the consequences of manifestly uneconomical outlays, one can reasonably deny that these outlays are investments. (Examples: government appropriations for wasteful "river projects" promoted by vote-conscious legislators; industrial construction projects that promise jobs for construction workers but no returns from operations; subsidies for educational programs in vocations where the chances for employment are minimal.) I have said most of this in Chapter 14; some outlays for schooling may be for immediate pleasure, some may be wasteful, and some may be really harmful. Any large educational program may include some items in these categories; if the portions that are unproductive (in the sense that no future returns can be expected from them) are not excessive, the total program will still merit the designation as investment.

CHAPTER 17

PRODUCTION FUNCTIONS:
THE CHOICE OF VARIABLES

IN THE PRECEDING CHAPTER the route from investments to returns was described with special attention to intermediate stops—intervening variables that seem to make the assumed causal connections more plausible. The possibilities of testing these connections empirically and of ascertaining and estimating the strength of various influences supposedly affecting the selected variables were viewed with great skepticism. Such skepticism, however, is out of tune with the econometric fashion of our time. Even if the hypotheses are only tentative, the proposed surrogates for the relevant theoretical constructs rather questionable, the empirical data notoriously unreliable, and the computed coefficients of correlation or regression often inconsistent and never stable over time—the urge to measure overpowers the most serious doubts about the significance of the results of measurement. Perhaps this is as it should be: a critical attitude is the hallmark of a truly scientific spirit but it should not make us stop trying.

In economics, an algebraic function that assembles the major factors assumed to contribute to a given result is called a production function. The present chapter is devoted to discussions of attempts to specify production functions, quantitative relations between inputs and outputs. But just what are the outputs here in question?

The Outputs

The four featured stops on the route from investments to returns were ability, capacity, performance, and earnings. In the language of the production function, the first three stops would be designated as intermediate products in the sequence of "stages of production" leading to the final product, earnings.[1] In principle it is possible to

---

[1] Some readers object to the materialism displayed in a formulation that refers to human ability as an "intermediate product" and to money earnings as a "final product." They are disgusted with the seeming insensitiveness to humanistic, cultural values. I wish to reassure sensitive readers that economics does recognize the existence and importance of intellectual, artistic, and spiritual satisfactions. Admittedly, theoretical analysis and empirical research of production functions are technical and lack humanism as well as entertainment value.

devise production functions for each intermediate product, which subsequently becomes an input in the production function of the next stage. In the sequence of steps in which human capital is produced and used, the specification and estimation of production functions is complicated, conceptually and, still more, operationally. Ability, as we have seen, is difficult to define, and no operational definition has been found that would allow unambiguous measurement. Capacity cannot be measured either, but only "rated" on the basis of arbitrary criteria that leave wide margins for highly subjective judgments. Performance is probably the first of the intermediate outputs that can, in special cases, be operationally defined.

Performance, however, acquires meaning only if the task (duty, action) to be performed is specified. Thousands, or perhaps millions, of different tasks are relevant in the production of earnings; it would be practically impossible to list all these tasks and to ascertain the performance of workers in their execution. Although particular employers may test the performance of their workers or job seekers in tasks relevant to the activities required in their particular production programs, researchers of "performance" can at best select a limited number of typical or characteristic tasks to be performed. General performance tests have been designed, for example, for typists, stenographers, and other occupations that demand standardized skills. In occupations that are subject to public supervision, licensing, certification, or other conditions of admission, examinations in special fields of knowledge (for example, law, accounting, medicine), to test the performance of the applicants in answering some supposedly relevant questions, have been devised. The extent to which performance in such *tests* is a good predictor of performance in the *occupation* the applicant wishes to enter is somewhat problematic. In most instances, the tested performance attests merely that certain minimum standards are being met, and it thus does not even attempt to measure anything closely related to the later performance for which the performer will be paid.

After all that has been said it looks as though we have to give up the idea that performance is a measurable output entering as an input in the production of earnings. In order to save the theoretical model as a basis for operational research we have to retreat to a more modest concept of performance: success in achievement tests related to school learning, verbal (vocabulary, grammar, reading, composition, etc.), quantitative (computation, algebra, geometry, etc.), or mastery of special subjects (physics, biology, economics, literature, etc.). To repeat what I said in earlier chapters, these tests, though sometimes called aptitude tests or even ability tests ("verbal ability," "reading ability," "mathematical ability"), are all nothing but achievement tests, where achievement is measured by performance on a particular examination or sequence of examinations.

Before we say more about school achievement, we should mention the possibility of another intermediate output on the way to earnings, the final product, or perhaps a byproduct of the final product. This intermediate output or byproduct, featured in some sociological models, is "occupational rank." The idea that occupational rank be considered an output of education, separate from earnings is perhaps associated with an observation of particular appeal to sociologists, namely, that some of the highest achievers in school and higher education do not become the recipients of the highest incomes. They prefer to enter professions paying less in money than in public prestige or in personal satisfaction, or those perhaps appealing to persons imbued with a sense of ethical mission and civic service. These persons in "high occupational ranks" with "high social status" are probably the scholars and scientists, the researchers and teachers on tertiary and sometimes secondary levels of education, the judges, the ministers of the church, and other respected professionals. They are not in the highest income brackets, indeed they earn much less than the business managers in large industrial or financial corporations. Rank correlations between academic achievement and occupational earnings would therefore "fail": hence, the analysts' desire to have "occupational rank" regarded as an output of the education system.

The recognition of earnings as the final output is in conformance with the economist's notion of returns to investments. It is, in a sense, the only production function that fits in with the theory of human capital. Costs, inclusive of earnings foregone, are to be compared with benefits or earnings attributable to the incurrence of these costs. This production function is not as simple as it may sound; on the cost side the estimates of earnings foregone complicate matters, and, on the benefit side the question of what portions of the earnings are really attributable to the educational investment is a major predicament.

Educational Production Functions

I have promised to say more about school achievement as output of educational and related inputs. Some twenty-five or thirty years ago very little could have been said about this subject, because the "educational production function" is a relatively recent subject of systematic research. It has become a rapidly growing specialty with researchers from several fields: psychology, sociology, education, and economics.

A survey of the major educational input-output studies, presented in 1975 by Elchanan Cohn,[2] reported on twenty-three studies completed between 1956 and 1975. Almost all of these studies—twenty-one of the twenty-three—took scores on achievement tests as the measure of output.[3] In a few exceptional instances the measure of output included some other indicators, such as "school holding power," that is, the percentage of students continuing their schooling, or the students' attitudes, educational plans, and expectations. The following "school inputs" were listed: school size, staff size, class size, classroom atmosphere, student-teacher ratio, instructional expenditures, instructional expenditures per student, number of instructional assignments per teacher, teachers' experience, teachers' salaries, teachers' degree level, teachers' verbal ability, teacher turnover, teachers' job satisfaction, teachers' race, quality of teachers' college, administrators' salaries, number of library books, science laboratory facilities, specific vocational courses, age of school building, students' attendance record, percentage of transferring students. The number of these different inputs of "school-service components" used as independent variables in any one analysis of educational production varied from one to eleven, with four variables as the mode. Fifteen of the studies employed multiple-regression analysis (eleven with a single equation, four with simultaneous equations); six employed correlation analysis, and two, factor analysis. (The major differences among these techniques will be briefly described later in this chapter.)

Another survey of educational production functions, presented by Richard Murnane, also in 1975, reported on only nine of the research undertakings included in Cohn's survey but described them in greater detail and with helpful comments about the techniques employed.[4] Murnane's observations on the studies by Eric Hanushek and Martin Katzman are especially instructive.[5] Before reporting on his own research, which is based on a variety of models individually designed

[2] Elchanan Cohn, *Input-Output Analysis in Public Education* (Cambridge, Mass.: Ballinger, 1975), pp. 29-49.

[3] Cohn is fully aware that achievement tests cannot be satisfactory substitutes or proxies for the "relevant outputs" of the educational process. He lists five categories of output: basic skills, vocational skills, creativity, attitudes, and "other outputs" (among these are intellectual and artistic "consumption benefits"). Ibid., pp. 22-24. These passages are reproduced in Cohn's textbook, *The Economics of Education* (Cambridge, Mass.: Ballinger, 1979), pp. 169-171.

[4] Richard J. Murnane, *The Impact of School Resources on the Learning of Inner City Children* (Cambridge, Mass.: Ballinger, 1975), pp. 5-30.

[5] Eric A. Hanushek, *Education and Race* (Lexington, Mass.: Heath, 1972); Martin

to test particular hypotheses, and on data obtained from many different sources, Murnane recites the lessons learned from earlier studies about the effects of schools and teachers on the test achievements of students. These lessons are that (1) "The unit of observation is the individual child." (2) "Longitudinal information on the progress of each child" is needed to focus on the "value added" by different school resources. (3) "Detailed information on individual classroom teachers" has to be "matched to the student data." (4) The children studied should be in stratified samples, that is, separated by race, school system, or other group characteristics if there is any presumption that the effects of school and teacher may be different on different groups. (5) The reliability of the data should be checked and improved by means of interviews with administrators of the schools. (6) Separate samples of children should be analyzed in order to allow "replicability of the research results."[6]

Murnane used, in his models and equations, up to sixteen independent variables. Still larger numbers of variables, assumed to affect student achievement, were used by Anita Summers and Barbara Wolfe in analyzing a rich source of data recorded by the School District of Philadelphia.[7] Their production functions include several variables taken as proxies for teacher quality, school quality, pupil motivation or effort (such as unexcused absences and lateness) and family background. Altogether twenty independent variables are given recognition, or even twenty-nine if "interactions" are taken into account by multiplying one variable by another. (For example, the number of unexcused absences is multiplied by family income.)[8]

Input: Years of Schooling; Output: Annual Earnings

It may come as a shock if I now proceed (or recede) from an educational production function, "explaining" students' test achieve-

T. Katzman, *The Political Economy of Urban Schools* (Cambridge, Mass.: Harvard University Press, 1971).

[6] Murnane, *Impact*, p. 30. — In fairness to several researchers in this area I must not fail to cite the careful review of techniques and conclusions in a volume prepared and published by the Rand Corporation. Harvey A. Averch, Stephen J. Carroll, Theodore S. Donaldson, Herbert J. Kiesling, and John Pincus, *How Effective is Schooling? A Critical Review and Synthesis of Research Findings* (Santa Monica, Cal.: Rand Corp., 1972). — For a more recent survey of the literature, with references to 152 titles, see Eric A. Hanushek, "Conceptual and Empirical Issues in the Estimation of Educational Production Functions," *Journal of Human Resources*, Vol. 14 (Summer 1979), pp. 351-388.

[7] Anita A. Summers and Barbara L. Wolfe, "Intradistrict Distribution of School Inputs to the Disadvantaged: Evidence for the Courts," *Journal of Human Resources*, Vol. 11 (Summer 1976), pp. 328-342; and also "Do Schools Make a Difference?" *American Economic Review*, Vol. 67 (September 1977), pp. 639-652.

[8] Summers and Wolfe, "Schools," p. 643.

ments as the output of up to twenty-nine input variables, to a production function that tries to explain annual earnings of people as the output of a single input variable, the number of years of schooling.

It seems unbelievably simplistic to specify a "production function" with years of schooling as the one and only independent variable and annual earnings as the dependent variable. Yet, many reports do in fact confine themselves to these two statistics, sometimes even without making a distinction between earnings from work and income from all sources. There is no need to express the relations in the form of an algebraic equation; one may group the population of working age according to years of schooling (or according to highest levels of school completed) and show for each group the average annual income per head. There is probably no country in the world in which such comparisons will not show that average incomes are higher for groups with more schooling.

Does this prove that longer schooling "produces" higher incomes? Of course not; several other explanations of the "correlation" are possible. Think, for example, of the hypothesis that social mobility is minimal and economic status is transferred from parents to children, so that rich families stay rich and poor families stay poor. Rich families can afford longer schooling for their children; poor families have to send their children to work as early as possible. The statistical comparison, showing that affluence and length of schooling go together, seems to "confirm" the hypothesis that those with larger incomes can buy, and do buy, more education.

Think of an alternative hypothesis, which explains higher earnings as the result of higher intelligence, greater ambition, and more diligence. The same three "determinants" of earnings determine also people's decisions about the appropriate length of schooling. By this hypothesis it is not the amount of schooling that explains the size of income and it is not the size of income that explains the amount of schooling, but both schooling and incomes are explained by the same variables, not included among the data. Available statistical data are perfectly consistent with the hypothesis.

Although these reflections may seem primitive, it can be instructive to elaborate on the theme.

Do the Data Tell the Story?

The data on average annual earnings of persons with different amounts of schooling leave no doubt that earnings and schooling are positively related: groups with more years of schooling have higher incomes than those with fewer years of schooling. The question of causality, however, is not answered by this observed relation. Although it is possible that the higher earnings are due entirely to improvements of working capacity through longer education, it is also possible that they are due entirely to other factors. Among such factors may be greater ability (either innate or acquired in early years) of those who continue school for more years,[9] or parents' incomes or socioeconomic status, or differences in working morale, diligence, effort, and various attitudes not acquired through additional schooling but predisposing the ambitious to submit to more schooling.

Assume that statistical data show that high-school graduates, or persons with twelve years of schooling, have on the average annual earnings of $14,250, whereas college graduates, or persons with sixteen years of school, have average annual earnings of $17,500. Are the differential earnings of $3,250 attributable to the college education? Does the increment in earnings measure the increase in productive capacity achieved through the added four years of study?

That this need not be the case can be easily understood with the help of a simple argument. Assume that the class of high-school graduates was composed of four groups of equal size with different working and learning capacities and, accordingly, different earnings: persons in Group A make $20,000 a year; in Group B, $15,000; in Group C, $12,000; and in Group D, $10,000. Thus, on the average, the annual income of high-school graduates will be $14,250. Next, assume that only persons of A and B capacity choose to go to college, to study for another four years. It is possible that their working capacities will be further enhanced as a result of the prolonged studies, but for the sake of the argument we assume that college does absolutely nothing for them: it neither increases nor reduces the working capacity, working morale, employability, and earning capacity of the graduates. Thus, persons of the A type will still make, despite the four more years of education, $20,000 a year, and persons of the B type, $15,000. Since no one from the other two groups has chosen to go to college, and the A and B groups are represented by equal numbers, the annual average income of the college graduates will be $17,500. In other words, the income differential of $3,250 is due entirely to the different *composition* of the group of college graduates.

This argument was not designed to deny the possible contribution of a college education to the working and earning capacity of the graduates. It was designed only to show that the record of actual differentials in earnings does not *prove* that additional education

[9] According to data for 1953, the average intelligence quotient, IQ, of college graduates was 120.5, and that of high-school graduates who did not go to college was only 106.8. Dael Wolfle, *America's Resources of Specialized Talent* (New York: Harper, 1954), p. 314.

contributes to earning capacity. The mere fact that the poorest prospects do not go on to college or, more generally, do not continue their education beyond the compulsory minimum, is enough to produce the statistical result that the "better educated" have higher earnings.

The discovery that the higher earnings recorded for persons with more schooling may be just a statistical fallacy—the fallacy of composition—does not give a deathblow to the theory that education creates human capital. The lesson that statistical correlations or regression coefficients do not prove anything should be well known to all; and just as they cannot prove the positive contribution of education to earnings, they cannot disprove it either. Investigators attempting to estimate the effects of schooling have to find a way to assess the influences of a large variety of other factors. The number of variables considered as eligible candidates for inclusion in the production function of earnings is quite large; the data available as possible statistical proxies range from fair to unacceptable or unobtainable; and the techniques employed for unscrambling the various influences are questionable. Attempts at unscrambling have to be made, nevertheless, if we are to say anything at all about the productive contribution of schooling.

Factor Analysis, Multiple Regression Analysis, Path Analysis

Unscrambling the effects of various factors upon a given outcome and estimating their relative contributions to the end result are tasks for which a variety of techniques have been developed. It happens that representatives of different disciplines prefer different techniques. Psychologists seem to favor factor analysis, economists regression analysis, and sociologists path analysis. The study of the effects of schooling and learning is within the domain of all three sciences—psychology, sociology, and economics—and some of those who profess these disciplines have, perhaps with undue delay and reluctance, realized that it may be helpful to understand what their fellow researchers from the other departments have been doing. For purposes of a broad overview we may be satisfied with a general idea of the alternative techniques.

Broadly speaking, the techniques of factor analysis, multiple regression analysis, and path analysis incorporate progressively stronger statements about the (possibly causal) links among variables. Factor analysis is a method of determining common elements among a number of variables from correlation matrices displaying the intercorrelations among variables.[10] It describes only correlation, not causation. Multiple regression is a technique to analyze the relations between a dependent variable and a set of two or more independent variables. Its purposes are said to be "either descriptive or inferential."[11] Path analysis is a particular application of multiple regression, often with the assumption (1) of a weak causal order among the variables, that is, of a likelihood that a change of any of the independent variables can produce a change in the dependent variable, and (2) of a causally closed relationship among the variables. Path analysis includes both direct and indirect causal effects.[12]

These definitions or descriptions may be quite unhelpful; more helpful, perhaps, is an indication of major applications of some of these techniques in the area of our research. Path analysis and simultaneous systems (including multistage regression analysis) are employed where dependent intervening variables are used in a model of complex causal relations that include both direct and indirect influences on the outcome. It is assumed, for example, that parental factors affect an individual's earnings not only directly but also indirectly through influencing the number of years spent at school, the quality of schooling, the ability to learn, the attitudes towards learning and towards performance, and the range of job opportunities. Such complex relationships can be modeled in systems of simultaneous equations. One possible form of such a system would be sets of recursive regression equations, representing a sequence of production functions for intermediate products where each may include the same input variable that joins with other factors in determining the output at two or more intermediate stages and perhaps also the ultimate product.[13] A serious difficulty with the use of regression equations is that they are often thoughtlessly specified in linear form where the theoretical model would call for other specifications.[14] An illustration of such misspecification will be offered later in this chapter.

---

[10] For a relatively simple explanation, see Arthur R. Jensen, *Bias in Mental Testing* (New York: Free Press, 1980), pp. 185-213.

[11] Norman H. Nie, C. Hadlai Hull, Jean G. Jenkins, Karin Steinbrenner, and Dale H. Bent, *Statistical Package for the Social Sciences*, 2d ed. (New York: McGraw-Hill, 1975), pp. 321-324.

[12] Ibid., pp. 383-384. See also Ching C. Li, *Path Analysis: A Primer* (Pacific Grove, Cal.: Boxwood Press, 1975).

[13] Several statements in this subsection may be out of reach of readers not trained in statistics. An attempt to provide brief definitions would not make matters more intelligible; full explanations would take too much space. Readers who do not fully comprehend the statistical comments in the text may be satisfied with a vague idea.

[14] This comment applies to single equations as well as to systems of equations, and also to path analysis.

Wanted: Good Proxies for Nonobservables

All quantitative analysis is hampered by the fact that some of the "casual" factors in a theoretical model have no observable counterpart in the empirical domain and that no measurable proxy can be found; for some other causal factors, acceptable proxies or clues may be conceived but, unfortunately, quite often no data can be obtained.

Think of the combined effects upon the product (earnings) of the number of hours worked, the intensity of the work (effort expended per hour), and the efficiency in using that effort. All three may be related to "education," both as inputs *in the process* of learning— studying for longer hours, with greater intensity (attention, concentration), and more efficiently—and *as effects* of learning—if educational programs have created or increased a love for hard work (more hours of work per week and year and greater effort expended per hour) and also skills and other knowledge making labor more efficient. Hours of work are operational concepts; efficiency per labor hour can be operationally defined if the product is measurable and if efficiency is broadly defined to "fudge" effort and efficient use of effort. Separation of effort expended per hour from efficiency in the use of effort, and imputation of product shares to these two factors, may be possible in mental experiments, but statistical operations with available data cannot yield this kind of information.[15]

These references to efficiency in the use of effort call for still other distinctions: efficiency may be increased through the use of physical tools and other equipment, through the use of skills embodied in the mind and/or body of the worker, or through the use of nonembodied knowledge. All these three efficiency raisers may be the result of the creation and dissemination of knowledge; hence they are pertinent to this study and, particularly, to this discussion on human capital. Whether any methods can be divised to obtain reliable empirical proxies for them and to separate clearly the contributions each has made to the product (earnings) is questionable.

If efficiency in the use of effort—or, more generally, in the use of inputs of labor and physical capital—is regarded as an effect of creation and dissemination of productive knowledge, it is perhaps justifiable to skip this intervening variable and use the accumulated

---

[15] Physical effort can conceivably be measured by advanced physiological devices; mental effort is thus far not measurable, neither through practical nor through conceivably feasible operations. Anyone who has learned improved strokes in swimming knows that he can now swim faster with less effort, thanks to greater efficiency. Anyone who has learned better techniques of mental arithmetic knows that he can now manipulate numbers in his head more speedily with less mental effort, thanks to more efficient mental processes.

stock of "knowledge capital" as an independent variable in a production function. From the theorist's point of view, a serious loss of
explanatory power of the abstract-theoretical model is involved in
the omission of average and incremental efficiency from the causal
chain. After all, not all new knowledge is practical, and not all practical knowledge is productive in the sense of reducing the input-
output ratios in the production of goods and services. Still, the researcher engaged in quantitative-empirical analysis may be glad to
get rid of an inconvenient intervening variable. Of course, stocks of
productive knowledge capital are not observable either, and still less
measurable, but their place in the production function may be taken
by a measurable surrogate, the accumulated cost of past investments
in knowledge. Just as stocks of physical capital may appear as independent variables in a production function, stocks of human capital—workers' knowledge and skills improving their earning capacity
and measured by the cost of their past investments in schooling and
training—may be assigned a place in that function. And for the part
of productive knowledge that is not embodied in either men or machines, the accumulated cost of past investments in research and
development may be appointed and accredited as surrogate of the
stock of nonembodied productive knowledge capital.

With regard to all these stock variables in the explanation of incomes, complicated problems of depreciation arise. Chapter 19 will
be devoted to a thorough discussion of these problems. We want to
concentrate here on the issue of the productive contribution of education.

Isolating the Effects of Schooling

Before all, let us be clear about the difference between schooling
and education; to equate the two is a baneful error. Schooling may
result in learning, but whether it does so depends on several conditions. The student's physical presence in school is surely not a
sufficient condition for his successful learning; but the statistics used
to "measure schooling" do not even report attendance—they merely
signify enrollment. Despite this obvious misreporting, educational
statisticians have succeeded in getting the term "educational attainment" accepted for "number of years enrolled in school." If attainment is to stand for anything near the common meaning of the word,
enrollment in school does not qualify as "attainment," at least not
in school systems that allow quasi-automatic promotion to the next
grade with little regard to genuine educational attainment. The theoretical causal connection is between "school learning" (or "school
education") and earning capacity. School attendance is an opera-

tional proxy for learning, and school enrollment is a proxy for attendance. The honest thing to do would be to replace the phrase educational attainment with "years enrolled in school" or "highest grade completed." The abbreviation "years of schooling" is acceptable with repeated warnings that it must not be confused with actual attendance and, still less, with learning.

Having duly noted that schooling does not necessarily result in learning and education, we should also recall that much education takes place outside school: in the home, in the church, in the army, in everyday life, and especially at work, on the job. Thus, just as not all schooling leads to education, not all education is obtained in school.

Another warning refers to the "product," the dependent variable of the production function: earnings or, more generally, income. Does it stand for actual or for expected income? for income before or after taxes? for income excluding or including receipts of transfer payments (such as unemployment benefits)? for income from all sources or only earnings from labor? for annual earnings from actual hours of work or standardized for full-time employment throughout the year? for earnings collected in cash and paychecks or for earnings adjusted for the value of learning opportunities on the job? for earnings received in a particular year or for an annual average of lifetime earnings or for a lifetime profile of earnings? These are some of the most widely known varieties of the dependent variable of our production function.

Now let us turn to the "independent" variables assumed to combine in determining the product. One may classify them in several categories. The most obvious category is composed of "personal characteristics" of the income earners, with "ability" as the most widely recognized variable. Some appraisers of the effects of schooling have used rough rules of thumb for the strength of influences of personal characteristics. Edward Denison, for example, assumed that two-fifths of the earnings differentials of persons with more schooling were due to their natural ability, energy, and similar personal qualities, whereas three-fifths were a result of their additional schooling.[16] Other analysts have tried to measure native ability and motivation by the student's class ranks and have found that rank accounted for one-fourth of the income differentials.[17] A most original analysis

[16] Edward F. Denison, "Measuring the Contribution of Education," in E[dward] A[ustin] G. Robinson and J[ohn] E. Vaizey, eds., The Economics of Education (London: Macmillan, 1966), p. 207.

[17] Dael Wolfle and Joseph Smith, "The Occupational Value of Education for Superior High-School Graduates," Journal of Higher Education, Vol. 27 (April 1956), pp. 201-213.

was made by Gary Becker.[18] He found samples of persons for whom intelligence quotients (IQ) and grades in primary school were on record, in addition to their incomes, years of schooling, and other data usually furnished by the census. Using the IQs for native ability and the grades in primary school for drive and ambition, Becker extracted the income differential that could with good conscience be attributed to additional years of schooling. (Critics may object to using IQs as proxies for native ability.)

The category of "personal-background variables" includes such factors as ethnic or racial extraction and geographic location, but the most widely researched variables are family influences. These influences have been investigated by sociologists, psychologists, educationists, and economists. (Some of their methods and findings were discussed above in Chapter 16, and additional observations will be made later in the present chapter.) Family influences operate on the individuals' early and later abilities, on the length and quality of their schooling, on their motivation and perseverance, on their choice of occupation, and also directly on their earnings and other incomes. The strength of these influences will vary greatly among different groups, and estimates will vary according to the models chosen by different analysts. The number of family variables available for inclusion is large (the most popular are father's occupation, father's schooling, mother's occupation, mother's schooling, parental income, and number of siblings), and the number of possible combinations is enormous. It is somewhat pretentious to designate these attempts to estimate the effects of all these factors—and, in the process, isolate the effects of the years of schooling—as "measurements"; they are more in the nature of illustrative exercises.

Postschool learning may be seen as a category by itself. Analyses of the effects of "training on the job" are theoretically impressive attempts to disentangle a convoluted web of influences on returns from investment in human self-improvement. (Chapter 20 will include a detailed discussion of the possibility of dissecting the combined effects of school and work experiences.) Jacob Mincer's analysis of job training started with the presumptions that "occupational ranks," determined by average earnings, could be taken as indicators of the amount of training required, and that increases in productivity with increasing work experience are more pronounced in jobs requiring more training.[19] These presumptions were supported by em-

[18] Gary S. Becker, *Human Capital* (New York: Columbia University Press, 1964), pp. 69-113; 2d ed. (1974), pp. 147-190.

[19] Jacob Mincer, "Investment in Human Capital and Personal Income Distribution," *Journal of Political Economy*, Vol. 66 (July-August 1958), pp. 298-301. For references to Mincer's later writings, see footnote 1 of Chapter 20.

pirical studies showing a strong correlation between occupational ranks and dispersion of incomes within each occupation. Still, the empirical basis of the theoretical life profiles of earnings, of investments in learning on the job, of increases in earning capacity due to such learning, and of eventual decreases in earning capacity due to gradual deterioration with age, is not sufficiently firm. In particular, the separation of returns to investment in postschool work from returns to investment in schooling remains speculative.

Researchers find it sometimes expedient for particular purposes to dispense with several of the variables, although they are regarded as significant determinants—for example, personal characteristics and family background—and to focus exclusively on school and postschool experience. In order to compare the "effects" of these two factors on the relative earnings of people of different race (or gender), one must not include race (or gender) as a dummy variable in a regression equation but, instead, run separate regressions for each group.[20] Different regression coefficients for schooling of white and black (or male and female) earners can raise important questions—even if the coefficients do not provide any answers regarding the causes of such differences.

A Parade of Variables and Models

In the preceding section, variables of several categories were mentioned as having been used, together with years of schooling, in functions determining the earnings of individuals. Many of the analysts have arranged the selected factors in a single equation and

---

[20] This was how Christopher Jencks and his associates set up their regression analysis when they studied the effects of race. Christopher Jencks et al., *Who Gets Ahead? The Determinants of Economic Success in America* (New York: Basic Books, 1979), Chap. 7, pp. 191-212. Many earlier researchers had included race or sex (or both) in a single equation as dummy variable(s) along with other variables presumed to explain earnings. Dummy variables affect only the constant term of the regression equation, not the coefficients of the other variables; and thus one does not learn how different are the elasticities of the product with respect to other inputs, such as schooling. Does additional schooling affect earnings *equally* for whites and nonwhites, for women and men, or are the "effects" of longer schooling upon earnings *different* for the different groups? No answer to this important question can be had from a regression equation with race, sex, or both as dummy variables. One wonders why so many researchers impose on their analysis such a naive constraint. Perhaps they are satisfied with a finding about how much "skin color" affects the variances from mean earnings; or perhaps they realize that their sample for nonwhites is too small to yield significant findings. If insufficient sample size is the reason, it would be better to admit the inadequacy of the available data than to proceed with an analysis that implicitly presumes that the effect of schooling upon earnings is the same for members of the different groups.

regressed the dependent variable on each of the independent variables. Others have arranged them in sets of recursive equations to accommodate the hypothesis that some of the factors influence the final product only indirectly through an intermediate product that is an input at another stage of the production process, whereas other factors influence it both directly and indirectly. We can get a useful conspectus of possible variables and arrangements by sketching a few of the many models proposed by researchers on the effects of schooling.[21]

In a model by the sociologist Otis Dudley Duncan, six variables jointly determine earnings and occupations of the individuals in a sample of white men, 25 to 34 years old. Four of the independent variables, all of them interrelated, are the individual's "early intelligence" (IQ before school), the father's education (school years), the father's occupation (rated in the order of prestige), and the number of siblings. All four variables influence the individual's education (number of years at school); and one of the four, early intelligence, influences (both directly and through education) "later intelligence" (AFQT [Armed Forces Qualification Test] scores, adjusted). The semifinal product, occupation in 1964, depends on the two intermediate variables, education and later intelligence, and on three of the original independent variables, the number of siblings, the father's occupation, and the father's education. The final product, earnings in 1964, depends on occupation, later intelligence, education, and father's education. All intermediate variables as well as the final dependent variable are also subject to unspecified variables coming from outside the system.[22]

A model by Lee Hansen, Burton Weisbrod, and William Scanlon, designed to estimate the influence of schooling on earnings of "low achievers," was applied to a sample of men, white and black, who

[21] In a recent survey of studies on economic returns on educational investments, Gordon Douglass distinguished "the early period, 1956-1965," in which returns were "almost surely overstated . . . since part of the income superiority attributed to education was the result of other factors"; the middle period, 1966-1972," based "on better data" and "better equipped to correct . . . estimates for the effects of age, social class, and unemployment"; and finally "recent studies, 1973-1977," sorting out "the influence of education from other variables that affect earnings, such as individual ability and family background." Gordon K. Douglass, "Economic Returns on Investments in Higher Education," Chap. 12 in Howard R. Bowen, Investment in Learning (San Francisco: Jossey-Bass, 1977), pp. 365-368. — The dating of the three periods is somewhat misleading: some of the innovations had been anticipated by earlier publications.

[22] Otis Dudley Duncan, "Ability and Achievement," Eugenics Quarterly, Vol. 15 (March 1968), pp. 1-11.

were rejected for service in the armed forces because of their low scores on the AFQT. The following nine independent variables were selected: "education" (years of schooling), achieved learning (AFQT scores, percentiles), life experience (age), postschool training (a dummy variable), color (dummy), marital status (dummy), divorce of parents (dummy), family size (dummy for five or more), non-South (dummy). The authors found that the returns to additional schooling were very low.[23] They were criticized on various grounds, especially for using age instead of years of postschool experience.[24] In response, the authors admit very substantial differences in the estimated effects of schooling upon earnings if "alternative experience measures" are used, to wit, "years since leaving school," "years since leaving school after age 14," and "years since leaving school after age 16." They conclude that "ideally, independent measures of both age and [years of work] experience would be obtained and introduced into models of the determinants of earnings."[25]

A model built by Herbert Gintis uses two sets of background variables, one for "abilities," the other for "social class," each being the result of ratings on the basis of several components; major variables are years of schooling and resulting cognitive achievements and noncognitive personality traits. The thrust of the analysis is to show that these noncognitive traits—perseverance, docility, industry, and ego control, rather than creativity, autonomy, and initiative—are the dominant influences on earnings.[26]

Zvi Griliches and William Mason equip their models of income determination with a rich complement of variables: age, color (dummy), schooling before military service (years), schooling increment after service (years), total schooling (years), intelligence (AFQT percentile), length of active military service (months), father's schooling (years), father's occupational status (rating), grown up in the South (dummy), grown up in large city (dummy), grown up in suburb of large city (dummy), now living in the South (dummy), now living in the West (dummy), now living in a standard metropolitan statistical area (dummy), length of time in current job (months), never

[23] W. Lee Hansen, Burton A. Weisbrod, and William J. Scanlon, "Schooling and Earnings of Low Achievers," American Economic Review, Vol. 60 (June 1970), pp. 409-418.

[24] Barry R. Chiswick, "Schooling and Earnings of Low Achievers: Comment," American Economic Review, Vol. 62 (September 1972), pp. 752-754.

[25] W. Lee Hansen, Burton A. Weisbrod, and William J. Scanlon, "Schooling and Earnings of Low Achievers: Reply," American Economic Review, Vol. 62 (September 1972), pp. 760-762.

[26] Herbert Gintis, "Education, Technology, and the Characteristics of Worker Productivity," American Economic Review, Vol. 61 (Suppl. May 1971), pp. 266-279.

married (dummy), current occupational status (rating). The dependent variable is actual income (weekly gross earnings). The researchers report on estimations from twelve regression equations with different combinations of independent variables; the coefficients estimated for incremental schooling (after military service) are invariably higher than for preservice schooling, but both schooling coefficients fall short of the coefficient for color and exceed by far the coefficient for postschool intelligence (AFQT scores). Indeed, the "net contribution [of this proxy for intelligence] to the explanation of the variance in the income of individuals is very small."[27]

A distinguishing feature of some of the models by William Sewell and Robert Hauser is the use of social-psychological variables, such as "encouragement," "plans," "aspirations," at certain stages of their path analysis. This was possible for the particular sample explored: a cohort of 1957 high-school seniors (twelfth year of school), followed through their early postschool careers. The authors' most elaborate model includes the following set of variables to "explain" earnings in 1967: father's education (years), mother's education (years), father's occupation (rating), average parental income (dollars), mental ability (IQ), high-school grades (school reports), teachers' encouragement (scored by student), parental encouragement (scored by student), friends' plans for college (scored by student), "educational aspirations" (student's own plans for college), "occupational aspirations" (reported by student in twelfth grade), "educational attainment" (years of schooling after high school), and "occupational attainment" (status in 1964). Although "educational aspirations" are highly significant predictors of "educational attainment" (after all, why should the seniors' plans not be carried out in most instances?), when it comes to the ultimate dependent variable, earnings, the social-psychological variables have not added very much to the explanation. Father's occupation, high-school grades, and IQ remain significant predictors of the attained occupational status of the son, and indirectly of his earnings. In the ultimate determination of earnings, schooling is still the most important single factor, even if it explains only a small part of the total variance in earnings.[28]

[27] Zvi Griliches and William M. Mason, "Education, Income, and Ability," *Journal of Political Economy*, Vol. 80 (May-June 1972, Part II), pp. S74-S103; the quoted clause is from p. S88.

[28] William H. Sewell and Robert M. Hauser, "Causes and Consequences of Higher Education: Models of the Status Attainment Process," *American Journal of Agricultural Economics*, Vol. 54 (December 1972), pp. 851-861. For a more elaborate report see the same authors' book, *Education, Occupation, and Earnings: Achievements in Early Career* (New York: Academic Press, 1975). — Mary Jean Bowman asks a crucial question: "When so little of diversity in earnings is explained by education, what is

A simple model by George Johnson and Frank Stafford is unique in several respects: it confines itself to five independent variables, it includes one designed to stand for quality of schooling, it takes not annual or weekly but hourly earnings as dependent variable, and it uses data from a "national probability sample of households," gathered by the Survey Research Center of the University of Michigan in one of their personal surveys. The five independent variables are school experience (years of schooling), work experience (years of potential employment, that is, age minus year in school minus 1), quality of school (expenditures of primary and secondary schools per student enrolled), grown up in urban area (dummy), urban residence in 1964 (dummy). The authors offered also an expanded model with three background variables, assumed to influence schooling: father's education, the number of siblings, and the number of siblings older than the respondent. One of the main purposes of the exercise was to see whether and how much the quality of schooling affected the outcome. Quality does matter, according to the authors, but its marginal returns diminish rapidly.[29]

Samuel Bowles and Valerie Nelson present a model in which four variables determine occupation and income in a set of recursive equations: first, genotypic intelligence and socioeconomic background jointly determine childhood intelligence (IQ at age 6); second, childhood intelligence together with the socioeconomic background determine schooling (years); and third and fourth, schooling together with childhood intelligence and the socioeconomic background determine occupation (the usual rating) on the one hand, and income on the other. Genotypic intelligence operates solely through childhood intelligence, but socioeconomic background is in all four equations, affecting childhood intelligence, years of schooling, occupation, and income. All regression coefficients are estimated separately

---

the justification for all the rate-of-return analyses?" This is her own answer: "In simplist terms, investment in schooling may yield a high rate of return if it shifts an individual's whole probability distribution of earnings sufficiently to the right, even though we can explain only a small part of the total variance in earnings." Mary Jean Bowman, "Through Education to Earnings?" *Proceedings of the National Academy of Education*, Vol.3 (Washington, D.C., 1976) pp. 252-253.

[29] George E. Johnson and Frank P. Stafford, "Social Returns to Quantity and Quality of Schooling," *Journal of Human Resources*, Vol. 8 (Spring 1973), pp. 139-155. — Among other studies of the effects of school quality are Lewis C. Solmon, "The Definition and Impact of College Quality," in Lewis C. Solmon and Paul J. Taubman, eds., *Does College Matter?* (New York: Academic Press, 1973), pp. 77-102; Paul Wachtel, *The Effect of School Quality on Achievement, Attainment, and Earnings* (New York: McGraw-Hill, 1974).

for four different age groups. The sample consists of white males of nonfarm background who in 1962 were in the experienced labor force. The major conclusion drawn by the authors is that the "intergenerational reproduction of economic inequality" is not explained by genetic inheritance of intelligence but may well be explained by socioeconomic background.[30]

Special Choices of Variables

In the preceding parade of models and variables one may have obtained the impression that analysts chose the variables for their models largely on the basis of their theories, hypotheses, or hunches. However, more often than not, the selections were not made under "free choice" but primarily because the researchers had no choice: they had to take what the records offered. Confined to whatever samples had been obtained (by, for example, the census of population, demographic surveys, records from school systems, from the air force, or other parts of the military establishment), and confined to the information obtained for these samples, the researchers had to make do with what there was. They sometimes mentioned what they would "ideally" like to have for testing their favorite hypotheses, but often their pride of accomplishment did not allow them to give sufficiently loud expression to their disappointment about the lack of adequate data.

In a good many instances, however, the specifications of the production functions are inconsistent with the analyst's own hypotheses. Some who expect that (discounted) earnings are a function of years of schooling and of measured ability (besides a constant and an uncorrelated random variable) fail to realize that a linear function "implies that schooling and ability are perfect substitutes in determining earnings. . . . More important, it implies that the marginal product of additional schooling is independent of ability."[31] This implication is surely not intended by the analysts, who probably expect and assume that additional schooling yields higher returns for abler individuals, that the opportunity cost of additional schooling also is higher for abler individuals, that the returns to (the more costly) additional schooling have to be higher for abler individuals if they are to have an economic incentive to make this investment

[30] Samuel Bowles and Valerie I. Nelson, "The 'Inheritance of IQ' and the Intergenerational Reproduction of Economic Inequality," *Review of Economics and Statistics*, Vol. 56 (February 1974), pp. 39-51.

[31] John C. Hause, "Ability and Schooling as Determinants of Lifetime Earnings, or If You're So Smart, Why Aren't You Rich" in F. Thomas Juster, ed., *Education, Income, and Human Behavior* (New York: McGraw-Hill, 1975), pp. 127-128.

in their earning capacity; and that in actual fact abler people do acquire more schooling than the less able.

As a relief from some of the unwanted implications of the (mis)specification of the production function, some analysts have chosen to replace the *level* of earnings (as dependent variable) by the *logarithm* of earnings. This change still does not adequately show the effects of more schooling on earnings of abler persons. John Hause, in his study of the "ability-schooling-earnings relationship," abandoned the crippling specification of a single production function and divided each of his four samples into five or six subsamples with different levels of schooling.[32]

To the two strategic independent variables—ability and schooling—Hause added somewhat unusual background variables, probably because the data happened to contain this information, and there was a chance that they might have some significance in the explanation of the outcome. Thus, the background variables for two of the samples include high or low social class (dummy) and marital status (dummy); another sample contains variables for type and region of school (dummies for private, parochial, and southeastern schools); and prolonged illness during or after the late teens (dummy) figures in his Swedish sample. One significant variable, absent from most other production functions of annual income, is the number of weeks worked during the year. Two interesting findings from Hause's analyses should here be mentioned: first, a strong indication of positive interaction between ability and schooling, which implies that the use of these strategic variables in a single regression equation is liable to result in false estimations of their influences; and second, strong support for the observation that, for subgroups with higher

[32] The four samples are described by F. Thomas Juster, in Appendix A of the volume cited, pp. 397-404. (1) A sample of 2,316 men who were among 75,000 carefully tested volunteers accepted in 1943 for training programs by the Army Air Force and among the 10,000 surveyed in 1955 by Robert L. Thorndike and Elizabeth P. Hagen, and among the 5,100 who responded with completed information to a resurvey in 1969 by the National Bureau of Economic Research (hence, known as the NBER-TH sample). (2) A sample of 343 individuals who were among a group of eighth-grade students in Connecticut whose IQs were tested in 1935 and whose earnings for 1950, 1955, 1960, and 1965 were obtained by questionnaire in a 1966 survey by Daniel C. Rogers. (3) A sample of 8,840 who were among some 14,000 male high-school juniors (11th grade) tested in 1960 for the "Project Talent" of the U.S. Office of Education and among those who responded to questionnaires about their employment and earnings in 1966. (4) A sample of 455 men in Sweden who were tested in 1938 when they were in third grade in Malmö, Sweden, and whose earnings were obtained from income-tax records in 1949, 1954, 1959, 1964, and 1968, with additional information from responses to questionnaires. These data were obtained and reported by Torsten Husén.

education levels, "IQ appears to have an effect [on earnings] that increases substantially over time. This tendency of ability to become more important as labor force experience increases is pervasive, but is weaker at lower levels of schooling."[33]

Working Hours and Leisure Time

Of all the earnings-production functions described so far in this chapter, only some of Hause's included among the input variables the number of weeks worked per year. In two other models, however, the output produced was weekly earnings or hourly earnings, and this made the question of how many weeks or hours the individuals in the sample worked during the year irrelevant. In discussions of schooling as accumulation of human capital affecting annual earnings, and of the returns to the investment in schooling, the problem of differences and changes in the allocation of time between work and leisure should not be overlooked. If one attempts to explain variances in annual earnings by differences in years of schooling and disregards hours and weeks worked during the year, one implicitly attaches zero values to the pleasures derived from different types of work and from leisure. If this statement sounds mysterious, a simple illustration may help clarify its meaning.

Assume that the average annual earnings of workers who attended only primary school are $10,800; of workers who completed twelve years of school, $14,000; and of those who graduated from college, $18,000. Assume further, for the sake of simplicity, that native intelligence and ability are the same for people in all three groups. Assume finally—what most statistical sources fail to divulge—that those in the first group work 48 hours a week (or 2,400 hours a year); those in the second group, 40 hours a week (or 2,000 hours a year); and those in the third group, 60 hours a week (or 3,000 hours a year). If we compare not only annual earnings but also hourly earnings, we find that people in the group with only primary schooling, earning $10,800 annually, made $4.50 per hour; that the high-school graduates, earning $14,000 annually, made $7.00 per hour; and that the college graduates, with annual earnings of $18,000, made only $6.00 per hour. The additional four years of education can be credited with an increment of annual earnings (over those of high-school graduates) of $4,000 but may be charged with effecting a reduction in hourly earnings from $7.00 to $6.00. Does it make better sense to compare annual or hourly earnings if we want to assess the effect of additional education?

[33] Hause, "Ability," p. 133.

There are arguments for both procedures. The higher earnings of the college graduates would be due to their working one hour and a half for each hour worked by high-school graduates. The difference in hourly earnings is negative, which would argue strongly against the use of annual earnings in an evaluation of the effect of additional education. On the other hand, perhaps the kind of work done by the college graduates is so enjoyable that they *want* to work more hours; they get more pleasure from working than from alternative uses of their time. This would argue against using hourly earnings; the difference in hourly earnings would fail to reflect the positive psychic-income differential.[34]

This problem has no unique solution, especially if we drop the assumption of equal ability. Not even if we knew the preference maps of all individuals would we be equipped for a meaningful exercise in welfare economics, for, more likely than not, the individuals' preferences (tastes) will be changed, along with their skills, by their additional education. If the relative appreciation of work and leisure—in the economists' language, "the elasticity of substitution between work and leisure"—has changed in the process of education, how can we evaluate the change in additional psychic income, particularly if more leisure time gave *additional* satisfaction before the change in tastes but *reduced* satisfaction after the change? We must be satisfied with recognizing the existence of this question, for we are not able to do much about answering it.

Incidentally, the assumption that more-educated people work longer hours, although it was made here only for the sake of illustration, does to some extent correspond with observation. Approximately one more year of school was found to be associated with one more hour per week worked, according to one investigator.[35] Other researchers have found even greater correlations between the amount

[34] Another effect of the additional schooling may be to make it *possible* for the more qualified to work longer hours. Those with less education may not have opportunities to work sixty hours a week even if they were willing to do so. (Elchanan Cohn suggested this point in a letter to me, dated 19 September, 1980.)

[35] T. Aldrich Finegan, "Hours of Work in the United States: A Cross-Sectional Analysis," *Journal of Political Economy*, Vol. 70 (September-October 1962), p. 460. The positive correlation between hours of work and years of education may have several explanations; for example, college graduates may have acquired a taste for more work, or people with such taste are more likely to go to college, or more qualified work requires larger workloads. Another explanation was suggested by Jacob Mincer: Even if tastes remain unchanged and work-load requirements are the same, the substitution effect of the higher wage rate may outweigh the wealth effect in the labor-supply function, causing the better-paid workers to substitute income for leisure, that is, work more hours.

of schooling completed and the number of hours worked per week and per year.[36] A more systematic approach to this problem was followed by Richard Eckaus, who estimated private returns to education "using incomes adjusted to a common annual hourly basis."[37] He adjusted the "observed individual incomes to a standard, 40-hour week, 50-week year income," or the income that could be earned in 2,000 hours of work. "The internal rates of returns [to investment in additional schooling] calculated on this . . . basis are most frequently lower and often drastically so. They reflect, in general, the tendency for annual hours of work to increase with the level of education."[38] The results, according to Eckhaus "suggest the possibility of over-investment in high-school education relative to other types of investment."[39]

Causes, Proxies, Cues, and Miscues

Any known technique of analysis will sometimes yield misleading "findings." An illustration of a serious miscue was presented above, in the subsection on "Do the Data Tell the Story," where it was shown how systematic features in the composition of groups can result in higher average (and median) earnings *attributed* to schooling even if not a single person in any group has had increased earnings *due* to schooling. Multiple-regression analysis will sometimes yield coefficients indicating a significant contribution of a certain factor to the outcome even when it is quite obvious that in actual fact its contribution was nil. The following example may reinforce this warning to those who in naive credulity accept the results of this kind of "empirical analysis."

Imagine that some enthusiasts contend that musical education contributes to earning capacity and propose to take the years of piano instruction as a factor determining lifetime earnings. If we could obtain the required data, we should expect a quite remarkable regression coefficient for the role of piano lessons in "producing" additional earnings. Not that the lessons would really produce any monetary returns, but they are associated with other factors that exert genuine influence. Individuals who have taken piano lessons for several years were probably raised in families with incomes high

[36] Jacob Mincer, *Schooling, Experience and Earnings* (New York: National Bureau of Economic Research, 1974), p. 121.

[37] Richard S. Eckaus, "Estimation of the Returns to Education with Hourly Standardized Incomes," in *Estimating the Returns to Education: A Disaggregated Approach* (Berkeley, Cal.: Carnegie Commission on Higher Education, 1973), pp. 1-9.

[38] Ibid., p. 7. Eckaus' procedure amounts to using wage rates, not earnings, (as has been called to my attention by Jacob Mincer).

[39] Ibid., p. 8.

enough to afford a piano and the payments to piano teachers; thus, parental income is "behind" the selected variable; in addition, extended piano lessons probably indicate strong parental pressures with regard to learning, not just to play the piano but also to develop verbal and quantitative skills; finally, extended piano lessons may indicate a high degree of discipline, industry, and perseverance, traits that are strong causal factors in earning capacity. These traits are not directly measurable, and no good proxies for them are readily available; hence, they are usually not among the variables in empirical earnings functions. If parental incomes and other parental influences are not included either, then the regression coefficient for piano lessons, substituting for these influences, will be relatively high. What from the point of view of causal theory is quite ridiculous may receive a high mark from quantitative empirical analysis.

If the preceding sentence were meant to imply a criticism of regression analysis or its use in research in our subject area, econometricians would object, and for good reasons. For they do not try to estimate the strength of selected factors as *causes* of the outcome but merely their reliability as *predictors* of the outcome. Piano lessons may not contribute to high incomes, but they may help to predict them.

The Places for Ability and Socioeconomic Background

Critical issues concerning mental ability and socioeconomic status were discussed in Chapters 15 and 16, and again in earlier sections of the present chapter. I come back to them once more to consider the question of their proper places in a production function or a system of sequential production functions, for it is puzzling to see the relative importance of mental ability (achievement-test scores) and socioeconomic status (variously concocted) estimated so differently in different empirical models.

Multiple regression analysis on the basis of single, linear equations cannot be expected to yield meaningful results. Since mental ability is always deputized by achievement-test scores, and since these scores are different at different stages of personal development (childhood, after primary school, after secondary school, etc.), but probably interrelated (though affected also by socioeconomic factors), it would make little sense to place them side by side in a single production function. It has been recognized in more recent research that multiple-stage regression analysis can produce superior (or less flawed) results.

In their "revised model of income determination" Griliches and Mason use four stages of "ability," the first one genetically inherited, the next three determined jointly by the preceding one and by family factors and incremental schooling. Ability, called also the human-capital variable, is unobservable but is assumed to affect achievement-test scores at each stage; the scores are, of course, affected also by exogenous error terms.[40]

Ability in the sense used in this context is not a constant or stable constitution of the mind, a natural endowment; instead, it is a growing (and, later in life, declining) ability to achieve. Thus, it does not involve a comparison with an age-related or school-year-related norm, and one can expect that almost every child after some years of learning will be abler than most preschool children. Even a young genius, in terms of age-related IQ, may not be able to solve differential equations before he has learned how to do it. In other words, the tests by which the growth of ability (as a result of family influences, schooling, training, and life experiences) can be sized up are not different for persons of different age, either in contents or in scores or scaling, and the achievements are not relative to some "standard intelligence." Scores on these tests are raw, independent of how others have performed.

Another Digression on Innate Intelligence

Having devoted a whole chapter to the controversial issue of nature versus nurture—innate versus acquired intelligence—and having endorsed, in the preceding section, the stage theory of intelligence development, I have severe scruples about returning once more to the subject of innate intelligence. I must confess that, in the course of writing these chapters, I have changed my mind several times. Instead of presenting my "latest" views on the subject and risking regret tomorrow, I shall resolve my dilemma by first reproducing what I drafted a few months ago and then stating why I no longer believe it to be correct:

It is accepted by many, perhaps most, specialists in education, sociology, and psychology that general mental abilities can be changed by schooling and learning.[41] No matter whether or not this is correct,

---

[40] Zvi Griliches and William M. Mason, "Education, Income, and Ability," *Journal of Political Economy*, p. S93. The authors supply both a graphical scheme and an algebraic sequence of the relationship assumed for the model. "Basically we have an unobservable ability or achievement (or human-capital) variable, which is augmented by schooling, and the stock of which is estimable (subject to error) via test scores. . . . We assume in this model that all of the influence of class and heredity is indirect, via the early-achievement variable."

[41] In a Swedish study, ability of the same cohort was tested in 1938 and 1939; while schooling as a rule raised the IQ, it did not do so for boys who completed only elementary school; as a matter of fact, they lost slightly in "ability." Torsten Husén, *Begöwning och miljö* (Stockholm: Victor Petterson, 1951), p. 131. Quoted from Mary Jean Bowman, "Through Education to Earnings?" in *Proceedings of the National Academy of Education*, Vol. 3 (Washington, D.C., 1976), p. 234.

will not the effects of the same education be different depending on the initial ability, or perhaps native intelligence, of the learner? Some of the controversies are ideological in nature. Those inclined to recognize a genetic origin of ability are contradicted by those who feel committed to discredit the genes and to give most or all of the credit to acquired elements of ability, that is, to environmental factors, such as the quality of upbringing in the home, the socioeconomic status of parents, neighbors, and classmates and, of course, schooling. This controversy cannot be settled, because no techniques have been found to separate innate from acquired ability.

This issue is all but irrelevant for the problem with which we are concerned. (See above, Chapter 15.) Only if we want to learn something about the productivity of earliest-childhood education might it be interesting to know something about innate ability, that is, the mental and physical capacities of a child at age zero. When we are concerned with the productivity of additional years of education beyond four or six years of elementary education, we need not know the division between innate and acquired ability. If we ask what the effects might be of prolonging elementary schooling by adding three grades for pupils who have had six years of schooling, all we need to know are the abilities of the sixth-graders, and it does not make any difference whether their abilities were innate or acquired in the first eleven or twelve years of their lives, including the first six years of school. Similarly, when we want to find the productivity of adding still another three years of school—grades 10 to 12—the analysis will merely need to apportion the contributions of the various factors, including ability after grade 9, no matter how much of the ability was innate and how much was acquired in the first fifteen years of life. Finally, in order to investigate the returns to an investment in college education, the factor "ability" would include all the mental and physical aptitudes acquired in the first seventeen or eighteen years of life, or in twelve years of school.

Ability, in the foregoing statement of my views of yesterday, was referred to as a "factor," although it was seen as a compound of many aptitudes. Do individuals with the same "ability" have to be equal in all the aptitudes that are included in the mixture? Can lower scores on some achievements be compensated for by higher scores on other achievements? Is the ability to "catch on," to grasp quickly, and to learn fast part of general ability? Do the achievement tests that are designed to measure general mental ability include scores for speed of comprehension and, to the extent that they do, how heavily are such speed scores weighted in comparison with accuracy, memory, and mastery? Assume that several persons have scored equally on achievement tests at age eleven, but that some of them are fast learners and others are hard workers; would we conclude that they would benefit equally from the next four years of schooling? I am now inclined to hold that easy learning, the ability to comprehend more quickly and to retain it more firmly, gives the fortunate individual who possesses it an advantage; and, futhermore, that this ability is, to a larger extent than other abilities, genetically determined.[42]

If this is right, it is not sufficient to build on the "preceding stage" of ability when the returns on additional schooling are estimated. Some dose of innate ability, an inherited natural endowment, may make a difference. The difference may be small enough to justify disregarding it ultimately, but the variable, though nonobservable, should not be omitted from models designed to assess the productive contribution of schooling.

A somewhat sophistical methodological reservation may be aired in this connection. In attempting to estimate the effects of additional capacity created by additional schooling, one should realize that the additions are fictitious magnitudes, not observable, since the lower earnings of the *same* persons, had they not improved their capacity through additional educational investment, can only be hypothesized. Of course, the *hypothetical* lower earnings of the *same*, but *hypothetically* less-schooled workers are replaced, in empirical analysis, by *observed* (estimated, reported) lower earnings of *different*, but *actually* less-schooled workers, on the assumption that people are sufficiently alike to allow us to take the earnings of the latter as the basis for the comparison. This assumption is usually considered legitimate.

Cohorts versus Cross Sections

Some empirical studies on the returns to schooling have used data on cohorts of people observed annually or at longer intervals. Such

[42] It is sometimes difficult to interpret the views on this subject held by others who have discussed the relative importance of ability for educational investment, on the one hand, and on earnings capacity, on the other. Gary Becker discussed the necessity and difficulty of separating the return on the investment and the premium resulting from "unskilled personal characteristics." Among the difficulties is the fact "that persons of superior ability and other personal characteristics would invest more in themselves" and "persons with more investment in schooling invest also more in other human capital." Gary S. Becker, *Human Capital* (New York: National Bureau of Economic Research, 1964), pp. 89 and 91. — Giora Hanoch gave considerable space to the significance of variables other than schooling. He had estimated a linear regression equation of earnings on 23 explanatory variables, but had many statistical and technical reservations: "The more important biases inherent in the estimated profiles and rates of return are those associated with ability. There is probably a significant positive correlation between ability to earn income—a combination of natural and acquired ability traits—and the level of schooling achieved. This obviously leads to a positive bias in the differentials between schooling levels and in rates of return to

longitudinal analyses of virtually the same groups of people growing up, moving from lower to higher schools and then from first jobs to subsequent ones with higher pay and larger earnings, may provide many important insights. Alas, until recently, the required data have been hard to come by. Census data did not include such things as intelligence quotients or parents' schooling and incomes; even the information on the respondents' schooling and incomes was not compiled until the 1930s, so that 1939 data, from the 1940 census, are the earliest that can be used for comparisons of education and income. With data from only one census, the researcher is confined to cross-section analysis, comparing education and income of different age groups and assuming that information about different people at various ages can be substituted for information about a given cohort of people growing older over the years.

The substitution of latitudinal for longitudinal data suffers from many disadvantages, though one advantage is that income figures need not be adjusted for inflation. On the other hand, the cross-section figures do not reflect the general increase in incomes over time due to the part of increased productivity that is not associated either with education or with prior ability. A rough adjustment for secular growth of productivity, however, can be made to the income data for different age groups to simulate the effect of such growth observed in cohort analysis. But no adjustment is possible for changes in relative scarcities of longer-schooled persons in different age groups. If in a particular census year the group of age 50 contains only 10 per cent college graduates whereas the group of age 30 contains 35 per cent college graduates, the scarcity value of better educated among the older persons would most likely be reflected in larger income differentials. The statistical results based on such data cannot help being deceiving. The point seems to me of sufficient importance to justify reproducing the argument in an earlier formulation of mine:

> The cross-section data [used by Gary Becker and others] on incomes of various age groups were from the 1940 and 1950 census figures, that is, from 1939 and 1949 incomes. The incomes of persons 40 years old were therefore the incomes of those who graduated from college in 1921 and 1931. Giora Hanoch (1965) has more recent data from the 1960 census, and they confirm Becker's results. Still, the 40-year-old income earners from that census graduated from college in 1942. At that time only 15 per cent of the college-age group were enrolled in college. I question whether in-

come differentials earned at a time when only 15 per cent of the eligible population went to college will be valid for a time when 50 per cent go to college.

The law of supply and demand is still in effect. Income differentials earned at a time when college graduates were scarce will not hold in times when graduates are plentiful. The Carnegie Commission on Higher Education believes that there is a satisfactory pecuniary return to investment in college education, and they explain their belief with an increase in demand for graduates. I grant that technological and organizational changes in our economy have resulted in increased demand for college-trained personnel, but I doubt that the expansion of demand can have matched the explosion of supply. Thus, I do not share the faith of my fellow analysts of the economics of tertiary education in the persistence of positive net returns. Indeed, I would not be surprised if future income data should show that the positive income differentials of our current graduates have vanished.[43]

Longitudinal analysis becomes possible if a series of censuses provides consistent information. The census of population, every ten years, would allow the researcher to assume that the forty-year-olds in one census are largely the same people as the thirty-year-olds in the preceding census. The *Current Population Reports*, appearing annually, allow the assumption of virtually unchanged groups just one year older than in the previous report. Thus, the annual data from 1939 to 1979 give us time series for each cohort over a period of forty years: the group of age 20 in 1939 would be the group of age 60 in 1979. This yields a major portion of their life-income profiles. Of course, the data are still deficient in many respects: incomes include more than just earnings from work: hours of work may vary greatly, and variables such as ability or parental socioeconomic status are not obtainable from census statistics.

When I say that longitudinal data are much more appropriate than latitudinal data for the estimation of life-earnings profiles, and when I explain this superiority with the argument that only a cohort moving through life can justify the assumption of a largely unchanged composition, I may turn attention away from the fact that the composition of groups with different amounts of schooling must be inherently different. Those with sixteen years of schooling are different

[43] Fritz Machlup, "Perspectives on the Benefits of Postsecondary Education," in Lewis C. Solmon and Paul J. Taubman, *Does College Matter?* (New York: Academic Press, 1973), pp. 356-357.

people than those with only twelve years, who in turn are different from those with only nine years of schooling. In order to know the effect of education upon earnings we would have to know how the *same* persons would have done with more and with less schooling. Since each person can live only one life (at least at the same period of time) this information is not even conceivably obtainable. To take groups of different composition for a comparison of the effects of different amounts of schooling is to assume that people are fundamentally alike although they have selected, or have been selected for, different educational careers.

Since these comments may be interpreted as rejections of the entire approach to the estimation of returns (and rates of return) to investment in human capital, it is fair to add another comment in support of its methodological validity. If the estimation of returns on the basis of past experiences of different—perhaps similar, but never equal—groups of persons is not intended to serve as justification of past or future investments but as *explanation of expectations* of persons considering investments in themselves or in their children, the use of other persons' experiences is both reasonable and rational. The statistical data and computations refer to a group with more schooling and another group with less schooling; and the findings are assumed to explain the investment decisions of a third group. There is nothing basically wrong with such speculations.

Production Function and "Human-Capital Approach"

Modern economic literature appears to be very fond of the term "approach"—approaches to solutions of all sorts of problems. One can find references to the "production-function approach" and to the "human-capital approach" to the determination of earnings and of the productive contributions of various factors. One may wonder whether these are rival approaches. They are not. There is no contradiction between the two; indeed, they are complementary and often so closely associated that they are merely two aspects of the same theoretical scheme.

If several factors (inputs) determine the product (earnings), it is logically impossible to estimate the contribution of one or two of them—the human capital embodied in the workers through their past schooling and training—separately from the contributions of the other factors. If a theorist selects, say, eight factors that he suspects of having affected the product (total earnings), and if two of these factors are regarded as human capital (accumulated through years of schooling and in-service training), he cannot ascertain the flow of earnings attributable to that capital unless the influences of the other six factors are estimated simultaneously.

Of course, not every production function contains capital variables. One can imagine production functions in which all inputs are current services and materials yielding current outputs without any time lag. Where time intervals between input and output are treated as strategic elements, the production function involves capital theory; and where certain inputs are services from durable producers' goods or, more generally, from accumulated capital stocks, capital theory is an integral part of the analysis; and if, finally, the stocks consist of investments embodied in human productive capacity, it is human capital that is part of the production function.[44]

That capital stocks are given roles as variables in production functions raises delicate conceptual and operational questions: is it the total stock of capital *available* or only the part actually *employed* in producing the current output that should figure in the production function? And if accumulated investments have formed the stock of capital, are all such investments, say, all expenditures for, and implicit costs of, schooling at all ages, at all levels, and of all types, included in the stock? And how are the problems of cumulative interest, gradual depreciation, and discounted returns to be treated? Some of these questions, dealt with in other chapters, may be beyond the scope of the production-function approach, though very much within that of capital theory.[45]

[44] It is perhaps in order to recall that the paradigmatic use of the "production-function approach" saw the product as a function of labor and *capital*. See Paul H. Douglas, *Theory of Wages* (New York: Macmillan, 1934).

[45] The first of the questions asked above referred to the difference between a stock of capital *available* and the part of it that is actually *used* in production. For the case of physical capital, this question has often been addressed. For example, when input-output analysis measured the input of capital by the total value of the capital stock on the books of the firms, regardless of the extent of its use—24 hours a day, 8 hours a day, intermittently, or not at all—several economists protested the validity of this procedure. The same protest may be raised in the case of human capital. If the individual investor in his own productive capacity decides to work longer or shorter work weeks, the degree of utilization of the capital embodied in his (her) person is implied in this decision, and the value of less or more leisure enjoyed is likely to be taken into account. The question is different, however, if "society" subsidizes additional schooling in order to accumulate human capital for use in the production of goods and services. If schooling affects aptitudes as well as attitudes, and if the school-effects on attitudes are adverse to hard work and disciplined effort, society may have to confront a problem of unused capacity: underutilized human capital. Schools that train people to require several periods of rest during relatively few hours of work produce only intermittently usable human capital. Subsequent training on the job with insistence on working discipline may have to offset the "training for rest and relaxation" that is provided in some school systems. (James Mill refused to send his son to school lest he learn how to loaf.)

CHAPTER 18

Productivity versus Credentials

A WIDE CHOICE of titles is available to announce the topic or problem to be discussed in this chapter. Listing some of the possible titles may not only help the reader see the range of semantic options but may also circumscribe the questions we have to probe regarding the effects of longer schooling. "Real Capacity versus Certification" comes closest to the title selected, but "Actual Improvement versus Easier Marketability" may even more sharply point up the contrast. Other possibilities are "Increasing Working Power versus Increasing Worker's Appeal," "Performance Effect versus Sheepskin Effect," or "Producing Greater Capacity or only Signals to Employers." Still another set of possibilities may be proposed, but with a warning that, although they seem to suggest the same question, they may actually refer to a different one: "Competence-Building Device versus Screening Device," "Efficiency Raiser versus Filter," or "Skill-Lifting Aid versus Sifting Aid." I shall presently explain why the last three titles are not necessarily equivalent to the six earlier ones; I should confess, however, that although I myself had concocted several of the phrases, it was only after a good deal of reflection that I detected a critical equivocation in the "screening debate."

The Meaning of Screening

To screen can mean, according to the dictionary, to shelter, protect, shut off, hide from view, conceal, sift, and project. Whereas all these meanings may color our understanding, "sifting" is the intended meaning here. It is not clear, however, who sifts, for what purposes, and by what criteria. In principle, every *school* has a filtering function, because there is no effective teaching without sorting out the pupils (or students) who have not yet grasped the latest lesson from those who have. A school must engage in sifting and sorting in the very process of carrying out its teaching function. On the other hand, a writer about the "screening device" may refer to *employers* who want to select among large numbers of job applicants the ones that look most promising; in this process they are aided by the school authorities' certification of the students' educational "attainments."

If we read that education serves a screening function, we cannot be sure which of the two functions is referred to, nor indeed if a relationship between the two is implied.

When Paul Taubman and Terence Wales ask whether differential earnings of workers reflect their differential *productivity* acquired by differential amounts of education or, instead, "discrimination in the job market" on the basis of school *credentials*, we know that they think of screening as a criterion in the employer's personnel selection that may not be, and often is not, a good indicator of the applicants' qualifications.[1] On the other hand, when some other writers discuss the sorting-out function that the school carries out as a part of its normal operation, we may be in doubt whether the allusion is to true grade-labeling or to discrimination in hiring on the basis of possibly deceptive signals.

Even if schools did not confer degrees and diplomas, did not furnish recommendations, evaluations, or transcripts of grades, and did not even certify the number of years completed by a student, they would still, if they wanted to do an effective job of teaching, have to sort students according to their progress in their studies. To let students proceed to advanced stages of learning a skill or subject before making sure they have mastered the preliminary stages would be a waste of time and effort. It is an inherent part of education to sort students according to their readiness for more advanced studies and their comparative qualifications for different disciplines or occupations.[2] This sorting or screening need not be connected with any credentials or signals to employers.

Having noted this important sorting function of schools, I may state that, according to my understanding of the issues, most writers in the screening debate are talking about credentialism, the use of school credentials in the hiring process and in the determination of the job seekers' rates of pay.

Conjunctive and Disjunctive Alternatives

The set of dichotomies proposed as possible titles for our present discussion seems to convey the relationship of disjunctive alternatives—either/or. This was evidently intended by some who asked whether the diploma certifying the high-school graduation or the bachelor's degree was not the very thing that assured positive pecuniary returns to extended schooling. Yet, we may ask in return,

[1] Paul Taubman and Terence Wales, *Higher Education and Earnings: College as an Investment and a Screening Device* (New York: McGraw-Hill, 1974), p. 171.

[2] Fritz Machlup, "Poor Learning from Good Teachers," *Academe* [Bulletin of the American Association of University Professors], Vol. 65, No. 6 (October 1979), p. 379.

why should the additional years of schooling that produce the certificates and diplomas not concomitantly produce real improvements
in the graduates' working capacity? Why should the question whether
the incremental education increases competence or provides credentials not be answered to the effect that it can do both? Successful
completion of college work at a reputable institution can signify both
that genuine training has been provided and that the graduate's train-
ability has been thereby certified.

Even if it is admitted that additional years of schooling increase
the productivity of the schooled individuals *and* secure them the
credentials that help them get better jobs and initiate careers with
higher lifetime earnings, the question arises how the combined effect
can be apportioned between the two components.[3] Lester Thurow
contends that in the queuing for jobs one's rank in the queue is
determined by school credentials, so that those equipped with diplomas are the first to get in.[4] No doubt, some employers will not
hire dropouts but only applicants who have completed high school;
and, surely, some firms reserve certain jobs for college graduates.
They do this, however, not in blind trust of the diploma, but because
they believe that the fact of having persevered and completed the
courses of study does signify something about the capability and
working habits of the better-schooled applicants. The screening of
job seekers by relying on school credentials is a perfectly rational
(cost-efficient) way for employers to select applicants for jobs.

By relying on school credentials in hiring, the employment offices
of business firms do not do anything that households would not do
every day when they rely on labels and trade names in buying household appliances and furnishings, wearing apparel and foods. The
question whether the buyers pay more for better quality or rather for
better-known trademarks and trade names is moot: they evidently
believe that the labels signal quality. Of course, they are sometimes
wrong and pay too much for the label; indeed, in some instances
they are so impressed with the label that they not only accept an
inferior product, but they are willing to pay more for it—at least in

---

[3] Taubman and Wales attempted to estimate, on the basis of empirical data, what
proportion of observed differences in earnings associated with schooling may be
attributed to schooling alone—that is, to capacity increases effected by additional
schooling—and what proportion may be due to the effect of credentials. For a critical
appraisal of their techniques and results see Mary Jean Bowman, "Through Education
to Earnings?" in the *Proceedings of the National Academy of Education*, Vol. 3 (1976),
pp. 265-269.

[4] Lester Thurow, "Education and Economic Equality," *The Public Interest*, Vol. 28
(Summer 1972), pp. 66-81; and *Generating Inequality* (New York: Basic Books, 1975).

the opinion of "experts," real or alleged. Still, there are not many economists who would propose that labeling, trademarks, and trade names be abolished. The question whether a producer gets his price differential for the better quality of his product or for his trade name is difficult to answer. The fact that some trade names and trademarks are valuable property rights suggests that part of the sales revenues are attributable to these intangible assets and, therefore, constitute returns to the producers' capital.[5]

This analogy helps us to see that any "sheepskin effect" of education may likewise be a source of income, conceptually separable from the earnings attributable to the improved labor services rendered by the graduate. Both sources of differential earnings, however, are intangible capital owned by human beings and inseparable from them, the one because it is embodied in the person, the other because it is legally not transferable or negotiable.

Is Credentialism Inconsistent with Human-Capital Theory?

Some analysts regard the "screening hypothesis" or "credentialism" as a "rival approach" to the human-capital approach.[6] Some waver between considering the two theories as rivals or complements.[7] This vacillation is understandable, because matters look quite different from the private and public points of view. For the private considerations of the individual job holder, it makes no difference whether he makes more money owing to his credentials or because he has really become a more competent worker. He has invested in himself and collects the returns on his investment; it is of no consequence to him, or to those who rely on his experience and make the same investment, whether the human capital thereby created

[5] In the United States, we have recently gone through an experience of reducing the monopoly power of trade names and proprietary designations for prescription drugs. Statutes provide that the druggist (chemist) filling prescriptions for pharmaceuticals must offer the buyer a choice between proprietary brands and generic alternatives. This is possible only where the generic drugs are sold with all ingredients accurately listed, so that the buyer or his physician can rely on the alternative products being close, if not perfect, substitutes. Such listing of ingredients is not possible for the labor services offered by human beings, and this lack of information reduces the substitutability of "unbranded labor" (workers without school credentials) for certified or trade-named labor.

[6] Barry R. Chiswick, "Schooling, Screening, and Income," in Lewis C. Solmon and Paul J. Taubman, eds., *Does College Matter?* (New York: Academic Press, 1973), pp. 154, 157-158.

[7] Mark Blaug, "The Empirical Status of Human-Capital Theory: A Slightly Jaundiced Survey," *Journal of Economic Literature*, Vol. 14 (September 1976), pp. 833 and 845-848.

consists in improved working capacity or in a certificate that helps employers to screen applicants for jobs and select the certified ones.[8]

For the considerations of welfare economists, policy advisers, and policymakers—in other words, from the point of view of "society"—there is a serious question: should "society" make these costly investments in additional schooling if it will serve mostly as a convenient device for the screening of job applicants and thus ease the tasks of employment officers of business corporations or government agencies? Or should such investments be made only if they pay for themselves through improved working capacity and increased productivity of the better educated? The answer seems rather obvious: there are cheaper ways to screen applicants for jobs. If job seekers cannot be tested in a day or two, they can be hired on probation and tried out for a few weeks or months. This would be a far less costly selection process than to rely on a diploma certifying the completion of four years of high school or college. It follows that investment in incremental schooling does not form human capital from the point of view of society if it serves chiefly the function of a filter.

If filtering and sorting of applicants for employment were really the main function of schooling beyond some point, it would surely be an exceedingly wasteful operation. Can it be credible that, in a free-enterprise society, employers would pay for that high cost of screening in the form of high wages and salaries of "certified" graduates of secondary schools and colleges? Large employers could organize their own testing and screening departments, and there would undoubtedly emerge firms specialized in testing and certifying the general and special qualifications of job seekers and, with free entry into the market, the screening industry would be sufficiently competitive to provide its services for a small fraction of the cost of schooling. That this industry does not exist is a weighty argument against the screening hypothesis.[9]

---

[8] In a similar vein, Mincer holds that the screening hypothesis does "not conflict with the fundamental notion of human capital—of forgoing current income for increased future earnings. For this general concept, it does not matter whether the increased marketability produced by schools is due to their affective, informational, or cognitive function." Jacob Mincer, "Human Capital and Earnings," in Douglas M. Windham, ed., *Economic Dimensions of Education* (Washington, D.C.: National Academy of Education, 1979), p. 27.

[9] "Indeed, if all schooling does is *sort* people on the basis of family background, ability, or affective behavior, there would be a strong incentive for specialized firms to develop to perform this service at a lower cost. That such firms have not arisen suggests that the "sorting effect" of schooling has a low market value." Barry R. Chiswick, "Schooling," p. 154. Similarly, "the characteristics for which schooling serves as a screen should be discoverable by means of direct interviewing and testing much more cheaply than by expenditures of many years and tens of thousands of

Some who are strongly impressed by the validity and relevance of the screening hypothesis have started to estimate what they call the "informational returns" to the "signal" that the investment in longer education creates for the labor market.[10] The question of estimating the benefits derived from the information obtained is, I submit, misplaced. If there are alternative techniques for securing certain flows of information, the value of any particular technique is determined by the cost of the least expensive alternative. The valuation of the information service rendered by educational investment can be of interest only if that service is a joint product, that is, inseparably joined with the improved labor services that the same investment generates.

My intuitive judgment prevents me from giving high odds in favor of the screening hypothesis to explain higher lifetime earnings of persons with more years of schooling. The reason is simple: credentials such as high-school diplomas or college degrees serve graduates chiefly for getting their first jobs. To retain these jobs, to be promoted and/or to secure still better-paying second and third jobs requires real working capacity. Employees who are no more competent than job seekers with only nine years of school will not forever secure earnings far in excess of their less schooled substitutes. To be sure, the school credentials may be helpful in getting a better first job; and a good first job may be a good start for a productive career. But it is difficult to believe that enhanced lifetime earnings can be attributed to nothing but school credentials.[11]

dollars on an average education. Markets for testing would surely spring up if such tremendous savings were possible; their absence is a strong argument against a 'pure' screening hypothesis." Jacob Mincer, "Human Capital," p. 28.

[10] Kenneth Wolpin is not among those who have concluded that the screening hypothesis has sustained empirical testing. On the other hand, he does hold that if schooling did serve as an efficient screen, it would "generally increase actual aggregate output. From a social perspective, schooling may have a positive gross social product independent of its productivity augmenting capacity." See Kenneth Wolpin, "Education and Screening," American Economic Review, Vol. 67 (December 1977), pp. 949-958. The quoted sentences are from p. 953.

[11] If graduates with diplomas and degrees are given preference to nongraduates in their first jobs, but do not acutally prove to be more qualified and more productive than "cheaper" nongraduates, the lack of differential qualifications would show itself later in their careers, and the earnings differentials would decline or vanish. If empirical studies show that differential earnings of the better-schooled employees actually increase over the years, one may conclude that they have proved their worth through superior performance—not just by the school credentials that may have helped them to secure their first job. On the basis of this argument, several writers have rejected the screening hypothesis. Barry R. Chiswick, "Schooling," pp. 151-159; Richard Layard and George Psacharopoulos, "The Screening Hypothesis and the Returns to Education," Journal of Political Economy, Vol. 82 (September-October 1974), pp.

Empirical Tests of the Screening Hypothesis

A voluminous literature has developed to explain the screening hypothesis and to elaborate on its implications.[12] What has given such a boost to a hypothesis that on theoretical grounds does not look so very plausible? "Empirical evidence" was the booster. Repeated tests with various data, latitudinal as well as longitudinal, seemed to confirm that the earnings of persons who had completed secondary school were much higher than those of persons who had left school one year earlier; similarly, earnings of college graduates were much higher than those of persons who had attended college for only three years. Employing the usual techniques of calculation, some researchers found that the rates of return to investment in the last year of high school and the last year of college were conspicuously higher than the rates to other one-year additions to schooling. Since the "last" years could not have contributed so much more to the working capacities of the graduates than other single years of schooling, it was plausible to infer that the difference was due to the certificate earned by those who stayed in school or college to the bitter end and earned the sweet credentials.

A more telling indication of the earning capacity of a school diploma or college degree might be provided by statistics differentiating between earnings of people with the same number of school years completed but with and without the graduation document. Instead of ascertaining the differential earnings of workers with twelve years of school over those with only eleven years, we should want to see any differentials for those who have twelve years of school *and* a high-school diploma above the earnings of others with twelve years of school but *no* diploma to show for them. I have not seen any such data, or findings based on such data; but even if they existed, they would not prove that any differential earnings recorded are entirely based on "credentialism." The failure of a student to earn his graduation diploma gives rise to a presumption that there was "something wrong," that the withholding of the diploma may signal some deficiencies in the student's ability, ambition, industry, cooperation, or reliability. The same suspicions may reasonably be entertained

985-998; George Psacharopoulos, "College Quality as a Screening Device?" *Journal of Human Resources*, Vol. 9 (Fall 1974), pp. 556-558.

[12] Stiglitz provided a sophisticated analysis of the effects of screening through credentials upon the allocation of resources to education, with possible implications on national income and inequality of income distribution. Joseph E. Stiglitz, "The Theory of 'Screening,' Education, and the Distribution of Income," *American Economic Review*, Vol. 65 (June 1975), pp. 283-300.

regarding a job applicant who has completed four years of college but has failed to earn a bachelor's degree.

If these considerations are sound, the significance of "mere credentialism" is much reduced. It still could be possible that most workers with only nine years of school would, if given a chance, be just as productive as those with twelve years; but there is some basis for the suspicion that of all who have completed twelve years of school, those who have failed to earn the graduation diploma may be less productive than the certified graduates.

Incidentally, the empirical data on differential returns and rates of return are not completely silent on questions of this sort, though the messages which the analysts read into them are sometimes ambiguous or unwarranted. Taubman and Wales worked with the largest available sample containing data that are considered acceptable proxies for family background, personal ability, school records, and earnings.[13] They divided the men of this sample into groups with different "educational attainment" or "levels," and compared their average earnings, their education-related earnings (that is, net earnings after eliminating the effects of other factors), and rates of return to educational investment. One such comparison was between those who "completed college," those who have "some college," and those who only completed high school. The earnings, and even the (much smaller) education-related earnings, were still higher for the groups with more years of education, but the rates of return to the investment in these additional years were lower. What seems important in the present context is the finding that the social rate of return (counting only pecuniary rewards, not deflated by the increase in the consumer price index) for those who invested in some college (one to three years only) was 14 per cent, whereas the rate of return for those who invested in completing college with a bachelor's degree was only 10 per cent. Thus, in their capacity as investors seeking money returns, college dropouts did better than college graduates (in the particular sample with data on earnings for 1955 and 1969).[14]

[13] This is the NBER-TH sample, compiled by the National Bureau of Economic Research, using an earlier study by Thorndike and Hagen. It consists of 70 per cent responses to a questionnaire sent in 1955 to 17,000 Army Air Force volunteers randomly chosen from 75,000 men tested in 1943. See Robert L. Thorndike and Elizabeth P. Hagen, *Ten Thousand Careers* (New York: Wiley, 1959). For a concise description, see F. Thomas Juster, "Appendix A: Basic Data," in F. Thomas Juster, ed., *Education, Income and Human Behavior*, A Report prepared for the Carnegie Commission on Higher Education and the National Bureau of Economic Research (New York: McGraw-Hill, 1975), pp. 397-404. The same volume contains the chapter by Paul Taubman and Terence Wales on "Education as an Investment and a Screening Device" (pp. 95-121).

[14] Taubman and Wales, "Education," p. 108.

This result does not seem to be consistent with the same authors' conclusions regarding the screening hypothesis. One could expect the effects of employers' excessive reliance on credentials to be reflected in higher rates of return to investment in college degrees relative to the rates earned by college dropouts (unless they dropped out early in the game). Taubman and Wales, however, sought to find evidence in support of their belief in the importance of the screening function of schools and colleges in very different sets of data: the "occupational distribution of individuals at various educational levels" compared with the hypothetical distribution they would expect if entry to the labor market and to the jobs desired were free rather than restricted by admission tickets in the form of diplomas.[15] The authors held that "high-paying occupations" are closed to job seekers without college education, a discriminatory restriction that raises the earnings of degree holders at the expense of the excluded, who lack, not the working capacity, but only the credentials. This redistribution of income "does not benefit society." Their conclusion: "Since we find screening to be important quantitatively, our conclusion that overinvestment in education has occurred is strengthened."[16]

The arguments as well as the empirical analysis of Taubman and Wales have been rejected by several critics. In a closely reasoned review, Mary Jean Bowman pointed to several flaws in the econometric procedures used, questioned whether their "manipulations of the occupational structure" could be "taken seriously," and found their theoretical models "internally inconsistent."[17] Among others who found the assessment of a substantial or significant screening effect of the diploma for graduation from high school or college either unsupported or disconfirmed by evidence is Richard Eckaus.[18] He showed that the large differentials in earnings of high-school graduates over those of early school leavers (dropouts) were only apparent in data for annual earnings but vanished when earnings were corrected for hours worked per year. Similarly, the apparent difference in internal rates of return to investment in four years of college and in only three years of college—a difference often "interpreted as possibly indicative of the 'union card' or 'certification effect' of a

[15] Ibid., p. 113.

[16] Ibid., pp. 118-119.

[17] Bowman, "Through Education," pp. 221-292, esp. pp. 225-226, 253-256, and 261-269.

[18] Richard S. Eckaus, "Estimation of the Returns to Education with Hourly Standardized Incomes" in Estimating the Returns to Education: A Disaggregated Approach (Berkeley, Cal.: Carnegie Commission on Higher Education, 1973), pp. 6-9.

college diploma"—disappears when the calculation is made with incomes standardized for hours of work per year. Eckaus concludes that "the 'union card' interpretation of the effect of the last year of college must now be put aside."[19]

Clarifications

Some of the above arguments and counterarguments may have been a little confusing, and it is not easy to judge comparative weights of the contradictory pieces of evidence for or against the screening hypothesis. Clarificaticns may be helpful.

We take it for granted that schooling does fulfil a filtering and sorting function: school administrators and teachers select the students to be promoted to higher grades and/or to be advised to proceed to more advanced studies; moreover, students engage in some self-selecting when they decide whether to continue schooling or to quit. To say this is not to contend that sorting is the *chief* function of schooling beyond some level, let alone, the *only* function actually fulfilled. The screening hypothesis supposes that students with more years of schooling, certified by graduation diplomas or college degrees, will get better jobs and receive higher lifetime earnings, not because the additional years of schooling have increased their capacity and improved their performance, but chiefly or solely because employers, trusting the school credentials, give certified graduates preference in employment, in promotion, and in rates of compensation.

What are the qualifications or traits of the students and job seekers that are supposedly attested to and duly certified by the diplomas or degrees? Three traits have been stressed by different observers: family background (social class), affective behavior (attitudes), and ability (aptitudes). Critics of bourgeois society have claimed that employers and school authorities, conspiring to maintain the given social structure, have undertaken to favor, and therefore to label, students who "come from the right homes" and, hence, are disposed to conserve the social order.[20] Critics of the functioning of competitive markets have suggested that employers discriminate against job seekers coming from "wrong families" and favor children of respectable and respected parentage.[21]

---

[19] Ibid., p. 6.

[20] Samuel Bowles and Herbert Gintis, *Schooling in Capitalist America: Educational Reform and the Contradictions of Economic Life* (New York: Basic Books, 1976). No specific quotations give expression to this view, but it is inherent in their main argument.

[21] Rejecting this hypothesis, Chiswick reports on research findings to the effect that in regression analysis the alleged influence of the father's schooling disappears if the mother's schooling is included as a separate variable. Chiswick, "Schooling," p. 153.

Employers could test for all three traits—societal, affective, and cognitive—relatively cheaply without reliance on school credentials. If such credentials are available, employers, private or public, will of course save the expense of operating testing departments or buying the services of testing agencies. But the idea that private employers in competitive industries would permanently overpay graduates of high schools or colleges just because of their credentials is not believable. If firms, trying to make profit under the pressure of competition, perceive or suspect that they could get equally capable employees without school credentials at considerably lower rates of pay, they surely would hire them—and any differentials in earnings attributable to school credentials would vanish. However, if almost all students complete twelve years of school, except those unwilling or unable to learn, the absence of a high-school diploma signals to employers a real difference in the attitudes and/or aptitudes of the dropouts. In this case, the preference given to those who have completed school is neither irrational nor arbitrary nor discriminatory: it takes account of a potentially real difference in the quality of labor.

We must guard against a misunderstanding: to state that those without a high-school diploma are likely to be less capable, less reliable, or less productive than those with a diploma is not to affirm that the four years of high school have increased the capability, reliability, or productivity of the students entering the labor market. If students completing nine years of school are coerced, pressured, or persuaded to study for three additional years, and if all but the rebels, the loafers, and the dimwitted conform with the rule that wants them to "sit out" three more years of schooling, they will probably earn preferred hiring and higher compensation than the nonconformers, the dropouts. Although this may prove that the conformers are more productive than the nonconformers, it does not prove that three extra years of schooling have increased the productivity of the conformers, that is, have made them perform better than they would have been capable of performing without the added schooling.

The difference is subtle and easily misunderstood. The fact that individuals who have graduated from secondary school receive higher earnings than those who have attended school for only nine years may be due to their greater capabilities and more desirable attitudes, but it is quite possible that they have had these capabilities and attitudes already at the end of nine years of schooling. In this case, the difference in earnings can be attributed to the difference in performance—not just to the high-school diploma—but not to the investment in the additional three years of schooling.

This is really a confusing conclusion: the credentials, or the signals they convey, may be trustworthy, in that the certified graduates with additional years of school attendance or college are really better performers than those who quit school years before; yet, it need not be the additional schooling that has given them the superior performing capacity—they may have been equally superior without these extra years at school.

Private Gain and Social Loss

We have observed before that matters look quite different from the private and public points of view. The possible "divergence between social and private demands for information" about workers' productive capacities was most rigorously analyzed by Kenneth Arrow for the case of "higher education as a filter."[22] In order to "make a dramatic and one-sided presentation of the screening model," Arrow assumes that college education "contributes in no way to superior economic performance; it increases neither cognition nor socialization. Instead, higher education serves as a screening device, in that it sorts out individuals of different abilities, thereby conveying information to the purchasers of labor."[23] This valuable information which the employer receives free of charge is a productive service "from the private viewpoint." Can it also have a social value?

Arrow shows that colleges may "serve really as a double filter, once in selecting entrants and once in passing or failing students."[24] To find out under what conditions the sorting function of the college can have a social value, Arrow considers first "the simplest model of production," where "all individuals are perfect substitutes in production with ratios given by their productivities."[25] By this he means

[22] Kenneth J. Arrow, "Higher Education as a Filter," *Journal of Public Economics*, Vol. 2 (July-August 1973), pp. 193-216. The quoted clause is on p. 199. Arrow does not say why he confines his analysis to the screening role of college, but it stands to reason that high school cannot do much sifting when as much as 90 per cent (or more) of the population in the relevant age group pass through that wide-meshed sieve.

[23] Ibid., p. 194. "Socialization" by education is "the acquisition of skills such as the carrying out of assigned tasks, getting along with others, regularity, punctuality, and the like . . ." (p. 193). Arrow remarks that "the socialization hypothesis is just as much a human capital theory as the cognitive skill acquisition hypothesis" (p.194). Workers' "socialization"—reinforcing discipline, reliability, working morale, and similar attitudes—improves their social as well as private productivity.

[24] Ibid., p. 195. A third filter is self-selection by applicants for admission to college. In actual fact, the screening by the college is effective only if strict standards are maintained. In many colleges, admission standards are practically nonexistent, and standards for completion and graduation have become so low that there is not much sifting left. In the prestige colleges all three stages of screening are effective.

[25] Ibid., p. 199.

that all products call for only one type of labor, though not all workers are equally fast, equally reliable, equally productive. It would be nice for individual producers to know which are the best workers, but if some sorting process, like the college filter, helped to channel more of the most productive workers to particular producers, other producers would obtain more workers of below-average quality. The allocation of selected workers to selective producers may be of private value to those concerned but of no social value, because for total production the distribution of workers among employers and products makes no difference. The production functions are such that for any output two workers of given efficiency are perfectly substitutable for four workers of half that efficiency or for one worker of twice that efficiency. With total output independent of how labor of different efficiency is distributed, sorting is without social value. If the sorting process is costly, "these costs are simply a social waste."[26] Depending on various conditions, there may be "a net gain in social output by abolishing college, and everybody could be made better off by doing so and redistributing income suitably."[27]

The case is different if production functions call for "complementary kinds of labor. Then education has a positive value in sorting out types of workers."[28] Total output can be "increased by successful filtering, provided, of course, that the cost of the filter is not too high."[29] Assuming that college identifies the individuals who have the qualifications for one type of labor (whereas those without these abilities cannot secure college admission and graduation), higher education will facilitate the allocation of that type of labor to the producers who need it. There is still "a divergence between private and social benefits in filtering, but . . . it is no longer true that the socially optimal level of college education is zero."[30]

When filtering through college may be socially valuable, there is still the question whether "on-the-job filtering" is not more effective or less expensive. "To the extent that the employer does filter and does so accurately, the value of the college filter is reduced."[31] On-the-job filtering has the advantage that job performance is more easily judged; "ability to pass [college] tests is [only] weakly related to ability to perform specific productive tasks."[32]

---

[26] Ibid.

[27] Ibid., p. 201.

[28] Ibid., p. 202.

[29] Ibid., p. 203.

[30] Ibid., p. 211. I am puzzled by Arrow's disregard of wage payments by piece rates, which might take care of many screening problems.

[31] Ibid., p. 215.

[32] Ibid.

Concluding Speculations

Assume it is true that extended schooling, especially college, has little value to society in the function of sifting and sorting possessors of productive abilities. Assume it is also true that its value in creating or reinforcing these abilities is quite uncertain. Contrast these assumptions with the presumption that the private value of academic credentials is considerable. Can this situation—if it is the situation in the United States in the 1980s—continue indefinitely, or is it liable to change?

Some of the hitherto patient students are likely to realize, sooner or later, that in the added years at school or in college they are not learning anything that makes them more efficient or more competent performers in the occupations for which market demand is strong. Recognizing that they are wasting time, they may drop out of school and try in some other way to demonstrate their high qualifications to employers, convincing them that certification of long-term school attendance is not the only signal of superior capacity. Employers may eventually learn to find qualified workers from the pool of early school-leavers, "dropouts" in present-day parlance.

It may be many years, however, until such a correction takes place. The fact that those with more years of schooling receive, on the average, better rates of compensation may keep most students at school and in college. It takes courage and self-confidence for able students to join the less competent dropouts, and risk unemployment or poorly paid employment, in the hope of devising other ways to signal their qualifications to possible employers or of being able to prove these qualifications in a low-paying job effectively enough to be promoted to a job commensurate with their capacities. Not many students may have the self-confidence to act on their suspicions about how little school can do for them, and to resist the high-pressure salesmanship of educators, politicians, and labor-union spokesmen, all trying to keep young people at school (and out of the labor market) as long as possible. If virtually everyone tells them about the large benefits of more years of schooling, and about the high risks of dropping out, students will not easily come to the decision to quit school and look for a job. Similarly, if employers have for years found that school credentials have been a reliable signal of superior qualifications, they may not readily turn to seeking exceptionally good workers from among the "dropouts."

What might eventually speed up the process of correcting the overestimation of the contribution extended schooling makes to the graduates' productive capacities—assuming that such overestimation is real and widespread—would be a period of severe glut in the market for "overqualified labor." When increasing numbers of job seekers who have earned the credentials certifying long years of school attendance find it hard to obtain the fine jobs they believe to have earned through their patience, their disappointment may become infectious and lead to younger cohorts' disenchantment with unnecessarily extended schooling. The superior workers among the early school-leavers may have to accept jobs with low pay and poor working conditions but prove to their supervisors that they deserve rapid advancement. If such upward mobility of laborers without school credentials becomes more frequent, more visible, and better publicized, credentialism may vanish. Such an optimistic prediction, however, may be entirely out of place—for it is quite possible that the analysts who deny the existence of credentialism have been right, and what does not exist cannot vanish.

CHAPTER 19

DEPRECIATION OF KNOWLEDGE STOCKS
AND HUMAN CAPITAL

THE AGENDA for this chapter is largely determined by what is to come after it. The next chapter will deal with profiles of outlays for learning and of receipts of earnings. The chapter after the next will deal with rates of return. Because rates of return are ratios of earnings to sums or "stocks" of capital, it seems clear that the present chapter has to be devoted to the discussion of stocks. The value of a stock increases by additions and appreciation and diminishes by withdrawals and depreciation. Since additions (investments) have been discussed all along and appreciation of previous accumulations is not a regular phenomenon (unless the stocks have to be currently revalued to adjust for price inflation), write-offs for withdrawals and depreciation are the "natural" subject of this chapter.

Stocks of knowledge are not necessarily stocks of human capital; nor do all stocks of human capital consist of stocks of knowledge. I have said this before and I shall presently clarify this statement. First, however, I want to make it clear why the problem of allowances for depreciation is inextricably connected with the theory of capital. Nonpermanence of resources is an attribute and, in some definitions, a characteristic of capital as a source of flows of services or benefits; and nonpermanence—depletion, exhaustion, deterioration, extinction—implies a concern with depreciation allowances if the flow of services or benefits is to be sustained. Thus, all capital accounting involves depreciation accounting. This has always been understood with regard to physical capital. Analysis of depreciation of human and other nonmaterial capital is a relatively recent item on the economist's agenda; it has been explored in only a few articles and chapters published during the last ten or fifteen years.

Stocks of Knowledge and Human Capital

In several statements in the first volume of this work I raised questions about the meaning of a "stock of knowledge." Several conceptual obstacles hinder, or even prevent, making good sense of this term. There is the difference between knowledge of "that which is known" and knowledge as "the state of knowing" and, as soon as one goes beyond a single mind or memory, the problem of additivity arises. There are, moreover, the difference between knowledge of enduring significance and knowledge of merely temporary, quickly vanishing relevance; the difference between knowledge important for many and knowledge of interest to only a few; and, of course, the difference between practical knowledge, which may help in the production of things wanted, and intellectual knowledge, spiritual knowledge, and pastime knowledge, all of which may be desired, regarded as valuable, and produced at a cost, and which may contribute to long-lasting flows of pleasures and satisfactions, without being instrumental in the production of things included in the usual national-income-and-product accounts.

In view of all these differences, one cannot reasonably identify, count, measure, or estimate the "stocks" of knowledge recorded on written or printed matter, or on disks and tapes, or stored in human memories. The situation is not much better regarding the flow of knowledge per period of time, say, per year, as long as one has no good idea of quantities of message units produced, transmitted, or received. Thus, neither flows nor stocks of knowledge can be measured as long as one cannot devise a reasonable unit of measurement. (See Volume I, Chapter 9.) The only somehow manageable makeshift is to use the "measuring rod of money" for expenditures and implicit costs incurred in knowledge-creating and knowledge-transmitting activities.[1]

A cost-accounting for annual flows of knowledge makes good sense; but how much of that flow becomes a valuable stock and how long that stock remains valuable is impossible to determine. If consumers, producers, and governments in the United States spent $136 billion on knowledge in 1958 and, say, $148 billion in 1959, and perhaps $166 billion in 1960, should we assume that some constant or variable portion of these amounts were costs of "investment" in knowledge, added to a previously accumulated stock of knowledge? Or should we classify the expenditures into investment, consumption, and intermediate production cost, and add the amounts of investment to the capital account?

I did make several classifications for the expenditures of 1958. I divided them according to who paid for them: government, $38 billion; business, $42 billion; and consumers, $56 billion. I divided

---

[1] Perhaps I should at this place join a specialist in information theory in warning the reader against "speculations revolving around the concept of information [in the sense of the mathematical theory of communication] as a tool for quantifying the 'amount of knowledge.' " Anatol Rapoport, "The Promise and Pitfalls of Information Theory," *Behavioral Science*, Vol. 1 (1956).

them according to branches of knowledge production (or knowledge industries): education, $60 billion; R and D, $11 billion; media of communication, $38 billion; information services, $18 billion; and information machines, $9 billion (and each of these I subdivided into subbranches.) Finally, I divided them into final product (investment or consumption), $109 billion, and intermediate product (current cost), $27 billion.[2] With a little more daring I might have attempted a rough division of the expenditures for knowledge as final product into investment and consumption. I intend to make these judgments in some of the subsequent volumes of the present work.

If I judge certain expenditures for creation and dissemination of knowledge to be investments, these would be gross investments of still undetermined service lives. They would be gross investments because some part of them, or possibly all of them, might be merely replacements of knowledge no longer serviceable and hence written off from the (imaginary) capital account. Moreover, for every investment one would have to judge how long the stream of services or benefits expected from it can be assumed to last and at what rate these returns would diminish or dwindle over time.

Knowledge as Consumption Capital

Certain expenditures for knowledge production are classified as consumption expenditures because the utility or satisfaction derived from them does not last long enough; the outlay does not create assets yielding streams of psychic benefits for more than a year. This is a rather arbitrary judgment; some cultural events and even mere entertainments may give a lifetime of pleasurable recollections. A circus performance may give a young child a joyful experience he or she will treasure all through life. An outstanding opera performance may be an unforgettable experience, an asset the appreciative beholder will not write off from the value of his stock of "consumer capital" as long as he lives. Yet, such grateful spectators and music fans are probably only small minorities among the entire audiences, and it would then not be appropriate to enter in the investment account the total box-office receipts plus subsidies from private and public funds as the value of additional consumption capital.

Similar considerations hold for expenditures on mass media of communication, both print and electronic media. The cost of news-

---

[2] Fritz Machlup, *The Production and Distribution of Knowledge in the United States* (Princeton: Princeton University Press, 1962), p. 361, based on Table IX-1, pp. 354-357.

papers and magazines as well as the cost of broadcasting operations will not be entered as new consumption capital even when the knowledge transmitted is new to many and long appreciated by a few. On the other hand, books placed on the shelves of public and private libraries could be regarded as gross additions to the stock of knowledge capital; and this is true also for purchases of radios and television sets and for new equipment and installations by broadcasting stations. Library collections of scholarly books and scientific journals may even be judged as stocks of *productive* knowledge capital, on the assumption that they contribute to the long-run productivity of many readers. On the other hand, these are not net additions to the stock since the knowledge transmitted may not remain useful forever. Most books and journal articles have "half-lives" of only a few years, as we have learned from citation indexes; hence, a rate of depreciation of such capital stocks has to be taken into account.

It has been an accepted convention among economists that the cost of schooling be considered an investment, a purchase of durable human wealth, not of knowledge consumed within a year. The question, however, whether this investment makes additions to the stock of productive capital or to the stock of consumption capital has not been given much attention. Perhaps the fear of being labeled as crass materialists, as philistines insensitive to cultural values, has kept some economists from stressing the distinction between capital (or wealth) that yields streams of psychic income and capital that aids in the production of other things and thus operates as some sort of multiplier in the production process. It is clear that a goodly portion of what we learn in school and college makes us more appreciative readers, more sensitive viewers of nature and art, more interesting conversationalists, without making us necessarily more efficient workers, more effective supervisors, or more resourceful managers in the production of goods and services. It follows that the effects of schooling upon productivity and its effects on only psychic benefits should be distinguished: whereas both increase our welfare, additions to productive human capital contribute not only to our income but also to faster rates of *increase* in income.

In making this statement, no value judgment is intended; but it is of significance to distinguish between addition and multiplication. Granting that welfare is increased both by additional physical goods and by additional cultural benefits, the economist cannot honestly be silent about the fact that an increase in human capacity to produce can have far greater effects upon total welfare because it may augment the flow of goods and services by a factor greater than 1.

There was a time when economists were anxious to distinguish between wealth and capital, with wealth as the wider concept including capital as that part of wealth that is instrumental in the production of other goods and services. A beautiful sculpture may yield an endless stream of benefits in the form of consumers' satisfaction; a lovely house may yield a stream of satisfactions to inhabitants, neighbors, and passers-by for hundreds of years. Such structures are part of our wealth, but they are not productive capital. It was perhaps semantic awkwardness to propose and adopt the term "consumption capital" for wealth yielding services that are not used as complementary factors in production processes.

Are these questions mere quibbles, semantic hairsplitting, purely academic disputations, or are they relevant to the interpretation of observed phenomena? If attempts are made to explain variations in observed growth rates of gross national product by changes in the stock of human capital, and to measure the stock of human capital as an explanatory variable in determining the rates of growth of factor productivity and final output, then it *is* significant that we use the appropriate theoretical concept and classify the data for the pertinent measurements in a way consistent with the theory. This is the reason why economists should reconsider the present convention of estimating a stock of human capital—adding gross investment and deducting depreciation—without sufficient regard to its division into "consumption capital" or productive capital.[3]

Depreciation of Capital, Physical and Human

In the official system of social accounts, durable real, or physical, capital goods acquired by business firms are shown, in the year in which they are produced, as "final" products, although they are destined to become instruments in the production of other goods

---

[3] The realization that many durable goods are consumer wealth rather than productive capital has probably contributed to the convention, adopted by our official national-product accountants, not to bother with gradual depreciation of consumer durables, but to write them off completely at the time of purchase. Even if passenger automobiles (not owned by business firms) may have service lives of more than ten years, they are regarded as fully consumed in the first year, with no addition made to the stock of "consumption capital." The continuing availability of these vehicles surely matters in estimates of national welfare, but may not matter very much in an accounting of stocks of productive capital. Perhaps dishwashing machines and air conditioners are better examples, because it can be argued that the possession of passenger cars raises workers' productivity by facilitating their transport to the places of work. Incidentally, that our official system of social accounts does not recognize expenditures for education as investments, to be written off over many years, implies that the knowledge and skills produced are assumed to be consumed at once, or that any stock of human capacity is depreciated by 100 per cent at the time of its creation.

and services in subsequent years. These expenditures, at market prices or factor cost, are taken to be *gross* investment, and hence part of *gross* national product; depreciation of existing stocks of capital goods is deducted to obtain *net* national product, which consists of *net* investment and consumption. The underlying theory is that some of gross capital formation is taken as merely replacing the part of the stock of real capital that has become worn-out, depleted, obsolete, or abandoned. The depreciation allowances, as reported by the firms that own and employ the capital goods, are included in the values of the goods and services produced with the help of the depreciating real capital assets, but they are deducted from the new gross investment expenditures when the new net capital formation is estimated.

Are the considerations that have led to these accounting procedures for physical capital applicable to human and other nonmaterial capital? Official social accounting has not thought so: neither gross investment nor net investment in human and other nonmaterial capital is included in GNP or NNP; some expenditures for knowledge production are shown as consumption, some as current cost of intermediate products, and some of the costs are omitted altogether. A large and growing group of economists, however, has been engaged in devising new systems of social accounting to accommodate a wider concept of national product, income, and welfare. They have taken account of knowledge production and of that portion of it that can be regarded as formation of human capital. For these emerging social-accounting systems the question of whether the principles developed for physical capital are applicable to nonmaterial capital becomes relevant. In particular, should expenditures for the production of knowledge in the minds of children, adolescents, and adults be treated as gross investments in human capital, and should they be subject to adjustments for depreciation of existing stocks of human capital? The knowledge in question, whether of the knowing-*what* or the knowing-*how* type, may depreciate over the years. Thus, there is a strong case for treating investment in human and other nonmaterial capital in ways analogous to the principles adopted for physical capital.

There are differences, however, conceptual and operational, but especially operational. The most important difference lies in the availability of recorded data: annual gross investments in physical capital, stocks of physical capital assets, and depreciation allowances for physical assets are all recorded in the books of business firms and reported to the tax authorities and other governmental agencies. No records exist of investments in human capital, gross or net, of stocks past or present, or of depreciation of human capital previously accumulated. In the absence of genuine data, empirical researchers have to develop—"invent" may be a more appropriate word—their numerical series from information about "distant relatives," pressed into service as proxies and subjected to a sequence of manipulations in accordance with algebraic models constructed to conform with rather bold hypotheses. The use of these (untestable, though quite plausible) hypotheses, makes the differences between physical and human capital accounting conceptual as well as operational.

That economists have to invent statistical series by applying heroic hypotheses and ingenious manipulations to figures that do not directly disclose what we want to know is exemplified (below in Chapter 20) by the account of Jacob Mincer's research. He showed how gross and net investment in human capital through training on the job, and depreciation of the accumulated stocks of human capital, could be estimated without a single genuine datum on any of these magnitudes. Another researcher on the same complex of interrelated concepts and measures, Sherwin Rosen, had this to say about the lack of data: "Knowledge embodied in a person is not directly observable, and it is necessary to estimate capital accumulation (in value terms) at each age as well as obsolescence and depreciation rates . . . [but,] in principle, rates of obsolescence and depreciation cannot be estimated as a 'pure' problem in measurement and in the absence of a model."[4]

Be this as it may, one has to recognize that a problem of accounting for depreciation exists for human as for physical capital, even if the data bases are very different. When stocks of human capital are estimated at different times, depreciation of earlier accumulations has to be estimated in the process. Not clear at this juncture, however, is whether we are more interested in the capital formation that takes place during a period of time (a year) or in the capital stock that exists at certain moments of time (at year's end). It is possible that certain problems require information on only one of these two magnitudes, the other serving only as an intermediate step in finding the desired one.

The Causes of Depreciation of Human Capital

All capital accounting can be done, in principle, in two ways: (1) One may compare the value of the total stock at two consecutive

[4] Sherwin Rosen, "Measuring the Obsolescence of Knowledge," in F. Thomas Juster, ed., *Education, Income, and Human Behavior*. A Report prepared for the Carnegie Commission on Higher Education and the National Bureau of Economic Research (New York: McGraw-Hill, 1975), p. 205.

moments of time and take the difference as a measure of the *net* capital formation that has taken place in the interval. (2) One may add up the (gross) investment expenditures over a period of time to arrive at the total of *gross* capital formation, deduct from it an estimate of the depreciation of the previously existing capital stock, and take the remainder as net capital formation.

These methods are rather obvious in the case of physical capital. In the case of human capital, however, the first method is inapplicable, because we do not have valuations of the stock of human capital at consecutive dates. The few attempts that have been made to arrive at the total value of the stock of human capital have been for a few selected dates, and results were usually arrived at by cumulating investments in human capital over some presumably appropriate period of time. Thus, researchers are confined to using the second method: It may cause moderate difficulties in selecting and estimating the expenditures and associated implicit costs that may normally be regarded as gross investment in human capital; and it involves the intricate problems of ascertaining the amount to be deducted from gross investment to account for the depreciation of previously existing stocks of human capital and thus to obtain the amount of net investment.

Depreciation, in one sense of the word, is a reduction of market values, ordinarily a result of anonymous market forces; in another sense, depreciation is the reduction of book values of assets decided upon by accountants using conventional rules or informed judgment to adjust financial accounts so that they reflect sound estimates of the present values of the assets in question. Neither an appropriate choice of rules nor a reasonable exercise of judgment is possible without analysis of the causes of, or reasons for, depreciation. These causes are different for different assets, and they are different also for different types of human capital. Assume that the human capital in question consists of mental and physical capacities embodied in individuals as a result of costly activities (investments) imparting useful knowledge. Such knowledge may be of the knowing-*what* type (cognitive) or of the knowing-*how* type (skills). Some causes of depreciation operate with equal strength on both types of knowledge; others, however, operate on one type more severely than on the other. I propose to distinguish four major categories of causes of depreciation of human capital formed through costly acquisition of knowledge: (1) elimination or termination of the carrier of the knowledge as participant in the production process; (2) deterioration of the carrier's mental or physical capacities, for example, loss of memory;

(3) obsolescence of the knowledge in question; and (4) decline in the scarcity value of the knowledge in question. A fifth category may be mentioned: (5) erosion of trained workers' skills through long interruptions of their employment. Let us discuss these categories in turn.

Termination

Human capital consisting of knowledge-based capacities of an individual is lost when the individual, the knowledge carrier, dies; when he retires at a stipulated age; when he retires prematurely because of illness, perhaps as a result of an accident, or because of a decisive preference for leisure; or when his employment is terminated by his employer.

If the concept of human capital is narrow, confined to capacities employed in production processes, the knowledge-carrier's retirement from the job and from the labor force calls for a complete write-off of the particular capital asset: it is depreciated to zero. If the concept is wide enough to include consumption capital, retirement from productive activity need not reduce the value of the individuals' knowledge to zero. Some of the retired persons' accumulated stocks of knowledge remain valuable for their consumption activities, for example, as they enjoy reading, participating in serious discussions, appreciating works of art, listening to serious music, teaching their grandchildren, and taking part in several other activities for which earlier investment in intellectual knowledge is essential.

As I have said in an earlier section, analysts and social accountants whose major interests are in economic growth and advances in factor productivity are apt to prefer the narrower concept of "productive" human capital. Consistency with this conception would require a rule of depreciation that reduces the value of knowledge-based capacity of retired persons to zero, and provides for systematic write-downs of human capital as employed workers approach retirement.

Deterioration

Deterioration of the mental or physical capacities of carriers of useful knowledge is a major cause of depreciating the stock of human capital. Note that I refer here to deterioration of the carriers of knowledge, not of the knowledge they carry (which will be discussed separately under the headings of obsolescence and reduction of scarcity value). The deterioration of knowledge carriers may be due to physiological or psychological changes, reducing their physical or mental powers. It may be a slowing down of reactions, a gradual or sudden loss of agility, or malfunctions of muscles or memory. The memory loss may be so complete as to result in the loss of a particularly rare piece of knowledge; in this case, not only the carrier of the knowledge but the knowledge itself may be lost to society—forgotten and perhaps irretrievable. Whereas this is probably an exceptional instance, the deterioration of mental and physical powers of aging persons is a normal process with which we all must reckon.

Evidence for the prevalence of deterioration of human capacities to perform is conclusive from medical statistics as well as from statistics of earnings from employment (or self-employment) of older persons. This does not mean that each and every member of the labor force shows signs of deterioration before retirement; indeed, a good many workers retire with unimpaired mental and physical strength. Still, they are a minority; the normal curve of performing and earning capacity shows a downward slope during the last years before the conventional retirement age.

It should be clear that this normal experience calls for adjustment of the book value of human capital. Depreciation rules must take account of the deterioration of capacity.[5]

Obsolescence

Obsolescence of knowledge is largely a consequence of the emergence of new knowledge, either of the cognitive sort (knowing *what*) or of performing skill (knowing *how*). Most often it is technological progress that makes existing production techniques obsolescent or obsolete. When a new method of production is developed that is superior to methods hitherto used, the knowledge of the superseded techniques and the know-how related to them lose value. They may become worthless at once; more frequently, however, the old techniques can still be used in competition with the new ones and may retain for some time a declining remainder of their original value.

The implications and consequences of obsolescence in cases of knowledge embodied in individual persons are different from those in which knowledge is embodied in particular machines and material

---

[5] A warning against a strange linguistic confusion may be in order. Some writers speak of depreciation as a cause of deterioration instead of the other way around. Deterioration is a physical or mental process, a reduction of the capacity to perform or to please; depreciation (derived from the Latin *precium*, price) is the market's or the accountants' reaction to deterioration, obsolescence, or other reductions in the usefulness of the asset in question. Among writers who have committed the error are Yoram Ben-Porath, "The Production of Human Capital and the Life-Cycle of Earnings," *Journal of Political Economy*, Vol. 75 (July-August 1967, Part I), pp. 352-365, and Sherwin Rosen, "Measuring," pp. 199-232. Rosen, for example, spoke of "obsolescence and depreciation" and "a combined deterioration rate," p. 207.

goods, and also those in which knowledge is not embodied in either persons or material goods. Hence, depreciation due to obsolescence may follow different rules for human capital, for other nonmaterial capital, and for physical capital. One should not assume that an obsolete machine, an obsolete machinist, and an obsolete technique in the manufacture of machinery, can all be treated, in economic analysis and national accounts, as if they were a single phenomenon to be examined with the aid of one theoretical model. The case of the obsolete machine or, in general, obsolescence of physical capital, can be left aside in the present discussion, because it has been sufficiently explored in the literature. This is not so in the cases of human capital and of nonembodied-knowledge capital. Obsolescence of nonembodied knowledge will be discussed first.

Obsolescence of Nonembodied Knowledge

Of the various classes of knowledge, obsolescence of *practical* knowledge will have the greatest practical importance; and of all types of practical knowledge, *technology* may be singled out as the one for which obsolescence is of principal significance. The technological knowledge most relevant in a discussion of obsolescence is that which was acquired at a cost, especially through *investments in research and development*. These investments are assumed to have built up a "stock of R and D" or "a stock of knowledge capital."

To refer to the knowledge built up as a result of R and D expenditures as "nonembodied" (disembodied)[6] technological change, usually called progress, is, in some sense, conceptually inaccurate; after all, knowledge is not floating around in space as a noncorporeal entity (or perhaps analogous to waves of light) but is always embodied in something, either brains or records on paper, tapes, or disks. The economically relevant difference lies in the attribution of the beneficial consequences of productive uses of the knowledge in question. Knowledge embodied in individual persons that increases their productivity may be paid for by higher wage rates (rentals of labor) earned by the knowledge carriers. Knowledge embodied in particular machines that increases the efficiency of these pieces of equipment may result in higher prices or rentals paid for them. Knowledge *not* embodied in either people or machines may increase the productivity of any or all factors of production; by increasing total output, it increases physical productivity per man, machine, or

---

[6] The term "disembodied" technological progress was introduced by Robert Solow in a paper published in 1959. See above, footnote 14 in Chapter 13.

acre of land although no change has occurred in the quality or make-up of these factors. Their *marginal* physical productivity (the increment in output due to the employment of an additional unit of input) may rise or fall in the process, because the technological change may be labor augmenting, capital augmenting, land augmenting, or "neutral," that is, the effects of a new technique may be equivalent to increases in supply of any or all of these factors.[7] What happens to the *value* of output in terms of money, and to the "revenue productivity" of the factors engaged in its production depends on the elasticity of demand for the product. If that elasticity is small (smaller than unity), total sales revenue declines as output increases, and the "marginal revenue products" of the employed factors become negative. This does not mean, however, that society will not benefit from the increase in total output; it only means that such benefits are harder to estimate, because the depressed prices of products in larger supply do not readily reveal the effects upon consumers' welfare. Conventional national-income accounting does not reflect the welfare increase due to nonembodied technological progress.

Some writers on this subject have compared disembodied technological knowledge to "manna from heaven [falling] on all men and machines."[8] The analogy may help us understand that men do not have to be retrained and machines do not have to be remodeled in order to become more efficient (produce more per unit of input) thanks to the new techniques, but if it leads us to think that this technological progress is available without effort or sacrifice, the manna analogy misleads. To be sure, *some* of the new ideas in technology or management may be costless, but a far greater part is the result of conscious effort and expense. One need not assume that all technological progress is due to investment (public or private) in R and D activities, or that all R and D expenditures succeed in producing improved techniques, but expansion of R and D generally leads to technological advance. Only in most exceptional cases will an increase in R and D expenditures lead to increased productivity in the same year; it may take several years for the results to be realized

[7] Economists have long distinguished between labor-saving, capital-saving, and neutral inventions. They have used labor/output, labor/capital, and capital/output ratios to characterize the effects but have differed in the definition of neutrality. For explanations see, for example, Roy G. D. Allen, *Macro-Economic Theory: A Mathematical Treatment* (London: Macmillan, 1967), Chap. 13; or Edwin Burmeister and A. Rodney Dobell, *Mathematical Theories of Economic Growth* (New York: Macmillan, 1970), pp. 65-66 and 90-91.

[8] Allen, *Macro-Economic Theory*, p. 254; similarly, p. 236.

in production and sales, and estimates of more than five years as the average lag seem quite plausible.[9] The existence of this lag is a cogent reason for regarding R and D expenditures as investments in future productivity. Investments build up capital stocks; investments in R and D build up a stock of nonmaterial capital in the form of nonembodied technology. (Of course, many of the new techniques may call

[9] Since writing these lines in the text I have seen empirical studies that arrived at much shorter lags of practical application behind the inception of applied research. The so-called "R and D lag" is commonly subdivided into the "gestation lag"—from the inception of a project of applied research to its completion—and the "application lag"—from the completion of the research to the practical (or "commercial") application of the innovation. John Rapoport decomposed the innovation process into five stages: applied research, specification, prototype or pilot plant, tooling and manufacturing facilities, and start-up of manufacturing. It stands to reason that the first two stages constitute the gestation lag, the other three the application lag. Rapoport estimates the sum of the two lags for innovations in electronics to average less than one and one-fourth years. His estimate of the total lag in the machinery industry is larger, though still less than two and one-half years. John Rapoport, "The Anatomy of the Product-Innovation Process: Cost and Time," and "The Time-Cost Trade-Off Function, Overlapping Stages, and the Timing Decision," in Edwin Mansfield et al., *Research and Innovation in the Modern Corporation* (New York: Norton, 1971), pp. 110-135, and 136-156. Leonore Wagner had also estimated very short R and D lags, for example, only about two years and seven months for durable-goods industries. Leonore U. Wagner, "Problems in Estimating Research and Development Investment and Stock," *American Statistical Association, Proceedings of the Business and Economic Statistics Section* (1968), pp. 189-198.

These estimates were endorsed by Pakes and Schankerman in a recent study, largely based on Wagner and Rapoport. The average R and D lag is taken to be between 1.2 and 2.5 years. Ariel Pakes and Mark Schankerman, "The Rate of Obsolescence of Patents, Research Gestation Lags, and the Private Rate of Return to Research Resources," in Zvi Griliches, ed., *R and D, Patents, and Productivity* (Chicago: University of Chicago Press, for the National Bureau of Economic Research, 1983).

My intuition militates against these estimates. Perhaps I am overly impressed by the frequent stories about excessive lags in the development of new types or models in aeronautics, weaponry, rocketry, space missiles, and pharmaceutical products. Perhaps I also overestimate the cost of projects that did not pan out and were abandoned. These projects had an R and D lag of infinity, or the expenditures for them had to be counted as part of the cost of successful innovations.

There are possible explanations for the findings of short lags. For example, the data in the cited studies came from very small samples (35 and 29 observations, respectively) of company-financed innovations and thus omitted notoriously longer-run projects financed by the government. Moreover, the technique of computing the "average" by considering the distribution of expenditures over the total period between start and finish will result in "short lags" if expenditures are heavier in the last stages. In many, perhaps most instances, the bulk of expenditures is incurred in the last year or two before the innovation is reduced to practice. If expenditures were incurred at a constant rate per year, the average lag would be one-half of the total period. The average lag is much shorter if expenditures are bunched near the end. I submit that this technique is misleading in that it takes the expenditures in the last stages to be

for new models of machines and new kinds of manpower training, in which case stocks of physical and human capital will be built up too.)

Sometimes the use of nonembodied technology is restricted. Although the new techniques are recorded in articles, books, or patent documents available to everybody, patents of invention may grant temporary monopolies restricting the making and selling of products for which the particular knowledge is used. In this case, this stock of knowledge—or, more correctly, the exclusive rights to its use— may have private value in excess of the historical cost incurred for the R and D that has led to the particular knowledge. If, on the other hand, the technological knowledge in question is not proprietary but public, easily accesssible and freely usable, and thus can be exploited without limit, its market value is zero; it does not represent private capital, and whether it ought to be regarded as social capital is an open question.[10] If society invests in the creation and dissemination

R and D expenditures, which in fact they are not. As Rapoport states (p. 114), "Stage 5 is *manufacturing start-up*. A number of things must be done before the production facility is ready to begin routine operation. Production workers must be trained. The assembly line or plant must be 'debugged' and procedures set up for manufacturing. Often some production must take place before an acceptable quality level is reached. The cost and time of these tasks is included in the stage 5." My point is that time elapsed in stages 4 and 5 must surely be counted in the lag of application behind expenditures for R and D, but most *expenditures* in these stages are not for R and D, and hence should not be included when the average lag for R and D expenditures is computed. According to Rapoport (p. 123), R and D expenditures constitute only about 50 per cent of the "total cost of the innovation process." The outlays for R and D were largely in the earlier stages of the innovation process, making for a longer, not a shorter, average R and D lag.

In a more recent piece of research, Edwin Mansfield found that in 1967 and 1977 only 34 per cent of R and D expenditures in manufacturing industries were for "projects lasting five or more years." Edwin Mansfield, "Basic Research and Productivity Increase in Manufacturing," *American Economic Review*, Vol. 70 (December 1980), Table 2, p. 870. If this seems to indicate that 66 per cent were for projects lasting less than five years, let us note that (1) the study was for company-financed R and D, excluding therefore the longer-term projects financed by the government, and (2) the data reflected the expectations of the management, not ex post experiences, which ordinarily show substantial cost overruns as well as time overruns. I have concluded that I had better stick to my estimate of an average R and D lag of five years or longer.

[10] If a novel technique, developed by privately or publicly financed R and D, is open to unrestricted exploitation by competing producers, the prices of their products will be too low to allow any rent to be paid for the new knowledge (the marginal cost of its use being zero). National-income-and-product accounts will not show any increase in total output, measured at market or factor prices, even if the physical output of the now more efficiently produced good is increased as a result of a process innovation. An increase in factor productivity can be computed only if the reduction in product prices is taken into account through the use of price-index figures in the calculation of real product. (In the case of product innovations, data on real output will show

of new technological knowledge, in the expectation that such investment will pay off in the form of increased or improved output, a good argument can be made for regarding that knowledge stock as nonmaterial capital, no matter whether or not the stream of benefits from its use is shown in national-product accounts as measured, measurable, or nonmeasurable output. If the benefits cannot be measured or estimated, their present value cannot possibly be ascertained, and the knowledge stock can be quantified only by the cumulated expenditures for R and D. In such a valuation of the knowledge stock, one may have to take account of the fact that some of the knowledge will be superseded; when superior techniques are developed and replace older ones, it may be unsound to count both the new and the old as valuable parts of the knowledge stock. Hence, ongoing obsolescence calls for appropriate depreciation of the particular assets in the nation's accounts.

In the case of proprietary knowledge or, more concretely, of restrictions on the use of patented techniques, the knowledge stock may be said to have private value, and this value, the capitalized value of future monopoly rents, may exceed the patentees' cumulated expenditures for R and D. Should, in this case, the private value of the monopoly rights be also taken as the value of the particular knowledge stock to society? An affirmative answer to this question would have the paradoxical implication that society prefers smaller outputs to larger ones when artificial scarcity can procure larger revenues to private holders of monopoly rights.[11]

Experts in social accounting who regard expenditures for R and D as investments in nontangible capital are satisfied with entering these outlays as gross capital formation; they do not try to calculate and capitalize social benefits above cost (consumer surpluses). Gradual obsolescence of parts of the inventory of productive knowledge will

---

nothing, and R and D will have no effect on measured factor productivity.) The social benefits derived from full utilization of new technological knowledge can perhaps be estimated by using models that include pre-innovation prices for the goods made less expensive by use of knowledge of the better processes. However, no proponent of extended systems of national or domestic welfare accounting has gone so far as to compute present values of future streams of social benefits that have no market value. Even the most progressive designers of product, income, and welfare accounts have settled for the backward look of treating the historical cost of R and D activities as a stock of nonmaterial capital.

[11] Questions of this sort are essential in the analysis of benefits and costs of patent protection, compulsory licensing, and public measures to safeguard the secrecy of undisclosed technological knowledge. A detailed discussion will be offered in Volume VI of this work.

be taken account of by way of successive write-offs of the historical cost incurred in building it up.[12]

Technology Developed in Stages

Even if it is agreed that depreciation of knowledge capital through obsolescence in the course of technical advance should be on the basis of historical cost (not of the higher present value of expected future benefits derived from it), there is still a question of including or excluding the historical cost of earlier stages in the research and development leading to the latest state of the arts. It seems to be generally agreed that invention of a production technique superior to an existing one makes the older one obsolete and that traditional accounting practice would indicate an appropriate "write-off" from the existing stock of technological knowledge. Thus, assuming that the cost of developing technique t_1 was written off when a superior technique, t_2, was invented, and that further R and D has now resulted in a still better technique, t_3, the cost of developing t_2 would be deducted from the value of the stock of human capital. I submit that this treatment of the effects of technological progress is questionable. The following example may show the possible error involved.

Assume that persistent R and D activities in a particular firm lead to the development of technique t_3, but do so in steps, encompassing successively the development of techniques t_1 and t_2. If t_1 and t_2 are not reduced to practice, but are considered only as steps in the development of t_3, no one would suggest that the cost of developing t_1 and t_2 be separated and regarded as wasted. It seems more logical to treat the entire R and D expenditures as the cost necessary for developing technique t_3.

This argument is neither vitiated nor weakened by the fact that the tax laws permit business firms to expense *all* R and D expenditures, successful or abortive, and thus not to record them as having generated a capital asset. Business-accounting practice need not dictate the conventions of social accounting. If economists agree that

[12] If cumulative expenditures on R and D in certain agricultural sectors (say, for hybrid corn) have amounted to 100 million dollars and have yielded social returns of 700 per cent per annum, this rate is meant to refer to the *historical cost* of the investment in the new knowledge. Social accountants would not reappraise and enter the particular knowledge-capital at a "present value" of 10,000 million dollars, reflecting a capitalization of the estimated social benefits at a going rate of interest of 7 per cent. — The illustration used in this footnote is based on the fact that Zvi Griliches once estimated a social rate of return to particular research outlays to have been 700 per cent per annum. Zvi Griliches, "Research Costs and Social Returns: Hybrid Corn and Related Innovations," *Journal of Political Economy*, Vol. 66 (October 1958), pp. 419-431.

the cost of creating and disseminating potentially practical knowledge should be regarded as formation of immaterial capital, all R and D expenditures constitute investment in the sense implied in the theory of immaterial or human capital. There is no good reason why the portion of R and D expenditures incurred in earlier stages leading to the latest technological advances should be deducted from the total investment, and only the expenditures for the last steps should be admitted as having formed the stock of present knowledge included in the present stock of capital.

These considerations should, of course, not be carried too far, lest all past costs of research and development, beginning perhaps with the invention of the wheel, be regarded as part and parcel of the present stock of intangible capital. Yet, is there a reasonable point at which to begin "counting in" all accumulations of knowledge assumed to be useful today? And is there a reasonable half-life of technological knowledge to guide us in deciding on the correct rate of depreciation to account for obsolescence? Views on these questions differ, but no economist, as far as I know, has undertaken to examine the present stock of currently used technological knowledge (not embodied in human beings or in physical goods) for its age composition or for components getting ready to be declared dead or withdrawn from further use.

The first question, where to begin the series of annual expenditures for R and D, has been "solved" in a very arbitrary, highly pragmatic way: the researchers begin with the year for which the first good statistical data are available. Thus, John Kendrick chose 1929 and 1948 as his "benchmarks" for the accumulation of R and D investments in "nonhuman intangible capital" because these were the beginnings of his statistical series of R and D expenditures.[13] Similarly, Nadiri and Bitros, in their study of R and D at the level of the firm (not the economy as a whole), began accumulating the firms' "stocks of research and development" in the first year for which the firms reported consistent data.[14]

---

[13] John W. Kendrick, *The Formation and Stocks of Total Capital* (New York: National Bureau of Economic Research, 1976).

[14] "Reliable estimates of the benchmark and depreciation rates for R and D at the individual firm are not available. We constructed the stock of R and D by assuming an arbitrary depreciation rate of 10% per annum for each firm. The 1965 R and D investment in constant dollars is used as the benchmark for those firms that did not report any figures prior to 1965, while for firms with more extended data, the first year of consistent reporting was chosen as the benchmark." M. Ishaq Nadiri and George C. Bitros "Research and Development Expenditures and Labor Productivity at the Firm Level: A Dynamic Model," in John W. Kendrick and Beatrice N. Vaccara, eds., *New Developments in Productivity Measurement and Analysis*, National Bureau of

The question regarding the appropriate annual rate of depreciation of the stock of productive technological knowledge, built up by accumulated R and D expenditures, has been answered less pragmatically and more inconsistently. Some economists, such as Edward Denison, have questioned the conceptual soundness of making any allowances for obsolescence of that knowledge stock.[15] According to Zvi Griliches, "the most common assumption has been of . . . no depreciation" due to obsolescence.[16] John Kendrick has proposed that in "capital stock calculations for basic research" no regard be given to obsolescence, whereas "stocks of applied research and development [be] estimated by the perpetual inventory method," with annual depreciation calculated by the "double-declining balance" formula applied up to the point "where straight-line depreciation of the net stock balance gives a larger annual depreciation."[17] Robert Eisner followed "with some misgivings . . . Kendrick on basic research and development but . . . used undelayed twenty-year, straight-line depreciation for the applied portion."[18] Eisner finds application of the straight-line method more realistic.[19] Griliches argues strongly

Economic Research, Studies in Income and Wealth, Vol. 44 (Chicago: University of Chicago Press, 1980), p. 394.

[15] Edward F. Denison, "Explanations of Declining Productivity Growth," Survey of Current Business, Vol. 59, No. 8, Part 2 (August 1979), p. 22, footnote 27.

[16] Zvi Griliches, "Returns to Research and Development Expenditures in the Private Sector," in John W. Kendrick and Beatrice N. Vaccara, eds., New Developments, p. 424.

[17] Kendrick, Formation and Stocks, pp. 60-61.

[18] Robert Eisner, "Total Incomes in the United States, 1959 and 1969," Review of Income and Wealth, Series 24, No. 1 (March 1978), p. 46.

[19] The straight-line method applies a constant percentage depreciation to original cost, the annual rate being determined by the reciprocal of the useful life of the asset. The declining-balance method applies a constant rate of depreciation, not to the

End of Year	Straight-line 10%		Declining Balance 10%		Declining Balance 15%		Declining Balance 20%	
	Write-off	Book Value	Write-off	Book Value	Write-off	Book Value	Write-off	Book Value
0	—	10,000	—	10,000	—	10,000	—	10,000
1	1,000	9,000	1,000	9,000	1,500	8,500	2,000	8,000
2	1,000	8,000	900	8,100	1,275	7,225	1,600	6,400
3	1,000	7,000	810	7,290	1,084	6,141	1,280	5,120
4	1,000	6,000	729	6,561	921	5,220	1,024	4,096
5	1,000	5,000	656	5,905	783	4,437	819	3,277
6	1,000	4,000	591	5,314	665	3,772	655	2,622
7	1,000	3,000	531	4,783	566	3,206	524	2,098
8	1,000	2,000	478	4,305	481	2,725	420	1,678
9	1,000	1,000	431	3,874	409	2,316	336	1,342
10	1,000	0	387	3,487	347	1,969	268	1,074

in favor of applying depreciation rates to stocks of knowledge accumulated through R and D activities, because of the "disappear-
ance" of techniques or products "from the currently utilized stock
of knowledge due to changes in external circumstances and the development of superior techniques or products by competitors." Griliches was inclined to accept a rate of 10 per cent as the appropriate
rate of obsolescence of the knowledge for which cumulated R and
D expenditures were the statistical proxy. Nevertheless, in his research on the returns to investments in R and D, Griliches omitted
depreciation and defended the omission as compensating for having
omitted R and D expenditures prior to 1957; thus, the unduly short
series of accumulations is supposed to make up for the failure to
deduct depreciation of the "cumulated R and D capital."[20] Pakes and
Schankerman concluded that a 10 per cent rate was far too low. They
may be right, but the basis for their finding is inordinately soft. They
based their calculations on statistics of renewals of patents of inventions in countries where fees for renewals are charged, and on
the argument that patentees would rationally decide not to renew
their patents when the "appropriable revenues" had "decayed" to a
level at which they were no longer paying for the renewal fee. Pakes
and Schankerman's "point estimate" of "the (average) decay rate"
was 25 per cent per annum; and they argued that the rate of decay
of revenues from patents would also be appropriate as the rate of
obsolescence for other technological innovations generated by research and development.[21] I submit that this proposed rate of
"obsolescence" includes a rate of nonviable inventions, that is, inventions that failed to become innovations.

Obsolescence of Human Knowledge Carriers

Most writers on depreciation of human and other nonmaterial
capital have failed to distinguish clearly among the different reasons
for making depreciation allowances; some analysts of human capital

---

original cost, but to the depreciated book value at the end of the preceding year; the
rate chosen is usually higher than the reciprocal of the useful service life. The double-
declining-balance method applies an annual rate of exactly twice the reciprocal of
the years of useful life. What these methods do to the annual depreciation allowances
and the year-end book values of an asset with a service life of ten years and an original
cost of $10,000 is shown in this tabulation.

[20] Griliches, "Returns," pp. 443-444.

[21] Pakes and Schankerman, "Rate of Obsolescence." The "empirical" basis of their
estimate is questionable, among other reasons because many of the patents that were
not renewed may never have generated any revenue for their owners. Zero revenues
cannot "decay." The patented inventions may not even have been used in actual

have used the same percentage rate of depreciation to take account of termination, deterioration, and obsolescence, all at once. That such indiscriminate treatment is inappropriate becomes clear as soon as one realizes that the usefulness and value of a piece of knowledge is not the same as the usefulness and value of the performing capacity of a knowledge carrier. The rate of obsolescence of a production technique and the rate of obsolescence of individuals with particular knowledge and know-how are different things. A few economists writing on the subject were thinking chiefly or solely of human beings whose schooling and training becomes obsolescent as younger individuals with more up-to-date knowledge in their heads come on the market.

Sherwin Rosen discusses the measurement of obsolescence in terms of people's usefulness in the economy. He finds that "obsolescence is obviously related to some concept of 'vintage,'" for example, the year of graduation. Those who finished school long ago acquired knowledge no longer accepted, learned skills no longer useful, and were taught by less efficient teaching methods than are used today. For all these reasons, more recent graduates of high schools and colleges are assumed to be superior to older ones, who have suffered obsolescence.[22] Of course, most graduates have an opportunity of obtaining postschool learning through work experience, which explains why the effects of obsolescence do not show up in the years during which workers increase their earning capacity. Still, what they learn at work is also subject to obsolescence and, consequently, the time comes when more-recent vintages of schooled and trained workers will perform better and earn more than the older vintages.[23] It is easy to cite examples of obsolescence of school learning and job training.[24]

---

production. After a few years, when the owner gives up the hope that the patent may be good for anything, he stops paying renewal fees.

[22] Rosen, "Measuring," p. 200. — Note that this statement refers to high-school and undergraduate, not postgraduate, studies. My own impression regarding these levels of schooling is that, except for students of natural sciences, engineering, and computer use, older vintages may be superior to more recent ones.

[23] Since Rosen deals with the knowledge and skills acquired by and embodied in human workers, his linking of obsolescence and deterioration is quite legitimate. The aging workers' capacity is reduced through obsolescence of previously acquired knowledge and skills and through decline in their powers to apply whatever they have learned.

[24] As to college graduates, those who majored in physics, biology, economics, or engineering some twenty or thirty years ago but have not kept up with the changes in these fields will find that recent graduates will be preferred for jobs where up-to-date knowledge in these disciplines is required. The same will hold true for holders of advanced degrees. Think of specialists in recombinant DNA research, with whom older Ph.D.s in genetics or developmental biology will not easily compete unless they have been working within the enchanted circle of gene splitters. Similar handicaps

Data on earnings are assumed to reflect the increase in work experience as well as the decline in its value through obsolescence and deterioration; though they reflect the augmentations and diminutions of the stock of human capital, they do not specify or reveal them.[25] The various influences on gross earnings of labor cannot be disentangled except on the basis of simplifying and quite arbitrary assumptions. Thomas Johnson, for example, assumed that the earnings function is continuous, "that the rate of return is constant for all investments in human capital, that the rates of depreciation [for any cause, obsolescence and all others] and [autonomous] growth [of capacity] are constant, and that the fraction of earning capacity invested in human capital is 1 while the individual is in school and declines linearly from an estimated value at the end of schooling to zero at the sixty-fifth birthday (assumed retirement)."[26] Using earnings data estimated by Giora Hanoch, and employing nonlinear regression, Johnson proceeds to estimate base-year earnings capacity at the individual's age when he makes the first decision to invest in himself, the return this individual will receive, the fraction of earnings capacity invested in training on the job immediately after schooling is completed, and the constant rate of depreciation for all causes (obsolescence plus all the others).[27] Jacob Moreh emphasizes that, contrary to Johnson, he uses in his model social rather than private

---

are being reported regarding older and recent vintages in various departments of engineering. As to job training, one may think of computer programmers when new generations of computers are installed or new advances in software development occur.

[25] Rosen mentions the possibility of "relative capital losses" without "absolute capital losses." He connects this with vintage effects of "innovations in teaching methods" making "exposures to learning environments more productive" through increasing "value added from given resource inputs" and thereby reducing the "private and social costs of learning." ("Measuring," p. 200.) This seems to mean that these improvements in teaching, while creating human capital for the better taught, inflict capital losses on older graduates, leaving the human capital for society as a whole unchanged. This notion, perhaps insufficiently thought out, invites elaboration and extension, for it would be equally applicable to the development of new production techniques making older ones obsolete. Those who invested in developing the knowledge now replaced by new knowledge suffer capital losses, while the owners of the new knowledge (if they are given monopoly rights) have their stocks of immaterial capital augmented. However, the notion of a balance between private capital gains and private capital losses should not lead us to the conclusion that the social returns to investment in new technological knowledge are zero. For a discussion of depreciation of social and private human capital see later in this chapter.

[26] Thomas Johnson, "Returns from Investments in Human Capital," *American Economic Review*, Vol. 60 (September 1970), p. 546.

[27] Ibid., pp. 547-550.

costs. He employs "deterioration . . . as a generic term covering all factors that reduce earning capacity with the passage of time, such as obsolescence of acquired training. . . ."[28] Assuming that gross investment in on-the-job training is positive throughout working life, Moreh sets out "to estimate the minimum rate of deterioration that fits a given costs and returns series" but admits that "this is not necessarily the true rate of deterioration."[29] For pragmatic reasons he joins others in applying "a uniform rate of *proportional* deterioration . . . to a given education level throughout schooling and working life."[30] The calculated minimum rates of "deterioration" for different groups of workers vary from 0 (for nonwhite males with eight years of schooling) to 12 per cent per year (for nonwhite males with five to seven years of schooling; for white males the rates range only between 3 and 4 per cent per year).[31] Nevertheless, Moreh uses at other places in his argument a uniform rate of 10 per cent per year for all educational levels.[32] In the absence of empirical evidence, our imagination has much leeway. In any case, since the suggested annual rates are assumed to cover depreciation of human capital, not just due to obsolescence of acquired skills and knowledge, but for all other reasons too, their soundness may be questioned also on conceptual grounds.

Decline in Scarcity Value

Obsolescence is closely related to substitution and competition. For both nonembodied technological knowledge and knowledge embodied in individual persons in the labor force, obsolescence depreciates the existing stocks of nonmaterial capital because superior knowledge emerges, competes with, and is substituted for, the previously existing knowledge. Yet, the new knowledge does not even have to be superior in order to be substitutable for the old; it often suffices that it is a suitable alternative. Where certain techniques, processes or products, are monopolized by a holder of patents of invention, development of an inferior technique, not covered by the earlier patent claims, enables a competing producer to make and sell an acceptable substitute for the patentee's product; the sales of the

---

[28] Jacob Moreh, "Human Capital: Deterioration and Net Investment," *Review of Income and Wealth*, Ser. 19 (September 1973), pp. 279-302.

[29] Ibid., p. 280. The reference to "given" costs and returns series calls for a reminder that these series are not really given but largely fabricated.

[30] Ibid., p. 281. Emphasis in the original.

[31] Ibid., Table 1, p. 286.

[32] Ibid., Table 3, p. 289.

new product may reduce the value of the first producer's proprietary knowledge. Similarly, where persons acquire knowledge and skills that are only imperfect substitutes of the knowledge and skills embodied in highly skilled workers, the scarcity value of the performing capacity of the earners of high "differential rents" may be effectively reduced.

Scarcity values of knowledgeable and skilled labor may be eroded when the supply of persons with the same knowledge and skills increases. The knowledge and skills of the newcomers do not have to be superior to those of the previously available workers; just "more of the same" or "more of almost the same" would have essentially the same effects. Private human capital consisting of some specific performing capacities can be effectively destroyed if the acquired qualifications become abundant, either through increases in supply or through reductions in demand.

To restate the case of depreciation due to increased supply: if more people learn a hitherto scarce skill, the value of the services in question declines and the human-capital stock of the earlier practitioners of the skill is depreciated. Thus—it should be repeated for emphasis because it has been overlooked in the literature—schooling and training of larger numbers of individuals in subjects or skills previously mastered by fewer people tend to reduce the scarcity value of the particular services and, thus, to result in a depreciation of the human capital of the previously privileged possessors of the now more widely distributed knowledge.

The common disregard of the problem of opposite changes in social and private stocks of human capital is surprising. It should not be hard to realize that the combined stocks of knowledge in the minds of the people may increase while the sum of private human capital represented by the earning capacities of the individual "knowers" is reduced in the process. This divergence of social from private income and wealth is an old story in economic theory, analyzed, for example, in connection with natural and artificial scarcity of particular goods and services. The breakup of monopoly positions may increase total real income but destroy the rents and reduce the capital of the monopolists. It is strange that the depreciation of private human capital is especially emphasized in the case of obsolescence of knowledge through the emergence of socially new superior knowledge but disregarded in the case of the loss of the scarcity value of knowledge through its wider dissemination and the consequent increase in the supply of the services of people equipped with that knowledge.

Erosion of Skills Through Work Interruptions

Termination of employment through retirement or death was the first on my list of causes of, or reasons for, depreciation of human capital; deterioration of physical or mental capacities through aging was the second. Akin to both, and yet different from them, is erosion of skills through interruption of employment.

Interruptions of employment may be involuntary; in periods of mass unemployment or sectoral unemployment skilled workers may experience an erosion of their special skills through extended non-use. The difference of this case from that of elimination of the job, or of the job holder, or of definite termination of his employment through retirement, voluntary or stipulated, is clear: interruption is not termination. Interruption is temporary, termination is final. The worker who is temporarily laid off does not leave the labor force, or even his occupation. His temporary inactivity, however, may, if the interruption lasts too long, reduce his capacity to perform. (This loss is sometimes overlooked when the social cost of long-term unemployment is estimated.)

Interruptions of employment may also be voluntary, for example, in the case of women quitting their jobs to deliver and raise children. Withdrawals of women from the labor force in order to stay home and care for their young children are quite common, and these gaps in their participation in the labor force "tend to erode acquired skills."[33] It is this skill erosion that makes the case of temporary withdrawals similar to deterioration of capacity through aging, but the difference between declining capacity while using one's skills at work and eroding skill through nonuse during long periods of not working is too obvious to call for an extended explanation.

Skill erosion through discontinuity of work experience probably plays a significant role in accounting for the notorious earnings differentials between sexes. "Close to half of the differences in wages [of men and women] emerging two decades following school were due to shorter accumulated work experience and to depreciation resulting from long gaps (usually when children were small) in participation [of women]."[34]

[33] Jacob Mincer, "Human Capital and Earnings," in Douglas M. Windham, ed., *Economic Dimensions of Education*, Report of a Committee of the National Academy of Education (Washington, D.C.: National Academy of Education, 1979), p. 17. — "More than half of the working women dropped out of the labor force when the first child was born and large numbers returned after the youngest child reached school age. In contrast, women without husbands and without children spend close to 90% of their working lives in the labor market." Mincer, p. 17.

[34] Ibid., p. 18. For a detailed analysis see Jacob Mincer and Solomon Polachek,

Jacob Mincer observes that the depreciation of the stock of human capital through skill erosion as women withdraw from the labor force in order to give maternal care to their young children may be offset by these mothers' investment in the human capital of their children.[35] The depreciation of the capital accumulated by the women's learning on the job and the formation of capital through preschool education of young children in the home are the joint result of their mothers' decision to quit their jobs and spend their time bringing up their children. The two capital accounts are very different, however, and it remains to be seen whether the pioneers in national welfare accounting will make provisions for the inclusion of the corresponding estimates.

Depreciation of Private and Social Human Capital

In the discussion of obsolescence of knowledge, accumulated either as human capital or as nonembodied knowledge capital, it was pointed out that private losses need not be net social losses, and that, indeed, society may gain while private owners of knowledge and skill may lose. More should be said about the question of human capital and its depreciation from private and social points of view, notwithstanding my rather skeptical remarks on "Private and Social Valuation" in Chapter 14 above.

From the private point of view, depreciation of human capital is a matter of rational calculation. One may understand this as a part of normative economics, offering precepts to individuals—chiefs of households, students, workers, managers of business—about optimal decision-making. Alternatively, and more in line with the intentions of most writers on the subject, one may understand the theories in question as parts of positive economics, constructing models of rational behavior—ideal types, not descriptive of real-life types—that can help explain observed phenomena, such as changes in school enrollments, wage differentials, income distribution, occupational structure, and other statistical observations. From the social point of view, one may find depreciation of human capital to serve several purposes: evaluative, in attempts to judge certain structural or institutional changes as good or bad for society as a whole; instrumental, in attempts to inform the development of public policy; and explanatory, in attempts to explain such things as changes in the

---

"Family Investment in Human Capital: Earnings of Women," *Journal of Political Economy*, Vol. 82 (March-April 1974, Part 2), pp. S76-S108.

[35] Mincer, "Human Capital and Earnings," p. 18.

growth of national product or in the rate of increase of labor productivity. With so many possible objectives in mind, one can understand that answers to the question of a "correct" formula for, and rate of depreciation of, stocks of human capital may be very different and appear inconsistent and even irreconcilable.

Risking a charge of repetitiousness, I want to go once more over the possible effects that a technological advance may have upon existing stocks of nonmaterial capital. Assume a new technique is developed by a business firm making heavy investments in R and D. If the new technique is superior to one previously patented and used by the same firm, it is possible that consumers will not—for several years—benefit from the innovation. The private stock of nonembodied knowledge capital may be regarded as having increased, because the exclusive rights to new patent claims will promise extended flows of monopoly rents to the innovative firm. If, however, the new inventions were made and patented by another firm, and if that firm will produce and sell in competition with the previously sole producer of the product, the latter's stock of nonmaterial capital will be depreciated and the newcomer's stock increased. Combined monopoly rents may be lower than those previously earned by the sole producer, so that their present value will be pared down; on the other hand, consumers are likely to benefit from lower prices. Whether or not this will be reflected in an increase in the social stock of nonmaterial capital is a still unresolved question. Now let us again change our assumptions and see what happens if the new technique is not reserved to its developer (who fails to secure patent rights) and that many competing producers exploit the new invention. The first producer's returns to his exclusive rights in his knowledge stocks will fall to zero, the competing investor in R and D generating the new knowledge will not have any returns to his investment and its present value to him is therefore nil, and the flock of new producers, using the new knowledge without any proprietary rights to it, will have no returns attributable to the generally available knowledge stocks. The consumers will be the winners.[36] Should the benefits accruing to them be capitalized and exhibited as a formation of social nonmaterial capital? Probably so, because otherwise the increase in

---

[36] Although opponents of the patent system may point to these winnings as "evidence" in support of their case, advocates of the system may counter by arguing that without it the new technique may never have come into being, since only expectations of patent rights, guaranteeing exclusivity in the use of the invention, induced the second firm to invest in R and D.

national product and factor productivity would remain "unexplained."

Similar considerations can be entertained with regard to human capital, private and social. Indeed, they have been presented above, particularly in Chapter 14. Three different situations were examined where investment in additional education created private human capital with returns in the form of differential earnings accruing to those with more schooling. Depending on whether their services were complementary or competitive with the services of workers with less schooling, the earnings of the latter would be increased or reduced. Thus, the stocks of human capital possessed by the less schooled would be appreciated or depreciated as a result of the supply of labor with more schooling. Even if the less schooled suffer absolute reductions in earnings, it is still possible that the gains exceed the losses and national product is increased. In this case, the social human capital formed through education should probably show a net increase.

Social accountants have disagreed on whether or not human capital should be included in the accounts. Although it is still disregarded in the conventional systems, more progressive analysts have decided in favor of inclusion; but they disagree on whether human capital should be shown at historical cost or at present value of expected returns. Conceptual soundness, operational feasibility, and internal consistency are some of the grounds on which the case for one or the other of the accounting principles has been argued. Among those who have pleaded for the present-value approach are Henry S. Houthakker,[37] Mary Jean Bowman,[38] Herman P. Miller,[39] John Graham and Roy Webb,[40] and Oli Havrylyshyn.[41] Among those who have

[37] Henry S. Houthakker, "Education and Income," *Review of Economics and Statistics*, Vol. 41 (February 1959), pp. 24-28.

[38] Mary Jean Bowman, "Human Capital: Concepts and Measures," in Selma J. Mushkin, ed., *The Economics of Higher Education* (Washington, D.C.: U.S. Department of Health, Education, and Welfare, 1962), pp. 69-92, esp. pp. 73, 75, 89; Mary Jean Bowman, "Postschool Learning and Human Resource Accounting," *Review of Income and Wealth*, Ser. 20 (December 1974), pp. 483-499.

[39] Herman P. Miller, "Lifetime Income and Economic Growth," *American Economic Review*, Vol. 55 (September 1965), pp. 834-844; Herman P. Miller and Richard A. Hornseth, *Present Value of Estimated Lifetime Earnings*, Technical Paper No. 16, U.S. Department of Commerce, Bureau of the Census, 1967.

[40] John W. Graham and Roy H. Webb, "Stocks and Depreciation of Human Capital: New Evidence from a Present-Value Perspective," *Review of Income and Wealth*, Ser. 25 (June 1979), pp. 200-224.

[41] Oli Havrylyshyn, *National Income Accounting and the Depreciation of Human*

used the historical-cost approach are Theodore W. Schultz,[42] Edward Denison,[43] Yoram Ben-Porath,[44] Sherwin Rosen,[45] John Kendrick,[46] and Robert Eisner.[47]

The "Correct" Rate of Depreciation

With all these differences in purposes, concepts, and theories, there is obviously not one "correct" formula and not one "correct" rate of depreciation; but the least one may ask for is that the choice of formula and rate be consistent with the purposes expressed, concepts employed, and theories adopted. For example, analysts endorsing a present-value approach to the estimation of capital stocks, and favoring periodic or even annual revaluations of all stocks of capital to reflect current expectations of future returns, need not concern themselves with separate estimations of depreciation. All causes of reduced contributions of capital stocks affect the future flows of income and, hence, their present values. It is chiefly for analysts who value capital stocks at historical cost to worry about adequate depreciation. Depreciation of capital stocks that are measured by accumulated investments is designed to adjust their book values so that some of the most obvious forces that diminish their productive contributions are taken into account.

Implied in the two approaches is a reversal of known and unknown, or given and dependent, variables. The present-value approach assumes that it is possible to know or estimate the future flows of income, and it undertakes to value the sources of these flows by capitalization. The historical-cost approach, on the other hand, starts from the known investments of the past and seeks to correct the values of the accumulated material and immaterial stocks (in-

---

Capital, Working Paper No. 6, Statistics Canada, Office of the Senior Adviser on Integration, 1978.

[42] Theodore W. Schultz, "Investment in Human Capital," American Economic Review, Vol. 51 (March 1961), pp. 1-17; also "Education and Economic Growth" in Sixtieth Yearbook of the National Society for the Study of Education, Nelson B. Henry, ed., Part II, Social Forces Influencing American Education (Chicago: University of Chicago Press, 1961), pp. 46-88.

[43] Edward Denison, "Measurement of Labor Input," in Output, Input and Productivity Measurement. Studies in Income and Wealth, Vol. 25, National Bureau of Economic Research (Princeton: Princeton University Press, 1961), pp. 347-372; also Why Growth Rates Differ (Washington, D.C.: Brookings Institution, 1967).

[44] Yoram Ben-Porath, "Production of Human Capital," pp. 352-365.

[45] Rosen, "Measuring," pp. 199-232.

[46] Kendrick, Formation and Stocks, esp. pp. 18-22.

[47] Eisner, "Total Incomes," pp. 41-70, esp. p. 52.

cluding embodied and nonembodied technological knowledge) for normal depreciation in order to obtain a firmer basis for estimations of future incomes.

Depreciation, in this case, may be a step in the prediction of earnings. (Of course, past experiences of the relationship between investments made and incomes received can be helpful in finding "appropriate" rates of capital depreciation.)

Several economists who have written about depreciation of human capital have, in their algebraic expositions and in their efforts at measurement, worked with a single depreciation rate that, in my opinion, is inconsistent with the various causes of depreciation. There have been suggestions of applying different depreciation rates to stocks of knowledge capital acquired at school and to those acquired in postschool learning on the job. This difference, however, is probably less systematic than differences inherent to the various causes that give rise to annual write-offs in the value of accumulated human capital. For example, the write-offs required by the limitation of the worker's service life may follow other rules than write-offs due to gradual deterioration of physical and mental capacities and those due to obsolescence of the acquired knowledge. These three reasons for depreciation relate to foreseeable and expected processes or occurrences: approaching retirement at a stated age, gradual deterioration of mental strength and vigor, and emergence of new knowledge superseding previously acquired knowledge. These are integral parts of rational expectations. Debilitating accidents or death before stipulated retirement are similarly predictable on the basis of actuarial calculations. Other causes of depreciation of human capital, such as reductions in the scarcity of the services available from the capital, are not predictable and therefore cannot be included in general rules of annual depreciation.

To understand the depreciation procedure appropriate to the limits of the worker's active service life, one has to bear in mind that retirement at a stated age need not coincide with the exhaustion of capacity to perform. It is quite possible that the person retiring at age sixty-five still has in him (or her) enough strength to continue rendering marketable services for several more years. Yet, if a retirement age has been stipulated by contract, custom, personal preference, or simply most likely expectation, the stream of earnings from performance is assumed to come to an end at the stated age. If, for example, an employee at age fifty-five invests in himself by taking courses in computer programming and electronic data processing, he will normally expect to receive pecuniary returns in this investment for ten years. Thus, the investment will have to be written off over that period, and the stock of human capital will depreciate year after year until it reaches zero at the end of the tenth year. The rate of depreciation appropriate to the approaching termination of the earning stream is not constant but rises from year to year, at a gradient depending on the going rate of interest. If there were no other reason for depreciation—neither obsolescence of skill nor depreciation of capacity—the stream of earnings would remain unchanged year after year, to terminate after the tenth year. Assume that the investment was exactly equal to the present value of the series of earnings, that is, to the sum of the discounted earnings expected during the ten years. The absolute discount is largest on the earnings to be received in the tenth and last year; hence, the present (or discounted) value of the earnings from that (most distant) year is the smallest. After one year, when only nine years of future earnings remain, the human capital has been reduced by only the present value of the earnings expected for the tenth year, the smallest amount in the series. After two years, when the earnings of only eight years remain in the expected stream of future receipts, the depreciation will be equal to the discounted value of earnings eight years away in the future. Thus, the annual depreciation will rise from age fifty-five to age sixty-four, when the present value of the last year's earnings will reflect a discount for only one year. In brief, the annual depreciation is lowest in the first year after the investment and highest in the last year before retirement.

Gradual deterioration of the worker's health, vigor, and performance was the second on my list of causes of depreciation of (or reasons for depreciating) human capital. It is not easy to find one rule that would fit all occupations. Sticking to the example of an individual investing in learning computer programming and data processing, one should think that a fifty-five-year-old person with such ambitions does not expect his health to give out and slow him down in the near future. He probably counts on staying mentally and physically agile for a few years and, if he must reckon with deterioration, he will assume it to start slowly and to accelerate only after several years. This expectation would call for increasing annual amounts of depreciation over the ten years. In other occupations, however, experience and expectations would surely be otherwise. Think of an opera singer, perhaps a coloratura soprano, investing at age fifty in learning new, highly demanding parts that require a flawless voice. Deterioration of the singing voice, especially female, sets in when the singer is in her forties and proceeds rapidly after she is over fifty years of age. A proper depreciation rate, accounting for deterioration in this occupation, would be very high in the first years after the investment; this human capital would have to be written off rapidly, so that annual depreciation in later years would be relatively small. Think now of surgeons or dentists in mid-career investing in learning new operations, new surgical or orthodontic techniques. The appropriate depreciation rates taking account of deteriorating health, vigor, and performance would largely depend on the age and physical condition of the particular individual. One can imagine that a modest annual depreciation at a constant rate, either by a straight-line or a declining-balance formula, would seem adequate. For large groups of people pursuing all sorts of occupations, it may be excessively cumbersome to attempt disaggregations required to fit a depreciation procedure to each subset characterized by occupation and age. It may well be that subsets calling for annual depreciation declining over the years and those calling for increasing depreciation will balance each other, so that a constant depreciation rate may be the "correct" procedure to account for gradual deterioration of mental and physical capacities of the members of large groups.

Let us turn to the third cause of depreciation on our list, obsolescence; and let us confine our discussion to human capital, omitting nonembodied productive knowledge. It is assumed that the emergence of new knowledge, and the competition from people in possession of it (that is, trained in the new know-*what* and know-*how*), reduces the value of the services of individuals equipped only with previously acquired knowledge skills. A variety of assumptions regarding the speed of obsolescence may seem reasonable. One can imagine that obsolescence is small in the beginning and increases over the years; or, alternatively, that it goes on at a given percentage rate, reducing the earnings from year to year by a given percentage and therefore by declining amounts; or, again differently, that the stream of earnings is reduced by a constant absolute amount per year, corresponding to the straight-line formula.

No a priori grounds seem to favor any one of these possibilities; and no empirical evidence has been mustered to support one of them more strongly than the others. For the sake of simplicity, one may prefer to depreciate the stock (which grows through additional gross investment) by a constant percentage rate, but it may seem more reasonable to increase that rate in times when R and D activities are especially heavy, since it stands to reason that more old knowledge becomes obsolete when more new knowledge is generated.

Numerical Illustrations

Numerical illustrations, based on different assumptions, will be presented in order to show the operation of different causes of depreciation. For the sake of comparability, all models will share some common features: (a) an investment in human capital is made by an individual at, or just before, age 55; (b) annual earnings in the first year will be $1,000; (c) annual earnings are received in one sum on the last day of each year; (d) the rate of interest is 10 per cent per annum; (e) expectations are entertained with certainty and no changes other than those assumed will occur during the ten-year period; (f) the value of human capital is entered on the imaginary accounts as of the first day of each year; and (g) annual depreciation is calculated on the last day of each year, immediately after receipt of the year's earnings and simultaneously with the valuation of the remaining stock of human capital.

Table 19.1 shows the effects of depreciation due to the approaching retirement at age 65; no other causes of depreciation exist no deterioration of capacity, no obsolescence of skills, no probability of accidents, illness, premature death, interruption of employment, or of a change in the scarcity of the services rendered. Hence, there is a series of ten years' undiminished earnings of $1,000 each, entirely attributable to the investment made at age 55.

Total returns to be collected over the ten years will be $10,000. The present value of the series of receipts is calculated by discounting each year's earnings at the assumed rate (10 per cent interest is 9.09 per cent discount per annum). Thus, at the beginning of the year the first year's earnings are worth $909, and the ultimate year's earnings (to be received on the day of retirement at age 65) have a present value (on the individual's 55th birthday) of $386. The series of constant receipts corresponds to a series of discounted values diminishing monotonically from $909 to $386. The source of this flow, the human capital, has a present value of $6,144 at the beginning of the first year. At the end of that year, the depreciation to be deducted from the beginning value of the stock of human capital must reflect the fact that only nine years' earnings remain; the second year's earnings will again have a discounted value of $909, but the earnings nine years away (to be collected on the day of retirement) will have a discounted value of $424. The sum of the discounted earnings of the remaining nine years will be $5,758, or $386 less than the original stock of human capital. It follows that the depreciation in the first year is $386. In the same fashion the figures for subsequent years are calculated and shown in Table 19.1.

Table 19.2 shows the effects of depreciation due to deterioration of the productive capacity as progressive impairment of the individual's health and vigor reduces his annual earnings by $100 a year. Thus, the returns, $1,000 in the first year, dwindle to $100 at the

TABLE 19.1

Depreciation of Human Capital Formed at Age 55: Constant Annual
Earnings until Fixed Retirement; Discounted Values (r = 0.10) at
Age 55; Values of Human Capital; and Annual Depreciation
Deducted

Age	Annual Earnings Not Discounted	Annual Earnings Discounted to Age 55	Human Capital at Beginning of Year	Depreciation at End of Year
55	$1,000	$909	$6,144	$386
56	1,000	826	5,758	424
57	1,000	751	5,334	467
58	1,000	683	4,867	513
59	1,000	621	4,354	564
60	1,000	564	3,790	621
61	1,000	513	3,169	683
62	1,000	467	2,486	751
63	1,000	424	1,735	826
64	1,000	386	909	909
	$10,000	$6,144		$6,144
	sum collected over ten years	present value at age 55		written off over ten years

end of the tenth year. Whether retirement is fixed at age 65 or later
is irrelevant in this case, because earnings from the particular investment come to a natural end as a result of deterioration of performing capacity. The sum of the series of earnings over the ten years
is $5,500 and its present value at the beginning of the first year is
$3,855. One year later, the sum of the remaining nine years' earnings
will be reduced to $4,500, the present value of which, at the begin-
ning of the second year, will be $3,241. Hence, the depreciation at
the end of the first year (after the receipt of the $1,000) is $614. By
the same method the consecutive years' stocks of human capital and
amounts of depreciation are calculated and shown in Table 19.2.

Tables 19.3 and 19.4 depict the effects of declining annual returns
from the investment in human capital if the decline, due to deterioration of capacity or to obsolescence of the knowledge or skill embodied in the individual, is not by constant amounts per year but at
increasing or decreasing rates. In Table 19.3, annual earnings decline

TABLE 19.2

Depreciation of Human Capital Formed at Age 55: Annual Earnings Declining by $100 a Year Because of Deterioration of Capacity; Discounted Values (r = 0.10) at Age 55; Values of Human Capital; and Annual Depreciation Deducted

Age	Annual Earnings Not Discounted	Annual Earnings Discounted to Age 55	Human Capital at Beginning of Year	Depreciation at End of Year
55	$1,000	$909	$3,855	$614
56	900	743	3,241	577
57	800	601	2,664	533
58	700	478	2,131	487
59	600	373	1,644	435
60	500	282	1,209	379
61	400	205	830	317
62	300	140	513	249
63	200	85	264	173
64	100	39	91	91
	$5,500	$3,855		$3,855
	sum collected over ten years	present value at age 55		written off over ten years

at first quite slowly but at an increasing rate. ($Y_t = 1,000 - 10 \times$ [t − 55], where Y_t stands for annual returns at age t, with t > 55.) In Table 19.4, annual earnings decline rapidly but at a decreasing rate ($Y_t = 1,000 \times 0.8^{(t-55)}$). With the rates of deterioration or obsolescence, assumed for cases described in Tables 19.3 and 19.4, earnings would not completely vanish by age 65, but they would be so small that the individual would not find it worthwhile to go on working. For simplicity, we assume that he chooses to retire. The values of human capital and annual write-off of depreciation are calculated by the methods explained for Table 19.2.

The series of annual amounts of depreciation, which showed a monotonic increase in Table 19.1 and a monotonic decrease in Table 19.2, behaves differently in Table 19.3: it first increases, then, after four years, begins to decrease. The reason for this turnaround is that two forces push in opposite directions; the amounts of depreciation

TABLE 19.3

Depreciation of Human Capital Formed at Age 55: Annual Earnings Declining, First Slowly but at a Rapidly Increasing Rate, Because of Deterioration of Capacity and Obsolescence of Skill; Discounted Values (r = 0.10) at Age 55; Values of Human Capital; and Annual Depreciation Deducted

Age	Annual Earnings Not Discounted*	Annual Earnings Discounted to Age 55	Human Capital at Beginning of Year	Depreciation at End of Year
55	$1,000	$909	$4,569	$281
56	990	818	4,288	562
57	960	721	3,726	588
58	910	622	3,138	595
59	840	522	2,543	586
60	750	423	1,957	555
61	640	328	1,402	498
62	510	238	904	420
63	360	153	484	311
64	190	73	173	173
	$7,150	$4,569		$4,569
	sum collected over ten years	present value at age 55		written off over ten years

* $Y_t = 1000 - 10 \times (t - 55)$; $t \geq 55$.

reflect the decline in earnings and the increase in discounts over the years. Since it is assumed, in Table 19.3, that annual earnings decline at first slowly, though at an increasing rate, the relative effect of the decline in earnings is, in the earlier years, weaker than that of the increasing discounts. This does not happen in Table 19.4, where depreciation exhibits the monotonic decline observed in Table 19.2.

Purposes of Depreciation Accounting

I have mentioned that the optimal choice of principles of depreciation accounting depends on the purposes pursued, but I have not yet offered sufficient support for this pronouncement. From the point of view of a profitable business firm it may be optimal to choose a method that will reduce tax payments to the government and dividend payments to stockholders; this is most easily accomplished by treating investments in nonmaterial knowledge capital not as in-

TABLE 19.4

Depreciation of Human Capital Formed at Age 55: Annual Earnings Declining, First Rapidly, though at a Decreasing Rate, Because of Deterioration of Capacity and Obsolescence of Skill; Discounted Values (r = 0.10) at Age 55; Values of Human Capital; and Annual Depreciation Deducted

Age	Annual Earnings Not Discounted*	Annual Earnings Discounted to Age 55	Human Capital at Beginning of Year	Depreciation at End of Year
55	$1,000	$909	$3,163	$646
56	800	661	2,517	551
57	640	481	1,966	444
58	512	318	1,522	359
59	409	254	1,163	293
60	328	185	870	242
61	262	134	628	197
62	210	98	431	167
63	168	71	264	142
64	134	52	122	122
	$4,463	$3,163		$3,163
	sum collected over ten years	present value at age 55		written off over ten years

* $Y_t = 1000 \times 0.8^{t-55}$; $t \geqslant 55$.

vestments but as current expense. In effect, the investment is completely written off at the time it is made. This falsifies the records somewhat—since the expenditures in question are really made for the sake of future production and future returns—but the procedure is perfectly legal and recommends itself also as good practice of conservative accounting—not to carry on the books assets that are not salable and cannot be counted upon to have any value in the case of the firm's liquidation.

Accounting principles designed to obtain an advantageous determination of taxable profits or an opportune determination of earnings distributable to stockholders are surely very different from principles of calculating the profitability of new investments. Individuals investing in their own earning capacities and firms investing in their future capacity to generate profits have to allow for the prospective decline and eventual termination of the returns to these investments.

These are, of course, considerations regarding individual persons and individual firms; they rest on their own expectations, perhaps rational, reasonable, and possibly realistic, but surely subjective. (Expectations about one's own future can never be anything but subjective.)

Models of how people think when they make decisions are designed to aid analysts in microeconomics. Models of investment in knowledge, of accumulation of nonmaterial capital, either of the embodied or the nonembodied type, contain as chief elements ideal-typical expectations and considerations regarding future returns to and depreciation of the productive capacity generated by the investment. These models are not designed as aids in the interpretation of observed behavior of *particular* persons or firms; instead, they are tools in the explanation of observations seen as effects of reactions that groups of (anonymous) people, showing some significant characteristics (for example, physicians, engineers, chemists, graduate students), have had or are likely to have to particular changes in external conditions.[48]

Finally, there are models used by analysts of aggregative economics (macroeconomics); these models are designed as tools in the explanation of changes in such global absolute magnitudes as national product and factor productivity, or in such global relative magnitudes as the size distribution of national income. Stocks of capital of the material and nonmaterial kind are essential components of these models, and depreciation of such stocks is an integral part of the analysis.

These reflections on the role of depreciation on various levels of economic analysis may create or reinforce the idea that depreciation is an indispensable notion in virtually every chapter of economic theory. Yet, to think so would be erroneous; there are many economic problems that can be adequately analyzed without regard to depreciation of capital. Among these are the problems of calculating *gross* national product and its components.

---

[48] To offer just one example, one may wish to theorize about the comparative effects on private investment in tangible and human capital if depreciation is or is not deductible from taxable income. Under present tax laws in the United States, depreciation of physical capital is allowed as a deduction, but depreciation on human capital is not, at least not explicitly. (Investment in training on the job is deductible in its entirety inasmuch as it is paid for in the form of lower earnings of either employees or employers; investment in university courses is deductible as business expense if paid for by employers, but not deductible if paid by the students unless they can prove that their incomes depend on it.

Gross National Product and Its Components

Gross national product includes gross investment, or gross capital formation. Almost all writers on social accounting have argued that net investment, or net capital formation, is the more important magnitude to calculate and, hence, depreciation has to be ascertained. To the extent that changes of national product over time are to be explained or predicted, it is certainly essential to know whether gross investment is just large enough to replace depleted, deteriorated, and obsolete parts of the capital stock—in which case net capital formation would be zero—or whether there is substantial net investment (net of the depreciation of the previous stocks) to provide the material and nonmaterial durables that will make productive factors more productive and generate future increases in total product. For this and similar purposes, the economist needs to know the size of gross capital formation *and* the amounts of capital depreciation to be deducted. These are not, however, the only concerns of economic analysis. For example, a descriptive analysis of national economic activity need not involve itself in a decomposition of gross investment into replacement and net investment.

A disaggregation of gross national product by type of product need not concern itself with the question of depreciation of capital stocks. If one is interested in the absolute and relative size of steel production, one need not ascertain how much of the annual output of steel went into the manufacture of new machines replacing machines retired because they were worn out or obsolete. If one is interested in the absolute and relative size of the production of textiles, it is not necessary to find out how many old clothes, bath towels, and curtains were discarded in the same year. Similarly, if we inquire into the annual cost of higher education, we can do so without asking how many former graduates of colleges and universities retired or died during the year. And if we want to ascertain the absolute and relative expenditures for R and D in any given years, we do not have to speculate about the obsolescence of previous technological knowledge.

No doubt, the problems of depreciation are relevant and essential for inquiries into wealth and capital, but they are not relevant or essential in calculations of the gross national product and, in particular, in calculations of the annual cost of total production of knowledge. If we want to know how much of its total resources a society devotes to knowledge production in any particular year, the relevant concept is not affected by changes in what anyone might consider the existing stock of knowledge. Indeed, I have tried to emphasize in my writings on the subject, in 1962 as well as in 1980 (in Volume I of this work), that I do not believe there is much sense in our attempting to obtain a total value of our stock of knowledge. There is good sense, however, in obtaining an idea of what portion of our productive services we devote annually to the production—creation and dissemination—of knowledge.

There is a legitimate interest in finding out how much people spent for television in a particular year. The figure that answers this question should include purchases of new television sets (both to replace outworn ones and to have multiple apparatuses), the cost of repair and maintenance services, the cost of the programs transmitted and of the operation of television stations, and investments in the expansion of such stations and their equipment. It would make no sense to reduce the total figure by an estimate of the depreciation of old equipment and appliances.

If we want to know how much was spent in a particular year on computers and calculators, the answer will not be affected by an estimate of depreciation of old installations and instruments. In other words, for any estimate of the GNP type, depreciation is irrelevant. Only estimates of the NNP type call for estimates of depreciation.

These considerations should not suggest that research on depreciation of capital is of minor significance. Discussions of national wealth and social capital cannot dispense with analyses of both additions and substractions, and the subtractions will include depreciation of technological knowledge, nonembodied or embodied in the country's labor force. However, those not interested in the stock concepts but only in annual flows and their breakdown into various categories need not bother with "correcting" these flows for diminutions in the value of any kind of stock. For the simple question of what portion of the nation's economic activity (measured in gross product) is devoted to the creation and dissemination of knowledge, the problem of depreciation of old knowledge is not relevant. (Incidentally, this "simple question" will occupy us in several volumes of this work.) Moreover, even a "welfare-oriented" system of national-income accounting may not be interested in depreciation of old knowledge owing to its being superseded by superior knowledge. If new knowledge is produced that will be enjoyable to have and/or helpful in producing (more or better) goods and services, people will be better off and need not bother about the fact that old knowledge has become "worthless" in the process.

CHAPTER 20

PROFILES OF LIFETIME LEARNING
AND EARNING

IN REPORTING about theoretical and empirical research on educational investment in human capital—both in school and on the job—it is important to distinguish between different objectives of the inquiries. To try to explain earnings (and, hence, differences in earnings) of individuals or small groups of persons in particular professions or occupations is one thing; it is another thing to attempt an explanation of observed patterns in the income distribution of a large population composed of persons in all sorts of occupations; and, assuming that one has succeeded in estimating the effects of human-capital accumulation on earnings (and differences in earnings), it is again another thing to try to calculate rates of return on investments in capacity improvements. It is possible to evaluate a research program as highly successful in attaining one of these objectives, or in yielding important insights relevant to it, without necessarily regarding the program as successful in reaching or approaching the other objectives.

Patterns in the Distribution of Earnings

The work of Jacob Mincer[1] should be recognized as particularly successful in explaining observed patterns in the distribution of earnings within very large groups of the population. "Successful" may mean, first, that the theoretical specification of the variables is considered plausible in light of general economic theory (in that the model includes factors that are regarded as causally most important in the determination of the outcome); second, that adequate empirical counterparts for selected variables are identified and obtained

[1] Jacob Mincer, "Investment in Human Capital and Personal Income Distribution," *Journal of Political Economy*, Vol. 66 (July-August 1958, pp. 281-302; "On-the-Job Training: Costs, Returns, and Some Implications," *Journal of Political Economy*, Vol. 70 (September-October 1962, Part 2), pp. 50-79; "The Distribution of Labor Incomes: A Survey with Special References to the Human Capital Approach," *Journal of Economic Literature*, Vol. 8 (March 1970), pp. 1-26; *Schooling, Experience, and Earnings* (New York: National Bureau of Economic Research, 1974); "Human Capital and Earnings," in Douglas M. Windham, ed., *Economic Dimensions of Education* (Washington, D.C.: National Academy of Education, 1979), pp. 1-31.

with an acceptable degree of accuracy; and third, that by means of appropriate statistical techniques a substantial part of the outcome (say, variances of observed earnings from average earnings) is statistically "accounted for" by the magnitudes included in the model. For example, if perhaps as much as one-half of the observed variances in earnings can be statistically "explained" by such variables as age, years of schooling, and years of experience in jobs that presumably provide valuable work experiences, the particular research may, according to the standards of many regression analysts, be regarded as successful.

To illustrate the third of these criteria of success, take a random sample of white men of the nonfarm population of all working ages and examine their earnings; only about 7 per cent of the differences in their annual earnings can be statistically explained by differences in the duration of their schooling. Next, take account also of differences in their work experiences, particularly in their postschool investments in learning on the job, and about one-third of the earnings differentials are explained. Then, take account also of the number of weeks the individuals in the group have worked during the years, and as much as one-half of the differences in annual earnings are explained.[2] If more factors are included, for example, IQ test scores, parental incomes or socioeconomic status, or other clues to mental and financial abilities, the "unexplained residual" of the variances in earnings may be further reduced.[3] Of course, no researcher can reasonably aspire to explain each and every deviation from the norm.

Recorded Data and Processed Numbers

The theoretical constructs, their empirical proxies or surrogates, the actual data, and the manipulations with the data should be briefly described here, so that the reader can appreciate the researcher's ingenuity in overcoming the difficulties inherent in his task. In an analysis of the contributions of different factors to a given outcome, the analyst's first demand is that each of the factors as well as the outcome can be independently ascertained. In the problem in ques-

[2] Mincer, Schooling, pp. 44 and 94.

[3] Readers versed in regression analysis will realize that the inclusion of additional variables, thought to be good surrogates for presumably effective causes, may reduce the previously estimated coefficients. Just as inclusion (into the model) of investment in work experience reduced drastically the explanatory power of investment in schooling, and inclusion of the number of weeks worked reduced the explanatory power of investment in job training, a fourth variable may reduce the values of the first three coefficients. Needless to say, additional variables should be included only if they are not in conflict with the theoretical model and do not obscure the theoretical interpretation of the featured variables.

tion—to ascertain the contributions that certain accumulations of human capital make to the investors' earnings—we should want independent records of investments in schooling, of investments in job training, and of earnings. Moreover, since the time intervals between investments and returns are of strategic importance, and since many people invest in job training over extended periods during which they also receive earnings, the researcher would need profiles of the individuals' lifetime investments in their earning capacity (and also of depreciation of their stocks of human capital) and profiles of their lifetime earnings.[4] Ideally, the analysis of investments and returns would call for a comparison between time series of earnings spread over forty to fifty years and the earners' net investments spread over an only slightly shorter period (beginning and ending earlier than the series of earnings).

Data of this sort are neither available nor even conceivably obtainable. The fundamental obstruction lies in the fact that most of the investments in human capital consist of earnings foregone, neither reported nor recorded by anybody, merely hypothetical values, never observed but at best inferred. Whatever records of earnings exist are only of net earnings actually collected, net of the values of the learning opportunities for which the holders of growth jobs pay in the form of accepting rates of money compensation lower than the rates received by holders of jobs that do not promise valuable work experience with higher earnings in the future.[5]

The Existence of Growth Jobs

Let me use a simple illustration to clarify the concept of what I have called "growth jobs." Assume that a person is paid $250 a week in a job that provides him with valuable learning experiences, whereas he could have earned $300 a week in an ordinary no-growth job. The appropriate adjustments of the raw data would call for raising

[4] "Indeed, the major reorientation that human capital analysis has provided for labor economists is the shift of focus from analysis of *current* earnings of groups to complete *lifetime* earnings profiles." Mincer, "Human Capital and Earnings," pp. 4-5. (Emphasis added.)

[5] Mincer reminds the reader repeatedly that the essential series consist of hypothetical numbers. For example, earnings of persons with certain amounts of schooling but no work experience, denoted by Y_s, represent "a hypothetical concept of earnings a person would receive after completion of schooling, if he did not incur any further growth-producing self-investments. Values of Y_s are not observable . . ." *Schooling*, pp. 47-48. Again, "If information were available on all variables and parameters for each individual i, the equation would represent a complete accounting . . . of the human capital characteristics entering into the formation of earnings. Of course, the availability of such information is not even conceivable." *Schooling*, p. 90.

the earnings from $250 to $300 and for entering the difference of $50—as an imaginary tuition fee—under the heading of investment in self-improvement. For the sake of consistency, a similar treatment would be required for someone who holds a part-time job that enables him to have part-time schooling. The earnings foregone should be added both to the earnings collected and to the investments made. Finally, a person of working age going to school or college full-time, without receiving any stipends, would forego full-time earnings; these potential full-time earnings ought to be included as hypothetical receipts in the lifetime earnings profile and charged to investments in human capital. Earnings profiles obtained with such procedures can hardly have great similarity with series of actual incomes received; and the corresponding investment profiles are also the results of purely hypothetical reasoning. In Mincer's research, the investment profile was not explicitly included; since the investments are estimates of unpaid parts of (hypothetical) gross earnings, it is possible to calculate their present value without actually developing the series of imaginary outlays.

A few more words to reinforce notions developed above. Jobs that provide opportunities for "learning by doing," and that therefore promise faster increases in earnings, attract applicants willing to work temporarily for lower rates of pay. Acceptance of this lower pay is tantamount to an investment in one's capacity.[6] This investment, however, is not directly observed but only inferred from "underpay" for some years and from especially rapid increases in pay in subsequent years, where both the low pay and the rapid increase are relative to more ordinary jobs. The investments implied in the years of relative underpay are intermingled with the earnings collected and can be disentangled from them only by adding to the actual pay the hypothetical worth of the prospect for increases in the future.

Cohorts, Time Series, and Cross-Sectional Data

All our talk about years of investment and years of earnings, especially profiles of lifetime earnings of individuals and large groups

---

[6] "If more learning, and hence a more steeply rising wage, is available in some jobs compared with others, all qualified workers would gravitate to such jobs if learning were thought to be costless. In consequence, entry wage levels in such jobs would be reduced relative to entry wages elsewhere for workers of the same quality, thereby creating opportunity investment costs in moving to such jobs. Thus, it is not merely training on the job (formal or informal), but also the processes of occupation choice that give rise to investments beyond schooling." Mincer, "Human Capital and Earnings," p. 6.

of individuals, may give the impression that we "observe" unchanging samples of people going through life as cohorts, being schooled, taking jobs, growing older, and eventually retiring. Yet, longitudinal series of data for unchanging groups of people are hard to come by. Statisticians are well trained in substituting for the needed time series latitudinal statistics for a given year but containing information about persons of all ages. In other words, hypothetical time series are fabricated from cross-sectional data.

The transformation of cross-sectional data into time series implies a strong resolution: Be it tacitly assumed that information about the conditions of Mr. Doe, age forty-four, Mr. Foe, age forty-five, and Mr. Hoe, age forty-six, all in the year 1978, can tell the story of the consecutive conditions of Mr. Roe, in 1976, 1977, and 1978, provided they all have had the same number of years in school (never mind which school, what teachers, what studies) and had left school in the same year to take a job (never mind what job). This assumption naturally is contrary to fact but statisticians (as well as theoreticians) are freehanded, and have to be if they want to get anywhere.

This does not mean that the transformation of latitudinal into longitudinal "data" is a sort of mischievous trickery. Such a fictitious time series may actually prove more reliable than a sequence of observations of the conditions of a virtually unchanged cohort, say, the cohort of which Messrs. Hoe and Roe, both of age forty-six in 1978, are members. With regard to life profiles of earnings, we should admit that a genuine time series of earnings of the members of a genuine cohort might suffer from even worse defects. The series may reflect temporary distortions, changes not relevant to the purpose at hand, effects of wage and price inflation, and various discontinuities of development and growth well-nigh inevitable in any long period of time.

A curve depicting lifetime earnings of individuals or groups would show rises and falls for a variety of reasons, some of which would be purely personal and others, related to general economic conditions. Among the personal factors accounting for a rise or series of rises in the earnings curve are (a) maturation, physiological and psychological; (b) the accumulation of life experience (sometimes free of explicit or even implicit costs); (c) school experience acquired in the past (when it caused entries on the investment account only if it occasioned actual outlays and/or foregone earnings); (d) increasing work experience, that is, learning by doing (which called for entries in the investment account); and (e) other sorts of job training, probably in the past (usually at a cost). With regard to general economic conditions, it should be clear that economy-wide productivity gains, booms, recessions, depressions, wage inflation, tax increases, and so forth, would introduce a great deal of noise into the information furnished by longitudinal data. Attempts to eliminate such noise may call for rather arbitrary decisions, particularly since the analyst's adjustments of the data depend on whether he considers the particular change in general economic conditions as permanent, long-lasting, or merely temporary. Whereas such judgments might be less arbitrary for data from a more distant past, they would be most arbitrary when based on conjectures about mere conjunctures that are subject to change within a relatively short time.

The effects of various personal factors on the series of net earnings received cannot be separated except on the basis of simplifying assumptions. Surely, life experiences, school experiences, and work experiences are essentially nonquantifiable components operating together in augmenting earning capacity; a causal allocation of the resulting earnings among these three kinds of experience looks like an impossible task. To make it possible, one assumes that age can serve as a proxy for life experience; the number of years at school, as a proxy for school experience; and the number of years in gainful employment, as a proxy for work experience; but one should not forget that these are only surrogates—and rather poor ones at that—for the respective "causes" of capacity, performance, and earnings. *Life experiences* in different environments or communities—urban or rural, elite or slum, integrated or segregated, wealthy or poor—are very different, and the same number of years spent in such different circumstances will hardly have the same effects on earning capacity. *School experiences* may depend on the type and quality of school, on the curricula available and actually selected, on the number of days per year in active attendance, and so on. *Work experiences* cannot help having different effects according to type of work, permanence of employment, number of hours per year, and many other things. If average returns to average investments in such different kinds of experiences were estimated, just what could be learned from such an exercise?

Earnings Differentials, Earnings Distribution,
and Rates of Return

The rhetorical question with which I ended the previous section, apparently inviting a negative response, would be justified only if the research in question were designed chiefly to throw light on rates of return of different kinds of educational investment. This was not the case. When I embarked on a description of Mincer's research, I distinguished among different possible objectives and indicated that his inquiry was intended to explain the statistical distribution of earnings. The research was successful in proving (or, more correctly, not disconfirming) that variances in earnings are largely determined by differences in the stocks of accumulated human capital. Estimation of rates of return on investments in different forms of human capital, though connected with the explanation of earnings differentials, is another story. There is more to say on earnings differentials before we can examine any implications of the findings for rates of return.

Three important principles of rational decision-making regarding human investment were formulated by Gary Becker. First, with finite lifetimes, investments made at an early age will produce returns for longer periods, and investments in self-improvement made late in life can yield benefits for only brief periods; it follows that total returns on given amounts of investments made at a higher age will tend to be smaller. Second, at any positive rate of discount, the present value of total future returns, even if their undiscounted sum were the same, is larger if the returns are received earlier. Third, the most important cost of self-improvement is the value of the individual's own time devoted to learning; since most people's time becomes more valuable as they become more experienced, more skilled, and more knowledgeable, the cost of investment in self-improvement will be higher the later in their lives the investment is made.[7] All three considerations are clear and strong arguments for making investments in human capital as early in life as possible.

Are these arguments heeded in most real-life situations? Parental influences seem to work in the right direction in that most parents try to warn their children against avoidable postponements in the acquisition of skills and cognitive knowledge. The children themselves often have strong time preferences, attaching great importance to present leisure (play) relative to study that promises future returns; this does not mean that they act irrationally, but it does frequently mean that the children will later in life regret their childish and immature schemes of preferences. The real trouble, however, lies with collective decisions, that is, chiefly decisions of the government, legislating about education, labor markets, wage rates, work incentives, and actually operating much of the existing school system. Since the rational legislator in a democratic society is apt to maxi-

---

[7] Gary S. Becker, *Human Capital* (New York: Columbia University Press, 1964; 2d ed., 1974), pp. 48, 50-58; 2d ed., pp. 64, 72-80. Similar propositions were formulated by Yoram Ben-Porath, "The Production of Human Capital and the Life Cycle of Earnings," *Journal of Political Economy*, Vol. 75 (July-August 1967), pp. 352-365. For a concise summary see Mincer, *Schooling*, pp. 13-14.

mize his chances for reelection, he probably considers preferences of voters who cannot calculate costs that they do not think they bear, and benefits that they do not realize. The result is that the rationality of public policy is confined to considerations of expected voting behavior of people who do not, and cannot, make benefit-and-cost analyses of public actions. I conclude that the general principle of efficient educational policy—that as much learning as possible be done as early in life as possible—are commonly violated by the kinds of government influence on the people's opportunities for schooling and work-training, chiefly by postponing the teaching of materials that could be taught earlier and by postponing entry into the job market. (This is not an objection to using the model of rational decision-making in examining, not only what "ought to be done," but also what actually is done by private individuals investing in their self-improvement.) Application of the wise rule, "the earlier you learn, the more you will earn," is, however, impeded not only by effects of government policies, but also by an economic principle, the law of increasing cost.

The human brain is not without limits and cannot possibly absorb an infinite amount of learning per hour, day, or week. Long before the point of maximum absorption is reached, serious inefficiencies will set in; and long before that, disutilities or pain costs of learning will have started to become very high; at a still earlier point, the opportunity costs of learning—chiefly foregone earnings and foregone leisure (sleep, fun, play)—will have become high enough to make further increments of human-capital formation too costly relative to the present valuation of the future benefits to be derived from them. Thus, increasing costs in the production of human capital reduce the application of the rule that speedy and early learning is much more valuable than slower or later learning.[8]

A valuable insight was gained by using lifetime profiles in the descriptive analysis of earnings and human-capital investments and, particularly, for ascertaining the time at which observed earnings may be assumed to reflect the accumulation of human capital through

---

[8] For technical reasons, some analysts—for example, Ben-Porath ("Production," p. 356), and Mincer (Schooling, p. 14)—presented graphs showing the marginal-cost curve of capital formation increasing all the way from the origin of the system of coordinates. Although it is not relevant to their argument, it should be pointed out that too little learning per unit of time may be so inefficient that the resulting capital formation is very costly, perhaps even infinite. One cannot learn the basic skills if only a few minutes per day or a few hours per week are devoted to the task; one will never learn a foreign language if only two hours a week are given to this endeavor. Thus, the cost of producing human capital is diminishing before it starts increasing. Too slow learning can be just as costly as too fast learning, or even more costly.

schooling. If many of the school leavers find employment in growth jobs, the part of the gross earnings they actually collect as wages will understate their potential earnings and, hence, their earning capacity. How long does it take for observed earnings to catch up with the imaginary tuition fees paid for the learning opportunities provided by the jobs? Mincer estimated that at the end of a period of between seven to nine years after leaving school and starting gainful employment, the returns on the past investment in self-improvement will equal the costs of current investment. He called this the "point of overtaking."[9] It is at this point in the profile of lifetime earnings that the data may show a minimum of distortion from postschool investment; it takes eight years, on the average, until returns from previous investments match the current new net investments in further improvements of capacity. The point of overtaking, about eight years after leaving school—whether that was at age fifteen, eighteen, twenty-two, or any other age—will be the one point at which observed (paid-out) earnings will reflect the returns on investment in schooling without admixtures of investment cost for, or returns from, postschool investment. This device enables the researcher to estimate rates of return on schooling, provided good estimates are available of the cost of schooling, of which earnings foregone by those above fifteen years of age are the largest part.

Optional School-Leaving Ages, Employment, and Retirement

Again, it may be helpful to go over some of the issues discussed in preceding sections in less technical language and with simple illustrations. I begin with a tabulation of four levels of schooling, the ages of starting and leaving each level, and the ages of starting and retiring from gainful employment. To simplify the exposition, I shall forget nursery school and kindergarten and assume that all children start elementary school at age six and complete it at age twelve. I assume further that secondary school is divided into two halves of three years each. Next I assume that persons with more schooling will retire later, but not sufficiently later to make up for their delayed start in gainful employment. Finally I assume that nobody dies before the stated age of retirement. None of these assumptions is essential to the argument; they all are made for purposes of illustration. (In the tabulation I have shortened the term "point of overtaking" to "checkpoint.")

It may have been more realistic to assume a time interval between leaving school and starting on a job, since we have become sadly aware of the fact that many school leavers, especially teenagers, have

[9] Mincer, *Schooling*, pp. 17-18, 34, 52, 64.

Highest level of school completed	Age at entering	Years in school			Age at leaving school and starting job	Age at checkpoint for earnings	Years in job of gainful employment	Age at retirement
		Previous	Additional	Cumulated				
Middle school (junior high school)	12	6	3	9	15	23	50	65
Upper school (senior high school)	15	9	3	12	18	26	49	67
Undergraduate school (college)	18	12	4	16	22	30	46	68
Postgraduate school (graduate school of arts and sciences, professional or vocational school)	22	16	6	22	28	36	42	70

a hard time finding employment and may have to suffer a year or several years of unemployment. This issue, though of extreme importance for our social, economic, and political conditions, and explained by many economists chiefly as the (carefully unadvertised) result of popular public policies (for example, minimum wage rates), lies outside the frame of reference of the analysis under discussion. With an interval between the school-leaving age and the job-starting age, various figures would be different from those tabulated, and the profiles of investments and earnings would be altered accordingly, but the formal analysis, or the procedural rules adopted, would not be affected.[10]

Each row in the table refers to persons who stop their formal education after completing the level of school named at left. The school-leaving age for those who have completed middle school is given as fifteen, which presupposes that compulsory school attendance does not go beyond that age (as it actually does in some of the states). The duration of the four levels of school is taken to be three years for each half of high school (secondary school), four years for college, and six years for graduate study (Ph.D., M.D., D.D.S., Dr. Eng., Dr. Ed., etc.). It is clear that most persons completing a particular level of school have several options available: they may continue to the next higher level of school, either for a terminal degree or for even more advanced studies; they may quit school and accept a growth job at relatively low pay (with different amounts of relative "underpay" and hence different amounts of investment in themselves); or they may take an ordinary no-growth ("dead-end") job at the standard wage (with gross earnings equal to net earnings, since no postschool investment is involved). The last option provides no increases in earnings over the years, so that the earnings at the checkpoint are the same as the starting wage at the first job immediately after leaving school.[11] If, on the other hand, employment is taken in jobs with learning opportunities and, hence, with postschool investment, the checkpoints for earnings that reflect just the returns on schooling—but not any earnings on postschool investment (because they match the cost of current investment)—are at ages twenty-

[10] Jacob Mincer advises me that "the observed differences between school leaving and the first job thereafter are, on average, small."

[11] To make this statement more realistic, one would have to take account of such pay increases as are general for the entire economy. Instead of talking about zero increases versus raises commensurate with acquired training, one would have to talk about across-the-board rates versus skill-related (or merit) rates of increase. (In time series fabricated from cross-section data this problem of across-the-board increases does not arise.)

three, twenty-six, thirty, and thirty-six, respectively, that is, eight years after the first postschool employment.

I have repeatedly modified the term "postschool investment" with the adjective "net" in order to take account of depreciation of human capital previously accumulated. Such depreciation occurs through losses of memory and declining skills. For the greater part of most persons' careers, net investment is positive, although it may be declining with advancing age. There comes a time, however, with retirement approaching, when the job holder finds additional learning unprofitable. With the aging worker's physical and mental powers declining, the net investment in his human capital becomes negative. Empirical evidence, inferred from the profiles of lifetime earnings, supports these theoretical deductions but, as we have seen in Chapter 19, the notion of depreciation of human capital is so problematic that it allows not much more than qualitative testing. For numerical answers we would need operational definitions in terms of clearly observable empirical proxies for the theoretical constructs involved. Neither the required definitions nor the data are likely to be forthcoming.

If virtuosos of applied research, combining their mastery of pure theory with their ingenuity in mathematical craftsmanship, succeed in squeezing several time series out from only one set of cross-section data, we cannot help being impressed. The cross-section data used in this exercise were of incomes received by people of different ages and with different years of schooling and different years of gainful employment. The hypothetical time series were of annual cost of schooling (expenditures plus earnings foregone), annual cost of job training (earnings foregone), annual depreciation of the human capital created by schooling and training (implicit in reduced earnings), and annual earnings corrected for the implicit cost of training. Not that these four time series were actually shown in dollar figures for each year, but they were used for calculating the returns to the human capital (gradually accumulated and gradually depreciated) by the income earners. Since all these numbers were produced from only one set of rather "soft" cross-sectional data subjected to highly esoteric transformation on the basis of specifications informed by pure theory, the findings should be treated with reserve by empiricists as well as theorists.

We should repeat, however, that the chief purposes of the research in question were to provide more satisfactory explanations of observed distributions of income and, perhaps only incidentally to that, better insights into the rates of return to investment in learning at schools and in jobs. The next chapter will be devoted to a survey of writings on rates of return to educational investment.

Investing in Future Options

Another word may be added here on the worth of future options that might explain some distortions in relative rates of return to consecutive investments in ever higher levels of education. The point is that these investment decisions have to be made at different points in one's career but, since it is ordinarily impossible to enter into any higher level before having completed the level below, the chance of going on to higher levels may be valued separately from the stream of differential earnings that can be expected by those who do not go on to the next level of schooling but, instead, enter the labor force.

In order to see the issue clearly, let us assume that all schooling is voluntary and that there are job opportunities for school leavers regardless of age and number of school years completed. For simplicity, let us assume seven levels of schooling: primary school, ending after grade 6; junior secondary, ending after grade 9; senior secondary, ending after grade 12; junior college, ending after "grade 14"; upper-division college, ending after "grade 16"; master's degree work, ending after "grade 18"; and doctor's degree work, ending after "grade 22." Students, having completed junior high school would, in considering investing in the next three years of schooling—senior high school—not only think of the differential earnings of high-school graduates over those who had taken jobs after the ninth grade, but they would think also of the "admission ticket" to college education (of a sort) that high-school graduation would give them, an "option" they could, after another three years of school, exercise. This option may be worth a premium even if, at the moment (that is, three years ahead) the pecuniary advantage of a college education should seem unattractive. (Remember, many people buy options for corporate stocks even when most financial analysts see little or no promise in the future earnings of the company in question.)

The worth of options to go on to higher levels of schooling may explain why some optimistic students may invest in any level of schooling even when currently reported returns to that investment seem unsatisfactory compared with returns to alternative uses of investible funds, and even if the current reports on the rates of return to the investment in the (optional) next level of schooling look relatively poor. Times may change, interest rates may come down, and additional schooling may eventually fetch higher returns than it seems to do at the moment. Hence, options are acquired.

CHAPTER 21

RATES OF RETURN TO INVESTMENT
IN EDUCATION

THIS CHAPTER is to serve a variety of purposes. I intend it to make a more explicit and didactic statement about the *size* of returns to capital and the *rate* of return; to report on findings from empirical research on rates of return to investment in learning; to question some of the theoretical and statistical premises of this kind of research, perhaps even to cast doubt regarding its basic presuppositions; and to provide a summary of several issues treated in the preceding chapters.

The Size and the Rate

In simplest terms, the size of returns means dollars and the rate means per cent. If the returns come in as a series of receipts, a flow over time—perhaps over a lifetime—they can be expressed in a single magnitude as a present (capitalized) value, where each future receipt is discounted at a given rate. If the returns are to be compared with a given stock of capital (or with a given flow of investments), and the quantitative relation between returns and capital (investment outlays) is to be shown, one does not use a *given* rate of discount, or rate of capitalization, but, instead, calculates the *internal* rate of return. This is the rate that reduces the expected future returns to a present value equal to the given accumulated stock of capital (the sum of investment outlays plus interest up to the present).[1]

Several implications of these statements are obvious, but others may be quite difficult to handle. It is easy to see that future outlays and receipts may have rather low present values because of the discounting. The undiscounted dollar figures of returns expected to

[1] Assume that there have been annual investment outlays over the past five years and further outlays are to be made in the next seven years; returns are expected to be received beginning in five years and continuing for forty-five years. The present value of the series of investments is calculated by adding interest to the past outlays and deducting discount from the future outlays, and summing the resulting items. The present value of the series of expected returns is calculated by discounting each receipt and totaling the discounted items. The internal rate of return is found by asking which rate would make the two present values equal to each other.

accrue in a distant future may be very high, but the discount may cut them down to rather small present values. Besides the discount, there will be greater risk and great uncertainty regarding returns in a distant future; the person considering investments in his working and earning capacity is likely to take account of the possibility that he may not live long enough, or not be able to work long enough, to collect and enjoy the earnings that an "average" individual can reasonably expect. This consideration suggests that a supplement to the discount applied to future earnings (reducing their present value further) would be justified.

More serious complications arise from the fact that investment outlays and expected returns are not independent of each other, in that the cost of self-improvement consists almost entirely of earnings foregone. The value of the time an investor in his own capacity devotes to learning is higher for abler and more self-confident individuals than for average persons. He may expect to derive high future returns from his additional learning efforts, but he also has the option to earn more than average compensations from present employment. Since the returns—earnings in later years—are discounted more heavily than the investments—earnings foregone now and in the near future—the internal *rate* of return may turn out to be quite low even if the *size* of the returns is conspicuously high.

It is not surprising, therefore, that the size of the returns to extended and advanced education may be very high, but the rate of return quite low. Similarly, we should readily comprehend statements that attribute increasing returns but decreasing rates of return to the same extension of the duration of schooling. Finally, if returns from alternative investments are compared and it is assumed, tacitly or explicitly, that the amounts (present values) of the investments are the same, that comparison is implicitly also of the *rate* of return.

Even Bad Investments May Have Positive Returns

We should beware of confusing relatively low returns, diminishing returns, and negative returns. About diminishing returns, we shall talk later in this chapter; about negative and low positive returns, a few reflections may be helpful now.

The case of negative returns is easy to comprehend: even without any discount on income accruing in the future, the gross sum of receipts resulting from certain "investments" may be less than zero. The implications of such negative returns should be clear: the persons, communities, or societies concerned are worse off than they would have been if they had never made this particular investment, and even worse off than if they had made no investment at all. That

is to say, the investment actually made is inferior not only to alternative investments (which might have yielded *some* benefits), but
also to states of affairs that would exist if the persons or societies
concerned had never possessed the resources required for the investment or had thrown them away or lost them instead of using
them for that particular project. In other words, the effects of the
unfortunate "investment" are downright harmful: they actually cut
into the incomes or benefits derived from other sources.[2]

What about the case of zero returns, where the chosen investments
do not make people poorer or richer than they would have been
without these or alternative investments? We may skip this case,
because the results are quite similar to those where returns are positive but smaller than the returns that could have been obtained from
other investments of the same size. In other words, certain outlays
designed to yield fair returns actually yield much less than equal
outlays would have secured in different investments. Thus, the returns to the particular investment are positive but inadequate in
comparison with the alternative investments that were foregone.[3]

The way to compare the social productivity or private profitability
of alternative investments is to calculate their internal rates of return.
For each of the alternatives one calculates the rate of discount, or
capitalization, that would make the present value of the flow of
revenues equal to the accumulated cost-value of the outlay (or flow
of outlays and sacrifices) that constitute the investment. To choose
the most productive or most profitable investment projects, one ranks
them in descending order of internal rates of return and then draws
a "cut-off" line dictated by the availability of investible capital funds.

This strategy of ranking investment projects by internal rates of
return and setting a "cut-off" line where the available funds are all

---

[2] As an illustration from the domain of real capital, one may imagine that a nation
invests in building up its chemical industry and that toxic wastes contaminate the
streams, the soil, and the air so that soon after operations have started the region is
made uninhabitable. (I trust my readers will forgive me for treating them to such a
horror story—merely to explain an economic concept.) To use a similarly gruesome
illustration from the domain of presumptive investment in human capital, one may
imagine that a nation invests in compelling all students to study economic theory for
a minimum of ten years, including two years each of the history of economic thought,
the writings of Marx and Lenin, mathematical economic theory, and econometrics;
that many of these abused students, as a result of their excessive learning efforts, go
mad (insane) or get mad (rebellious) and destroy all university buildings, power plants,
and steel mills.

[3] If the opportunity cost of capital funds were deducted from the returns, the *net*
revenues would be negative; but for simplicity we will look at the positive revenues
undiminished by the theoretical (implicit) cost of capital funds.

used for the most profitable projects is not generally accepted. There is an extensive literature about the desirability of discriminating in favor of certain projects or programs regarded as especially meritorious though below the strategic "cut-off" line. One group of writers favors governmental projects over private ones, partly because governments can, as a rule, borrow funds at interest rates lower than those charged to private investors. Others argue that the lives of private savers and investors are limited, whereas the state or the nation will live forever—a difference that (because expectations of mortality influence savers' "time preference") justifies higher private than public discount rates.

I am not much impressed with these arguments; whenever an investment project stands to be thrown out, rejected as returning too little for the private sector, its advocates would push it as a good project for the public sector, where its meager rate of return would still be "satisfactory." There may be reasons to favor certain governmental programs, but such reasons would be found in some assured extra nonprivate or external benefits expected from the investment, that is, in the belief that the total social benefits will exceed the private ones thanks to some "third-party benefits" that do not enter the calculations of private investors. Arguments of this sort can make economic sense and deserve consideration. But discrimination in the rate-of-return standard of selection is apt to result in investment decisions inconsistent with the economic principle of optimizing the use of scarce resources.

The Stock of Human Capital and the Returns

Educational investment designed to yield material and pecuniary returns may consist in outlays made and earnings foregone for the purpose of creating, through processes of teaching, training, and learning, a *skill* and a *will* to perform certain activities more effectively than the same individuals would be able to do without that investment. Such investment does not create material durable goods; it creates an otherwise nonexistent human capacity to perform, in other words, human capital.

Conceptual tools described and examined in the first chapter of this part—Chapter 12—can now be put to use in this discussion of valuations of stocks of human capital and calculations of the rates of return they are expected to yield. If *past* investments in human capacity have resulted in an accumulated stock of human capital, one asks whether and how this stock can be measured or appraised. If *new* investments in human capacity are expected to produce a flow of incremental incomes in the future, one asks for the numerical relationship of these future increments in earnings to the investment outlays. The look backward shows the integral of the past investments minus earned depreciation plus cumulated interest up to the present. The look forward shows a picture that can be interpreted in at least two ways. The expected stream of returns attributed to the improvement of productive capacity—improved labor power—can be capitalized (discounted) at the rate applied to other current investments; in this way the present value of the stream of returns, that is, its capital value, is calculated. Alternatively, one can calculate the internal rate of capitalization (discount) that would reduce the expected increments of income to the investment outlay supposed to create them.

Only if all expectations entertained in the past had been completely right, and no changes whatever had occurred in the economy, and only if all expectations for the future were entertained with a rare degree of certainty and confidence could the stock of human capital measured by *past* outlays or sacrifices be equal to the stock of human capital measured by *future* income differentials. In analogy to the write-offs of tangible capital assets that have been scrapped, there should be "write-offs" of past investments in human capital to take account of persons who have been withdrawn from active service because of disabling illness or accident, retirement, or death, or whose acquired skills or cognitive knowledge have become obsolete. Only active members of the labor force can be regarded as embodiments of human capital by an analyst who confines his estimates to material or pecuniary benefits.[4] In analyses that include the psychic incomes of the retired, say, the greater enjoyment of literature, music, and other arts by educated pensioners, or that put a value on the effect of the educational services the retired may render to their grandchildren, retirement is not assumed to terminate the stream of benefits from past investment in human capital.

Write-offs from human capital valued on the basis of past investment outlays are appropriate not only in order to take account of withdrawals of the skilled from active service but also for other reasons. For example, it would be quite unreasonable to expect that, in a world of change, the skills, aptitudes, and attitudes acquired by past investments should be precisely those demanded now and in the future. Undoubtedly many bad investments have been made, with the result that the capitalization of expected future additions

---

[4] Pensioners who use their earlier training in financial analysis to play the securities markets (stocks, bonds, forward options, etc.) and succeed in making money from such activity may be considered self-employed members of the labor force. (A searching question from Mary Huber induced me to add this qualification.)

to earnings (attributable to the improvements of labor power) cannot show a present value equal to the stock of human capital measured by past investments. Thus, human capital, valued by past investments, can hardly earn a yield equal to the yields expected from current investment made with supposedly better knowledge of things to come.

If one asks what rate of return has been obtained from past investments in human capital, one takes the backward look. But who takes that look? The private investor, curious to see how well or how badly he has done? The economist who, if he relies on statistical data, can only look into the past and report his findings in an essay in social and economic history? The economist as Inspector General of Society, trying to judge whether its investments in human capital have been doing well? Or the economist as advisor of the government, trying to apply past investment experience to current investment planning for future returns? If he wants to make this sort of judgment or give this sort of advice, is it prudent to take all educational investments together as a global magnitude instead of trying to disaggregate it by type of education or by different vocational or academic curricula?

Different Returns from Different Fields of Study

It is reported that lawyers have on the average much higher earnings than priests; that truck drivers earn more than most college professors; that certified accountants earn more than archaeologists; that electricians earn more than musicians; and that plumbers earn more that school teachers. Yet, in each of these pairs the higher earner has spent fewer years in schools or in advanced studies. If research findings were disaggregated by field of study and occupation, we would surely see that the rates of return to investment in different kinds of schooling, studying, and training differ drastically.

Instances of extraordinarily high returns in certain occupations may be taken as indications of general underinvestment in the educational preparation required for the occupations in question. Such underinvestment may sometimes be attributed to lack of foresight by those who failed to choose these careers, giving the smarter or luckier ones who did choose them nice windfall profits from their investments. Another cause for exceptionally high rates of return to investment in specialized schooling or training may be the existence of entrance barriers either to the occupations or to the education required for them. It is possible, of course, that the scarcity of people in the best-paying careers is not artificial, not due to restrictions on entry (imposed by professional organizations, trade unions, or government) but natural, a scarcity of special talents. Investigators should be able to identify the past or present conditions that explain the excess demand for, or undersupply of, particular skills and the consequent high rates of return to the investment in acquiring them.[5] In any case, if one calculates the capital value of flows of differential earnings that reflect the scarcity value of the services in question, one may consider the owners of the intangible resources as having made attractive "human-capital gains."

At the other extreme, there are many instances of human-capital losses, instances in which the present capital value of the flow of differential earnings is below the historical cost of the educational investment. (It may even be zero.) The evident overinvestment and overcrowding may be due to ignorance, excessive optimism, or large nonpecuniary attractions of the particular occupations. Low or zero rates of return to the educational investment of actors and musicians may be attributed to the strong appeal or even fascination that performing in the arts has for many. More generally, however, propaganda and misinformation may have pushed too many young people into prolonged schooling, and excessive optimism may have steered them into schooling that taught the wrong skills (or wrong attitudes). Unforeseen changes in market demand for different skills may play the main role in causing a condition of oversupply in particular occupations. Where the unlucky investors have suffered capital losses in pecuniary terms, one can only hope that they get at least some compensatory intellectual satisfaction out of their past efforts at improving themselves.

With good and bad investments thrown together in one aggregate mass of "investment in education" or "investment in human capital," does it make much sense to calculate an average rate of return? Analysts of the accumulation of, and returns to, physical capital rarely bother to calculate average returns to an aggregate composed of past investments in agriculture, mining, manufacturing industry, transportation, communication, housing, national defense, and all the rest. No economist assumes that decisions to invest in airplane manufacturing and in zipper manufacturing—to have these two stand for all industry branches from A to Z—can be explained by the average rate of return to past investment in industry as a whole. If some diligent statisticians were to come forth with findings concerning average returns to the total stock of physical capital, what

[5] See, for example, the pioneering investigation on the rates of return in the education of medical doctors, lawyers, and certified accountants, by Milton Friedman and Simon Kuznets, *Income from Independent Professional Practice* (New York: National Bureau of Economic Research, 1945).

significance would these numbers have? I can conceive of a few problems for which the results of such a study might be pertinent.[6] For most purposes, however, disaggregated studies are needed.

A similar argument can be made with regard to human capital. A rate of return that averages the pecuniary results of any and all investments in education is not very helpful. Decisions to go to university and study no matter what, whether it be theology, engineering, Sanskrit, cybernetics, or musicology, may perhaps be rationally made on the basis of intellectual curiosity and love of knowledge for its own sake; however, if the decision is to be made with a view to high pecuniary returns, information is needed about differential earnings in careers making use of particular acquired abilities.[7] Governmental decisions to subsidize and promote higher education regardless of the fields studied may be justified on cultural grounds, in support of an affluent society appreciating the finer things in life; but if the decisions are to be made with a view to advances in productive capacity and economic growth, information about the productive contributions of different occupations will be needed.

The need for inquiries into comparative returns from different courses of study is widely recognized. Such inquiries are relatively scarce because pertinent statistical data are hard to come by.[8] Most of the empirical work on rates of return to additional years of education has been done with data from the census of population. The census data in the United States provide information on several variables fundamental to the theory—annual income, sex, age, and years of schooling—but no information on *what* was taught or learned. Hence, from this source only the number of years of undifferentiated schooling is available.

---

[6] Comparative studies of the productivity of capital or of the productive efficiency in the use of capital in different countries may perhaps disregard the "mix" of capital invested in different sectors, industries, or branches. I am thinking of the kind of research done by Abram Bergson, for example, for his book *Planning and Productivity under Soviet Socialism* (New York: Columbia University Press, 1968).

[7] ". . . an over-all, average private rate of return to university education is perfectly compatible with negative rates of return to certain fields of study at certain low-quality institutions." Mark Blaug, "The Empirical Status of Human-Capital Theory: A Slightly Jaundiced Survey," *Journal of Economic Literature*, Vol. 14 (September 1976), p. 842.

[8] One of the earlier studies of comparative returns was by Bruce W. Wilkinson, "Present Values of Lifetime Earnings for Different Occupations," *Journal of Political Economy*, Vol. 74 (November-December 1966), pp. 566-572. A more comprehensive study was done by Richard S. Eckaus, *Estimating the Returns to Education: A Disaggregated Approach* (Berkeley, Cal.: Carnegie Commission on Higher Education, 1973).

Private Rates of Return in the United States

Let us now look at some of the findings of empirical research on rates of return to investment in incremental education.[9] Gary Becker used several census years (1939, 1949, 1956, and 1958) in his calculations for the United States; his results from the different sets of data were, of course, not all the same, but they were similar enough to give us some confidence in their order of magnitude. The private rates of return, before accounting for differences in native qualities, were quite stable for college education: for the four different sets of data, the rates were between 12.4 and 14.8 per cent per annum.[10] Thus, an investment in four years of college yielded an annual return of about 13 per cent over the average working life of the graduate. We must not forget, however, that the differential earnings become positive only after several years. Ten years after graduation the rate of return is still negative.[11] Let us also note that the annual return of 13 per cent refers to estimated lifetime earnings of persons who went to school almost half a century ago.

The rates of return to high-school education in the United States were, according to Becker's estimates, rising over the years, from 16 per cent in 1939 to 28 per cent in 1958. He suggested two explanations for this increase. With regard to the 16 per cent rate in 1939, he pointed out that the returns compare earnings of high-school graduates with earnings of persons with only nine years of school, and that the rates of return were calculated without taking account of ability, either native or ninth-graders'. We know that the percentage of youngsters completing the twelfth grade greatly increased after 1939, so that now practically only the least talented, least motivated, and most handicapped fail to complete high school.[12] It stands to reason, therefore, that much of the differential earnings is really due to differences in ambition and ability of the ninth-graders going on to high school, not to the high-school education they receive. As a second explanatory factor, Becker points to a notorious shift in the demand for labor away from less schooled to better educated. Less educated persons are becoming unemployable at the minimum wages imposed by legislation, trade unions, modern business ethics, and business-prestige considerations. High-school ed-

[9] This and the subsequent section are taken, with some alterations and insertions, from my book, *Education and Economic Growth* (Lincoln: University of Nebraska Press, 1970; reprinted New York: New York University Press, 1975), pp. 43-49.

[10] Gary S. Becker, *Human Capital* (New York: Columbia University Press, 1964; 2d ed. 1974), 1st ed., p. 128; 2d ed., p. 206.

[11] Ibid., 1st ed., p. 112; 2d ed., p. 190.

[12] Ibid., 1st ed., p. 129; 2d ed., p. 207.

ucation is becoming a condition of employment even where it contributes little to the skills required for the jobs in question.

Becker's pioneering calculations were followed by many others, using similar or different techniques. Giora Hanoch used data for 1959 and rather different estimating procedures for sorting out the effects of extraneous factors on personal earnings. For male whites in the northern United States he obtained an average rate of return to investment in high school (against only eight or nine years of school) of 16 per cent; and in college (against high school) of 10 per cent.[13] More recent analyses have arrived at much lower estimates, partly by using different bodies of data, partly by using different regression equations, and partly by using comparisons of wage rates rather than annual earnings (or, what comes to the same thing, by standardizing annual earnings by the number of hours worked per year). Jacob Mincer states that "the average rate of return to *schooling* varies between 7% and 11% in various bodies of data."[14] Further reductions have recently been reported, reflecting a significant decline, in the 1970s, of the differentials in the earnings of persons with more years of school attendance. I postpone presenting these findings until later in this chapter, after a brief survey of research findings for developing countries and, especially, after an examination of the question of diminishing returns to investment in education, for it is in connection with this question that some of the empirical research seems particularly relevant.

Rates of Return in Developing Countries

The preceding account related to the situation in the United States, and the figures reported are the *private* rates of return to educational investment. Similar calculations have been made for many other countries, though the statistical bases were much weaker. A few of the findings may be summarized here.

A study of Bogota, Colombia, calculated semiprivate, or "partially social," rates of return. "Partially social" means that the costs to the government were added to the costs to the students and their families, but the benefits included no additional benefits to society over and above the income differentials earned by the educated.[15] The reported partially social rates of return for men in Bogota were only

[13] Giora Hanoch, "An Economic Analysis of Earnings and Schooling," *Journal of Human Resources*, Vol. 2 (Summer 1967), pp. 324-325.

[14] Jacob Mincer, "Human Capital and Earnings," in Douglas M. Windham, ed., *Economic Dimensions of Education* (Washington, D.C.: National Academy of Education, 1979), p. 13.

[15] For a more comprehensive explanation see the comments at the end of this section.

15 per cent per annum for primary education, but 27 per cent for
secondary education, and 35 per cent for vocational training, yet
only 3 per cent for higher education. The returns were rather different
for women: a zero rate of return for primary education, 14 per cent
for secondary school, 40 per cent for vocational training, and 4 per
cent for university education.[16] The zero return for primary school
indicates that women without any schooling were getting the same
kinds of jobs as women who had attended primary school. The return
of 40 per cent obtained on investment in vocational training was
probably a result of the foreign-language skills acquired by typists
and secretaries.[17] The extremely low rate of return reported for higher
education, 3 per cent for men, may still prove too high if *social* costs
are correctly counted, since the calculation disregarded the fact that
one-half of the university graduates left the country. (Emigration does
not necessarily increase the loss of the investment of the nation that
has subsidized the education. The loss to the nation would be even
greater if the "overeducated" stayed home, unemployed or under-
employed.)[18] The *private* rates of return for university education are
probably much higher, since the emigrants' earnings abroad—especially in the United States—greatly exceed the earnings of the
graduates who have remained in the home country.

   In more developed countries, the partially social rates of return
from higher education are higher: 12 per cent in Chile[19] and 20 per
cent in Venezuela.[20] In Mexico, the private rate of return from higher
education was found to be 40 per cent.[21] For India, on the other hand,
the social rate of return to "education in general" for men was reported to be less than 16 per cent, and for secondary education alone
was no more than 10 or 12 per cent.[22] A more recent and more
detailed study, on the basis of 1961 data, shows social rates for

   [16] Theodore Paul Schultz, *Returns to Education in Bogota, Colombia* (Santa Monica,
Cal.: Rand Corp., 1968), p. 36.
   [17] Ibid., p. 29.
   [18] This question was addressed before. See Chapter 14, the section on "Social Justice
and Social Waste," particularly footnote 24.
   [19] Arnold Harberger and Marcelo Selowsky, *Key Factors in Economic Growth in
Chile*, mimeographed (Chicago, Ill., 1966).
   [20] Carl Shoup, *The Fiscal System of Venezuela* (Baltimore: Johns Hopkins University
Press, 1959).
   [21] Martin Cornoy, "Rates of Return to Schooling in Latin America," *Journal of
Human Resources*, Vol. 2 (Summer 1967), Table 7, p. 368.
   [22] Arnold C. Harberger, "Investment in Men versus Investment in Machines: The
Case of India," in C. Arnold Anderson and Mary Jean Bowman, eds., *Education and
Economic Development* (Chicago: Aldine, 1965); A. M. Nalla Gounden, "Investment
in Education in India," *Journal of Human Resources*, Vol. 2 (Summer 1967), Table
2, p. 352.

primary education as low as 13.7 per cent, for secondary education 12.4 per cent, and for college education 7.4 per cent. The private rate of return to the college graduate, compared with the illiterate, was only 15.2 per cent, and the social rate 12.3 per cent.[23] The author of one of the Indian studies reminds us of the very high rates of return on investment in physical capital (machines): they were between 17 and 26 per cent, much higher than the yields from human capital.[24]

The inconsistent shifts of focus on private, partially social, and social rates of return call for a reminder of the essential differences in the treatment of two pecuniary items: public subsidies to education, which tend to reduce private costs below social costs, and income taxes, which tend to reduce private gross returns below social returns. In calculating partially social returns only, the public cost of education is added to the private cost, which makes the partially social rates of return lower than the private. If income-tax rates, or other imposts on earnings, are high relative to the public share in the cost of education, social rates of return may conceivably exceed private rates. With low income taxes and large public subsidies to education, private rates of return will be significantly higher than social rates.[25]

Diminishing Returns

A few idiosyncratic economists reject the notion of marginal productivity, or efficiency of productive factors, no matter whether it is applied to land, labor, or capital. In general, however, the conception is accepted as fundamental at all levels of economic analysis. Yet, those who accept it forget sometimes that the marginal efficiency of any factor is, given the supply of cooperating factors and the demand for its product, a function of its quantity. The relative scarcity of any factor, and the marginal contribution it can make to output, will, other things remaining largely unchanged, diminish as its supply or availability increases beyond some point. This is probably an inescapable fact of life, a fundamental principle. It holds for both capital and investment, the former considered as a stock at a moment of time, the latter as a flow per unit of time. Other things being unchanged, increments to the capital stock and enlargements of the

[23] Mark Blaug, Richard Layard, and Maureen Woodhall, The Causes of Graduate Unemployment in India (London: Allen Lane, Penguin, 1969), Table 10.1

[24] Harberger, "Investment in Men," p. 29.

[25] For a comprehensive survey of the literature on country studies see George Psacharopoulos, Returns to Education: An International Comparison (Amsterdam: Elsevier, 1973).

investment outlays per period will be subject to diminishing additions to output—diminishing returns.

How does the "law of diminishing returns" apply to investment in human capital and, especially, to education? We must recall the distinction between several ways to invest in additional education: (1) to increase the number of *people* (the percentage of certain age groups) who are compelled or persuaded to attend secondary or tertiary school, (2) to increase the number of *years* a given number of people go to school, and (3) to increase the number of dollars (of given purchasing power) spent per student/year to improve the *quality* or the ingredients of schooling. The first of these investment opportunities relates to social rather than private choices. The private investor in schooling—the student himself or his parent or benefactor—choosing among various educational options would not normally consider changes in total numbers enrolled, although he may be persuaded by a "social trend," either to join it or to worry about the consequences for his own future career. The second and the third of the investment opportunities present both social and private choices. The private investor in educational capital will consider the possible differential earnings (and other benefits) and the additional costs of going to school for additional years and of selecting a more expensive school.

Statistical studies of earnings and costs associated with additional years of schooling relate necessarily to the past. As discussed earlier, there is no good reason to expect that past experiences will remain relevant for the future, especially if social and economic conditions change drastically. Nonetheless, we cannot afford to disregard the past if it is the only source of numerical information. In any case, it is interesting to see whether application of modern estimation techniques to the statistical data at our disposal yields findings that indicate whether or not the law of diminishing returns has been operating. In the case of the returns to investment where inputs can be measured only in terms of money and where differential money incomes are considered the only measurable outputs, we shall have to focus on percentage rates of return. Let us look at the findings reported by empirical researchers.

The evidence is confusing, which is not surprising once one realizes the variety of conceptual and statistical difficulties. Wage ratios between skilled and unskilled labor may change in one direction while the ratios of annual earnings change in the other; earnings differentials in favor of skilled labor may increase while returns (net of costs) may decrease, or vice versa; rates of returns to college education may be below those to secondary education, although either of the two may increase or decrease from one cohort to another, and so forth. Too many ratios and rates, adjustments and manipulations are involved to afford a clear or consistent picture of "actual" developments. Still, what have the analysts concluded from their empirical research?

Empirical Research on Changing Rates of Return

Gary Becker interpreted his data as showing significant reductions in rates of return to both high-school and college education between 1900 and 1940, followed by a sequence of increases up to 1960. These variations were evidently associated with increases in the numbers of graduates. As to the returns to longer education, the private rates of return to high-school graduation increased (on the basis of earnings unadjusted for differential ability) from 16 per cent in 1939 to 20 per cent in 1949, to 25 per cent in 1956, and to 28 per cent in 1958. The rates of return to college graduation fluctuated in these twenty years, first falling from 14.8 per cent to 12.4 per cent, then rising again to 14.8 per cent.[26] Incidentally, Becker's finding of an increase (by one-fourth) of the rates of return to high-school education from

[26] Becker, *Human Capital*, 1st ed., pp. 128 and 134; 2d ed. pp. 206 and 212. The following paragraph attempts to explain the earlier period: "If the data before 1940 can be considered representative, which is questionable, rates of return on both high-school and college education declined rather significantly during the first forty years of the century, and then stopped declining and even rose during the next twenty years. Since at least the relative number of college graduates increased more rapidly after 1940 and since mortality declined more rapidly before, these very different trends would probably be explained by less rapid shifts in the demand for educated persons during the earlier period: advances in knowledge and shifts in demand for final products may have been less favorable to educated persons then." (1st ed., p. 134; 2d ed., p. 212). Regarding the second period Becker proposed these explanations: "The movements in rates since 1939 were the net result of several changes with different effects. The substantial advance in technology and knowledge would tend to increase rates of return on education, even if the advance was 'neutral' ... and even if the advance was itself an effect of education. Demand for well-educated persons has also risen since 1939 because of a shift in government and business toward complicated military hardware and systematic research. On the other hand, a growth in the relative number of highly educated persons would, by itself, reduce rates of return on education. . . . [T]he number of college and high-school graduates has increased at about the same rate since 1939, so there is apparently little reason from the supply side to expect much decline in percentage earning differentials between them. Yet these changes in supply would produce a decline in the rate of return from college education. For the earnings of college and high-school graduates would decline relative to less-educated persons, and thus absolute earning differentials between college and high-school graduates would decline even if percentage differentials were unchanged. And a decline in absolute differentials would lower the rate of return from college unless costs declined by an equal amount." (1st ed., pp. 129-130; 2d ed., pp. 207-208).

1939 to 1949 seems to be contradicted by Mincer's finding that "there was a significant (about ⅓) drop in the rate [of return to schooling] between 1939 and 1949."[27] In a lecture, delivered in 1967 and reproduced in 1975 in the second edition of his book, Becker offered a fascinating discussion of two approaches to "Human Capital and the Personal Distribution of Income."[28] The two approaches are graphically described by means of supply and demand curves, supply depicting the opportunities to obtain schooling, and demand the eagerness to get it, where quantity is shown on the horizontal axis and price (the cost including foregone earnings) on the vertical axis. The "egalitarian approach" assumes essentially that differences in ability count less than differences in opportunities (barriers due to ignorance, poverty, prejudice); thus, there may be a single negatively declining demand curve, but several different supply curves for investment in human capital. The "elite approach" assumes that abilities differ, which implies that there is a set of different demand curves for educational investment, whereas opportunities are relatively equal and therefore best pictured in a single (positively rising) supply curve. "The 'egalitarian' approach implies that the marginal rate of return is lower the larger the amount invested in human capital, while the 'elite' approach implies the opposite relation. Marginal rates of return appear to decline in the United States as years of schooling increase. . . ."[29]

Giora Hanoch, having found that the data (from the 1960 census) differed significantly according to sex, color, and geographic region, calculated separate rates of return to different years of schooling for males of different color and region. For male whites in the North his estimates yielded (as I mentioned earlier in this chapter) the following rates of return to investment in additional years of schooling: for completion of high school (as against merely 8 or 9 years of school) 16 per cent; for completion of college (as against merely 12 years of school) 10 per cent; and for those with 1 year or more of postgraduate study (as against only 16 years of school and college) 7 per cent. He concluded that "the higher the amount of schooling, the lower the marginal internal rate" of return.[30]

Richard Eckaus, in the early 1970s, recalculated internal rates of return with incomes standardized for hours of work per year. This standardization changed matters considerably. The rate of return to high-school completion (as compared with only 8 years of school)

---

[27] Mincer, "Human Capital and Earnings," p. 13.
[28] Becker, *Human Capital*, 2d ed., pp. 94-144.
[29] Ibid., p. 113.
[30] Giora Hanoch, "An Economic Analysis," pp. 324-326.

was reduced to as little as 4 per cent; the rate for college graduation (as compared with 12 years of school) came out as 12 per cent; and the rate for 1 or more years of graduate study (as against college graduation) was only 4.5 per cent. A considerable come-down, indeed. Eckaus concluded that possibly "there were more high school educated people than were 'required' in the labor force," and that perhaps "the compulsory attendance requirements at high school ages may contribute to a relative excess supply of high school educated persons."[31]

Richard Freeman, writing in 1975, had data at his disposal that reflected the deterioration of economic conditions in the United States in the early 1970s. He found the following changes during the preceding twenty years. The labor force included 7.9 per cent persons with college degrees in 1952, 12.6 per cent in 1969, and 15.6 per cent in 1974. Between 1969 and 1974, the starting salaries of college graduates had declined in real terms at annual rates of between 2.2 and 4.1 per cent (the last figure applying to graduates in physical sciences and mathematics). Between 1969 and 1972, the ratio of average incomes of college graduates to high-school graduates in the age group 25 to 34 had declined by 11.5 per cent, and the ratio to elementary-school graduates in the age group 35 to 44 had fallen by 15.6 per cent. The placement of college graduates had become difficult: "Twenty-four per cent of employed male graduates and twenty-two per cent of female graduates in these classes [1972] ended up in areas 'not at all related' to their college studies compared to about ten per cent of the starting graduates" in the class of 1958. Freeman calculated that the rate of return to college education had declined from 11.5 per cent in 1969 to 8.5 per cent in 1974.[32]

Finis Welch reported in 1979 that "there is some evidence that during the early 1970's earnings of young college graduates fell relative to earnings of high-school graduates." He saw the explanation in the following developments: "In the eight years from March 1967 to March 1975, the (18-64 year-old) civilian labor force grew 21 per cent . . . [while] numbers of participants with [only] 5-8 years of schooling fell 32 per cent and numbers with 1-3 years of high school fell by 5 per cent. . . . [The] number of high school graduates grew 35 per cent, and both for those with 1-3 years of college and for college graduates the number of persons in the civilian labor force

[31] Richard S. Eckaus, Estimating, p. 9.

[32] Richard B. Freeman, "Overinvestment in College Training," Journal of Human Resources, Vol. 9 (Summer 1975), Table 4; and The Declining Economic Value of Higher Education and the American Social System (New York: Aspen Institute Program on Education for a Changing Society, 1976).

jumped an astonishing 64 per cent."[33] No wonder, then, that the scarcity value of improved labor began to decline.

In Mark Blaug's view, "in general, private rates of return tend to decline monotonically with additional years of schooling, thus implying a chronic tendency on the part of individuals to over-invest in their education as a function of the acquisition of previous schooling."[34]

Qualifications

I plead guilty of having been selective in citing and quoting. I have chosen statements supporting the view that diminishing returns have been operative in reducing the pecuniary earnings of persons with more years of schooling relative to those with less schooling. My skepticism regarding the validity of econometric exercises of this sort is not reduced, however, when the results seem to confirm my intuitive judgment.

A major caveat is required, no matter how seriously we take the findings or any message they may convey regarding the economic value of education. Economic analysis is not confined to pecuniary incomes or to material goods; it includes choices and decisions that take account of satisfactions from nonmaterial goods. Education beyond some point may not yield a sufficient flow of incremental marketable services, or a sufficient flow of incremental earnings received in money, but it may still yield additional pleasures. The rate of return to education beyond grade 9 or beyond grade 12 may be quite low, or even zero, if it encompasses only differential pecuniary incomes, but it may still be quite high if all intellectual and aesthetic gratifications of the educated are counted in.

The nonpecuniary returns "may" be high, but I am not convinced that they really are for many, perhaps the majority, of the "investors." I suspect that "college graduate" or "schooled for 16 years" is not always the same as "educated." The "intellectual and aesthetic gratifications of the educated" are significant chiefly for those who have become avid readers of serious literature, assiduous listeners of serious music, frequent patrons of theaters and concerts, regular visitors to museums and art galleries. Whatever data we have on cultural activities of this sort indicate that the population of "users" is much smaller than that of college graduates. Of course, intellectual discernment and aesthetic sensibility can be brought also to more pop-

[33] Finis Welch, "Effects of Cohort Size in Earnings; The Baby-Boom Babies' Financial Bust." Discussion Paper 146 (Los Angeles: University of California, January 1979), pp. 1-2.

[34] Blaug, "Empirical Status," p. 840.

ular activities, such as travel, conversation, and even politics; but we have no data to indicate the special contribution that college makes to the gratification derived from these pursuits.

The reminder that the customary calculations of rates of return from investment in education disregard the nonpecuniary benefits, and that purely psychic returns may be significant, may serve to explain why rates of return may be lower for investment in schooling than for investment in physical capital: the nonmeasured returns can make up the difference. Although probably many investors in education are disappointed by the poor money returns (or even disgruntled if parents, friends, and propagandists have misled them by promises of high pecuniary rewards), others may be quite satisfied, in that they made their investment decisions on the conscious assumption that a part of the return will come not in money but in the form of other satisfactions.

Still another consideration may explain why the rates of pecuniary returns may in some countries be systematically lower for human capital than for physical or financial capital assets. A very special risk, which may be substantial for physical and financial assets, does not usually exist for human capital: the risk of confiscation. Such a risk may exist in countries with strong anticapitalist mentality and high propensity to nationalize (socialize) private property. Human capital, by definition not separable from the bodies and brains of the owners, is not in any danger of being taken over by the state. Similar differences in risk may be observed where people may wish (or be forced) to emigrate but are not permitted to take their physical property with them and/or to transfer their financial assets to any foreign country. Although their physical and financial assets have to be left behind, the knowledge they have accumulated through educational investment will go with them. Thus, in an important sense, human capital is "safer" than capital in other forms, safer from governmental seizures and foreign-exchange restrictions. That safer assets carry smaller effective yields in terms of money is an old story.[35]

[35] This was the hypothesis offered in explanation of the observation that few Jews owned farm land. George Stigler and Gary Becker attributed this hypothesis to a statement by Reuben Kessel: ". . . since Jews have been persecuted so often and forced to flee to other countries, they have not invested in immobile land, but in mobile human capital . . . that would automatically go with them." George J. Stigler and Gary S. Becker, "De Gustibus Non Est Disputandum," *American Economic Review*, Vol. 67 (March 1977), p. 76. Stigler, in a letter to me, ventured the guess that phrases such as "he escaped only with his wits" go back several centuries. Of course, the experience of these escapees would not *necessarily* have induced "rational" expectations by others, causing them to prefer investing in human capital at rates of return lower than are obtainable from seizable assets. Still, an "asset preference" in favor of nonseizable human capital is quite plausible.

No proposition about the real world ever holds without qualification. Since human capital created by investment in schooling and training is not homogeneous but often highly specific, the owners of particularly scarce knowledge capital may incur the risk of not being allowed to emigrate, whereas those with less specific qualifications may get their "exit visa." To be sure, the acquired knowledge is not separated from the individuals who have acquired it, but the carriers of that valuable knowledge may be forbidden to leave. They "know too much," in the opinion of the authoritarian officials, to be allowed to export their specific human capital and to use it abroad.

Complementarity

Some teachers of economics have modeled the role of physical capital in the production process by imagining a universal tool or machine that can do everything in every technological process.[36] Helpful as such a model may be for the comprehension of some economic relations, it may be a hindrance in making students grasp other economic relations. The imaginary universal tool allows us to dodge the problem of complementarity of different capital goods: generators, motors, turbines, transmissions, transformers, boilers, tubes, pipes, cables, drills, hammers, screws, nails, and thousands of other hardware, tools, appliances, instruments, machines have to be available in required proportions. It would not do to have generators but no motors, hammers but no nails, electric power but no cables, and so forth.

Similar conditions exist concerning the stock of human capital. It is true that human resources are less "specific" than physical ones. Some people may be good in work of every sort, or they can quickly learn to be good in whatever is demanded, in manual or mental labor. By and large, however, people are specialized or, at least, relatively more suitable for some kind of work than for another. The stock of human capital, embodying the learning and training of people, accumulated over short and long periods of time, is composed of many different types of abilities and skills. In view of the existing complementarities, the stock can be valuable—that is, can yield high returns—only if the different forms of human capital are available in proportions that match the technological or organizational requirements of the place and the time. And, as times change, requirements are likely to change.

Complementarity exists also between physical and human capital.

<hr>

[36] Most of the text in this subsection was used in my *Lecture on Theory of Human Capital* (Islamabad: Pakistan Institute of Development Economics, 1982), pp. 25-27.

The best farm machines will do little good if there are no mechanics to maintain them, keep them in good repair. Skilled electricians will do little good where there is no electricity. Tailors need fabrics, needles, and thread in order to be useful. Computer centers need hardware, the computers, and software, the programs provided by programmers. Enough of such examples, the message is clear. There is need for a complex matching of different forms of physical capital and different forms of human capital. The question is who will do the matching and how. A competitive-market mechanism with mobile labor and flexible wage rates could probably do a reasonably good job, but actual labor markets are not so constituted. However poorly the matching problem can be solved in noncompetitive and inefficient labor markets, an efficient allocation of resources by central-planning agencies is even less likely.

The essential moral of my discussion of complementarity is, however, that outlays intended to create human capital will in fact prove to have done so only if they result in the right mixture of human aptitudes and attitudes formed through the educational effort. And what is right or wrong in this context is not a matter of value judgment but will depend on conditions beyond the control of individuals, groups, cartels, commissions, legislatures, and governments.

national aggregates, classification of writings on, 323-324; prices, profits, and interest rates, classification of writings on, 323-324; technological change, classification of writings on, 323-324; trends and fluctuations, classification of writings on, 323-324

forward-exchange markets, 58-62; and interest differentials, 61; banks as hedgers in, 59; hedgers in, 59; in Goschen, 285; principle of interest parity in, 60; role of information in, 60-61

Fox, Harold G., 359

Frank, Philipp, 232 n.21

Freeman, Richard B., 399, 441 n.4, 605

free riders, 122, 329; and knowledge, 161; and user fees, 133-134; exclusion of, 133-134; problem of, 146 n.51

Freiburg School, 221 n.12

Frenkel, Jacob A., 62 n.32, 391

Freud, Sigmund, 225 n.18

Frey, Bruno S., 393

Friedman, James W., 368, 371, 376

Friedman, Milton, 276 n.30, 301, 369, 385, 386, 397, 421

Frisch, Ragnar, 43

Friss, Istvan, 394

Frydman, Roman, 280 n.36, 282 n.37

futures markets, 52-62; in Moore, 286

Gabor, Andre, 378

Galbraith, John Kenneth, 49

Gallaway, Lowell E., 372

gambling: classification of writings on, 317, 319; in Samuelson, 287

games: in Lamberton, 290 n.15; of chance, in Bernoulli, 15-16, 284

game theory, 198-300; and decision theory, classification of writings on, 325; and public-good valuation, 137; as analytical technique, 299 n.41; classification of writings on, 325; in Bernouilli, 298; in *Index of Economic Journals*, 299 n.41; in Morgenstern, 298; in Neumann, 298; in Samuelson, 287; in Schotter and Schwödiauer, 299; in Shubik, 298-299; vs. theories of "conjectural variations," 45

Garfield, Eugene, 409 n.66

Gates, D. J., 376

Gauss, Karl Friederich: in Schumpeter, 286 n.2

genetic endowment and conscious improvement, 453-454

Gibbard, Allan, 353

Gibson, William F., 385

Gilfillan, Seabury Colum, 359, 365

Gill, Shlomo, 376

Gintis, Herbert, 397, 457 n.16, 507, 532 n.20

Girshick, Meyer A., 366

Gladwin, Thomas N., 362

Glennan, Thomas K., Jr., 340

Goddard, Haynes C., 345

Goldberg, Victor P., 371

Goldfarb, Robert S., 400

Goldhar, Joel D., 346

Goldman, William, 343

Goldschmidt, Yaagov, 349

Gonedes, Nicholas J., 110 n.68, 388

Goodhart, Charles A. E., 319 n.1, 352

goods: experience, nonconsumer, and search, advertising of, 48; mixed, and user fees, 132; mixed, vs. social goods, 132-133; nonsocial, 133; private, prices as indicators for in planning, 196, 198-199; private vs. public in planning, 196, 198; semiprivate and semipublic, 157-158

Gore, Daniel, 345

Goschen, George Joachim, 62 n.32, 284, 390

Gould, John P., 347

Gounden, A. M. Nalla, 600 n.22

government: and the public good, 127 n.9; as advertiser, 48; as decisionmaker, 121-128, 247; information services, classification of writings on, 315, 317; measures, and optimum output, 123 n.3, 124; monopoly, and electronic mass media, 316; regulation of advertising, 51; spending on education, 447

Grabowski, Henry G., 341

Graham, Benjamin, 364

Graham, John W., 409 n.5, 564

Gramlich, Edward M., 340

Granger, Clive W. J., 364, 365, 378

Granick, David, 395

Library of Congress Cataloging in Publication Data

Machlup, Fritz, 1902-
   The economics of information and human capital.

   (Knowledge, its creation, distribution, and economic
   significance ; v. 3)
   Includes bibliographical references and index.
   1. Information theory in economics. 2. Human capital.
I. Title. II. Series: Machlup, Fritz, 1902-
Knowledge, its creation, distribution, and economic
significance ; v. 3.
AZ505.M28 vol. 3 [HB133]   001s [331]   83-42588
ISBN 0-691-04233-0